English Drama
and Theatre,
1800-1900

AMERICAN LITERATURE, ENGLISH LITERATURE, AND WORLD LITERATURES IN ENGLISH: AN INFORMATION GUIDE SERIES

Series Editor: Theodore Grieder, Curator, Division of Special Collections, Fales Library, New York University, New York, New York

Associate Editor: Duane DeVries, Associate Professor, Polytechnic Institute of New York, Brooklyn, New York

Other books on English literature in this series:

ENGLISH DRAMA TO 1660 (EXCLUDING SHAKESPEARE)—*Edited by Frieda Elaine Penninger*

ENGLISH DRAMA, 1660-1800—*Edited by Frederick M. Link*

ENGLISH DRAMA, 1900-1950—*Edited by E.H. Mikhail*

CONTEMPORARY DRAMA IN AMERICA AND ENGLAND, 1950-1970—*Edited by Richard H. Harris**

ENGLISH FICTION, 1660-1800—*Edited by Jerry C. Beasley**

ENGLISH FICTION, 1800-1850—*Edited by Duane DeVries**

ENGLISH FICTION, 1900-1950 (2 volumes)—*Edited by Thomas J. Rice**

ENGLISH NOVEL, 1851-1900—*Edited by Robert Schweik and Albert Dunn**

THE ENGLISH LITERARY JOURNAL TO 1900—*Edited by Robert B. White, Jr.*

ENGLISH PROSE, PROSE FICTION, AND CRITICISM TO 1660—*Edited by S.K. Heninger, Jr.*

OLD AND MIDDLE ENGLISH POETRY TO 1500—*Edited by Walter H. Beale*

ENGLISH POETRY, 1500-1660—*Edited by S.K. Heninger, Jr.**

ENGLISH POETRY, 1600-1800—*Edited by Donald C. Mell**

ENGLISH ROMANTIC POETRY, 1800-1835—*Edited by Donald H. Reiman**

VICTORIAN POETRY, 1835-1900—*Edited by Ronald E. Freeman**

ENGLISH POETRY, 1900-1950—*Edited by Emily Ann Anderson**

*in preparation

The above series is part of the
GALE INFORMATION GUIDE LIBRARY

The Library consists of a number of separate series of guides covering major areas in the social sciences, humanities, and current affairs.

General Editor: Paul Wasserman, Professor and former Dean, School of Library and Information Services, University of Maryland

Managing Editor: Denise Allard Adzigian, Gale Research Company

English Drama and Theatre, 1800-1900

A GUIDE TO INFORMATION SOURCES

Volume 12 in the American Literature, English Literature, and World Literatures in English Information Guide Series

L.W. Conolly

Associate Professor of English
University of Alberta
Edmonton, Alberta

J.P. Wearing

Associate Professor
Department of English
University of Arizona

Gale Research Company
Book Tower, Detroit, Michigan 48226

Library of Congress Cataloging in Publication Data

Conolly, Leonard W
    English drama and theatre, 1800-1900

    (American literature, English literature, and
world literatures in English ; v.12) (Gale information
guide library)
    Includes index.
    1. English drama—19th century—Bibliography.
2. English drama—19th century—History and criticism—
Bibliography. 3. Theatre—Great Britain—History—
Bibliography. I. Wearing, J. P., joint author.
II. Title.
Z2014.D7C72 [PR721] 016.822'7'08 73-16975
ISBN 0-8103-1225-5

VITAE

L.W. Conolly is currently associate professor of English at the University of Alberta. He received his B.A. and Ph.D. degrees from the University of Wales and his M.A. degree from McMaster University, Hamilton, Ontario. He has received several awards from the Canada Council and one from the American Council of Learned Societies.

Conolly is the author of THE CENSORSHIP OF ENGLISH DRAMA 1737-1824 (San Marino, 1976) and cofounder and coeditor of NINETEENTH CENTURY THEATRE RESEARCH (with Professor Wearing). He has published numerous articles on English drama and theatre in British, Canadian, and American journals. Conolly is currently president of the Association for Canadian Theatre History.

J.P. Wearing is associate professor in the department of English at the University of Arizona and received his Ph.D. from the University of Wales. He formerly taught at the University of Alberta, where he was also an Izaac Walton Killam Memorial Post-Doctoral Fellow. He edited THE COLLECTED LETTERS OF SIR ARTHUR PINERO (1974) and is the author of the LONDON STAGE 1890-1899: A CALENDAR OF PLAYS AND PLAYERS (1976). He is coeditor and cofounder of NINETEENTH CENTURY THEATRE RESEARCH (with L.W. Conolly) and has written numerous articles on nineteenth- and twentieth-century English drama and theatre. He is currently working on AMERICAN AND BRITISH THEATRE BIOGRAPHY: A DIRECTORY and THE LONDON STAGE 1900-1909: A CALENDAR OF PLAYS AND PLAYERS.

CONTENTS

Contents

Contents

Contents

ACKNOWLEDGMENTS

We wish to thank Paula Pranka and Bonnie Dewart, both of the University of Alberta, for their assistance in the preparation of some parts of this work. We are also very grateful to Barbara Conolly for her help in proofreading and to Linda Stoddart for so carefully and cheerfully typing a difficult manuscript. Professor Conolly gratefully acknowledges a University of Alberta research grant which enabled him to visit the Harvard Theatre Collection. Professor Wearing gratefully acknowledges the research assistance and support provided by the University of Arizona.

INTRODUCTION

In this bibliography we have attempted to provide comprehensive, though not exhaustive, coverage of all important aspects of nineteenth-century English drama and theatre. The work is divided into the ten chapters indicated in the table of contents.

In chapter 1 we have included mainly works published between 1800 and 1900, although some studies published after 1900 are, in an important sense, "contemporary" and are therefore included in this section.

Chapter 2 includes works published up to the beginning of 1974, and also lists doctoral dissertations. Here, as in other chapters where doctoral dissertations are listed, the University Microfilms order number is given as it appears in DISSERTATION ABSTRACTS.* (For British and some American and Canadian dissertations this is not possible; they are usually available only from the library of the university which granted the degree.)

Chapter 3 considers 110 authors, dividing each author's bibliography into the following six sections--I Collected Works; II Acted Plays--Principal Titles; IIa Unacted Plays; III Bibliographies; IV Biography; V Critical Studies; VI Journals and Newsletters--although not all of these categories are required in all cases. We have not attempted to give in this section a complete listing of all nineteenth-century plays and playwrights, as Allardyce Nicoll has done in in his invaluable handlists (items 298 and 321, below). Our list is, however, intended to include all important nineteenth-century English playwrights as well as many lesser, but still representative, names. We have not included any playwrights' nondramatic works; for these the reader should consult the NEW CAMBRIDGE BIBLIOGRAPHY OF ENGLISH LITERATURE 1800-1900 (item 2456) or other volumes in the Gale Information Guide Library.

For each play listed in chapter 3 we have given the full title as found on the

---

*Order from Xerox University Microfilms, P.O. Box 1764, Ann Arbor, Michigan 48106.

title page of the edition consulted, the place, the publisher and date of publication, and the theatre and date of the first production. The edition cited is not necessarily the first (or the only), but it is usually the one to be found in the Readex Microprint collection of ENGLISH AND AMERICAN DRAMA OF THE 19TH CENTURY (see item 2517). This is the most comprehensive collection of nineteenth-century plays available; and although consulting it involves all the inconveniences of the microprint form, it is, nonetheless, the only large-scale collection which is likely to be reasonably accessible to most researchers. We have indicated with an asterisk (*) those individual plays listed in sections II and IIa of chapter 3 which are not yet to be found in the Readex collection. In addition, we have also listed some individual plays which were produced but never published and exist only in manuscript form in the British Library. Such plays are designated LC. A partial catalog of them is given in item 2436, below. The other major collection of nineteenth-century manuscript plays is the Larpent Collection at the Huntington Library, for which see item 2401. Plays listed from this collection are designated LA.

We have also thought it worthwhile to annotate the editions of the plays we list in chapter 3. Sometimes the annotation indicates only that the edition consulted contains, besides the text of the play, basic information such as is included in most nineteenth-century acting editions--stage directions, scene plans, property lists, cast lists, and so on. Often, surprisingly useful additional information is discovered. Critical introductions, memoirs or biographical sketches of playwrights or actors, prefaces on censorship or copyright legislation, dedications, complaints about audiences or managers, manuscript notes: these and other matters appear, where appropriate, in our annotations.

We have given the full title of each play (from the title page) so that the reader might better appreciate the kinds of plays favored and specialized in by particular writers. The titles frequently indicate genre (burletta, melodrama, etc.) and length of the play, and thus provide valuable information.

Some playwrights who belong partly in the nineteenth century, but whose most important output lies in the eighteenth or twentieth centuries, have been excluded from chapter 3: Frederick Reynolds, George Colman the Younger, Charles Dibdin the Elder, J.M. Barrie, George Bernard Shaw, and Stephen Phillips, for example. Non-English writers whose work was influential in England (e.g., Ibsen) are also, with some exceptions, omitted.

Chapters 4, 5, and 6 are self-explanatory.

In chapter 7, as in chapter 3, we have had to omit some important people. Non-English performers who appeared on the English stage only occasionally, like Rachel, Mde. Ristori, Tommaso Salvini, and Charles Fechter, have been left out entirely. One or two others, like Sarah Bernhardt, have been given only cursory treatment.

It is important to point out that in chapters 8, 9, and 10, as with all chapters which include nineteenth-century theatrical studies, readers should also consult the excellent bibliography by Arnott and Robinson, ENGLISH THEATRICAL LITERATURE 1559-1900 (item 2458), which gives a more detailed and comprehensive coverage of contemporary material than we have space for.

All items in all chapters are listed chronologically. Cross-references have been kept to a minimum, but the index will enable users to find all items relevant to a particular subject or person.

Our aim in compiling this bibliography has been to give extensive and representative coverage of primary and secondary materials important in the study of nineteenth-century English drama and theatre. We hope that it will be accepted by student and scholar alike as a convenient and reliable starting point for any project in the area we have covered. Those readers wishing to locate works published since the end of 1973 are encouraged to consult the bibliography published annually in NINETEENTH CENTURY THEATRE RESEARCH (item 3232), where significant additions and corrections to ENGLISH DRAMA AND THEATRE, 1800-1900 will also be published.

ABBREVIATIONS

ABC	AMERICAN BOOK COLLECTOR	EIC	ESSAYS IN CRITICISM
AL	AMERICAN LITERATURE	ELH	JOURNAL OF ENGLISH LITERARY HISTORY
AN&Q	AMERICAN NOTES AND QUERIES	ELT	ENGLISH LITERATURE IN TRANSITION (1880-1920)
AQ	AMERICAN QUARTERLY	EM	ENGLISH MISCELLANY
BB	BULLETIN OF BIBLIOG-RAPHY	EMD	AN ENGLISH MISCELLANY
BMQ	BRITISH MUSEUM QUAR-TERLY	ETJ	EDUCATIONAL THEATRE JOURNAL
BNYPL	BULLETIN OF THE NEW YORK PUBLIC LIBRARY	EUQ	EMORY UNIVERSITY QUARTERLY
BuR	BUCKNELL REVIEW	Expl	EXPLICATOR
CE	COLLEGE ENGLISH	FMLS	FORUM FOR MODERN LANGUAGE STUDIES
CLAJ	COLLEGE LANGUAGE ASSOCIATION JOUR-NAL	FSUS	FLORIDA STATE UNIVER-SITY STUDIES
DA	DISSERTATION ABSTRACTS	GM	GENTLEMAN'S MAGAZINE
DR	DALHOUSIE REVIEW	HAB	HUMANITIES ASSOCIA-TION BULLETIN
DramS	DRAMA SURVEY	HLB	HARVARD LIBRARY BULLETIN
DUJ	DURHAM UNIVERSITY JOURNAL	HLQ	HUNTINGTON LIBRARY QUARTERLY

Abbreviations

HudR	HUDSON REVIEW	PBSA	PAPERS OF THE BIBLIO-GRAPHICAL SOCIETY OF AMERICA
JEGP	JOURNAL OF ENGLISH AND GERMANIC PHILOLOGY	PLL	PAPERS ON LANGUAGE AND LITERATURE
KSJ	KEATS-SHELLEY JOURNAL	PMLA	PUBLICATIONS OF THE MODERN LANGUAGE ASSN. OF AMERICA
KSMB	KEATS-SHELLEY MEMORIAL BULLETIN		
LC	Lord Chamberlain's Collection of Plays	PQ	PHILOLOGICAL QUAR-TERLY
LCh	LIBRARY CHRONICLE	PULC	PRINCETON UNIVERSITY LIBRARY CHRONICLE
MD	MODERN DRAMA	PURBA	PUNJAB UNIVERSITY RESEARCH BULLETIN, ARTS
MLN	MODERN LANGUAGE NOTES		
MLQ	MODERN LANGUAGE QUARTERLY	QJS	QUARTERLY JOURNAL OF SPEECH
MLR	MODERN LANGUAGE REVIEW	QQ	QUEEN'S QUARTERLY
MLS	MODERN LANGUAGE STUDIES	QR	QUARTERLY REVIEW
		REL	REVIEW OF ENGLISH LITERATURE
MP	MODERN PHILOLOGY	RES	REVIEW OF ENGLISH STUDIES
N&Q	NOTES AND QUERIES		
NCTR	NINETEENTH CENTURY THEATRE RESEARCH	RLC	REVUE DE LITTERATURE COMPAREE
NEQ	NEW ENGLAND QUARTERLY	RS	RESEARCH STUDIES
		SAQ	SOUTH ATLANTIC QUARTERLY
OJES	OSMANIA JOURNAL OF ENGLISH STUDIES (Osmania University, Hyderabad)	SEL	STUDIES IN ENGLISH LITERATURE, 1500-1900
OSUTCB	OHIO STATE UNIVERSITY THEATRE COLLECTION BULLETIN	ShN	SHAKESPEARE NEWSLETTER
		SIR	STUDIES IN ROMANTICISM

SLRJ	ST. LOUIS UNIVERSITY RESEARCH JOURNAL	UCSLL	UNIVERSITY OF COLORADO STUDIES IN LANGUAGE AND LITERATURE
SM	SPEECH MONOGRAPHS		
SoR	SOUTHERN REVIEW	UMSE	UNIVERSITY OF MISSISSIPPI STUDIES IN ENGLISH
SP	STUDIES IN PHILOLOGY		
SR	SEWANEE REVIEW	UR	UNIVERSITY REVIEW (Kansas City, Missouri)
TA	THEATER ANNUAL		
TDR	TULANE DRAMA REVIEW	URLB	UNIVERSITY OF ROCHESTER LIBRARY BULLETIN
ThQ	THEATRE QUARTERLY	UTQ	UNIVERSITY OF TORONTO QUARTERLY
ThR	THEATRE RESEARCH		
ThS	THEATRE SURVEY	VN	VICTORIAN NEWSLETTER
TLS	TIMES LITERARY SUPPLEMENT	VP	VICTORIAN POETRY
		VS	VICTORIAN STUDIES
TN	THEATRE NOTEBOOK	WCircle	WORDSWORTH CIRCLE
TQ	TEXAS QUARTERLY	WHR	WESTERN HUMANITIES REVIEW
TS	THEATRE STUDIES (formerly OSUTCB)	WVUPP	WEST VIRGINIA UNIVERSITY PHILOLOGICAL PAPERS
TSE	TULANE STUDIES IN ENGLISH		
		YR	YALE REVIEW
TSL	TENNESSEE STUDIES IN ENGLISH	YULG	YALE UNIVERSITY LIBRARY GAZETTE

Chapter 1

CONTEMPORARY HISTORY AND CRITICISM

For a more extensive listing of contemporary history and criticism, including many items of a more esoteric nature than given here, readers should consult Arnott and Robinson's invaluable ENGLISH THEATRICAL LITERATURE 1559-1900 (item 2458, below), especially the sections headed "Government Regulation of the Theatre," "The Morality of the Theatre," and "General History."

1   Hill, Rowland. A WARNING TO PROFESSORS, CONTAINING APHO-
     RISTIC OBSERVATIONS ON THE NATURE AND TENDENCY OF PUBLIC
     AMUSEMENTS. London: Printed by Joseph Hartnell, 1805. viii, 76 p.

     A warning (about the evils of the stage) which prompted
     several responses and some controversy in the first decade of
     the century.

2   Hunt, Leigh. CRITICAL ESSAYS ON THE PERFORMERS OF THE LONDON
     THEATRES: INCLUDING GENERAL OBSERVATIONS ON THE PRACTISE
     AND GENIUS OF THE STAGE. London: John Hunt, 1807. xiv, 229 p.

3   Plumptre, James. FOUR DISCOURSES ON SUBJECTS RELATING TO THE
     AMUSEMENT OF THE STAGE: PREACHED AT GREAT ST. MARY'S
     CHURCH, CAMBRIDGE, ON SUNDAY SEPTEMBER 25, AND SUNDAY
     OCTOBER 2, 1808; WITH COPIOUS SUPPLEMENTARY NOTES. Cam-
     bridge, Eng.: F.C. and J. Rivington, 1809. xv, 184 p.

     An important and influential defense of properly regulated
     drama and theatre.

4   [Frere, Benjamin]. THE ADVENTURES OF A DRAMATIST, ON A
     JOURNEY TO THE LONDON MANAGERS. 2 vols. London: Lacking-
     ton, Allen & Co., 1813. vi, 204; 204 p.

     The memoirs of an unsuccessful and frustrated playwright.

5   Lawrence, James. "Dramatic Emancipation, or Strictures on the State of the Theatres. . . . " PAMPHLETEER, 2, no. 4 (1813), 370-95.

          An antimonopoly tract.

6   Dramaticus. AN IMPARTIAL VIEW OF THE STAGE, FROM THE DAYS OF GARRICK AND RICH TO THE PRESENT PERIOD: OF THE CAUSES OF ITS DEGENERATED AND DECLINING STATE, AND SHEWING THE NECESSITY OF A REFORM IN THE SYSTEM, AS THE ONLY MEANS OF GIVING STABILITY TO THE PRESENT PROPERTY OF THE TWO WINTER THEATRES. London: Chapple, 1816. vii, 26 p.

          Dramaticus' view of the condition of the two patent theatres is far from impartial, but he does give an interesting account of the various ailments afflicting the theatre at the beginning of the century.

7   Sutor, Alexander. AN ESSAY ON THE STAGE: IN WHICH THE ARGUMENTS IN ITS BEHALF, AND THOSE AGAINST IT, ARE CONSIDERED: AND ITS MORALITY, CHARACTER, AND EFFECTS ILLUSTRATED. Aberdeen, Scot.: Printed by D. Chalmers & Co., 1820. ix, 166 p.

          After much zealous argument the author, a surgeon by profession, concludes that "he who continues under the teaching of the Stage, by every lesson he learns, is fitting himself for wrath against the day of wrath--for the execution of the sentence of a just, holy, and jealous God; and if he continue under its deceitful influence, loses his immortal soul" (p. 150).

8   Dwight, Timothy. AN ESSAY ON THE STAGE: IN WHICH THE ARGUMENTS IN ITS BEHALF, AND THOSE AGAINST IT, ARE CONSIDERED; AND ITS MORALITY, CHARACTER AND EFFECTS ILLUSTRATED. London: Sharp, Jones & Co., 1824. ix, 166 p.

          In which a Yale president attacks the theatre.

9   [Hazlitt, William]. THE SPIRIT OF THE AGE. London: Henry Colburn, 1825. 424 p.

          Views on, among others, Byron, Southey, Leigh Hunt, James Sheridan Knowles.

10   [Ryan, Richard]. DRAMATIC TABLE TALK; OR SCENES, SITUATIONS, & ADVENTURES, SERIOUS & COMIC, IN THEATRICAL HISTORY & BIOGRAPHY. 3 vols. London: John Knight & Henry Lacey, 1825-30.

          An "assemblage of curious and interesting facts . . . combining, in each page, research and gaiety. . . . " Brief essays on miscellaneous theatre subjects, some of nineteenth-century interest.

11   [Collier, John Payne]. PUNCH AND JUDY, WITH ILLUSTRATIONS
      DESIGNED AND ENGRAVED BY GEORGE CRUIKSHANK. ACCOM-
      PANIED BY THE DIALOGUE OF THE PUPPET-SHOW, AN ACCOUNT OF
      ITS ORIGIN, AND OF PUPPET-PLAYS IN ENGLAND. London: S. Pro-
      wett, 1828. 111 p.

      Cruikshank's splendid illustrations helped this work go through
      several nineteenth-century editions.

12   Great Britain. REPORT FROM THE SELECT COMMITTEE ON DRAMATIC
      LITERATURE; WITH MINUTES OF EVIDENCE. House of Commons, 2
      August 1832.

      The most easily accessible edition of this valuable repository
      of information on the early nineteenth-century theatre is in
      BRITISH PARLIAMENTARY PAPERS: STAGE AND THEATRE I
      (Shannon: Irish University Press, 1968). This collection also
      contains other reports and legislation relating to the nineteenth-
      century theatre.

13   Thackeray, Thomas James. ON THEATRICAL EMANCIPATION, AND THE
      RIGHTS OF DRAMATIC AUTHORS. London: C. Chapple, 1832. 47 p.

      An antimonopoly tract, with reference to French practices.

14   Place, Francis. A BRIEF EXAMINATION OF THE DRAMATIC PATENTS.
      London: Printed by Baylis and Leighton, 1834. 12 p.

      An attack on the monopoly by one of its fiercest opponents,
      this essay is reprinted from MONTHLY MAGAZINE, March,
      1834.

15   Bennett, John B. THE EVIL OF THEATRICAL AMUSEMENTS, STATED
      AND ILLUSTRATED IN A SERMON, PREACHED IN THE WESLEYAN-
      METHODIST CHAPEL, LOWER ABBEY-ST., ON SUNDAY, NOVEMBER 4,
      1838; WITH AN APPENDIX. Dublin: John Fannin and Co., 1838. iv,
      48 p.

      A diatribe against the theatre, citing much biblical authority.
      The appendix quotes other writers who have denounced the
      theatre. See John Calcraft's reply, below, item 17.

16   Styles, John. THE STAGE: ITS CHARACTER AND INFLUENCE. 4th ed.,
      rev. London: Thomas Ward, 1838. vi, 210 p.

      An antitheatre tract originally published in 1806 as AN
      ESSAY ON THE CHARACTER, IMMORAL, AND ANTI-
      CHRISTIAN TENDENCY OF THE STAGE. In 1838 Styles
      still felt that the "moral evils of a Theatre, against which
      the work was originally directed, are . . . little abated."

17 Calcraft, John William [John William Cole]. A DEFENCE OF THE
STAGE, OR AN INQUIRY INTO THE REAL QUALITIES OF THEATRICAL
ENTERTAINMENTS, THEIR SCOPE AND TENDENCY. Dublin: Milliken
and Son, 1839. viii, 175 p.

> A reply to Bennett's sermon (above, item 15). Calcraft quotes
> and refers to an impressive number of authorities, religious and
> secular.

18 [Tomlins, F.G.]. THE PAST AND PRESENT STATE OF DRAMATIC ART
AND LITERATURE; ADDRESSED TO AUTHORS, ACTORS, MANAGERS
AND THE ADMIRERS OF THE OLD ENGLISH DRAMA. London: C.
Mitchell, 1839. 32 p.

> The "present degradation" of the stage is "entirely owing to
> its having been converted into a monopoly one hundred and
> seventy-nine years since. . . . " This was a common ex-
> planation of the problems of the theatre in the first half of
> the nineteenth century--but see Cooke's essay, below, item
> 19.

19 Cooke, James. THE STAGE. ITS PRESENT STATE, AND PROSPECTS
FOR THE FUTURE. London: J. Pattie, [1840]. 16 p.

> Cooke argues that the "present degradation" of the drama is
> owing to "high prices, the daily increase of sectarianism;
> neglect of the great models of stage literature; and want of
> union and self respect amongst the professors of the art" (p.5).

20 Tomlins, F.G. A BRIEF VIEW OF THE ENGLISH DRAMA, FROM THE
EARLIEST PERIOD TO THE PRESENT TIME, WITH SUGGESTIONS FOR
ELEVATING THE PRESENT CONDITION OF THE ART. London: C.
Mitchell, 1840. viii, 152 p.

21 _____. THE NATURE AND STATE OF THE ENGLISH DRAMA: A
LECTURE. London: C. Mitchell, 1841. 24 p.

22 _____. THE RELATIVE VALUE OF THE ACTED AND UNACTED DRAMA:
A LECTURE . . . REPRINTED FROM THE MONTHLY MAGAZINE. London: C. Mitchell, 1841. 14 p.

23 Horne, Richard Hengist. A NEW SPIRIT OF THE AGE. 2 vols. London:
Smith, Elder & Co., 1844.

> Views on, among others, Douglas Jerrold, Leigh Hunt, James
> Sheridan Knowles, Macready, and Bulwer-Lytton.

23a Robson, William. THE OLD PLAY-GOER. London: Joseph Masters,
1846. xi, 252 p.

A lament for the decline of the theatre, with most of the
blame placed on the managers.

24   Dramaticus. THE STAGE AS IT IS. London: F. Newton, 1847. iii,
24 p.

> An idiosyncratic view of the London stage, with some reasons
> for its low ebb. Dramaticus also discusses the leading actors
> and actresses (with Macready receiving a good measure of
> attention) and proposes the establishment of a national theatre.

25   Chapman, J.K., ed. A COMPLETE HISTORY OF THEATRICAL ENTER-
TAINMENTS, DRAMAS, MASQUES, AND TRIUMPHS, AT THE ENGLISH
COURT, FROM THE TIME OF KING HENRY THE EIGHTH TO THE PRES-
ENT DAY INCLUDING THE SERIES OF PLAYS PERFORMED BEFORE
HER MAJESTY AT WINDSOR CASTLE, CHRISTMAS 1848-9. . . . Lon-
don: John Mitchell, [1849]. 86, 11 p.

> Written in true "Court circular" style, this book is largely
> interesting for its factual details, notably the series of play-
> bills reproduced as an appendix. Performers in the theatricals
> at Windsor included Charles Kean, Charles Mathews, Buck-
> stone, William Farren, Vandenhoff, and Mrs. Keeley.

26   Powell, Thomas. THE LIVING AUTHORS OF ENGLAND. New York:
Appleton, 1849. 316 p.

> Brief essays on, among others, J.W. Marston, Knowles,
> Bulwer-Lytton, Boucicault, and Douglas Jerrold.

27   An Old Playgoer [Brook Bridges Parlby]. DESULTORY THOUGHTS
ON THE NATIONAL DRAMA. London: Onwhyn, 1850. iii, 62 p.

> These are desultory and digressive thoughts indeed on the
> perennial "doom and gloom" state of the English theatre.
> The Old Playgoer aims at examining "whether there have
> not been, and still are, such various antagonistic causes at
> work, as to render it almost a wonder that the drama has
> not sustained a total wreck."

28   Scott, Walter. "The Drama." THE MISCELLANEOUS PROSE WORKS OF
SIR WALTER SCOTT. Edinburgh: Adam and Charles Black, 1851. I,
575-615.

> The final paragraphs explain the damage suffered by the theatre
> from the maintenance of the monopoly enjoyed by the patent
> theatres.

29   Donne, William Bodham. ESSAYS ON THE DRAMA AND ON POPULAR
AMUSEMENTS. 2nd ed. London: Tinsley and Jones, 1863. 256 p.

Essays reprinted from QUARTERLY REVIEW, WESTMINSTER REVIEW, and FRAZER'S MAGAZINE. One essay is on Charles Kemble.

30 A HANDY-BOOK ON THE LAW OF THE DRAMA AND MUSIC: BEING AN EXPOSITION OF THE LAW OF DRAMATIC COPYRIGHT, COPYRIGHT IN MUSICAL COMPOSITIONS, DRAMATIC COPYRIGHT IN MUSIC, AND INTERNATIONAL COPYRIGHT IN THE DRAMA AND MUSIC; THE LAW FOR REGULATING THEATRES; THE LAW AFFECTING THEATRES; AND THE LAW RELATING TO MUSIC, DANCING, AND PROFESSIONAL ENGAGEMENTS; WITH THE STATUTES, FORMS, &C., REFERRING THERETO. London: T.H. Lacy, 1864. viii, 80 p.

A valuable description of the law and the theatre at mid-century.

31 [Mackintosh, Matthew]. STAGE REMINISCENCES: BEING RECOLLECTIONS, CHIEFLY PERSONAL, OF CELEBRATED THEATRICAL & MUSICAL PERFORMERS DURING THE LAST FORTY YEARS. Glasgow: James Hedderwick & Son, 1866. 236 p.

The author, a stage carpenter, originally published these essays in the GLASGOW WEEKLY CITIZEN. There are chapters on Edmund Kean, Madame Vestris, Charles Mathews, Andrew Ducrow, and other theatre personalities and events.

32 Morley, Henry. THE JOURNAL OF A LONDON PLAYGOER FROM 1851 TO 1866. London: Routledge, 1866. 384 p.

A series of reviews of productions on the London stage from 1851 to 1866. Contains much incidental information on the contemporary nature and condition of the theatre.

33 Fitzgerald, Percy Hetherington. PRINCIPLES OF COMEDY AND DRAMATIC EFFECT. London: Tinsley Bros., 1870. 368 p.

34 Hodder, George. MEMORIES OF MY TIME, INCLUDING PERSONAL REMINISCENCES OF EMINENT MEN. London: Tinsley Bros., 1870. xx, 420 p.

Includes memories of, among others, Jerrold, Frances Kelly, Knowles, Macready, and Charles Kean.

35 "Q" [Thomas Purnell]. DRAMATISTS OF THE PRESENT DAY. London: Chapman and Hall, 1871. vii, 140 p.

Purnell's papers originally appeared in ATHENAEUM and deal perceptively, if briefly, with Bulwer-Lytton, Westland Marston, F.C. Burnand, Boucicault, John Oxenford, Robertson, Taylor, and Reade. Many of Purnell's judgments are substantiated with judicious quotation, an uncommon feature in nineteenth-century dramatic criticism.

36 Taylor, Tom. THE THEATRE IN ENGLAND: SOME OF ITS SHORT-COMINGS AND POSSIBILITIES. London: British and Colonial Publishing Co., 1871. 12 p.

37 Maggin, William. A GALLERY OF ILLUSTRIOUS LITERARY CHARACTERS (1830-1838). Draws. Daniel Maclise. Ed. William Bates. London: Chatto and Windus, 1873. 239 p.

Portraits and brief critical surveys of the work of, among others, J.B. Buckstone, Bulwer-Lytton, Theodore Hook, Leigh Hunt, and James Sheridan Knowles.

38 Fitzgerald, Percy. THE BOOK OF THEATRICAL ANECDOTES. London: Routledge, [1874]. 128 p.

A series of miscellaneous anecdotes of limited interest and value.

39 Martin, [Sir] Theodore. ESSAYS ON THE DRAMA. London: Privately printed, 1874. [v], 331 p.

A collection of essays on various aspects of the theatre, such as contemporary interpretations of Shakespeare, the Theatres Bill 1865, and the general state of drama. These pieces originally appeared in periodicals such as PALL MALL GAZETTE, QUARTERLY REVIEW, FRASER'S MAGAZINE, and DUBLIN UNIVERSITY MAGAZINE.

40 Hollingshead, John. THEATRICAL LICENSES. London: Chatto and Windus, 1875. 24 p.

Letters reprinted from the DAILY TELEGRAPH and TIMES describing (and protesting against) anomalies and injustices in the licensing of theatres and plays.

41 Neville, Henry G. THE STAGE, ITS PAST AND PRESENT IN RELATION TO FINE ART . . . BEING THE SUBJECT OF A LECTURE. London: Richard Bentley and Son, 1875. xvi, 96 p.

42 Godwin, George. ON THE DESIRABILITY OF OBTAINING A NATIONAL THEATRE NOT WHOLLY CONTROLLED BY THE PREVAILING POPULAR TASTE. London: Wyman & Sons, 1878. 32 p.

An earnest and persuasive argument for a government-subsidized theatre "where the glories of our past writers might be enjoyed and new poetical and thoughtful works fittingly brought forward."

43   Planche, J.R. SUGGESTIONS FOR ESTABLISHING AN ENGLISH ART
      THEATRE. London: Wyman & Sons, 1879. 12 p.

> Detailed suggestions for implementing proposals made by
> George Godwin (item 42) and others for establishing a Na-
> tional Theatre.

44   Cook, Dutton. A BOOK OF THE PLAY: STUDIES AND ILLUSTRATIONS
      OF HISTRIONIC STORY, LIFE, AND CHARACTER. 3rd ed., rev. Lon-
      don: Sampson Low, Marston, Searle, & Rivington, 1881. viii, 391 p.

> A miscellany of jottings first published in 1876, mainly his-
> torical, on various subjects, such as "Foot-Lights," "Stage
> Whigs," and "Real Horses." A curious and entertaining
> source of theatre history.

45   Fitzgerald, Percy. THE WORLD BEHIND THE SCENES. London: Chatto
      and Windus, 1881. 320 p.

> Chapters on stage mechanism, spectacles, actors, theatres,
> and authors. Packed with information about the nineteenth-
> century stage, but lacking an index.

46   Lennox, William Pitt. PLAYS, PLAYERS AND PLAYHOUSES AT HOME
      AND ABROAD WITH ANECDOTES OF THE DRAMA AND THE STAGE.
      2 vols. London: Hurst and Blackett, 1881. viii, 303; viii, 271 p.

> A superficial history; includes European theatre.

47   Archer, William. ENGLISH DRAMATISTS OF TO-DAY. London:
      Sampson Low, Marston, Searle and Rivington, 1882. 387 p.

> An important and influential book for its time, this deals
> with major and up-and-coming dramatists. Included among
> these perceptive studies are Gilbert, Grundy, H.A. Jones,
> and Pinero.

48   Fitzgerald, Percy. A NEW HISTORY OF THE ENGLISH STAGE FROM
      THE RESTORATION TO THE LIBERTY OF THE THEATRES, IN CONNEC-
      TION WITH THE PATENT HOUSES. 2 vols. London: Tinsley Bros.,
      1882. xii, 437; viii, 463 p.

> The last section of volume 2 (pp. 371-432) deals with the
> first half of the nineteenth century. Fitzgerald was one of
> the first theatre historians to recognize the value of Lord
> Chamberlain's papers, which he uses extensively in this study.

49   Kemble, Frances Anne. NOTES UPON SOME OF SHAKESPEARE'S PLAYS.
      London: Richard Bentley & Son, 1882. 169 p.

> On MACBETH, HENRY VIII, THE TEMPEST, and ROMEO
> AND JULIET.

50   Morris, Mowbray. ESSAYS IN THEATRICAL CRITICISM. London:
Remington, 1882. 226 p.

51   Thornell, J. Higden, ed. THE BILL OF THE PLAY: AN ILLUSTRATED
RECORD OF THE CHIEF DRAMAS, PLAYS, OPERAS BOUFFE, ETC.,
PRODUCED OR REVIVED DURING THE YEAR 1881. WITH A SHORT
STORY OF THE PLOT, A CRITICAL ANALYSIS OF THE PIECE AND THE
ACTORS, AND THE FULL CAST, AND DATE OF PRODUCTION. WITH
NUMEROUS ILLUSTRATIONS BY HAL LUDLOW. London: Pictorial
World Office, [1882]. 116 p.

52   Cook, Dutton. NIGHTS AT THE PLAY: A VIEW OF THE ENGLISH
STAGE. London: Chatto and Windus, 1883. xvi, 480 p.

> Cook selects 155 of his reviews from the PALL MALL GAZETTE
> and the WORLD, covering the period 1867-81, with the purpose
> of giving a representative survey of the theatre, drama, and ac-
> tors of the time. He recognizes the limitations of only one opin-
> ion, but rightly points out that reviews are one of the few ways
> in which we can recall the abilities of actors. Foreign produc-
> tions in London during the period are excluded.

53   _____. ON THE STAGE: STUDIES OF THEATRICAL HISTORY AND
THE ACTOR'S ART. 2 vols. London: Sampson Low, 1883. viii, 287;
iv, 332 p.

> Rather than attempting a formal theatre history, Cook tries
> to "supply a genuine guide to the character and economy of
> scenic illusion in England, an account of the growth and de-
> velopment of the actor's art amongst us and of our system of
> theatrical exhibition."

54   "The English Stage." QUARTERLY REVIEW, 155 (April 1883), 354-88.

> A review article which also incorporates comment on the con-
> temporary stage. The books under review are Percy Fitz-
> gerald, A NEW HISTORY OF THE ENGLISH STAGE, (item
> 48); F.A. Kemble's NOTES UPON SOME OF SHAKESPEARE'S
> PLAYS, (item 49); Archer's ENGLISH DRAMATISTS OF TO-
> DAY (item 47); and Helen Faucit's LETTERS ON SOME OF
> SHAKESPEARE'S FEMALE CHARACTERS (originally published
> in BLACKWOOD'S MAGAZINE, later in book form; see item
> 57).

55   Kendal, Madge. THE DRAMA: A PAPER READ AT THE CONGRESS OF
THE NATIONAL ASSOCIATION FOR THE PROMOTION OF SOCIAL
SCIENCE, BIRMINGHAM, SEPTEMBER 1884. 4th ed. London: David

Bogue, [1884]. 24 p.

A controversial essay in its time.

56 Day, W.C. BEHIND THE FOOTLIGHTS; OR, THE STAGE AS I KNEW IT. London and New York: Frederick Warne & Co., 1885. iv, 191 p.

Miscellaneous theatrical anecdotes, engagingly illustrated by G.B. Le Fanu.

57 Faucit, Helen. ON SOME OF SHAKESPEARE'S FEMALE CHARACTERS: OPHELIA, JULIET, PORTIA, IMOGEN, DESDEMONA, ROSALIND, BEATRICE. Edinburgh and London: Blackwood, 1885. ix, 443 p.

Helen Faucit's insights into roles with which she was, as she says, "especially identified." An enlarged edition was published in 1891 with Hermione added to the list of characters in the title.

58 Geary, W.N.M. THE LAW OF THEATRES AND MUSIC-HALLS INCLUDING CONTRACTS AND PRECEDENTS OF CONTRACTS. . . WITH HISTORICAL INTRODUCTION BY JAMES WILLIAMS. . . . London: Stevens and Sons, 1885. xii, 230 p.

Includes an appendix of national statutes, and of London and provincial acts and regulations; an important source for information on the theatre and the law.

59 Lamb, Charles. THE ART OF THE STAGE AS SET OUT IN LAMB'S DRAMATIC ESSAYS WITH A COMMENTARY BY PERCY FITZGERALD. London: Remington, 1885. v, 277 p.

Worth reading. Of interest is Fitzgerald's commentary in which he attempts to formulate into a systematic theory Lamb's principles as they emerge in the essays.

60 Archer, William. ABOUT THE THEATRE: ESSAYS AND STUDIES. London: T. Fisher Unwin, 1886. iii, 350 p.

One of Archer's earlier examinations of the state of English drama from several aspects. The papers are anthologized from Archer's work in THEATRE, WESTMINSTER REVIEW, NINETEENTH CENTURY, DRAMATIC REVIEW, and other journals.

61 Brereton, Austin. SHAKESPEAREAN SCENES AND CHARACTERS: WITH DESCRIPTIVE NOTES ON THE PLAYS, AND THE PRINCIPAL SHAKESPEAREAN PLAYERS, FROM BETTERTON TO IRVING. London: Cassell, 1886. 96 p.

Illustrated.

62   Hanley, Peter. A JUBILEE OF PLAYGOING. London: Tinkler and Hillhouse, 1887. 113 p.

>Originally published in 1883 as RANDOM RECOLLECTIONS OF THE STAGE; informal observations on performances and performers over a fifty-year period.

63   Vedder, Paul. THE PLAYGOERS' POCKET BOOK: THE DRAMATIC YEAR, 1886. WITH DESCRIPTIONS AND ILLUSTRATIONS OF ALL THE MOST IMPORTANT NEW PLAYS OF THE YEAR; COPIES OF MANY OF THE PLAY-BILLS, AND A RECORD OF DRAMATIC EVENTS. London: J. & R. Maxwell, [1887]. 136 p.

>Also contains portraits of some actors; a selective summary of the year's activity.

64   Coleman, John. PLAYERS AND PLAYWRIGHTS I HAVE KNOWN. 2 vols. London: Chatto and Windus, 1888. 329; 397 p.

>Reminiscences of Macready, Charles Kean, Ellen Tree, Samuel Phelps, Charles Mathews, Madame Vestris, Ben Webster, Charles Reade, Tom Taylor, T.W. Robertson, and others. Several lesser lights of the nineteenth-century theatre are also discussed. Coleman himself was much involved in the London and provincial theatre both as an actor and manager.

65   Doran, John. "THEIR MAJESTIES' SERVANTS." ANNALS OF THE ENGLISH STAGE FROM THOMAS BETTERTON TO EDMUND KEAN. Ed. and rev. Robert W. Lowe. 3 vols. London: John C. Nimmo, 1888.

>Most of volume 3 deals with the nineteenth century. Lowe's edition of this important early history (first published in 1864) is the best available.

66   Vedder, Paul. THE PLAYGOERS' POCKET-BOOK: THE DRAMATIC YEAR, 1887. WITH DESCRIPTIONS AND ILLUSTRATIONS OF ALL THE NEW PLAYS OF THE YEAR; COPIES OF MANY OF THE PLAY-BILLS, AND A COMPLETE RECORD OF DRAMATIC EVENTS. London: Spencer Blackett, [1888]. 144 p.

>Although only slightly longer than Vedder's previous annual (item 63), this work aims at being a more comprehensive coverage of the year's events and is certainly more profusely illustrated.

67   Headlam, Stewart D. THE FUNCTION OF THE STAGE. London: Frederick Verinder, 1889. 37 p.

>A defense of the stage, and an attack on some of its legal restrictions, written by an ex-clergyman.

68   Martin, Sir Theodore. ESSAYS ON THE DRAMA: SECOND SERIES.
      London: Privately printed, 1889. [vi], 350 p.

          A further series of Martin's essays reprinted from BLACK-
          WOOD'S, NINETEENTH CENTURY, QUARTERLY REVIEW,
          and ST. JAMES'S GAZETTE. His subjects include Rachel,
          Macready, Irving's 1879 production of THE MERCHANT OF
          VENICE, the Meiningen Company (1881 visit to London), and
          theatrical reform, among others. See item 39.

69   Fitzgerald, Percy. MUSIC-HALL LAND. AN ACCOUNT OF THE NA-
      TIVES, MALE AND FEMALE, PASTIMES, SONGS, ANTICS, AND GEN-
      ERAL ODDITIES OF THAT STRANGE COUNTRY. London: Ward and
      Downey, [1890]. vi, 90 p.

          With illustrations by Alfred Bryan.

70   Jerome, Jerome K[lapka]. STAGE-LAND: CURIOUS HABITS AND CUS-
      TOMS OF ITS INHABITANTS. Illus. J. Bernard Partridge. New York:
      Henry Holt, 1890; rpt. Bath: Cedric Chivers, 1972. 158 p.

          A less-than-serious look at some stock characters of the
          nineteenth-century stage.

71   Adams, William Davenport. A BOOK OF BURLESQUE. SKETCHES OF
      ENGLISH STAGE TRAVESTIE AND PARODY, BY WILLIAM DAVENPORT
      ADAMS. WITH PORTRAITS OF F.C. BURNARD, W.S. GILBERT, AND
      G.R. SIMS. London: Henry and Co., 1891. vi, 220 p.

72   Lamb, Charles. THE DRAMATIC ESSAYS OF CHARLES LAMB: EDITED
      WITH AN INTRODUCTION AND NOTES BY BRANDER MATTHEWS.
      London: Chatto and Windus, 1891. 265 p.

          This delightful collection of essays is drawn from the "Elia"
          pieces.

73   Scott, Clement William. THIRTY YEARS AT THE PLAY, AND DRAMATIC
      TABLE TALK. London: Railway and General Automatic Library, [1891].
      246 p.

74   Irving, Henry. THE DRAMA: ADDRESSES BY HENRY IRVING. London:
      Heinemann, [1892]; rpt. New York: Blom, 1969. 164 p.

          Contains Irving's lectures, "The Stage As It Is," delivered
          at Edinburgh, 1881; "The Art of Acting," Harvard, 1885;
          "Four Great Actors" (Burbage, Betterton, Garrick, and Kean),
          Oxford, 1886; "The Art of Acting," Edinburgh, 1891.

75   Walkley, A.B. PLAYHOUSE IMPRESSIONS. London: T. Fisher Unwin,

1892. viii, 261 p.

A miscellany of dramatic criticism, reprinted from SPEAKER, NATIONAL OBSERVER, and STAR. Apart from more general topics, Walkley touches on Shakespeare, Ibsen, H.A. Jones, Grundy, Pinero, Bernhardt, and Irving.

76   Knight, Joseph. THEATRICAL NOTES. London: Lawrence & Bullen, 1893; rpt. New York: Blom, 1971. xvi, 321 p.

A collection of material Knight had previously published in ATHENAEUM, covering the period 1874 to 1879.

77   Archer, William. THE THEATRICAL "WORLD" FOR 1893. 1894; rpt. New York: Blom, 1969. xxxv, 307 p.

Reprints of Archer's articles for WORLD. An invaluable account and record of the London stage which is continued in Archer's companion volumes (see items 80, 84, 86, 88). The later volumes also include playbills of major productions and revivals for each season.

78   Hunt, Leigh. DRAMATIC ESSAYS: SELECTED AND EDITED, WITH NOTES AND AN INTRODUCTION, BY WILLIAM ARCHER AND ROBERT W. LOWE. London: Walter Scott, 1894. xlvii, 241 p.

Archer declares Hunt to be "the finest English dramatic critic . . . the first writer of any note who made it his business to see and report upon all the principal theatrical events of the day," and selects criticism from Hunt's CRITI-CAL ESSAYS (1807) and from Hunt's contributions to TATLER. This selection, therefore, covers the major theatrical figures of the first three decades of the century.

79   Archer, William, and Robert W. Lowe, eds. DRAMATIC ESSAYS [OF] WILLIAM HAZLITT. London: Walter Scott, 1895. xxx, 231 p.

Contains "all of Hazlitt's theatrical essays that have any abiding interest for the general reader" (introduction, p. xxvii).

80   Archer, William. THE THEATRICAL "WORLD" OF 1894: WITH AN INTRODUCTION BY GEORGE BERNARD SHAW AND A SYNOPSIS OF PLAYBILLS OF THE YEAR BY HENRY GEORGE HIBBERT. 1895; rpt. New York: Blom, 1971. xxxiii, 417 p.

See items 77, 84, 86, 88.

81   Jones, Henry Arthur. THE RENASCENCE OF THE ENGLISH DRAMA: ESSAYS, LECTURES, AND FRAGMENTS RELATING TO THE MODERN

ENGLISH STAGE, WRITTEN AND DELIVERED IN THE YEARS 1883-94. London: Macmillan, 1895. xiv, 343 p.

> Jones's collection of essays is central to his own work as well as reflecting the current theatrical climate. Jones's aims in writing these pieces were threefold: 1) to establish drama as an art, separating it from popular entertainment; 2) to establish the right of the dramatist to write freely what he chooses; 3) to fight "for sanity and wholesomeness, for largeness and breadth of view."

82 Stuart, Charles Douglas, and A.J. Park. THE VARIETY STAGE: A HISTORY OF THE MUSIC HALLS FROM THE EARLIEST PERIOD TO THE PRESENT TIME. London: T. Fisher Unwin, [1895]. xii, 255 p.

> An interesting account, but lacking documentation and, less forgivably, illustrations.

83 À Beckett, Arthur W. GREENROOM RECOLLECTIONS. Bristol: J.W. Arrowsmith; London: Simpkin, Marshall, Hamilton, Kent and Co., [1896]. ix, 296 p.

84 Archer, William. THE THEATRICAL "WORLD" OF 1895: WITH A PREFATORY LETTER BY ARTHUR W. PINERO, AND A SYNOPSIS OF PLAYBILLS OF THE YEAR BY HENRY GEORGE HIBBERT. 1896; rpt. New York: Blom, 1971. xxxix, 445 p.

> See items 77, 80, 86, 88.

85 Forster, John, and George Henry Lewes. DRAMATIC ESSAYS: REPRINTED FROM THE "EXAMINER" AND THE "LEADER," WITH NOTES AND AN INTRODUCTION BY WILLIAM ARCHER AND ROBERT W. LOWE. London: Walter Scott, 1896. xliv, 284 p.

> Forster's essays from the EXAMINER are taken from the issues of 1835 to 1838, Lewes's from the LEADER, 1850-54. Both deal with the major figures of the period--Macready and Charles Kean, for example--as well as with a host of other theatrical subjects. Archer's introductory biographies are also well worth reading.

86 Archer, William. THE THEATRICAL "WORLD" OF 1896: WITH AN INTRODUCTION "ON THE NEED FOR AN ENDOWED THEATRE" BY WILLIAM ARCHER AND A SYNOPSIS OF PLAYBILLS OF THE YEAR BY HENRY GEORGE HIBBERT. 1897; rpt. New York: Blom, 1971. lxi, 423 p.

> See items 77, 80, 84, 88.

87 Filon, Augustin. THE ENGLISH STAGE. BEING AN ACCOUNT OF

THE VICTORIAN DRAMA. Trans. from French by Frederic Whyte. Intro. Henry Arthur Jones. London: John Milne; New York: Dodd, Mead, & Co., 1897; rpt. London and New York: Blom, 1969. 319 p.

> A substantial and interesting introduction by Jones, followed by a critical survey of the major plays, playwrights, and actors of the Victorian theatre, nonetheless valid for having been written by a Frenchman.

88 Archer, William. THE THEATRICAL "WORLD" OF 1897: WITH AN INTRODUCTION BY SYDNEY GRUNDY AND A SYNOPSIS OF PLAY-BILLS OF THE YEAR BY HENRY GEORGE HIBBERT. 1898; rpt. New York: Blom, 1969. xxviii, 452 p.

> See items 77, 80, 84, 86.

89 Strong, A.A. DRAMATIC AND MUSICAL LAW: BEING A DIGEST OF THE LAW RELATING TO THEATRES AND MUSIC HALLS AND CON-TAINING CHAPTERS ON THEATRICAL CONTRACTS, THEATRICAL MUSIC AND DANCING AND EXCISE LICENCES, DRAMATIC AND MUSICAL COPYRIGHT, &C. WITH AN APPENDIX CONTAINING THE ACTS OF PARLIAMENT RELATING THERETO AND THE REGULATIONS OF THE LONDON COUNTY COUNCIL AND THE LORD CHAMBERLAIN. London: "The Era" Publishing Office, 1898. xi, 155 p.

> Another valuable source of information on the theatre and the law.

90 Syle, L. Dupont. ESSAYS IN DRAMATIC CRITICISMS WITH IMPRES-SIONS OF SOME MODERN PLAYS. New York: W.R. Jenkins, 1898. [ix], 161 p.

> Syle's essays deal with such general topics as an endowed theatre and the future of the drama, and although written from an American viewpoint, contain references to English and continental drama. His impressions, which first appeared in the SAN FRANCISCO EXAMINER, consist of reviews of American performances of English plays.

91 Archer, William. STUDY & STAGE: A YEAR-BOOK OF CRITICISM. London: Grant Richards, 1899. xi, 250 p.

> This work is a continuation of Archer's THEATRICAL WORLD series (see item 77), but also includes articles on literary topics. The miscellany is drawn from Archer's contributions to WORLD, DAILY CHRONICLE, ACADEMY, and OUTLOOK.

92 Grein, J.T. DRAMATIC CRITICISM. 5 vols. London: J. Long, 1899-1905.

> Anthologies of Grein's drama reviews.

93   Scott, Clement. THE DRAMA OF YESTERDAY & TO-DAY. 2 vols.
      London and New York: Macmillan, 1899. xviii, 607; x, 581 p.

      Reminiscences of the London stage from 1840 to the 1890's
      by one of the leading critics who became an avowed anti-
      Ibsenite. Scott's remarks, therefore, favor things past and
      sentimental, although there is useful material here, such as
      playbills and letters.

94   Walkley, A.B. FRAMES OF MIND. London: Grant Richards, 1899.
      viii, 286 p.

      A miscellany of articles selected and reprinted from Walkley's
      work for the DAILY CHRONICLE, SPEAKER, STAR, and COS-
      MOPOLIS. The selection on the "Playhouse" covers such
      subjects as HAMLET, RICHARD III, DR. FAUSTUS, Pinero,
      Shaw, Bernhardt, and Dan Leno.

95   [Arnold, W.T., et al.]. THE MANCHESTER STAGE 1880-1900: CRITI-
      CISMS REPRINTED FROM "THE MANCHESTER GUARDIAN." Westminster,
      Eng.: Archibald Constable, [1900]. 241 p.

      This useful collection of theatre reviews provides interesting
      provincial reactions to leading London performers. Thus there
      are reports of Irving in THE MERCHANT OF VENICE, Bern-
      hardt in LA DAME AUX CAMELIAS, Mrs. Campbell and
      George Alexander in THE SECOND MRS. TANQUERAY, and
      many more.

96   Courtney, W.L. THE IDEA OF TRAGEDY IN ANCIENT AND MODERN
      DRAMA: THREE LECTURES DELIVERED AT THE ROYAL INSTITUTION
      FEBRUARY, 1900: WITH A PREFATORY NOTE BY A.W. PINERO. West-
      minster, Eng.: Constable, 1900; rpt. New York: Russell and Russell, 1967.
      xii, 132 p.

      This is a wide-ranging discussion of the nature of tragedy
      from the Greeks to the twentieth century. In his third lec-
      ture devoted to the nineteenth century, Courtney concentrates
      on Ibsen's work, but mentions others, notably Pinero.

97   Grein, J.T. PREMIERES OF THE YEAR. London: John Macqueen, 1900;
      rpt. New York: Blom, 1971. 275 p.

      A collection of Grein's reviews, from 21 May 1899 to 15
      July 1900.

98   Tarpey, W.K. "English Dramatists of To-Day." CRITIC, 37 (1900), 117-
      31.

      Tarpey, in his brief survey of contemporary dramatists, sees
      Pinero as the most important, followed by H.A. Jones. There

are brief references to "J.O. Hobbes," H.V. Esmond, Shaw, R.C. Carton, Grundy, Haddon Chambers, and L.N. Parker.

99   Jones, Henry Arthur. "The Drama in the English Provinces." NINE-TEENTH CENTURY, 49 (1901), 431-44.

Deals mainly with "the transition in the provinces from the stock company to our present system of travelling companies moving from town to town and playing only one piece"--and the consequences of this transition.

100   Clapp, Henry Austin. REMINISCENCES OF A DRAMATIC CRITIC: WITH AN ESSAY ON THE ART OF HENRY IRVING. Boston and New York: Houghton Mifflin, 1902. ix, 241 p.

Clapp's reminiscences stem from his time as a critic with the BOSTON DAILY ADVERTISER and include pieces on British artists who visited Boston. In addition to the essay on Irving, there are sections on J.L. Toole, Charles Mathews, E.A. Sothern, and Charles Fechter.

101   Brown, T. Allston. A HISTORY OF THE NEW YORK STAGE FROM THE FIRST PERFORMANCE IN 1732 TO 1901. 3 vols. New York: Dodd, Mead & Co., 1903; rpt. New York: Blom, 1964.

Useful in checking on the appearance of English plays and players in New York.

102   Archer, William. REAL CONVERSATIONS. London: Heinemann, 1904. xiii, 254 p.

A series of "faithful reproductions" of conversations originally printed in PALL MALL MAGAZINE. Representing the theatrical profession are Pinero, Mrs. Craigie ("J.O. Hobbes"), Stephen Phillips, Gilbert, and George Alexander.

103   Beers, Henry A. "The English Drama of To-Day." NORTH AMERICAN REVIEW, 180 (1905), 746-57.

Beers's thesis is that "the dramatic output of the last quarter-century outweighs that of any other quarter-century since 1700"--with Pinero classed as "the foremost English play-writer of to-day."

104   Craig, Edward Gordon. THE ART OF THE THEATRE, TOGETHER WITH AN INTRODUCTION . . . PREFACE BY R. GRAHAM ROBERTSON. Edinburgh and London: T.N. Foulis, 1905. 54 p.

Contains reproductions of Craig's designs.

105 Shaw, G[eorge] Bernard. DRAMATIC OPINIONS AND ESSAYS: CON-
TAINING AS WELL A WORD ON THE DRAMATIC OPINIONS AND
ESSAYS OF G. BERNARD SHAW BY JAMES HUNEKER. 2 vols. New
York: Brentano's, 1906. xix, 447; vii, 466 p.

> A collection of Shaw's inimitable reviews for SATURDAY
> REVIEW, which are always enjoyable, often informative, and
> sometimes perverse.

106 Walkley, A.B. DRAMA AND LIFE. London: Methuen, [1907]; rpt.
Freeport, N.Y.: Books for Libraries, 1967. viii, 331 p.

> A series of essays on a variety of theatrical subjects.

107 Hamilton, Clayton. THE THEORY OF THE THEATRE: AND OTHER
PRINCIPLES OF DRAMATIC CRITICISM. London: Grant Richards, 1910.
248 p.

> Hamilton's theory of drama and the theatre is somewhat
> clouded by his writing, a mixture of the academic and euphu-
> istic. To illustrate his theory he draws examples from a wide
> range of drama, including the English nineteenth century.

108 Spence, E.F. OUR STAGE AND ITS CRITICS: BY E.F.S. OF "THE
WESTMINSTER GAZETTE". London, 1910. xv, 296 p.

109 Craig, Edward Gordon. ON THE ART OF THE THEATRE. London:
Heinemann, 1911. xix, 296 p.

> For those who can tolerate Craig's eccentric style and ap-
> proach, there is much of interest both about the contemporary
> theatre and Craig's own theories. The book is well illustrated
> with selections from Craig's own designs for scenery and cos-
> tumes.

110 Frohman, David. MEMORIES OF A MANAGER: REMINISCENCES OF
THE OLD LYCEUM AND OF SOME PLAYERS OF THE LAST QUARTER
CENTURY. London: Heinemann, 1911. xvii, 235 p.

> Frohman's reminiscences are interesting mainly for their first-
> hand account of the appearances of English plays and players
> on the New York stage.

111 Hale, Edward Everett. DRAMATISTS OF TO-DAY: ROSTAND, HAUPT-
MANN, SUDERMANN, PINERO, SHAW, PHILLIPS, MAETERLINCK:
BEING AN INFORMAL DISCUSSION OF THEIR SIGNIFICANT WORK.
6th ed. 1911; rpt. Freeport, N.Y.: Books for Libraries, 1969. v,
284 p.

> The range of the work is indicated in the subtitle. How-

ever, the discussion of the various plays is casual, lacking
any useful discernment.

112 Russell, Sir Edward R. THE THEATRE AND THINGS SAID ABOUT IT:
A PAPER READ BEFORE THE LITERARY AND PHILOSOPHICAL SOCIETY
OF SOUTHPORT ON THE 2ND MARCH, 1911. Liverpool: Henry Young
and Sons, 1911. 33 p.

113 Armstrong, Cecil Ferard. SHAKESPEARE TO SHAW: STUDIES IN THE
LIFE'S WORK OF SIX DRAMATISTS OF THE ENGLISH STAGE. London:
Mills & Boon, 1913; rpt. Freeport, N.Y.: Books for Libraries, 1968.
v, 330 p.

> Chapters on Shakespeare, Congreve, Sheridan, Robertson,
> Pinero, and Shaw. Written in a chatty manner, it lacks
> critical incisiveness and is often muddle-headed.

114 Howe, P.P. DRAMATIC PORTRAITS. London: Martin Secker, 1913;
rpt. Port Washington, N.Y.: Kennikat Press, 1969. 264 p.

> Howe attempts, with varying degrees of success, to examine
> the purely theatrical aspects of the work of Pinero, Jones,
> Wilde, Barrie, and others.

115 Jones, Henry Arthur. THE FOUNDATIONS OF A NATIONAL DRAMA:
A COLLECTION OF LECTURES, ESSAYS AND SPEECHES, DELIVERED
AND WRITTEN IN THE YEARS 1896-1912 (REVISED AND CORRECTED,
WITH ADDITIONS). New York: George H. Doran; London: Chapman
& Hall, [1913]. xviii, 358 p.

> Jones discusses important topics like the foundation of a
> National Theatre (which he supported) and censorship (which
> he opposed).

116 Poel, William. SHAKESPEARE IN THE THEATRE. London and Toronto:
Sidgwick and Jackson, 1913. 247 p.

> Poel's radical views on Shakespearean production are reprinted
> from NATIONAL REVIEW, WESTMINSTER REVIEW, ERA, and
> NEW AGE.

117 Grundy, Sydney. THE PLAY OF THE FUTURE, BY A PLAYWRIGHT OF
THE PAST. A GLANCE AT "THE FUTURE OF THE THEATRE" BY JOHN
PALMER. [London]: S. French, 1914. 41 p.

118 Arnold, Matthew. LETTERS OF AN OLD PLAYGOER: WITH AN
INTRODUCTION BY BRANDER MATHEWS. Publications of the Dramatic
Museum of Columbia University, ser. 4, no. 4. New York: 1919.
54 p.

Reprinted from PALL MALL GAZETTE.

119 Terry, Ellen. FOUR LECTURES ON SHAKESPEARE. EDITED WITH AN
INTRODUCTION BY CHRISTOPHER ST. JOHN. London: Martin Hopkinson, 1921. 201 p.

120 Archer, William. THE OLD DRAMA AND THE NEW: AN ESSAY IN
RE-VALUATION. Boston: Small, Maynard, 1923. viii, 396 p.

This work was originally a series of lectures "giving a mere
outline of the course of theatrical history." Archer, as ever,
is full of sound judgments on the nineteenth century, which
is covered in lectures 9-12. Some of his earlier opinions are
modified and toned down (for example, on Pinero), but his
basic assessments remain the same.

120a Newton, Henry Chance. CUES AND CURTAIN CALLS; BEING THE
THEATRICAL REMINISCENCES OF H. CHANCE NEWTON ("CARADOS"
OF THE "REFEREE"). Intro. Sir Johnston Forbes-Robertson. London:
John Lane, 1927. xiv, 306 p.

121 Drinkwater, John, ed. THE EIGHTEEN-SEVENTIES. ESSAYS BY
FELLOWS OF THE ROYAL SOCIETY OF LITERATURE. Cambridge: At
the University Press, 1929. xiv, 284 p.

Contains Pinero on "The Theatre in the 'Seventies'" (a dis-
cussion of Robertson, Gilbert, James Albery, Wills, and H.J.
Byron) and Granville-Barker on "Tennyson, Swinburne,
Meredith--and the Theatre."

122 Archer, William. PLAY-MAKING: A MANUAL OF CRAFTSMANSHIP.
4th ed. London: Chapman and Hall, 1930. xvi, 323 p.

Archer's manual expounds some of his theory of drama by
examining the various elements which constitute a play. His
argument is illustrated by examples drawn from contemporary
playwrights and their works. The book first appeared in 1912.

123 Beerbohm, Max. AROUND THEATRES. 2 vols. New York: Knopf,
1930.

These two volumes contain generous selections from Beerbohm's
inimitable contributions to SATURDAY REVIEW, for which he
was dramatic critic from 1898 to 1910.

124 De La Mare, Walter, ed. THE EIGHTEEN-EIGHTIES. ESSAYS BY
FELLOWS OF THE ROYAL SOCIETY OF LITERATURE. Cambridge: At

the University Press, 1930. xxviii, 271 p.

Contains G.K. Chesterton on Gilbert and Sullivan and Granville-Barker on "The Coming of Ibsen," a general survey of the theatre of the 1880's.

125 Agate, James, ed. THE ENGLISH DRAMATIC CRITICS. AN ANTHOLOGY, 1660-1932. London: A. Barker, [1932]; rpt. New York: Hill and Wang, [1958]. xii, 370 p.

A collection comparable in scope to Ward's (item 127).

126 Drinkwater, John, ed. THE EIGHTEEN-SIXTIES. ESSAYS BY FELLOWS OF THE ROYAL SOCIETY OF LITERATURE. Cambridge: At the University Press, 1932. x, 282 p.

Contains Harley Granville-Barker on "Exit Planché--Enter Gilbert."

127 Ward, A.C., ed. SPECIMENS OF ENGLISH DRAMATIC CRITICISM XVII-XX CENTURIES. World's Classics, no. 498. London: Oxford University Press, 1945. x, 355 p.

There is a generous and representative selection from the nineteenth century.

128 Hazlitt, William. LIBOR AMORIS AND DRAMATIC CRITICISMS: WITH AN ESSAY OF INTRODUCTION BY CHARLES MORGAN. London: Peter Nevill, 1948. 426 p.

A lengthy but unscholarly anthology of Hazlitt's dramatic criticism.

129 Shaw, G[eorge] B[ernard]. OUR THEATRES IN THE NINETIES. 3 vols. London: Constable, 1948. [Standard Edition].

Despite all Shaw's prejudices and verbiage, these reviews garnered from SATURDAY REVIEW are indispensable reading.

130 Houtchens, Lawrence Huston, and Carolyn Washburn Houtchens, eds. LEIGH HUNT'S DRAMATIC CRITICISM 1808-1831. New York: Columbia University Press, 1949. xiii, 347 p.

A scholarly edition of "the best of Hunt's uncollected essays on the drama," culled largely from EXAMINER and TATLER.

131 Sprague, Arthur Colby, and Bertram Shuttleworth, eds. THE LONDON THEATRE IN THE EIGHTEEN-THIRTIES. London: Society for Theatre Research, 1950. vii, 86 p.

Excerpts from the Charles Rice manuscript, Harvard Theatre

Collection. Rice was an enthusiastic amateur critic; presented here are his views on performances at seven London
theatres from the summer of 1836 to the summer of 1837.
The editors provide notes, a brief bibliography, and a useful
index.

132   Matthews, Brander, ed. PAPERS ON PLAYMAKING. Preface. Harry T.
Wells. New York: Hill and Wang, 1957. viii, 312 p.

There are essays by Pinero (on Stevenson as a dramatist),
Gilbert ("A Stage Play"), and Matthews (on Gilbert).

133   Brown, Eluned. "A Note on Henry Crabb Robinson's Reactions to J.P.
Kemble and Edmund Kean." TN, 13 (1958-59), 14-18.

Extracts from Robinson's diary. See item 138.

134   Nagler, A.M. A SOURCE BOOK IN THEATRICAL HISTORY (SOURCES
OF THEATRICAL HISTORY). New York: Dover Publications, 1959.
xxiii, 611 p.

First published in 1952 as SOURCES OF THEATRICAL HISTORY,
this collection of contemporary documents includes about sixty
pages on the nineteenth century, with comment on actors,
actresses, costume, theatre architecture, audiences, and other
theatrical matters.

135   Matthews, John F. SHAW'S DRAMATIC CRITICISM (1895-98). New
York: Hill and Wang, 1959. viii, 306 p.

A useful collection of fifty-four essays drawn from Shaw's
contributions to SATURDAY REVIEW, and also included in
OUR THEATRES IN THE NINETIES (item 129).

136   Laurence, Dan H., ed. BERNARD SHAW: COLLECTED LETTERS 1874-
1897. London: Reinhardt, 1965. xxii, 877 p.

An excellently edited edition of Shaw's correspondence, which
is invaluable for much incidental information and comment on
the contemporary theatre. See also item 143.

137   Manvell, Brian. "Cartoons of Theatrical Interest Appearing in VANITY
FAIR." TN, 19 (1965), 126-33.

Illustrated, with a list of numerous theatrical people who were
caricatured in VANITY FAIR.

138   Brown, Eluned, ed. THE LONDON THEATRE 1811-1866. SELECTIONS
FROM THE DIARY OF HENRY CRABB ROBINSON. London: Society for
Theatre Research, 1966. 227 p.

The editor supplies a substantial introduction, useful notes, and a list of plays referred to in Robinson's diary.

139   Beerbohm, Max. MORE THEATRES 1898-1903: WITH AN INTRODUC-
TION BY RUPERT HART-DAVIS. New York: Taplinger, 1969. 624 p.

A further selection of Beerbohm's SATURDAY REVIEW pieces.
See item 123.

140   _____. LAST THEATRES 1904-1910: WITH AN INTRODUCTION BY
RUPERT HART-DAVIS. London: Hart-Davis, 1970. 553 p.

See items 123, 139.

141   Robinson, J.W., ed. THEATRICAL STREET BALLADS: SOME NINETEENTH-
CENTURY STREET BALLADS ABOUT THE THEATRE. London: Society for
Theatre Research, 1971. 111 p.

As George Speaight says in a foreword, "This collection . . .
illustrates vividly the place that the theatre played in the
popular mind during the nineteenth century." The editor
supplies a substantial introduction, useful notes, and a list
of works cited in this amusing and instructive volume.

142   Rowell, George, ed. VICTORIAN DRAMATIC CRITICISM. London:
Methuen, 1971. xxvi, 372 p.

Not just Victorian criticism, but the whole nineteenth century.
An extensive and very useful selection. Eighteen critics are
represented, and the editor gives brief but helpful biographical
notes on each. The essays are organized under five main
headings: actors, theatres and audiences, drama, pantomime
and music hall, and the critic on his craft. While there is
a brief, useful introduction, the book is not indexed and
hence much information cannot be easily located.

143   Laurence, Dan H., ed. BERNARD SHAW: COLLECTED LETTERS 1898-
1910. London: Reinhardt, 1972. xxiv, 1,017 p.

See also item 136.

144   Reiman, Donald H., ed. THE ROMANTICS REVIEWED: CONTEMPO-
RARY REVIEWS OF BRITISH ROMANTIC WRITERS. 9 vols. New York
and London: Garland, 1972.

"Contains all contemporary British periodical reviews of the
first (or other significant early) editions from 1793 to 1824
of works by William Wordsworth, Samuel Taylor Coleridge,
George Gordon Byron (6th Baron Byron), Percy Bysshe Shelley,
and John Keats." An invaluable anthology of reviews repro-
duced in facsimile.

145   Morgan, Peter F., ed. THE LETTERS OF THOMAS HOOD. Toronto:
      University of Toronto Press, 1973. xxviii, 703 p.

>   Includes letters to Bulwer-Lytton, Lord Byron, Dickens,
>   Jerrold, and Mark Lemon, as well as much background
>   information.

146   Nelson, Alfred L., and Gilbert B. Cross, eds. DRURY LANE JOURNAL:
      SELECTIONS FROM JAMES WINSTON'S DIARIES 1819-1827. London:
      Society for Theatre Research, 1974. xv, 176 p.

>   The diaries of Drury Lane's acting manager, splendidly edited
>   and indexed; the diaries "give us an eyewitness account of
>   the London theatrical scene during the first third of the nine-
>   teenth century. . . . Winston touched the lives of most of
>   the prominent literary and theatrical personalities of his day,
>   many of whom are mentioned in these pages."

Chapter 2

MODERN HISTORY AND CRITICISM

147 Brown, Calvin. "The Later English Drama." Ph.D. Dissertation, University of Colorado, 1899.

148 Broadbent, R.J. A HISTORY OF PANTOMIME. London: Simpkin, Marshall, & Co., [1901]; rpt. New York: Blom, 1964. 226 p.

> Fewer than fifty pages on the nineteenth century, with one short chapter on Grimaldi. No illustrations; no index.

149 _____. STAGE WHISPERS. London: Simpkin, Marshall, Hamilton, Kent & Co., 1901. 184 p.

> Eleven essays on miscellaneous theatrical subjects, some relevant to the nineteenth century, e.g., "A History of Theatrical Costume." The treatment is superficial.

150 Hooper, W. Eden. THE STAGE IN THE YEAR 1900. A SOUVENIR, BEING A COLLECTION OF PHOTOGRAVURE PLATES PORTRAYING THE LEADING PLAYERS AND PLAYWRIGHTS OF THE DAY AND A HISTORY OF THE STAGE DURING THE VICTORIAN ERA. 2 vols. London: Spottiswoode, 1901. xiv, 280; iv, 184 p.

> Includes lengthy survey of the Victorian stage by Joseph Knight and over one hundred portraits, each with a brief biography by Hooper.

151 Gosse, Edmund. "The Revival of Poetic Drama." ATLANTIC MONTHLY, 90 (1902), 156-66.

> With some reference to nineteenth-century verse dramatists.

152 Fitzgerald, Percy. THE GARRICK CLUB. London: Elliot Stock, 1904. xix, 252 p.

> Contains anecdotes about and portraits of numerous nineteenth-century theatrical members of the club.

153 Nicholson, Watson. THE STRUGGLE FOR A FREE STAGE IN LONDON. London: Constable, 1906; rpt. New York: Blom, 1966. xii, 475 p.

"The subject of this volume is the story of the long struggle to free London of the theatrical monopoly, a struggle which began almost within the lifetime of the second Charles himself, and culminated in the parliamentary act of 1843" (preface). This is the standard work on the complex but vitally important monopoly disputes of the early nineteenth century.

154 Darbyshire, Alfred. THE ART OF THE VICTORIAN STAGE. NOTES AND RECOLLECTIONS. London and Manchester: Sherrat & Hughes, 1907; rpt. New York: Blom, 1969. [viii], 182 p.

Essays on Charles Kean, Phelps, Calvert, Irving, "Robertsonian and Modern Drama," and some interesting observations on theatre architecture from the point of view of safety regulations.

155 Child, Harold. "Nineteenth-Century Drama." THE CAMBRIDGE HISTORY OF ENGLISH LITERATURE. Ed. A.W. Ward and A.R. Waller. Cambridge: At the University Press, 1907-16. xiii, part 2, 255-74.

A brief introductory survey.

156 Borsa, Mario. THE ENGLISH STAGE OF TO-DAY. TRANSLATED FROM THE ORIGINAL ITALIAN AND EDITED WITH A PREFATORY NOTE BY SELWYN BRINTON. London and New York: John Lane, 1908. xi, 317 p.

A study admired by William Archer as "not only a wide but a minute survey of the Stageland of to-day and yesterday" (preface).

157 G., G. M. THE STAGE CENSOR: AN HISTORICAL SKETCH 1554-1907. London: Sampson Low, Marston & Co., 1908. 128 p.

There is a short, very sketchy, chapter on nineteenth-century theatrical censorship.

158 McNeill, William Everett. "A History of the English Drama from 1788 to 1832, with Special Reference to Theatrical Conditions." Ph.D. Dissertation, Harvard University, 1909.

159 Sharp, R. Farquharson. A SHORT HISTORY OF THE ENGLISH STAGE FROM ITS BEGINNINGS TO THE SUMMER OF THE YEAR 1908. London: Walter Scott, 1909. [viii], 355 p.

The study is concerned primarily with theatres and actors.

There are chapters on the leading actors of the nineteenth
century and on provincial, Scottish, and Dublin theatres.
There is a good index, but no bibliography or illustrations.

160 Wood, Alice I. Perry. THE STAGE HISTORY OF SHAKESPEARE'S KING
RICHARD THE THIRD. New York: Columbia University Press, 1909; rpt.
New York: AMS Press, 1965. xii, 187 p.

Includes a chapter "From Garrick to Irving--1741-1897."

161 Carter, Huntly. THE NEW SPIRIT IN DRAMA AND ART. London:
Frank Palmer, 1912. x, 270 p.

162 Dukes, Ashley. MODERN DRAMATISTS. London: Frank Palmer, 1912;
rpt. Freeport, N.Y.: Books for Libraries, 1967. vi, 310 p.

Dukes's is a selective survey of the state of European drama
at the turn of the century. He makes no apologies for his
somewhat arbitrary and dogmatic stances.

163 Elton, Oliver. A SURVEY OF ENGLISH LITERATURE 1780-1830. 2
vols. London: Edward Arnold, 1912. xv, 456; xii, 475 p.

Volume two includes some literary discussion of the plays of
Southey, Byron, and Shelley as well as a brief survey of other
drama of the early nineteenth century.

164 Oliver, D.E. THE ENGLISH STAGE: ITS ORIGINS AND MODERN
DEVELOPMENTS. London: John Ouseley, [1912]. xv, 152 p.

The nineteenth-century material is of an introductory nature
only.

165 Palmer, John. THE CENSOR AND THE THEATRES. London: T. Fisher
Unwin, 1912. 307 p.

This is primarily an account, by a staunch opponent of the
censorship, of the Report of the 1909 Joint Select Committee
of the House of Lords and the House of Commons on Stage
Plays (Censorship). Many leading figures of the late nineteenth-
century theatre gave evidence before this committee.

166 Andrews, Charlton. THE DRAMA TO-DAY. Philadelphia and London:
J.B. Lippincott, 1913. 236 p.

This is a survey of American and European drama as well as
British, but there is a substantial chapter devoted to the
British drama, with discussion of the leading playwrights at
the turn of the century.

167   Armstrong, Cecil Ferrard. SHAKESPEARE TO SHAW: STUDIES IN THE LIFE'S WORK OF SIX DRAMATISTS OF THE ENGLISH STAGE. London: Mills & Boon, [1913]; rpt. Freeport, N.Y.: Books for Libraries, 1968. v, 330 p.

> There are chapters on Robertson and Pinero.

168   Fowell, Frank, and Frank Palmer. CENSORSHIP IN ENGLAND. London: Frank Palmer, 1913; rpt. New York: Blom, 1969; New York: Burt Franklin, 1970. xii, 390 p.

> A history of theatre censorship from the beginnings to the early twentieth century. Appendices include a table of play licenses granted and refused, 1852–1912, and extracts from the 1843 Theatres Act.

169   Jackson, Holbrook. THE EIGHTEEN NINETIES. A REVIEW OF ART AND IDEAS AT THE CLOSE OF THE NINETEENTH CENTURY. London: Grant Richards, 1913; rpt. Harmondsworth: Penguin, 1950. 368 p.

> Includes a chapter on "The Higher Drama."

170   Chandler, Frank Wadleigh. ASPECTS OF MODERN DRAMA. New York: Macmillan, 1914; rpt. St. Clair Shores, Mich.: Scholarly Press, 1971. viii, 494 p.

> This work consists of a series of public lectures which examine the contemporary drama by theme rather than by author. Dramatists mentioned include Granville-Barker, Bjornson, Brieux, Hauptmann, Ibsen, H.A. Jones, Maeterlinck, Stephen Phillips, Pinero, Shaw, Strindberg, Sudermann, Chekhov, and Wilde. The public nature of these lectures renders them less incisive than they might have been.

171   Hamilton, Clayton. STUDIES IN STAGECRAFT. New York: Holt, 1914. 298 p.

> This study contains a good deal of discussion of some late nineteenth-century playwrights and the conditions and conventions of the Victorian theatre.

172   Henderson, Archibald. THE CHANGING DRAMA: CONTRIBUTIONS AND TENDENCIES. New York: Holt, 1914. xvi, 321 p.

> The aim of this work is an evaluation of the theatre and drama "as the symbol of a general movement in human consciousness" rather than a treatment of individual dramatists and movements. This approach results in theoretical generalities rather than specifics, assertion instead of discussion. Moreover, Henderson fails to cite and document his sources, thus limiting what usefulness the book has.

173 McLeod, Malcolm. "French Influence on English Drama during the First Forty Years of the Nineteenth Century." Ph.D. Dissertation, Harvard University, 1914.

174 Schelling, Felix E. ENGLISH DRAMA. London: Dent; New York: Dutton, 1914. [vii], 341 p.

> There is an outline of the nineteenth century in chapter twelve, "English Drama since Sheridan."

175 Sowers, William L. "Influences upon the English Drama and the English Stage, 1865-1896." Ph.D. Dissertation, Harvard University, 1914.

176 Cooke, Margaret W. "Schiller's ROBBERS in England." MLR, 11 (1916), 156-75.

> Discusses the influence of DIE RAUEBER on English plays of the Romantic period.

177 Dye, William S. A STUDY OF MELODRAMA IN ENGLAND FROM 1800-1840. State College, Pa.: Nittany Printing and Publishing Co., 1919. 54 p.

178 Harbeson, William Page. "The Elizabethan Influence on the Tragedy of the Late 18th and Early 19th Centuries." Ph.D. Dissertation, University of Pennsylvania, 1920.

179 Thaler, Alvin. "Milton in the Theatre." SP, 17 (1920), 269-307.

> Includes discussion of several nineteenth-century productions.

180 Odell, George C.D. SHAKESPEARE FROM BETTERTON TO IRVING. 2 vols. London: Constable, 1920; rpt. New York: Blom, 1963.

> Odell's book is essential for an understanding of nineteenth-century Shakespearean production methods.

181 Sharp, R. Farquharson. "Travesties of Shakespeare's Plays." THE LIBRARY, 4th series, 1 (1920), 1-20.

> Discusses nineteenth-century parodies of Shakespeare.

182 White, Newman I. "The English Romantic Writers as Dramatists." SR, 30 (1922), 206-15.

> An unconvincing attempt to explain the Romantics' failure to achieve success as dramatists. "The spirit of great drama," we are told, "rests at the centre of human nature and can be evoked only by a deep knowledge of humanity." The Roman-

tics apparently lacked this knowledge and were therefore
doomed to failure as dramatists.

183   Agate, James. WHITE HORSE AND RED LION: ESSAYS IN GUSTO.
       London: Collins, 1924. 273 p.

       Contains an essay, "An Old Actor," on John Philip Kemble.

184   Baring, Maurice. PUNCH AND JUDY & OTHER ESSAYS. London:
       Heinemann, 1924. x, 370 p.

       Baring wrote essays on a number of subjects related to the
       nineteenth-century stage, e.g. Sarah Bernhardt, Gilbert and
       Sullivan, Mrs. Patrick Campbell, and THE CENCI.

185   Morgan, A.E. TENDENCIES OF MODERN ENGLISH DRAMA. London:
       Constable, 1924. 320 p.

       There are short chapters on Early Victorians, Robertson, Late
       Victorians (mainly Grundy), Jones, and Pinero.

186   Disher, M[aurice] Willson. CLOWNS AND PANTOMIMES. London: Cons-
       table, 1925; rpt. New York and London: Blom, 1968. xx, 344 p.

       A sweeping survey from the Greeks to the early twentieth
       century. As far as the nineteenth century is concerned, the
       book is largely superseded by David Mayer's study (item 384),
       but as with other books by Disher this one contains many in-
       teresting illustrations.

187   Beaumont, Cyril W. THE HISTORY OF HARLEQUIN. London: C.W.
       Beaumont, 1926; rpt. New York: Blom, 1967. 156 p.

       There are two short chapters on English harlequins and
       numerous illustrations.

188   Brinton, Crane. THE POLITICAL IDEAS OF THE ENGLISH ROMANTI-
       CISTS. London: Oxford University Press, 1926. 242 p.

       Includes some concise comments on political aspects of Byron's
       plays.

189   Darton, F.J. Harvey. VINCENT CRUMMLES: HIS THEATRE AND HIS
       TIMES. London: Wells Gardner Darton, 1926. lxx, 230 p. Illus.

       In addition to extrapolating the theatrical portions of NICHO-
       LAS NICKLEBY, Darton provides a brief outline of the provin-
       cial circuits (notably at Portsmouth, Kent, Bristol, Bath, Nor-
       wich, and York) and the general repertory system.

190 Landa, M.J. THE JEW IN DRAMA. London: P.S. King & Son, 1926.
340 p.

> This is an interesting study, with considerable discussion of
> the Jew as he appeared in many nineteenth-century plays.
> There is also an appendix, "Edmund Kean Not a Jew."

191 Stokoe, F.W. GERMAN INFLUENCE IN THE ENGLISH ROMANTIC
PERIOD, WITH SPECIAL REFERENCE TO SCOTT, COLERIDGE, SHELLEY
AND BYRON. Cambridge: At the University Press, 1926. xii, 202 p.

> Comparatively little of this study is related directly to the
> drama, but it provides a good general background to the re-
> lationship between the German and English Romantic drama.

192 Thompson, Alan Reynolds. "A Study of Melodrama as a Dramatic
Genre." Ph.D. Dissertation, Harvard University, 1926.

193 Watson, Ernest Bradlee. SHERIDAN TO ROBERTSON: A STUDY OF
THE NINETEENTH-CENTURY LONDON STAGE. Cambridge, Mass.:
Harvard University Press, 1926; rpt. New York: Blom, 1963. xv,
485 p.

> This first serious and comprehensive history of the nineteenth-
> century theatre is still a standard work. There are several
> illustrations, a bibliography, and full index.

194 Cunliffe, John W. MODERN ENGLISH PLAYWRIGHTS. A SHORT
HISTORY OF THE ENGLISH DRAMA FROM 1825. New York and London: Harper, 1927. x, 260 p.

> The opening chapter presents a sketchy and unsympathetic
> survey of the nineteenth-century theatre. There follow brief
> discussions of Robertson, Gilbert, Jones, Pinero, and Wilde,
> and lengthier sections on Shaw, Barrie, Galsworthy, Granville-
> Barker, and Hankin.

195 Newton, H. Chance. CRIME AND THE DRAMA: OR, DARK DEEDS
DRAMATIZED. London: Stanley Paul, 1927. 284 p.

> A descriptive, rather than scholarly or critical, account of
> the dramatization of criminal incidents and types. Topics
> include Jack Sheppard, Jonathan Wilde, Dick Turpin, pirates,
> slave dramas, treason, rebellion, and foreign imports of simi-
> larly dastardly drama.

195a White, Henry Adelbert. SIR WALTER SCOTT'S NOVELS ON THE
STAGE. New Haven: Yale University Press; London: Oxford University
Press, 1927. 259 p.

White recounts the plots of various adaptations and also gives brief stage histories; generally the method is descriptive rather than critical.

196 Odell, George C.D. ANNALS OF THE NEW YORK STAGE. 15 vols. New York: Columbia University Press, 1927-49.

This monumental work is invaluable for tracing the fortunes of English plays and players on the New York stage.

197 Balmforth, Ramsden. THE PROBLEM-PLAY AND ITS INFLUENCE ON MODERN THOUGHT AND LIFE. London: George Allen & Unwin, 1928. 155 p.

"The purpose of this book is to show how deeply Problem-Plays have influenced, and may influence, the public mind not only on sex and marriage problems, but also on social, ethical, and religious problems" (preface). A worthy aim, but almost impossible to realize.

198 Bowley, Victor E.A. "English Versions of Victor Hugo's Plays." FRENCH QUARTERLY, 10 (1928), 86-98.

Includes a list of English plays, 1827-1904, founded on those of Hugo.

198a Nag, U.C. "The English Theatre of the Romantic Period." NINE-TEENTH CENTURY AND AFTER, 104 (1928), 384-98.

This is a brief and heavily footnoted history of the theatre during the Romantic period. It says little about Romantic drama and contains nothing which cannot be found in standard histories.

199 Rubinstein, H.F. THE ENGLISH DRAMA. London: Ernest Benn, 1928. 80 p.

Includes half-a-dozen pages on the nineteenth century.

200 Thompson, Alan Reynolds. "Melodrama and Tragedy." PMLA, 43 (1928), 810-35.

The discussion includes references to nineteenth-century plays.

201 Thompson, L.F. KOTZEBUE: A SURVEY OF HIS PROGRESS IN EN-GLAND AND FRANCE PRECEDED BY A CONSIDERATION OF THE CRITI-CAL ATTITUDE TO HIM IN GERMANY. Paris: Libraire Ancienne Honoré Champion, 1928. 174 p.

The study includes a useful survey of nineteenth-century

English productions of Kotzebue's plays.

202 Wray, Edith. "English Adaptations of French Drama Between 1780 and 1815." MLN, 43 (1928), 87-90.

The list includes about fifty early nineteenth-century plays.

203 Thorndike, Ashley H. ENGLISH COMEDY. New York: Macmillan, 1929. vii, 635 p.

Over one hundred pages are devoted to nineteenth-century comedy, with some discussion of all the major comic dramatists from O'Keeffe to Shaw.

204 Dickinson, Thomas H. THE CONTEMPORARY DRAMA OF ENGLAND. Rev. ed. Boston: Little, Brown, 1931. 355 p.

In addition to early chapters devoted to the general development of the Victorian theatre, this fairly adequate, though not profound, study includes chapters on H.A. Jones, Pinero, Barrie, Shaw, and later dramatists.

205 Ellehauge, Martin. STRIKING FIGURES AMONG MODERN ENGLISH DRAMATISTS: WITH AN INTRODUCTORY ESSAY ON MAETERLINCK. Copenhagen: Levin and Munksgaard, 1931. 151 p.

Although Ellehauge's rather brief book is devoted largely to playwrights of the early twentieth century, it contains a suggestive chapter on Barrie. Reissued in a limited edition by Folcroft Library Editions, 1971, 322 p.

206 Miller, Anna Irene. THE INDEPENDENT THEATRE IN EUROPE, 1887 TO THE PRESENT. New York: Ray Long and Richard R. Smith, 1931. xi, 435 p.

There is a long chapter on the establishment and development of the Independent Theatre movement in England. Bibliography.

207 Mackechnie, Samuel. POPULAR ENTERTAINMENT THROUGH THE AGES. London: Sampson, Low, Marston & Co., [1931]. xvi, 240 p.

An extensively illustrated work with discussion of nineteenth-century music hall, pantomime, and circus.

208 Norenilis, Alma C. "Dramatic Criticism in Nineteenth Century Periodicals 1800-1830, and Its Influence on Contemporary Drama." Ph.D. Dissertation, University of London, 1931.

209 Sawyer, Newell W. THE COMEDY OF MANNERS FROM SHERIDAN
TO MAUGHAM. Philadelphia: University of Pennsylvania Press, 1931.
vii, 275 p.

> Although a considerable portion of this book is devoted to
> Robertson, Gilbert, Wilde, Pinero, Jones, and other play-
> wrights, it does not satisfactorily come to grips with the
> overall topic. Criticism gives way to plot-telling, and
> textual evidence is scanty. There is, however, an exten-
> sive bibliography.

210 Ellehauge, Martin. "The Initial Stages in the Development of the English Problem-Play." ENGLISCHE STUDIEN, 66 (1931-32), 373-401.

> A discussion of the origins of the "problem play" and its
> development by Gilbert, Grundy, Pinero, H.A. Jones, and
> Wilde.

211 Byrne, Muriel St. Clare. "Stalls and Places in the Orchestra." TLS,
24 November 1932, p. 888.

> Interesting notes on the introduction of stalls in London
> theatres, beginning in the 1820's.

212 Donegan, Sylvia Eugenie. "The Failure of the Poetical Drama in the
Victorian Period, With Special Attention to Browning, Bulwer-Lytton,
and Tennyson." Ph.D. Dissertation, Boston University, 1932.

213 Dubois, Arthur E. "The Beginnings of Tragic Comedy in the Drama of
the Nineteenth Century." Ph.D. Dissertation, Johns Hopkins University,
1932.

214 Wilson, A.E. PENNY PLAIN TWOPENCE COLOURED: A HISTORY OF
THE JUVENILE DRAMA. Foreword. Charles B. Cochran. London:
Harrap, 1932; rpt. New York and London: Blom, 1969. 118 p.

> The first book on the subject. It is generously illustrated,
> although not in color, and there are two useful appendices--
> one a list of publishers of juvenile drama, the other a list of
> plays published by William West between 1811 and 1831.
> Wilson also provides a short list of newspaper and periodical
> articles on the subject.

215 Bleackley, Horace. JACK SHEPPARD . . . WITH AN EPILOGUE ON
JACK SHEPPARD IN LITERATURE AND DRAMA . . . BY S.M. ELLIS.
Edinburgh and London: W. Hodge, 1933. xiv, 260 p.

> Ellis refers to a number of nineteenth-century plays based on
> the life of Sheppard, the notorious eighteenth-century criminal.

216 Perugini, Mark Edward. THE OMNIBUS BOX: BEING DIGRESSIONS AND ASIDES ON SOCIAL AND THEATRICAL LIFE IN LONDON AND PARIS, 1830-1850. London: Jarrolds, 1933. 287 p.

> Forty-eight plates.

217 Christensen, France. "Three Romantic Poets and the Drama," Ph.D. Dissertation, Harvard University, 1934.

218 Covert, Marjorie A. "Realism in the Prose Theatre of France and England, 1890-1910." Ph.D. Dissertation, University of Wisconsin, 1934.

219 Dubois, Arthur E. "Shakespeare and 19th-Century Drama." ELH, 1 (1934), 163-96.

> As much a wide-ranging and sympathetic analysis of nineteenth-century drama as an essay on Shakespeare.

220 Thouless, Priscilla. MODERN POETIC DRAMA. Oxford: Blackwell, 1934. iii, 204 p.

> Although this book concentrates mainly on poetic drama of the first thirty years of the twentieth century, it contains a useful, though short, general introduction which surveys poetic drama in the nineteenth century and a chapter on Stephen Phillips.

221 Lawrence, W.J. OLD THEATRE DAYS AND WAYS. London: Harrap, 1935. 256 p.

> A readable hodgepodge of theatre history with interesting illustrations.

222 Pellizzi, Camillo. ENGLISH DRAMA: THE LAST GREAT PHASE. Trans. from Italian by Rowan Williams. Foreword. Orlo Williams. London: Macmillan, 1935. ix, 306 p.

> Chapter 2, "The Middle Classes at the Theatre," is a survey of nineteenth-century English drama. Intended for an uninformed Italian audience, it is no more than a useful summary for the beginner.

223 Wilson, A.E. KING PANTO. THE STORY OF PANTOMIME. New York: Dutton, 1935. 262 p.

> A general, popular history of pantomime, with a number of nineteenth-century illustrations.

224   Arthur, George. FROM PHELPS TO GIELGUD. London: Chapman and
      Hall, 1936; rpt. New York: Blom, 1972. 256 p.

        This is more reminiscence than history. There is a brief
        introduction by John Gielgud, ten plates, and a facsimile
        of an Irving-Arthur letter.

225   Boas, Frederick S. FROM RICHARDSON TO PINERO: SOME INNOVA-
      TORS AND IDEALISTS. London: John Murray, 1936. vii, 292 p.

        Contains a chapter on "Edmund Kean in His Heroic Parts,"
        a reconsideration of Kean's place in the history of the English
        stage.

226   Nicoll, Allardyce. THE ENGLISH THEATRE: A SHORT HISTORY.
      London: Nelson, 1936. xi, 252 p.

        One introductory chapter on the nineteenth century.

227   Reynolds, Ernest. EARLY VICTORIAN DRAMA (1830-1870). Cambridge,
      Eng.: Heffer, 1936; rpt. New York: Blom, 1956. vii, 163 p.

        This is a fairly short but serious study in which the theatre,
        as well as the drama, is considered. Actors are, however,
        relegated to an appendix. There is an interesting appendix
        on "The Dramatization of Fiction in the Mid-Nineteenth
        Century," a good bibliography, and an adequate index.

228   Disher, M[aurice] Willson. WINKLES AND CHAMPAGNE: COMEDIES
      AND TRAGEDIES OF THE MUSIC HALL. London: B.T. Batsford, 1938.
      xii, 147 p.

        This is a general history of the music hall with some splendid
        illustrations, some in color.

229   Grauel, George E. "The Decline of Tragedy in the Early Nineteenth
      Century." Ph.D. Dissertation, University of St. Louis, 1938.

230   Ball, Robert Hamilton. THE AMAZING CAREER OF SIR GILES OVER-
      REACH. Princeton: Princeton University Press; London: Oxford Univer-
      sity Press, 1939. ix, 467 p.

        The study contains considerable information on nineteenth-
        century productions of Massinger's play, including performances
        by both Keans, Cooke, Phelps, and Junius Brutus Booth. Illus-
        trated.

231   Girard, Clet A. "The Equestrian Drama of the Nineteenth Century."
      Ph.D. Dissertation, Louisiana State University, 1939.

232 Merriam, Harold G. EDWARD MOXON: PUBLISHER OF POETS. New
York: Columbia University Press, 1939. vii, 223 p.

>   Includes discussion of Moxon's affairs with some nineteenth-
>   century playwrights, e.g., Knowles and Talfourd.

233 Troesch, Helen D. "The Negro in English Dramatic Literature on the
Stage and a Bibliography of Plays with Negro Characters." Ph.D.
Dissertation, Western Reserve University, 1940.

234 Disher, M[aurice] Willson. FAIRS, CIRCUSES AND MUSIC HALLS. London:
William Collins, 1942. 48 p.

>   A brief though useful pictorial history which demonstrates the
>   connections among and evolution of village fairs, circuses,
>   and music halls. There is a considerable emphasis on the
>   nineteenth century.

235 Eaton, Julia. "Classic and Popular Elements in English Comedy of the
Eighteenth and Nineteenth Centuries." Ph.D. Dissertation, Cornell
University, 1943.

236 Irwin, Joseph J. "Dramatizations of English Novels on the Nineteenth
Century English Stage." Ph.D. Dissertation, University of Iowa, 1943.

237 Williams, Charles D. "A Note on Pollock's Plays." N&Q, 185 (1943),
347-48.

>   Williams catalogs the various plays offered by Ben Pollock, a
>   publisher of toy theatres. See corrections to this article by Williams
>   and others in N&Q, 186 (1944), 27, 168; 187 (1944), 233-34, 285.

238 Morice, Gerald. "Long Live the Juvenile Drama." N&Q, 186 (1944),
157-58; 187 (1944), 253-55.

>   Morice gives further information on "Pollock's" toy theatre-
>   shop in Hoxton and the possibility of its closure. There are
>   numerous references to newspaper reports following up this
>   item and giving interesting details about the death throes of
>   this business.

239 Williams, Charles D. "A Note on H.G. Clarke Productions." N&Q,
186 (1944), 19-20.

>   Williams contributes a brief history of Clarke, publisher of
>   many "penny plain, twopence coloured." See also N&Q,
>   186 (1944), 79, 212, 231.

240 Morice, Gerald. "Victorian Toy Theatres, Parlour Pastimes and Pursuits, and Street Games." N&Q, 187 (1944), 157-59.

> This is a ragbag contribution of notes on various aspects of toy theatres, compiled mainly from manufacturers' advertisements.

241 Williams, Charles D. "A Note on Toy Theatre Lighting." N&Q, 187 (1944), 212.

> Williams offers some personal conjectures on what form lighting took for toy theatres. See also N&Q, 188 (1945), 20-21, 86.

242 _____. "A Note on Wells Gardner Darton & Co. Ltd." N&Q, 187 (1944), 232-33.

> A brief history of a toy theatre publishing firm. See also N&Q, 187 (1944), 305-6; 188 (1945), 41.

243 Wilson, A.E. PANTOMIME PAGEANT. London: Stanley Paul, [1945]. 136 p.

> Interesting for the extensive quotation from a number of nineteenth-century sources.

244 Stone, M.W. "Juvenile Drama and J.H. Jameson." TN, 1 (1945-47), 5-6.

> Jameson was an early publisher of juvenile drama; Stone includes a list of the plays he published.

245 _____. "William Blake and the Juvenile Drama." TN, 1 (1945-47), 41.

> Stone demonstrates that Blake did not work as a designer for William West, the publisher of juvenile drama, as has commonly been supposed.

246 _____. "Juvenile Drama Publishers--The Dyers." TN, 1 (1945-47), 80.

> Early nineteenth-century publications.

247 Agate, James. THOSE WERE THE NIGHTS. London: Hutchinson, [1946]. xi, 145 p.

> Agate's anthology of theatre reviews and the like are culled from the NEWS CHRONICLE, DAILY TELEGRAPH, EVENING STANDARD, STAGE, and STAR. He covers many significant

productions, actors, and events in the period 1887 to 1906.

248   Ervine, St. John. "The Victorian Theatre." FORTNIGHTLY, n.s. 160 (1946), 353-59.

This is a general review-essay on the salient features of Victorian theatre, prompted by the first publication of Nicoll's HISTORY OF LATE NINETEENTH CENTURY DRAMA (See item 321).

249   Scott, Harold. THE EARLY DOORS: ORIGINS OF THE MUSIC HALL. London: Nicholson and Watson, 1946. 259 p.

A detailed and illustrated history of music hall with a song index, a general index, and a bibliography.

250   Downer, Alan S. "Mr. Dangle's Defense: Acting and Stage History." ENGLISH INSTITUTE ESSAYS, 1946. New York: Columbia University Press, 1947. 159-90.

Partly a history of stage history, partly an addition to stage history (e.g. an analysis of Macready's MACBETH), partly a defense of stage history--a valuable study.

251   Eastman, Fred. CHRIST IN THE DRAMA: A STUDY OF THE INFLU-ENCE OF CHRIST ON THE DRAMA OF ENGLAND AND AMERICA: THE SHAFFER LECTURES OF NORTHWESTERN UNIVERSITY, 1946. New York: Macmillan, 1947; rpt. Freeport, N.Y.: Books for Libraries, 1972. xiii, 174 p.

Of peripheral interest to major concerns of this bibliography. However, the book includes a chapter on Shaw. The study as a whole is rather too short for its subject and is not very penetrating.

252   Evans, Bertrand. GOTHIC DRAMA FROM WALPOLE TO SHELLEY. Berkeley and Los Angeles: University of California Press, 1947. viii, 257 p.

Evans's study is designed to redress the distorted impression that Gothic literature is to be found solely in Gothic fiction. He examines in some detail the roots and development of the genre and concentrates on Ann Radcliffe, "Monk" Lewis, and Joanna Baillie as well as discussing plays by Wordsworth, Scott, Shelley, and Byron. An appendix lists Gothic plays comprehensively from 1768 to 1810, and representatively to 1823.

253   Macqueen-Pope, W. CARRIAGES AT ELEVEN: THE STORY OF THE EDWARDIAN THEATRE. London: Hutchinson, 1947; rpt. London: Hale, 1972. 232 p.

Includes discussion of many nineteenth-century performers and managers whose careers began in the Victorian era. There are numerous plates.

254 Pallette, Drew B. "The Development of Late-Victorian Drama, as Seen in London Periodicals, 1879-93." Ph.D. Dissertation, Harvard University, 1947.

255 Tyrwhitt-Drake, Garrard. THE ENGLISH CIRCUS AND FAIR GROUND. 2nd ed. London: Methuen, 1947. xiv, 215 p.

With a chapter on nineteenth-century circuses.

256 Mander, Raymond, and Joe Mitchenson. "MARIA MARTEN--An Early Version." TN, 2 (1947-48), 38-39.

At the Lincoln theatre, 27 October 1830.

257 Baker, Seymour O. "The English Farce from 1800-1880." Ph.D. Dissertation, Harvard University, 1948.

258 Rulfs, Donald J. "Beaumont and Fletcher on the London Stage 1776-1833." PMLA, 63 (1948), 1245-64.

259 Walton, Thomas. "Notes for a History of Juvenile Drama." TN, 3 (1948-49), 64-66.

260 Disher, Maurice Willson. BLOOD AND THUNDER: MID-VICTORIAN MELODRAMA AND ITS ORIGINS. London: Frederick Muller, 1949. 280 p.

A useful survey, interestingly illustrated, but short on scholarship.

261 Rulfs, Donald J. "Reception of the Elizabethan Playwrights on the London Stage 1776-1833." SP, 46 (1949), 54-69.

The period from 1790 to 1810 saw a "perceptible decline in interest," but the period 1810 to 1833 brought a "decided renewal of interest in the old plays." This is a well-documented article which is very instructive about early nineteenth-century theatrical tastes.

262 Vardac, A. Nicholas. STAGE TO SCREEN: THEATRICAL METHOD FROM GARRICK TO GRIFFITH. Cambridge, Mass.: Harvard University Press, 1949; rpt. New York: Blom, 1968. xxvi, 283 p.

Vardac examines the relationship between eighteenth- and

nineteenth-century production techniques and film techniques; an unusual and illuminating approach to theatre history.

263 Wilson, A.E. THE STORY OF PANTOMIME. London: Home and Van Thal, 1949. 142 p.

Another Wilson popular history.

264 Seaton-Reid, D. "An Early West Sheet?" TN, 4 (1949-50), 36-37.

The essay discusses a sheet of characters from the juvenile version of John Millingen's THE BEEHIVE (Lyceum, 19 January 1811). See items 265, 279.

265 Spencer, H.D. "A West Artist." TN, 4 (1949-50), 37-38.

Concerning a C. Tompkins whose signature appears on some West portraits ca. 1817-19.

266 Downer, Alan S. THE BRITISH DRAMA: A HANDBOOK AND BRIEF CHRONICLE. New York: Appleton-Century-Crofts, 1950. x, 397 p.

A chapter on "The Decline of the Drama" deals with the nineteenth century; included are a few rather uninspiring illustrations and a basic reading list of criticism and plays.

267 Macqueen-Pope, W. THE MELODIES LINGER ON: THE STORY OF MUSIC HALL. London: W.H. Allen, 1950. 459 p.

This is an interesting general history with several illustrations.

268 Sprague, Rosemary. "The Victorian Scene on the London Stage 1843-1883." Ph.D. Dissertation, Western Reserve University, 1950.

269 Taylor, Aline Mackenzie. NEXT TO SHAKESPEARE: OTWAY'S "VENICE PRESERV'D" AND "THE ORPHAN" AND THEIR HISTORY ON THE LONDON STAGE. Durham, N.C.: Duke University Press, 1950; rpt. New York: AMS Press, 1966. viii, 328 p.

Includes considerable detail on nineteenth-century productions.

270 Seaton-Reid, D. "Early West Plates." TN, 5 (1950-51), 42-43.
Rare 1811 plates of juvenile drama.

271 Spencer, H.D. "The Juvenile Drama Artists: William Heath's Early Sheets." TN, 5 (1950-51), 43-44.

272 Enkvist, Nils Erik. CARICATURES OF AMERICANS ON THE ENGLISH

STAGE PRIOR TO 1870. Helsingfors, 1951; rpt. Port Washington, N.Y.: Kennikat Press, 1968. 168 p.

273 Finch, Ernest B. "The Mid-Victorian Theatre as Seen by Its Critics, 1850-1870." Ph.D. Dissertation, Cornell University, 1951.

274 Hudson, Lynton. THE ENGLISH STAGE 1850-1950. London: Harrap, 1951. 223 p.

> A readable account of familiar material, lacking in documentation, bibliography, and index.

275 R., S. [Sybil Rosenfeld]. "Bills of the Play." N&Q, 196 (1951), 321-23.

> A description of the author's collection of Victorian playbills.

276 Short, Ernest. SIXTY YEARS OF THEATRE. London: Eyre & Spottiswoode, 1951. vii, 402 p.

> Mainly popular twentieth-century theatre history, but Irving and some of his contemporaries are included. Material from the same author's THEATRICAL CAVALCADE (1942) and FIFTY YEARS OF VAUDEVILLE (1946) is reprinted in this work.

277 Stoakes, J.P. "English Melodrama: Forerunner of Modern Social Drama." FLORIDA STATE UNIVERSITY STUDIES, 3 (1951), 53-62.

> Not a very penetrating study.

278 White, Eric Walter. THE RISE OF THE ENGLISH OPERA. Intro. Benjamin Britten. New York: Philosophical Library, 1951. 335 p.

> Includes a good deal of information on opera in the nineteenth-century English theatre.

279 Seaton-Reid, D. "A Portrait of William West." TN, 6 (1951-52), 43-44.

> The early nineteenth-century publisher of juvenile drama.

280 South, R.J. "Changes in the Interpretation of Shakespeare in the Second Half of the Nineteenth Century: The Treatment of the Plays by the Theatres and Dramatic Critics." Ph.D. Dissertation, London University, 1951-52.

281 Brook, Donald. THE ROMANCE OF THE ENGLISH THEATRE. London: Rockliff, 1952. 222 p.

> There are two general chapters on the nineteenth century and numerous plates.

282 Clinton-Baddeley, V.C. THE BURLESQUE TRADITION IN THE ENGLISH
THEATRE AFTER 1660. London: Methuen, 1952; rpt. London: Methuen
Library Reprints, 1973. xvi, 152 p.

> A study of "the chief ingredients of English theatrical bur-
> lesque," with attention to Thomas Dibdin, Planché, Gilbert,
> and other nineteenth-century figures. There are several
> plates, a short bibliography, and two indexes.

283 Hobson, Harold. VERDICT AT MIDNIGHT: SIXTY YEARS OF DRAMAT-
IC CRITICISM. London: Longmans, 1952. viii, 199 p.

> This is an interesting reexamination of contemporary critical
> judgments in the light of subsequent theatrical history. Hob-
> son pieces together long extracts from first night reviews with
> his own and other (later) critics' opinions. The whole forms
> a readable and informed history from the 1890's onwards.

284 Pulling, Christopher. THEY WERE SINGING AND WHAT THEY SANG
ABOUT. London: Harrap, 1952. 276 p.

> The songs and singers of the music hall, mainly Victorian.
> Several hundred songs are listed and discussed. Illustrated.

285 STUDIES IN ENGLISH THEATRE HISTORY IN MEMORY OF GABRIELLE
ENTHOVEN. London: Society for Theatre Research, 1952. [vii],
133 p.

> Contains five essays relating to the nineteenth-century theatre:
> James Laver, "Gabrielle Enthoven, O.B.E., and the Enthoven
> Theatre Collection"; Norma Hodgson, "Sarah Baker, 1736/7-
> 1816, 'Governess-General of the Kentish Drama'"; St. Vincent
> Troubridge, "Theatre Riots in London"; "A Bristol Theatre Royal
> Inventory [1829]"; and Barry Jackson, "Barnstorming Days."

286 Speaight, George. "Pope in the Toy Theatre." TN, 7 (1952-53), 62-
63.

> Plagiarism from Pope's ILIAD in a juvenile version of George
> Almar's THE CEDAR CHEST.

287 Hanson, Frank Burton. "London Theatre Audiences of the Nineteenth
Century." Ph.D. Dissertation, Yale University, 1953. 464 p.
(DA#71-20642)

288 Troubridge, St. Vincent. "Fitzball and Elliston: or, How to Submit a
Play in 1820." TN, 7 (1953), 64-65.

The article is based mainly on a letter from Fitzball to
Elliston, offering the latter a play, and as such throws interesting light on how such matters were managed.

289 Stone, M.W. "Shakespeare and the Juvenile Drama." TN, 8 (1953-
54), 65-66.

Early nineteenth-century juvenile drama adapted from Shakespeare.

290 Bair, George Eldridge. "The Plays of the Romantic Poets: Their Place
in Dramatic History." Ph.D. Dissertation, University of Pennsylvania,
1954. 211 p. (DA#54-3058)

An attempt to examine the closet drama of Southey, Coleridge,
Wordsworth, Byron, Keats, Shelley, and Scott in the light of
current theatrical conditions.

291 Clinton-Baddeley, V.C. ALL RIGHT ON THE NIGHT. London: Putnam, 1954. 243 p.

An engrossing study of "Georgian playhouse manners" (i.e.
audience behavior) covering the years 1737-1843. There are
some fine illustrations and two useful indexes.

292 Disher, M[aurice] Willson. MELODRAMA: PLOTS THAT THRILLED. London: Rockliff, 1954. xiv, 210 p.

Discusses the development of the genre from the mid-
nineteenth to the mid-twentieth century and includes
American plays and film. The book's main strength lies
in its excellent and numerous plates and illustrations. It
is well-indexed, with a separate index to all plays mentioned.

293 Kernodle, George R. "Stage Spectacle and Victorian Society." QJS,
40 (1954), 31-36.

By examining a number of differing plays (CASTLE SPECTRE,
FAUST, CAMILLE, UNDER THE GASLIGHT, FASHION, and
RICHARD II), Kernodle demonstrates how stage effects "were
well devised expressions of certain recurrent themes of the
isolated individual and his conflict with the social sanctions
of the time."

294 Mandeville, Gloria E. "A Century of Melodrama on the London Stage,
1790-1890." Ph.D. Dissertation, Columbia University, 1954.

295 Mears, Richard M. "Serious Verse Drama In England, 1812-1850."

Ph.D. Dissertation, University of North Carolina, 1954. 185 p.

296 Guest, Ivor. "Parodies of Giselle on the English Stage (1841-1871)."
TN, 9 (1954-55), 38-46, 79.

With notes by St. Vincent Troubridge.

297 Mander, Raymond, and Joe Mitchenson. HAMLET THROUGH THE AGES:
A PICTORIAL RECORD FROM 1709. Ed. and intro. Herbert Marshall.
2nd ed., rev. and enl. London: Rockliff, 1955. xvii, 158 p.

Includes several nineteenth-century illustrations. Originally
published in 1952.

298 Nicoll, Allardyce. A HISTORY OF ENGLISH DRAMA 1660-1900.
VOLUME IV, EARLY NINETEENTH CENTURY DRAMA 1800-1850. 2nd
ed. Cambridge: At the University Press, 1955. x, 668 p.

Two-thirds of this work (originally published in 1930) consist
of appendices on the theatres and plays of the period.
Nicoll's handlist of plays, arranged by author, is a basic and
indispensable reference tool. See also items 321, 431, and
2429. For corrections to the handlist see below, items
2403-5, 2408-9, 2411-13, 2416, 2430, 2435.

299 Stanton, Stephen S. "English Drama and the French Well-Made Play,
1815-1915." Ph.D. Dissertation, Columbia University, 1955. 370 p.
(DA#55-1114)

Scribe and Sardou's influence on Taylor, Boucicault, Robertson, Gilbert, Pinero, Wilde, and Shaw.

300 Wong, Helen Har Lin. "The Late Victorian Theatre as Reflected in THE
THEATRE, 1878-1897." Ph.D. Dissertation, Louisiana State University,
1955. 226 p. (DA#55-1385)

THE THEATRE was an influential and highly regarded
theatrical periodical.

301 Macqueen-Pope, W. NIGHTS OF GLADNESS. London: Hutchinson,
1956. 268 p.

This is a not-too-accurate history of the musical play in all
its manifestations, and is clearly not directed at the serious
student of drama.

302 Rowell, George. THE VICTORIAN THEATRE: A SURVEY. London:
Oxford University Press, 1956. xiv, 203 p.

Actually covers 1792-1914. This is a concise and intelligent
survey by a leading theatre scholar. There are several good

illustrations, a select list of plays, and a bibliography. One
of the best introductions available.

303 Trewin, J.C. VERSE DRAMA SINCE 1800. Cambridge, Eng.: National
Book League, 1956. 27 p.

This is a brief but well-written survey of 150 years of verse
drama with a short bibliography of plays and critical studies.

304 Speaight, George. "The M.W. Stone Collection." TN, 11 (1956-57),
62-63.

Juvenile drama in the Enthoven Collection.

305 Edwards, Charlene Frances. "The Tradition for Breeches in the Three
Centuries that Professional Actresses Have Played Roles on the English-
speaking Stage." Ph.D. Dissertation, University of Denver, 1957.

306 Kochman, Andrew John, Jr. "Realism in the Early and Middle Nineteenth Century British Theatre." Ph.D. Dissertation, University of
Wisconsin, 1957. 464 p. (DA#57-1110)

Some attention is given to Phelps, C. Kean, Fechter, Boucicault, Bancroft, and Robertson.

307 Maher, M.A. "The Literary Drama in the First Half of the Nineteenth
Century." Ph.D. Dissertation, University of Leeds, 1957.

308 Mander, Raymond, and Joe Mitchenson. A PICTURE HISTORY OF THE
BRITISH THEATRE. London: Hulton Press, 1957. 160 p.

There are over five hundred plates with substantial sections
on the nineteenth-century theatre; an admirable collection.

309 Morris, Harry Caesar. "Nineteenth and Twentieth Century Criticism of
Shakespeare's Problem Comedies." Ph.D. Dissertation, University of
Minnesota, 1957.

310 Highfill, Philip H. "Edmund Simpson's Talent Raid on England in 1818."
TN, 12 (1957-8), 83-91, 130-40; 13 (1958-59), 7-14.

Deals with a recruiting trip to England by the stage manager
of the Park Street Theatre, New York.

311 Grieder, Theodore G., Jr. "The French Revolution in the British Drama:
A Study in British Popular Literature of the Decade of Revolution." Ph.D.
Dissertation, Stanford University, 1958.

312 Jones, David Llewellyn. "Stage Reform and Tragedy in the English Romantic Period." Ph.D. Dissertation, Harvard University, 1958. 172 p.

313 Shattuck, Charles H., ed. BULWER AND MACREADY: A CHRONICLE OF THE EARLY VICTORIAN THEATRE. Urbana: University of Illinois Press, 1958. [viii], 278 p.

> Bulwer-Macready-John Forster correspondence, 1836-66, expertly edited. The letters mainly concern Bulwer-Lytton's career as a playwright, but also give valuable insights into early Victorian theatre practices. The editor provides an excellent introduction, very full notes, eight plates, and a good index.

314 Hollis, Hastell Filmore. "An Acting History of CORIOLANUS." Ph.D. Dissertation, University of Denver, 1959.

315 Insch, A. "English Blank Verse Tragedy, 1790-1825." Ph.D. Dissertation, University of Durham, 1959.

316 Kahan, Stanley. "Pre-Victorian Melodrama." Ph.D. Dissertation, University of Wisconsin, 1959. 538 p. (DA#59-00176)

317 Kroll, Daniel Ronald. "HAMLET from Edwin Booth to Laurence Olivier: Some Changing Interpretations Reflecting Changes in Culture and the Tastes of Audience." Ph.D. Dissertation, Columbia University, 1959. 269 p. (DA#59-2584).

318 Macomber, Philip Alan. "The Iconography of London Theatre Auditorium Architecture, 1660-1900." 2 vols. Ph.D. Dissertation, Ohio State University, 1959. 644 p. (DA#59-05864)

319 Matlaw, Myron. "Persiflage on the Nineteenth-Century Stage." ETJ, 11 (1959), 212-21.

> Nineteenth-century burlesques of Sheridan's PIZARRO and THE STRANGER.

320 Merchant, W. Moelwyn. SHAKESPEARE AND THE ARTIST. London: Oxford University Press, 1959. xxx, 254 p.

> An extensively illustrated study of Shakespeare and the visual arts, with considerable attention given to nineteenth-century scenic design.

321 Nicoll, Allardyce. A HISTORY OF ENGLISH DRAMA 1660-1900.

VOLUME V, LATE NINETEENTH CENTURY DRAMA 1850-1900. 2nd ed.
Cambridge: At the University Press, 1959. vi, 901 p.

> There are two hundred pages of erudite history and uneven
> criticism, followed by seven hundred pages of indispensable
> lists of theatres and plays. Nicoll's handlist of plays is a
> massive and vital contribution to theatre scholarship. Orig-
> inally published in 1946. See also items 298, 431, and
> 2429.

322   Paulus, Gretchen. "Ibsen and the English Stage, 1889-1903." Ph.D.
Dissertation, Radcliffe College, 1959.

323   Burton, E.J. THE BRITISH THEATRE: ITS REPERTORY AND PRACTICE
1100-1900. London: Herbert Jenkins, 1960. 271 p.

> A guide for producers and designers, with information on
> nineteenth-century plays.

324   Guest, Ivor. THE DANCER'S HERITAGE: A SHORT HISTORY OF
BALLET. London: Adam and Charles Black, 1960. xii, 156 p.

325   Heilman, Robert B[echtold]. "Tragedy and Melodrama: Speculations on
Generic Form." TQ, 3, no. 2 (1960), 36-50.

> This conjectural essay, while short, is wide-ranging and
> attempts to clarify what constitutes tragedy; the author con-
> signs the tag "literature of disaster" to melodrama. While
> not specifically directed towards the nineteenth century, some
> of Heilman's observations on the characteristics of melodrama
> are useful and stimulating. His argument is more fully devel-
> oped in his later book. See item 367.

326   Ganzel, Dewey. "Patent Wrongs and Patent Theatres: Drama and the
Law in the Early Nineteenth Century." PMLA, 76 (1961), 384-96.

> An important article on the Report of the 1832 Select Com-
> mittee on Dramatic Literature and the 1843 Theatres Act,
> dealing with the monopoly of the patent theatres, censorship,
> and dramatic copyright.

327   Weales, Gerald. RELIGION IN MODERN ENGLISH DRAMA. Philadelphia: University of Pennsylvania Press, 1961. xv, 317 p.

> Although primarily concerned with religious drama in the
> twentieth century, Weales traces the roots of the genre to
> the nineteenth century and has interesting observations to
> make, especially with regard to H.A. Jones.

328 Halpé, A. "Poetry and the Theatre, 1800-1850: A Study of the Place of Dramatic Poetry in the English Theatre during the First Half of the Nineteenth Century, with Particular Reference to the Verse Drama of the Theatre." Ph.D. Dissertation, Bristol University, 1961-62.

329 Meisel, Martin. "Political Extravaganza: A Phase of Nineteenth-Century British Theatre." ThS, 3 (1962), 19-31.

> An interesting and persuasive article, pointing out that "politics, both topical and general, had an important place in the nineteenth-century English theatre." Examples are given from several plays with particular emphasis on W.S. Gilbert's and Arthur à Beckett's HAPPY LAND.

330 Schroeder, Neil Rolf. "AS YOU LIKE IT in the English Theatre 1740-1955." Ph.D. Dissertation, Yale University, 1962. 260 p. (DA#55-7524)

> Among other productions, the author examines those with Macready and Helen Faucit.

331 Soliman, A.G. "The Movement of Naturalism in the Late Nineteenth Century English Drama." Ph.D. Dissertation, University of Liverpool, 1962.

332 Wiesen, Pearl. "TWELFTH NIGHT: A Stage History." Ph.D. Dissertation, University of Wisconsin, 1962. 396 p. (DA#63-00628)

333 Byers, William Franklin. "The Nineteenth Century English Farce and Its Influence on George Bernard Shaw," Ph.D. Dissertation, Columbia University, 1963. 273 p. (DA#64-5046)

> Interesting for its examination of the various forms of farce and their common characteristics.

334 Grube, Max. THE STORY OF THE MEININGER. EDITED BY WENDELL COLE AND TRANSLATED BY ANN MARIE KOLLER. Coral Gables, Fla.: University of Miami Press, 1963. xviii, 121 p.

> An important study of this influential company, originally published in 1926 as GESHICHTE DER MEININGER. See also items 343 and 2883.

335 Hanratty, Jerome. "Melodrama--Then and Now: Some Possible Lessons from the Nineteenth Century." REL, 4, no. 2 (1963), 108-14.

> Hanratty suggests that contemporary melodramatists have something to learn from their nineteenth-century predecessors--especially regarding language and craftmanship.

336   Meisel, Martin. SHAW AND THE NINETEENTH-CENTURY THEATRE. Princeton: Princeton University Press, 1963. xii, 477 p.

> This is primarily a book about Shaw, but the author discusses the relationship between Shaw and the nineteenth-century popular theatre in order to demonstrate how Shaw used "the conventions, modes, techniques, and genres" of that theatre in his own plays. There are some interesting illustrations and a good bibliography and index.

337   Clunes, Alec. THE BRITISH THEATRE. London: Cassell, 1964. 188 p.

> Clunes provides a good introductory survey of nineteenth-century theatres, acting and drama, and his book is attractively illustrated.

338   Kostandi, F.M. "A Reconsideration of Henry Arthur Jones, Pinero, Wilde and Synge, with Special Reference to Ibsen." Ph.D. Dissertation, University of Manchester, 1964.

> Kostandi sees Ibsen as an all-pervading theatrical giant, and ascribes to him considerable influence. However, his arguments and evidence concerning Pinero, for example, are factually wrong and completely misleading.

339   Tsai, Andre Tii-Kang. "The British Nautical Drama, 1824-1843." Ph.D. Dissertation, Ohio State University, 1964. 264 p. (DA#65-3934)

> Tsai examines twenty-five plays to give an overall view of this genre. He concentrates on the works of Edward Fitzball and Douglas Jerrold.

340   Booth, Michael R. "The Drunkard's Progress: Nineteenth-Century Temperance Drama." DR, 44 (1964-65), 205-12.

> Booth argues: "Nowhere is temperance propaganda more extreme or more violent than in nineteenth-century melodrama." He surveys several such plays in this interesting essay.

341   _____. ENGLISH MELODRAMA. London: Herbert Jenkins, 1965. 223 p.

> Attempts to "show generally what melodrama was, how it developed from about 1790 to 1900, and how it is related to previous drama and its social and theatrical background." This is the standard work on English melodrama; included are an annotated bibliography and numerous plates and line drawings.

342 Bradbrook, M.C. ENGLISH DRAMATIC FORM: A HISTORY OF ITS DEVELOPMENT. London: Chatto & Windus, 1965. 205 p.

> In which the period from Dryden to Yeats is dismissed as totally lacking in "imaginative activity."

343 Byrne, Muriel St. Clare. "What We Said about the Meiningers in 1881." ESSAYS AND STUDIES, 18 (1965), 45-72.

> An analysis of contemporary reviews of the Meiningers' 1881 season at Drury Lane. See also items 334 and 2883.

344 Coleman, William S.E. "Shylock from Dogget to Macready." Ph.D. Dissertation, University of Pittsburgh, 1965. 292 p. (DA#66-8112)

> "This dissertation presents a history of the London productions of William Shakespeare's THE MERCHANT OF VENICE prior to the end of the Patent Law in 1843." Nineteenth-century interpretations include those by G.F. Cooke, Kean, William Dowton, Charles Kemble, and Macready.

345 Donohue, Joseph Walter. "Toward the Romantic Concept of Dramatic Character: RICHARD III and MACBETH in Criticism and Performance, 1740-1820." Ph.D. Dissertation, Princeton University, 1965. 261 p. (DA#66-4991).

> See Donohue's later book, item 390.

346 McInnes, Edward. "Naturalism and the English Theatre." FMLS, 1 (1965), 197-206.

> A useful survey of the varied critical receptions and reactions to naturalism (supported by newspaper accounts and the like). McInnes also gives some account of the movement's proponents, the adverse effects of naturalistic drama produced subsequently to Ibsen, and the theatrical conditions which militated against the rapid adoption of the movement in England.

347 Mander, Raymond, and Joe Mitchenson. BRITISH MUSIC HALL. London: Studio Vista, 1965. 208 p.

> A brief survey of music hall from eighteenth-century beginnings to the early 1960's followed by 301 plates, over half of which relate to the nineteenth century. There is a foreword by John Betjeman.

348 Mayer, David, III. "Dandyism in Regency Pantomime." TN, 19 (1965), 90-100.

> A cogent discussion of the way in which Dandyism was treated satirically in pantomimes in the early decades of the nineteenth century. Illustrated.

349 Stavisky, Aron Y. "Victorian Shakespeare Criticism." Ph.D. Dissertation, New York University, 1965. 195 p.

350 Harris, A.J. "KING LEAR in the Theatre: A Study of the Play Through the Performances of Garrick, Kean, Macready, Irving, Gielgud, and Scofield." Ph.D. Dissertation, Birmingham University, 1965-66.

351 Adlard, John. "Poetry and the Stage-Doors of the Nineties." REL, 7, no. 4 (1966), 50-60.

> This is an interesting though brief survey of the manner in which ballet in the music halls became a significant subject for certain poets in the 1890's.

352 Carter, Rand. "The Architecture of English Theatres 1760-1860." Ph.D. Dissertation, Princeton University, 1966.

353 Downer, Alan S. "Mr. Congreve Comes to Judgement." HAB, 17, no. 2 (1966), 5-12.

> Discusses Macready's 1842 production of LOVE FOR LOVE (the promptbook and contemporary reviews of the play) and Wallack's New York 1852 production.

354 Ehrstine, John W. "The Drama and Romantic Theory: The Cloudy Symbols of High Romance." RS, 34 (1966), 85-106.

> This article evaluates the dramatic output of the Romantics in the light of Romantic criticism of drama--"just as Romantic plays seem to be closet dramas, their criticism of drama seems closet criticism," since the Romantic poets viewed drama in a particularly undramatic way, being more intent on "the drama of the mind."

355 Fletcher, Richard M. ENGLISH ROMANTIC DRAMA 1795-1843: A CRITICAL HISTORY. New York: Exposition Press, 1966. 226 p.

> Aims at a reassessment of Romantic drama as "more vibrant, more vital--and more artistic--than it generally is acknowledged to be" (preface). Fletcher deals with Coleridge, Wordsworth, Shelley, and Byron, as well as figures like Sheil, Knowles, Talfourd, Bulwer-Lytton, and Browning, and discusses their plays in a theatrical context. This is an important study of early nineteenth-century theatre and drama; it has a substantial bibliography, but, unfortunately, no index.

356 Booth, Michael R. "Queen Victoria and the Theatre." UTQ, 36 (1966-67), 249-58.

A useful, straightforward account of Victoria's interest in
the theatre, rightly demonstrating her influence in helping
to restore the status of the theatre and so, indirectly, im-
proving the content of drama.

357 Speaight, George. "Juvenile Drama and Puppetry Research." TN, 21
(1966–67), 24–26.

A survey of research developments.

358 Findlater, Richard. BANNED! A REVIEW OF THEATRICAL CENSOR-
SHIP IN BRITAIN. London: MacGibbon & Kee, 1967. 238 p.

A general history which relies heavily on secondary sources.

359 Rahill, Frank. THE WORLD OF MELODRAMA. University Park and
London: Pennsylvania State University Press, 1967. xviii, 334 p.

A study of French, English, and American melodrama. It
is a careful, scholarly book, valuable for putting melodrama
in an international context.

360 Taylor, John R. THE RISE AND FALL OF THE WELL-MADE PLAY.
London: Methuen; New York: Hill and Wang, 1967. 175 p.

A rather superficial survey of Scribe, Robertson, H.A. Jones,
Pinero, Shaw, Wilde.

361 Troubridge, St. Vincent. THE BENEFIT SYSTEM IN THE BRITISH ISLES.
London: Society for Theatre Research, 1967. 172 p.

An authoritative survey, amply documented, of the benefit
system as it operated in the English theatre from the 1680's
to the 1880's.

362 Stokes, J.A.A. "The Non-Commercial Theatres in London and Paris in
the Late Nineteenth Century and the Origins of the Irish Literary Theatre
and Its Successors." Ph.D. Dissertation, University of Reading, 1967–
68.

363 Eastman, Arthur M. A SHORT HISTORY OF SHAKESPEAREAN CRITI-
CISM. New York: Random House, 1968. xxiv, 418 p.

Contains a good section on nineteenth-century criticism.

364 Ellis, Theodore Richard, III. "The Dramatist and the Comic Journal in
England, 1830-1870." Ph.D. Dissertation, Northwestern University,
1968. 396 p. (DA#69-1827)

An examination of dramatists who also wrote for humorous journals, particularly Douglas Jerrold, Tom Taylor, H.J. Byron, F.C. Burnand, Robertson, and Gilbert.

365 Hartnoll, Phyllis. A CONCISE HISTORY OF THE THEATRE. London: Thames and Hudson, 1968. 288 p.

An eminently readable short account of the history of world theatre, with two chapters on the nineteenth century. Adequately illustrated.

366 Hatcher, Joe Branch. "G.B.S. on the Minor Dramatists of the Nineties." Ph.D. Dissertation, University of Kansas, 1968. 268 p. (DA#68-17391)

An examination of Shaw's SATURDAY REVIEW criticisms of H.A. Jones, Pinero, Henry James, Wilde, Sudermann, Boucicault, Robertson, and Sardou.

367 Heilman, Robert Bechtold. TRAGEDY AND MELODRAMA: VERSIONS OF EXPERIENCE. Seattle and London: University of Washington Press, 1968. iii, 326 p.

See item 325.

368 Moore, Edward Mumford. "Changes in Shakespearean Production from the Age of Irving to Granville-Barker." Ph.D. Dissertation, Harvard University, 1968. 174 p.

369 Nelson, James Malcolm. "The Growth of Social Criticism in the Theatre in England from 1840 to 1890." Ph.D. Dissertation, University of Toronto, 1968.

370 Roston, Murray. BIBLICAL DRAMA IN ENGLAND FROM THE MIDDLE AGES TO THE PRESENT DAY. Evanston, Ill.: Northwestern University Press, 1968. 335 p.

Includes a chapter on the nineteenth century, with some discussion of the censorship problem.

371 Saxon, A.H. ENTER FOOT AND HORSE: A HISTORY OF HIPPODRAMA IN ENGLAND AND FRANCE. New Haven and London: Yale University Press, 1968. xiv, 249 p.

A thoroughly well-documented and readable account of this phenomenon of popular theatre. Illustrated.

372 Scrimgeour, Gary James. "Drama and the Theatre in the Early Nineteenth Century." Ph.D. Dissertation, Princeton University, 1968.
555 p. (DA#69-10521)

Examines the period 1790-1830, which is viewed as "the
greatest single period of change in the English dramatic
tradition since the late sixteenth century."

373 Salerno, Henry F. "The Problem Play: Some Aesthetic Considerations."
ELT, 11 (1968), 195-205.

Salerno considers the chief characteristics of the "problem
play," with special attention to Pinero (THE SECOND MRS.
TANQUERAY), Shaw, Barrie, and Galsworthy.

374 Trewin, J.C. THE POMPING FOLK IN THE NINETEENTH-CENTURY
THEATRE. London: Dent, 1968. xvii, 230 p.

An interesting collection of extracts from the writings of
many of the leading figures of the nineteenth-century theatre;
the collection serves as a good introduction to the theatrical
flavor of the period.

375 Felice, James de. "The London Theatrical Agent." TN, 23 (1968-69),
87-94.

An interesting examination of the business conducted by three
early nineteenth-century agents at a time when competition
among actors for employment was severe.

376 Scrimgeour, Gary J[ames]. "Nineteenth-Century Drama." VS, 12
(1968-69), 91-100.

An interesting review-article which surveys the then current
state of nineteenth-century theatre scholarship.

377 Bartholomeusz, Dennis. MACBETH AND THE PLAYERS. Cambridge:
At the University Press, 1969. xv, 302 p.

"What this study investigates is another approach to Shake-
speare--the player's," and to this end Bartholomeusz examines
performances of Macbeth and Lady Macbeth from the sixteenth
century to the present. About one-third of the work is devoted to detailed examination and reconstruction of the roles
as performed by leading nineteenth-century stars, such as
Kemble, Macready, Irving, and Ellen Terry. For this task,
primary materials have been drawn upon, notably promptbooks
and contemporary accounts of the performances. In short,
this is an invaluable study of acting and staging techniques.
Appendix I lists performances of MACBETH, together with
players and theatres.

378   Baum, Joan Mandell. "The Theatrical Compositions of the Major English Romantic Poets." Ph.D. Dissertation, Columbia University, 1969. 296 p. (DA#69-17573)

     A study of the attempts of Wordsworth, Coleridge, Byron, Shelley, and Keats to write for the stage.

379   Carlisle, Carol Jones. SHAKESPEARE FROM THE GREENROOM: ACTORS' CRITICISMS OF FOUR MAJOR TRAGEDIES. Chapel Hill: University of North Carolina Press, 1969. 493 p.

     Opinions on HAMLET, OTHELLO, KING LEAR, and MACBETH from several nineteenth-century actors.

380   Glenn, George David. "THE MERRY WIVES OF WINDSOR on the Nineteenth Century Stage." Ph.D. Dissertation, University of Illinois, 1969. 268 p. (DA#69-15309)

     Using original production promptbooks, Glenn examines productions by English and American dramatists--Frederick Reynolds, Madame Vestris, James H. Hackett, Charles Dickens, Charles Kean, Augustin Daly, H.B. Tree. Glenn regards these productions as representative of the varying managerial attitudes towards Shakespeare, and a valuable examination of their diverse practices.

381   Jansen, Kenneth Edward. "The Ibsen Movement in England: Ibsen Misunderstood." Ph.D. Dissertation, Ohio University, 1969. 167 p. (DA#70-15282)

     This essay centers on an examination of the English Ibsenites (H.A. Jones, Pinero, Granville-Barker, Galsworthy, and Shaw) and concludes they "were closer to the optimistic and humanistic view of the enlightenment than to Ibsen's modern sensibility." It is, however, muddle-headed to refer to some of these dramatists as self-styled Ibsenites.

382   Mander, Raymond, and Joe Mitchenson. MUSICAL COMEDY: A STORY IN PICTURES. Foreword. Noel Coward. London: Peter Davies, 1969. 64 p. Text only.

     An extensively illustrated survey from the 1890's to the 1960's.

383   Mattson, Marylu Catherine. "Censorship and the Victorian Drama." Ph.D. Dissertation, University of Southern California, 1969. 426 p. (DA#69-9034)

     Extends to 1909.

384   Mayer, David. HARLEQUIN IN HIS ELEMENT: THE ENGLISH PANTO-

MIME, 1806-1836. Cambridge, Mass.: Harvard University Press, 1969. xvii, 400 p.

> This exhaustive study of an important period in the history of English pantomime is extensively illustrated and fully documented. There are two appendices ("Pantomime Trickwork," "Pantomime Music"), a list of sources, and detailed indexes.

385   Spanabel, Robert Roy.   A Stage History of HENRY THE FIFTH: 1583-1859."   Ph.D.   Dissertation, Ohio State University, 1969.   307 p. (DA#69-22213)

> Chapters 4 and 5 of this dissertation are devoted to productions by John Philip Kemble, Macready, Samuel Phelps, and Charles Kean. The account is based on acting editions, together with manuscript materials, newspaper reviews, and promptbooks.

386   Speaight, George.   THE HISTORY OF THE ENGLISH TOY THEATRE. London: Studio Vista, 1969.   224 p.

> An authoritative study with numerous illustrations, including some impressive color plates. Appendices list publishers of juvenile drama (more extensive than Wilson's list, item 214), plays published as juvenile drama, and public collections (in Britain and the United States) of juvenile drama. The book was first published in 1946 as JUVENILE DRAMA: THE HISTORY OF THE ENGLISH TOY THEATRE (London: MacDonald).

387   Trewin, J.C.   "The Romantic Poets in the Theatre."   KSMB, 20 (1969), 21-30.

> A helpful introductory essay.

388   Olshen, B.N.   "Early Nineteenth-Century Revisions of LOVE FOR LOVE."   TN, 24 (1969-70), 164-75.

> Examining several editions of the play, Olshen demonstrates how various revisions reflected changes in taste and manners. There is also a list of productions of LOVE FOR LOVE, 1800-1828, with cast details.

389   Raafat, Z.M.   "The Influence of Scribe and Sardou upon English Dramatists in the Nineteenth Century, with Special Reference to Pinero, Jones, and Wilde."   Ph.D.   Dissertation, University of London, 1969-70.

390   Donohue, Joseph W.   DRAMATIC CHARACTER IN THE ENGLISH ROMANTIC AGE.   Princeton: Princeton University Press, 1970.   xiii, 402 p.

An important study of the Romantic concept of dramatic
character. The author's extensive Bibliographical Note is
a very useful feature of the book, and the illustrations in
the text are as valuable as they are plentiful.

391 Driver, Tom S. ROMANTIC QUEST AND MODERN QUERY: A HIS-
TORY OF THE MODERN THEATRE. New York: Delacorte Press, 1970.
xviii, 493 p.

Early chapters on "The Well-Made Play" and "The Revolution
in Theatrical Means" make this book of interest to students
of the nineteenth-century theatre.

392 Herring, Paul D. "Nineteenth-Century Drama." MP, 68 (1970), 83-90.

A useful review article surveying four anthologies of nineteenth-
century drama which appeared in the late sixties.

393 McReynolds, Doris Janet. "Image of the Theatre in Victorian Literature."
Ph.D. Dissertation, University of Minnesota, 1970. 242 p. (DA#71-
8249)

394 Simon, Elliott Martin. "The Theatrical Evolution of the Edwardian
Problem-Play: A Study of the Changes in the Dramatic Conventions of
English Melodrama 1890-1914." Ph.D. Dissertation, University of Michi-
gan, 1970. 375 p. (DA#71-4730)

The discussion refers in part to H.A. Jones and Pinero.

395 Southern, Richard. THE VICTORIAN THEATRE: A PICTORIAL SURVEY.
Newton Abbot: David & Charles, 1970. 112 p.

396 Speaight, George. PUNCH & JUDY: A HISTORY. Rev. ed. London:
Studio Vista, 1970. 160 p.

This splendidly illustrated history includes an 1854 Punch
and Judy text, a bibliography, and a good index. It was
first published in 1955 as THE HISTORY OF THE ENGLISH
PUPPET THEATRE (London: Harrap).

397 Williams, Clifford John. THEATRES AND AUDIENCES. A BACK-
GROUND TO DRAMATIC TEXTS. London: Longman, 1970. 122 p.

An illustrated basic introduction with a short chapter on
"Regency to 1914."

398 Kimberley, M.E. "The Nineteenth-Century 'Proprietary' Acting Editions
of Shakespeare." Ph.D. Dissertation, Birmingham University, 1970-71.

399   Barish, Jonas A.   "Antitheatrical Prejudice in the Nineteenth Century."
       UTQ, 40 (1970-71), 277-99.

       This article is not what it might have been since it examines
       antitheatrical prejudice in secondary sources (for example,
       MANSFIELD PARK). While literature can often reflect an
       age, this is not necessarily so, and there are many other
       areas Barish could have examined to discuss this topic. As
       it stands, the piece is interesting, though diffuse, given its
       terms of reference.

400   McCarthy, Sean.   "Frank Matcham's Early Career."   TN, 25 (1970-71),
       103-8, 152-57; 26 (1971-72), 64-71.

       An account of this theatre architect's "formative years 1879-
       1892," dealing with Matcham's designs for several London
       and provincial theatres. Illustrated.

401   Stephens, J. Russell.   "William Bodham Donne: Some Aspects of His
       Later Career as Examiner of Plays."   TN, 25 (1970-71), 25-32.

       Donne's career as deputy examiner and examiner (from 1849-
       74) was one of the longest, and he consequently exercised
       considerable influence in the theatre.

402   Burke, John David.   "The Stage History of the London Productions of
       George Farquhar's THE RECRUITING OFFICER, 1706-1964."   Ph.D.
       Dissertation, Ohio State University, 1971.   491 p.   (DA#72-15182)

       The nineteenth-century production is that by Charles Kemble
       in 1829.

403   Cross, Beverly Gilbert.   "Nineteenth Century Domestic Drama as Theatri-
       cal Communication."   Ph.D. Dissertation, University of Michigan, 1971.
       314 p.   (DA#72-14830)

       A sympathetic examination of the genre on its own terms and
       set against prevailing theatrical conditions.

404   Donohue, Joseph W., ed.   THE THEATRICAL MANAGER IN ENGLAND
       AND AMERICA: PLAYER OF A PERILOUS GAME. PHILIP HENSLOWE,
       TATE WILKINSON, STEPHEN PRICE, EDWIN BOOTH, CHARLES WYND-
       HAM. Princeton: Princeton University Press, 1971. xii, 216 p.

       Essays by various hands, the one on Wyndham being by
       George Rowell. The editor provides a thoughtful intro-
       ductory essay on "The Theatrical Manager and the Uses
       of Theatrical Research."

405 Lott, Nelda Jackson. "The Tragedies of Scott, Lamb and Coleridge: Their Elizabethan Heritage." Ph.D. Dissertation, University of Southern Mississippi, 1971. 163 p. (DA#72-09080)

406 Nichols, Arthur Richard. "A History of the Staging of Thomas Southerne's THE FATAL MARRIAGE and OROONOKO on the London Stage from 1694 to 1851." Ph.D. Dissertation, University of Washington, 1971. 234 p. (DA#72-7399)

407 Richards, Kenneth, and Peter Thomson, eds. ESSAYS ON NINETEENTH CENTURY BRITISH THEATRE: THE PROCEEDINGS OF A SYMPOSIUM SPONSORED BY THE MANCHESTER UNIVERSITY DEPARTMENT OF DRAMA. London: Methuen, 1971. ix, 195 p.

A valuable miscellany of essays covering diverse aspects of the theatre and drama--the Theatre Royal, Hull, Charles Kean, Colman the Younger, Byron's tragedies, farce, G.H. Lewes as playwright, the first production of THE IMPORTANCE OF BEING EARNEST, Dr. Henniquin, and nineteenth-century productions of Shakespeare.

408 Senelick, Laurence. "A Brief Life and Times of the Victorian Music-Hall." HLB, 19 (1971), 375-98.

A useful short survey of this particular facet of the theatre. Illustrated.

409 Speaight, George. "The Toy Theatre." HLB, 19 (1971), 307-13.

A short, lucid, illustrated history of the toy theatre (juvenile drama) with specific reference to the Harvard holdings in this field.

410 Brown, John Russell. "Originality in Shakespeare Production." TN, 26 (1971-72), 107-15.

Includes discussion of some nineteenth-century views (e.g. by Hazlitt and Macready).

411 Carlson, Marvin. "Montigny, Laube, Robertson: The Early Realists." ETJ, 24 (1972), 227-36.

In the 1850's and 1860's Germany, France, and England each "produced an innovative theatre with a manager who encouraged . . . a degree of realism hitherto unknown and thereby provided an important model for later producers."

412 Chiang, Oscar Ching-Kuan. "Idealism in Plays Written by Early Nineteenth Century Poets." Ph.D. Dissertation, St. John's University, 1972.

271 p. (DA#72-21716)

This study examines the dramatic output of Southey, Coleridge, Wordsworth, Byron, Shelley, and Keats "to identify their common idealistic features on the assumption that all these early Romantic poets had expressed their didactic, revolutionary or philosophical ideas in their plays."

413 Findlater, Richard. "The Playwright and His Money." ThQ, 2, no. 8 (1972), 44-56.

414 Guest, Ivor. THE ROMANTIC BALLET IN ENGLAND: ITS DEVELOPMENT, FULFILMENT AND DECLINE. London: Pitman, 1972. 176 p.

First published in 1954 (London: Phoenix House), this second edition has a new introduction. The book is a history of "the great flowering of ballet in the 1830s and 1840s." Some useful appendices include a list of ballet masters at the King's Theatre (later Her Majesty's) 1770-1881, ballets given at the King's 1772-1881, principal dancers and choreographers at the King's 1750-1881, and a selected list of ballets given at other London theatres 1791-1865. There are many illustrations.

415 Mackie, Wade Craven. "The Evolution of the Long Run in the Theatres of London, 1800-1870." Ph.D. Dissertation, Indiana University, 1972. 152 p. (DA#73-2733)

This study concludes that the long run developed earlier than had been previously thought and that it had a deleterious effect on resident stock companies, the multiple-playbill, the number of productions from the traditional repertory, and benefits. It stimulated the growth of actors' salaries and new theatres.

416 Morice, Gerald, and George Speaight. "New Light on the Juvenile Drama." TN, 26 (1972), 115-21.

A reprinting of an 1850 interview between Henry Mayhew (the litterateur and social historian) and William West, publisher of toy theatres.

417 Otten, Terry. THE DESERTED STAGE: THE SEARCH FOR DRAMATIC FORM IN NINETEENTH-CENTURY ENGLAND. Athens: Ohio University Press, 1972. ix, 178 p.

Otten has no use for the "popular" nineteenth-century theatre which he dismisses out-of-hand. His sole interest is in the "experimental dramas composed by major poets" and to this end he selects works by Shelley, Byron, Tennyson, and Browning which illustrate both their traditional and innovative approaches to drama. This rather constrictive approach will be found controversial by many.

417a Rosenberg, Marvin. THE MASKS OF KING LEAR. Berkeley and Los Angeles: University of California Press, 1972. viii, 431 p.

Includes discussion of many nineteenth-century productions.

418 Stephens, John Russell. "Dramatic Censorship During the Reign of Victoria." Ph.D. Dissertation, University of Wales, 1972. 455 p.

A comprehensive study of Victorian theatrical censorship drawing extensively on manuscript sources.

419 Stokes, John. RESISTIBLE THEATRES: ENTERPRISE AND EXPERIMENT IN THE LATE NINETEENTH CENTURY. London: Paul Elek, 1972. [viii], 203 p.

The core of this work is three essays, on E.W. Godwin, Herkomer and Bayreuth, and the Independent Theatre. Stokes sees in each case "a triadic relationship between text, staging and organisation, which ultimately determines the nature of the result."

420 Warner, Frederick Elliott. "The Burletta in London's Minor Theatres During the Nineteenth Century, with a Handlist of Burlettas." Ph.D. Dissertation, Ohio State University, 1972. 170 p. (DA#73-11601)

421 Weisberg, Lynne Beth Willing. "'Ibsen and English Criticism': Early Critical Reactions to Ibsen in England and Their Aftermath in Modern Ibsenism." Ph.D. Dissertation, University of Michigan, 1972. 198 p. (DA#73-11294)

A study of Ibsen criticism which sees a division into two camps--the aesthetic stance of Archer and the sociopolitical of Shaw. The thesis then traces the modern successors of Archer and Shaw.

422 Whaley, Frank Leslie, Jr. "A Descriptive Compendium of Selected Historical Accessories Commonly Used as Stage Properties." Ph.D. Dissertation, Florida State University, 1972. 577 p. (DA#73-4710)

One of the eight epochs into which the study is divided is the nineteenth century. There are also eight categories of accessories: food, table service, firemakers and illuminating devices, tobacco, arms, writing materials, toilet articles, and luggage.

423 Brockett, Oscar G., and Robert R. Findlay. CENTURY OF INNOVA-
     TION: A HISTORY OF EUROPEAN AND AMERICAN THEATRE AND
     DRAMA SINCE 1870. Englewood Cliffs, N.J.: Prentice Hall, 1973.
     xiv, 826 p.

       Wide-ranging, well-illustrated general survey.

424 Clarke, Mary, and Clement Crisp. BALLET: AN ILLUSTRATED HIS-
     TORY. London: A. & C. Black, 1973. 245 p.

425 Donohue, Joseph. "Burletta and the Early Nineteenth-Century English
     Theatre." NCTR, 1 (1973), 29-51.

       A scholarly, wide-ranging attempt to define exactly what
       constitutes burletta.

426 Elsom, John. EROTIC THEATRE. London: Secker and Warburg, 1973.
     xv, 269 p.

       A discussion of the treatment of sex in the theatre in two
       periods--1890 to 1910, and 1950 to the 1970's. Illustrated.

427 Jennings, Ann S. "The Reactions of London's Drama Critics to Certain
     Plays by Henrik Ibsen, Harold Pinter and Edward Bond." Ph.D. Dis-
     sertation, Florida State University, 1973. 257 p. (DA#73-24262)

428 Leacroft, Richard. THE DEVELOPMENT OF THE ENGLISH PLAYHOUSE.
     London: Eyre, Methuen, 1973. xiii, 354 p.

       Architectural development of the theatre from the beginnings
       to the early twentieth century. Illustrated.

429 Mander, Raymond, and Joe Mitchenson. PANTOMIME: A STORY IN
     PICTURES. Foreword. Danny La Rue. New York: Taplinger, 1973.
     56 p.

       An extensively illustrated history of pantomime from the
       early eighteenth century to the 1970's.

430 Mayer, David. "The Pantomime of the Poor." PANTO!, no. 2 (Christ-
     mas 1973), 2-11.

       Extracts from Henry Mayhew's LONDON LABOUR AND THE
       LONDON POOR describing the experiences of a Penny-Gaff
       clown in the mid-nineteenth century.

431 Nicoll, Allardyce. ENGLISH DRAMA 1900-1930: THE BEGINNINGS
     OF THE MODERN PERIOD. London and New York: Cambridge Univer-
     sity Press, 1973. x, 1,083 p.

This book extends Nicoll's monumental history to 1930 and includes the twentieth-century output of nineteenth-century dramatists. The handlist of plays is immensely useful, again complementing the earlier lists. Indispensable. See also items 298, 321, and 2429.

432 Pitman, Rosalind. "William Archer and 'Peer Gynt.'" N&Q, 20 (July 1973), 255-57.

Quotes in full a letter from Archer to Quiller-Couch expressing the former's opinion of PEER GYNT. The critical apparatus used to date the letter also provides useful background information.

433 Smith, James L. MELODRAMA. London: Methuen, 1973. 96 p.

A helpful introduction to the genre, with a bibliography and an index of titles discussed or referred to.

434 Speaight, George. "Was There Ever an American Toy Theatre?" NCTR, 1 (1973), 89-93.

American publications were not original, but closely adapted from English predecessors.

435 Stephens, J.R. "JACK SHEPPARD and the Licensers: The Case Against Newgate Plays." NCTR, 1 (1973), 1-13.

A good, scholarly account of the productions and censorship of a striking example of Newgate drama. Much material from the Lord Chamberlain's correspondence is quoted.

436 Booth, Michael R. "A Defence of Nineteenth-Century English Drama." ETJ, 26 (1974), 5-13.

A strong and important essay demonstrating "the significance of theatrical as well as literary criteria" in judging nineteenth-century drama, and illustrating the drama's "intrinsic interest and consequence," and even its "relevance" to "life and theatre in the 1970s."

437 Cheshire, D.F. MUSIC HALL IN BRITAIN. Newton Abbot, Devonshire, Eng.: David & Charles, 1974. 112 p.

An interesting and well-illustrated series of extracts from contemporary sources relating to the history of music hall, 1843-1923. In addition to the development of music hall entertainment itself, Cheshire includes comment on the audiences, the law and music hall, and finance.

Chapter 3

INDIVIDUAL AUTHORS

The entries for each author in this chapter are divided into six sections--I
Collected Works; II Acted Plays; IIa Unacted Plays; III Bibliographies;
IV Biography; V Critical Studies; VI Journals and Newsletters. Not all
of these categories are required in all cases. Titles in section II are chronological by date of performance; in section IIa they are chronological by date
of publication.

The majority of the editions of individual plays cited in sections II and IIa are
to be found in the Readex Microprint collection of nineteenth-century plays
(for details of which see item 2517, below). Those editions which are NOT
at present available in the Readex collection are marked with an asterisk (*).
Some plays exist only in manuscript form; the designation LC indicates that
such plays are located in the Lord Chamberlain's plays at the British Library.
For a partial catalog of the Lord Chamberlain's plays see below, item 2436.

Many of the plays listed here were published in series in the nineteenth century.
Where appropriate and where possible we have given the series name and volume
number or the number of the play in the series (e.g. Dicks' Standard Plays, no.
1006). Bibliographical information for many of these series will be found in
chapter 5, below.

For additional notes on this chapter see the Introduction, above, p. xiii.

À BECKETT, GILBERT ABBOTT (1811-56)

II Acted Plays—Principal Titles

438 THE MAN WITH THE CARPET BAG: A FARCE IN ONE ACT. (Victoria,
29 September 1834.) London: William Strange, n.d. 24 p.

> Contains cast list of first London production.

439   MAN-FRED: A BURLESQUE BALLET OPERA IN ONE ACT. (Strand, 26 December 1834.) London: Cumberland, n.d. 19 p.

        An acting edition with cast lists of the Strand and Victoria productions, and "Remarks" on the play by D--G [George Daniel].

440   "The Postillion of Lonjumean: A Burletta." (St. James's, 13 March 1837.)

        A manuscript promptcopy (22 leaves), located in New York Public Library.

441   THE ASSIGNATION; OR, WHAT WILL MY WIFE SAY: A DRAMA IN TWO ACTS. (St. James's, 29 September 1837.) London: William Strange; New York and Philadelphia: Turner and Fisher, 1837. 37 p.

        An acting edition with a cast list of the first London production.

442   THE ARTIST'S WIFE: A PETITE COMEDY IN TWO ACTS. (Haymarket, 28 July 1838.) London: Chapman and Hall, n.d. 24 p.

        An acting edition with a cast list of the first London production.

443   THE CHIMES: A GOBLIN STORY OF SOME BELLS THAT RANG AN OLD YEAR OUT AND A NEW YEAR IN: A DRAMA IN FOUR QUARTERS. With Mark Lemon. (Adelphi, 19 February 1844.) The Acting National Drama, vol. 11, no. 115. London: National Acting Drama Office, n.d. 44 p.

        An acting edition with a cast list of the first London production. The play is adapted from Dickens.

444   DON CAESAR DE BAZAN: A DRAMA IN THREE ACTS. With Mark Lemon. (Princess's, 8 October 1844.) London: W. Barth, n.d. 39 p.

        An acting edition with a cast list of the first London production.

445   ST. GEORGE AND THE DRAGON: A NEW GRAND EMPIRICAL EXPOSITION IN TWO ACTS. With Mark Lemon. (Adelphi, 24 March 1845.) The Acting National Drama, vol. 12, no. 119. London: National Acting Drama Office, n.d. 24 p.

        An acting edition with a cast list of the first London production.

446 PETER WILKINS; OR, THE LOADSTONE ROCK AND THE FLYING
INDIANS: AN EXTRA EXTRAVAGANT EXTRAVAGANZA IN TWO ACTS.
With Mark Lemon. (Adelphi, 9 April 1846.) The Acting National
Drama, vol. 12. London: National Acting Drama Office, n.d. 21 p.

> An acting edition with a cast list of the first London pro-
> duction.

447 THE CASTLE OF OTRANTO: A ROMANTIC EXTRAVAGANZA IN ONE
ACT. (Haymarket, 24 April 1848.) The Acting National Drama, vol.
14. London: National Acting Drama Office, n.d. 31 p.

> An acting edition with a cast list of the first London pro-
> duction.

IV Biography

448 À Beckett, Arthur William. THE À BECKETTS OF "PUNCH". Westminster: Constable, 1903; rpt. Detroit: Singing Tree Press, 1969.
334 p.

> Some attention (but not much) paid to À Beckett the play-
> wright.

ALBERY, JAMES (1838-89)

I Collected Works

449 Albery, Wyndham, ed. THE DRAMATIC WORKS OF JAMES ALBERY:
TOGETHER WITH A SKETCH OF HIS CAREER, CORRESPONDENCE
BEARING THEREON, PRESS NOTICES, CASTS, ETC. 2 vols. London:
Davies, 1939. cxiv, 762; vii, 886 p.

> Volume one: TWO ROSES; COQUETTES; TWEEDIE'S RIGHTS;
> APPLE BLOSSOMS; FORGIVEN; ORIANA; THE WILL OF
> WISE KING KINO; MARRIED; FORTUNE; WIG AND GOWN;
> PRIDE. Volume two: THE SPENDTHRIFT; THE MAN IN
> POSSESSION; THE SPECTRE KNIGHT; THE GOLDEN WREATH;
> JACKS AND JILLS; DR. DAVY; PICKWICK; PINK DOMINOS;
> THE CRISIS; DUTY; THE OLD LOVE AND THE NEW; WHERE'S
> THE CAT?; LITTLE MISS MUFFIT; FEATHERBRAIN; WELCOME
> LITTLE STRANGER; CHISELLING; NO. 20 OR THE BASTILLE
> OF CALVADOS; THE VICAR; THE JESUITS; GENEVIEVE.
> The whole edition contains much useful information and criti-
> cal apparatus, and is indispensable for the study of Albery.

II Acted Plays—Principal Titles

450 TWO ROSES: A COMEDY IN THREE ACTS. (Vaudeville, 4 June 1870) Sergel's Acting Drama, no. 288. New York: 1881. 39 p.

> An acting edition with cast lists of the first London and New York productions.

451 *TWO ROSES: AN ORIGINAL COMEDY IN THREE ACTS. London and New York: French, n.d. 66 p.

> An acting edition with a cast list of the first London production.

452 "The Pink Dominos: A Comedy in Three Acts." (Criterion, 31 March 1877.)

> Manuscript promptcopy, located in New York Public Library.

453 JINGLE: A FARCE IN ONE ACT. (Lyceum, 8 July 1878.) No publication details. 36 p.

> An acting copy.

454 DUTY: COMEDY IN FOUR ACTS (ADAPTED FROM VICTORIEN SARDOU'S COMEDY "LES BOURGEOIS DE PONT ARCY"). (Prince of Wales's, 27 September 1879.) London and New York: French, n.d. 75 p.

> An acting edition with a cast list of the first London production.

ALMAR, GEORGE (b. 1802)

II Acted Plays—Principal Titles

455 THE ROVER'S BRIDE; OR, THE BITTERN'S SWAMP: A ROMANTIC DRAMA IN TWO ACTS. (Surrey, 30 October 1830.) London: Cumberland, n.d. 47 p.

> An acting edition with a cast list of the first London production and "Remarks" by D--G [George Daniel].

456 PEDLAR'S ACRE; OR, THE WIFE OF SEVEN HUSBANDS: A DRAMA IN TWO ACTS. (Surrey, 22 August 1831.) Cumberland's Minor Theatre, vol. 5. London: Cumberland, n.d. 52 p.

> An acting edition with a cast list of the first London production and "Remarks" by D--G [George Daniel].

457 THE TOWER OF NESLE; OR, THE CHAMBER OF DEATH: AN HISTORI-
CAL DRAMA IN THREE ACTS. (Surrey, 17 September 1832.) Cumberland's Minor Theatre, vol. 6, no. 50. London: G.H. Davidson, n.d.
51 p.

> An acting edition with a cast list of the first London pro-
> duction and "Remarks" by D--G [George Daniel].

458 THE KNIGHTS OF ST. JOHN! OR, THE FIRE BANNER! A ROMANTIC
DRAMA IN TWO ACTS. (Sadler's Wells, 26 August 1833.) New British
Theatre, no. 93. London: Duncombe, n.d. 38 p.

> An acting edition with a cast list of the first London pro-
> duction; this copy is a promptbook with a few manuscript
> notes (New York Public Library).

459 THE CLERK OF CLERKENWELL; OR, THE THREE BLACK BOTTLES: A
ROMANTIC DRAMA IN TWO ACTS. (Sadler's Wells, 27 January 1834.)
Cumberland's Minor Theatre, vol. 7. London: Cumberland, n.d. 54 p.

> An acting edition with a cast list of the first London pro-
> duction and "Remarks" by D--G [George Daniel].

460 THE SEVEN SISTERS; OR, THE GREY MAN OF TOTTENHAM! AN
HISTORICAL DRAMA IN TWO ACTS. (Sadler's Wells, 29 July 1835.)
London: Duncombe, n.d. 40 p.

> An acting edition with a cast list of the first London pro-
> duction.

461 THE BULL-FIGHTER; OR, THE BRIDAL RING: A ROMANTIC DRAMA
IN THREE ACTS. (Surrey, 8 October 1838.) Cumberland's Minor
Theatre, vol. 14. London: Cumberland, n.d. 39 p.

> An acting edition with a cast list of the first London pro-
> duction and "Remarks" by D--G [George Daniel].

462 OLIVER TWIST: A SERIO-COMIC BURLETTA IN THREE ACTS. (Surrey,
19 November 1838.) [London: Dicks, n.d.] 26 p.

> An acting edition with a cast list of the first London pro-
> duction. The play is adapted from Dickens.

463 JANE OF THE HATCHET; OR, THE SIEGE OF BEAUVAIS: A MELO-
DRAMA IN TWO ACTS. (Surrey, 20 (?) July 1840.) London: Duncombe, n.d. 34 p.

> An acting edition with cast lists of productions at the Surrey
> and Queen's (where, according to this edition, the play re-
> ceived its first production on 12 July 1840).

ARNOLD, SAMUEL JAMES (1774-1852)

II Acted Plays—Principal Titles

464 AULD ROBIN GRAY: A PASTORAL ENTERTAINMENT IN TWO ACTS. (Haymarket, 29 July 1794.) London: George Goulding, 1794. 55 p.

> This edition includes a brief prefatory note by Arnold and a cast list of the first London production.

465 THE VETERAN TAR: A COMIC OPERA IN TWO ACTS. (Drury Lane, 29 January 1801.) London: J. Barker, 1801. 39 p.

> In a preface Arnold acknowledges some debt to a French play, LE PETIT MATELOT, and thanks the performers for their efforts; also a cast list of the first London production.

466 "FOUL DEEDS WILL RISE": A MUSICAL DRAMA. (Haymarket, 18 July 1804.) London: Barker and Son, 1804. 47 p.

> In a preface Arnold complains of the unfair reception of his play and objects to the management's withdrawal of it; also a cast list of the first London production.

467 MAN AND WIFE; OR, MORE SECRETS THAN ONE. A COMEDY IN FIVE ACTS. (Drury Lane, 5 January 1809.) London: Richard Phillips, 1809. 90 p.

> In a note Arnold thanks the performers for their efforts in making the play a success; cast list of the first London production.

468 DEVIL'S BRIDGE: AN OPERA IN THREE ACTS. (Lyceum, 6 May 1812.) New York: D. Longworth, 1817. 57 p.

> Includes a cast list of the New York production.

469 THE WOODMAN'S HUT: A MELO-DRAMATIC ROMANCE IN THREE ACTS. (Drury Lane, 12 April 1814.) London: Miller, 1814. 46 p.

> In a prefatory note Arnold thanks the performers and dedicates the play to Miss Kelly "as a sincere mark of his [Arnold's] admiration of her talents, and of his high respect for the virtues which so eminently distinguish her character in private life." Also a cast list of the first London production.

470 THE MAID AND THE MAGPYE; OR, WHICH IS THE THIEF? A MUSICAL ENTERTAINMENT IN TWO ACTS. (Lyceum, 28 August 1815.) London: Miller, 1815. 52 p.

Adapted from Caigniez's LA PIE VOLEUSE, as Arnold explains
in a prefatory note--in which he also gives his customary
thanks to the performers; cast list of the first London production.

471   FREE AND EASY: A MUSICAL FARCE IN TWO ACTS. (English Opera
House, 16 September 1816.) Cumberland's British Theatre, vol. 42.
London: Cumberland, n.d. 50 p.

An acting edition with cast lists of Opera House and Covent
Garden productions and "Remarks" by D--G [George Daniel].

BAILLIE, JOANNA (1762-1851)

I Collected Works

472   A SERIES OF PLAYS: IN WHICH IT IS ATTEMPTED TO DELINEATE THE
STRONGER PASSIONS OF THE MIND: EACH PASSION BEING THE
SUBJECT OF A TRAGEDY AND A COMEDY. 3 vols. London: T.
Cadell, Junior, and W. Davies, 1798-1812. [Imprint for volume 3 is
Longman, Hurst, Rees, Orme, and Brown.]

Volume one: Introductory Discourse (Baillie's theory of
drama); COUNT BASIL; THE TRYAL; DE MONTFORT.
Volume two: THE ELECTION; ETHWALD, PART FIRST;
ETHWALD, PART SECOND; THE SECOND MARRIAGE.
Volume three: ORRA; THE DREAM; THE SIEGE; THE
BEACON. This SERIES OF PLAYS went through several
editions in the early nineteenth-century. Only DE MONT-
FORT, THE ELECTION, and THE BEACON appear to have
been acted (see below, items 476, 478, 479).

473   MISCELLANEOUS PLAYS, BY JOANNA BAILLIE. London: Longman,
Hurst, Rees & Orme, 1804. xix, 438 p.

Contents include: RAYNER: A TRAGEDY, THE COUNTRY
INN: A COMEDY, and CONSTANTINE PALEOLOGUS; OR,
THE LAST OF THE CAESARS: A TRAGEDY. CONSTANTINE
was probably acted in Liverpool in 1808.

474   DRAMAS, BY JOANNA BAILLIE. 3 vols. London: Longman, Rees,
Orme, Brown, Green, & Longman, 1836.

"The first volume comprises a continuation of the series of
Plays on the stronger Passions of the Mind, and completes
all that I intended to write on the subject. . . . The two
following volumes will complete the whole of my Dramatic
Works" (author's preface). Volume one contains ROMIERO:

A TRAGEDY; THE ALIENATED MANOR: A COMEDY; HENRI-
QUEZ: A TRAGEDY; THE MARTYR: A DRAMA. Volume two
contains THE SEPARATION: A TRAGEDY; THE STRIPLING: A
TRAGEDY; THE PHANTOM: A DRAMA; ENTHUSIASM: A COM-
EDY. Volume three includes WITCHCRAFT: A TRAGEDY IN
PROSE; THE HOMICIDE: A TRAGEDY; THE BRIDE: A DRAMA;
THE MATCH: A COMEDY. All but HENRIQUEZ (Drury Lane,
19 March 1836) and THE SEPARATION (Covent Garden, 24 Feb-
ruary 1836) were unacted. The DRAMAS are available in the
Readex microprint collection.

475 THE DRAMATIC AND POETIC WORKS OF JOANNA BAILLIE. 2nd ed.
London: Longman, Brown, Green, and Longman, 1851. xxii, 847 p.

With a short "Life of Joanna Baillie."

II Acted Plays—Principal Titles

476 *DE MONTFORT: A TRAGEDY IN FIVE ACTS. (Drury Lane, 29 April
1800.) The British Theatre, vol. 24. London: Longman, Hurst, Rees,
Orme and Brown, n.d. 95 p.

With remarks by Mrs. Inchbald.

477 THE FAMILY LEGEND: A TRAGEDY. (Edinburgh, 29 January 1810;
Drury Lane, 29 April 1815.) 2nd ed. Edinburgh: John Ballantyne,
1810. xii, 96 p.

"The following play is not offered to the Public as it is
acted in the Edinburgh Theatre, but is printed from the original copy which I gave to the Theatre" (author's preface).
The preface also relates the historical incidents on which the
play is based. The Readex Collection also has a New York
1810 edition of the play.

478 *THE BEACON: A SERIOUS MUSICAL DRAMA IN TWO ACTS. (Edinburgh, 1815?) New York: D. Longworth, 1812. 36 p.

479 *THE ELECTION: A COMEDY IN FIVE ACTS. (English Opera House,
7 June 1817.) Philadelphia: M. Carey, 1811.

IIa Unacted Plays

480 *BASIL: A TRAGEDY. Philadelphia: M. Carey, 1811. 208 p.

481 *ORRA: A TRAGEDY IN FIVE ACTS. New York: Longworths, 1812.
71 p.

482   *THE SIEGE: A COMEDY IN FIVE ACTS. New York: Longworths,
      1812. 67 p.

483   THE MARTYR: A DRAMA IN THREE ACTS. London: Longman, Rees,
      Orme, Brown, and Green, 1826. xvii, 78 p.

      In a lengthy preface Baillie explains, among other things,
      that "the subject of this piece is too sacred, and therefore
      unfit for the stage."

484   THE BRIDE: A DRAMA IN THREE ACTS. London: Henry Colburn, 1828.
      x, 112 p.

      With a preface by Baillie speaking of the necessity of
      spreading the Christian faith, especially to Ceylon.

IV Biography

485   Carswell, Donald. SIR WALTER: A FOUR-PART STUDY IN BIOGRAPHY
      (SCOTT, HOGG, LOCKHART, JOANNA BAILLIE). London: John
      Murray, 1930. ix, 293 p.

      Deals with Scott's relationship with Baillie, and includes a
      portrait of her.

V Critical Studies

486   Badstuber, Alfred. JOANNA BAILLIES PLAYS ON THE PASSIONS.
      Wien and Leipzig: Wilhelm Braumueller, 1911. xi, 119 p.

      A critical survey of the plays, in German. See also E.
      Ziegenrucker's JOANNA BAILLIES PLAYS (Hamburg, 1909)
      and R.C. Pieszczek's JOANNA BAILLIE (Berlin, 1910), both
      in German.

487   Meynell, Alice. "Joanna Baillie." THE SECOND PERSON SINGULAR
      AND OTHER ESSAYS. London: Oxford University Press, 1922. Pp. 56-61.

      A sympathetic comment on Baillie's plays, with particular
      praise for THE TRIAL.

488   Carhart, Margaret S. THE LIFE AND WORK OF JOANNA BAILLIE.
      New Haven: Yale University Press, 1923; rpt. New York: Archon
      Books, 1970. 215 p.

      A straightforward but far from exhaustive account of Baillie's
      career. Bibliography.

489   Norton, M.   "The Plays of Joanna Baillie."   RES, 23 (1947), 131–43.

>   A review of Baillie's dramatic theories and methods with the
>   aim of demonstrating how largely, though not completely, she
>   was free from Shakespearean influence.

490   Insch, A.G.   "Joanna Baillie's DE MONTFORT in Relation to Her Theory
of Tragedy."   DUJ, 54 (1961–62), 114–20.

>   A discussion of Baillie's tragic theory as expounded in her
>   1798 SERIES OF PLAYS (item 472).   Insch concludes that DE
>   MONTFORT fails to be good tragedy, partly because Baillie's
>   theory "kept interfering with her practice," and partly be-
>   cause "she was not skilled enough to exploit the slight plot
>   with sufficient dramatic force."

BARNETT, CHARLES ZACHERY (fl. 1840)

II Acted Plays—Principal Titles

491   THE YOUTHFUL DAYS OF WILLIAM THE FOURTH; OR, BRITISH TARS
IN 1782: AN HISTORICAL DRAMA IN TWO ACTS.   (Royal Pavilion,
27 June 1831.)   Duncombe's British Theatre, vol. 8, no. 63.   London:
Duncombe, n.d.   24 p.

>   An acting edition with a cast list of the first London produc-
>   tion and a brief prefatory note by the author ("The piece was
>   written, rehearsed, and acted in the short space of four days!").

492   CAESAR BORGIA: THE SCOURGE OF VENICE!   AN HISTORICAL
DRAMA IN THREE ACTS.   (Royal Pavilion, 8 August 1831.)   Duncombe's
British Theatre, vol. 11.   London: Duncombe, n.d.   28 p.

>   An acting edition with a cast list of the first (?) London
>   production.

493   THE LOSS OF THE ROYAL GEORGE; OR, THE FATAL LAND BREEZE:
A NAUTICO-DOMESTIC DRAMA IN TWO ACTS.   (Royal Pavilion, 8
June 1835.)   Duncombe's British Theatre, vol. 42.   London: Duncombe,
n.d.   46 p.

>   An acting edition with a cast list of a Sadler's Wells produc-
>   tion of October 1840 (here cited as the first).

493a   OLIVER TWIST; OR, THE PARISH BOY'S PROGRESS: A DOMESTIC
DRAMA IN THREE ACTS.   (Royal Pavilion, 21 May 1838.)   Duncombe's
British Theatre, vol. 29.   London: Duncombe, n.d.   38 p.

>   An acting edition with a cast list of the first London produc-

tion. Adapted from Dickens.

494 THE DREAM OF FATE; OR, SARAH THE JEWESS: A DRAMA IN TWO
ACTS. (Sadler's Wells, 20 August 1838.) The New British Theatre, no.
239. London: Lacy, n.d. 38 p.

> An acting edition with a cast list of the first London produc-
> tion.

495 FARINELLI: A SERIO COMIC OPERA IN TWO ACTS. (Drury Lane, 8
February 1839.) Duncombe's British Theatre, vol. 33. London: Duncombe, n.d. 46 p.

> An acting edition with a cast list of the first London produc-
> tion. Music by J. Barnett is not included.

496 THE BOHEMIANS OF PARIS: A ROMANTIC DRAMA IN THREE ACTS.
(Surrey, 27 November 1843.) London: Lacy, n.d. 52 p.

> An acting edition with a cast list of the first London produc-
> tion.

497 A CHRISTMAS CAROL; OR, THE MISER'S WARNING! A DRAMA IN
TWO ACTS. (Surrey, 5 February 1844.) Duncombe's British Theatre,
vol. 48. London: Duncombe, n.d. 26 p.

> An acting edition with a cast list of the first London produc-
> tion. The play is adapted from Dickens's story.

498 DON CAESAR DE BAZAN! OR, MARITANA THE GYPSY! A DRAMA
IN THREE ACTS. (Surrey, 21 October 1844.) Duncombe's British
Theatre, vol. 51. London: Duncombe, n.d. 48 p.

> An acting edition with a cast list of the first London produc-
> tion; based on a play by Dumanoin and Dennery.

BARNETT, MORRIS (1800-1856)

II Acted Plays—Principal Titles

499 THE BOLD DRAGOONS: AN ORIGINAL COMIC DRAMA IN TWO
ACTS. (Adelphi, 9 February 1820.) Lacy's Acting Edition, vol. 9.
London: Lacy, n.d. 29 p.

> An acting edition with a cast list of the first London produc-
> tion.

500 TACT! OR, THE WRONG BOX: A FARCE IN TWO ACTS. (Queen's, 14 February 1821.) Duncombe's British Theatre, vol. 13. London: Duncombe, n.d. 34 p.

An acting edition with a cast list of the first London production.

501 MRS. G--, OF "THE GOLDEN PIPPIN": A MUSICAL PIECE IN TWO ACTS. (Queen's, 14 March 1831.) Duncombe's British Theatre, vol. 8. London: Duncombe, n.d. 26 p.

An acting edition with a cast list of the first London production.

502 THE SPIRIT OF THE RHINE: A PETITE OPERA IN TWO ACTS. (Queen's, 22 September 1835.) Duncombe's British Theatre, vol. 19. London: Duncombe, n.d. 26 p.

An acting edition with a cast list of the first London production.

503 THE YELLOW KIDS: A FARCE IN ONE ACT. (Adelphi, 19 October 1835.) Duncombe's British Theatre, vol. 18. London: Duncombe, n.d. 22 p.

An acting edition with a cast list of the first London production.

504 MONSIEUR JACQUES: A MUSICAL DRAMA IN ONE ACT (St. James's, 13 January 1836.) Duncombe's British Theatre. London: Duncombe, n.d. 23 p.

An acting edition with a cast list of the first London production. The play is adapted from Cogniard's LE PAUVRE JACQUES.

505 THE SERIOUS FAMILY: A COMEDY IN THREE ACTS. (Haymarket, 30 October 1849.) French's Standard Drama, no. 79. New York: French, n.d. 48 p.

An acting edition with cast lists of the first London and New York productions. A brief editorial introduction claims that the play's popularity "exceeded the attraction of Macready or the Keans in their best characters." The Readex copy is a promptbook with manuscript notes (New York Public Library).

506 SARAH THE CREOLE; OR, A SNAKE IN THE GRASS: A DRAMA IN FIVE ACTS. (Olympic, 27 October 1852.) Lacy's Acting Edition, vol. 31. London: Lacy, n.d. 51 p.

An acting edition with a cast list of the first London production (with the title of SARAH BLANGE).

BARRYMORE, WILLIAM (d. 1845)

II Acted Plays—Principal Titles

507 THE DOG OF MONTARGIS; OR, THE FOREST OF BONDY: A MELODRAMA IN TWO ACTS. (Covent Garden, 30 September 1814.) Lacy's Acting Edition, vol. 43. London: Lacy, n.d.

> An acting edition with a cast list of the first London production. The play is adapted from Pixérécourt's LE CHIEN DE MONTARGIS.

508 WALLACE: THE HERO OF SCOTLAND: AN HISTORICAL DRAMA IN THREE ACTS. (Royal Amphitheatre, 6 October 1817.) Spencer's Boston Theatre, no. 48. Boston: William V. Spencer, n.d. 30 p.

> An acting edition with the cast lists of five American productions. This edition also contains a memoir of J.B. Howe with an engraving of him as Wallace.

509 TRIAL BY BATTLE; OR, HEAVEN DEFEND THE RIGHT: A MELODRAMATIC SPECTACLE IN TWO ACTS. (Coburg, 11 May 1818.) London: Duncombe, n.d. 43 p.

> An acting edition with cast lists of the first and an 1831 London production. The Readex copy is a promptbook with manuscript notes (New York Public Library).

510 EL HYDER, THE CHIEF OF THE GHAUT MOUNTAINS: A GRAND EASTERN MELO-DRAMATIC SPECTACLE IN TWO ACTS. (Coburg, 7 December 1818.) Lacy's Acting Edition, vol. 6. London: Lacy, n.d. 25 p.

> An acting edition with a cast list of the first London production (9 November according to this edition).

511 GILDEROY; OR, THE BONNIE BOY: A MELODRAMA IN TWO ACTS. (Coburg, 25 June 1822.) London: Thomas Richardson, n.d. 54 p.

> An acting edition with a cast list of the first London production and introductory comments on Barrymore and his play.

512 THE SECRET: A FARCE IN ONE ACT. (Royal Amphitheatre, 11 May 1824.) Lacy's Acting Edition, vol. 48. London: Lacy, n.d. 24 p.

> An acting edition with cast lists of two London productions

and "Remarks" by D--G [George Daniel].

513 THE QUEEN BEE; OR, HARLEQUIN AND THE FAIRY HIVE. (Drury Lane, 26 December 1828.) London: W. Kenneth, 1828. 16 p.

> Includes a cast list of the first London production.

BAYLY, THOMAS HAYNES (1797-1839)

II Acted Plays—Principal Titles

514 PERFECTION; OR, THE LADY OF MUNSTER: A COMEDY IN ONE ACT. (Drury Lane, 25 March 1830.) Dicks' Standard Plays, no. 276. London: Dicks, n.d. 8 p.

> An acting edition with a cast list of a Haymarket production, 9 January 1833; this copy is a promptbook with a few manuscript notes (New York Public Library).

515 HOW DO YOU MANAGE? A FARCE IN ONE ACT. (Adelphi, 9 February 1835.) London: W. Strange, 1836. 21 p.

> An acting edition with a cast list of the first London production.

516 WHY DON'T SHE MARRY? A MUSICAL BURLETTA IN TWO ACTS. (Olympic, 9 February 1835.) London: W. Strange, 1836. 20 p.

> An acting edition with a cast list of the first London production.

517 A GENTLEMAN IN DIFFICULTIES: AN ENTIRELY ORIGINAL FARCE IN ONE ACT. (Olympic, 28 September 1835.) London: W. Strange, 1836. 24 p.

> An acting edition with a cast list of the first London production.

518 COMFORTABLE SERVICE: AN ENTIRELY ORIGINAL FARCE IN ONE ACT. (Olympic, 16 November 1835.) London: W. Strange, 1836. 21 p.

> An acting edition with a cast list of the first London production.

519 ONE HOUR; OR, THE CARNIVAL BALL: AN ORIGINAL BURLETTA IN ONE ACT. (Olympic, 12 January 1836.) Dicks' Standard Plays, no. 906. London: Dicks, n.d. 11 p.

An acting edition with a cast list of the first London production.

520 FORTY AND FIFTY: A FARCE IN ONE ACT. (Olympic, 2 March 1836.) The Acting National Drama, vol. 4. London: Chapman and Hall, n.d. 15 p.

With a dedication to John Liston and a cast list of the first London production.

521 THE BARRACK-ROOM: A MUSICAL BURLETTA IN TWO ACTS. (Olympic, 7 November 1836.) London: W. Strange, 1837. 24 p.

An acting edition with a cast list of the first London production and a dedication to Madame Vestris.

522 THE LADDER OF LOVE: A MUSICAL DRAMA IN ONE ACT. (Olympic, 16 December 1837.) London: W. Strange, n.d. 27 p.

An acting edition with a cast list of the first London production.

523 THE CULPRIT: AN ORIGINAL FARCE IN ONE ACT. (St. James's, 18 January 1838.) London: Chapman and Hall, 1838. 21 p.

An acting edition with a cast list of the first London production.

524 YOU CAN'T MARRY YOUR GRANDMOTHER: AN ORIGINAL PETITE COMEDY IN TWO ACTS. (Olympic, 1 March 1838.) London: Webster & Co., n.d. 28 p.

An acting edition with a cast list of the first London production; this copy is a promptbook with a very few manuscript notes (New York Public Library).

525 THE BRITISH LEGION: A BURLETTA IN ONE ACT. (St. James's, 7 May 1838.) The Acting National Drama, vol. 4. London: Chapman and Hall, n.d. 20 p.

With a cast list of the first London production and a few manuscript notes.

IV Biography

526 Lang, Andrew. "Thomas Haynes Bayly." ESSAYS IN LITTLE. London: Henry and Co., 1891. 36-50.

This is mainly a discussion of Bayly's songs and poems, with

only a brief reference to the plays; but there is some biographical information.

BEAZLEY, SAMUEL (1786-1851)

II Acted Plays—Principal Titles

527 THE BOARDING-HOUSE; OR, FIVE HOURS AT BRIGHTON: A MUSICAL
FARCE IN TWO ACTS. (Lyceum, 26 August 1811.) London: C. Chapple, 1816. 39 p.

> Includes a cast list of the first London production.

528 IS HE JEALOUS? AN OPERETTA IN ONE ACT. (English Opera House,
2 July 1816.) London: John Miller, 1816. 33 p.

> Includes a cast list of the first London production.

529 MY UNCLE: AN OPERETTA IN ONE ACT. (English Opera House, 23
June 1817.) London: John Miller, 1817. 29 p.

> Includes a cast list of the first London production.

530 JEALOUS ON ALL SIDES; OR, THE LANDLORD IN JEOPARDY! A
COMIC OPERA IN TWO ACTS. (English Opera House, 19 August 1818.)
London: William Fearman, 1818. 43 p.

> Includes a cast list of the first London production.

531 THE STEWARD; OR, FASHION AND FEELING: A COMEDY IN FIVE
ACTS. (Covent Garden, 15 September 1819.) London: John Lowndes,
1819. xi, 83 p.

> The play is based on Holcroft's THE DESERTED DAUGHTER
> from which, Beazley explains in a preface, the "revolting
> situations" have been expunged; cast list of the first London
> production.

532 IVANHOE; OR, THE KNIGHT TEMPLAR. (Covent Garden, 2 March
1820.) London: W. Smith, 1820. 72 p.

> Includes a cast list of first London production; the play is
> adapted from Scott's novel.

533 LOVE'S DREAM: A PETITE OPERA IN TWO ACTS. (English Opera
House, 5 July 1821.) London: John Lowndes, 1821. 35 p.

> Includes a cast list of the first London production; based on

Scribe's LA SOMNAMBULE.

534 THE LOTTERY TICKET AND THE LAWYER'S CLERK: A FARCE. (Drury Lane, 13 December 1826.) London: C. Chapple, 1827. 32 p.

Includes a cast list of the first London production.

BERNARD, WILLIAM BAYLE (1807-75)

II Acted Plays—Principal Titles

535 "The Four Sisters; or, Woman's Worth and Woman's Ways: A Petite Comedy in One Act." (Strand, 13 May 1832.)

A manuscript copy with forty-four leaves (New York Public Library).

536 THE CONQUERING GAME: A PETITE COMEDY IN ONE ACT. (Olympic, 28 November 1832.) Duncombe's British Theatre, vol. 36. London: Duncombe, n.d. 24 p.

An acting edition with a cast list of the first London production and a dedication to Charles Mathews.

537 THE NERVOUS MAN AND THE MAN OF NERVE: A FARCE IN TWO ACTS. (Drury Lane, 26 January 1833.) Modern Standard Drama, no. 36. New York: William Taylor, n.d. 45 p.

An acting edition with cast lists of the first London and Park Theatre, New York, productions, and an editorial introduction ("Great dramatic skill is shown in the whole construction of this piece").

538 LUCILLE; OR, THE STORY OF THE HEART: A DRAMA IN THREE ACTS. (English Opera House, 4 April 1836.) Lacy's Acting Edition, vol. 28, no. 420. London: Lacy, n.d. 37 p.

With a cast list of the first London production and a dedication to Bulwer-Lytton upon whose PILGRIMS OF THE RHINE the play is based.

539 THE FARMER'S STORY: A DOMESTIC DRAMA IN THREE ACTS. (English Opera House, 13 June 1836.) London and New York: French, n.d. 45 p.

An acting edition with a cast list of the first London production.

540 ST. MARY'S EVE; OR, A SOLWAY STORY: AN ORIGINAL DOMESTIC
DRAMA IN TWO ACTS. (Adelphi, 1 January 1838.) London: Lacy,
n.d. 39 p.

> An acting edition with cast lists of Adelphi and Haymarket
> productions; this copy is a promptbook with manuscript notes.

541 MARIE DUCANGE: AN ORIGINAL DOMESTIC DRAMA IN THREE ACTS.
(Lyceum, 29 May 1841.) London: Lacy, n.d. 48 p.

> An acting edition with a cast list of the first London produc-
> tion.

542 THE ROUND OF WRONG; OR, A FIRESIDE STORY: AN ORIGINAL
DRAMA IN TWO ACTS. (Haymarket, 19 December 1846.) London:
The Acting National Drama, vol. 13, no. 139. National Acting Drama
Office, n.d. 46 p.

> With a cast list of the first London production.

543 THE PASSING CLOUD: A ROMANTIC DRAMA IN TWO ACTS. (Drury
Lane, 8 April 1850.) Modern Standard Drama, no. 85. New York:
William Taylor, n.d. 59 p.

> An acting edition with a cast list of the first London produc-
> tion and a brief editorial introduction.

544 A STORM IN A TEA CUP: A COMEDIETTA IN ONE ACT. (Princess's,
20 March 1854.) Lacy's Acting Edition, no. 200. London: Lacy, n.d.
20 p.

> With a cast list of the first London production.

545 THE EVIL GENIUS: AN ORIGINAL COMEDY IN THREE ACTS. (Haymarket, 8 March 1856.) London: Lacy, n.d. 68 p.

> An acting edition with a cast list of the first London produc-
> tion.

546 A LIFE'S TRIAL: AN ORIGINAL DRAMA IN THREE ACTS. (Haymarket,
19 March 1857.) Lacy's Acting Edition, vol. 30, no. 436. London:
Lacy, n.d. 48 p.

> With a cast list of the first London production.

547 THE TIDE OF TIME: AN ORIGINAL COMEDY IN THREE ACTS. (Haymarket, 13 December 1858.) Lacy's Acting Edition, vol. 38. London:
Lacy, n.d. 53 p.

> With a cast list of the first London production.

BLANCHARD, EDWARD LEMAN (1820-89)

II Acted Plays—Principal Titles

548 THE ARTFUL DODGE: A FARCE IN ONE ACT. (Olympic, 21 February 1842.) London: Lacy, n.d. 23 p.

> An acting edition with a cast list of the first London production.

549 PORK CHOPS; OR, A DREAM OF HOME: A FARCICAL EXTRAVA-GANZA FURNISHED WITH A DRAMATIC SCENE BY MR. W.R. BEVERLY AND A MUSICAL SAUCE BY MR. CAULCOTT IN ONE ACT. (Olympic, 13 February 1843.) London: Lacy, n.d. 12 p.

> An acting edition with a cast list of the first London production.

550 FAITH, HOPE, AND CHARITY! OR, CHANCE AND CHANGE! A DOMESTIC DRAMA IN THREE ACTS. (Surrey, 7 July 1845.) London: Duncombe, n.d. 55 p.

> An acting edition with a cast list of the first London production, and a preface by Blanchard.

551 ADAM BUFF; OR, THE MAN WITHOUT A ------! A FARCE IN ONE ACT. (Surrey, 4 March 1850.) London: Duncombe/Lacy, n.d. 24 p.

> An acting edition with a cast list of the first London production.

552 CHERRY & FAIR STAR; OR, THE SINGING APPLE, THE TALKING BIRD, AND THE DANCING WATERS: A GRAND COMIC CHRISTMAS AN-NUAL. (Sadler's Wells, 26 December 1861). London: Music-Publishing Co., n.d. 16 p.

> Libretto with a cast list of the first London production.

553 HARLEQUIN AND THE HOUSE THAT JACK BUILT; OR, OLD MOTHER HUBBARD AND HER WONDERFUL DOG. (Drury Lane, 26 December 1861.) London: Music-Publishing Co., n.d. 24 p.

> An acting edition with a cast list of an unspecified production.

554 *RIQUET WITH THE TUFT; OR, HARLEQUIN & OLD MOTHER SHIPTON: AN ENTIRELY NOVEL, ORIGINAL, BURLESQUE, GROTESQUE, METRI-CAL, MUSICAL, MAGICAL, GRAND COMIC CHRISTMAS PANTOMIME. (Princess's, 26 December 1862.) London: Music-Publishing Co., n.d.

20 p.

Libretto with a cast list of the first London production.

IV Biography

555 Scott, Clement, and Cecil Howard. THE LIFE AND REMINISCENCES
OF E.L. BLANCHARD WITH NOTES FROM THE DIARY OF WM. BLANC-
HARD. 2 vols. London: Hutchinson, 1891. xv, 736 p.

An autobiography in diary form covering the years 1844–89,
and giving an interesting record of the London stage. Supplemented by voluminous notes and an appendix containing a
sketch of Blanchard's father, Blanchard's letters, and ephemera.

BOUCICAULT, DION (ca. 1820/22-90)

I Collected Works

556 Nicoll, Allardyce, and F. Theodore Cloak, eds. FORBIDDEN FRUIT &
OTHER PLAYS. America's Lost Plays, vol. 1. Princeton: Princeton
University Press, 1940. viii, 313 p.

Contains: FORBIDDEN FRUIT; LOUIS XI; DOT; THE FLYING
SCUD; MERCY DODD; and ROBERT EMMET. A scholarly
edition with a separate introduction to each play giving a
brief history and the provenance of the text reprinted.

557 Krause, David, ed. THE DOLMEN BOUCICAULT: WITH AN ESSAY BY
THE EDITOR ON THE THEATRE OF DION BOUCICAULT AND THE
COMPLETE AUTHENTIC TEXTS OF BOUCICAULT'S THREE IRISH PLAYS.
Dublin: Dolmen Press, 1964. 253 p.

Texts of THE COLLEEN BAWN; OR, THE BRIDES OF GARRY-
OWEN; ARRAH NA POGUE; OR, THE WICKLOW WEDDING;
and THE SHAUGHRAUN. Krause bases his texts on the acting
editions published by Lacy, French, and Dicks. There are
cast lists of the first productions and a bibliography of works
by and about Boucicault. Krause's essay is a useful introduction to Boucicault's life and works.

II Acted Plays—Principal Titles

558 *LONDON ASSURANCE: A COMEDY IN FIVE ACTS, WITH THE STAGE
BUSINESS, CAST OF CHARACTERS, COSTUMES, RELATIVE POSITIONS,
&C., AS PERFORMED AT THE PARK THEATRE. (Covent Garden, 4

March 1841.) French's Standard Drama, no. 27. New York: [1854].
71 p.

An acting edition with an unabridged text.

559 LONDON ASSURANCE: A COMEDY IN FIVE ACTS: AS PERFORMED
AT THE PARK THEATRE. French's Standard Drama, no. 27. New York:
n.d. 71 p.

A promptcopy, interleaved with manuscript notes, and including an "Editorial Introduction" and a cast list of the
first New York production.

560 "London Assurance: A Comedy in Five Acts."

A typescript with each act paginated separately. Original
located in New York Public Library.

561 LONDON ASSURANCE: A COMEDY IN FIVE ACTS. London: 1841.
vii, 86 p.

A promptbook, interleaved with manuscript notes, and including a preface by Boucicault and a cast list of the first
London performance.

562 *LONDON ASSURANCE: A COMEDY IN FIVE ACTS: ACTING VER-
SION OF THE YALE UNIVERSITY DRAMATIC ASSOCIATION (INCOR-
PORATED): WITH AN INTRODUCTION BY WILLIAM LYON PHELPS.
New Haven, Conn.: 1910. xx, 87 p.

The introduction deals briefly with Boucicault's life and the
play. The text has been cut in several places, mainly to
shorten its playing time.

563 LONDON ASSURANCE: THE FULL ORIGINAL TEXT ADAPTED FOR
THE MODERN STAGE AND EDITED BY RONALD EYRE: WITH AN
INTRODUCTION BY PETER THOMSON. London: Methuen, 1971.
xxiv, 87 p.

The text is the original 1841 version, but also shows the
alterations made by Eyre for the Royal Shakespeare Company's
revival (Aldwych, 23 June 1970). There is also a useful,
brief biographical introduction.

564 THE OLD GUARD: A DRAMA IN ONE ACT. (Princess's, 9 October
1843.) Minor Drama, no. 29. New York: John Douglas, 1848. 20 p.

A promptbook with numerous manuscript notes and an editorial introduction.

565 USED UP: A PETITE COMEDY IN TWO ACTS. With Charles Mathews. (Haymarket, 6 February 1844.) London: National Acting Drama Office, n.d. 33 p.

   An acting edition with a cast list of the first London production.

566 CAESAR DE BAZAN; OR, LOVE AND HONOUR! A DRAMA IN THREE ACTS. With Benjamin Webster. (Adelphi, 14 October 1844.) London: Webster, n.d. 40 p.

   An acting edition with a cast list of the first London production.

567 OLD HEADS & YOUNG HEARTS: A COMEDY IN FIVE ACTS. (Haymarket, 18 November 1844.) 2nd ed. London: National Acting Drama Office, n.d. 80 p.

   An acting edition with a cast list of the first London production. The Readex collection also includes French's edition, no. 62 (New York, n.d.), 73 p., which contains cast lists of London and American productions and an editorial introduction. This copy also has numerous manuscript notes.

568 *THE KNIGHT OF ARVA: A COMIC DRAMA IN TWO ACTS. (Haymarket, 22 November 1848.) New York: French, n.d. 28 p.

   An acting edition with several cast lists of productions in England and America.

569 THE QUEEN OF SPADES: A DRAMA IN TWO ACTS. ADAPTED FROM "LA DAME DE PIQUE". (Drury Lane, 29 March 1851.) London: Lacy, n.d. 30 p.

   An acting edition with a cast list of the first London production.

570 THE CORSICAN BROTHERS: A DRAMATIC ROMANCE IN THREE ACTS: AS FIRST PERFORMED AT THE PRINCESS'S THEATRE UNDER THE MANAGEMENT OF CHARLES KEAN. (Princess's, 24 February 1852.) London: J.K. Chapman, n.d. 40 p.

   An acting edition with a cast list of the first London production.

571 FAUST AND MARGUERITE: A MAGICAL DRAMA IN THREE ACTS: AS PERFORMED AT THE PRINCESS'S THEATRE . . . [BY] . . . CHARLES KEAN. (Princess's, 19 April 1854.) London: J.K. Chapman, n.d. 40 p.

A note at the end of this copy (located in Yale University Library) indicates it was Kean's own.

572   "Louis XI." (Princess's, 13 January 1855.)

A manuscript promptbook, located in Harvard University. The Readex collection also includes the Nicoll and Cloak text, item 556.

573   THE COLLEEN BAWN; OR, THE BRIDES OF GARRYOWEN: A DOMESTIC DRAMA IN THREE ACTS. (Laura Keene's, New York, 28 March 1860; Adelphi, 10 September 1860.) Standard Drama, no. 356. London and New York: French, n.d. 42 p.

An acting edition with the cast list for the first New York production.

574   THE OCTOROON; OR, LIFE IN LOUISIANA: A PLAY IN FOUR ACTS. (Winter Garden, N.Y., 6 December 1859; Adelphi, 18 November 1861.) London and New York: French, n.d. 43 p.

An acting edition with a cast list of the first New York production. The Readex collection also contains a second, different copy, which is a promptbook, interleaved with manuscript notes and including cast lists of two other American productions.

575   *THE OCTOROON; OR, LIFE IN LOUISIANA. Miami, Fla., 1969. 40 p.

A reprint of an unspecified acting edition, with cast lists of two early American productions.

576   DOT. (Winter Garden, N.Y., 14 September 1859; Adelphi, 14 April 1862.) No publication details. 33 p.

A promptbook, with manuscript notes. The Readex collection also includes a version of DOT printed from item 556.

577   JESSIE BROWN; OR, THE RELIEF OF LUCKNOW: A DRAMA IN THREE ACTS. (Wallack's, New York, 22 May 1858; Drury Lane, 15 September 1862.) Dicks' Standard Plays, no. 473. London: Dicks, n.d. 16 p.

An acting edition, with a cast list of the first New York production. The Readex collection also includes a second copy, a promptbook (32 p.) with numerous manuscript notes.

578   THE POOR OF NEW YORK: A DRAMA IN FIVE ACTS. (Princess's, 1 August 1864; as THE STREETS OF LONDON, Wallack's, New York, 8 December 1857.) Standard Drama, no. 189. New York: French, n.d. 45 p.

An acting edition with a cast list of the first New York production. The Readex collection contains a second copy of this edition, interleaved with numerous manuscript notes; the title has been altered to THE STREETS OF NEW YORK.

579 ARRAH-NA-POGUE; OR, THE WICKLOW WEDDING: AN IRISH DRAMA IN THREE ACTS. (Dublin, 7 November 1864; Princess's, 23 March 1865.) Acting Plays, no. 365. New York: De Witt, n.d. 53 p.

An acting edition, with cast lists of the first productions in Dublin and London. The Readex collection also includes another promptbook with manuscript notes.

580 *RIP VAN WINKLE, AS PLAYED BY JOSEPH JEFFERSON. (Adelphi, 4 September 1865.) New York, 1895; rpt. New York: AMS, 1969. 199 p.

Jefferson's acting version of the famous story with an introduction outlining the history of this version and Boucicault's hand in it.

581 *THE LONG STRIKE: A DRAMA IN FOUR ACTS. (Lyceum, 15 September 1866.) Standard Drama, no. 360. New York: French, n.d. 38 p.

An acting edition.

582 THE FLYING SCUD: A DRAMA IN [TWO] ACTS. (Holborn, 6 October 1866.) No publication details. 55 p.

A printed promptbook with numerous manuscript notes. The Readex collection also includes the version from item 556.

583 FOUL PLAY: A DRAMA IN FOUR ACTS. (Holborn, 28 May 1868.) Chicago: Dramatic Publishing Co., n.d. 33 p.

An acting edition with a cast list of the first London production. The Readex collection also contains a printed promptbook with numerous manuscript notes.

584 AFTER DARK: A DRAMA OF LONDON LIFE IN 1868, IN FOUR ACTS. (Princess's, 12 August 1868.) London, n.d. 39 p.

An acting edition with sketches of scenes.

585 FORMOSA: ("THE MOST BEAUTIFUL"); OR, THE RAILROAD TO RUIN: A DRAMA OF MODERN LIFE IN FOUR ACTS. (Drury Lane, 5 August 1869.) No publication details. 44 p.

An acting edition, with details of scenery and a cast list of the first London production.

586 *KERRY; OR, NIGHT AND MORNING. (Prince's, Manchester, 7 September 1871; Gaiety, London, 19 November 1871.) Intro. Hilary Berrow. IRISH UNIVERSITY REVIEW 3, no. 1 (1973), 31-50.

> The National Library of Ireland manuscript text of Bouci- cault's play, first performed as NIGHT AND MORNING in Manchester in 1871.

587 THE SHAUGHRAUN: AN ORIGINAL DRAMA IN THREE ACTS: ILLUS- TRATIVE OF IRISH LIFE AND CHARACTER. (Wallack's, New York, 14 November 1874; Drury Lane, 4 September 1875.) No publication details. 26 p.

> A [Dicks] acting edition with a cast list of the first New York production. The Readex collection also contains a promptbook, interleaved with numerous manuscript notes.

588 *THE SHAUGHRAUN: AN ORIGINAL DRAMA IN THREE ACTS. Lon- don and New York: French, n.d. 64 p.

> An acting edition with sketches of the scenes and cast lists of the first productions in London and New York.

589 THE O'DOWD. (Booth's, New York, 17 March 1873; as DADDY O'DOWD, Adelphi, 21 October 1880.) London and New York: French, 1909. 52 p.

> An acting edition with a cast list of the first London produc- tion.

590 [DADDY O'DOWD]. No publication details. Each act numbered sepa- rately--17, 29, 31 p.

> A promptbook (located in Princeton University Library) with numerous manuscript notes.

591 BELLE LAMAR. (As FIN MACCOUL, Booth's, New York, 10 August 1874; as BELLE LAMAR, Elephant and Castle, 2 February 1887.) [New York, 1874.]

> A promptbook (located in New York Public Library) with numerous manuscript notes and part pieces.

IV Biography

592 "Mr. Dion Boucicault on Himself." THEATRE, n.s. 3 (November 1879), 186-88.

A hostile review of Boucicault's RESCUED and a charge that he is a mere poseur.

593 "Mr. Boucicault Again." THEATRE, n.s. 3 (December 1879), 248-50.

A sarcastic attack on Boucicault's published defense of himself and his work.

594 Boucicault, Dion. "Leaves from a Dramatist's Diary." NORTH AMERICAN REVIEW, 149 (1889), 228-36.

A group of random accounts about various aspects of Boucicault's life.

595 Downer, Alan S. "The Case of Mr. Lee Moreton." TN, 4 (1950), 44-45.

Brief details of one or two incidents connected with Boucicault's use of his pseudonym, Lee Moreton.

596 Orr, Lynn E. "Dion Boucicault and the Nineteenth Century Theatre: A Biography." Ph.D. Dissertation, Louisiana State University, 1953. 241 p.

597 Faulkner, Seldon. "The OCTOROON War." ETJ, 15 (1963), 33-38.

An account of Boucicault's legal battles over the New York production of THE OCTOROON in 1859.

598 Folland, Harold F. "Lee Moreton: The Debut of a Theatre Man." TN, 23 (1968-69), 122-29.

Boucicault's early acting career (under the name of Moreton) in Brighton, Bristol, and Hull.

599 Johnson, Albert E. "Real Sunlight in the Garden: Dion Boucicault as a Stage Director." ThR, 12, no. 2 (1972), 119-25.

A short account of Boucicault's excellent ability as a director; draws on primary materials by way of illustration.

600 Roman, Diane P., and Mary T. Hamilton. "Boucicault and the Anne Jordan Affair." JOURNAL OF IRISH LITERATURE, 1, no. 2 (1972), 120-27.

Concerning a relationship Boucicault enjoyed in 1863 with one of his company's actresses.

601 Johnson, Albert E. "Dion Boucicault Learns to Act." PLAYERS, 48

(1973), 78-85.

> An account of Boucicault's acting career in the late 1830's, which found him in provincial and minor London theatres.

V Critical Studies

602 "Mr. Boucicault and Mr. Barnum." SATURDAY REVIEW, 61 (1 May 1886), 607-8.

> A review of THE JILT, which gives opportunity for some assessment of Boucicault's talents.

603 "Dion Boucicault." CRITIC (New York), 9, no. 143 (September 1886), 145-56.

> Merely a dip into some features of Boucicault's work.

604 Walsh, Towsend. THE CAREER OF DION BOUCICAULT. New York: Dunlap Society, [1915]; rpt. New York: Blom, 1967. xviii, 224 p.

> A somewhat anecdotal work on Boucicault's life and work, written in the genial fashion so common in earlier theatrical histories. However, it does contain a useful survey of the main points of Boucicault's career and lists Boucicault's appearances in Dublin and his dramatic works. The book is partially documented but has no index.

605 Maclysaght, W. DEATH SAILS THE SHANNON: THE AUTHENTIC STORY OF "THE COLLEEN BAWN." Tralee: The Kerryman, 1953. 136 p.

> An account of the murder of Ellen Hanley in 1819, an event which formed the basis for Boucicault's play, THE COLLEEN BAWN.

606 Rohrig, Gladys May. "An Analysis of Certain Acting Editions and Promptbooks of Plays by Dion Boucicault." Ph.D. dissertation, Ohio State University, 1956. 208 p. (DA#00-20715)

607 Hunter, Jack W. "Some Research Problems in a Study of THE CORSICAN BROTHERS." OSUTCB, 9 (1962), 6-22.

> A discussion of the technical problems of staging THE CORSICAN BROTHERS, which conjectures how the lateral trap door was constructed. A brief history of the play and its productions is also given.

608   Ritchie, Harry M. "The Influence of Melodrama on the Early Plays of Sean O'Casey." MD, 5 (1962-63), 164-73.

> An account of Boucicault's influence on O'Casey, in which Ritchie argues O'Casey adapted the melodramatic formula for his own purposes. He incidentally gives some useful pointers on Boucicault's dramatic skills.

609   Hunter, Jack W. "THE CORSICAN BROTHERS: Its History and Technical Problems Related to the Production of the Play." Ph.D dissertation, Ohio State University, 1963.

610   Faulkner, Seldon. "The Great Train Scene Robbery." QJS, 50 (1964), 24-28.

> An account of the similarity between Daly's UNDER THE GASLIGHT and Boucicault's AFTER DARK, which led to a court case in New York in 1868. The crux of the case (which Boucicault lost) was the alleged plagiarism of a "train scene."

610a   Enkvist, Nils Erik. "THE OCTOROON and English Opinions of Slavery." AQ, 8 (1965), 166-70.

611   Harrison, Allie Cleveland. "The Dramatic Theories of Dion Boucicault: A Study of Statements on Dramaturgy in His Published Essays." Ph.D. Dissertation, University of Kansas, 1967. 363 p. (DA#68-06917).

611a   Hogan, Robert. DION BOUCICAULT. New York: Twayne, 1969. 146 p.

> A general introduction to Boucicault's life and work, with a useful bibliography.

BROOKS, CHARLES WILLIAM SHIRLEY (1816-74)

II Acted Plays—Principal Titles

612   *THE WIGWAM: A BURLETTA IN ONE ACT. (Lyceum, 25 January 1847.) Dicks' Standard Plays, no. 1,004. London: Dicks, n.d. Pp. numbered 11-21.

> An acting edition with a cast list of the first London production.

613   THE CREOLE; OR, LOVE'S LETTERS: AN ORIGINAL DRAMA IN THREE ACTS. (Lyceum, 8 April 1847.) London, n.d. 48 p.

An acting edition with some manuscript notes, a preface, and
a cast list of the first London production. The Readex collection includes a second edition published by Lacy (London,
n.d.), 48 p.

614 ANYTHING FOR A CHANGE: A PETITE COMEDY IN ONE ACT.
(Lyceum, 7 June 1848.) London and New York: French, n.d. 22 p.

An acting edition with a cast list of the first London production.

615 THE DAUGHTER OF THE STARS: A DRAMA IN TWO ACTS. (Strand,
5 August 1850.) London: Lacy, n.d. 36 p.

An acting edition with a dedication to Angus B. Reach and
a cast list of the first London production.

616 THE EXPOSITION: A SCANDINAVIAN SKETCH, CONTAINING AS
MUCH IRRELEVANT MATTER AS POSSIBLE: IN ONE ACT. (Strand, 28
April 1851.) London: Lacy, n.d. 22 p.

An acting edition with a cast list of the first London production.

617 *TIMOUR THE TARTAR! OR, THE IRON MASTER OF SAMARKAND-BY-
OXUS: AN EXTRAVAGANZA. (Olympic, 26 December 1860.) London:
Lacy, n.d. 36 p.

An acting edition with a cast list of the first London production.

IV Biography

618 Jerrold, Blanchard. "Shirley Brooks." GENTLEMAN'S MAGAZINE,
236 (May 1874), 561-69.

An affectionate memoir.

619 Layard, George Somes. A GREAT "PUNCH" EDITOR: BEING THE LIFE,
LETTERS AND DIARIES OF SHIRLEY BROOKS. London: Pitman, 1907.
xi, 599 p.

A somewhat verbose and digressive biography, illustrated with
many of Brooks's letters and other material.

BROUGH, ROBERT BARNABAS (1828-60)

II Acted Plays—Principal Titles

620 THE ENCHANTED ISLE; OR, "RAISING THE WIND" ON THE MOST
APPROVED PRINCIPLES: A DRAMA WITHOUT THE SMALLEST CLAIM
TO LEGITIMACY, CONSISTENCY, PROBABILITY, OR ANYTHING ELSE
BUT ABSURDITY; IN WHICH WILL BE FOUND MUCH THAT IS UNAC-
COUNTABLY COINCIDENT WITH SHAKESPEARE'S "TEMPEST." With
William Brough. (Amphitheatre, Liverpool, 1848; Adelphi, 20 November
1848.) Acting National Drama, no. 152. London: Webster, n.d.
32 p.

An acting edition with cast lists of London productions.

621 CAMARALZAMAN AND BADOURA; OR, THE PERI WHO LOVED THE
PRINCE: AN EXTRAVAGANT ARABIAN NIGHT'S ENTERTAINMENT IN
TWO ACTS. With William Brough. (Haymarket, 26 December 1848.)
Acting National Drama, vol. 15. London: Webster, n.d. 40 p.

An acting edition with a cast list of the first London production.

622 THE SPHINX: A "TOUCH FROM THE ANCIENTS" IN ONE ACT.
With William Brough. (Haymarket, 9 April 1849.) Acting National
Drama, vol. 15. London: Webster, n.d. 33 p.

An acting edition with a cast list of the first London production.

623 THE LAST EDITION OF IVANHOE, WITH ALL THE NEWEST IMPROVE-
MENTS: AN EXTRAVANGANZA IN TWO ACTS. With William
Brough. (Haymarket, 1 April 1850.) Acting National Drama, vol. 16.
London: Webster, n.d. 43 p.

An acting edition with a cast list of the first London production.

624 THE SECOND CALENDAR; AND THE QUEEN OF BEAUTY, WHO HAD
A FIGHT WITH THE GENIE: AN EXTRAVANGANZA IN TWO ACTS.
With William Brough. (Haymarket, 26 December 1850.) Acting Na-
tional Drama; no. 175. London: Webster, n.d. 46 p.

An acting edition with a dedication to J.B. Buckstone and
a cast list of the first London production.

625 MEDEA; OR, THE BEST OF MOTHERS, WITH A BRUTE OF A HUSBAND:
A BURLESQUE IN ONE ACT. (Olympic, 14 July 1856.) London: Lacy,
n.d. 35 p.

An acting edition with a cast list of the first London production.

626 MASANIELLO; OR, THE FISH'OMAN OF NAPLES: A FISH TALE IN ONE ACT. (Olympic, 2 July 1857.) London: Lacy, n.d. 42 p.

An acting edition with a dedication to Mrs. Alfred Wigan and a cast list of the first London production.

627 THE SIEGE OF TROY: A BURLESQUE IN ONE ACT. (Olympic, 27 December 1858.) London: H. Barclay, n.d. 47 p.

An acting edition with a cast list of the first London production.

628 ALFRED THE GREAT; OR, THE MINSTREL KING: AN HISTORICAL EXTRAVAGANZA. (Olympic, 26 December 1859.) London: Lacy, n.d. 48 p.

An acting edition with a cast list of the first London production.

IIa Unacted Plays

629 A CRACKER BON-BON FOR CHRISTMAS PARTIES: CONSISTING OF CHRISTMAS PIECES, FOR PRIVATE REPRESENTATION, AND OTHER SEASONABLE MATTER IN PROSE AND VERSE. London: W. Kent, 1861. 99 p.

The Christmas "pieces" are KING ALFRED AND THE CAKES, WILLIAM TELL, and ORPHEUS AND EURYDICE.

IV Biography

630 Archer, Thomas. "Robert Brough." THE POETS AND THE POETRY OF THE NINETEENTH CENTURY: CHARLES KINGSLEY TO JAMES THOMSON. Ed. Alfred H. Miles. London: Routledge, 1905. Pp. 331-34.

A brief biographical sketch, mainly with references to Brough's poetic output.

BROUGH, WILLIAM (1826-70)

II Acted Plays--Principal Titles. See also plays with Robert Brough, above.

631 PERDITA; OR, THE ROYAL MILKMAID, BEING THE LEGEND UPON

WHICH SHAKESPEARE IS SUPPOSED TO HAVE FOUNDED HIS "WINTER'S TALE": A NEW AND ORIGINAL BURLESQUE. (Lyceum, 15 September 1856.) London: Lacy, n.d. 39 p.

An acting edition with a cast list of the first London production.

632　THE AREA BELLE: A FARCE IN ONE ACT. With Andrew Halliday. (Adelphi, 7 March 1864.) Sergel's Acting Drama, no. 93. Chicago: Sergel, n.d. 12 p.

An acting edition with a cast list of the first London production.

633　THE FIELD OF THE CLOTH OF GOLD: AN ORIGINAL GRAND HISTORICAL EXTRAVAGANZA. (Strand, 11 April 1868.) London: Lacy, n.d. 44 p.

An acting edition with a cast list of the first London production.

BROUGHTON, FREDERICK W. (1851-94)

II Acted Plays—Principal Titles

634　WITHERED LEAVES: A COMEDIETTA IN ONE ACT. (Theatre Royal, Sheffield, 5 April 1875; Terry's, 31 October 1892.) London: French, n.d. 26 p.

An acting edition with a cast list of the Sheffield production.

635　RUTH'S ROMANCE: A SUMMER EVENING'S SKETCH. (Theatre Royal, Bath, 6 March 1876; Strand, 1879.) London and New York: French, n.d. 30 p.

An acting edition with cast lists of productions at Bath and London.

636　SUNSHINE: AN ORIGINAL COMEDY IN ONE ACT. (Theatre Royal, Bristol, 5 January 1880; Theatre Royal, Bradford, 5 May 1880; Strand, 2 June 1884.) London and New York: French, n.d. 19 p.

An acting edition with a cast list of the Bradford production.

637　THE BAILIFF: A DOMESTIC COMEDY IN ONE ACT. (Theatre Royal, Bath, 5 April 1890; Royalty, 17 May 1890.) London and New York: French, n.d. 18 p.

An acting edition with cast lists of the productions in Bath and London.

BROWNING, ROBERT (1812-89)

I Collected Works

638 DRAMAS. 2 vols. in 1. Boston: Houghton Mifflin, 1883. 384; 251 p.

Omits STRAFFORD; no editorial matter.

639 Rolfe, William J., and Heloise E. Hersey, eds. "A BLOT IN THE 'SCUTCHEON" AND OTHER DRAMAS BY ROBERT BROWNING. New York: Harper, 1887. 245 p.

The other dramas are COLOMBE'S BIRTHDAY and A SOUL'S TRAGEDY. The editors supply a general introduction and critical comments and notes on each play.

640 Rinder, Frank, ed. "A BLOT IN THE 'SCUTCHEON" AND OTHER POETIC DRAMAS BY ROBERT BROWNING. London: Walter Scott, [1896]. xix, 367 p.

Includes A BLOT IN THE 'SCUTCHEON, THE RETURN OF THE DRUSES, COLOMBE'S BIRTHDAY, THE FLIGHT OF THE DUCHESS, LURIA, A SOUL'S TRAGEDY, and CHRISTMAS-EVE AND EASTER-DAY. The editor's introduction offers no justification for classifying THE FLIGHT OF THE DUCHESS and CHRISTMAS-EVE AND EASTER-DAY as dramas.

641 _____. "PIPPA PASSES" AND OTHER POETIC DRAMAS BY ROBERT BROWNING. London: Walter Scott, 1896. xxiv, 372 p.

Includes PAULINE, PARACELSUS, STRAFFORD, PIPPA PASSES, and KING VICTOR AND KING CHARLES. The editor does not indicate in what sense he sees PAULINE as a drama.

642 Wise, Thomas J., ed. BELLS AND POMEGRANATES. FIRST SERIES. London: Ward, Lock & Co., 1896. xiv, 326 p.

A collection of the first five BELLS AND POMEGRANATES pamphlets (1841-43), containing (in addition to the DRAMATIC LYRICS) PIPPA PASSES, KING VICTOR AND KING CHARLES, THE RETURN OF THE DRUSES, and A BLOT IN THE 'SCUTCHEON. Brief notes and a bibliography are supplied by the editor.

643 _____. BELLS AND POMEGRANATES. SECOND SERIES. London: Ward, Lock & Co., 1897. x, 283 p.

A collection of the final three BELLS AND POMEGRANATES pamphlets (1844-46), containing (in addition to DRAMATIC

ROMANCES AND LYRICS) COLOMBE'S BIRTHDAY, LURIA,
and A SOUL'S TRAGEDY.

644 Browning, Oscar, ed. DRAMAS BY ROBERT BROWNING. London:
Routledge, 1898. xl, 480 p.

Includes PARACELSUS, PIPPA PASSES, KING VICTOR AND
KING CHARLES, COLOMBE'S BIRTHDAY, A BLOT IN THE
'SCUTCHEON, THE RETURN ON THE DRUSES, LURIA, A
SOUL'S TRAGEDY, and STRAFFORD. The editor's introduc-
tion is biographical; no introductory material or notes are sup-
plied for the plays.

645 Bates, Arlo, ed. "A BLOT IN THE 'SCUTCHEON," "COLOMBE'S
BIRTHDAY," "A SOUL'S TRAGEDY" AND "IN A BALCONY." Boston:
D.C. Heath, 1904. xxxviii, 305 p.

There is an ample introduction, brief notes, a bibliography,
and a glossary.

646 Waugh, Arthur, ed. THE POEMS & PLAYS OF ROBERT BROWNING
1833-1844. Everyman's Library. London: Dent; New York: Dutton,
1906. xxi, 662 p.

Contains PARACELSUS, STRAFFORD, PIPPA PASSES, KING
VICTOR AND KING CHARLES, THE RETURN OF THE DRUSES,
A BLOT IN THE 'SCUTCHEON, and COLOMBE'S BIRTHDAY.

647 Commins, Saxe, ed. THE POEMS AND PLAYS OF ROBERT BROWNING.
New York: Modern Library, 1934. xvii, 1223 p.

Omits STRAFFORD and KING VICTOR AND KING CHARLES.
The editor's introduction contains a very brief summary of
Browning the playwright.

648 King, Roma A., et al., eds. THE COMPLETE WORKS OF ROBERT
BROWNING. WITH VARIANT READINGS & ANNOTATIONS. Athens:
Ohio University Press, 1969- .

Volume one (1969) has PARACELSUS; volume two (1970) has
STRAFFORD; volume three (1971) has PIPPA PASSES, KING
VICTOR AND KING CHARLES, and THE RETURN OF THE
DRUSES; Volume 4 (1973) has A BLOT IN THE 'SCUTCHEON,
COLOMBE'S BIRTHDAY, and LURIA. Authoritative texts with
useful editorial notes.

649 Jack, Ian, ed. POETICAL WORKS 1833-1864. London: Oxford University Press, 1970. xvi, 952 p.

Contains PARACELSUS and PIPPA PASSES.

II Acted Plays—Principal Titles

650 *STRAFFORD: AN HISTORICAL TRAGEDY. (Covent Garden, 1 May 1837.) London: Longman, 1837. vi, 132 p.

> Details of other performances of this play may be found on page three of the Broughton bibliography (item 673).

651 *Hickey, Emily H., ed. STRAFFORD: A TRAGEDY. Intro. Samuel R. Gardiner. London: George Bell, 1884. xvi, 93 p.

652 *Wilson, Agnes, ed. STRAFFORD: A TRAGEDY. London: Blackie, 1901. xliv, 112 p.

653 *George, Hereford B., ed. STRAFFORD: A TRAGEDY. Oxford: Clarendon Press, 1908. xviii, 93 p.

654 *Hampden, John, ed. STRAFFORD: A TRAGEDY. London: Nelson, 1929. 93 p.

655 A BLOT IN THE 'SCUTCHEON: A TRAGEDY IN THREE ACTS. (Drury Lane, 11 February 1843.) London: Edward Moxon, 1843. 16 p.

> Includes a cast list of the first London production. The text is from BELLS AND POMEGRANATES, no. 5 (see item 642). For a brief record of further performances of this play see page 8 of the Broughton bibliography (item 673).

656 *A BLOT IN THE 'SCUTCHEON. New York: Hearst's International Library, 1916. 54 p.

657 *A BLOT IN THE 'SCUTCHEON. London: Jarrold. 1923. 89 p.

658 *Wilson, Thomas F., Jr. "Robert Browning's A BLOT IN THE 'SCUTCHEON: An Edition with Variant Readings and Annotations." Ph.D. Dissertation, Ohio University, 1971.

659 *COLOMBE'S BIRTHDAY: A PLAY IN FIVE ACTS. (Haymarket, 25 April 1853.) London: Edward Moxon, 1844. 20 p.

> The text is from BELLS AND POMEGRANATES, no. 6 (see item 643). For a brief record of further performances of this play see page 9 of the Broughton bibliography (item 673).

660 *IN A BALCONY. (Prince's Hall, London, 28 November 1884.) Pub-

lished in Browning's MEN AND WOMEN. (London: Chapman and Hall, 1855.)

> For other performances of this play see page 13 of the Broughton bibliography (item 673).

661 IN A BALCONY: A DRAMA IN ONE ACT. Chicago: Dramatic Publishing Co., n.d. 35 p.

662 *PIPPA PASSES. (Boston, 23 May 1899.) London: Edward Moxon, 1841. 16 p.

> The text is from BELLS AND POMEGRANATES, no. 1 (see item 642). For a brief record of further performances of this play see page 4 of the Broughton bibliography (item 673).

663 *Symons, Arthur, ed. PIPPA PASSES. London: Heinemann, 1906. viii, 83 p.

664 *Irvine, A.L., ed. PIPPA PASSES. London: Humphrey Milford, 1924. 84 p.

> For several other editions of PIPPA PASSES see pages 4 and 5 of the Broughton bibliography (item 673).

665 *THE RETURN OF THE DRUSES: A TRAGEDY IN FIVE ACTS. (Boston, 25 March 1902.) London: Edward Moxon, 1843. 20 p.

> The text is from BELLS AND POMEGRANATES, no. 4 (see item 642). For the text of the Boston production see item 666.

666 *Porter, Charlotte, ed. STAGE VERSION OF BROWNING'S TRAGEDY, THE RETURN OF THE DRUSES. New York: Thomas Y. Crowell, 1903. viii, 56 p.

> As performed "for the first time on any stage."

667 *A SOUL'S TRAGEDY. (London Stage Society, 13 March 1904.) London: Edward Moxon, 1846 [with LURIA]. 32 p.

> The text is from BELLS AND POMEGRANATES, no. 8 (see item 643).

IIa Unacted Plays

668 KING VICTOR AND KING CHARLES: A DRAMA. London: Edward Moxon, 1842. 20 p.

The text is from BELLS AND POMEGRANATES, no. 2 (see item 642).

669 *LURIA. London: Edward Moxon, 1846 [with A SOUL'S TRAGEDY]. 32 p.

The text is from BELLS AND POMEGRANATES, no. 8 (see item 643).

670 *PARACELSUS. London: Effingham Wilson, 1835. xii, 216 p.

671 *Denison, Cristina Pollock. THE PARACELSUS OF ROBERT BROWNING. New York: Baker and Taylor, 1911. x, 239 p.

The text of the play with a lengthy introduction on Paracelsus the man and his philosophy. There is also a "General Review of the Poem Bringing Out the Most Significant Passages," and a glossary of words and allusions.

III Bibliographies

672 Furnival, Frederick, J. A BIBLIOGRAPHY OF ROBERT BROWNING FROM 1833 TO 1881. London: Truebner, 1883. 170 p.

Superseded in many respects by the Broughton bibliography (item 673); but there is a still-valuable section on Browning's acted plays (here taken to be STRAFFORD, A BLOT IN THE 'SCUTCHEON, and COLOMBE'S BIRTHDAY), giving reviews of early performances.

673 Broughton, Leslie Nathan, Clark Sutherland Northup, and Robert Pearsall. ROBERT BROWNING: A BIBLIOGRAPHY, 1830-1950. Ithaca, N.Y.: Cornell University Press, 1953. xiv, 446 p.

An excellent bibliography. There is no separate section on the drama, but each play is indexed. Many entries are annotated, and there are separate sections for primary and secondary materials. The bibliography is especially useful for tracing reviews of various performances of the plays.

IV Biography

674 Orr, Mrs. Sutherland. LIFE AND LETTERS OF ROBERT BROWNING. New ed. Rev. Frederic G. Kenyon. Boston and New York: Houghton Mifflin, 1908. xvii, 431 p.

675 Hood, Thurman L., ed. LETTERS OF ROBERT BROWNING COLLECTED

BY THOMAS J. WISE. New Haven: Yale University Press, 1933. xx, 389 p.

Includes some letters to Macready and occasional references to the plays.

676 Griffin, W. Hall, and Harry Christopher Minchin. THE LIFE OF ROBERT BROWNING. WITH NOTICES OF HIS WRITINGS, HIS FAMILY, & HIS FRIENDS. 3rd ed. London: Methuen, 1938. xi, 344 p.

The standard biography with one chapter on "Browning and the Drama" and numerous other references to the plays.

677 Cramer, Maurice Browning. "Browning's Friendship and Fame before Marriage (1833-1846)." PMLA, 55 (1940), 207-30.

A survey of various friendships enjoyed by Browning, including those with Macready and Talfourd.

678 De Vane, William Clyde, and Kenneth Leslie Knickerbocker, eds. NEW LETTERS OF ROBERT BROWNING. London: John Murray, 1951. vi, 413 p.

Includes several letters to Macready and many references to the plays. The letters are well-edited with substantial annotations.

679 Ward, Maisie. ROBERT BROWNING AND HIS WORLD: THE PRIVATE FACE (1812-1861). New York: Holt, Rinehart and Winston, 1967. xv, 335 p.

Includes a chapter on Browning and Macready.

V Critical Studies

680 Pancoast, Henry S. "LURIA: Its Story and Motive." POET LORE, 1 (1889), 553-60; 2 (1890), 19-26.

681 Robertson, Alice Kent. "The Tragic Motive of IN A BALCONY." POET LORE, 2 (1890), 310-14.

682 Fairfax, Walter. ROBERT BROWNING AND THE DRAMA. London: Reeves & Turner, 1891. 20 p.

Extravagant praise for Browning as one of "the world's pitiably few great dramatists."

683 Porter, Charlotte. "Dramatic Motive in Browning's STRAFFORD." POET LORE, 5 (1893), 515-26.

684 Chadwick, John White. "Browning's LURIA." POET LORE, 6 (1894), 251-64.

A good critical introduction to the play.

685 Buck, J.D. BROWNING'S "PARACELSUS" AND OTHER ESSAYS. Cincinnati: Robert Clarke, 1897. 101 p.

686 Fotheringham, James. STUDIES OF THE MIND AND ART OF ROBERT BROWNING. 4th ed. London: Marshall, 1900. xxviii, 576 p.

Chapter 7 is a twenty-page survey of the plays.

687 [Notes on the First Performance of THE RETURN OF THE DRUSES.] POET LORE, 14 (1902), 141-43.

The Boston Browning Society production, 25 March 1902.

688 Dowden, Edward. ROBERT BROWNING. London: Dent; New York: Dutton, 1904. xvi, 404 p.

There are two chapters on Browning, "The Maker of Plays."

689 [Early American Productions of COLOMBE'S BIRTHDAY]. POET LORE, 15, no. 4 (1904), 135-36.

Boston, 16 February 1854; Philadelphia, 31 March 1854.

690 [A BLOT IN THE 'SCUTCHEON]. POET LORE, 16, no. 3 (1905), 152-55.

Notes on New York and Boston performances, 1905.

691 Herford, C.H. ROBERT BROWNING. Edinburgh and London: Blackwood, 1905. xiii, 314 p.

Includes a brief section on the plays.

692 Lambuth, David Kelley. "PIPPA PASSES on the Stage." POET LORE, 18 (1907), 107-12.

A sympathetic review of a New York 1907 production.

693 Elliott, G.R. "Shakespeare's Significance for Browning." ANGLIA, 32 (1909), 90-162.

Part of this essay (pp. 125-41) discusses the relationships among LURIA, THE RETURN OF THE DRUSES, and OTHELLO; A BLOT IN THE 'SCUTCHEON and ROMEO AND JULIET and

MUCH ADO ABOUT NOTHING; STRAFFORD and the history
plays; KING VICTOR AND KING CHARLES and LEAR.

694   Orr, Mrs. Sutherland. A HANDBOOK TO THE WORKS OF ROBERT
       BROWNING. London: G. Bell, 1910. xv, 420 p.

       Includes plot summaries of the plays.

695   Lounsbury, Thomas R. THE EARLY LITERARY CAREER OF ROBERT
       BROWNING. New York: Charles Scribner's Sons, 1911. vii, 205 p.

       This study contains a good discussion of the stage histories of
       A BLOT IN THE 'SCUTCHEON and STRAFFORD.

696   Phelps, William Lyon. "Browning as Dramatist." YR, 1 (1912), 551-67.

697   Tupper, James W. "A SOUL'S TRAGEDY: A Defence of Chiappino."
       ENGLISCHE STUDIEN, 44 (1912), 361-74.

698   Harrington, Vernon C. BROWNING STUDIES. Boston: Richard G.
       Badger; Toronto: Copp Clark, 1915. ix, 391 p.

       Includes short chapters on most of the plays (but not STRAF-
       FORD); they are of a very introductory nature.

699   Clarke, George Herbert. "Browning's A BLOT IN THE 'SCUTCHEON:
       A Defence." SR, 28 (1920), 213-27.

       The play "is worth so much more as a work of high creative
       art than as a theatrical performance"; however, as Clarke also
       shows, A BLOT has been well received by theatre critics.
       The article usefully summarizes previous criticism of the play.

700   Russell, Frances Theresa. "Browning's Account with Tragedy." SR, 31
       (1923), 86-99.

       Includes some discussion of the tragic elements in A BLOT IN
       THE 'SCUTCHEON, IN A BALCONY, THE RETURN OF THE
       DRUSES, LURIA, and STRAFFORD.

701   Gwathmey, E.M. "THE RETURN OF THE DRUSES: A Critical Study,"
       WILLIAM AND MARY LITERARY MAGAZINE, 33 (1926), 327-33.

702   Somervell, D.C. "An Early Victorian Tragedy." LONDON MERCURY,
       16 (1927), 170-78.

       STRAFFORD is called "a very good play, one of the major

works of one of the major poets."

703 Page, Howard Gordon. "PARACELSUS: A Critical Study of Browning's Immortal Poem." POETRY REVIEW, 22 (1931), 360-73.

Sees PARACELSUS as "reflective" rather than "dramatic."

704 Boas, Frederick S. "Robert Browning's PARACELSUS, 1835-1935." QR, 265 (1935), 280-95.

Boas argues that PARACELSUS may not appropriately be seen as a drama, and contends: "The series of long monologues in PARACELSUS indicates what was to be a permanent weakness in his [Browning's] craftmanship as a writer of plays."

705 Dubois, Arthur E. "Robert Browning, Dramatist." SP, 33 (1936), 626-55.

A lengthy but not especially illuminating survey of Browning's plays, with particular attention to the "tragic comedy" element in them.

706 Charlton, H.B. "Browning as Dramatist." BULLETIN OF THE JOHN RYLANDS LIBRARY, 23 (1939), 33-67.

A solid introductory essay with analyses of all of the plays except PARACELSUS.

707 Purcell, J.M. "The Dramatic Failure of PIPPA PASSES." SP, 36 (1939), 77-87.

The "failure" arises principally out of faulty characterization.

708 Ariail, J.M. "Is PIPPA PASSES a Dramatic Failure?" SP, 37 (1940), 120-29.

A reply to Purcell's essay (item 707).

709 Faverty, Frederic E. "The Source of the Jules-Phene Episode in PIPPA PASSES." SP, 28 (1941), 97-105.

Parallels between PIPPA PASSES and Bulwer-Lytton's popular success, THE LADY OF LYONS.

710 Reese, Gertrude. "Robert Browning and A BLOT IN THE 'SCUTCHEON." MLN, 63 (1948), 237-40.

Concerning Dickens' high opinion of the play.

711 Greer, Louise. BROWNING AND AMERICA. Chapel Hill: University of North Carolina Press, 1952. xiv, 355 p.

> Valuable for information on performances of Browning's plays in the United States. The playbill for Lawrence Barrett's 1884 revival of A BLOT IN THE 'SCUTCHEON is reproduced.

712 McCormick, James Patton. "Robert Browning and the Experimental Drama." PMLA, 68 (1953), 982-91.

> A survey of Browning's failures as a playwright, and an analysis of the "experimental plays," PIPPA PASSES and A SOUL'S TRAGEDY.

713 Glen, Margaret Eleanor. "The Meaning and Structure of PIPPA PASSES." UTQ, 24 (1954-55), 410-26.

714 De Vane, William Clyde. A BROWNING HANDBOOK. 2nd ed. New York: Appleton-Century-Crofts, 1955. xii, 594 p.

> Valuable sections on individual plays, giving publication and textual details, information on genesis, composition, sources and influences, and, where appropriate, stage history.

715 Johnson, Charles E. "The Dramatic Career of Robert Browning: A Survey and Analysis." Ph.D. Dissertation, Duke University, 1958. 277 p.

716 Barnett, Howard A. "Robert Browning and the Drama: Browning's Plays Viewed in the Context of the Victorian Theatre: 1830-1850." Ph.D. Dissertation, Indiana University, 1959. 348 p.

717 Wilkinson, D.C. "The Need For Disbelief: A Comment on PIPPA PASSES." UTQ, 29 (1959-60), 139-51.

> A discussion and criticism of "the general trend . . . to overestimate PIPPA PASSES."

718 Hulcoop, J.F. "Robert Browning, 'Maker of Plays' and Poet: A Study of His Concepts and Practice of Drama and of Their Relation to His Concepts and Practice of Poetry; With a Chronology of His Early Literary Career, 1832-1846." Ph.D. Dissertation, London University, 1960-61.

719 Honan, Park. BROWNING'S CHARACTERS: A STUDY IN POETIC TECHNIQUE. New Haven,Conn.: Yale University Press, 1962. xiv, 327 p.

> Includes two substantial sections on the plays, headed "Character for the Stage" (STRAFFORD, KING VICTOR AND KING CHARLES, THE RETURN OF THE DRUSES, A BLOT IN THE 'SCUTCHEON, COLOMBE'S BIRTHDAY) and "Character for

the Study" (PIPPA PASSES, A SOUL'S TRAGEDY, LURIA).
Excellent discussion of the plays.

720 Orel, Harold. "Browning's Use of Historical Sources in STRAFFORD."
SIX STUDIES IN NINETEENTH-CENTURY ENGLISH LITERATURE AND
THOUGHT. Ed. Harold Orel and George G. Worth. Lawrence: Uni-
versity of Kansas Publications, 1962. 23-37.

721 McCall, John. "Browning's Uncloseted Dramas." IOWA ENGLISH
YEARBOOK, no. 8 (1963), 51-55.

722 Kramer, Dale. "Character and Theme in PIPPA PASSES." VP, 2 (1964),
241-49.

723 Drew, Philip, ed. ROBERT BROWNING: A COLLECTION OF CRITICAL
ESSAYS. London: Methuen, 1966. ix, 278 p.

Contains Edgar Stoll's "Browning's IN A BALCONY."

724 PAPERS OF THE BROWNING SOCIETY. 3 vols. Nendeln, Liechten-
stein: Kraus Reprint, 1966.

The papers (1881-91) cover a wide range of Browning studies,
including the plays. The volumes unfortunately lack an index
and even a table of contents.

725 Patrick, Michael D. "The Dramatic Techniques of Robert Browning."
Ph.D. Dissertation, University of Missouri, 1966. 273 p. (DA#67-948)

726 Williams, Ioan M. BROWNING. London: Evans Brothers, 1967.
160 p.

Includes a useful introduction to the plays.

727 King, Roma A. THE FOCUSING ARTIFICE: THE POETRY OF ROBERT
BROWNING. Athens: Ohio University Press, 1968. xxiii, 288 p.

There is a useful chapter on the plays, with a brief analysis
of each. The author argues that the plays show "the alienation of his [Browning's] characters and the meaninglessness of
their lives in the absence of traditional values" (p. 62).
Early nineteenth-century dramatic convention did not suit
Browning's "revolutionary concept of action in character."

728 Korg, Jacob. "A Reading of PIPPA PASSES." VP, 6 (1968), 5-19.

"PIPPA PASSES is not concerned with moral positions, but

rather with the phenomenon of the sudden recovery of moral awareness and, hence, free will."

729   Otten, Terry. "What Browning Never Learned from Bulwer-Lytton." RE-SEARCH STUDIES, 37 (1969), 338-42.

       A response to Faverty's essay (item 709) about the relation-ship between PIPPA PASSES and THE LADY OF LYONS, which Otten finds superficial.

730   Brestensky, Dennis F. "A Funny Thing Happened on the Way to a Play." MLS, 1 (1971), 3-8.

       On PIPPA PASSES.

731   Saradhi, K.P. "Browning and the Early Nineteenth Century Theatre." OJES, 8 (1971), 19-30.

732   _____. "Browning's THE RETURN OF THE DRUSES: 'Action in Charac-ter' Versus 'Character in Action.'" OJES, 8 (1971), 53-65.

733   Smith, Charles William. "A Critical Introduction to Robert Browning's STRAFFORD." Ph.D. Dissertation, University of Maryland, 1971. 322 p. (DA#72-1692)

734   Abbot, Craig. "Revisions in the 'Second Edition' of A BLOT IN THE 'SCUTCHEON." BROWNING NEWSLETTER, no. 8 (Spring 1972), 53-55.

735   Kincaid, Arthur. "IN A BALCONY--Reflections by the Director." BROWNING SOCIETY NOTES, 2 (1972), 17-20.

       Performances in Oxford and London, 1970 and 1971.

736   Kincaid, Margaret. "IN A BALCONY Design." BROWNING SOCIETY NOTES, 2 (1972), 15-17.

       See item 735.

VI Journals and Newsletters

737   BROWNING NEWSLETTER. Waco, Tex.: Baylor University, Armstrong Browning Library, 1968-- . Semiannual.

       Includes an annual review of research activities.

738   BROWNING SOCIETY NOTES. London: Browning Society, 1970-- .

       Three times a year.

BUCHANAN, ROBERT (1841-1901)

I Collected Works

739   THE DRAMA OF KINGS. London: Strahan, 1871. xiii, 471 p.

>Contains BUONAPARTE; OR, FRANCE AGAINST THE TEUTON, NAPOLEON FALLEN, and THE TEUTON AGAINST PARIS, together with "Dedication," "Prologue," "Choric Interludes," "Epilude," "Notes," and "On Mystic Realism: A Note for the Adept."

II Acted Plays—Principal Titles

740   *THE NINE DAYS' QUEEN. (Gaiety, 22 December 1880.) LC.

741   *THE SHADOW OF THE SWORD. (Theatre Royal, Brighton, 9 May 1881; Olympic, 8 April 1882.) LC.

742   *LADY CLARE. (Globe, 11 April 1883.) LC.

743   ALONE IN LONDON. (Olympic, 2 November 1885.)

>No publication details. Each act numbered separately. A manuscript promptbook, located in New York Public Library.

744   *SOPHIA. (Vaudeville, 12 April 1886.) LC.

745   *JOSEPH'S SWEETHEART. (Vaudeville, 8 March 1888.) LC.

746   * A MAN'S SHADOW. (Haymarket, 12 September 1889.) LC.

747   *MISS TOMBOY. (Vaudeville, 20 March 1890.) LC.

748   SWEET NANCY: A COMEDY IN THREE ACTS. (Lyric, 12 July 1890.) London and New York: French, 1914. 76 p.

>An acting edition with cast lists of two London productions, 1890 and 1896.

749   *AN ENGLISH ROSE. (Adelphi, 2 August 1890). LC.

750   *THE BLACK DOMINO. (Adelphi, 1 April 1893). LC.

751   *THE CHARLATAN. (Haymarket, 18 January 1894). LC.

IIa Unacted Plays

752   *NAPOLEON FALLEN: A LYRICAL DRAMA. 2nd ed. London: Strahan, 1871. viii, 151 p.

> Contains a preface to the second edition, a prefatory note,
> and "War-Song, January 1871"; the first and third items were
> omitted in the first edition. .

IV Biography

753   "Robert William Buchanan." ATHENAEUM, no. 3842 (15 June 1901),
760-61.

> Obituary notice.

754   Jay, Harriett. ROBERT BUCHANAN: SOME ACCOUNT OF HIS LIFE,
HIS LIFE'S WORK AND HIS LITERARY FRIENDSHIPS. London: T. Fisher
Unwin, 1903; rpt. New York: AMS, 1970. xii, 324 p.

> This biography of Buchanan is suffused with adulation from
> his adopted sister-in-law, Harriett Jay. The worth of the
> book must be carefully weighed against this fact, although
> Miss Jay attempts to allow Buchanan to speak for himself as
> much as possible, largely through memoirs, diary entries, and
> the like. The chapter devoted to Buchanan's playwriting is
> straightforward, although the general caveat still applies.

V Critical Studies

755   Murray, Henry. ROBERT BUCHANAN: A CRITICAL APPRECIATION AND
OTHER ESSAYS. London: Philip Wellby, 1901. 254 p.

756   Fairchild, Hoxie N. "The Immediate Source of THE DYNASTS." PMLA,
67 (1952), 43-64.

> A lengthy and conclusive study of the influence of Buchanan
> on Hardy, more particularly demonstrating that the immediate
> source of THE DYNASTS is THE DRAMA OF KINGS.

757   Cassidy, John A. "The Original Source of Hardy's DYNASTS." PMLA,
69 (1954), 1085-1100.

> Cassidy extends Fairchild's study (item 756) and demonstrates

that the inspiration and substance of Buchanan's DRAMA OF KINGS was Victor Hugo's LA LEGENDE DES SIECLES.

BUCKSTONE, JOHN BALDWIN (1802-79)

II Acted Plays—Principal Titles

758 LUKE THE LABOURER; OR, THE LOST SON: A DOMESTIC DRAMA IN TWO ACTS. (Adelphi, 17 October 1826.) 2nd ed. London: William Kenneth, 1828. 63 p.

Includes cast lists for productions of 1826 and 1827.

759 THE MAY QUEEN: A DOMESTIC DRAMA IN TWO ACTS. (Adelphi, 9 October 1828.) London: William Strange, 1834. 43 p.

An acting edition with a cast list of the first London production and a dedication to Charles Mathews.

760 ISABELLE; OR, WOMAN'S LIFE: A DRAMA IN THREE ACTS. (Adelphi, 27 January 1834.) London: William Strange, 1835. 64 p.

An acting edition with a cast list of the first London production and a dedication to Richard John Smith.

761 MARRIED LIFE: A COMEDY IN THREE ACTS. (Haymarket, 20 August 1834.) London: William Strange, 1834. 66 p.

Includes a cast list of the first London production, a brief prefatory note and a dedication to William Farren; the Readex copy is a promptbook (in the New York Public Library) with extensive manuscript annotations, including one and a half pages of property description.

762 AGNES DE VERE; OR, THE WIFE'S REVENGE: A DRAMA IN THREE ACTS. (Adelphi, 10 November 1834.) London: William Strange, 1836. 32 p.

Includes a cast list of the first London production, a dedication to Mrs. Keeley, and an "Advertisement" explaining that the play's successful run was interrupted by Mrs. Yates's "interesting disposition," i.e., her pregnancy.

763 SINGLE LIFE: A COMEDY IN THREE ACTS. (Haymarket, 23 July 1839.) [London: Chapman & Hall, 1839?] 58 p. [Title page of this copy lacking.]

An acting edition with a cast list of the first London production; the Readex copy is a promptbook (in the New York

Public Library) with a few manuscript notes.

764 JACK SHEPPARD: A DRAMA IN FOUR PARTS. (Adelphi, 28 October 1839.) London: Webster, n.d. 72 p.

An acting edition with a cast list of the first London production; the Readex copy is a promptbook (in the New York Public Library) with a few manuscript notes and some pages deleted.

765 THE GREEN BUSHES; OR, A HUNDRED YEARS AGO: AN ORIGINAL DRAMA IN THREE ACTS. (Adelphi, 27 January 1845.) New York: French, n.d. 50 p.

An acting edition with cast lists for the first London and subsequent American productions.

766 THE FLOWERS OF THE FOREST, A GYPSY STORY: AN ORIGINAL DRAMA IN THREE ACTS. (Adelphi, 11 March 1847.) French's Standard Drama, no. 267. New York and London: French, n.d. 53 p.

An acting edition with cast lists of the first London and subsequent North American productions.

767 AN ALARMING SACRIFICE: A FARCE IN ONE ACT. (Haymarket, 12 July 1849.) London and New York: French, n.d. 18 p.

An acting edition with cast lists of the first London and subsequent American productions.

IV Biography

768 Gressman, Malcolm George. "The Career of John Baldwin Buckstone." Ph.D. Dissertation, Ohio State University, 1963. 205 p. (DA#64-07016)

V Critical Studies

769 Brokaw, John Wilkie. "The Farces of John Baldwin Buckstone." Ph.D. Dissertation, Indiana University, 1970. 410 p. (DA#71-0628)

BULWER-LYTTON, EDWARD GEORGE (1803-73)

I Collected Works

770 THE POETICAL AND DRAMATIC WORKS OF SIR EDWARD BULWER

LYTTON. 5 vols. London: Chapman and Hall, 1852-54.

Volume four contains THE DUCHESS DE LA VALLIERE, THE
LADY OF LYONS, and RICHELIEU; volume five includes
MONEY and NOT SO BAD AS WE SEEM.

771 THE DRAMATIC WORKS OF THE RIGHT HON. LORD LYTTON. 2nd
ed. London: Routledge, [1873?]. 496 p.

Includes THE DUCHESS DE LA VALLIERE, RICHELIEU,
MONEY, THE LADY OF LYONS, and NOT SO BAD AS
WE SEEM. There is no editorial matter.

772 BULWER'S PLAYS: BEING THE COMPLETE DRAMATIC WORKS OF LORD
LYTTON. New York: De Witt, [1875]. 396 p.

An acting edition prepared "From the original text, as produced under the supervision of the author and Mr. Macready."
The plays are THE LADY OF LYONS, MONEY, RICHELIEU,
THE RIGHTFUL HEIR, WALPOLE, NOT SO BAD AS WE SEEM,
and THE DUCHESS DE LA VALLIERE.

773 THE WORKS OF EDWARD BULWER LYTTON (LORD LYTTON). 9 vols.
New York: Collier, [1882?].

Volume nine contains the plays listed in item 772 with the
addition of DARNLEY.

774 DRAMAS AND POEMS. Boston: Roberts Brothers, 1889. vi, 454 p.

Contains a brief biographical preface, nineteen poems, and
THE LADY OF LYONS, RICHELIEU, and MONEY.

II Acted Plays—Principal Titles

775 THE DUCHESS DE LA VALLIERE: A PLAY IN FIVE ACTS. (Covent
Garden, 4 January 1837.) 2nd ed. London: Saunders and Otley, 1836.
xviii, 178 p.

There is a lengthy preface by Bulwer-Lytton dealing mainly
with his treatment of the historical circumstances on which
the play is based.

776 THE LADY OF LYONS; OR, LOVE AND PRIDE: A PLAY IN FIVE ACTS.
(Covent Garden, 15 February 1838.) London and New York: French,
n.d. 60 p.

An acting edition with a cast list of the first London production and a brief preface; the Readex copy is a promptbook
(in the New York Public Library) interleaved with manuscript

notes. (The Readex Collection also contains a Princeton promptbook with manuscript notes.)

777 RICHELIEU; OR, THE CONSPIRACY: A PLAY IN FIVE ACTS. (Covent Garden, 7 March 1839.) Modern Standard Drama, no. 4. New York: Douglas, n.d. 96 p.

An acting edition with a brief editorial introduction and a preface by the author; the Readex copy is a promptbook (in the New York Public Library) interleaved with manuscript notes.

778 RICHELIEU: A NEW VERSION OF SIR EDWARD BULWER-LYTTON'S PLAY OF THE SAME NAME BY ARTHUR GOODRICH. TOGETHER WITH LORD LYTTON'S ORIGINAL TEXT. Intro. Clayton Hamilton. New York and London: Appleton, 1930. xvi, 263 p.

779 THE SEA-CAPTAIN; OR, THE BIRTHRIGHT: A DRAMA IN FIVE ACTS. (Haymarket, 31 October 1839.) London: Saunders and Otley, 1839. viii, 112 p.

Includes a cast list of the first production and a brief preface by the author.

780 MONEY: A COMEDY IN FIVE ACTS. (Haymarket, 8 December 1840.) 2nd ed. London: Saunders and Otley, 1840. 158 p.

781 NOT SO BAD AS WE SEEM; OR, MANY SIDES TO A CHARACTER: A COMEDY IN FIVE ACTS. (Devonshire House, 14 May 1851.) New York: Harper and Bros., 1851. vi, 166 p.

Includes a cast list of the Devonshire House production.

782 THE RIGHTFUL HEIR: A DRAMA IN FIVE ACTS. (Lyceum, 3 October 1868.) London: John Murray, 1868. 62 p.

Includes a cast list of the first London production and a brief preface; the Readex copy is a promptbook (in the Princeton University Library) interleaved with manuscript notes.

783 THE HOUSE OF DARNLEY. (Court, 6 October 1877.)

For published text see item 773.

784 *JUNIUS BRUTUS; OR, THE HOUSEHOLD GODS. (Princess's, 26 February 1885.) LC.

IIa Unacted Plays

785 WALPOLE; OR, EVERY MAN HAS HIS PRICE: A COMEDY IN RHYME
IN THREE ACTS. De Witt's Acting Plays, no. 91. New York: De Witt,
n.d. 34 p.

III Bibliographies

786 Dickson, Sarah. "The Bulwer-Lytton Collection." PULC, 8 (1946), 28-
32.

> A brief description of the Princeton collection which contains
> many playbills of Bulwer-Lytton's plays.

IV Biography

787 Cooper, Thompson. LORD LYTTON: A BIOGRAPHY. London and New
York: Routledge, 1873. vi, 158 p.

> A sketchy biography with a very brief chapter on the plays.

788 THE LIFE, LETTERS AND LITERARY REMAINS OF EDWARD BULWER,
LORD LYTTON. BY HIS SON. 2 vols. London: Kegan Paul, Trench
& Co., 1883. xii, 369; viii, 392 p.

> Bulwer-Lytton's unfinished autobiography occupies volume one;
> his son does the rest. The work is illustrated, but there is no
> index.

789 Escott, T.H.S. EDWARD BULWER, FIRST BARON LYTTON OF KNEB-
WORTH. A SOCIAL, PERSONAL, AND POLITICAL MONOGRAPH.
London: Routledge, 1910. viii, 348 p.

> This biography is undocumented and contains only a few pages
> on the plays.

790 Frost, William Alfred. BULWER LYTTON: AN EXPOSURE OF THE
ERRORS OF HIS BIOGRAPHERS. London: Lynwood & Co., 1913.
120 p.

> Purports to rectify errors in previous biographies, including
> those by Bulwer-Lytton's son (item 788), Cooper (item 787),
> and Escott (item 789).

V Critical Studies

790a Fitzgerald, Percy. "THE LADY OF LYONS." GM, 267 (1889), 136-
41.

791 Bell, E.G. INTRODUCTION TO THE PROSE ROMANCES, PLAYS AND COMEDIES OF EDWARD BULWER, LORD LYTTON. Chicago: Walter M. Hill, 1914. 401 p.

There is a section of about one hundred pages given to the plays, but the bulk of it is plot summary.

792 Qualia, Charles B. "French Dramatic Sources of Bulwer-Lytton's RICHE-LIEU." PMLA, 42 (1927), 177-84.

Parallels between RICHELIEU and two French plays, Hugo's CROMWELL and Delavigne's LOUIS XI (plays which Bulwer-Lytton may or may not have known).

793 Ewing, Majl. "The Dramas of Bulwer Lytton: A Study in the Early Victorian Stage." Ph.D. Dissertation, University of Virginia, 1929.

794 Lytton, the Earl of. BULWER-LYTTON. London: Home and Van Thal, 1948. 111 p.

The main concern of this study by Bulwer-Lytton's grandson is the novels, but there is a useful introductory chapter on the plays.

795 Shattuck, Charles H. "E.L. Bulwer and Victorian Censorship." QJS, 34 (1948), 65-72.

An interesting account of public opposition to THE DUCHESS DE LA VALLIERE (on moral and religious grounds) and THE LADY OF LYONS (on political grounds), with quotations from numerous contemporary reviews.

796 Ganzel, Dewey. "Bulwer and His Lady." MP, 58 (1960-61), 41-52.

A well-researched study of the source, manuscript, production, and reception of THE LADY OF LYONS.

797 Peterson, W.M. "The Dramatic Work of Bulwer-Lytton." Ph.D Dissertation, Bristol University, 1969-70.

BUNN, ALFRED (1798-1860)

II Acted Plays—Principal Titles

798 KENILWORTH: A DRAMA IN TWO ACTS. (Covent Garden, 8 March 1831.) Lacy's Acting Edition, vol. 98. London: Lacy, n.d. 35 p.

With cast lists of three London productions and "Remarks" by

D--G [George Daniel]. The play is a revised version of
T.J. Dibdin's dramatization of Scott's novel.

799 THE MINISTER AND THE MERCER: A COMEDY IN FIVE ACTS. (Drury
Lane, 8 February 1834.) London: John Miller, 1834. vi, 85 p.

Includes a cast list of the first London production and an
interesting note by Bunn with a copy of a letter he sent
to the Lord Chamberlain regarding licensing difficulties encountered with the play (which is adapted from Scribe's
BERTRAND ET RATON).

800 THE BOHEMIAN GIRL: [AN OPERA]. With M.W. Balfe. (Drury Lane,
27 November 1843.) New York: New York Printing Co., 1870. 36 p.

Includes a cast list of an unspecified production.

801 THE DAUGHTER OF ST. MARK: A GRAND OPERA SERIA IN THREE
ACTS. With M.W. Balfe. (Drury Lane, 27 November 1844.) London:
W.S. Johnson, n.d. v, 46 p.

Includes a cast list of the first London production and an introductory note by Bunn.

802 A NEW AND ORIGINAL OPERA IN THREE ACTS ENTITLED THE EN-
CHANTRESS. With M.W. Balfe. (Drury Lane, 14 May 1845.) Philadelphia: King and Baird, 1852. 40 p.

Includes a cast list of a Chestnut Street Theatre, Philadelphia,
production.

IV Biography

803 Bunn, Alfred. THE STAGE: BOTH BEFORE AND BEHIND THE CURTAIN.
3 vols. London: Richard Bentley, 1840.

The memoirs of one of the nineteenth-century theatre's most
colorful and controversial figures.

V Critical Studies

804 Urwin, G.G. "Bunn and His Influence in the Theatre." Ph.D. Dissertation, London University, 1955-56.

805 _____. "Alfred Bunn 1796-1860: A Revaluation." TN, 11 (1956-57),
96-102.

Individual Authors

BYRON, LORD GEORGE GORDON (1788-1824)

I Collected Works

806 Coleridge, Ernest Hartley, ed. THE WORKS OF LORD BYRON. PO-
ETRY. Rev. and enl. ed. 7 vols. London: John Murray; New York:
Charles Scribner's Sons, 1904–5.

> This is the best collected edition of Byron's plays. There are
> informative introductions to each play and useful annotations.
> Volume 4 has MANFRED and MARINO FALIERO; volume 5
> has SARDANAPALUS, THE TWO FORCARI, CAIN, HEAVEN
> AND EARTH, WERNER, and THE DEFORMED TRANSFORMED;
> volume 7 has bibliographical details on editions of the plays,
> including translations.

807 THE POETICAL WORKS OF LORD BYRON. London: Oxford University
Press, 1952. x, 923 p.

> First published in 1904, this edition contains Byron's address
> spoken at Drury Lane on 10 October 1812 and the plays
> listed in item 806.

II Acted Plays—Principal Titles

808 *MARINO FALIERO, DOGE OF VENICE: AN HISTORICAL TRAGEDY
IN FIVE ACTS: WITH NOTES. THE PROPHECY OF DANTE, A POEM.
(Drury Lane, 25 April 1821.) London: John Murray, 1821. xxi, 261 p.

809 WERNER: A TRAGEDY. (New York, 16 December 1828; Bristol, 13
January 1830; Drury Lane, 15 December 1830.) London: John Murray,
1823. viii, 188 p.

> The Readex copy is Macready's promptbook, interleaved with
> manuscript notes (at the Princeton University Library). There
> is a brief preface by Byron.

810 *Spevack, Marvin, ed. WERNER: A TRAGEDY. A FACSIMILE OF THE
ACTING VERSION OF WILLIAM CHARLES MACREADY. Munich: Wilhelm Fink Verlag, 1970.

811 SARDANAPALUS, A TRAGEDY. (Drury Lane, 10 April 1834.) THE TWO
FOSCARI, A TRAGEDY. (Covent Garden, 7 April 1837.) CAIN, A
MYSTERY. London: John Murray, 1821. viii, 439 p.

> There are notes and a preface to each play as well as Byron's
> own brief general preface. There is no recorded performance
> of CAIN. See also items 816–17, below.

812   *Bartholomew, James Reece. "Byron's SARDANAPALUS: A Manuscript Edition." Ph.D. Dissertation, University of Texas, 1964. 275 p. (DA#64-11776)

813   MANFRED: A DRAMATIC POEM. (Covent Garden, 29 October 1834.)
London: John Murray, 1817. 80 p.

IIa   Unacted Plays

814   *HEAVEN AND EARTH: A MYSTERY. London: Benbow, 1823. 35 p.

First published in the LIBERAL, no. 2 (1822), 165–206,
available in the Readex Collection.

815   *THE DEFORMED TRANSFORMED: A DRAMA. London: J. & H. L.
Hunt, 1824. 88 p.

816   *Mortenson, Robert Lawrence. "Lord Byron's CAIN, A MYSTERY: A
Variorum Edition." Ph.D. Dissertation, University of Pennsylvania, 1964.
975 p. (DA#64-11025)

817   *Steffan, Truman Guy. LORD BYRON'S "CAIN." TWELVE ESSAYS
AND A TEXT WITH VARIANTS AND ANNOTATIONS. Austin and
London: University of Texas Press, 1968. xviii, 509 p.

The most authoritative text and a most meticulous study of
the play. It includes background to the play, a survey of
CAIN criticism from Byron's contemporaries to the present, a
twenty-page bibliography, a thorough index and tables on
such matters as the "Number of Times in Act III each Foot is
Irregular." See also items 811 and 816, above.

III Bibliographies

818   Wise, Thomas James. A BIBLIOGRAPHY OF THE WRITINGS IN VERSE
AND PROSE OF GEORGE GORDON NOEL, BARON BYRON. 2 vols.
London: Dawsons of Pall Mall, 1963. xxx, 139; xxiv, 131 p.

Contains detailed bibliographical information on all of the
plays. Originally published in 1933 for private circulation
only.

819   Santucho, Oscar J. "A Comprehensive Bibliography of Secondary Materials in English: George Gordon, Lord Byron." Ph.D. Dissertation, Baylor University, 1968. 418 p. (DA#68-15816)

IV Biography

820   Prothero, Rowland E., ed. THE WORKS OF LORD BYRON. LETTERS
       AND JOURNALS. Rev. and enl. ed. 6 vols. London: John Murray,
       1902-4.

> The detailed index in volume 6 leads to numerous references
> to Byron's thoughts on drama and the theatre, as well as
> essential information on the plays.

821   Murray, John, ed. LORD BYRON'S CORRESPONDENCE. CHIEFLY
       WITH LADY MELBOURNE, MR. HOBHOUSE, THE HON. DOUGLAS
       KINNAIRD, AND P.B. SHELLEY. 2 vols. London: John Murray, 1922.

> These letters were not accessible to Prothero when he pre-
> pared his edition of the LETTERS AND JOURNALS (item 820).
> They include further views and information on the plays.

822   Quennell, Peter, ed. BYRON: A SELF-PORTRAIT. LETTERS AND
       DIARIES 1798-1824. 2 vols. New York: Charles Scribner's Sons, 1950.

> Contains hitherto unpublished letters.

823   Marchand, Leslie A. BYRON: A BIOGRAPHY. 3 vols. New York:
       Knopf, 1957.

> The best of numerous Byron biographies. The work is im-
> mensely detailed and contains scores of references to the
> plays--easily traceable through an ample index.

824   _____. BYRON'S LETTERS AND JOURNALS. THE COMPLETE AND
       UNEXPURGATED TEXT OF ALL THE LETTERS AVAILABLE IN MANU-
       SCRIPT AND THE FULL PRINTED VERSION OF ALL OTHERS. Vol. 1:
       IN MY HOT YOUTH, 1798-1810; vol. 2, FAMOUS IN MY TIME,
       1810-1812; vol. 3, ALAS! THE LOVE OF WOMEN! London: John
       Murray, 1973-- .

> The definitive edition; in progress.

V Critical Studies

824a   Gerard, William. BYRON RE-STUDIED IN HIS DRAMAS. BEING A
       CONTRIBUTION TOWARDS A DEFINITIVE ESTIMATE OF HIS GENIUS.
       London: F.V. White, 1886; rpt. Folcroft, Pa.: Folcroft Press, 1970.
       229 p.

825   Gower, F. Leveson. "Did Byron Write WERNER?" NINETEENTH CEN-
       TURY, 46 (1899), 243-50.

The author believes that WERNER was written by Gower's grandmother.

826 Pudbres, Anna. "Lord Byron, the Admirer and Imitator of Alfieri." ENGLISCHE STUDIEN, 33 (1904), 40-83.

A general discussion of Byron's enthusiasm for the plays of Alfieri followed by a detailed analysis of MARINO FALIERO and its relationship to LA CONGIURA DE PAZZI, and briefer accounts of SARDANAPALUS and THE TWO FOSCARI. The author's general conclusion is that "Bryon's over-great admiration of Alfieri's works did but lead to the pernicious result of considerably hampering the poet's genius by not allowing his originality, his own forcible diction, his mastery over language to have their own way."

827 Chew, Samuel C. THE DRAMA OF LORD BYRON. A CRITICAL STUDY. Baltimore: Johns Hopkins University Press, 1915; rpt. New York: Russell and Russell, 1964. viii, 181 p.

Still the most substantial discussion of Byron's plays. There are chapters on "The Drama of the Romantic Period" and "Byron and the Contemporary Drama," as well as extended analyses of all the plays. Three appendices are given: "Byron and the Dramatic Unities," "MANFRED and FAUST," and "Shakespearean Echoes in MARINO FALIERO." No index or bibliography.

828 Brooke, Stopford. "Byron's CAIN." HIBBERT JOURNAL, 18 (1919), 74-94.

A defense and analysis of CAIN in terms of Christian orthodoxy.

829 Goode, Clement Tyson. BYRON AS CRITIC. Weimar: R. Wagner John, 1923; rpt. New York: Haskell House, 1964. 312 p.

Contains useful summaries of Byron's critical theories and judgments about drama and acting taken largely from his letters and journals.

830 Briscoe, Walter A., ed. BYRON THE POET. London: Routledge, 1924; rpt. New York: Haskell House, 1967. xvi, 287 p.

Includes "Byron on the Stage," a twenty-page essay, with "opinions specially contributed by Sir Squire Bancroft and William Archer." There are brief comments on Byron's amateur acting followed by a survey of the plays. The bulk of the essay seems to be the editor's work; Bancroft's and Archer's views are brief--and negative.

831   Chew, Samuel C.   BYRON IN ENGLAND.   HIS FAME AND AFTER-
       FAME.   London: John Murray, 1924.   x, 415 p.

       Chew discusses at some length the reception of CAIN; the
       other plays are less fully dealt with.   There is a fifty-page
       bibliography of Byron studies.   Chew's book is to some extent
       superseded by Rutherford's volume (item 886).

832   Babcock, R.W.   "The Inception and Reception of Byron's CAIN."   SAQ,
       26 (1927), 178-88.

       Not much more than a series of short quotations about CAIN
       from Byron's letters and journals and other obvious contempo-
       rary sources.

833   King, Lucille.   "The Influence of Shakespeare on Byron's MARINO
       FALIERO."   STUDIES IN ENGLISH (University of Texas), no. 11, (1933),
       48-55.

       "For incident and characterization Byron was influenced
       by JULIUS CAESAR, but most of the similarities in phrase-
       ology . . . are from MACBETH."

834   Calvert, William J.   BYRON: ROMANTIC PARADOX.   Chapel Hill:
       University of North Carolina Press, 1935; rpt. New York: Russell &
       Russell, 1962.   xiii, 235 p.

       Chapter seven, entitled "Drama and Propaganda," discusses
       Byron's theories about playwriting (e.g. his devotion to the
       Unities) as well as the plays themselves.

835   Motter, T.H. Vail.   "Byron's WERNER Re-Estimated: A Neglected
       Chapter in Nineteenth Century Stage History."   THE PARROTT PRESENTA-
       TION VOLUME.   Ed. Hardin Craig.   Princeton, N.J.:   Princeton Uni-
       versity Press, 1935.   243-75.

       Motter poses this question: "How was it possible for the
       author of CAIN, or of MANFRED, of MARINO FALIERO,
       or of SARDANAPAULUS, to write a play which should be
       bad enough to catch and hold the interest of nineteenth-
       century playgoers for nearly three generations?"   He an-
       swers it with an impressive discussion of theatrical, textual,
       and literary aspects of the play.

836   Erdman, David V.   "Byron's Stage Fright: The History of His Ambition
       and Fear of Writing for the Stage."   ELH, 6 (1939), 219-43.

       The author uses a "bit of modern psychological understanding"
       to try to explain the "obvious contradiction between Byron's
       professed aim to reform the English stage and his vociferously
       professed intention to keep his own plays off the English stage."

He concludes that Byron's professed disinterest in his plays'
reception was a rationalization of their failure on the stage.

837 Johnson, Edward D. H. "A Political Interpretation of Byron's MARINO
FALIERO." MLQ, 3 (1942), 417-25.

A discussion of the play in relationship to Byron's enthusiasm
for Italian revolutionaries and distaste for English radicals.
Because he was an eighteenth-century Whig as far as England
was concerned, and a nineteenth-century liberal on the continent, Byron failed to achieve "a consistent political philosophy" in MARINO FALIERO.

838 Evans, Bertrand. "Manfred's Remorse and Dramatic Tradition." PMLA,
62 (1947), 752-73.

Evans places the characteristics of Byron's hero in the Gothic
tradition in English drama beginning with Horace Walpole's
MYSTERIOUS MOTHER (1768).

838a Rainwater, Frank Palmer. LORD BYRON: A STUDY OF THE DEVELOP-
MENT OF HIS PHILOSOPHY WITH SPECIAL EMPHASIS UPON THE
DRAMA. Nashville: Privately printed, 1949. 41 p.

839 Knight, G. Wilson. "The Plays of Lord Byron." TLS, 3 February 1950,
p. 80.

A plea for greater recognition of "the most important poetic
dramas in English between the seventeenth century and our
own time."

840 Bebbington, W.B. "THE TWO FOSCARI." ENGLISH, 9 (1953), 201-6.

In fact, very little about THE TWO FOSCARI; mainly general
and simplistic comment on Byron's alleged inability to write
plays.

841 Norman, Arthur. "Dialogue in Byron's Dramas." N&Q, 199 (1954),
304-6.

842 Scott, Noel. "Byron and the Stage." QR, 293 (1955), 496-503.

Contemporary reviews of some of the plays from the WINDSOR
AND ETON EXPRESS AND GENERAL ADVERTISER.

843 Harrison, John William. "The Imagery of Byron's Romantic Narratives
and Dramas." Ph.D. Dissertation, University of Colorado, 1958. 148 p.
(DA#59-00829).

844 Quinlan, Maurice J. "Byron's MANFRED and Zoroastrianism." JEGP, 57 (1958), 726-38.

> The influence of Zoroastrianism, most evident in the character of Arimanes, does not alter accepted interpretations of Manfred so much as it "serves to emphasize the fundamental conflict between good and evil in the main character."

845 Knight, G. Wilson. "Shakespeare and Byron's Plays." SHAKESPEARE JAHRBUCH, 95 (1959), 82-97.

> "Despite his rejection of Shakespearean influence in surface style, Shakespearean affinities are clearly apparent"--particularly in MANFRED, CAIN, MARINO FALIERO, and SARDANAPALUS.

846 Klein, John W. "Byron's Neglected Plays." DRAMA, n.s., no. 63 (1961), 34-36.

> A plea for their revival, particularly MARINO FALIERO.

847 Rutherford, Andrew. BYRON: A CRITICAL STUDY. Edinburgh and London: Oliver & Boyd, 1961. xiv, 253 p.

> Chapter five contains a lengthy assessment of MANFRED.

848 Dobrée, Bonamy. BYRON'S DRAMAS. Nottingham: Nottingham University Press, 1962. 24 p.

> The Byron Foundation Lecture, 1962.

849 Marshall, William H. THE STRUCTURE OF BYRON'S MAJOR POEMS. Philadelphia: University of Pennsylvania Press, 1962. 191 p.

> One chapter on MANFRED; another on CAIN and HEAVEN AND EARTH.

850 Thorslev, Peter L. THE BYRONIC HERO. TYPES AND PROTOTYPES. Minneapolis: University of Minnesota Press, 1962. 228 p.

> Pays some attention to the plays, especially CAIN and MANFRED. There is also an interesting chapter on the Gothic villain in drama.

851 Butler, Maria Hogan. "An Examination of Byron's Revision of MANFRED, Act III." SP, 60 (1963), 627-36.

852 Chatterton, Roylance Wayne. "Lord Byron's Dramas: An Attempt to Reform the English Stage." Ph.D. Dissertation, University of Utah, 1963. 318 p. (DA#63-04363)

853 Morokoff, Gene Emerson. "A Critical Study of Byron's MANFRED."
Ph.D. Dissertation, University of Illinois, 1963. 252 p. (DA#64-02931)

854 West, Paul, ed. BYRON. A COLLECTION OF CRITICAL ESSAYS.
Englewood Cliffs, N.J.: Prentice-Hall, 1963. 175 p.

> Includes Paul West on the plays, pp. 50-64. This essay is
> reprinted from his BYRON AND THE SPOILER'S ART (Lon-
> don: Chatto & Windus, 1960), pp. 100-120. "The plays
> really amount to prodigious soliloquies set out as drama. . . .
> States of mind intrigue him; events hardly at all."

855 Cooke, M.G. "The Restoration Ethos of Byron's Classical Plays."
PMLA, 79 (1964), 569-78.

> A convincing argument that Byron was indebted to Restora-
> tion heroic tragedy: with SARDANAPALUS, to Dryden's
> ALL FOR LOVE; and with MARINO FALIERO, to Otway's
> VENICE PRESERVED.

856 Ehrstine, John W. "An Analysis of Byron's Plays." Ph.D. Dissertation,
Wayne State University, 1964. 301 p. (DA#68-06628)

857 Joseph, M.K. BYRON THE POET. London: Gollancz, 1964. 352 p.

> One chapter on the plays, divided into four parts: 1. MAN-
> FRED; 2. "The Search for Form"; 3. "The Drama of Politics";
> 4. "The Drama of Theology."

858 Mellon, John Paul. "Byron's MANFRED: A Study of Sources and Ideas."
Ph.D. Dissertation, University of Pittsburgh, 1964. 197 p. (DA#64-
05213)

859 Thompson, James Roy. "Studies in the Drama of Lord Byron." Ph.D.
Dissertation, University of Cincinnati, 1964. 225 p. (DA#64-11991)

862 Coleman, Ronald Gregg. "Cosmic Symbolism in Byron's Dramas." Ph.D.
Dissertation, Vanderbilt University, 1965. 308 p. (DA#64-10465)

860 Vanderbeets, Richard. "A Note on Dramatic Necessity and the Incest
Motif in MANFRED." N&Q, 209 (1964), 26-28.

> The author argues that the incest motif arises as much out of
> Byron's use of the Gothic tradition and the Faust legend as
> it does out of his incestuous relationship with his half-sister.

861 Bhalla, Alok. "Two Voices in Byron's MANFRED." EMD, 3 (1965),
19-32.

The two voices are Manfred's: "a voice of heroic rebellion [against a universe of recognized values] and a voice expressing the absurdity and pointlessness of human existence."

863 Hassler, Donald M. "MARINO FALIERO, the Byronic Hero, and Don Juan." KSI, 14 (1965), 55-64.

864 Elledge, W. Paul. "Imagery and Theme in Byron's CAIN." KSJ, 15 (1966), 49-57.

865 Knight, G. Wilson. BYRON AND SHAKESPEARE. New York: Barnes & Noble, 1966. xvi, 381 p.

No substantial discussion of Byron's plays, but many fleeting references.

866 Lehn, Gertrude Lydia. "The Development of Byron as a Dramatist." Ph.D. dissertation, Harvard University, 1966.

867 Thompson, P.W. "Byron and Edmund Kean--A Comment." ThR, 8, no. 1 (1966), 17-19.

Kean's performance of Richard III influenced a stage direction in WERNER. This leads Thompson to the tentative conclusion that Byron, despite his protestations to the contrary, intended WERNER for the stage.

868 Whitmore, Allen Perry. "The Major Characters of Lord Byron's Dramas." Ph.D. Dissertation, University of Colorado, 1966. 153 p. (DA#67-10021)

869 Lim, Paulino Marquez. "The Style of Byron's Plays." Ph.D. Dissertation, University of California, 1967. 193 p. (DA#68-03272)

870 McGann, Jerome J. "Byron, Teresa, and SARDANAPALUS." KSMB, 18 (1967), 7-22.

A close analysis of the character of Myrrha in SARDANAPALUS and her resemblance to Teresa Guiccioli, allegedly the life-model for Myrrha.

871 Michaels, Leonard. "Hail, Muse, Et Cetera: An Essay on Narrative Pattern, Costume, and the Idea of the Self in Byron's CAIN and His Tales." Ph.D. Dissertation, University of Michigan, 1967. 135 p. (DA#67-17815)

872 Thompson, James R. "Byron's Plays and DON JUAN: Genre and Myth." BuR, 15, no. 3 (1967), 22-38.

> A discussion of Byron's plays and DON JUAN as responses to what seemed to Byron "an increasingly meaningless universe." These works constitute his "alternate methods of dealing with the absurdity of modern experience."

873 Caruthers, Clifford Mack. "A Critical Study of the Plays of Lord Byron." Ph.D. Dissertation, University of Missouri, 1968. 212 p. (DA#68-12487)

874 McGann, Jerome J. "Byronic Drama in Two Venetian Plays." MP, 66 (1968), 30-44.

> A defense of MARINO FALIERO and THE TWO FOSCARI both as drama and poetry. McGann persuasively refutes earlier allegations that the two plays are failures.

875 _____. FIERY DUST: BYRON'S POETIC DEVELOPMENT. Chicago and London: University of Chicago Press, 1968. xiv, 324 p.

> Includes extended discussion of several of the plays.

876 Manning, Peter J. "Byron and the Stage." Ph.D. Dissertation, Yale University, 1968. 363 p. (DA#69-13357)

877 Mortenson, Robert. "Byroniana: 'Remarks on CAIN' Identified." HLB, 16 (1968), 237-41.

> Comments on an anonymous early nineteenth-century pamphlet at Harvard.

878 _____. "Byron's Letter to Murray on CAIN." LCh, 34 (1968), 94-99.

879 Nurmi, Martin K. "The Prompt Copy of Charles Kean's 1838 Production of Byron's SARDANAPALUS." SERIF, 5, no. 2 (1968), 3-13.

> Discussion of Kean's promptbook at Kent State University.

880 Barker, Kathleen. "The First English Performance of Byron's WERNER." MP, 66 (1968-69), 342-44.

> Macready's production at the Theatre Royal, Bristol, 13 January 1830.

881 Kahn, Arthur D. "Seneca and SARDANAPALUS: Byron, the Don Quixote of Neo-Classicism." SP, 66 (1969), 654-71.

> Kahn shows that Seneca "provided the chief model and source

for Byron's play and that Seneca's influence pervades every page of SARDANAPALUS."

882   Michaels, Leonard. "Byron's CAIN." PMLA, 84 (1969), 71-78.

A discussion of the structure of a "very interesting, if not very good, play."

883   Mortenson, Robert. "The Copyright of Byron's CAIN." PBSA, 63 (1969), 5-13.

An interesting discussion of the legal issues surrounding the copyright of CAIN and William Benbow's pirated edition of 1822.

884   Osterberg, Oliver Sinclaire. "Proteus: Form and Idea in Three Metaphysical Dramas of George Gordon Noel, Lord Byron." Ph.D. Dissertation, University of Minnesota, 1970. 629 p. (DA#71-08252)

Discusses CAIN, MANFRED, and THE DEFORMED TRANSFORMED.

885   Reisner, Thomas A. "Cain: Two Romantic Interpretations." CULTURE, 31 (1970), 124-43.

A discussion of Byron's play and Blake's GHOST OF ABEL.

886   Rutherford, Andrew, ed. BYRON: THE CRITICAL HERITAGE. New York: Barnes & Noble, 1970. xviii, 513 p.

There is a very useful section on contemporary reaction to Byron's plays, with selections from the views of major writers and critics of the 1820's.

887   Stringham, Scott. "I DUE FOSCARI: From Byron's Play to Verdi's Opera." WVUPP, 17 (1970), 31-40.

888   Goldstein, Stephen L. "Byron in Radical Tradition: A Study in the Intellectual Backgrounds and Controversiality of CAIN." Ph.D. Dissertation, Columbia University, 1971. 222 p.

889   Luke, K. McCormick. "Lord Byron's MANFRED: A Study of Alienation from Within." UTR, 40 (1971), 15-26.

"In MANFRED the Byronic hero is as always ill-starred, fated to suffer, alienated. But in this play the dramatically operative alienation of the hero is not from society, as in CHILDE HAROLD and DON JUAN: rather it is alienation within himself." The essay is a straightforward critical discussion of

MANFRED with no reference to the other plays.

890 Tillotson, Marcia. "Byron's Tragedies." Ph.D. Dissertation, University of Chicago, 1971. 221 p.

891 Ashton, Thomas L. "The Censorship of Byron's MARINO FALIERO." HLQ, 36 (1972), 27–44.

892 Jump, John D. BYRON. London and Boston: Routledge & Kegan Paul, 1972. xiv, 200 p.

> Includes a brief assessment of MANFRED and a longer discussion of CAIN; the other plays are mentioned in passing only.

893 Kushwaha, M.S. "Byron the Dramatist: A Reappraisal." PURBA, 3 (1972), (1972), 113–20.

894 Taborski, Boleslaw. BYRON AND THE THEATRE. Salzburg: Institute für Englische Sprache und Literatur, 1972. 395 p.

895 Carr, Sherwyn T. "Bunn, Byron and MANFRED." NCTR, 1 (1973), 15–27.

> A detailed examination of the text used by Bunn for the 1834 Covent Garden production.

VI Journals and Newsletters

896 THE BYRON JOURNAL. London: Byron Society, 1973-- . Annual.

BYRON, HENRY JAMES (1834-84)

II Acted Plays—Principal Titles

897 THE MAID AND THE MAGPIE; OR, THE FATAL SPOON! A BURLESQUE BURLETTA FOUNDED ON THE OPERA OF "LA GAZZA LADRA." (Strand, 11 October 1858.) London: Lacy, n.d. 36 p.

> An acting edition with a cast list of the first London production.

898 ALADDIN; OR, THE WONDERFUL SCAMP: AN ORIGINAL BURLESQUE EXTRAVAGANZA IN ONE ACT. (Strand, 1 April 1861.) London: Lacy, n.d. 42 p.

An acting edition with a cast list of the first London production.

899 GEORGE DE BARNWELL: A BURLESQUE PANTOMIME OPENING. (Adelphi, 26 December 1862.) London: Lacy, n.d. 34 p.

900 THE ROSEBUD OF STINGINGNETTLE FARM; OR, THE VILLANOUS SQUIRE AND THE VIRTUOUS VILLAGER: BEING AS DOMESTIC A DRAMA AS CAN BE PERFORMED IN A QUARTER OF AN HOUR. (Adelphi, 9 September 1863.) London: Nassau Steam Press, 1862. 12 p.

An acting edition with a cast list.

901 1863; OR, THE SENSATIONS OF THE PAST SEASON WITH A SHAMEFUL REVELATION OF LADY SOMEBODY'S SECRET: A COMICAL CONGLOMERATIVE ABSURDITY IN ONE ACT. (St. James's, 26 December 1863.) London: Lacy, n.d. 30 p.

An acting edition with a cast list of the first London production.

902 LA SONNAMBULA! OR, THE SUPPER, THE SLEEPER, AND THE MERRY SWISS BOY: AN ORIGINAL OPERATIC BURLESQUE EXTRAVAGANZA. (Prince of Wales's, 15 April 1865.) London: Lacy, n.d. 36 p.

An acting edition with a cast list of the first London production.

903 WAR TO THE KNIFE: AN ORIGINAL COMEDY IN THREE ACTS. (Prince of Wales's, 10 June 1865.) London: Lacy, n.d. 31 p.

An acting edition with a cast list of the first London production.

904 LUCIA DI LAMMERMOOR; OR, THE LAIRD, THE LADY, AND THE LOVER: A NEW AND ORIGINAL OPERATIC BURLESQUE EXTRAVAGANZA: FOUNDED ON DONIZETTI'S POPULAR OPERA, AND CONSEQUENTLY VERY UNLIKE THE ROMANCE. (Prince of Wales's, 25 September 1865.) London and New York: French, n.d. 35 p.

An acting edition with a cast list of the first London production.

905 THE LANCASHIRE LASS; OR, TEMPTED, TRIED AND TRUE: A DOMESTIC MELODRAMA IN FOUR ACTS AND A PROLOGUE. (Alexandra, Liverpool, 28 October 1867; Queens, 24 July 1868.) Chicago: Dramatic Publishing Co., n.d. 45 p.

An acting edition with cast lists of productions in Liverpool and London.

906 BLOW FOR BLOW: AN ORIGINAL DRAMA IN A PROLOGUE AND THREE ACTS. (Holborn, 5 September 1868.) London: French, n.d. 53 p.

> An acting edition with a cast list of the first London production. The Readex collection also includes Sergel's acting edition (Chicago: n.d., 41 p.) with cast lists of the first London and Boston productions.

907 CYRIL'S SUCCESS: A COMEDY IN FIVE ACTS. (Globe, 28 November 1868.) Chicago and New York: Sergel, n.d. 46 p.

> An acting edition with cast lists of the first London and Boston productions.

908 NOT SUCH A FOOL AS HE LOOKS: A FARCICAL DRAMA IN THREE ACTS. (Theatre Royal, Manchester, 4 December 1868; Globe, 23 October 1869.) Chicago: Sergel, n.d. 32 p.

> An acting edition with cast lists of London and New York productions.

909 UNCLE DICK'S DARLING: A DOMESTIC DRAMA IN THREE ACTS. (Gaiety, 13 December 1869.) New York: Sergel, n.d. 29 p.

> An acting edition with a cast list of the first London production.

910 THE PROMPTER'S BOX: A STORY OF THE FOOTLIGHTS AND THE FIRESIDE: AN ORIGINAL DOMESTIC DRAMA IN FOUR ACTS. (Adelphi, 23 March 1870.) London and New York: French, n.d. 48 p.

> An acting edition with a cast list of the first London production.

911 EURYDICE; OR, LITTLE ORPHEUS AND HIS LUTE: A GRAND BURLESQUE EXTRAVAGANZA, BEING A SECOND EDITION OF "ORPHEUS AND EURYDICE; OR, THE YOUNG GENTLEMAN WHO CHARMED THE ROCKS." (Strand, 24 April 1871.) London: Lacy, n.d. 39 p.

> An acting edition with a cast list of the first London production.

912 DAISY FARM: A DOMESTIC DRAMA IN FOUR ACTS. (Olympic, 1 May 1871.) Acting Drama, no. 286. Chicago: Sergel, 34 p.

> An acting edition with a cast list of the first London production.

913 PARTNERS FOR LIFE: AN ORIGINAL COMEDY IN THREE ACTS.
(Globe, 7 October 1871.) London and New York: French, n.d. 48 p.

An acting edition with a cast list.

914 OLD SOLDIER: AN ORIGINAL COMEDY IN THREE ACTS (Strand, 25
January 1873.) London and New York: French, n.d. 40 p.

An acting edition with a cast list of the first London production. Title page reads OLD SOLDIER, while the correct
running title is OLD SOLDIERS.

915 FINE FEATHERS: AN ORIGINAL MODERN DRAMA IN THREE ACTS
AND A PROLOGUE. (Globe, 26 April 1873.) London and New York:
French, n.d. 60 p.

An acting edition with a cast list of the first London production.

916 OLD SAILORS: ORIGINAL COMEDY IN THREE ACTS. (Strand, 19
October 1874.) London and New York: French, n.d. 42 p.

An acting edition with a cast list of the first London production.

917 "OUR BOYS": AN ORIGINAL MODERN COMEDY. (Vaudeville, 16
January 1875.) Chicago: Dramatic Publishing Co., n.d. 59 p.

An acting edition with a cast list of the first London production.

918 WEAK WOMAN: A NEW AND ORIGINAL COMEDY IN THREE ACTS.
(Strand, 6 May 1875.) London and New York: French, n.d. 43 p.

An acting edition with a cast list of the first London production.

919 MARRIED IN HASTE: AN ORIGINAL COMEDY IN FOUR ACTS. (Haymarket, 2 October 1875.) London and New York: French, n.d. 52 p.

An acting edition with cast lists of the first London and New
York productions.

920 £20 A YEAR--ALL FOUND; OR, OUT OF A SITUATION REFUSING
TWENTY: BEING AN APROPOS SKETCH, WITH A MORAL FOR SER-
VANTS AND MISTRESSES. (Folly, 17 April 1876.) London and New
York: French, n.d. 18 p.

An acting edition with a cast list of the first London production.

921 "COURTSHIP"; OR, THE THREE CASKETS: A COMEDY IN THREE ACTS.
(Court, 16 October 1879.) London and New York: French, n.d. 48 p.

An acting edition with a cast list of the first London production.

922 BOW BELLS: AN ORIGINAL COMIC DRAMA IN THREE ACTS.
(Royalty, 4 October 1880.) London and New York: French, n.d. 48 p.

An acting edition with a cast list of the first London production.

V Critical Studies

923 Wrey, Peyton. "Notes on Popular Dramatists: Mr. H.J. Byron." LON-
DON SOCIETY, 26 (August 1874), 121-29.

In this generalized article Wrey holds that Byron possesses
great potential, but that to date (after many plays) he has
yet to write a durable play. Byron's faults are his too-
easy facility with words and his cynicism.

CARTON, RICHARD CLAUDE [RICHARD CLAUDE CRITCHETT] (1857-1928)

II Acted Plays—Principal Titles

924 SUNLIGHT AND SHADOW: A NEW ORIGINAL MODERN PLAY IN
THREE ACTS. (Avenue, 1 November 1890.) London and New York:
French, 1900. 57 p.

An acting edition with a cast list of the first London production.

925 LIBERTY HALL: AN ORIGINAL DRAMA IN FOUR ACTS. (St. James's,
3 December 1892.) London and New York: French, 1900. 76 p.

An acting edition with a cast list of the first London production.

926 WHEELS WITHIN WHEELS. (Court, 25 May 1899.)

Typescript, located in New York Public Library.

927 LADY HUNTWORTH'S EXPERIMENT: AN ORIGINAL COMEDY IN
THREE ACTS. (Criterion, 26 April 1900.) London and New York:
French, 1904. 75 p.

An acting edition with a cast list of the first London production.

928 *MR. HOPKINSON: AN ORIGINAL FARCE IN THREE ACTS. (Avenue, 21 February 1905.) London and New York: French, 1908. 119 p.

> An acting edition with a cast list of the first London production.

929 *PUBLIC OPINION: A FARCE IN THREE ACTS. (Wyndham's, 10 October 1905.) London and New York: French, 1913. 155 p.

> An acting edition with a cast list of the first London production.

930 *MR. PREEDY AND THE COUNTESS: AN ORIGINAL FARCE IN THREE ACTS. (Criterion, 13 April 1909.) London and New York: French, 1911. 155 p.

> An acting edition with a cast list of the first London production.

931 *THE BEAR LEADERS: A FARCE IN FOUR ACTS. (Comedy, 1 December 1912.) London and New York: French, 1913. 182 p.

> An acting edition with a cast list of the first London production.

V Critical Studies

932 "Mr. R.C. Carton at Home." ERA, 4 February 1893, p.11.

> An informal interview, covering various aspects of Carton's life and works.

CHAMBERS, CHARLES HADDON (1860-1921)

II Acted Plays—Principal Titles

933 THE OPEN GATE: AN ORIGINAL DOMESTIC DRAMA IN ONE ACT. (Comedy, 28 March 1887.) London and New York: French, n.d. 18 p.

> An acting edition with a cast list of the first London production. The Readex collection also includes a World Acting Drama Edition (Chicago: n.d. 18 p.).

934 CAPTAIN SWIFT: A COMEDY IN FOUR ACTS. (Haymarket, 20 June 1888.) London and New York: French, 1902. 69 p.

> An acting edition with a cast list of the first London production.

935 THE IDLER: A PLAY IN FOUR ACTS. (Lyceum, New York, 11 November 1890; St. James's, 26 February 1891.) London and New York: French, 1902. 64 p.

> An acting edition with a cast list of the first London production. The Readex collection also includes a typescript, located in New York Public Library.

936 *JOHN-A-DREAMS. (Haymarket, 8 November 1894). LC.

937 THE TYRANNY OF TEARS: A COMEDY IN FOUR ACTS (Criterion, 6 April 1899.) Boston: Baker, 1902. v, 152 p.

> An acting edition with an introductory note by Alice Brown.

938 *THE AWAKENING: A PLAY IN FOUR ACTS. (St. James's, 6 February 1901.) London: Heinemann, 1902. 160 p.

> Includes a cast list of the first London production.

939 *PASSER-BY: A PLAY IN FOUR ACTS. (Wyndham's, 29 March 1911.) London: Duckworth, 1913. 139 p.

> An acting edition with a cast list of the first London production.

CHELTNAM, CHARLES SMITH (b. 1823)

II Acted Plays—Principal Titles

940 MRS. GREEN'S SNUG LITTLE BUSINESS: AN ORIGINAL FARCE IN ONE ACT. (Strand, 16 January 1865.) London: Lacy, n.d. 18 p.

> An acting edition with a cast list of the first London production.

941 EDENDALE: AN ORIGINAL DRAMA IN THREE ACTS. (Charing Cross, 19 June 1869.) London: Lacy, n.d. 42 p.

> An acting edition with a cast list of the first London production.

942 LEATHERLUNGS THE GREAT: HOW HE STORM'D, REIGN'D, AND MIZZLED: AN ENTIRELY NEW AND ORIGINAL EXTRAVAGANZA. (Adelphi, 1 July 1872.) London and New York: French, n.d. 32 p.

> An acting edition with a cast list of the first London production.

COLERIDGE, SAMUEL TAYLOR (1772-1834)

I Collected Works

943   Coleridge, Derwent, ed.   THE DRAMATIC WORKS OF SAMUEL TAYLOR
COLERIDGE.   New ed.   London: Edward Moxon, 1852.

>   Contains REMORSE, ZAPOLYA, THE PICCOLOMINI, and
>   THE DEATH OF WALLENSTEIN.   There is a short general
>   introduction by the editor.

944   Shedd, W.G.T., ed.   THE COMPLETE WORKS OF SAMUEL TAYLOR
COLERIDGE.   7 vols.   New York: Harper & Bros., 1884.

>   REMORSE, ZAPOLYA, THE PICCOLOMINI, and THE DEATH
>   OF WALLENSTEIN are printed in volume seven.

945   Coleridge, Ernest Hartley, ed.   THE COMPLETE POETICAL WORKS OF
SAMUEL TAYLOR COLERIDGE.   INCLUDING POEMS AND VERSIONS
OF POEMS NOW PUBLISHED FOR THE FIRST TIME.   2 vols.   Oxford:
Clarendon Press, 1912.   xxvi, 492; viii, 493-1,198 p.

>   Includes THE FALL OF ROBESPIERRE (written in collaboration
>   with Southey), OSORIO, THE PICCOLOMINI, THE DEATH
>   OF WALLENSTEIN, REMORSE, ZAPOLYA, and, printed for
>   the first time, THE TRIUMPH OF LOYALTY.   At present this
>   is the best available edition of Coleridge's plays.

946   Coburn, Kathleen, general ed.   THE COLLECTED WORKS OF SAMUEL
TAYLOR COLERIDGE.   London and Princeton: Routledge & Kegan Paul
and Princeton University Press, 1969-- .

>   A meticulously edited and probably definitive edition, but it
>   will be some time before the plays appear in this edition.

II Acted Plays—Principal Titles

947   THE TRIUMPH OF LOYALTY: AN HISTORIC DRAMA IN FIVE ACTS.
(Drury Lane, 7 February 1801.)

>   Includes a cast list of the Drury Lane production; the Readex
>   copy is reproduced from the text published by E.H. Coleridge
>   (item 945).

948   *OSORIO: A TRAGEDY, AS ORIGINALLY WRITTEN IN 1797 . . .
NOW FIRST PRINTED FROM A COPY RECENTLY DISCOVERED BY THE
PUBLISHER, WITH THE VARIORUM READINGS OF "REMORSE" AND A
MONOGRAPH ON THE HISTORY OF THE PLAY IN ITS EARLIER AND

LATER FORM. . . . London: J. Pearson, 1873. xxii, 204 p.

> See item 949, below.

949 REMORSE: A TRAGEDY IN FIVE ACTS. (Drury Lane, 23 January 1813.) London: W. Pople, 1813. viii, 72 p.

> With a cast list of the first London production and an interesting preface by Coleridge in which he contrasts the unfair treatment of his play by Sheridan following its composition in 1797 with the help and courtesy he received from Whitbread and Arnold prior to the 1813 production. The play's original 1797 title was OSORIO (item 948).

950 ZAPOLYA: A CHRISTMAS TALE IN TWO PARTS. (Surrey, 1818.) London: Fenner, 1817. 128 p.

> With a prefatory note by Coleridge explaining that this "dramatic poem is in humble imitation of the Winter's Tale of Shakespear." The play was adapted for the Surrey production by T.J. Dibdin.

IIa Unacted Plays

951 *THE FALL OF ROBESPIERRE: AN HISTORIC DRAMA. Cambridge: W.H. Lunn and J. and J. Merrill, 1794. 37 p.

> Acts two and three were written by Southey, although his name does not appear on the title page.

952 THE PICCOLOMINI; OR, THE FIRST PART OF WALLENSTEIN: A DRAMA IN FIVE ACTS. TRANSLATED FROM THE GERMAN OF FREDERICK SCHILLER. London: Longman and Rees, 1800. vi, 214 p.

> With a brief preface by Coleridge.

953 THE DEATH OF WALLENSTEIN: A TRAGEDY IN FIVE ACTS. TRANSLATED FROM THE GERMAN OF FREDERICK SCHILLER. London: Longman and Rees, 1800. ix, 157 p.

> With a short preface by Coleridge on Schiller's plays and on the difficulties of translation.

III Bibliographies

954 Shepherd, Richard Herne. THE BIBLIOGRAPHY OF COLERIDGE. A BIBLIOGRAPHICAL LIST ARRANGED IN CHRONOLOGICAL ORDER OF THE PUBLISHED AND PRIVATELY PRINTED WRITINGS IN VERSE AND PROSE OF SAMUEL TAYLOR COLERIDGE, INCLUDING HIS CONTRIBU-

TIONS TO ANNUALS, MAGAZINES AND PERIODICAL PUBLICA-
TIONS . . . REVISED, CORRECTED, AND ENLARGED BY COLONEL
W.F. PRIDEAUX. London: Frank Hollings, 1900. x, 95 p.

955 Haney, John Louis. A BIBLIOGRAPHY OF SAMUEL TAYLOR COLE-
RIDGE. Philadelphia: Printed for private circulation, 1903; rpt. Folcroft, Pa.: Folcroft Press, 1969. xv, 144 p.

A wide-ranging bibliography of primary and secondary materials,
supplementing Shepherd (item 954). But on primary works
Wise is more reliable (item 956).

956 Wise, Thomas J. A BIBLIOGRAPHY OF THE WRITINGS IN PROSE AND
VERSE OF SAMUEL TAYLOR COLERIDGE. London: Bibliographical
Society, 1913. x, 316 p.

Wise published a supplement to this detailed bibliography in
1919.

957 Kennedy, Virginia Wadlow. SAMUEL TAYLOR COLERIDGE: A SELECTED
BIBLIOGRAPHY OF THE BEST AVAILABLE EDITIONS OF HIS WRITINGS,
OF BIOGRAPHIES AND CRITICISMS OF HIM, AND OF REFERENCES
SHOWING HIS RELATIONS WITH HIS CONTEMPORARIES. FOR STU-
DENTS AND TEACHERS. Baltimore, Md.: Enoch Pratt Free Library, 1935.
vii, 151 p.

IV Biography

958 Chambers, E.K. SAMUEL TAYLOR COLERIDGE: A BIOGRAPHICAL
STUDY. Oxford: Clarendon Press, 1950. xvi, 373 p.

A standard biography in which there are several references
to the plays but no extended discussion of them.

959 Griggs, Earl Leslie, ed. COLLECTED LETTERS OF SAMUEL TAYLOR
COLERIDGE. 6 vols. Oxford: Clarendon Press, 1956-71.

The definitive edition.

960 Coburn, Kathleen, ed. THE NOTEBOOKS OF SAMUEL TAYLOR COLE-
RIDGE. London: Routledge & Kegan Paul, 1957-- .

A multivolume collection, expertly edited, with copious
notes and indexes.

V Critical Studies

961 Campbell, J. Dykes. "Coleridge's OSORIO and REMORSE." ATHENAE-

UM, 5 April 1890, pp. 445-46.

A discussion of textual problems in early editions of REMORSE.

962 Morrill, Dorothy I. "Coleridge's Theory of Dramatic Illusion." MLN, 42 (1927), 436-44.

More illuminating discussion of this complex issue can be found in items 967 and 972.

963 Hamilton, Marie Padgett. "Wordsworth's Relation to Coleridge's OSORIO." SP, 34 (1937), 429-37.

Connections between OSORIO and THE IDIOT BOY, THE BLIND HIGHLAND BOY, and RUTH.

964 Logan, Sister Eugenia, ed. A CONCORDANCE TO THE POETRY OF SAMUEL TAYLOR COLERIDGE. Saint Mary-of-the-Woods, Ind.: Privately printed, 1940. xvi, 901 p.

The plays are included.

965 Ashe, Dora Jean. "Byron's Alleged Part in the Production of Coleridge's REMORSE." N&Q, 198 (1953), 33-36.

The author argues that it is unlikely, as has sometimes been suggested, that Byron used his influence to persuade the Drury Lane management to accept REMORSE

966 _____. "Coleridge, Byron and Schiller's DER GEISTERSEHER." N&Q, 201 (1956), 436-38.

The article deals in part with the relationship between OSORIO and Schiller's prose tale.

967 Fogle, R.H. "Coleridge on Dramatic Illusion." TDR, 4, no. 4 (1960), 33-44.

A description and analysis of Coleridge's theory.

968 Bouslog, Charles S. "Coleridge's Marginalia in the Sara Hutchinson Copy of REMORSE." BNYPL, 65 (1961), 333-38.

969 Jackson, J.R. de J. "The Influence of the Theatre on Coleridge's Shakespearean Criticism." Ph.D. Dissertation, Princeton University, 1961. 236 p. (DA#61-04790)

970 Woodring, Carl R. "Two Prompt Copies of Coleridge's REMORSE." BNYPL, 65 (1961), 229-35.

Promptbooks for the London 1813 production and the 1814 productions in Philadelphia and Baltimore.

971 Fox, Arnold B. "Political and Biographical Background of Coleridge's OSORIO." JEGP, 61 (1962), 258-67.

A reading of OSORIO as an attack on the Pitt ministry, with Osorio as Coleridge's brother, George.

972 Jackson, J.R. de J. "Coleridge on Dramatic Illusion and Spectacle in the Performance of Shakespeare's Plays." MP, 62 (1964), 13-21.

An interesting explanation of Coleridge's dissatisfaction with contemporary productions of Shakespeare: "Coleridge was confronted with a stage which relied heavily on what approaches a theatrical trompe l'oeil; he was convinced that this mode of theatre was both inferior to and destructive of the effects of Shakespeare."

973 Banks, Thomas Wilson. "The Dramatic Career of Samuel Taylor Coleridge." Ph.D. Dissertation, Emory University, 1966. 399 p. (DA#67-00761)

974 Zall, P.M. "Coleridge's Unpublished Revisions to OSORIO." BNYPL, 71 (1967), 516-23.

Revisions made in a manuscript copy of the play now at the Huntington Library, revisions not included in E.H. Coleridge's collations in his edition of the POETICAL WORKS (item 945).

975 Ball, Patricia M. "The Waking Dream: Coleridge and the Drama." THE MORALITY OF ART: ESSAYS PRESENTED TO G. WILSON KNIGHT. Ed. D.W. Jefferson. London: Routledge, 1969. 165-74.

The author concentrates on REMORSE and ZAPOLYA in order to explore Coleridge's dramatic theory.

976 Jackson, J.R. de J. COLERIDGE: THE CRITICAL HERITAGE. New York: Barnes & Noble, 1970. xiii, 660 p.

Included are contemporary comments on THE FALL OF ROBESPIERRE, WALLENSTEIN, REMORSE, and ZAPOLYA.

COYNE, JOSEPH STIRLING (1803-68)

II Acted Plays—Principal Titles

977 THE QUEER SUBJECT: A FARCE IN ONE ACT. (Adelphi, 28 November

1836.) The Acting National Drama, vol. 1. London: Chapman and Hall, 1837. 13 p.

> With a cast list of the first London production and a lengthy memoir of the actor John Reeve.

978 VALSHA; OR, THE SLAVE QUEEN: A DRAMA IN THREE ACTS. (Adelphi, 30 October 1837.) London: Chapman and Hall, n.d. 36 p.

> An acting edition, but there is no cast list; the Readex copy is a promptbook with manuscript notes (New York Public Library).

979 HOW TO SETTLE ACCOUNTS WITH YOUR LAUNDRESS: AN ORIGINAL FARCE IN ONE ACT. (Adelphi, 26 July 1847.) Dicks' Standard Plays, no. 1006. London: Dicks, n.d.

> An acting edition with a cast list of the first London production.

980 THE HOPE OF THE FAMILY: AN ORIGINAL COMEDY IN THREE ACTS. (Haymarket, 3 December 1853.) London: Lacy, n.d. 41 p.

> An acting edition with a cast list of the first London production; the Readex copy is a promptbook with manuscript notes (New York Public Library).

981 THE SECRET AGENT: A COMEDY IN TWO ACTS. (Haymarket, 10 March 1855.) Lacy's Acting Edition, vol. 18. London: Lacy, n.d. 40 p.

> With a cast list of the first London production.

982 THE MAN OF MANY FRIENDS: AN ORIGINAL COMEDY IN THREE ACTS. (Haymarket, 1 September 1855.) London: Lacy, n.d. 40 p.

> An acting edition with a cast list of the first London production.

983 THE LOVE-KNOT: A COMEDY IN THREE ACTS. (Drury Lane, 8 March 1858.) Spencer's Boston Theatre, no. 163. Boston: William V. Spencer, n.d. 39 p.

> An acting edition with a cast list of the first London production; the Readex copy is a promptbook with manuscript notes (New York Public Library).

984 THE WOMAN IN RED: A DRAMA IN THREE ACTS AND A PROLOGUE. (Victoria, 28 March 1864.) Sergel's Acting Drama, no. 136. Chicago: Dramatic Publishing Co., n.d. 38 p.

With cast lists of the Victoria and St. James's productions.

CRAVEN, HENRY THORNTON [HENRY THORNTON] (1818-1905)

II Acted Plays—Principal Titles

985 DONE BROWN: A FARCE IN ONE ACT. (Adelphi, Edinburgh, 1845.)
London: Lacy, n.d. 20 p.

> An acting edition with a cast list of the first Edinburgh production.

986 BLETCHINGTON HOUSE; OR, THE SURRENDER! AN HISTORICAL
DRAMA IN THREE ACTS. (City of London, 20 April 1846.) New British Theatre, no. 447. London: n.d. 43 p.

> An acting edition with a cast list of the first London production.

987 BOWL'D OUT; OR, A BIT OF BRUMMAGEN: A FARCE IN ONE ACT.
(Princess's, 9 July 1860.) London: Lacy, n.d. 21 p.

> An acting edition with a cast list of the first London production.

988 THE CHIMNEY CORNER: AN ORIGINAL DOMESTIC DRAMA IN TWO
ACTS. (Olympic, 21 February 1861.) London: Lacy, n.d. 36 p.

> An acting edition with a cast list of the first London production, and interleaved with manuscript notes.

989 MIRIAM'S CRIME: A DRAMA IN THREE ACTS. (Strand, 9 October
1863.) London: Lacy, n.d. 39 p.

> An acting edition with a cast list of the first London production; interleaved with manuscript notes.

990 MILKY WHITE: AN ORIGINAL SERIO-COMIC DRAMA IN TWO ACTS.
(Prince of Wales's, Liverpool, 20 June 1864; Strand, 28 September 1864.) London: Lacy, n.d. 44 p.

> An acting edition with cast lists of the first Liverpool and London productions.

991 MEG'S DIVERSION: A DRAMA IN TWO ACTS. (Royalty, 17 October
1866.) London: Lacy, n.d. 54 p.

> An acting edition with a cast list of the first London production; interleaved with some manuscript notes.

CROSS, JOHN [JAMES?] C. (d. 1810)

I Collected Works

992 THE DRAMATIC WORKS OF J.C. CROSS, STAGE MANAGER OF THE SURREY THEATRE, CONTAINING A COMPLETE COLLECTION OF THE MOST FAVORITE BALLETS, SPECTACLES, MELO-DRAMAS, &C. PERFORMED AT THE ABOVE THEATRE. 2nd ed. 2 vols. London: Thomas Tegg, 1812.

> A collection of twelve of Cross's dramatic pieces. Volume one also contains a "Short Sketch of the Royal Circus." A cast list is given for each play. The plays are: THE ROUND TOWER; BLACKBEARD; CORA; JULIA OF LOUVAIN; LOUISA OF LOMBARDY; OUR NATIVE LAND; SIR FRANCIS DRAKE, AND IRON ARM; THE FALSE FRIEND; THE CLOUD KING; RINALDO RINALDINI; THE FIRE KING; HALLOWEEN. This edition is available in the Readex collection.

DALE, FELIX [H.C. MERIVALE] (1839-1906)

II Acted Plays—Principal Titles

993 *SIX MONTHS AGO: A COMEDIETTA IN ONE ACT. (Olympic, 26 July 1867.) Lacy's Acting Edition, no. 1144. London: Lacy, n.d. 17 p.

994 *HE'S A LUNATIC: A FARCE IN ONE ACT. (Queen's, 24 October 1867.) London: Lacy, n.d. 20 p.

> An acting edition with a cast list of the first London production.

995 A SON OF THE SOIL: A ROMANTIC PLAY IN THREE ACTS (FOUNDED ON THE "LION AMOUREUX" OF RONSARD). (Court, 4 September 1872.) London and New York: French, n.d. 48 p.

> An acting edition with a cast list of the first London production.

996 *ALONE: AN ORIGINAL COMEDY DRAMA IN THREE ACTS. With J.P. Simpson. (Court, 25 October 1873.) Acting Edition, no. 1531. London and New York: French, n.d. 38 p.

> With a cast list of the first London production.

997 A HUSBAND IN CLOVER: A FARCE IN ONE ACT. (Lyceum, 26 December 1873.) New York Drama, vol. 1, no. 8. New York: Wheat and Cornett, n.d. Pages numbered 23-28.

> An acting edition, with a cast list of the first London production.

998 THE WHITE PILGRIM: A TRAGEDY IN FOUR ACTS. (Court, 14 February 1874.) London and New York: French, n.d. 48 p.

> An acting edition with a cast list of the first London production.

999 PEACOCK'S HOLIDAY: A FARCICAL COMEDY IN TWO ACTS: FOUNDED ON THE "VOYAGE DE M. PERRICHON." (Court, 16 April 1874.) London and New York: French, n.d. 34 p.

> An acting edition with a cast list of the first London production.

1000 THE LADY OF LYONS MARRIED AND SETTLED: A VAUDEVILLE IN THREE SCENES. (Gaiety, 5 October 1878.) London and New York: French, n.d. 28 p.

> An acting edition with a cast list.

IIa Unacted Plays

1001 *FLORIEN: A TRAGEDY IN FIVE ACTS, AND OTHER POEMS. London: Remington, 1884. 163 p.

> A library edition.

DANCE, CHARLES (1794-1863)

II Acted Plays—Principal Titles

1002 A MATCH IN THE DARK: COMEDIETTA IN ONE ACT. (Olympic, 21 February 1833.) London: John Miller, 1836. 31 p.

> Includes cast lists of the Olympic and Queen's productions.

1003 THE BEULAH SPA: A BURLETTA IN TWO ACTS. (Olympic, 18 November 1833.) London: John Miller, 1833. 56 p.

> Includes a cast list of the first London production.

1004 PLEASANT DREAMS: A FARCE. (Covent Garden, 24 May 1834.) London: John Miller, 1834. 43 p.

> With a cast list of the first London production.

1005 ADVICE GRATIS: A FARCE IN ONE ACT. (Olympic, 29 September 1837.) London: Chapman and Hall, n.d. 23 p.

> An acting edition with a cast list of the first London production.

1006 THE BENGAL TIGER: A FARCE IN ONE ACT. (Olympic, 18 December 1837.) London: Chapman and Hall, 1838. 24 p.

> An acting edition with a cast list of the first London production; the Readex copy is a promptbook, interleaved with manuscript notes (New York Public Library).

1007 NAVAL ENGAGEMENTS: A COMEDY IN TWO ACTS. (Olympic, 3 May 1838.) London: Chapman and Hall, n.d. 35 p.

> An acting edition with a cast list of the first London production; the Readex copy is a promptbook, interleaved with a few manuscript notes (New York Public Library).

1008 DELICATE GROUND; OR, PARIS IN 1793: A COMIC DRAMA IN ONE ACT. (Lyceum, 27 November 1849.) London: S.G. Fairbrother, n.d. 31 p.

> With a cast list of the first London production.

1009 A MORNING CALL: AN ORIGINAL COMEDIETTA IN ONE ACT. (Drury Lane, 17 March 1851.) London: S.G. Fairbrother, n.d. 22 p.

> With a cast list of the first London production; the Readex copy is a promptbook (New York Public Library).

1010 MARRIAGE A LOTTERY: A COMEDY IN TWO ACTS. (Strand, 20 May 1858.) De Witt's Acting Plays, no. 249. New York: De Witt, n.d. 27 p.

> With a cast list of the first London production.

DIBDIN, CHARLES (1768-1833)

II Acted Plays—Principal Titles

1011 THE GREAT DEVIL; OR, THE ROBBER OF GENOA: A MELO-DRAMA IN TWO ACTS. (Sadler's Wells, 17 August 1801.) Cumberland's Minor

Theatre, vol. 14. London: Cumberland, n.d. 22 p.

>An acting edition with a cast list of the first London production and "Remarks" by D--G [George Daniel].

1012 THE WILD MAN; OR, THE WATER PAGEANT: A MELO-DRAMATIC ROMANCE IN ONE ACT. (Sadler's Wells, 22 May 1809.) London: Richardson and Clarke, n.d. 36 p.

>An acting edition with a cast list of the first London production and "Remarks" by W.T. Moncrieff.

1013 THE FARMER'S WIFE: A COMIC OPERA IN THREE ACTS. (Covent Garden, 1 February 1814.) London: G. & S. Robinson, 1814. 80 p.

>With a cast list of the first London production.

1014 MY SPOUSE AND I: AN OPERATICAL FARCE IN TWO ACTS. (Drury Lane, 7 December 1815.) London: Whittingham and Arliss, 1815. 44 p.

>With a cast list of the first London production; the Readex collection also has a second edition of this play.

1015 LIFE IN LONDON; OR, THE LARKS OF LOGIC, TOM, AND JERRY: AN EXTRAVAGANZA IN THREE ACTS. (Olympic, 12 November 1821.) 2nd ed. London: John Lowndes, 1822. 40 p.

>With a cast list of the first London production.

IV Biography

1016 Speaight, George, ed. PROFESSIONAL & LITERARY MEMOIRS OF CHARLES DIBDIN THE YOUNGER. London: Society for Theatre Research, 1956. x, 175 p.

>Covers Dibdin's theatrical career from 1797 to 1830.

DIBDIN, THOMAS JOHN (1771-1841)

II Acted Plays—Principal Titles

1017 IL BONDOCANI; OR, THE CALIPH ROBBER: A COMIC OPERA IN THREE ACTS. (Covent Garden, 15 November 1800.) London: Longman and Rees, 1801. 45 p.

>With a cast list of the first London production.

1018 THE CABINET: A COMIC OPERA IN THREE ACTS. (Covent Garden, 9 February 1802.) London: Longman, Hurst, Rees and Orme, 1805. 88 p.

   With a cast list of the first London production.

1019 FAMILY QUARRELS: A COMIC OPERA IN THREE ACTS. (Covent Garden, 18 December 1802.) London: Longman, Hurst, Rees and Orme, 1805. 74 p.

   With a cast list of the first London production.

1020 [THE] ENGLISH FLEET IN 1342: AN HISTORICAL COMIC OPERA IN THREE ACTS. (Covent Garden, 13 December 1803.) London: Longman, Hurst, Rees and Orme, 1805. 63 p.

   With a cast list of the first London production.

1021 VALENTINE AND ORSON: A ROMANTIC MELO-DRAMA. (Covent Garden, 3 April 1804.) London: Barker and Son, 1804. 50 p.

   With a cast list of the first London production.

1022 THIRTY THOUSAND; OR, WHO'S THE RICHEST? A COMIC OPERA IN THREE ACTS. (Covent Garden, 10 December 1804.) London: Barker and Son, 1804. 75 p.

   With a cast list of the first London production and a brief introduction by Dibdin.

1023 TWO FACES UNDER A HOOD: A COMIC OPERA IN THREE ACTS. (Covent Garden, 17 November 1807.) London: Appleyards, n.d. 80 p.

   With a cast list of the first London production.

1024 HARELEQUIN HOAX; OR, A PANTOMIME PROPOSED: A COMIC EX-TRAVAGANZA. (Lyceum, 16 August 1814.) 2nd ed. London: Whittingham and Arliss, 1815. 28 p.

   With a cast list of the first London production.

1025 DON GIOVANNI; OR, A SPECTRE ON HORSEBACK? A COMIC, HEROIC, OPERATIC, TRAGIC, PANTOMIMIC, BURLETTA-SPECTACULAR EXTRAVAGANZA IN TWO ACTS. (Royal Circus, 26 May 1817.) London: John Miller, 1818. 32 p.

   With a cast list of the first London production.

1026 THE HEART OF MID-LOTHIAN; OR, THE LILY OF ST. LEONARD'S: A MELO-DRAMATIC ROMANCE IN THREE ACTS. (Surrey, 13 January 1819.) 2nd ed. London: Robert Stodart, 1819. vi, 66 p.

> With a cast list of the first London production and a brief introduction by Dibdin. The play is based on Scott's novel.

1027 IVANHOE; OR, THE JEW'S DAUGHTER: A ROMANTIC MELO-DRAMA IN THREE ACTS. (Surrey, 20 January 1820.) Spencer's Boston Theatre, no. 196. Boston: William V. Spencer, n.d. 44 p.

> An acting edition with cast lists for the first London and three subsequent American productions. The play is based on Scott's novel.

1028 THE FATE OF CALAS [sic]: A TRAGIC MELODRAMA IN THREE ACTS. (Surrey, 3 April 1820.) London: C. Lowndes, 1820. 42 p.

> With a cast list of the first London production.

1029 SUIL DHUV, THE COINER: A MELO-DRAMATIC ROMANCE IN THREE ACTS. (Sadler's Wells, 14 January 1828.) London: G.H. Davidson, n.d. 47 p.

> An acting edition with a cast list of the first London production and "Remarks" by D--G [George Daniel].

1030 THE BANKS OF THE HUDSON; OR, THE CONGRESS TROOPER: A TRANSATLANTIC ROMANCE IN THREE ACTS. (Coburg, 26 December 1829.) Cumberland's Minor Theatre, vol. 4. London: Cumberland, n.d. 44 p.

> An acting edition with a cast list of the first London production and "Remarks" by D--G [George Daniel].

IV Biography

1031 THE REMINISCENCES OF THOMAS DIBDIN. 2 vols. London: Henry Colburn, 1827. xii, 446 p.; xi, 431 p.; rpt. in 1 vol. New York: AMS Press, 1970.

V Critical Studies

1032 Sandoe, James. "Some Notes on the Plays of T.J. Dibdin." UCSLL, ser. B, 1 (1940), 205-20.

> Corrections and additions to Nicoll's hand list (item 298).

1033 "Master of Melodrama. The Centenary of Thomas Dibdin. From Gothic to the Crime Play." TLS, 20 September 1941, p. 470.

A brief survey of Dibdin's achievements as a playwright.

DICKENS, CHARLES (1812-70)

I Collected Works

1034 Shepherd, Richard Herne, ed. THE PLAYS AND POEMS OF CHARLES DICKENS, WITH A FEW MISCELLANIES IN PROSE. 2 vols. London: W.H. Allen, 1882.

This edition does not include O'THELLO. There is a substantial introduction by the editor entitled "Charles Dickens as a Dramatist, Actor and Poet."

1035 MISCELLANEOUS PAPERS . . . AND PLAYS AND POEMS. 2 vols. The Gadshill Edition, vols. 35 and 36. London: Chapman & Hall; New York: Charles Scribner's Sons, [1908].

Volume two contains all the plays included in the Nonesuch Edition (item 1036) with the exception of O'THELLO.

1036 Waugh, Arthur, et al, eds. THE NONESUCH DICKENS. COLLECTED PAPERS. 2 vols. Bloomsbury, Eng.: Nonesuch Press, 1937.

Volume 2 contains the plays: O'THELLO (a fragment, for family performance); THE STRANGE GENTLEMAN; THE VILLAGE COQUETTES; IS SHE HIS WIFE? OR, SOME-THING SINGULAR!; THE LAMPLIGHTER (printed from the Forster manuscript); MR. NIGHTINGALE'S DIARY; NO THOROUGHFARE.

1037 COMPLETE PLAYS AND SELECTED POEMS OF CHARLES DICKENS. London: Vision Press, 1970. 245 p.

Brief foreword and all the plays except O'THELLO.

II Acted Plays—Principal Titles

1038 THE STRANGE GENTLEMAN: A COMIC BURLETTA IN TWO ACTS. (St. James's, 29 September 1836.) Dicks' Standard Plays, no. 466. London: Dicks, [1883?]. 14 p.

An acting edition with a cast list of the first London production.

1039 THE VILLAGE COQUETTES: AN OPERATIC BURLETTA IN TWO ACTS.
(St. James's, 6 December 1836.) Dicks' Standard Plays, no. 467. London: Dicks, [1883?].

> An acting edition with a cast list of the first London produc-
> tion.

1040 IS SHE HIS WIFE? OR, SOMETHING SINGULAR: A COMIC BURLETTA
IN ONE ACT. (St. James's, 6 March 1837.) Dicks' Standard Plays,
no. 470. London: Dicks, [1883?]. 9 p.

> An acting edition with a cast list of the first London produc-
> tion. The Readex collection also has a Boston 1877 acting
> edition.

1041 MR. NIGHTINGALE'S DIARY: A FARCE IN ONE ACT. (Devonshire
House, 27 May 1851.) Boston: James R. Osgood, 1877. 96 p.

> Includes a cast list for the first production.

1042 NO THOROUGHFARE: A DRAMA IN FIVE ACTS AND A PROLOGUE.
With Wilkie Collins. (Adelphi, 26 December 1867.) [New York: De
Witt, 1873.] 40 p.

> An acting edition with a cast list of the first London produc-
> tion.

IIa Unacted Plays

1043 THE LAMPLIGHTER: A FARCE IN ONE ACT. No publication details.
11 p.

1044 *THE LAMPLIGHTER: A FARCE IN ONE ACT AND AS A SHORT STORY.
Preface. William Lyon Phelps. New York: Appleton, 1926. viii,
84 p.

> The text of the play and the short story which Dickens based
> on the play.

III Bibliographies

1045 Eckel, John C. THE FIRST EDITIONS OF THE WRITINGS OF CHARLES
DICKENS. THEIR POINTS AND VALUES. London: Maggs Bros.; New
York: Maurice Inman, 1932. xvi, 272 p.

> Revised and enlarged from the 1913 first edition. Biblio-
> graphical descriptions are included for each of the plays.
> Eckel also includes Dickens's prologue to J. Westland Mars-
> ton's THE PATRICIAN'S DAUGHTER (see item 1502) and Wilkie

Collins' THE FROZEN DEEP and THE LIGHTHOUSE to which
Dickens made some contributions. The bibliography was published in a limited edition of 750 copies.

1046 Pierce, Dorothy. "Special Bibliography: The Stage Versions of Dickens's
Novels." BULLETIN OF BIBLIOGRAPHY AND DRAMATIC INDEX, 16
(1936-39), 10, 30-32, 52-54.

Lists scores of adaptations giving the author of each play and
the place and date of performance in England and America.

1046a Miller, William. THE DICKENS STUDENT AND COLLECTOR. A LIST
OF WRITINGS RELATING TO CHARLES DICKENS AND HIS WORKS,
1836-1945. London: Chapman and Hall, 1946. xii, 351 p.

Includes a chapter on various dramatic representations of
Dickens's works.

1047 Gold, Joseph. THE STATURE OF DICKENS. A CENTENARY BIBLIO-
GRAPHY. Toronto: University of Toronto Press for the University of
Manitoba Press, 1971. xxix, 238 p.

Contains 3,625 items. A valuable bibliography of Dickens
criticism, but the lack of annotations and an inadequate index
seriously impair it. As for the plays, the only way of tracing
what has been written about them is to read through virtually
the whole bibliography.

IV Biography

1048 Ley, J.W.T. "Dickens and Douglas Jerrold: A Well-Loved Friend."
DICKENSIAN, 13 (1917), 117-21, 153-56.

1049 Woollcott, Alexander. MR. DICKENS GOES TO THE PLAY. New York
and London: G.P. Putnam's Sons, 1922; rpt. Port Washington, N.Y.:
Kennikat Press, 1967. xii, 239 p.

Largely superseded by the Johnson anthology (item 1051); there
are, however, some interesting illustrations.

1050 Johnson, Edgar. CHARLES DICKENS: HIS TRAGEDY AND TRIUMPH.
2 vols. New York: Simon and Schuster, 1952.

A valuable critical biography, which includes discussion of
the plays.

1051 Johnson, Edgar, and Eleanor Johnson, eds. THE DICKENS THEATRICAL
READER. Boston and Toronto: Little, Brown & Co., 1964. xiv, 370 p.

A generous selection of Dickens' fiction, periodical writings, letters, and speeches covering many aspects of amateur and professional theatre from 1833 to 1868. Illustrated, but no index (which would have been very useful).

1052 House, Madeline, and Graham Storey, eds. THE LETTERS OF CHARLES DICKENS. Oxford: Clarendon Press, 1965-- .

This magnificent collection of letters, meticulously indexed, allows one to trace Dickens' thoughts on his plays as well as on the theatre and drama generally. Appendix G, volume one describes the Lord Chamberlain's copies of THE STRANGE GENTLEMAN, THE VILLAGE COQUETTES and IS SHE HIS WIFE?

1053 Forster, John. THE LIFE OF CHARLES DICKENS. 2 vols. London: Dent, 1966.

With notes and introduction by A.J. Hoppé; this is a good edition of Forster's famous biography, first published in three volumes, 1872-74.

V Critical Studies

1054 Cook, Dutton. "Charles Dickens as a Dramatic Critic." LONGMAN'S MAGAZINE, 2 (May 1883), 29-42.

1055 Pemberton, T. Edgar. CHARLES DICKENS AND THE STAGE. A RECORD OF HIS CONNECTION WITH THE DRAMA AS PLAYWRIGHT, ACTOR AND CRITIC. London: George Redway, 1888. 260 p.

1056 "Charles Dickens's Acting in THE LIGHTHOUSE." DICKENSIAN, 5 (1909), 91-94.

A review from the ILLUSTRATED TIMES of 21 July 1855 of a performance at Campden House, Kensington, in which Dickens played the part of Aaron Gurnock.

1057 Fitz-Gerald, S.J. Adair. DICKENS AND THE DRAMA, BEING AN ACCOUNT OF CHARLES DICKENS'S CONNECTION WITH THE STAGE AND THE STAGE'S CONNECTION WITH HIM. New York: Charles Scribner's Sons, 1910. xxiv, 352 p.

Some discussion of Dickens as an actor and a playwright, but the bulk of the book deals with stage adaptations of Dickens's novels. There are several good illustrations.

1058 Wade, H. Gerald. "With 'Boz' in Montreal." DICKENSIAN, 12 (1916), 249-51.

> Brief comments on Dickens' acting at the Old Queen's Theatre, May 1842.

1059 Matchett, Willoughby. "Dickens and Pinero." DICKENSIAN, 15 (1919), 19-23.

> Discusses the influence, general and particular, of Dickens on Pinero.

1060 Fitz-Gerald, S.J. Adair. "Charles Dickens and the St. James's Theatre." DICKENSIAN, 16 (1920), 67-76.

> Details of productions of THE STRANGE GENTLEMAN, THE VILLAGE COQUETTES, and IS SHE HIS WIFE? at St. James's.

1061 Stuart, E.A.G. "The Dickens Amateurs." N&Q, (1922), 308.

> A cast list for a performance of EVERY MAN IN HIS HUMOUR.

1062 Amerongen, J.B. Van. THE ACTOR IN DICKENS. A STUDY OF THE HISTRIONIC AND DRAMATIC ELEMENTS IN THE NOVELIST'S LIFE AND WORKS. New York: Appleton, 1927. x, 301 p.

> Covers much the same ground as the books by Pemberton and Fitz-Gerald, but Amerongen has done his research more thoroughly.

1063 [Dexter, Walter]. "Dickens's Correspondence With John Hullah: Some New Light on His Early Dramatic Work." DICKENSIAN, 29 (1933), 257-65; 30 (1934), 17-22.

> Hullah wrote the music for Dickens' early plays.

1064 D., W. [Walter Dexter]. "A Stage Aside: Dickens's Early Dramatic Productions. I, THE STRANGE GENTLEMAN, September, 1835." DICKENSIAN, 33 (1937), 81-85.

> Contemporary reviews of the play.

1065 _____. "A Stage Aside: Dickens's Early Dramatic Productions. II, THE VILLAGE COQUETTES, December, 1836." DICKENSIAN, 33 (1937), 163-72.

> Contemporary reviews of the play, including the full text of Forster's EXAMINER review, 11 December 1836.

1066 _____. "A Stage Aside: Dickens's Early Dramatic Productions. III, IS SHE HIS WIFE? March, 1837." DICKENSIAN, 33 (1937), 254-56.

> Contemporary reviews of the play, plus a reproduction of the playbill for the performance of 13 March 1837.

1067 _____. "A Stage Aside: Dickens's Early Dramatic Productions. IV, THE LAMPLIGHTER." DICKENSIAN, 34 (1938), 55-62.

> Dickens' tours established a precedent for high-quality productions in the provinces.

1068 _____. "For One Night Only: Dickens's Appearance as an Amateur Actor." DICKENSIAN, 35 (1939), 231-41; 36 (1940), 20-30, 90-102, 129-35, 193-201; 37 (1941), 7-11.

> This series of articles includes reproductions of several playbills as well as other illustrations, and the final article gives a complete list of Dickens' performances with plays, theatres, and dates.

1069 Churchill, R.C. "Dickens, Drama and Tradition." SCRUTINY, 10 (1941-42), 358-75.

> A misleading title, for the article concerns itself principally with the novels.

1070 Paterson, Andrew. "Dickensian Mysteries from Montreal." DICKENSIAN, 38 (1942), 17-22.

> Confusion over the name of the theatre where Dickens first acted in Montreal.

1071 _____. "The Amateur Theatricals in Montreal: Contemporary Criticism of Dickens's First Public Appearances as an Actor." DICKENSIAN, 38 (1942), 72-74.

> Reviews from the MONTREAL HERALD, 27 May 1842, and the MONTREAL GAZETTE, 30 May 1842.

1072 _____. "The Montreal Theatre and Another Mystery." DICKENSIAN, 38 (1942), 85-86.

> Further details about Dickens' 1842 acting in Montreal.

1073 Morley, Malcolm. "Early Dickens Drama in America." DICKENSIAN, 44 (1948), 153-57.

> Adaptations of Dickens' novels on the New York stage, 1837-41.

1074 _____. "American Theatrical Notes and Boz." DICKENSIAN, 44 (1948), 187-93.

> Dickens and the Boston and New York theatres during the novelist's 1842 visit.

1075 Staples, Leslie C. "Dickens and Macready's 'Lear.'" DICKENSIAN, 44 (1948), 78-80.

> The text of Dickens' review of October 1849.

1076 Morley, Malcolm. "Theatre Royal, Montreal." DICKENSIAN, 45 (1949), 39-44.

> A brief history of the theatre with some discussion of Dickens' performances there in May 1842.

1077 Fawcett, F. Dubrez. DICKENS THE DRAMATIST ON STAGE, SCREEN AND RADIO. London: W.H. Allen, 1952. xiii, 278 p.

> A useful survey of the history of Dickens' plays and the adaptations of his novels. Appendices include a list of productions of "the most noteworthy adaptations" of the novels and a list of characters played by Dickens in amateur theatricals, 1833-48. The book is interestingly illustrated.

1078 Fielding, K.J. "The Dramatisation of EDWIN DROOD." TN, 7 (1952-53), 52-58.

> Abortive attempts by Dickens, Jr., and Boucicault to stage a version of the novel.

1079 Highet, Gilbert. PEOPLE, PLACES AND BOOKS. New York: Oxford University Press, 1953. x, 277 p.

> Contains "Dickens as Dramatist," but the author is interested in drama in the novels, not the plays.

1080 Morley, Malcolm. "Plays and Sketches by Boz." DICKENSIAN, 52 (1956), 81-88.

> A general survey of Dickens' career as a dramatist, including adaptations of his works by others and his collaboration with other playwrights.

1081 Rosenberg, Marvin. "The Dramatist in Dickens." JEGP, 59 (1960), 1-12.

> A critical survey of the plays with particular emphasis on THE LAMPLIGHTER and NO THOROUGHFARE.

1082 Harvey, P.D.A. "Charles Dickens as Playwright." BMQ, 24 (1961), 22-25.

> The licensing manuscripts of THE VILLAGE COQUETTES, THE STRANGE GENTLEMAN, and IS SHE HIS WIFE?, the first two of which show alterations in Dickens's hand. A page from THE VILLAGE COQUETTES is reproduced.

1083 Lazenby, Walter Sylvester. "Stage Versions of Dickens's Novels in America to 1900." Ph.D. Dissertation, Indiana University, 1962. 335 p. (DA#62-05049)

1084 Morley, Malcolm. "Dickens Goes to the Theatre." DICKENSIAN, 59 (1963), 165-71.

> Dickens at the Richmond and Margate theatres.

1085 Tillotson, Kathleen, and Nina Burgis. "Dickens at Drury Lane." DICKENSIAN, 65 (1969), 81-83.

> Identifies Dickens as the author of a review of an adaptation of Donizetti's opera LA FAVORITA and a farce by Edward and John Maddison Morton, MY WIFE'S COME, which appeared in the EXAMINER, 21 October 1843. The opera and farce were performed at Drury Lane on 18 October 1843.

1086 Tomlin, E.W.F., ed. CHARLES DICKENS 1812-1870. London: Weidenfeld and Nicolson, 1969. 288 p.

> Contains Emlyn Williams essay, "Dickens and the Theatre," a superficial survey of Dickens as a playwright and actor. Williams is mainly concerned with Dickens' readings.

1087 Fulkerson, Richard Paul. "The Dickens Novel on the Victorian Stage." Ph.D. Dissertation, Ohio State University, 1970. 378 p. (DA#70-26286)

1088 Collins, Philip. DICKENS: THE CRITICAL HERITAGE. London: Routledge & Kegan Paul, 1971. xxi, 641 p.

> The plays are, unfortunately, excluded.

VI Journals and Newsletters

1089 THE DICKENSIAN. London: Dickens Fellowship, 1905-- . Three times a year.

1090 DICKENS STUDIES. Boston: Emerson College, 1965-69. Annual.

1091 DICKENS STUDIES ANNUAL. Carbondale and Edwardsville: Southern Illinois University Press; London and Amsterdam: Feffer and Simons, 1970-- .

> A substantial annual publication.

1092 DICKENS STUDIES NEWSLETTER. Carbondale, Ill.: Dickens Society, 1970-- . Quarterly.

> A checklist of recent Dickens studies is published in each issue.

DIMOND, WILLIAM (1780?-1836?)

II Acted Plays—Principal Titles

1093 THE SEA-SIDE STORY: AN OPERATIC DRAMA IN TWO ACTS. (Covent Garden, 12 May 1801.) 2nd ed. London: Barker and Son, 1801. 59 p.

> Includes a prefatory note by the author and a cast list of the first London production.

1094 THE HERO OF THE NORTH: AN HISTORICAL PLAY. (Drury Lane, 19 February 1803.) 7th ed. London: Barker and Son, 1803. 87 p.

> There is a preface by the author explaining how the "fierce spirit of revolution" of the times restricted the political content of the play; cast list of the first London production.

1095 THE HUNTER OF THE ALPS: A DRAMA, INTERSPERSED WITH MUSIC. (Haymarket, 3 July 1804.) 4th ed. London: J. Barker, n.d. 39 p.

> Includes a cast list of the first London production; the music was composed by M. Kelly.

1096 THE FOUNDLING OF THE FOREST: A PLAY IN THREE ACTS. (Haymarket, 10 July 1809.) London: Longman, Hurst, Rees, and Orme, 1809. 72 p.

> Includes a cast list of the first London production.

1097 GUSTAVUS VASA, THE HERO OF THE NORTH: AN HISTORICAL OPERA. (Covent Garden, 29 November 1810.) New ed. London: J. Barker, 1811. 83 p.

> The play is adapted from THE HERO OF THE NORTH (item 1094); there are cast lists of the first London and other productions.

1098 THE BROTHER AND SISTER: A PETIT OPERA IN TWO ACTS. (Covent Garden, 1 February 1815.) New York: E. Murden, 1822. 36 p.

> Includes a cast list of a New York production.

1099 THE BROKEN SWORD: A GRAND MELO-DRAMA, INTERSPERSED WITH SONGS, CHORUSSES, &C. (Covent Garden, 7 October 1816.) 2nd ed. London: J. Barker, 1816. 43 p.

> There is a note by the editor describing melodrama as "nearly as trivial as the Pantomime"; cast list of the first London production.

1100 THE LADY AND THE DEVIL: A MUSICAL DRAMA IN TWO ACTS. (Drury Lane, 3 May 1820.) London: R.S. Kirby, 1820. 44 p.

> There is a brief prefatory note by the author and a cast list of the first London production; this copy is a promptbook (New York Public Library). Music by M. Kelly.

1101 NATIVE LAND; OR, THE RETURN FROM SLAVERY: AN OPERA IN THREE ACTS. (Covent Garden, 10 February 1824.) London: R.S. Kirby, 1824. viii, 73 p.

> There is a cast list of the first London production and a preface by Dimond containing an interesting defense of English opera.

1102 THE NYMPH OF THE GROTTO; OR, A DAUGHTER'S VOW! AN OPERA IN THREE ACTS. (Covent Garden, 15 January 1829.) London: R.S. Kirby, 1839. iv, 73 p.

> Includes a cast list of the first London production and a preface in which Dimond expresses his dissatisfaction with the casting. The music is by Signor Liverati and A. Lee.

1103 STAGE STRUCK; OR, THE LOVES OF AUGUSTUS PORTARLINGTON AND CELESTINA BEVERLEY: A FARCE IN ONE ACT. (English Opera House, 12 November 1835.) London and New York: French, n.d. 22 p.

> An acting edition. The Readex copy is a promptbook (New York Public Library) with several deletions and a few notes.

ESMOND, H.V. [HENRY VERNON JACK] (1869-1922)

II Acted Plays—Principal Titles

1104 IN AND OUT OF A PUNT: A DUOLOGUE CONTAINING AN IN-

FALLIBLE RECEIPT FOR MARITAL HAPPINESS BY ONE WHO HAS TRIED IT. (Pavilion, Brighton, 25 February 1896; St. James's, 9 March 1896.) London and New York: French, 1902. 12 p.

>An acting edition with a cast list of the first Brighton production.

1105 *ONE SUMMER'S DAY. (Comedy, 16 September 1897.) London and New York: French, 1900. 63 p.

>An acting edition with a cast list of the first London production. The Readex collection includes a typescript, located in New York Public Library.

1106 *THE WILDERNESS: A COMEDY IN THREE ACTS. (St. James's, 11 April 1901.) London and New York: French, 1901. 65 p.

>An acting edition with a cast list of the first London production.

1107 *WHEN WE WERE TWENTY-ONE: A COMEDY IN FOUR ACTS. (Comedy, 2 September 1901.) London and New York: French, 1903. 80 p.

>An acting edition with a cast list of the first London production.

1108 *BILLY'S LITTLE LOVE AFFAIR: COMEDY IN THREE ACTS. (Criterion, 2 September 1903.) London and New York: French, 1904. 82 p.

>An acting edition with a cast list of the first London production.

1109 *HER VOTE: A COMEDY IN ONE ACT. (Terry's, 13 May 1909.) London and New York: French, 1910. 8 p.

>An acting edition with a cast list of the first London production.

1110 *ELIZA COMES TO STAY: A FARCE IN THREE ACTS. (Criterion, 12 January 1913.) London and New York: French, 1913. 79 p.

>An acting edition with a cast list of the first London production.

1111 *THE LAW DIVINE: A COMEDY IN THREE ACTS. (Wyndham's, 29 August 1918.) London and New York: French, 1922. 72 p.

>An acting edition with a cast list of the first London production and a photograph of the set.

FALCONER, EDMUND (1815-79)

II Acted Plays—Principal Titles

1112 EXTREMES; OR, MEN OF THE DAY: A COMEDY IN THREE ACTS. (Lyceum, 26 August 1858.) London: Lacy, n.d. 72 p.

> An acting edition with a cast list of the first London production and a preface by Falconer on the play's composition; interleaved, with some manuscript notes.

1113 NEXT OF KIN: AN ORIGINAL COMIC DRAMA IN TWO ACTS. (Lyceum, 9 April 1860.) London: Lacy, n.d. 26 p.

> An acting edition with a cast list of the first London production.

1114 DOES HE LOVE ME? A COMEDY IN THREE ACTS. (Haymarket, 23 June 1860.) London and New York: French, n.d. 48 p.

> An acting edition with a cast list of the first London production.

1115 PEEP O' DAY; OR, SAVOUREEN DEELISH: A DRAMA IN FOUR ACTS. (Lyceum, 9 November 1861.) Standard Drama, no. 349. New York: French, n.d. 44 p.

> An acting edition with several cast lists and a "Memoir of Frank E. Aiken." Title page wrongly attributes the play to Edward Falconer, and the running title is "Peep O' Day Boys."

FIELD, MICHAEL [KATHLEEN HARRIS BRADLEY (1846-1913) AND EDITH EMMA COOPER (1862-1914)]

I Collected Works

(In the instance of Field, these include only two or three plays.)

1116 CANUTE THE GREAT; THE CUP OF WATER. London: George Bell, n.d. 170 p.

> With a preface and a note.

1117 CALLIRRHOE; FAIR ROSAMUND. London: George Bell, n.d. 204 p.

> With a preface; available in the Readex collection. The Readex collection also includes a separate copy of FAIR ROSAMUND (London: 1897, lxxv p.).

1118 THE FATHER'S TRAGEDY; WILLIAM RUFUS; LOYALTY OR LOVE? London: George Bell, [1885]. iv, 312 p.

> With prefaces to each play.

1119 THE ACCUSER; TRISTAN DE LEONOIS; A MESSIAH. London: Sidgwick and Jackson, 1911. viii, 235 p.

> A library edition with a preface.

1120 THE TRAGEDY OF PARDON; DIANE. London: Sidgwick and Jackson, 1911. 251 p.

> A library edition.

1121 DEIRDRE; A QUESTION OF MEMORY; AND RAS BYZANCE. London: Poetry Bookshop, 1918. 171 p.

> A library edition.

II Acted Plays—Principal Titles

1122 A QUESTION OF MEMORY: A PLAY IN FOUR ACTS. (Opera Comique, 27 October 1893.) London: E. Mathews and J. Lane, 1893. 48 p.

> A privately printed acting edition with a preface and a note of the text.

IIa Unacted Plays

1123 BELLEROPHÔN [AND OTHER POEMS] BY ARRAN AND ISLA LEIGH. London: Kegan Paul, 1881. 181 p.

> Arran and Isla Leigh were the pseudonyms of Bradley and Cooper before Michael Field was chosen.

1124 BRUTUS ULTOR. London: George Bell, [1886]. vii, 78 p.

> With a preface "To the People of England" and a note on sources.

1125 THE TRAGIC MARY. London: George Bell, 1890. ix, 261 p.

> With a preface and note on the play.

1126 STEPHANIA: A TRIALOGUE. London: E. Mathews and J. Lane, 1892. [iii], 100 p.

1127 ATTILA, MY ATTILA! A PLAY. London: E. Mathews, 1896. 107 p.

With a brief preface on the nature of tragedy.

1128 *THE WORLD AT AUCTION. London: Hacon and Ricketts, 1898. 116 p.

A special limited edition of 210 copies.

1129 ANNA RUINA. London: David Nutt, 1899. 101 p.

1130 NOONTIDE BRANCHES: A SMALL SYLVAN DRAMA INTERSPERSED WITH SONGS AND INVOCATIONS. [Oxford]: H. Daniel, printer, [1899]. 45 p.

A privately printed, limited edition.

1131 *THE RACE OF LEAVES. London: Hacon and Ricketts, 1901. 85 p.

A special edition.

1132 *JULIA DOMNA. London: Hacon and Ricketts, 1903. 53 p.

A limited edition of 240 copies.

1133 *BORGIA: A PERIOD PLAY. London: Bullen, 1905. 187 p.

A library edition.

1134 *QUEEN MARIAMNE. London: Sidgwick and Jackson, 1908. 142 p.

A library edition.

1135 *IN THE NAME OF TIME: A TRAGEDY. London: Poetry Bookshop, 1919. 93 p.

A library edition.

IV Biography

1136 Sturgemoore, T., and D.C. Sturgemoore, eds. WORKS AND DAYS: FROM THE JOURNAL OF MICHAEL FIELD. London: Murray, 1933. xxii, 338 p.

This selection from Field's journal reveals much about the two women and their associations, often with such significant figures as Browning, Meredith, Wilde, Moore, and Ruskin. The journal entries are supplemented by extracts from Field's correspondence.

V Critical Studies

1137 Sturgeon, Mary. MICHAEL FIELD. London: Harrap, [1921]. 245 p.

> The greater part of this very sympathetic study is devoted to
> Field's plays, although the author prefers to rely on extensive
> quotation rather than close analysis in her discussions. There
> are also chapters devoted to the lyrics, biographical informa-
> tions, and a bibliography. Unfortunately there is no index.

1138 Smith, Logan Pearsall, "Michael Field." DIAL, 78 (1925), 115-22.

> Brief personal reminiscences. Insignificant.

1139 Biederstedt, Joan. "The Poetic Plays of Michael Field." Ph.D. dissertation, Loyola University, Chicago, 1964.

FITZBALL, EDWARD (1792-1873)

II Acted Plays—Principal Titles

1140 THE INNKEEPER OF ABBEVILLE; OR, THE HOSTLER AND THE ROBBER:
A MELO-DRAMA IN TWO ACTS. (Norwich, 1822; Surrey, 1826.)
London: John Lowndes, 1822. 26 p.

> Includes a cast list of the first London production.

1141 PEVERIL OF THE PEAK; OR, THE DAYS OF KING CHARLES II: A
MELO-DRAMATIC ROMANCE IN THREE ACTS. (Surrey, 6 February
1823.) London: John Lowndes, n.d. 48 p.

> Includes a cast list of the first London production; the play
> is adapted from Scott.

1142 THE FLOATING BEACON; OR, THE NORWEGIAN WRECKERS: A MELO-
DRAMA IN TWO ACTS. (Surrey, 19 April 1824.) London: John Lowndes, n.d. 24 p.

> There is a cast list of the first London production, and a
> brief prefatory note by the author.

1143 THE PILOT; OR, A STORM AT SEA: A NAUTICAL BURLETTA. (Adelphi, 31 October 1825.) London: Simpkin and Marshall, 1825. 53 p.

> Includes a cast list of the first London production. Adapted
> from Cooper's novel.

1144 THE FLYING DUTCHMAN; OR, THE PHANTOM SHIP: A NAUTICAL DRAMA IN THREE ACTS. (Adelphi, 1 January 1827.) French's American Drama, no. 6. New York: French, n.d. 35 p.

An acting edition with a cast list of the National Theatre, New York, production.

1145 THE INCHCAPE BELL: A NAUTICAL BURLETTA IN TWO ACTS. (Surrey, 26 May 1828.) London: Cumberland, n.d. 38 p.

An acting edition with a cast list of the first London production and "Remarks" by D--G [George Daniel].

1146 THE RED ROVER; OR, THE MUTINY OF THE DOLPHIN: A NAUTICAL DRAMA IN TWO ACTS. (Adelphi, 9 February 1829.) London: Cumberland, n.d. 46 p.

An acting edition with cast lists of Adelphi productions of 1828 and 1831 and "Remarks" by D--G [George Daniel]. The Readex copy is a promptbook with manuscript notes. Adapted from Cooper's novel.

1147 JONATHAN BRADFORD! OR, THE MURDER AT THE ROAD-SIDE INN: A DRAMA IN THREE ACTS. (Surrey, 12 June 1833.) London: Lacy, n.d. 37 p.

An acting edition with a cast list of the first London production; the Readex copy is a promptbook with manuscript notes.

1148 PAUL CLIFFORD: A MUSICAL DRAMA IN THREE ACTS. (Covent Garden, 28 October 1835.) Cumberland's British Theatre. London: Lacy, n.d. 44 p.

An acting edition with a cast list of the first London production. Adapted from Bulwer-Lytton's novel.

1149 ZAZEZIZOZU! OR, DOMINOES! CHESS!! AND CARDS!!! A MUSICAL EXTRAVAGANZA IN TWO ACTS. (Covent Garden, 4 April 1836.) London: Duncombe, n.d. 30 p.

An acting edition with a cast list of the first London production.

1150 THALABA, THE DESTROYER: A MELO-DRAMA IN THREE ACTS. (Covent Garden, 21 November 1836.) London: Cumberland, n.d. 48 p.

An acting edition with a cast list of a Royal Coburg production and "Remarks" by D--G [George Daniel].

1151 THE DAUGHTER OF THE REGIMENT: A DRAMA IN TWO ACTS. (Drury Lane, 30 November 1843.) Dicks' Standard Plays, no. 761. London: Dicks, n.d. 14 p.

> An acting edition with a cast list of the first London production.

1152 MARITANA: A GRAND OPERA IN THREE ACTS. (Drury Lane, 15 November 1845.) London: W.S. Johnson, n.d. 33 p.

> There is a brief introductory note by the author; the Readex copy is a promptbook with manuscript notes. The music was composed by W.V. Wallace.

1153 PETER THE GREAT: AN HISTORICAL MELODRAMA IN THREE ACTS. (Astley's, 26 July 1852.) London: Duncombe, n.d. 35 p.

> An acting edition with a cast list of the first London production.

1154 THE MILLER OF DERWENT WATER: A DRAMA IN THREE ACTS. (Olympic, 2 May 1853.) Clyde, Ohio: Ames' Publishing Co., n.d. 27 p.

> An acting edition with a cast list of the first London production and one at Clyde, Ohio, 21 September 1871.

IV Biography

1155 THIRTY-FIVE YEARS OF A DRAMATIC AUTHOR'S LIFE. 2 vols. London: T.C. Newby, 1859. x, 308; 414 p.

> Fitzball's memoirs.

GILBERT, SIR WILLIAM SCHWENCK (1836-1911)

I Collected Works

1156 ORIGINAL PLAYS. London: Chatto and Windus, 1876. 348 p.

> Contents: THE WICKED WORLD, PYGMALION AND GALATEA, CHARITY, THE PRINCESS, THE PALACE OF TRUTH, TRIAL BY JURY. There is a brief note by Gilbert together with cast lists.

1157 ORIGINAL PLAYS: SECOND SERIES. London: Chatto and Windus, 1881. 338 p.

> Contents: BROKEN HEARTS, ENGAGED, SWEETHEARTS, GRETCHEN, DAN'L DRUCE, TOM COBB, H.M.S. PINA-

FORE, THE SORCERER, THE PIRATES OF PENZANCE. With
cast lists.

1158 ORIGINAL COMIC OPERAS. London: Chappell, [1891?]. Var. pag.

Contents: Libretti only of THE SORCERER, H.M.S. PINA-
FORE, PIRATES OF PENZANCE, IOLANTHE, PATIENCE,
PRINCESS IDA, THE MIKADO, TRIAL BY JURY. Some cast
lists included.

1159 ORIGINAL PLAYS: THIRD SERIES. London: Chatto and Windus, 1895.
453 p.

Contents: COMEDY AND TRAGEDY, FOGGETY'S FAIRY,
ROSENCRANTZ AND GUILDENSTERN, PATIENCE, PRINCESS
IDA, THE MIKADO, RUDDIGORE, THE YEOMEN OF THE
GUARD, THE GONDOLIERS, THE MOUNTEBANKS, UTOPIA
LIMITED. With cast lists.

1160 SAVOY OPERAS: WITH ILLUSTRATIONS IN COLOUR BY W. RUSSELL
FLINT. London: Bell, 1909. xv, 208 p.

Libretti of THE PIRATES OF PENZANCE, PATIENCE, PRIN-
CESS IDA, THE YEOMEN OF THE GUARD. With cast lists
of the original productions and revivals, and a foreword on
the history of each piece by Gilbert.

1161 IOLANTHE AND OTHER OPERAS: WITH ILLUSTRATIONS IN COLOUR
BY W. RUSSELL FLINT. London: Bell, 1910. ix, 224 p.

Libretti and cast lists of the original productions and revivals
of IOLANTHE, THE MIKADO, RUDDIGORE, THE GONDO-
LIERS.

1162 ORIGINAL PLAYS: FOURTH SERIES. London: Chatto and Windus,
1911. 475 p.

Contents: THE FAIRY'S DILEMMA, THE GRAND DUKE, HIS
EXCELLENCY, THE GENTLEMAN IN BLACK, BRANTING-
HAME HALL, CREATURES OF IMPULSE, RANDALL'S THUMB,
THE FORTUNE-HUNTER, THESPIS. With some cast lists. An
expanded version was printed in 1920; see item 1163.

1163 ORIGINAL PLAYS: FOURTH SERIES. London: Chatto and Windus,
1920. 499 p.

Contents: THE FAIRY'S DILEMMA, THE GRAND DUKE, HIS
EXCELLENCY, "HASTE TO THE WEDDING," FALLEN FAIRIES,
THE GENTLEMAN IN BLACK, BRANTINGHAME HALL, CREA-
TURES OF IMPULSE, RANDALL'S THUMB, THE FORTUNE-

HUNTER, THESPIS, THE HOOLIGAN, TRYING A DRAMATIST.
With cast lists.

1164 THE SAVOY OPERAS: BEING THE COMPLETE TEXT OF THE GILBERT
AND SULLIVAN OPERAS AS ORIGINALLY PRODUCED IN THE YEARS
1875-1896. London: Macmillan, 1926. 698 p.; rpt. London and New
York: Macmillan, 1962. 660 p.

> Contents: TRIAL BY JURY, THE SORCERER, H.M.S. PINA-
> FORE, THE PIRATES OF PENZANCE, PATIENCE, IOLANTHE,
> PRINCESS IDA, THE MIKADO, RUDDIGORE, THE YEOMEN
> OF THE GUARD, THE GONDOLIERS, UTOPIA LIMITED, THE
> GRAND DUKE. Libretti only.

1165 SELECTED OPERAS: SECOND SERIES. London: Macmillan, 1928.
200 p.

> Libretti only of H.M.S. PINAFORE, THE PIRATES OF PEN-
> ZANCE, IOLANTHE, THE MIKADO.

1166 Allen, Reginald, ed. THE FIRST NIGHT GILBERT AND SULLIVAN:
CONTAINING COMPLETE LIBRETTOS OF THE FOURTEEN OPERAS,
EXACTLY AS PRESENTED AT THEIR PREMIERE PERFORMANCES: TO-
GETHER WITH FACSIMILES OF THE FIRST-NIGHT PROGRAMMES. [New
York]: Heritage Press, 1958. xxi, 465 p.

> A limited edition of 1,500 copies with a foreword by Bridget
> D'Oyly Carte, with introductions to each piece, cast lists,
> and other critical apparatus.

1167 THE SAVOY OPERAS: I: WITH AN INTRODUCTION BY DAVID CECIL
AND NOTES ON THE OPERAS BY DEREK HUDSON. London: Oxford
University Press, 1962. xix, 396 p.

> Libretti of: TRIAL BY JURY, THE SORCERER, H.M.S. PINA-
> FORE, THE PIRATES OF PENZANCE, PATIENCE, IOLANTHE,
> PRINCESS IDA, THESPIS.

1168 THE SAVOY OPERAS: II: WITH AN INTRODUCTION BY BRIDGET
D'OYLY CARTE AND NOTES ON THE OPERAS BY DEREK HUDSON.
London: Oxford University Press, 1963. xv, 423 p.

> Libretti of: THE MIKADO, RUDDIGORE, THE YEOMEN OF
> THE GUARD, THE GONDOLIERS, UTOPIA LIMITED, THE
> GRAND DUKE.

1169 Stedman, Jane W., ed. GILBERT BEFORE SULLIVAN: SIX COMIC
PLAYS BY W.S. GILBERT. London: Routledge & Kegan Paul, 1967.
xii, 270 p.

Contents: NO CARDS, AGES AGO, OUR ISLAND HOME,
A SENSATIONAL NOVEL, HAPPY ARCADIA, EYES AND NO
EYES. This is a scholarly edition of the German Reed Entertainments of Gilbert, with a lengthy introduction and appendices on "Texts and Variants in Gilbert's German Reed Entertainments," and "The Entertainments of Charles Matthews and
Mr. and Mrs. Howard Paul." There is also a glossary and
notes to the texts, a selected bibliography, and an index. An
admirable and well-produced book.

II Acted Plays—Principal Titles

1170 A NEW AND ORIGINAL EXTRAVANGANZA ENTITLED DULCAMARA;
OR THE LITTLE DUCK AND THE GREAT QUACK. (St. James's, 29
December 1866.) London: Strand Printing and Publishing Co., 1866.
34 p.

An acting edition with a cast list of the first London production; many manuscript notes.

1171 THE MERRY ZINGARA; OR, THE TIPSY GIPSY & THE PIPSY WIPSY: A
WHIMSICAL PARODY ON THE "BOHEMIAN GIRL." (Royalty, 21 March
1868.) London: Phillips, n.d. 41 p.

An acting edition with a cast list of the first London production.

1172 THE PRINCESS: A WHIMSICAL ALLEGORY (BEING A RESPECTFUL PER-
VERSION OF MR. TENNYSON'S POEM). (Olympic, 8 January 1870.)
London: Lacy, n.d. 44 p.

An acting edition with a cast list of the first London production.

1173 THE PALACE OF TRUTH: A FAIRY COMEDY IN THREE ACTS. (Haymarket, 19 November 1870.) London: Lacy, n.d. 55 p.

An acting edition with a cast list of the first London production.

1174 RANDALL'S THUMB: AN ORIGINAL COMEDY IN THREE ACTS. (Court,
25 January 1871.) Standard Drama, no. 363. New York: French, n.d.
42 p.

An acting edition with cast lists of the first London and New
York productions.

1175 *CREATURES OF IMPULSE: A MUSICAL FAIRY TALE IN ONE ACT.
(Court, 15 April 1871.) London: Lacy, n.d. 20 p.

An acting edition with a cast list of the first London production.

1176 PYGMALION AND GALATEA: AN ENTIRELY ORIGINAL MYTHOLOGICAL COMEDY IN THREE ACTS. (Haymarket, 9 December 1871.) London and New York: French, n.d. 36 p.

An acting edition with a cast list of the first London production. The Readex collection also includes an American acting edition (Chicago: n.d., 46 p.).

1177 *THESPIS; OR, THE GODS GROWN OLD: AN ENTIRELY ORIGINAL GROTESQUE OPERA, IN TWO ACTS. (Gaiety, 26 December 1871.) London, n.d. 42 p.

Libretto only, with a cast list of the first London production.

1178 *Rees, Terence, ed. THESPIS: A GILBERT & SULLIVAN ENIGMA. London: Dillon's University Bookshop, 1964. vii, 150 p.

"The present edition is an attempt to get as close as possible to that which was actually performed at the Gaiety Theatre in 1871 under the author's personal supervision. We have therefore incorporated at the appropriate places such additional pieces of dialogue as we find by report to have been spoken on that occasion but which are omitted from the 1911 text. In order to make the missing lines fit, it has sometimes been necessary to supply some words of our own." In addition, Rees provides a lengthy introduction which gives a full history of the various aspects of the production of the pieces.

1179 *THE WICKED WORLD: AN ENTIRELY ORIGINAL FAIRY COMEDY IN THREE ACTS AND ONE SCENE. (Haymarket, 4 January 1873.) Standard Drama, no. 364. London and New York: French, n.d. 42 p.

An acting edition with two cast lists.

1180 CHARITY: A PLAY IN FOUR ACTS. (Haymarket, 3 January 1874.) New York: Happy Hours, n.d. 45 p.

An acting edition with a cast list of the first London production.

1181 SWEETHEARTS: AN ORIGINAL DRAMATIC CONTRAST IN TWO ACTS. (Prince of Wales's, 7 November 1874.) London and New York: French, n.d. 20 p.

An acting edition with a cast list of the first London production.

1182 TRIAL BY JURY. With Arthur Sullivan. (Royalty, 25 March 1875.) No
publication details. 16 p.

Libretto only, with a cast list.

1183 TOM COBB; OR, FORTUNE'S TOY: AN ENTIRELY ORIGINAL FARCI-
CAL COMEDY IN THREE ACTS. (St. James's, 24 April 1875.) London
and New York: French, n.d. 32 p.

An acting edition with a cast list of the first London production.

1184 BROKEN HEARTS: AN ENTIRELY ORIGINAL FAIRY PLAY IN THREE
ACTS. (Court, 9 December 1875.) London and New York: French,
[1875]. 35 p.

An acting edition; interleaved, with manuscript notes.

1185 DAN'L DRUCE, BLACKSMITH: A NEW AND ORIGINAL DRAMA IN
THREE ACTS. (Haymarket, 11 September 1876.) London and New York:
French, n.d. 42 p.

An acting edition with a cast list of the first London production.

1186 ENGAGED: AN ENTIRELY ORIGINAL FARCICAL COMEDY IN THREE
ACTS. (Haymarket, 3 October 1877.) London and New York: French,
n.d. 48 p.

An acting edition with a cast list of the first London production, and a note by Gilbert (that the play be acted "with the
most perfect earnestness and gravity throughout"); interleaved,
with manuscript notes.

1187 THE SORCERER: AN ORIGINAL MODERN COMIC OPERA IN TWO
ACTS. With Arthur Sullivan. (Opera Comique, 17 November 1877.)
London: Chappell, n.d. 40 p.

Revised libretto, with two London cast lists.

1188 H.M.S. PINAFORE; OR, THE LASS THAT LOVED A SAILOR: AN EN-
TIRELY ORIGINAL NAUTICAL COMIC OPERA IN TWO ACTS. With
Arthur Sullivan. (Opera Comique, 25 May 1878.) London: Chappell,
n.d. 32 p.

Libretto only, with three London cast lists.

1189 THE PIRATES OF PENZANCE; OR, THE SLAVE OF DUTY: AN ENTIRELY
ORIGINAL COMIC OPERA IN TWO ACTS. With Arthur Sullivan.
(Bijou, Paignton, 30 December 1879; Fifth Avenue, New York, 31

December 1879; Opera Comique, 3 April 1880.) London: Chappell,
n.d. 32 p.

> Libretto only, with several cast lists. The Readex collection
> also includes an American libretto (Philadelphia: c. 1880,
> 39 p.).

1190 AN ENTIRELY NEW AND ORIGINAL AESTHETIC OPERA IN TWO ACTS
ENTITLED PATIENCE; OR, BUNTHORNE'S BRIDE! With Arthur Sullivan.
(Opera Comique, 23 April 1881.) London: Chappell, n.d. 40 p.

> Libretto only, with a cast list of the first London production.
> The Readex collection also includes a promptbook (Philadel-
> phia (?): 1881, 42 p.) which has extensive manuscript notes.

1191 IOLANTHE; OR, THE PEER AND THE PERI: A NEW AND ORIGINAL
COMIC OPERA IN TWO ACTS. With Arthur Sullivan. (Savoy, 25
November 1882.) Philadelphia: J.M. Stoddart, 1882. 47 p.

> Libretto only, with a cast list of the New York production.
> The Readex collection also includes a vocal score, published
> c. 1882, 155 p.

1192 A RESPECTFUL OPERATIC PER-VERSION OF TENNYSON'S "PRINCESS"
IN THREE ACTS, ENTITLED PRINCESS IDA; OR, CASTLE ADAMANT.
With Arthur Sullivan. (Savoy, 5 January 1884.) London: Chappell,
n.d. 47 p.

> Libretto only, with a cast list of the first London production.

1192a AN ENTIRELY NEW AND ORIGINAL JAPANESE OPERA IN TWO ACTS
ENTITLED THE MIKADO; OR, THE TOWN OF TITIPU. With Arthur
Sullivan. (Savoy, 14 March 1885.) London: Chappell, n.d. 46 p.

> Libretto only, with a cast list of an 1895 London production.
> The Readex collection also includes a libretto published in
> Boston (n.d., 46 p.) which includes music for two songs,
> "Hearts Do Not Break" and "Tit-Willow."

1193 AN ENTIRELY ORIGINAL SUPERNATURAL OPERA IN TWO ACTS EN-
TITLED RUDDIGORE; OR, THE WITCH'S CURSE! With Arthur Sullivan.
(Savoy, 22 January 1887.) London: Chappell, n.d. 46 p.

> Libretto only, with a cast list of the first London production.

1194 A NEW AND ORIGINAL OPERA IN TWO ACTS ENTITLED THE YEOMEN
OF THE GUARD; OR, THE MERRYMAN AND HIS MAID. With Arthur
Sullivan. (Savoy, 3 October 1888.) London: Chappell, n.d. 48 p.

> Libretto only, with a cast list of the first London production.
> The Readex collection also includes another edition (London:

1912, 54 p.).

1195 THE GONDOLIERS; OR, THE KING OF BARATARIA. With Arthur Sullivan. (Savoy, 7 December 1889.) Rev. ed. London: Chappell, n.d.
49 p.

> Libretto only. The Readex collection also includes a printed
> promptbook (47 p.) with extensive manuscript notes.

1196 AN ORIGINAL COMIC OPERA IN TWO ACTS ENTITLED UTOPIA
LIMITED; OR, THE FLOWERS OF PROGRESS. With Arthur Sullivan.
(Savoy, 7 October 1893.) London and New York: Chappell, n.d.
50 p.

> Libretto only, with a cast list of the first London production.

1197 THE GRAND DUKE; OR, THE STATUTORY DUEL: A COMIC OPERA IN
TWO ACTS. With Arthur Sullivan. (Savoy, 7 March 1896.) London:
Chappell, 1896. 54 p.

> Libretto only, with cast lists. The Readex collection also
> includes another libretto (Boston: 1896, 55 p.).

1198 *AN ORIGINAL OPERA IN TWO ACTS ENTITLED FALLEN FAIRIES; OR,
THE WICKED WORLD. With Edward German. (Savoy, 15 December
1909.) London: Chappell, 1909. 50 p.

> Libretto only, with a cast list of the first London production.

III Bibliographies

1199 Searle, Townley. A BIBLIOGRAPHY OF SIR WILLIAM SCHWENCK
GILBERT WITH BIBLIOGRAPHICAL ADVENTURES IN THE GILBERT &
SULLIVAN OPERAS: AND WITH AN INTRODUCTION BY R.E. SWART-
WOUT. London: [T. Searle], 1931; rpt. New York: Franklin, 1968.
107 p.

> A bibliography of Gilbert's works, works wrongly attributed
> to him, and books and articles about him. Many entries are
> embellished with personal comment, anecdote, and other read-
> able background information.

1200 DuBois, Arthur E. "Additions to the Bibliography of W.S. Gilbert's Contributions to Magazines." MLN, 47 (1932), 308-14.

> Supplements Searle's listings. See item 1199.

1201 Halton, F.J. "THE GILBERT AND SULLIVAN OPERAS": A CONCOR-
DANCE. New York: Bass Publishers, [1935]. 183 p.

1202 Dunn, George E. A GILBERT & SULLIVAN DICTIONARY. London: Allen and Unwin, 1936. 175 p.

1203 Leyburn, James G. "Words by W.S. Gilbert." YULG, 17, no. 3 (1943), 53-54.

>   A short account of Yale Library acquisitions of Gilbert first editions, typescript, and manuscript letters.

1204 Allen, Reginald. "William Schwenck Gilbert: An Anniversary Survey." TN, 15 (1961), 118-28.

>   A short account of Gilbert's work and career, with a table of productions to 1911 and a useful bibliographical guide to published plays.

1205 Rollins, Cyril, and R. John Witts, comps. THE D'OYLY CARTE OPERA COMPANY IN GILBERT AND SULLIVAN OPERAS: A RECORD OF PRODUCTIONS 1875-1961. London: Michael Joseph, 1962. xii, 186, xxvi p.

>   This is a thoroughly scholarly work which documents every aspect of the production of Gilbert and Sullivan's joint works in both London and the provinces. An indispensable reference tool.

1206 Allen, Reginald. W.S. GILBERT: AN ANNIVERSARY SURVEY AND EXHIBITION CHECKLIST WITH THIRTY-FIVE ILLUSTRATIONS. Charlottesville: Bibliographical Society of the University of Virginia, 1963. 83 p.

>   A checklist of the Grolier Club exhibition of Gilbert materials held in New York in 1961 and drawn from the Gilbert and Sullivan collection in the Pierpoint Morgan Library. Also includes a brief account of Gilbert's career and details of productions and publications of plays.

IV Biography

1207 Gilbert, W[illiam] S[chwenck]. A LETTER ADDRESSED TO THE MEMBERS OF THE DRAMATIC PROFESSION IN REPLY TO MISS HENRIETTA HODSON'S PAMPHLET. London: Privately printed, 1877. 18 p.

>   A personal dispute between the actress and Gilbert, but interesting also for what it reveals of author-actor relationships in the late nineteenth century. See item 2829.

1208 _____. "William Schwenck Gilbert: An Autobiography." THEATRE, n.s. 1 (April 1883), 217-24.

>   A brief cataloging of Gilbert's work down to 1883 with a

few incidental side comments; little personal biography.

1209 "W.S. Gilbert at Home." CRITIC (New York), 19 (1891), 310.

A short descriptive note on Gilbert's home at Graeme's Dyke.

1210 Pearson, Hesketh. GILBERT AND SULLIVAN: A BIOGRAPHY. London: Hamish Hamilton, 1935; rpt. Freeport, N.Y.: Books for Libraries, 1971. 317 p.

Pearson's biography is eminently readable, although scholars will find it too full of anecdote and undocumented fact.

1211 Bulloch, John Malcolm. "W.S. Gilbert's Father." N&Q, 171 (1936), 435-39.

A brief biographical note on Gilbert's father and a list of his books.

1212 Sullivan, Herbert, and Newman Flower. SIR ARTHUR SULLIVAN: HIS LIFE, LETTERS & DIARIES. 2nd ed. London: Cassell, 1950. ix, 306 p.

Although this affectionate biography (first published in 1927) centers on Sullivan, it contains much information about Gilbert, several of whose letters to Sullivan are quoted.

1213 Baily, Leslie. THE GILBERT & SULLIVAN BOOK. Rev. ed. New York: Coward-McCann, [1957]. xvi, 475 p.

This is the most detailed biographical history of both Gilbert and Sullivan and their respective work. Baily's book is lavishly illustrated, and he quotes freely from such source material as letters, diaries, playbills, newspaper reports, and so forth. If anything detracts from the work, it is Baily's predilection for pursuing the smallest detail, so that the narrative lacks purposeful direction.

1214 Pearson, Hesketh. GILBERT: HIS LIFE AND STRIFE. London: Methuen, 1957. 276 p.

Mainly useful for its collection of Gilbert's correspondence, which, among other things, throws light on the quarrel between Gilbert and Sullivan. However, the book lacks documentation.

V Critical Studies

1215 Adams, W. Davenport. "Mr. Gilbert as a Dramatist." BELGRAVIA,

(October 1881), 438-48.

A short assessment of Gilbert's achievement to 1881, with
some critical examination of his chief qualities.

1216 Marshall, A.F. "The Spirit of Gilbert's Comedies." MONTH, 55
(October 1885), 254-62.

A brief attempt to demonstrate the nature of Gilbert's ability
as a comic writer in order that he might be better appreci-
ated. Marshall sees Gilbert as more than simply a "popular"
writer.

1217 Fitzgerald, P. THE SAVOY OPERA AND THE SAVOYARDS. London:
Chatto and Windus, 1894. xv, 248 p.

1218 Bulloch, J.M. "The Work of W.S. Gilbert." BOOK BUYER (New
York), 17 (January 1899), 565-72.

Attempts to define, fairly generally, Gilbert's achievements
as a librettist, humorist, rhymer, and stage manager.

1219 Beerbohm, Max. "Mr. Gilbert's Rentrée (and Mine)." SATURDAY RE-
VIEW, 97 (14 May 1904), 619-20.

An antipathetical review of Gilbert's THE FAIRY'S DILEMMA
written in characteristic Beerbohm style. Beerbohm's main
criticism is of the creaking machinery of Gilbert's humor.

1220 Browne, Edith A. W.S. GILBERT. London: John Lane, 1907. x,
96 p.

1221 Sichel, Walter. "The English Aristophanes." FORTNIGHTLY REVIEW,
n.s. 90 (October 1911), 681-704.

A review of the major features of Gilbert's work with extensive examples. However, it is long on rhetoric and short on
analysis.

1222 Cellier, Francois, and Cunningham Bridgeman. GILBERT AND SULLIVAN
AND THEIR OPERAS: WITH RECOLLECTIONS AND ANECDOTES OF
D'OYLY CARTE & OTHER FAMOUS SAVOYARDS. London: Pitman,
1914; rpt. New York: Blom, 1970. xxiii, 443 p.

Cellier's reminiscences, which comprise less than half this
book, were compiled by Bridgeman in similar anecdotal and
sentimental vein. The work is mainly valuable because Cellier
was D'Oyly Carte's musical director. Also valuable are the
cast lists to be found in the text and in an appendix. The
latter comprises a chronological list of all operas produced at

the Opera Comique and the Savoy from 1877-1909, together with casts.

1223 Newman, Ernest. "The Gilbert and Sullivan Operas." LIVING AGE, 303 (1919), 433-36.

Newman attempts to account for the success of the Gilbert and Sullivan partnership, pointing to Gilbert's verbal pyrotechnics and Sullivan's ability to accentuate key words with the salient point of the musical line.

1224 Rowland-Brown, H. "The Gilbertian Idea." CORNHILL MAGAZINE, n.s. 52 (April 1922), 503-12.

A useful article for its quotations from one of Gilbert's notebooks in which he sketched out ideas about "topsy-turvydom." The article itself fails to put the material to good use.

1225 Baring, Maurice. "Gilbert and Sullivan." FORTNIGHTLY REVIEW, n.s. 112 (September 1922), 422-36.

A rather extravagant eulogy on the two men's combined genius.

1226 Lytton, Henry A. THE SECRETS OF A SAVOYARD. London: Jarrolds, [1922]. 191 p.

An autobiography which covers the many Gilbert and Sullivan roles Lytton played.

1227 Walbrook, H.M. GILBERT & SULLIVAN OPERA: A HISTORY AND A COMMENT: WITH A FOREWORD BY SIR HENRY WOOD. London: F.V. White, 1922. 156 p.

A brief survey of each opera with some useful historical information, but little criticism.

1228 Wilkinson, Clennell. "Gilbert and Sullivan." LONDON MERCURY, 5 (1922), 494-505.

A not too scholarly definition of Gilbert and Sullivan's qualities in the face of a decline in their popularity. See also a letter on this article, LM, 5 (1922), 643.

1229 Dark, Sidney, and Rowland Grey. W.S. GILBERT: HIS LIFE AND LETTERS. London: Methuen, 1923; rpt. New York: Blom, 1972. ix, 269 p.

With only little in the way of biography, this is more a genial survey of Gilbert's work, with liberal extracts from plays, supplemented by letters. There are appendices on the lost Bab Ballads, production details, and published editions of works.

1230 Fitzgerald, S.J.A. THE STORY OF THE SAVOY OPERA. London: Stanley Paul, 1924. xx, 238 p.

1231 Wilson, A.C. "W.S. Gilbert." MANCHESTER QUARTERLY, 51 (1925), 277-97.

Wilson defines Gilbertian humor, but his discussion is much too generalized to be penetrating.

1232 Godwin, A.H. GILBERT & SULLIVAN: A CRITICAL APPRECIATION OF THE "SAVOY OPERAS": WITH AN INTRODUCTION BY G.K. CHESTERTON. London and Toronto: Dent, 1926. xx, 300 p.

Among the earlier books this appreciation is, indeed, more critical than most, and is worth dipping into. However, there is no index to aid the reader, and Godwin's chapters follow no significant arrangement.

1233 Hamilton, Edith. "W.S. Gilbert: A Mid-Victorian Aristophanes." THEATRE ARTS MONTHLY, 11 (October 1927), 781-90.

Uses lengthy quotations from both Gilbert and Aristophanes to parallel similar comic devices.

1234 Goldberg, Isaac. THE STORY OF GILBERT AND SULLIVAN: OR THE "COMPLEAT" SAVOYARD. London: John Murray, 1928; rpt. New York: AMS, 1970. xviii, 588 p.

Goldberg's "story" is a leisurely and extensive account of both men's lives and careers, separately and jointly. His critical evaluations, however, are not very profound, and much information, although interesting, is undocumented. Goldberg includes "A Gilbert Miscellany"--a collection of Gilbert's poetry and prose, reprinted mainly from FUN. There is also a short annotated bibliography.

1235 Perry, Henry Ten Eyck. "The Victorianism of W.S. Gilbert." SR, 34 (1928), 302-9.

Sees Gilbert as representing the spirit of the age and limiting his ridicule of foibles to that "permitted by Englishmen to Englishmen, not to outsiders."

1236 DuBois, Arthur E. "W.S. Gilbert, Practical Classicist." SR, 37 (1929), 94-107.

A discussion of Gilbert as a pragmatist who "wanted to do something greatly serious, but he was a capable business man and, because he was willing to sacrifice art for business, he made an art of business."

1237 Quiller-Couch, Sir Arthur. STUDIES IN LITERATURE: THIRD SERIES. Cambridge: At the University Press, 1929. vii, 264 p.

Quiller-Couch's chatty musings about Gilbert are to be found on pp. 217-40.

1238 Lambton, Gervase. GILBERTIAN CHARACTERS AND A DISCOURSE ON W.S. GILBERT'S PHILOSOPHY IN THE SAVOY OPERAS: WITH A PRE-FACE BY VISCOUNT CECIL OF CHELWOOD. London: Philip Allan, 1931. 118 p.

A superficial survey of both characters and philosophy.

1239 Granville-Barker, Harley. "Exit Planché--Enter Gilbert." LONDON MERCURY, 25 (March, April 1932), 457-666; 558-73.

A review of some aspects of Planché's contribution to drama, and seeing Gilbert as his successor. Gilbert's advance was to bring a fresh vigor to burlesque and extravanganza, adding also sharpness and bite.

1240 Kendal, Madge. "W.S. Gilbert." CORNHILL MAGAZINE, n.s. 75 (September 1933), 303-16.

Personal reminiscences of Gilbert by this famous actress who acted in several of his plays. Gives some idea of how the plays were performed.

1241 Rickett, Edmond. "Certain Recollections of W.S. Gilbert: The Author of The Mikado et al. was a Difficult Director." NEW YORK TIMES, 1 April 1934, Section 10, pp. 1-2.

A short personal account of Gilbert's autocracy. Rickett knew Gilbert from 1904 onwards and composed and arranged some music for him. He thus had the opportunity to witness Gilbert's methods at first hand.

1242 "Two Victorian Humorists: Burnand and the Mask of Gilbert." TLS, 21 November 1936, pp. 935-36.

This article, prompted by the centenary of the births of F.C. Burnand and Gilbert, takes a brief look at some of the characteristics of the two men's humor.

1243 Vandiver, E.P., Jr. "W.S. Gilbert and Shakespeare." SHAKESPEARE ASSOCIATION BULLETIN, 13 (1938), 139-45.

Indicates some of Gilbert's borrowings from Shakespeare.

1244 Troubridge, St. Vincent. "Gilbert and Planché." N&Q, 180 (1941), 200-205.

A listing of Gilbert's notable borrowings from Planché.

1245 _____. "Gilbert's Sources." N&Q, 180 (1941), 224.

A note suggesting that a speech in IOLANTHE derives from a speech made by C.J. Mathews.

1246 _____. "Gilbert and Planché." N&Q, 181 (1941), 17-18.

Three further parallels between Gilbert and Planché.

1247 Parrott, Ian. "Arthur Sullivan (1842-1900)." MUSIC AND LETTERS, 23 (1942), 202-10.

An interesting evaluation of the positive qualities of Sullivan's music. Parrott sees his achievements as being in the field of melody and orchestration, although he recognizes there are many bad lapses. Frequent reference made to the Gilbert and Sullivan operas.

1248 Purdy, Claire Lee. GILBERT AND SULLIVAN: MASTERS OF MIRTH AND MELODY. New York: Julian Messner, 1946. 276 p.

Biographically and critically, this is a simplistic book. Its tone seems more appropriate to schoolchildren than anyone else, especially when plots are recounted. Strangely enough, there is an extensive bibliography, although, in keeping with the rest of the book, the critical section is labeled "A List of the Best Books . . . ."

1249 Boas, Guy. "The Gilbertian World and the World of To-day." EN-GLISH 7 (1948), 5-11.

A general, nostalgic account of Gilbert, his life, work, and qualities.

1250 Darlington, W.A. THE WORLD OF GILBERT AND SULLIVAN. New York: Crowell, 1950; rpt. Freeport, N.Y.: Books for Libraries, 1970. xiii, 209 p.

Darlington's purpose is to fill in "the social or political back-ground against which each opera was seen and understood in its own time." This he does in eminently readable fashion,

although knowledgeable readers might well be irritated by
some of the particulars explained. There is also a dictionary
index of opera characters.

1251 Farnsworth, Dean B. "Satire in the Works of W.S. Gilbert." Ph.D.
Dissertation, University of California, 1950. 196 p.

1252 Jacobs, Arthur. GILBERT AND SULLIVAN. London: Max Parrish,
1951. 66 p.

An elementary illustrated survey of the partnership.

1253 Williamson, Audrey. GILBERT & SULLIVAN OPERA: A NEW ASSESS-
MENT. London: Rockliff, 1953. xii, 292 p.

The literary and musical assessment of the operas falls somewhat short of the author's intention: it lacks rigorous execu-
tion, often rambling in the side-roads of plot-telling. More
useful are Williamson's accounts of past performances and
productions, with hints on "how to do it." These help the
reader in the study to visualise how the printed word becomes
the living performance.

1254 Stedman, Jane W. "William S. Gilbert: His Comic Techniques and
Their Development." Ph.D. Dissertation, University of Chicago, 1955. 139 p.

1255 Troubridge, St. Vincent. "Another Gilbert Borrowing." TN, 10 (1955-
56), 20-21.

Gilbert's THE GRAND DUKE and Tom Taylor's A DUKE IN
DIFFICULTIES.

1256 Hall, Robert A., Jr. "The Satire of THE YEOMEN OF THE GUARD."
MLN, 73 (1958), 492-97.

A convincing analysis of the opera which the author sees as
Gilbert mocking his own work, "Gilbert's satire on Gilbertian
tomfoolery." As such, it occupies a special position in the
Savoy canon.

1257 Hughes, Gervase. THE MUSIC OF ARTHUR SULLIVAN. London: Macmillan, 1960. viii, 180 p.

Although written by an avowed Sullivan enthusiast, who sees
Gilbert's contribution to the partnership as very subordinate,
this book examines the musical quality of Sullivan's work in
generally not too technical terms. As such, it is a useful
counterweight in balancing the partnership.

1258 Mander, Raymond, and Joe Mitchenson. A PICTURE HISTORY OF GILBERT AND SULLIVAN. London: Vista Books, 1962. 160 p.

> This book, through a wide variety of photographs and drawings, illustrates the life and work of Gilbert, Sullivan, Richard D'Oyly Carte, and their associates. Part IV is of particular interest: it illustrates chronologically the changes in production which have taken place in each opera over the years.

1259 Moore, Frank Leslie, comp. CROWELL'S HANDBOOK OF GILBERT AND SULLIVAN. New York: Thomas and Crowell, 1962. [vii], 264 p.

> This is essentially a book of information on the operas, furnishing dramatis personae; lists of songs and choruses; synopses; together with biographical essays on Gilbert, Sullivan, Carte, and other miscellaneous information.

1260 Ellis, James Delmont. "The Comic Vision of W.S. Gilbert." Ph.D. Dissertation, State University of Iowa, 1964. 424 p. (DA#64-7915)

> Ellis's examination of Gilbert's vision covers the Savoy operas, the Bab Ballads, and his sixty other stage works. Gilbert mocked enduring affectations and hence his humor remains fresh; in addition, he set on end Victorian behavior--"the disparity between personal desire and public necessity."

1261 Hammond, John W. "Gilbert's TRAIL BY JURY." Expl, 23 (1964), item 34.

> Hammond succinctly argues that "internal evidence indicates that Gilbert intended this libretto to be an inversion of Oliver Goldsmith's poem 'The Hermit.'"

1262 Jones, John B. "In Search of Archibald Grosvenor: A New Look at Gilbert's PATIENCE." VP, 3 (1965), 45-53.

> A contribution to the literary detection game of discovering prototypes for Bunthorne and Grosvenor.

1263 Randall, David A. "Gilbert and Sullivan's PRINCESS IDA." PBSA, 59 (1965), 322-26.

> A brief discussion of the variants between the English libretto and the first American libretto. In the latter "two entire songs, and two verses of other songs, differ in both matter and meter from the English libretto." These are reproduced in the article.

1264 _____. "THE GONDOLIERS." PBSA, 59 (1965), 193-98.

> A useful account of the differences between the English and

American libretti. Since, for copyright purposes, the latter had to be dispatched to the United States some time before the date fixed for simultaneous production in both countries, it contains portions of unrevised text.

1265 Revitt, Paul J. "Gilbert and Sullivan: More Seriousness than Satire." WHR, 19 (1965), 19-34.

Revitt's central thesis is that underlying Gilbert's topsy-turvydom and "manufactured logic is the Victorian principle that departure from the established order is fatal." He also devotes a considerable portion of his article to a discussion of Sullivan's contribution. However, neither portion offers radically new insights into the partnership.

1266 Stanton, Stephen S. "Ibsen, Gilbert, and Scribe's BATAILLE DE DAMES." ETJ, 17 (1965), 24-30.

Stanton seeks to demonstrate the similarities of plot in BATAILLE and ENGAGED, although this task is not very extensively fulfilled.

1267 Jones, John Bush. "Gilbert and Sullivan's Serious Satire: More Fact than Fancy." WHR, 21 (1967), 211-24.

A rebuttal on factual and critical grounds of Revitt's article, item 1265.

1268 _____. "The Printing of THE GRAND DUKE: Notes Toward a Gilbert Bibliography." PBSA, 61 (1967), 335-42.

A full account and discussion of the variants of THE GRAND DUKE in an attempt to point the difficulties of accurate bib-liographical work regarding the Gilbert canon. Jones also indicates some rules and considerations for such a task.

1269 _____. "Gilbertian Humor: Pulling Together a Definition". VN, 33 (1968), 28-31.

"It is, then, this method of humor-through-logic that is the real basis for that topsy-turvy comic inversion we call Gil-bertian."

1270 Stedman, Jane W. "The Genesis of PATIENCE." MP, 66 (1968), 48-58.

An analysis of an early draft of two-thirds of Act I of PATI-ENCE to demonstrate Gilbert's modus operandi. The draft (twenty-one pages, now located in the British Library) is printed in full with extensive annotations.

1271 Cole, David William. "W.S. Gilbert's Contribution to the Freedom of the Stage." Ph.D. Dissertation, University of Wisconsin, 1970. 260 p. (DA#70-24686)

> A discussion of Gilbert's successful treatment on stage of religious, moral, and political themes which violated Victorian taboos.

1272 Ellis, James. "The Unsung W.S. Gilbert." HLB, 18 (1970), 109-40.

> An examination of some fifty-six uncollected Bab Ballads. There is an occasional reference to Gilbert's dramatic work, usually demonstrating his use of the ballads as source material.

1273 Head, Thomas Garrett. "Contract to Please: A Study of the Plays of W.S. Gilbert." Ph.D. Dissertation, Stanford University, 1970. 139 p. (DA#71-12916)

> "Melodrama was the favorite dramatic form of the nineteenth century, and because W.S. Gilbert always thought of himself as a popular dramatist with a contract to please all classes of society, his plays are quite often written as melodramas." Special attention to GRETCHEN, BROKEN HEARTS, and THE NE'ER-DO-WEEL, as well as Gilbert's relationship with E.A. Sothern in writing the latter.

1274 Jones, John Bush. W.S. GILBERT: A CENTURY OF SCHOLARSHIP AND COMMENTARY: FOREWORD BY BRIDGET D'OYLY CARTE. New York: New York University Press, 1970. xix, 321 p.

> A useful collection of essays on Gilbert, aimed at providing an historical and critical overview of the works. Items 1208, 1221, 1233, 1235, 1237, 1262, 1263, 1264, 1268, and 1270 of this bibliography are among the articles included.

1275 Stedman, Jane W. "From Dame to Woman: W.S. Gilbert and Theatrical Transvestism." VS, 14 (1970), 27-46.

> Stedman devotes over half of her article to a discussion of the nineteenth-century theatrical traditions of men playing female roles and vice versa. With this background she examines the consequences (often awkward) of Gilbert's decision that "on artistic principles, no man should play a woman's part and no woman a man's."

1276 _____. "The New Gilbert Lyrics." BNYPL, 74 (1970), 629-33.

> Stedman provides a brief history of the publication adventures of Gilbert's short musical play, OUR ISLAND HOME, the third of Gilbert's German Reed Entertainments. She also supplies three hitherto "lost" lyrics.

1277 Cole, David W. "Gilbert's IOLANTHE." Expl, 29 (1971), item 68.

Cole elucidates the allusion in the lines "He shall end the cherished rights / You enjoy on Wednesday nights," pointing out that the House of Lords did not meet on Wednesday evenings.

1278 Helyar, James, ed. GILBERT AND SULLIVAN: PAPERS PRESENTED AT THE INTERNATIONAL CONFERENCE HELD AT THE UNIVERSITY OF KANSAS IN MAY 1970. Lawrence: University of Kansas Libraries, 1971. [vi], 228 p.

These very interesting papers cover many aspects of Gilbert and Sullivan criticism and scholarship and are written by some of the foremost academics in the field.

1279 Boyer, Robert D. "No Offense Intended: W.S. Gilbert and the Victorian Public." TS, no. 18 (1971-72), 65-74.

A brief account of some of the ways in which Gilbert attempted to make the Victorian theatre, in all its aspects, a place of propriety and respectability.

1280 Lawrence, Elwood P. "'The Happy Land': W.S. Gilbert as Political Satirist." VS, 15 (1971-72), 161-83.

Lawrence investigates at considerable length the stage history and political satire of the piece. He also deals with the initial censorship of and public response to the satire, and briefly attempts to place the play in the wider context of the Gilbert canon.

1281 Ayre, Leslie. THE GILBERT AND SULLIVAN COMPANION. London and New York: W.H. Allen, 1972. 485 p.

This companion is arranged alphabetically and provides information on every aspect of productions down to the present day. It is preceded by a short biographical history of Gilbert and Sullivan.

1282 Hardwick, Michael. THE OSPREY GUIDE TO GILBERT AND SULLIVAN. Reading, England: Osprey, 1972. 284 p.

This guide is the sort of work readers are likely to dip into to refresh their memories rather than to read cover to cover. It has an alphabetical list of characters, summaries of the operas together with brief production histories, an index of first lines of songs, a glossary to the operas, and a useful discography and bibliography.

1283 Thompson, Hilary. "The Savoy Opera as Metatheatre: A Study of Characterization in the Libretti of W.S. Gilbert." Ph.D. Dissertation, University of Alberta, 1972. iii, 240 p.

> This thesis explores the notion that "it is in his use of characters, not as imitations of human beings but as metaphors, that Gilbert anticipates the theatre of the absurd."

1284 Baily, Leslie. GILBERT AND SULLIVAN AND THEIR WORLD. London: Thames and Hudson, 1973. 128 p.

> A generously illustrated introductory volume.

1285 Henshaw, N.W. "Gilbert and Sullivan Through a Glass Brightly." TQ 16, no. 4 (1973), 48-65.

> "Logical absurdity and empty syllogism . . . are the very foundation of Gilbert's indomitable good humor. In his world, when absurd principles are carried to their logical conclusions, they are found to provide their own solutions to all the difficulties they have caused." Although Henshaw's observations are not radically startling, he does pay more than usual attention to Sullivan's contribution.

1286 Parrott, Ian. "IOLANTHE." MUSIC REVIEW 34, no. 1 (1973), 55-57.

> Parrott regards IOLANTHE as, musically, "an almost flawless masterpiece" and analyses the music briefly to demonstrate that claim. Although interesting, the article is scarcely extensive enough to substantiate the contention.

1287 Smith, Patrick J. "W.S. Gilbert and the Musical." YALE THEATRE 4, no. 3 (1973), 20-26.

> A very superficial survey.

1288 Walmisley, Guy H., and Claude A. Walmisley. TIT-WILLOW; OR NOTES AND JOTTINGS ON GILBERT AND SULLIVAN OPERAS. No publication details. 151 p.

> The subtitle accurately describes this work, which serious students will find too elementary to be of much use. Plot-outlines are mixed in with brief stage histories and notes on references in the operas. This material is adequately and more fully covered elsewhere.

VI Journals and Newsletters

1289 THE GILBERT AND SULLIVAN JOURNAL. London: Gilbert and Sullivan Society, 1925-30.

GRUNDY, SYDNEY (1848-1914)

II Acted Plays—Principal Titles

1290 A LITTLE CHANGE: A FARCE IN ONE SCENE. (Haymarket, 13 July 1872.) London and New York: French, n.d. 23 p.

An acting edition.

1291 THE SNOWBALL: A FARCICAL COMEDY IN THREE ACTS. (Strand, 2 February 1879.) London and New York: French, n.d. 45 p.

An acting edition with a cast list of the first London production; interleaved, with manuscript notes.

1292 IN HONOUR BOUND: AN ORIGINAL PLAY IN ONE ACT. (Prince of Wales's, 25 September 1880.) New York: H. Roorbach, n.d. 19 p.

An acting edition.

1293 THE GLASS OF FASHION: AN ORIGINAL COMEDY IN FOUR ACTS. (Grand, Glasgow, 26 March 1883; Globe, 8 September 1883.) London and New York: French, 1898. 60 p.

An acting edition with a cast list.

1294 THE SILVER SHIELD: AN ORIGINAL COMEDY IN THREE ACTS. (Strand, 19 May 1885.) London and New York: French, 1898. 56 p.

An acting edition with cast lists of two London productions.

1295 A FOOL'S PARADISE: AN ORIGINAL PLAY IN THREE ACTS. (Prince of Wales's, Greenwich, 7 October 1887, as THE MOUSETRAP; Gaiety, 12 February 1889.) London and New York: French, 1898. 64 p.

An acting edition with a cast list of the London production. The Readex collection also includes a second French's acting edition (London and New York: 1898, 57 p.).

1296 *THE DEAN'S DAUGHTER: A PLAY IN FOUR ACTS. With F.C. Philips. (St. James's, 13 October 1888.) London: Trischler, 1891. x, 140 p.

A library edition, with extracts of press reviews of the original production.

1297 A PAIR OF SPECTACLES: A COMEDY IN THREE ACTS, ADAPTED FROM THE FRENCH. (Garrick, 22 February 1890.) London and New York: French, 1898. 57 p.

An acting edition with a cast list of the first London production.

1298 AN ORIGINAL LIGHT ENGLISH OPERA IN THREE ACTS ENTITLED HADDON HALL. (Wolverhampton, 29 December 1892; Savoy, 24 September 1892.) London: Chappell, 1892. 51 p.

> Libretto only, with a cast list of the first London production. The Readex collection includes the vocal score (London: c. 1892, 169 p.).

1299 SOWING THE WIND: AN ORIGINAL PLAY IN FOUR ACTS. (Comedy, 30 September 1893.) No publication details. 68 p.

> A privately printed promptbook.

1300 "A BUNCH OF VIOLETS": A PLAY IN FOUR ACTS. (Haymarket, 25 April 1894.) International Edition, no. 47. London and New York: French, 1901. 57 p.

> An acting edition with a cast list of the first London production.

1301 THE NEW WOMAN: AN ORIGINAL COMEDY IN FOUR ACTS. (Comedy, 1 September 1894.) London: Privately printed, 1894. 104 p.

> An acting edition.

1302 THE LATE MR. CASTELLO: AN ORIGINAL FARCE IN THREE ACTS. (Comedy, 28 December 1895.) London and New York: French, 1901. 52 p.

> An acting edition with a cast list of the first London production.

V Critical Studies

1303 "A Gossip with Sydney Grundy." ERA, 8 October 1892, p. 11.

> An informal interview covering various aspects of Grundy's life and work.

1304 Watson, Malcolm. "Mr. Grundy and the Critics." THEATRE, 33 (October 1894), 161-64.

> Watson sees Grundy as belonging to the school of the well-made play, and possessing "a deep-rooted fondness for the old order of things." He also discusses Grundy's relationship with critics, especially his attack upon them for their indifference.

HAINES, JOHN THOMAS (1799?-1843)

II Acted Plays—Principal Titles

1305 THE IDIOT WITNESS; OR, A TALE OF BLOOD: A MELO-DRAMA IN
THREE ACTS. (Coburg, 6 October 1823.) Duncombe's British Theatre,
vol. 5. London: Duncombe, n.d. 24 p.

>An acting edition with cast lists of two London productions.

1306 JACOB FAITHFUL; OR, THE LIFE OF A THAMES WATERMAN! A
DOMESTIC LOCAL DRAMA IN THREE ACTS. (Victoria, 16 December
1834.) Duncombe's British Theatre, vol. 16. London: Duncombe, n.d.
50 p.

>An acting edition with a cast list of a Surrey (?) production.
>Adapted from Marryat's novel.

1307 MY POLL AND MY PARTNER JOE: A NAUTICAL DRAMA IN THREE
ACTS. (Surrey, 31 August 1835.) Lacy's Acting Edition, vol. 71.
London: Lacy, n.d. 51 p.

>With a playbill reproduction for the Surrey performance and
>"Remarks" by D--G [George Daniel].

1308 THE OCEAN OF LIFE; OR, EVERY INCH A SAILOR: A NAUTICAL
DRAMA IN THREE ACTS. (Surrey, 4 April 1836.) Lacy's Acting Edition, vol. 69. London: Lacy, n.d. 57 p.

>With a cast list of the first London production and "Remarks"
>by D--G [George Daniel].

1309 RICHARD PLANTAGENET: AN HISTORICAL DRAMA IN THREE ACTS.
(Victoria, 1 December 1836.) Cumberland's Minor Theatre, vol. 14.
London: Cumberland, n.d. 57 p.

>An acting edition with a cast list of the first London produc-
>tion.

1310 ANGELINE: AN ORIGINAL DRAMA IN ONE ACT. (St. James's, 29
September 1837.) Acting National Drama, no. 37. London: Chapman
and Hall, n.d. 19 p.

>With a cast list of the first London production.

1311 THE FACTORY BOY: A DRAMA IN THREE ACTS. (Surrey, 8 June
1840.) London: J. Pattie, n.d. 50 p.

>An acting edition.

1312 THE WIZARD OF THE WAVE; OR, THE SHIP OF THE AVENGER: A LEGENDARY NAUTICAL DRAMA IN THREE ACTS. (Victoria, 7 September 1840.) London: J. Pattie, n.d. 54 p.

> An acting edition with a cast list of the first London production.

1313 RUTH; OR, THE LASS THAT LOVES A SAILOR: A NAUTICAL AND DOMESTIC DRAMA IN THREE ACTS. (Victoria, 23 January 1843.) London: Lacy, n.d. 49 p.

> An acting edition with a reproduction of the playbill for the first London production.

HAYNES, JAMES (1788-1851)

II Acted Plays—Principal Titles

1314 CONSCIENCE; OR, THE BRIDAL NIGHT: A TRAGEDY IN FIVE ACTS. (Drury Lane, 21 February 1821.) London: Hurst, Robinson & Co., 1821. vi, 94 p.

> Includes an author's preface in which he thanks the performers for their efforts; cast list of the first London production.

1315 DURAZZO: A TRAGEDY IN FIVE ACTS. (Covent Garden, November 1838.) London: Hurst, Robinson & Co., 1823. 148 p.

> A brief note by Haynes explains that he withdrew the play from Drury Lane and Covent Garden theatres "rather than descend to the solicitations or submit to the delays which Managers would impose upon literary persons."

1316 MARY STUART: AN HISTORICAL TRAGEDY. (Drury Lane, 22 January 1840.) London: James Ridgway, 1840. 103 p.

> There is a cast list of the first London production, a dedication to Macready, and a brief introduction by Haynes. The Readex collection also contains a promptbook of this play with manuscript notes.

HAZLEWOOD, COLIN HENRY (1823-75)

II Acted Plays—Principal Titles

1317 *THE BONNET BUILDER'S TEA PARTY (Strand, 22 May 1854). LC.

1318 JENNY FOSTER THE SAILOR'S CHILD; OR, THE WINTER ROBIN: IN TWO ACTS. (Britannia, October 1855.) London and New York: French, n.d. 29 p.

An acting edition with a cast list of the first London production.

1319 WAITING FOR THE VERDICT; OR, FALSELY ACCUSED: A DOMESTIC DRAMA IN THREE ACTS. (City of London, 29 January 1859.) London and New York: French, n.d. 48 p.

An acting edition with a cast list of the first London production; interleaved, with manuscript notes.

1320 *THE LIFE OF A WEAVER. (Britannia, 28 November 1859.) LC.

1321 *OUR LOT IN LIFE; OR, BRIGHTER DAYS IN STORE. (Britannia, 22 April 1862.) LC.

1322 *CAST ON THE MERCY OF THE WORLD; OR, DESERTED AND DE-CEIVED. (Britannia, 13 October 1862.) LC.

1323 *THE DOWNFALL OF PRIDE. (Britannia, 27 June 1864). LC

1324 *THE CASTAWAY; OR, LIFE'S THORNY PATH AND THE ORPHAN'S HIGHBORN HUSBAND. (Britannia, 12 March 1866.) LC.

1325 THE LOST WIFE; OR, A HUSBAND'S CONFESSION: A DOMESTIC DRAMA IN THREE ACTS. (Britannia, 7 August 1871.) London: Lacy, 1871. 36 p.

An acting edition with a cast list of the first London production.

1326 LADY AUDLEY'S SECRET: AN ORIGINAL VERSION OF MISS BRAD-DON'S POPULAR NOVEL IN TWO ACTS. (Olympic, 25 June 1877.) [London and New York]: French, n.d. 30 p.

An acting edition with a cast list of the first London production.

HOBBES, JOHN OLIVER [MRS. PEARL MARY TERESA CRAIGIE] (1867-1906)

II Acted Plays—Principal Titles

1327 *"JOURNEYS END IN LOVERS MEETING." With George Moore. (Daly's, 5 June 1894.) LC.

1328 THE AMBASSADOR: A COMEDY IN FOUR ACTS. (St. James's, 2 June 1898.) London: Unwin, 1898. xiii, 152 p.

> An acting edition with a cast list of the first London production and a preface.

1329 THE WISDOM OF THE WISE: A COMEDY IN THREE ACTS. (St. James's, 22 November 1900.) New York: F.A. Stokes, 1900. 136 p.

> An acting edition.

1330 *THE FLUTE OF PAN: A COMEDY IN FOUR ACTS. (Shaftesbury, 12 November 1904.) London: T. Fisher Unwin, 1904. 211 p.

> An acting edition.

IIa Unacted Plays

1331 OSBERN AND URSYNE: A DRAMA IN THREE ACTS. London and New York: John Lane, 1900. 95 p.

> An acting edition.

IV Biography

1332 THE LIFE OF JOHN OLIVER HOBBES: TOLD IN HER CORRESPONDENCE WITH NUMEROUS FRIENDS: WITH A BIOGRAPHICAL SKETCH BY HER FATHER, JOHN MORGAN RICHARDS, AND AN INTRODUCTION BY THE RIGHT REV. BISHOP WELLDON, DEAN OF MANCHESTER. London: John Murray, 1911. xviii, 381 p.

> This work consists almost entirely of Hobbes's letters, strung together with a little informative narrative. The biographical sketch is highly subjective and of little use.

1333 Clarke, Isabel C. SIX PORTRAITS: MADAME DE STAEL: JANE AUSTEN: GEORGE ELIOT: MRS. OLIPHANT: JOHN OLIVER HOBBES (MRS. CRAIGIE): KATHERINE MANSFIELD. London: Hutchinson 1935; rpt. Freeport, N.Y.: Books for Libraries, 1967. 289 p.

> A straightforward, sympathetic biography.

JEROME, JEROME K[LAPKA] (1859-1927)

II Acted Plays—Principal Titles

1334 BARBARA: A PLAY IN ONE ACT. (Globe, 19 June 1886). New

York: Dicks, n.d. 22 p.

> An acting edition.

1335 SUNSET: A PLAY IN ONE ACT. (Comedy, 13 February 1888.)
Chicago: Sergel, n.d. 32 p.

> An acting edition with a cast list of the first London production.

1336 *THE PASSING OF THE THIRD FLOOR BACK: AN IDLE FANCY IN A
PROLOGUE, A PLAY AND AN EPILOGUE. (St. James's, 1 September
1903.) London: Hurst and Blackett, 1910. 212 p.

> An acting edition with several photographs.

IV Biography

1337 Jerome, Jerome K[lapka]. ON THE STAGE--AND OFF. THE BRIEF CA-
REER OF A WOULD-BE ACTOR. New York: Henry Holt, 1891. vi, 170 p.

> An amusing account of Jerome's less-than-outstanding acting
> career.

1337a _____. MY LIFE AND TIMES. New York: Harper, 1926. 318 p.

V Critical Studies

1338 Faurot, Ruth Marie. JEROME K. JEROME. New York: Twayne,
1974. 200 p.

> A general consideration of Jerome's life and work, including
> his career as a playwright and amateur actor. A selected
> bibliography is included.

JERROLD, DOUGLAS (1803-57)

I Collected Works

1339 THE WORKS OF DOUGLAS JERROLD. WITH AN INTRODUCTORY
MEMOIR BY HIS SON, W. BLANCHARD JERROLD. 4 vols. London:
Bradbury, Evans & Co., n.d.

> This collection does not contain any plays.

1340 THE WRITINGS OF DOUGLAS JERROLD. 8 vols. London: Bradbury
and Evans, 1851-58.

Volume seven, COMEDIES (1853), contains BUBBLES OF THE
DAY (Covent Garden, 25 February 1842), TIME WORKS
WONDERS (Haymarket, 26 April 1845), THE CATSPAW (Haymarket, 9 May 1850), THE PRISONER OF WAR (Drury Lane,
1 March 1842), RETIRED FROM BUSINESS (Haymarket, 3 May
1851), and ST. CUPID; OR, DOROTHY'S FORTUNE (Prin-
cess's, 22 January 1853); volume eight, COMEDIES AND
DRAMAS (1854), contains THE RENT DAY (Drury Lane, 25
January 1832), NELL GWYNNE; OR, THE PROLOGUE (Co-
vent Garden, 9 January 1833), THE HOUSEKEEPER (Haymar-
ket, 17 July 1833), THE WEDDING GOWN (Drury Lane, 2
January 1834), THE SCHOOLFELLOWS (Queen's, 16 February
1835), DOVES IN A CAGE (Adelphi, 18 December 1835),
THE PAINTER OF GHENT (Strand, 25 April 1836), and
BLACK-EY'D SUSAN; OR, ALL IN THE DOWNS (Surrey, 8
June 1829).

II Acted Plays—Principal Titles

1341 PAUL PRY: A COMEDY IN TWO ACTS. (Coburg, 27 November 1827.)
London: Lacy, n.d. 30 p.

> An acting edition with a cast list of the first London produc-
> tion.

1342 FIFTEEN YEARS OF A DRUNKARD'S LIFE: A MELODRAMA IN THREE
ACTS. (Coburg, 24 November 1828.) French's Standard Drama, no.
347. New York: French, n.d. 32 p.

> An acting edition with cast lists for some London and New
> York productions.

1343 BLACK EYED SUSAN; OR, ALL IN THE DOWNS: A NAUTICAL DRAMA
IN TWO ACTS. (Surrey, 8 June 1829.) New York: R.H. Elton, 1830.
30 p.

> Includes a cast list for the Park Theatre, New York, produc-
> tion.

1344 THE MUTINY AT THE NORE: A NAUTICAL DRAMA IN THREE ACTS.
(Royal Pavilion, 7 June 1830.) London: Cumberland, n.d. 48 p.

> An acting edition with cast lists for three London productions
> and "Remarks" by D--G [George Daniel].

1345 THE BRIDE OF LUDGATE: A COMIC DRAMA IN TWO ACTS. (Drury
Lane, 8 December 1831.) London: Cumberland, n.d. 47 p.

> An acting edition with a cast list of the first London produc-
> tion and "Remarks" by D--G [George Daniel]; D--G also has
> a memoir of Cooper, the actor.

1346 THE RENT DAY: A DOMESTIC DRAMA IN THREE ACTS. (Drury Lane, 25 January 1832.) Philadelphia: R.H. Lenfestey, n.d. 52 p.

> An acting edition with cast lists for London and Philadelphia productions; this copy is a promptbook with manuscript notes.

1347 BEAU NASH, THE KING OF BATH: A COMEDY IN THREE ACTS. (Haymarket, 16 July 1834.) Dicks' Standard Plays, no. 554. London: Dicks, n.d. 18 p.

> An acting edition.

1348 THE PRISONER OF WAR: A COMEDY IN TWO ACTS. (Drury Lane, 8 February 1842.) Lacy's Acting Edition, vol. 27. London: Lacy, n.d. 49 p.

1349 TIME WORKS WONDERS: A COMEDY IN FIVE ACTS. (Haymarket, 26 April 1845.) London: Punch Office, 1845. 76 p.

III Bibliographies

1350 "Thersites." "Douglas Jerrold." ERA, 18 February 1893, p. 11.

> A bibliographical listing of thirty-five plays by Jerrold, with performance dates. See also correspondence on this article, ERA, 4 March 1893, p. 12, and 18 March 1893, p. 11.

IV Biography

1351 Jerrold, Blanchard. THE LIFE AND REMAINS OF DOUGLAS JERROLD. London: W. Kent, 1859. xvi, 420 p.

> A biography by Jerrold's son.

V Critical Studies

1352 Jerrold, Walter. DOUGLAS JERROLD, DRAMATIST AND WIT. 2 vols. London, New York, and Toronto: Hodder and Stoughton, 1914. xi, 672 p.

> Some considerable attention is given to Jerrold the playwright. An appendix lists (incompletely) the plays, and the work is illustrated and indexed.

1353 Ley, J.W.T. "Douglas Jerrold." DICKENSIAN, 15 (1919), 82-86.

> A review article of Walter Jerrold's study (item 1352).

1354 Atkinson, Colin Bernard. "The Plays of Douglas Jerrold." Ph.D. Dissertation, New York University, 1971. 351 p. (DA#72-13334)

1355 Kelly, Richard M. DOUGLAS JERROLD. New York: Twayne, 1972. 168 p.

> A general introduction to Jerrold and his work with a fairly short and superficial chapter devoted to the plays. There is a useful bibliography of works by and about Jerrold.

JERROLD, M.W. BLANCHARD (1827-84)

II Acted Plays—Principal Titles

1356 COOL AS A CUCUMBER: A FARCE IN ONE ACT. (Lyceum, 24 March 1851.) New York: French, n.d. 18 p.

> An acting edition with three cast lists; interleaved, with manuscript notes.

1357 BEAU BRUMMELL, THE KING OF CALAIS: A DRAMA IN TWO ACTS. (Lyceum, 11 April 1859.) London: Lacy, n.d. 36 p.

> An acting edition with a cast list of the first London production.

1358 CUPID IN WAITING: A COMEDY IN THREE ACTS. (Royalty, 22 July 1871.) London: Lacy, n.d. 42 p.

> An acting edition with a cast list of the first London production.

JONES, HENRY ARTHUR (1851-1929)

I Collected Works

1359 REPRESENTATIVE PLAYS: EDITED, WITH HISTORICAL, BIOGRAPHICAL, AND CRITICAL INTRODUCTIONS BY CLAYTON HAMILTON. 4 vols. London: Macmillan, 1926.

> Contents: volume one: THE SILVER KING, THE MIDDLE-MAN, JUDAH, THE DANCING GIRL; volume two: THE CRUSADERS, THE TEMPTER, THE MASQUERADERS, THE CASE OF REBELLIOUS SUSAN; volume three: MICHAEL AND HIS LOST ANGEL, THE LIARS, MRS. DANE'S DEFENCE, THE HYPOCRITES; volume four: DOLLY REFORMING HERSELF, THE DIVINE GIFT, MARY GOES FIRST, THE GOAL, GRACE MARY. This edition includes Jones's major works, together with brief introductions and cast lists.

II Acted Plays—Principal Titles

1360 HEARTS OF OAK: A DOMESTIC DRAMA IN TWO ACTS. (Theatre Royal, Exeter, 29 May 1879.) London and New York: French, n.d. 30 p.

> An acting edition with a cast list of the Exeter production.

1361 *THE SILVER KING: A DRAMA IN FIVE ACTS. With Henry Herman. (Princess's, 16 November 1882.) London and New York: French, 1907. 175 p.

> An acting edition with cast lists of the first London and New York productions.

1362 SAINTS AND SINNERS: A NEW AND ORIGINAL DRAMA OF MODERN ENGLISH MIDDLE-CLASS LIFE IN FIVE ACTS. (Prince of Wales's, Greenwich, 17 September 1884; Vaudeville, 25 September 1884.) London: Macmillan, 1891. xxix, 142 p.

> The Macmillan uniform edition with a cast list of the first London production, a preface, and an appendix on religion and the stage.

1363 SWEET WILL: A COMEDY IN ONE ACT. (Covent Garden, 5 March 1887; Shaftesbury, 25 July 1890.) London and New York: French, n.d. 24 p.

> An acting edition with a cast list of the first London production.

1364 WEALTH. (Haymarket, 27 April 1889.) No publication details. Var. pag.

> A typescript, located in New York Public Library.

1365 *THE MIDDLEMAN: A PLAY IN FOUR ACTS. (Shaftesbury, 27 August 1889.) London and New York: French, 1907. 127 p.

> An acting edition with cast lists of the first London and New York productions, and a dedicatory letter to E.S. Willard.

1366 JUDAH: AN ORIGINAL PLAY IN THREE ACTS. (Shaftesbury, 21 May 1890.) London and New York: Macmillan, 1894. xxiii, 104 p.

> The Macmillan uniform edition with a cast list of the first London production, and a preface by Joseph Knight.

1367 THE DANCING GIRL: A DRAMA IN FOUR ACTS. (Haymarket, 15 January 1891.) London and New York: French, 1907. 119 p.

An acting edition with a cast list of the first productions
in London and New York, and a dedication to H.B. Tree.

1368 THE CRUSADERS: AN ORIGINAL COMEDY OF MODERN LONDON
LIFE. (Avenue, 2 November 1891.) London: Macmillan, 1893. xii,
115 p.

The Macmillan uniform edition with a cast list of the first
London production and preface by William Archer.

1369 THE BAUBLE SHOP. (Criterion, 26 January 1893.) No publication
details. Var. pag.

A typescript, located in New York Public Library.

1370 THE TEMPTER: A TRAGEDY IN VERSE IN FOUR ACTS. (Haymarket,
20 September 1893.) London and New York: French, 1893. [iii],
108 p.

An acting edition with a cast list of the first London production. The Macmillan uniform edition (London: 1898, xxii,
113 p.) contains a preface by Jones on the performance of
the play and on drama generally.

1371 THE MASQUERADERS: A PLAY IN FOUR ACTS. (St. James's, 28
April 1894.) London: Macmillan, 1899. ix, 113 p.

The Macmillan uniform edition with a cast list of the first
London production. The Readex collection also includes a
privately printed prompt copy (London: Chiswick Press, c.
1894, 84 p.), inscribed by Jones to Traill.

1372 THE CASE OF REBELLIOUS SUSAN: A COMEDY IN THREE ACTS.
(Criterion, 3 October 1894.) London: Macmillan, 1901. x, 118 p.

The Macmillan uniform edition with a preface to "Mrs.
Grundy."

1373 THE TRIUMPH OF THE PHILISTINES AND HOW MR. JORGEN PRESER-
VED THE MORALS OF MARKET PEWBURY UNDER VERY TRYING CIR-
CUMSTANCES: A COMEDY IN THREE ACTS. (St. James's, 11 May
1895.) London: Chiswick Press, 1895. 83 p.

A privately printed promptbook, inscribed by Jones to Traill.
The Readex collection includes a second copy of this edition,
interleaved with manuscript notes.

1374 MICHAEL AND HIS LOST ANGEL: A PLAY IN FIVE ACTS. (Lyceum,
15 January 1896.) London and New York: Macmillan, 1896. xxiv,
107 p.

The Macmillan uniform edition with a preface by Joseph
Knight and an author's note (on the brief run of the play).
The Readex collection also includes a privately printed
promptbook (London: Chiswick Press, 1895, 82 p.).

1375 THE ROGUE'S COMEDY: A PLAY IN THREE ACTS. (Garrick, 21 April
1896.) London: Macmillan, 1898. ix, 118 p.

The Macmillan uniform edition with a cast list of the first
London production.

1376 THE PHYSICIAN: AN ORIGINAL PLAY IN FOUR ACTS. (Criterion,
25 March 1897.) London and New York: French, c. 1899. 105 p.

An acting edition with a cast list of the first London production.

1377 THE LIARS: AN ORIGINAL COMEDY IN FOUR ACTS. (Criterion, 6
October 1897.) London: Chiswick Press, 1897. 91 p.

A privately printed promptbook.

1378 THE MANOEUVRES OF JANE: AN ORIGINAL COMEDY IN FOUR
ACTS. (Haymarket, 29 October 1898.) London and New York: French,
1905. 124 p.

An acting edition with a cast list of the first London production.

1379 MRS. DANE'S DEFENCE: A PLAY IN FOUR ACTS. (Wyndham's, 2
October 1900.) London and New York: Macmillan, 1905. 127 p.

The Macmillan uniform edition with a cast list of the first
London production.

1380 *WHITEWASHING JULIA: AN ORIGINAL COMEDY IN THREE ACTS.
(Garrick, 2 March 1903.) London: Chiswick Press, 1903. 98 p.

A privately printed promptbook.

1381 *THE HEROIC STUBBS: A COMEDY OF A MAN WITH AN IDEAL: IN
FOUR ACTS. (Terry's, 24 January 1906.) London: Chiswick Press,
1906. 99 p.

A privately printed promptbook.

1382 *THE HYPOCRITES: A PLAY IN FOUR ACTS. (Hudson, New York, 30
August 1906; Hicks's, 27 August 1907.) London and New York: French,
1908. 169 p.

An acting edition with cast lists of the first London and New York productions and a dedication to G.P. Baker.

1383 *DOLLY REFORMING HERSELF: A COMEDY IN FOUR ACTS. (Haymarket, 3 November 1908.) London: French, 1910. 112 p.

An acting edition with a cast list of the first London production, press reviews, and a dedication to Ethel Irving.

1384 *MARY GOES FIRST: A COMEDY IN THREE ACTS AND AN EPILOGUE. (Playhouse, 18 September 1913.) London: Bell, 1913. 100 p.

An acting edition with a cast list of the first London production, and a dedication to Marie Tempest.

IV Biography

1385 Blathwayt, Raymond. "Lions in their Dens: Henry Arthur Jones." IDLER, 4 (August 1893), 67-80.

An interview with Jones, briefly covering his life, career, and methods of playwriting.

1386 Hamilton, J. Angus. "Henry Arthur Jones." MUNSEY'S MAGAZINE (New York), 9 (1894), 174-78.

A short resumé of Jones's career, with some biographical information of a gossipy, mundane nature.

1387 "Henry Arthur Jones, Dramatist: Self-Revealed; a Conversation on the Art of Writing Plays with Archibald Henderson." NATION AND ATHE-NAEUM, 38 (December 1925), 349-50; 398-99.

1388 "Henry Arthur Jones." LONDON MERCURY, 19 (February 1929), 340-43.

An obituary notice which includes an extract from Jones's will in which he expressed what his ideals had been and how he felt he had largely failed in them.

1389 Jones, Doris Arthur. TAKING THE CURTAIN CALL: THE LIFE AND LETTERS OF HENRY ARTHUR JONES. New York: Macmillan, 1930. xx, 397 p.

The English edition has only the subtitle for its title. This is still the only extensive biography of Jones, illustrated with many letters. There are useful appendices listing Jones's plays (with dates of production and revival), other writings, a questionnaire on Jones's techniques, and a genealogical table.

1390 Thompson, Marjorie. "Henry Arthur Jones and Wilson Barrett: Some
Correspondence, 1879-1904." TN, 11 (1957), 42-50.

V Critical Studies

1391 Bettany, W.A. Lewis. "The Drama of Modern England, as Viewed by
Mr. H.A. Jones." THEATRE, 22 (October 1893), 203-9.

> A strongly antipathetical review of Jones's ability to reflect
> English society of the period. More assertive than reasoned.

1392 Bulloch, J.M. "Henry Arthur Jones." BOOK BUYER, ser. 3, 16
(1898), 225-29.

> A brief survey of Jones' career to 1897, for which a biblio-
> graphy is also given. Bulloch sees Jones as more important
> than Pinero or Grundy on the grounds that Jones "not only
> practises [dramatic art], he preaches as well."

1393 Beerbohm, Max. "This Inimpedible Mr. Jones." SATURDAY REVIEW,
90 (13 October 1900), 458-59.

> A review of MRS. DANE'S DEFENCE which is also both a
> spirited defense of Jones as a dramatist and an attack on
> critics for their failure to appreciate his abilities.

1394 Dickinson, Thomas H. "Henry Arthur Jones and the Dramatic Renascence."
NORTH AMERICAN REVIEW, 202 (November 1915), 757-68.

> Dickinson accounts for Jones's reception as being the result of
> holding up the mirror of nature too closely to the middle
> classes. The remainder of the article is devoted to surveying
> Jones as an evangelist of dramatic art.

1395 Wauchope, George Armstrong. "Henry Arthur Jones and the Social
Drama." SR, 29 (1921), 147-52.

> A very brief and generalized attempt to account for the
> rise of drama in the 1890's and at placing Jones in the
> forefront of that rise.

1396 Shorey, Paul. HENRY ARTHUR JONES. New York, 1925.

> Reprinted from THE TREND.

1397 Allen, Percy. "Henry Arthur Jones." FORTNIGHTLY REVIEW, n.s.
125 (May 1929), 692-99.

> A general review of the major aspects of Jones's plays and
> dramatic theory.

1398 Cordell, Richard A. HENRY ARTHUR JONES AND THE MODERN
DRAMA. New York: Long and Smith, 1932. xi, 265 p.

> Generally Cordell's study is eminently readable and sound,
> although he is clearly an ardent Jones enthusiast. He deals
> at length with Jones's major works as well as touching on his
> minor contributions, his dramatic theories, and other services
> to drama. The whole is sensibly placed in the context of
> nineteenth- and early twentieth-century drama.

1399 Northend, Majorie. "Henry Arthur Jones and the Development of the
Modern English Drama." RES, 18 (1942), 448-63.

> Northend argues that Jones's chief contribution to drama was
> his ability to compromise "between giving the public what
> they wanted, and making them appreciate better things."
> This made him, with Ibsen, a primary force in the renascence
> of drama.

1400 Shine, Hill, ed. BOOKER MEMORIAL STUDIES: EIGHT ESSAYS ON
VICTORIAN LITERATURE IN MEMORY OF JOHN MANNING BOOKER
1881-1948. Chapel Hill: University of North Carolina Press, 1950.
xiv, 183 p.

> This anthology contains an essay, "Science in the Dramas of
> Henry Arthur Jones," by J.O. Bailey, which examines in
> detail the plays of Jones's middle period to demonstrate Jones's
> use of science in motivating his characters.

JONES, J. WILTON (1853-97)

II Acted Plays—Principal Titles

1401 ON AN ISLAND: A DRAMATIC SKETCH IN WATER-COLOUR. (Theatre Royal, Bradford, 8 March 1879; Vaudeville, 4 February 1882). London and New York: French, n.d. 19 p.

> An acting edition with a cast list of the first Bradford pro-
> duction.

1402 THE GRAND CHRISTMAS PANTOMIME ENTITLED CINDERELLA; OR
HARLEQUIN, THE WICKED DEMON, THE GOOD FAIRY, AND THE
LITTLE GLASS SLIPPER! (Prince's, Manchester, 18 December 1880.)
Manchester: Guardian Letterpress and Lithographic Works, 1880. 16 p.

> An acting edition with a cast list of the Manchester produc-
> tion.

1403 IN AN ATTIC: COMEDIETTA IN ONE ACT. (St. James's, 25 March 1895.) London and New York: French, n.d. 17 p.

> An acting edition with a cast list of the first London production.

KEATS, JOHN (1795-1821)

I Collected Works

1404 Forman, H. Buxton, ed. THE POETICAL AND OTHER WRITINGS OF JOHN KEATS. REVISED WITH ADDITIONS BY MAURICE BUXTON FORMAN. INTRODUCTION BY JOHN MASEFIELD. 8 vols. New York: Scribner's, 1938-39; rpt. New York: Phaeton Press, 1970.

> Volume five contains the plays, OTHO THE GREAT (acted at St. Martin's Theatre, London, 26 November 1950) and KING STEPHEN (unacted). Each play is prefaced by brief, but useful, editorial notes, and variant readings are given for many lines in each play. Volume five also contains Keats's theatrical reviews.

III Bibliographies

1405 Macgillivray, J.R., ed. KEATS: A BIBLIOGRAPHY AND REFERENCE GUIDE, WITH AN ESSAY ON KEATS' REPUTATION. Toronto: University of Toronto Press, 1949. lxxxi, 210 p.

IV Biography

1406 Rollins, Hyder Edward, ed. THE LETTERS OF JOHN KEATS, 1814-1821. 2 vols. Cambridge, Mass.: Harvard University Press, 1958. xxii, 442; xiii, 440 p.

> A carefully edited and well-indexed collection in which there are many references to the theatre and Keats's own plays.

1407 Bate, Walter Jackson. JOHN KEATS. Cambridge, Mass.: Harvard University Press, 1964. xvii, 732 p.

> The standard biography.

V Critical Studies

1408 Hewlett, Dorothy. "OTHO THE GREAT." KSMB, 4 (1952), 1.

> Hewlett makes brief comments on the play's first production at St. Martin's theatre, 26 November 1950.

1409 Jones, Leonidas M. "Keats's Theatrical Reviews in the CHAMPION." KSJ, 3 (1954), 55-65.

> Identification and discussion of the reviews.

1410 Slote, Bernice. KEATS AND THE DRAMATIC PRINCIPLE. Lincoln: University of Nebraska Press, 1958. [vii], 229 p.

> A comprehensive study of Keats's relationship with the theatre, the dramatic elements in his poetry, and his two plays.

1411 Beaudry, Harry Richard. "The English Theatre and John Keats." Ph.D. Dissertation, Duke University, 1968. 277 p. (DA#69-3885)

> An examination of Keats as a dramatic critic, playgoer, and playwright.

KEMBLE, CHARLES (1775-1854)

II Acted Plays—Principal Titles

1412 *THE POINT OF HONOUR: A COMEDY IN THREE ACTS. (Haymarket, 15 July 1800.) Cumberland's British Theatre, vol. 28. London: Cumberland, n.d. 44 p.

> An acting edition with "Remarks" by D--G [George Daniel].

1413 *THE WANDERER; OR, THE RIGHTS OF HOSPITALITY: A DRAMA IN THREE ACTS. (Covent Garden, 12 January 1808.) London: Appleyards, 1808. 64 p.

> The play is an adaptation of Kotzebue's EDUARD IN SCHOTTLAND. A revised version appeared at Covent Garden, 26 November 1829, as THE ROYAL FUGITIVE.

1414 *PLOT AND COUNTERPLOT; OR, THE PORTRAIT OF CERVANTES; A FARCE IN TWO ACTS. (Haymarket, 30 June 1808.) London: Cumberland, n.d. 39 p.

> An acting edition with "Remarks" by D--G [George Daniel].

KENNEY, JAMES (1780-1849)

II Acted Plays—Principal Titles

1415 RAISING THE WIND: A FARCE IN TWO ACTS. (Covent Garden, 5 November 1803.) London: Longman and Rees, 1803. 37 p.

> Includes a cast list of the first London production.

1416 MATRIMONY: A PETIT OPERA IN TWO ACTS. (Drury Lane, 20 November 1804.) 3rd ed. London: Longman, Hurst, Rees and Orme, 1804. iv, 46 p.

   There is a preface by Kenney and a cast list of the first London production.

1417 FALSE ALARMS; OR, MY COUSIN: A COMIC OPERA IN THREE ACTS. (Drury Lane, 12 January 1807.) London: Longman, Hurst, Rees and Orme, 1807. 86 p.

   There is a preface by Kenney and a cast list of the first London production.

1418 ELLA ROSENBERG: A MELO-DRAMA IN TWO ACTS. (Drury Lane, 19 November 1807.) London: Longman, Hurst, Rees and Orme, 1807. 41 p.

   Includes a cast list of the first London production.

1419 BLIND BOY: A MELO-DRAMA IN TWO ACTS. (Covent Garden, 1 December 1807.) London: Longman, Hurst, Rees and Orme, 1808. 36 p.

   Includes a cast list of the first London production.

1420 THE WORLD! A COMEDY IN FIVE ACTS. (Drury Lane, 31 March 1808.) London: Longman, Hurst, Rees and Orme, 1808. 94 p.

   Includes a cast list of the first London production.

1421 TURN OUT! A MUSICAL FARCE IN TWO ACTS. (Lyceum, 7 March 1812.) 2nd ed. London: Sharpe and Hailes, 1812. 47 p.

   Includes a cast list of the first London production.

1422 LOVE, LAW, AND PHYSIC: A FARCE IN TWO ACTS. (Covent Garden, 20 November 1812.) Dublin: T. Charles, 1821. 34 p.

   Includes a cast list of the first London production.

1423 THE PORTFOLIO; OR, THE FAMILY OF ANGLADE: A DRAMA IN TWO ACTS. (Covent Garden, 1 February 1816.) London: Longman, Hurst, Rees, Orme and Brown, 1816. 52 p.

   Includes a cast list of the first London production.

1424 SWEETHEARTS AND WIVES: [A COMIC OPERA] IN THREE ACTS. (Haymarket, 7 July 1823.) The Acting American Theatre. Philadelphia: A.R. Poole, n.d. 66 p.

   Includes a cast list of a Philadelphia production in 1825; this copy is a promptbook (New York Public Library).

1425 SPRING AND AUTUMN; OR, MARRIED FOR MONEY: A COMIC
DRAMA IN TWO ACTS. (Haymarket, 6 September 1827.) Dicks' Standard Plays, no. 708. [London: Dicks], n.d. 14 p.

> An acting edition with a cast list of the first London produc-
> tion.

1426 THE SICILIAN VESPERS: AN HISTORICAL TRAGEDY. (Surrey, 21
September 1840.) London: John Miller, 1840. 66 p.

> Includes a cast list of the first London production.

KNOWLES, JAMES SHERIDAN (1784-1862)

I Collected Works

1427 THE DRAMATIC WORKS OF JAMES SHERIDAN KNOWLES. 3 vols.
London: Edward Moxon, 1841-43.

> Contents: volume one: CAIUS GRACCHUS, VIRGINIUS,
> WILLIAM TELL, ALFRED THE GREAT, THE HUNCHBACK;
> volume two: THE WIFE, THE BEGGAR OF BETHNAL GREEN,
> THE DAUGHTER, THE LOVE-CHASE, WOMAN'S WIT; volume
> three: THE MAID OF MARIENPORT, LOVE, JOHN OF
> PROCIDA, OLD MAIDS, THE ROSE OF ARAGON. There
> are cast lists for each play; this edition is in the Readex
> collection.

1428 THE DRAMATIC WORKS OF JAMES SHERIDAN KNOWLES. New ed. in
1 vol. London: Routledge, Warnes, & Routledge, 1859. vi, 448; 457 p.

> Plays are as in the Moxon edition (item 1427) with the addi-
> tion of THE SECRETARY. There is a portrait of Knowles, a
> brief introduction, and cast lists.

1429 Harvey, Frances, ed. VARIOUS DRAMATIC WORKS OF JAMES SHERI-
DAN KNOWLES. NOW FIRST COLLECTED AND PRIVATELY PRINTED
FOR JAMES MCHENRY. 2 vols. London: Privately printed, 1874.

> Includes fragments and other previously unpublished material.
> Only twenty-five copies printed; included in the Readex
> collection.

II Acted Plays—Principal Titles

1430 CAIUS GRACCHUS: A TRAGEDY IN FIVE ACTS. (Belfast, 13 February
1815; Drury Lane, 18 November 1823.) Glasgow: J. Ridgway, 1823.
101 p.

Includes a dedication to John Patterson (who first suggested that Knowles write the play) and a word of thanks to Macready and Elliston for their help.

1431 VIRGINIUS: A TRAGEDY IN FIVE ACTS. (Glasgow, 1820; Covent Garden, 17 May 1820.) London: James Ridgway, 1820. 85 p.

Includes a preface, a dedication to Macready, and a cast list of the Covent Garden production.

1432 WILLIAM TELL: A PLAY IN FIVE ACTS. (Drury Lane, 11 May 1825.) London: Thomas Dolby, n.d. 83 p.

Includes a cast list of the first London production; this copy is a promptbook (New York Public Library with some manuscript notes.

1433 THE HUNCHBACK: A PLAY IN FIVE ACTS. (Covent Garden, 5 April 1832.) London: Moxon, 1832. 118 p.

Includes a preface and cast list of the first London production; also included in the Readex collection is a New York edition of 1882.

1434 THE WIFE; A TALE OF MANTUA: A PLAY IN FIVE ACTS. (Covent Garden, 24 April 1833.) 3rd ed. London: Moxon, 1833. 120 p.

Includes a preface and a cast list of the first London production; the Readex copy is a promptbook (New York Public Library) with extensive manuscript notes.

1435 THE LOVE-CHASE: A COMEDY IN FIVE ACTS. (Haymarket, 9 October 1837.) London: Music-Publishing Co., n.d. 64 p.

An acting edition with a cast list of the first London production; also includes "Remarks" and a memoir of Miss Elphinstone, the actress, by D--G [George Daniel].

1436 WOMAN'S WIT; OR, LOVE'S DISGUISES: A PLAY IN FIVE ACTS. (Covent Garden, 23 May 1838.) London: Moxon, 1838. 120 p.

Includes a prefatory note by Knowles and a cast list of the first London production; the Readex copy is a promptbook (New York Public Library) with manuscript notes.

IV Biography

1437 "Sheridan Knowles." BLACKWOOD'S EDINBURGH MAGAZINE, 94 (1863), 429-47.

An obituary, including a critical survey of a few of Knowles's better-known plays.

1438 Knowles, Richard Brinsley. THE LIFE OF JAMES SHERIDAN KNOWLES. London: Privately printed for James McHenry, 1872. xi, 177 p.

> A limited edition of twenty-five copies.

V Critical Studies

1439 Meeks, Leslie Howard. SHERIDAN KNOWLES AND THE THEATRE OF HIS TIME. Bloomington, [Ind.]: Principia Press, 1933. ix, 239 p.

> A comprehensive account of Knowles's career. It is thorough and well-documented, and an appendix gives a list of performances of THE HUNCHBACK, the playbill for Knowles's New York benefit in April 1835, and receipts for some American productions of his plays. There is a bibliography of Knowles's work.

LEMON, MARK (1809-70)

II Acted Plays—Principal Titles

1440 THE P.L.; OR, 30, STRAND! A BURLETTA IN ONE ACT. (Strand, 25 April 1836.) London: Duncombe, n.d. 20 p.

> An acting edition with a cast list of the first London production.

1441 ARNOLD OF WINKELRIED; OR, THE FIGHT OF SEMPACH! A DRAMA IN FIVE ACTS. (Surrey, 25 July 1836.) London: Duncombe, n.d. 49 p.

> An acting edition with a cast list of the first London production.

1442 A FAMILIAR FRIEND: A FARCE IN ONE ACT. (Olympic, 8 February 1840.) London: James Pattie, n.d. 23 p.

> An acting edition with a cast list of the first London production.

1443 THE GENTLEMAN IN BLACK: A FARCE IN ONE ACT. (Olympic, 9 September 1840.) Dicks' Standard Plays, no. 776. London: Dicks, n.d. 16 p.

> An acting edition with a cast list of the first London production.

1444 WHAT WILL THE WORLD SAY? A COMEDY IN FIVE ACTS. (Covent Garden, 25 September 1841.) London: R. Bryant, 1841. 128 p.

> Includes a cast list of the first London production; the Readex

copy is a promptbook with some manuscript notes.

1445 GRANDFATHER WHITEHEAD: AN ORIGINAL DRAMA IN TWO ACTS. (Haymarket, 31 September 1842.) London: Webster, n.d. 32 p.

An acting edition with a cast list of the first London production.

1446 HEARTS ARE TRUMPS: A DOMESTIC DRAMA IN THREE ACTS. (Strand, 30 July 1849.) Acting National Drama 162. London: National Acting Drama Office, n.d. 36 p.

1447 THE RAILWAY BELLE: A FARCE IN ONE ACT. (Adelphi, 20 November 1854.) Lacy's Acting Edition, no. 247. London: Lacy, n.d. 19 p.

With a cast list of the first London production.

IV Biography

1448 Hatton, Joseph. WITH A SHOW IN THE NORTH: REMINISCENCES OF MARK LEMON. . . . TOGETHER WITH MARK LEMON'S REVISED TEXT OF FALSTAFF. London: Wm. H. Allen, 1871. 284 p.

An account of some of Lemon's activities as an amateur actor.

V Critical Studies

1449 Adrian, Arthur A. MARK LEMON: FIRST EDITOR OF PUNCH. London: Oxford University Press, 1966. xiv, 241 p.

Adrian concentrates on Lemon and PUNCH, but some attention is given to Lemon the playwright and amateur actor. An appendix lists his plays and operas.

LEWES, GEORGE HENRY ["SLINGSBY LAWRENCE"] (1817-78)

II Acted Plays—Principal Titles

1450 THE NOBLE HEART: A TRAGEDY IN THREE ACTS. (Theatre Royal, Manchester, 16 April 1849; Olympic, 19 February 1850.) London: Chapman and Hall, 1850. 47 p.

An acting edition with a preface by Lewes to Arthur Helps (on the stupidities of some aspects of the censorship) and a cast list of the London production. The Readex collection also includes a second copy (Spencer's Boston Theatre, no. 173. Boston: Spencers, [185-- ?]. 39 p.).

1451 THE GAME OF SPECULATION: A COMEDY IN THREE ACTS. (Lyceum, 2 October 1851.) London: Lacy, n.d. 44 p.

> An acting edition with a cast list of the first London production.

1452 A CHAIN OF EVENTS: A DRAMATIC STORY, IN EIGHT ACTS. With Charles Mathews. (Lyceum, 12 April 1852.) London: Lacy, n.d. 84 p.

> An acting edition with a cast list of the first London production.

1453 A STRANGE HISTORY: A DRAMATIC TALE IN EIGHT CHAPTERS. With Charles Mathews. (Lyceum, 29 March 1853.) London: Lacy, n.d. 64 p.

> An acting edition with a cast list of the first London production.

1454 A COZY COUPLE: A FARCE IN ONE ACT. (Lyceum, April 1854.) London: Lacy, n.d. 28 p.

> An acting edition with a cast list of the first London production.

1455 BUCKSTONE'S ADVENTURE WITH A POLISH PRINCESS: AN ORIGINAL FARCE IN ONE ACT. (Haymarket, 4 July 1855.) London: Lacy, n.d. 24 p.

> An acting edition with a cast list of the first London production. There are some manuscript notes and deletions.

V Critical Studies

1456 Hirshberg, Edgar W. "George Henry Lewes as Playwright and Dramatic Critic." Ph.D. Dissertation, Yale University, 1951. 184 p.

LEWIS, DAVID LEOPOLD (1828-90)

II Acted Plays—Principal Titles

1457 THE BELLS: A DRAMA IN THREE ACTS (ADAPTED FROM "THE POLISH JEW," A DRAMATIC STUDY [BY] MM. ERCKMANN-CHATRIAN). (Lyceum, 25 November 1871.) London and New York: French, n.d. 30 p.

> An acting edition with a cast list of the first London production; with some manuscript notes and deletions.

LEWIS, MATTHEW GREGORY (1775-1815)

II Acted Plays—Principal Titles

1458 *THE CASTLE SPECTRE: A DRAMA IN FIVE ACTS. (Drury Lane, 14 December 1797.) London: J. Bell, 1798. vi, 103 p.

> This popular play went through eight editions in 1798.

1459 *THE TWINS; OR, IS IT HE OR HIS BROTHER? (Drury Lane, 8 April 1799.)

> For publication details of this play see below, item 1478.

1460 *THE EAST INDIAN: A COMEDY IN FIVE ACTS. (Drury Lane, 22 April 1799.) 2nd ed. London: J. Bell, 1800. 87 p.

1461 ADELMORN, THE OUTLAW: A ROMANTIC DRAMA IN THREE ACTS. (Drury Lane, 4 May 1801.) 2nd ed. London: J. Bell, 1801. x, 101 p.

> Includes a lengthy preface by Lewis in which he defends his play against a number of criticisms; there is also a cast list of the first London production.

1462 ALFONSO, KING OF CASTILLE: A TRAGEDY IN FIVE ACTS. (Covent Garden, 15 January 1802.) London: J. Bell, 1801. vii, 111 p.

> Includes a preface by Lewis explaining why he chose to publish his play before it was acted. The Readex collection also has a second edition (1802) with a cast list of the first London production.

1463 THE HARPER'S DAUGHTER; OR, LOVE AND AMBITION: A TRAGEDY IN FIVE ACTS. (Covent Garden, 4 May 1803.) Philadelphia: M. Carey, 1813. 76 p.

> With a cast list of a Philadelphia (?) production.

1464 RUGANTINO; OR, THE BRAVO OF VENICE: A GRAND ROMANTIC MELODRAMA IN TWO ACTS. (Covent Garden, 18 October 1805.) 2nd ed. London: J.F. Hughes, 1806. vii, 55 p.

> With a preface by Lewis and a cast list of the first London production.

1465 THE WOOD DAEMON; OR, "THE CLOCK HAS STRUCK": A GRAND ROMANTIC MELO-DRAMA IN THREE ACTS. (Drury Lane, 1 April

1807.) London: J. Scales, n.d. 30 p.

With a cast list of the first London production.

1466 ADELGITHA; OR, THE FRUITS OF A SINGLE ERROR: A TRAGEDY IN
FIVE ACTS. (Drury Lane, 30 April 1807.) London: J.F. Hughes, 1806.
x, 127 p.

With a preface by Lewis explaining the historical basis of
the play.

1467 VENONI; OR, THE NOVICE OF ST. MARK'S: A DRAMA IN THREE
ACTS. (Drury Lane, 1 December 1808.) London: Longman, Hurst,
Rees, and Orme, 1809. 103 p.

With a preface by Lewis ("This will probably be the last of
my dramatic attempts. The act of composing has ceased to
amuse me. . . . ") and a cast list of the first London production. Two versions of the third act are printed.

1468 RAYMOND AND AGNES, THE TRAVELERS BENIGHTED; OR, THE
BLEEDING NUN OF LINDENBERG: AN INTERESTING DRAMA IN TWO
ACTS. (Norwich, 22 November 1809.) French's Acting Drama, no. 191.
New York: French, n.d. 24 p.

An acting edition with cast lists of several London and New
York productions. Peck (item 1476) lists this work as "spu-
rious."

1469 TIMOUR THE TARTAR: A GRAND ROMANTIC MELO-DRAMA IN TWO
ACTS. (Covent Garden, 29 April 1811.) London: Lowndes and Hobbs,
[1811]. 56 p.

With a preface by Lewis ("This trifle was written merely to
oblige Mr. Harris, who prest me very earnestly to give him
a Spectacle, in which Horses might be introduced. . . . ")
and a cast list of the first London production.

1470 ONE O'CLOCK! OR, THE KNIGHT OF THE WOOD DAEMON: A
GRAND MUSICAL ROMANCE IN THREE ACTS. (Lyceum, 1 August
1811.) London: Lowndes and Hobbs, [1811]. 79 p.

With a cast list of the first London production.

1471 RICH AND POOR: A COMIC OPERA IN THREE ACTS. (Lyceum, 22
July 1812.) 2nd ed. London: C. Chapple, 1814. 80 p.

With a brief preface by Lewis and a cast list of the first
London production.

IIa Unacted Plays

1472 *VILLAGE VIRTURES: A DRAMATIC SATIRE IN TWO PARTS. London:
J. Bell, 1796. 45 p.

1473 *THE MINISTER: A TRAGEDY IN FIVE ACTS. TRANSLATED FROM
THE GERMAN OF SCHILLER BY M.G. LEWIS. 2nd ed. London: J.
Bell, 1798.

1474 *ROLLA; OR, THE PERUVIAN HERO: A TRAGEDY IN FIVE ACTS.
TRANSLATED FROM THE GERMAN OF KOTZEBUE BY M.G. LEWIS.
London: J. Bell, 1799.

IV Biography

1475 [Baron-Wilson, Margaret]. THE LIFE AND CORRESPONDENCE OF M.G.
LEWIS . . . WITH MANY PIECES IN PROSE AND VERSE, NEVER BE-
FORE PUBLISHED. 2 vols. London: Henry Colburn, 1839.

> Superseded by Peck's biography (item 1475a).

1475a Peck, Louis Francis. A LIFE OF MATTHEW G. LEWIS. Cambridge,
Mass.: Harvard University Press, 1961. ix, 331 p.

> An excellent biography which includes a lengthy and thorough
> study of Lewis's plays. The discussion is well documented,
> and there are bibliographies of primary and secondary sources.

V Critical Studies

1476 _____. "M.G. Lewis and the Larpent Catalogue." HLQ, 5 (1941–42),
382–84.

> Points out that "six Larpent manuscripts included in the
> CATALOGUE [item 2401, below] . . . should be added
> to Lewis's list."

1477 ADELSPERGER, W. "Aspects of Staging in ADELGITHA." OSUTCB,
no. 7 (1960), 14–34.

1478 Guthke, Karl S. "M.G. Lewis' THE TWINS." HLQ, 25 (1962), 189–
223.

> The first publication of the play (from the licensing manu-
> script in the Huntington Library) and a short critical intro-
> duction.

1479 _____. "F.L. Schroeder, J.F. Regnard, and M.G. Lewis." HLQ, 27
(1963), 79-82.

>Discusses the sources of THE TWINS.

LOVELL, GEORGE WILLIAM (1804-78)

II Acted Plays—Principal Titles

1480 THE PROVOST OF BRUGES: A TRAGEDY. (Drury Lane, 10 February
1836.) London: John Macrone, 1836. 98 p.

>Includes a preface, a dedication to W.C. Macready, and
>a cast list of the first London production.

1481 LOVE'S SACRIFICE; OR, THE RIVAL MERCHANTS: A PLAY IN FIVE
ACTS. (Covent Garden, 12 September 1842.) London: Davidson, n.d.
72 p.

>An acting edition, with a preface, a dedication to John
>Vandenhoff, and "Remarks" by D--G [George Daniel].

1482 THE WIFE'S SECRET: AN ORIGINAL PLAY IN FIVE ACTS. (Park
Theatre, New York, 12 October 1846; Haymarket, 17 January 1848.)
London and New York: French, n.d. 62 p.

>An acting edition with a cast list of the first London produc-
>tion; the Readex copy is a promptbook with manuscript notes.

1483 LOOK BEFORE YOU LEAP; OR, WOOINGS AND WEDDINGS: A
COMEDY IN FIVE ACTS. (Haymarket, 29 October 1846.) London:
National Acting Drama Office, n.d. 83 p.

>An acting edition with a preface by the author and a cast
>list of the first London production; the Readex copy is a
>promptbook with manuscript notes.

V Critical Studies

1484 Dunkel, Wilbur D. "The Career of George W. Lovell." TN, 5 (1950-
51), 52-59.

>Claims that Lovell "wrote highly actable plays which kept
>alive original playwrighting at the nadir of the English
>theatre."

LOVER, SAMUEL (1797-1868)

I Collected Works

1485 COLLECTED WRITINGS. 10 vols. The Treasure Trove Edition. Boston: Little, Brown, 1901-3.

1486 THE WORKS OF SAMUEL LOVER. 6 vols. New Library Edition. Boston: Little, Brown, 1902.

> Volume five contains some of the plays: THE WHITE HORSE OF THE PEPPERS, RORY O'MORE, THE GREEK BOY, THE HAPPY MAN, THE HALL PORTER, MACCARTHY MORE. There is a biographical and critical introduction by J.J. Roche.

II Acted Plays—Principal Titles

1487 *THE BEAU IDEAL (Olympic, 9 November 1835.) LC.

1488 RORY O'MORE: A COMIC DRAMA IN THREE ACTS. (Adelphi, 29 September 1837.) London: Chapman and Hall, n.d. 51 p.

> An acting edition with a cast list of the first London production.

1489 THE WHITE HORSE OF THE PEPPERS. A COMIC DRAMA IN TWO ACTS. (Haymarket, 26 May 1838.) The Minor Drama, no. 18. New York: Berford, 1847. 44 p.

> An acting edition with a short editorial introduction and cast lists of Haymarket and Park theatre, New York, productions. The Readex collection also contains a promptbook (Princeton University Library), interleaved with manuscript notes.

1490 THE HAPPY MAN: AN EXTRAVAGANZA IN ONE ACT. (Haymarket, 20 May 1839.) London: Chapman and Hall, n.d. 20 p.

> An acting edition with a cast list of the first London production; the Readex copy is a promptbook (New York Public Library), interleaved with manuscript notes.

1491 THE HALL PORTER: A COMIC DRAMA IN TWO ACTS. (English Opera House, 26 July 1839.) London: Chapman and Hall, n.d. 31 p.

> An acting edition with a cast list of the first London production.

1492 THE GREEK BOY: A MUSICAL DRAMA IN TWO ACTS. (Covent Garden, 29 September 1840.) London: Sherwood, Gilbert, and Piper, n.d. 33 p.

> An acting edition with a cast list of the first London production and a dedication to Madame Vestris.

1493 IL PADDY WHACK IN ITALIA: AN OPERETTA IN ONE ACT. (English Opera House, April 1841.) Duncombe's British Theatre, no. 346. London: Duncombe, n.d. 30 p.

> An acting edition with a cast list of the first London production.

1494 BARNEY THE BARON: A FARCE IN ONE ACT. (Adelphi, 16 February 1857.) Dicks' Standard Drama, no. 323. [London: Dicks, n.d.] 8 p.

> An acting edition with a cast list of an unspecified production.

1495 MACCARTHY MORE; OR, POSSESSION NINE POINTS OF THE LAW: A COMIC DRAMA IN TWO ACTS. (Lyceum, 1 April 1861.) London and New York: French, n.d. 38 p.

IV Biography

1496 Bernard, Bayle. THE LIFE OF SAMUEL LOVER, R.H.A., ARTISTIC LITERARY, AND MUSICAL, WITH SELECTIONS FROM HIS UNPUBLISHED PAPERS AND CORRESPONDENCE. 2 vols. London: H.S. King, 1874. xxii, 348; viii, 205 p.

1497 Symington, Andrew James. SAMUEL LOVER: A BIOGRAPHICAL SKETCH, WITH SELECTIONS FROM HIS WRITINGS AND CORRESPONDENCE. London: Blackie & Son, 1880. 256 p.

MALTBY, C. ALFRED (d. 1901)

II Acted Plays—Principal Titles

1498 JUST MY LUCK: AN ENTIRELY ORIGINAL FARCE. (Olympic, 1 May 1852.) London and New York: French, n.d. 15 p.

> An acting edition with a cast list of the first London production.

1499 SHOULD THIS MEET THE EYE: AN ORIGINAL FARCE IN ONE ACT. (Lyceum, 10 June 1872.) London and New York: French, n.d. 20 p.

An acting edition with a cast list of the first London production.

1500 TAKEN BY STORM: AN ORIGINAL COMEDIETTA. (Avenue, November 1884.) London and New York: French, n.d. 14 p.

An acting edition with a cast list of the first London production.

MARSTON, JOHN WESTLAND (1819-90)

I Collected Works

1501 THE DRAMATIC AND POETICAL WORKS OF WESTLAND MARSTON. 2 vols. London: Chatto and Windus, 1876. 360; 395 p.

Contents: volume one: STRATHMORE, MARIE DE MERANIE, LIFE FOR LIFE, A LIFE'S RANSOM, THE PATRICIAN'S DAUGHTER, ANNE BLAKE; volume two: DONNA DIANA, THE FAVOURITE OF FORTUNE, PURE GOLD, THE WIFE'S PORTRAIT, A HARD STRUGGLE, BOROUGH POLITICS, Dramatic Scenes and Fragments, Sonnets, General Poems. As Marston states in his preface, some of these works received considerable revision after their first production or publication, and are here printed in revised form.

II Acted Plays—Principal Titles

1502 THE PATRICIAN'S DAUGHTER: A TRAGEDY IN FIVE ACTS. (Drury Lane, 10 December 1842; Sadler's Wells, 26 August 1846.) 4th ed. Enlarged and adapted for representation. London: C. Mitchell, 1843. 86 p.

An acting edition with a dedication to W.C. Macready, a preface, the preface to the first edition, and a cast list of the first London production. The Readex collection also includes a Lacy acting edition (London: n.d., 48 p.).

1503 BOROUGH POLITICS: A COMIC DRAMA IN TWO ACTS. (Haymarket, 27 June 1846.) National Acting Drama, no. 132. London: Webster, n.d. 24 p.

An acting edition with a cast list of the first London production.

1504 THE HEART AND THE WORLD: A PLAY IN FIVE ACTS. (Haymarket, 4 October 1847.) London: C. Mitchell, 1847. 85 p.

An acting edition with a preface and a cast list of the first London production.

1505 STRATHMORE: A TRAGIC PLAY IN FIVE ACTS. (Haymarket, 20 June 1849.) London: C. Mitchell, 1849. x, 91 p.

An acting edition with a dedication to Sir William Allan, a preface, and a cast list of the first London production.

1506 PHILIP OF FRANCE AND MARIE DE MÉRANIE: A TRAGEDY IN FIVE ACTS. (Olympic, 4 November 1850.) London: C. Mitchell, 1850. xi, 84 p.

An acting edition with a dedication to Helen Faucit, a preface, and a cast list of the first London production.

1507 ANNE BLAKE: A PLAY IN FIVE ACTS. (Princess's, 28 October 1852.) Boston Theatre, no. 57. Boston: Spencer, n.d. 35 p.

An acting edition with cast lists of productions in London, Boston, and New York. The Readex collection also includes a different copy (London: 1852, 68 p.) which has a dedication to Mr. and Mrs. Charles Kean and a preface.

1508 A LIFE'S RANSOM: A PLAY IN FIVE ACTS. (Lyceum, 16 February 1857.) London: C. Mitchell, 1857. xvi, 50 p.

An acting edition with a dedication to Forbes Winslow, a cast list of the first London production, and a "Preface; including Remarks on the Principles of the Poetic Drama."

1509 A HARD STRUGGLE: A DOMESTIC DRAMA IN ONE ACT. (Lyceum, 1 February 1858.) Boston Theatre, no. 161. Boston: Spencer, n.d. 21 p.

An acting edition with cast lists of British and American productions; interleaved, with manuscript notes. The Readex collection also has a Lacy acting edition (London: n.d., 28 p.), which includes a cast list of the first London production. This copy is also interleaved with manuscript notes.

1510 *THE WIFE'S PORTRAIT: A HOUSEHOLD PICTURE UNDER TWO LIGHTS. (Haymarket, 10 March 1862.) Acting Edition, no. 806. London: Lacy, n.d. 30 p.

With a cast list of the first London production.

1511 PURE GOLD: A PLAY IN FOUR ACTS. (Sadler's Wells, 9 November 1863.) London: Lacy, n.d. 66 p.

An acting edition with a cast list of the first London production; interleaved, with manuscript notes.

1512 *DONNA DIANA. (Princess's, 2 January 1864). LC. See item 1501.

1513 *THE FAVOURITE OF FORTUNE. (Haymarket, 2 April 1866.) LC. See item 1501.

1514 *LIFE FOR LIFE. (Lyceum, 6 March 1869.) LC. See item 1501.

1515 *UNDER FIRE. (Vaudeville, 1 April 1885.) LC.

IV Biography

1516 "The Late Westland Marston: Recollections by a Friend." PALL MALL GAZETTE, 59 (10 January 1890), 2.

1517 "Dr. Westland Marston." ATHENAEUM, no. 3246 (11 May 1890), 57-58.

V Critical Studies

1518 Clarke, Herbert E. "John Westland Marston." THE POETS AND THE POETRY OF THE NINETEENTH CENTURY: FREDERICK TENNYSON TO ARTHUR HUGH CLOUGH. Ed. Alfred H. Miles. London: Routledge, 1905. 611-16.

A short biographical and critical account of the man and his work.

1519 Wood, Lawrence A. "John Westland Marston, LL.D., Neo-Elizabethan Dramatist in the Victorian Age." Ph.D. Dissertation, Western Reserve University, 1955. 256 p.

1520 Thomson, Fred C. "A Crisis in Early Victorian Drama: John Westland Marston and the Syncretics." VS, 9 (1965-66), 375-98.

A close, scholarly discussion of Marston's THE PATRICIAN'S DAUGHTER which Thomson views as an experimental tragic verse drama which "failed because of an ambivalent commitment to the implications" of Syncretism. (The later theory was a "science of coalition" which "endeavoured to unite and harmonize what was true, from whatever source, filtering out the false and prejudiced.")

MATHEWS, CHARLES JAMES (1803-78)

For Mathews as actor and manager, see items 2983-86.

II Acted Plays—Principal Titles

1521 MY WIFE'S MOTHER: A COMIC DRAMA IN TWO ACTS. (Haymarket, 3 July 1833.) Lacy's Acting Edition, vol. 23. London: Lacy, n.d. 36 p.

>   Includes a cast list of the first London production.

1522 TRUTH: A ROMANTIC DRAMA IN ONE ACT. (Adelphi, 10 March 1834.) Acting National Drama, vol. 3. London: Chapman and Hall, [1838]. vi, 23 p.

>   With a cast list of the first London production and a "Biographical Sketch" of Mathews by B.W. (unidentified).

1523 THE HUMPBACKED LOVER: AN INTERLUDE IN ONE ACT. (Olympic, 7 December 1835.) London: Cumberland, n.d. 31 p.

>   An acting edition with a cast list of the first London production and with "Remarks" and a memoir of Mathews by D--G [George Daniel].

1524 WHY DID YOU DIE? A PETITE COMEDY IN ONE ACT. (Olympic, 20 November 1837.) Acting National Drama, vol. 2. London: Chapman and Hall, n.d. 28 p.

>   With a cast list of the first London production.

1525 THE RINGDOVES: A FARCE IN ONE ACT. (Olympic, 11 December 1837.) Acting National Drama, vol. 3. London: National Acting Drama Office, n.d. 28 p.

>   With a cast list of the first London production.

1526 BLACK DOMINO: A MUSICAL BURLETTA IN ONE ACT. (Olympic, 18 January 1838.) Acting National Drama, vol. 3. London: Chapman and Hall, 1838. 31 p.

>   With a cast list of the first London production; the play is adapted from Scribe's LE DOMINO NOIR.

1527 PATTER VERSUS CLATTER: A FARCE IN ONE ACT: (Olympic, 21 May 1838.) Lacy's Acting Edition, vol. 118. London and New York: French, n.d. 22 p.

With an incomplete cast list for the first London production.

1528 MARRIED FOR MONEY: A COMEDY IN THREE ACTS. (Drury Lane, 10 October 1855.) Lacy's Acting Edition, vol. 117. London and New York: French, n.d. 44 p.

With a cast list of the first London production.

1529 A BULL IN A CHINA SHOP: A COMEDY IN TWO ACTS. (Boston, 1864.) Spencer's Universal Stage, no. 26. Boston: Charles H. Spencer, n.d. 25 p.

An acting edition with cast lists of two Boston productions and a memoir of the American actor Charles R. Thorne, Jr.

1530 MY AWFUL DAD: A COMEDY IN TWO ACTS. (Gaiety, 13 September 1875.) Lacy's Acting Edition, vol. 117. London and New York: French, n.d. 53 p.

With a cast list of the first London production.

MERITT, PAUL (d. 1895)

II Acted Plays—Principal Titles

1531 GLIN GATH; OR, THE MAN IN THE CLEFT: A DRAMA IN FOUR ACTS. (Grecian, 1 April 1872.) London and New York: French, n.d. 44 p.

An acting edition with a cast list of the first London production.

1532 LINKED BY LOVE: A DOMESTIC COMEDY IN THREE ACTS. (Grecian, 19 July 1872.) London and New York: French, n.d. 32 p.

An acting edition with a cast list of the first London production. Also known under the title THAD; OR, LINKED BY LOVE.

1533 "BRITISH BORN": A NEW AND ORIGINAL DRAMA OF NATIONAL AND DOMESTIC INTEREST IN A PROLOGUE AND THREE ACTS. With Henry Pettitt. (Grecian, 17 October 1872.) London and New York: French, n.d. 48 p.

An acting edition with a cast list of an unspecified production.

1534 CHOPSTICKS AND SPIKINS: A FARCE. (Grecian, 25 September 1873.) London and New York: French, n.d. 20 p.

>An acting edition with a cast list of the first London production.

1535 *VELVET AND RAGS: A SPANISH ROMANCE OF THE PRESENT DAY: PROLOGUE AND THREE ACTS. With George Conquest. (Grecian, 6 April 1874.) London and New York: French, n.d. 46 p.

>An acting edition with a cast list of the first London production.

1536 *HAND & GLOVE; OR, PAGE 13 OF THE BLACK BOOK: A DRAMA IN THREE ACTS. With George Conquest. (Grecian, 25 May 1874.) London and New York: French, n.d. 42 p.

>An acting edition with a cast list of an unspecified production.

1537 THE WORD OF HONOUR: A JERSEY LOVE STORY: AN ORIGINAL DRAMA IN THREE ACTS. (Grecian, 22 October 1874.) London and New York: French, n.d. 28 p.

>An acting edition with a cast list of the first London production.

1538 THE GOLDEN PLOUGH: A NEW AND ENTIRELY ORIGINAL MELODRAMATIC ROMANCE IN FOUR ACTS. (Adelphi, 11 August 1877.) London and New York: French, n.d. 48 p.

>An acting edition with a cast list of the first London production.

IV Biography

1539 "Death of Paul Meritt." ERA, 13 July 1895, p. 9.

>Obituary notice.

MILNER, HENRY M.

II Acted Plays—Principal Titles

1540 BARMECIDE; OR, THE FATAL OFFSPRING: A DRAMATICK ROMANCE IN THREE ACTS. (Drury Lane, 3 November 1818.) London: Richard White, 1818. ix, 52 p.

>With a cast list of the first London production and a preface

outlining the historical basis of the play and thanking the
performers; the Readex copy is a promptbook (New York
Public Library) with some manuscript notes.

1541 JEW OF LUBECK; OR, THE HEART OF A FATHER: A SERIOUS DRAMA
IN TWO ACTS. (Drury Lane, 11 May 1819.) 2nd ed. London: J.
Lowndes, 1818. 27 p.

Includes a cast list for the first London production, a preface
by the author and a dedication to Stephen Kemble; the Readex
copy is a promptbook (New York Public Library) with manuscript notes, including a cast list for an unspecified production
of the play.

1542 THE BANDIT OF THE BLIND MINE: A MELODRAMA IN THREE ACTS.
(Coburg, 15 October 1821.) New British Theatre, no. 314. London:
Lacy, n.d. 29 p.

An acting edition with a cast list of the first London production.

1543 FRANKENSTEIN; OR, THE MAN AND THE MONSTER: AN ORIGINAL
MELODRAMA IN TWO ACTS. (Coburg, 18 August 1823.) Duncombe's
British Theatre, vol. 2. London: Duncombe, n.d. 28 p.

An acting edition with a cast list of the first London production (3 July 1826 according to this edition). The play is
adapted from Mary Shelley's romance and was performed under
the title FRANKENSTEIN; OR, THE DEMON OF SWITZER-
LAND.

1544 ALONZO THE BRAVE AND THE FAIR IMOGINE; OR, THE SPECTRE
BRIDE! A LEGENDARY ROMANTIC MELO-DRAMA IN TWO ACTS.
(Coburg, 19 June 1826.) Duncombe's British Theatre, vol. 2. London:
Duncombe, n.d. 28 p.

An acting edition with a cast list of an unspecified production; the Readex copy is a promptbook (New York Public
Library) with a few manuscript notes.

1545 MAZEPPA: A ROMANTIC DRAMA IN THREE ACTS. (Royal Amphitheatre, 4 April 1831.) London: Music Publishing Co., n.d. 52 p.

An acting edition with a cast list of the first London production and "Remarks" by D--G [George Daniel]; the Readex
copy is a promptbook (New York Public Library) with extensive manuscript notes and scene plans.

1546 GUSTAVUS THE THIRD; OR, THE MASKED BALL! AN HISTORICAL DRAMA IN THREE ACTS. (Royal Victoria, 8 November 1833.) Duncombe's British Theatre, vol. 13. London: Duncombe, n.d. 30 p.

> An acting edition with cast lists of three London productions.

MITFORD, MARY RUSSELL (1787-1855)

I Collected Works

1547 THE DRAMATIC WORKS OF MARY RUSSELL MITFORD. 2 vols. London: Hurst and Blackett, 1854.

> Contents: volume one: Introduction, RIENZI, FOSCARI, JULIAN, CHARLES I; volume two: SADAK AND KALASTRADE, INEZ DE CASTRO, GASTON DE BLONDEVILLE (unacted, available in the Readex collection), OTTO OF WITTELSBACH (unacted, available in the Readex collection), and DRAMATIC SCENES (various short unacted pieces, available in the Readex collection).

II Acted Plays—Principal Titles

1548 JULIAN: A TRAGEDY IN FIVE ACTS. (Covent Garden, 15 March 1823.) London: G. and W.B. Whittaker, 1823. xii, 81 p.

> Includes a dedication to Macready, a short preface, and a cast list of the first London production.

1549 THE FOSCARI: A TRAGEDY. (Covent Garden, 4 November 1826.) London: G.B. Whittaker, 1826. iv, 78 p.

> Includes a short preface (saying, among other things, that the play "was not only completed, but actually presented to Covent Garden Theatre before the publication of Lord Byron's well-known drama") and a cast list of the first London production.

1550 RIENZI: A TRAGEDY IN FIVE ACTS. (Drury Lane, 9 October 1828.) London: John Cumberland, 1828. vii, 66 p.

> Includes a preface and a cast list of the first London production.

1551 CHARLES THE FIRST: AN HISTORICAL TRAGEDY IN FIVE ACTS. (Victoria, 2 July 1834.) London: Duncombe, 1834. vi, 80 p.

> With a preface (in which the suppression of the play in 1825 is discussed) and a cast list of the first London production.

1552 SADAK AND KALASRADE; OR, THE WATERS OF OBLIVION: A
ROMANTIC OPERA IN TWO ACTS. (English Opera House, 20 April
1835.) London: Printed by S.G. Fairbrother, n.d. iv, 31 p.

> Includes a short preface and a cast list of the first London
> production.

1553 INEZ DE CASTRO: A TRAGEDY IN FIVE ACTS. (City of London, 12
April 1841.) Dicks' Standard Plays, no. 672. [London: Dicks, n.d.]
20 p.

> An acting edition with a cast list of the first London produc-
> tion.

III Bibliographies

1554 Sadleir, Michael. XIX CENTURY FICTION: A BIBLIOGRAPHICAL
RECORD BASED ON HIS OWN COLLECTION. 2 vols. London and
Los Angeles: Constable and University of California Press, 1951.

> The section on Mitford contains bibliographical information
> on the plays, although the section is not complete.

IV Biography

1555 RECOLLECTIONS OF A LITERARY LIFE; AND SELECTIONS FROM MY
FAVOURITE POETS AND PROSE WRITERS BY MARY RUSSELL MITFORD.
New ed. London: Richard Bentley, 1859. xii, 516 p.

> This is mainly a collection of Mitford's opinions of several
> writers, but there is also some autobiographical content. The
> first edition of the RECOLLECTIONS appeared in 1852.

1556 L'Estrange, Rev. A.G., ed. THE LIFE OF MARY RUSSELL MITFORD
. . . RELATED IN A SELECTION FROM HER LETTERS TO HER FRIENDS.
3 vols. London: Richard Bentley, 1870.

1557 Chorley, Henry, ed. LETTERS OF MARY RUSSELL MITFORD, SECOND
SERIES. 2 vols. London: R. Bentley & Son, 1872.

1558 L'Estrange, Rev. A.G., ed. THE FRIENDSHIPS OF MARY RUSSELL
MITFORD AS RECORDED IN LETTERS FROM HER LITERARY CORRESPON-
DENTS. 2 vols. London: Hurst and Blackett, 1882.

1559 Roberts, W.J. MARY RUSSELL MITFORD: THE TRAGEDY OF A BLUE
STOCKING. London: Andrew Melrose, 1913. 391 p.

> There are several illustrations in this biography and some

discussion of Mitford's dramatic career (especially her relations with Macready). There is virtually no documentation
and no index. The title on the book's cover is THE LIFE
AND FRIENDSHIPS OF MARY RUSSELL MITFORD.

1560 Hill, Constance. MARY RUSSELL MITFORD AND HER SURROUNDINGS.
London and New York: John Lane, 1920. xiv, 387 p.

Includes several illustrations and portraits.

1561 Johnson, R. Brimley, ed. THE LETTERS OF MARY RUSSELL MITFORD.
London: John Lane, 1925. ix, 236 p.

1562 Astin, Marjorie. MARY RUSSELL MITFORD: HER CIRCLE AND HER
BOOKS. London: N.Douglas, 1930. 160 p.

1563 Watson, Vera. MARY RUSSELL MITFORD. London: Evans Brothers,
[1949]. xv, 324 p.

A straightforward biography, scantly documented, with some
discussion of the plays.

1564 Miller, Betty, ed. ELIZABETH BARRETT TO MISS MITFORD: THE UN-
PUBLISHED LETTERS OF ELIZABETH BARRETT BARRETT TO MARY RUSSELL
MITFORD. London: John Murray, 1954. xviii, 284 p.

The letters cover the years 1836-46; by 1836 most of Mitford's dramatic work was finished and these letters rarely
speak of drama or the theatre.

1565 Lewis, Jenny. "Mary Russell Mitford Letters." BMQ, 29 (1965), 6-10.

Unpublished letters (1844-54) in the British Library.

MONCRIEFF, WILLIAM THOMAS (1794-1857)

I Collected Works

1566 SELECTIONS FROM THE DRAMATIC WORKS OF WILLIAM THOMAS
MONCRIEFF. 3 vols. London: H. Lacy, 1851.

II Acted Plays—Principal Titles

1567 GIOVANNI IN LONDON; OR, THE LIBERTINE RECLAIMED: AN
OPERATIC EXTRAVANGANZA IN TWO ACTS. (Olympic, 26 December
1817.) London: Cumberland, n.d. 48 p.

An acting edition with cast lists of Drury Lane and Covent
Gardens productions (both 1827) and "Remarks" by D--G
[George Daniel].

1568 WANTED A WIFE; OR, A CHEQUE ON MY BANKER: A COMEDY IN
FIVE ACTS. (Drury Lane, 3 May 1819.) London: John Lowndes, 1819.
68 p.

With a preface and cast list of the first London production.

1569 THE LEAR OF PRIVATE LIFE! OR, FATHER AND DAUGHTER: A
DOMESTIC MELO-DRAMA IN THREE ACTS. (Coburg, 27 April 1820.)
London: T. Richardson, n.d. 52 p.

An acting edition with a cast list of the first London production. The Readex copy is a promptbook (New York Public
Library) with manuscript notes.

1570 TOM AND JERRY; OR, LIFE IN LONDON: A BURLETTA OF FUN,
FROLIC, AND FLASH IN TWO ACTS. The Minor Drama, no. 157.
(Adelphi, 26 November 1821.) New York: French, n.d. 28 p.

An acting edition with cast lists of three American productions.

1571 THE CATARACT OF THE GANGES; OR, THE RAJAH'S DAUGHTER: A
GRAND ROMANTIC MELO-DRAMA IN TWO ACTS. (Drury Lane, 27
October 1823.) London: Simpkin & Marshall, 1823. 50 p.

With a cast list of the first London production and a preface:
"Mr. Elliston expressing a wish to have an After-piece written,
in which Horses and a Cataract could be introduced, occa-
sioned the construction of this Spectacle. . . ."

1572 THE SPECTRE BRIDEGROOM; OR, A GHOST IN SPITE OF HIMSELF: A
FARCE IN TWO ACTS. (Drury Lane, 2 July 1827.) London: Cumberland, n.d. 32 p.

An acting edition with cast lists of two Drury Lane productions and "Remarks" by D--G [George Daniel].

1573 EUGENE ARAM; OR, ST. ROBERT'S CAVE: A DRAMA IN THREE ACTS.
(Surrey, 8 February 1832.) 2nd ed. Richardson's New Minor Drama,
no. 32. London: Thomas Richardson, [1832]. 32 p.

An acting edition with a cast list of the first London production and "Remarks" [by George Daniel].

MORTON, JOHN MADDISON (1811-91)

I Collected Works

1574 COMEDIETTAS AND FARCES. New York: Harper & Brothers, 1886.
171 p.

> Contents: BOX AND COX (Lyceum, 1 November 1847);
> FIRST COME, FIRST SERVED; PEPPERPOT'S LITTLE PETS;
> AFTER A STORM COMES A CALM; EXPRESS!; TAKEN
> FROM THE FRENCH; DECLINED--WITH THANKS; and a
> short introductory essay on Morton. Of these plays, only
> BOX AND COX is recorded among Morton's plays in Nicoll's
> hand lists (items 298 and 321 above).

II Acted Plays—Principal Titles

1575 MY HUSBAND'S GHOST: A FARCE IN ONE ACT. (Haymarket, 26
April 1836.) Lacy's Acting Edition, vol. 93. London: Lacy, n.d.
25 p.

> With a cast list of the first London production and "Remarks"
> by D--G [George Daniel].

1576 CHAOS IS COME AGAIN; OR, THE RACE-BALL! A FARCE IN ONE
ACT. (Covent Garden, 19 November 1838.) Acting National Drama,
vol. 6. London: Chapman and Hall, n.d. 20 p.

> With a cast list of the first London production.

1577 A THUMPING LEGACY: AN ORIGINAL FARCE IN ONE ACT. (Drury
Lane, 11 February 1843.) London: S.G. Fairbrother, n.d. 24 p.

> An acting edition with a cast list of the first (?) London
> production.

1578 THE MOTHER AND CHILD ARE DOING WELL: A FARCE IN ONE ACT.
(Adelphi, 24 February 1845.) New York: Dick & Fitzgerald, n.d.
23 p.

> An acting edition with cast lists of the first London and a
> Park Theatre, New York, production.

1579 LEND ME FIVE SHILLINGS: A FARCE IN ONE ACT. (Haymarket, 19
February 1846.) Lacy's Acting Edition, vol. 30. London and New York:
French, n.d. 29 p.

> With a cast list of the first London production.

1580 DONE ON BOTH SIDES: A FARCE IN ONE ACT. (Lyceum, 24 February 1847.) Lacy's Acting Edition, vol. 26. London and New York: French, n.d. 36 p.

> With a cast list of the first London production.

1581 JOHN DOBBS: A FARCE IN ONE ACT. (Strand, 23 April 1849.) Lacy's Acting Edition, vol. 7. London and New York: French, n.d. 22 p.

> With a cast list of the first London production.

1582 WHERE THERE'S A WILL THERE'S A WAY: A COMIC DRAMA IN ONE ACT. (Strand, 6 September 1849.) Duncombe's British Theatre, vol. 7. London: Duncombe, n.d.

> An acting edition with a cast list of the first London production.

1583 WOODCOCK'S LITTLE GAME: A COMEDY FARCE IN TWO ACTS. (St. James's, 6 October 1864.) De Witt's Acting Plays, no. 11. New York: De Witt, n.d. 26 p.

> With cast lists for the first London and a Wallack's Theatre, New York, production.

OXENFORD, JOHN (1812-77)

II Acted Plays—Principal Titles

1584 DER FREISCHUTZ: A GRAND ROMANTIC OPERA IN FOUR ACTS. (English Opera House, 23 July 1824.) London: Lacy, n.d. 33 p.

> Includes a playbill for a production at Astley's, 2 April 1866; the music by Weber.

1585 MY FELLOW CLERK: A FARCE IN ONE ACT. (English Opera House, 20 April 1835.) London: Miller, 1835. 23 p.

> Includes a cast list of the first London production and a dedication to S.J. Arnold.

1586 THE DICE OF DEATH! A DRAMA IN THREE ACTS. (English Opera House, 14 September 1835.) Duncombe's British Theatre, vol. 28. London: Duncombe, n.d. 38 p.

> An acting edition with a cast list of the first London production; this copy is a promptbook (New York Public Library) with a few manuscript notes.

1587 TWICE KILLED: A FARCE. (Olympic, 26 November 1835.) Chicago: Dramatic Publishing Company, n.d. 16 p.

> An acting edition with cast lists of the first London and a New York production.

1588 A DAY WELL SPENT: A FARCE IN ONE ACT. (English Opera House, 4 April 1836.) London: Miller, 1836. 24 p.

> An acting edition with a cast list of the first London production and a dedication to the actor B. Wrench.

1589 THE RAPE OF THE LOCK: A BURLETTA IN TWO ACTS. (Olympic, 27 March 1837.) London: W. Strange, n.d. 33 p.

> An acting edition with a cast list of the first London production.

1590 NO FOLLOWERS: A BURLETTA IN ONE ACT. (Strand, 4 September 1837.) London: W. Strange, 1837. 27 p.

> An acting edition with a cast list of the first London production.

1591 A QUIET DAY: A FARCE IN ONE ACT. (Olympic, 12 October 1837.) London: W. Strange, 1837. 28 p.

> An acting edition with a cast list of the first London production. (According to Nicoll and the NEW CBEL, the play was unacted; neither lists Strange's edition, which indicates that the play was performed.)

1592 DOCTOR DILWORTH: A FARCE IN ONE ACT. (Olympic, 15 April 1839.) New York: French, n.d. 18 p.

> An acting edition with cast lists for the first London and four American productions (New York, Boston, Albany, St. Louis); this copy is a promptbook (New York Public Library), interleaved with manuscript notes.

1593 THE REIGNING FAVOURITE: A DRAMA IN THREE ACTS. (Strand, 9 October 1849.) Lacy's Acting Edition (n.s.), vol. 1. London: Lacy, n.d. 27 p.

> With a cast list of the first London production.

1594 A LEGAL IMPEDIMENT: A FARCE IN ONE ACT. (Olympic, 28 October 1861.) Lacy's Acting Edition, vol. 53. London: Lacy, n.d. 22 p.

With a cast list of the first London production.

1595 NEIGHBOURS: A NEW COMEDY IN TWO ACTS. (Strand, 10 November 1866.) Lacy's Acting Edition, vol. 73. London: Lacy, n.d. 33 p.

With a cast list of the first London production.

PALMER, T.A. (1838-1905)

II Acted Plays—Principal Titles

1596 TOO LATE TO SAVE; OR, DOOMED TO DIE: A STORY OF OLD PARIS: DRAMA IN FOUR ACTS. (Theatre Royal, Exeter, 1861.) London and New York: French, n.d. 36 p.

An acting edition with a cast list of the Exeter production.

1597 AMONG THE RELICS: A COMEDY-DRAMA IN THREE ACTS. (Theatre Royal, Plymouth, 22 November 1869.) London and New York: French, n.d. 49 p.

An acting edition with a cast list of the Plymouth production, and extracts from press reviews.

1598 RELY ON MY DISCRETION: AN ORIGINAL FARCE. (Royalty, 17 January 1870.) London and New York: French, n.d. 24 p.

An acting edition with three cast lists.

1599 "INSURED AT LLOYDS": DRAMA IN FOUR ACTS. (Queen's, Manchester, 5 November 1870; Theatre Royal, Plymouth, 4 October 1875.) No publication details. 55 p.

An acting edition with a cast list of the first Plymouth production.

1600 A DODGE FOR A DINNER: A FARCE IN ONE ACT. (Strand, 28 December 1872.) London and New York: French, n.d. 23 p.

An acting edition with a cast list of the first London production.

1601 THE LAST LIFE: A DRAMA IN THREE ACTS, ADAPTED FROM ONE OF MRS. S.C. HALL'S STORIES OF IRISH LIFE. (Theatre Royal, Greenwich, 9 February 1874.) London and New York: French, n.d. 38 p.

An acting edition with a cast list of the first London production.

1602 *EAST LYNNE. (Theatre Royal, Nottingham, 19 November 1874.)
Acting Edition, no. 1542. [London: French, n.d.] 44 p.

1603 WOMAN'S RIGHTS: A COMEDIETTA. (Grand, Douglas, August 1882.)
London and New York: French, n.d. 24 p.

> An acting edition with a cast list of the Douglas production.

PAYNE, JOHN HOWARD (1791-1852)

I Collected Works

1604 Hislop, Codman, and W.R. Richardson, eds. TRIAL WITHOUT JURY &
OTHER PLAYS. America's Lost Plays, vol. 5. Princeton: Princeton
University Press, 1940; rpt. Bloomington: Indiana University Press, 1964.
xvii, 264 p.

> Includes MOUNT SAVAGE; THE BOARDING SCHOOLS; OR,
> LIFE AMONG THE LITTLE FOLKS; THE TWO SONS-IN-LAW;
> MAZEPPA; OR, THE WILD HORSE OF TARTARY; THE SPAN-
> ISH HUSBAND; OR, FIRST AND LAST LOVE. There is a
> short general introduction by the editors and a brief note to
> each play.

1605 _____. THE LAST DUEL IN SPAIN & OTHER PLAYS. American's Lost
Plays, vol. 6. Princeton: Princeton University Press, 1940; rpt. Bloomington: Indiana University Press, 1964. 265 p.

> Includes WOMAN'S REVENGE; THE ITALIAN BRIDE; ROMU-
> LUS, THE SHEPHERD KING; THE BLACK MAN; OR, THE
> SPLEEN. There are brief editorial notes to each play.

IV Biography

1606 Hanson, Willis T. THE EARLY LIFE OF JOHN HOWARD PAYNE, WITH
CONTEMPORARY LETTERS HERETOFORE UNPUBLISHED. Boston: Printed
for members of the Bibliophile Society, 1913. 226 p.

> Covers the period up to 1813 when Payne left America for
> England.

1607 Harrison, Gabriel. JOHN HOWARD PAYNE, DRAMATIST, POET,
ACTOR, AND AUTHOR OF "HOME SWEET HOME!" Rev. ed. Philadelphia: J.B. Lippincott, 1885. 404 p.

> The study includes a list of Payne's plays, but no details of
> performance.

1608 Chiles, Rosa Pendleton. JOHN HOWARD PAYNE: AMERICAN POET, ACTOR, PLAYWRIGHT, CONSUL AND THE AUTHOR OF "HOME, SWEET HOME." Washington, [D.C.]: Columbia Historical Society, 1930. 89 p.

> Superseded by Overmyer's book (item 1609).

1609 Overmyer, Grace. AMERICA'S FIRST HAMLET. Washington Square: New York University Press, 1957. 439 p.

> A substantial biography with some detailed discussion of Payne's close acquaintance with the English theatre; bibliography.

V Critical Studies

1610 Gilbert, Vedder Morris. "The Stage Career of John Howard Payne, Author of 'Home, Sweet Home.'" NORTHWEST OHIO QUARTERLY, Winter 1950-51, pp. 59-74.

> A general survey; includes an annotated bibliography.

1611 Saxon, A.H. "John Howard Payne, Playwright with a System." TN, 24 (1969-70), 79-84.

> A defense of Payne's work as an adapter and translator.

PEAKE, RICHARD BRINSLEY (1792-1847)

II Acted Plays—Principal Titles

1612 AMATEURS AND ACTORS: A MUSICAL FARCE IN TWO ACTS. (English Opera House, 29 August 1818.) London: William Fearman, 1818. 46 p.

> Includes a cast list of the first London production and a series of acknowledgments of Peake.

1613 THE DUEL; OR, MY TWO NEPHEWS: A FARCE IN TWO ACTS. (Covent Garden, 18 February 1823.) London: Miller, 1823. 52 p.

> Includes a cast list of the first London production and a prefatory note by the author.

1614 AMERICANS ABROAD; OR, NOTES AND NOTIONS: A FARCICAL COMEDY IN TWO ACTS. (English Opera House, 3 September 1824.) Dicks' Standard Plays, no. 589. London: Dicks, n.d. 15 p.

> With a cast list of the first London production (under the title of JONATHAN IN ENGLAND).

1615 COMFORTABLE LODGINGS; OR, PARIS IN 1750: A FARCE IN TWO
ACTS. (Drury Lane, 10 March 1827.) Cumberland's British Theatre,
vol. 29. London: Cumberland, n.d. 36 p.

> An acting edition with cast list of Drury Lane and Adelphi
> productions and "Remarks" by D--G [George Daniel]; the
> Readex copy is a promptbook (New York Public Library).

1616 THE "MIDDLE TEMPLE"; OR, WHICH IS MY SON? A FARCE IN ONE
ACT. (English Opera House, 27 June 1827.) London: Chapman and
Hall, n.d. 19 p.

> With a cast list of the first London production (given in this
> edition as July 1828).

1617 THE CHANCERY SUIT! A COMEDY IN FIVE ACTS. (Covent Garden,
30 November 1830.) London: Edward Bull, 1831. 86 p.

> Includes a cast list of the first London production.

1618 THE CHAIN OF GOLD; OR, A DAUGHTER'S DEVOTION: A ROMANTIC
DRAMA IN THREE ACTS. (Adelphi, 29 September 1834.) Dicks' Standard Plays, no. 694. London: Dicks, n.d. 18 p.

> An acting edition with a cast list of the first London produc-
> tion.

1619 COURT AND CITY: A COMEDY IN FIVE ACTS. (Covent Garden, 17
November 1841.) Cumberland's British Theatre, vol. 42. London: Cumberland, n.d. 72 p.

> An acting edition with "Remarks" by D--G [George Daniel].
> The Readex copy is a promptbook (New York Public Library),
> interleaved with manuscript notes. The play is based on
> Steele's THE TENDER HUSBAND and Mrs. Sheridan's THE
> DISCOVERY.

1620 TEN THOUSAND A YEAR: A DRAMA IN THREE ACTS. (Adelphi, 29
March 1844.) Cumberland's Minor Theatre, vol. 16. London: Cumberland, n.d. 48 p.

> An acting edition with a cast list of the first London produc-
> tion ('given in this edition as 1842) and "Remarks" as a
> "Memoir of Mr. Wright" by D--G [George Daniel].

1621 THE TITLE DEEDS: AN ORIGINAL COMEDY IN THREE ACTS. (Adelphi,
21 June 1847.) The Acting National Drama, vol. 14. London: National Acting Drama Office, n.d. 60 p.

> An acting edition with a cast list of the first London production.

PETTITT, HENRY (1848-93)

II Acted Plays—Principal Titles

1622 GOLDEN FRUIT. (East London, 14 July 1873.) No publication details. Var. pag.

A manuscript promptbook, located in New York Public Library.

1623 NECK OR NOTHING: A NEW AND ORIGINAL DRAMA IN THREE ACTS. With George Conquest. (Grecian, 3 August 1876.) London and New York: French, n.d. 42 p.

An acting edition with a cast list of the first London production.

1624 *TAKEN FROM LIFE. (Adelphi, 31 December 1881.) LC.

1625 *THE HARBOUR LIGHTS. With G.R. Sims. (Adelphi, 23 December 1885.) LC.

1626 THE BELLS OF HASLEMERE: A ROMANTIC DRAMA IN FOUR ACTS. With Sydney Grundy. (Adelphi, 28 July 1887.) No publication details. Var. pag.

A prompt typescript, located in New York Public Library. The title is derived from a playbill included in the typescript.

III Bibliographies

1627 O'Creon, Tim. "Henry Pettitt's Plays." ERA, 13 January 1894, p. 11.

A bibliography of Pettitt's plays with dates of performances.

IV Biography

1628 "Death of Henry Pettitt." ERA, 30 December 1893, p. 11.

Obituary notice.

V Critical Studies

1629 "A Day with Henry Pettitt." ERA, 10 September 1892, p. 9.

An informal interview, covering various aspects of Pettitt's life and work.

PHILIPS, WATTS (1825-74)

II Acted Plays—Principal Titles

1630 THE DEAD HEART: AN HISTORICAL DRAMA IN THREE ACTS. (Adelphi, 10 November 1859.) Standard Drama, no. 238. New York: French, n.d. 44 p.

> An acting edition with cast lists of two New York productions.

1631 HIS LAST VICTORY: AN ORIGINAL DRAMA IN TWO ACTS. (St. James's, 21 June 1862.) London: Lacy, n.d. 36 p.

> An acting edition with a cast list of the first London production.

1632 CAMILLA'S HUSBAND: AN ORIGINAL DRAMA IN THREE ACTS. (Olympic, 22 November 1862.) London: Lacy, n.d. 44 p.

> An acting edition with a cast list of the first London production.

1633 PAUL'S RETURN: AN ORIGINAL COMEDY IN THREE ACTS. (Princess's, 15 February 1864.) London: Lacy, n.d. 46 p.

> An acting edition with a cast list of the first London production; interleaved, with numerous manuscript notes.

1634 THEODORA: ACTRESS AND EMPRESS: AN ORIGINAL HISTORICAL DRAMA IN FIVE ACTS. (Surrey, 9 April 1866.) London: Lacy, n.d. 64 p.

> An acting edition with a cast list of the first London production.

1635 LOST IN LONDON: A DRAMA IN THREE ACTS. (Adelphi, 16 March 1867.) Universal Stage, no. 1. Boston: Spencer, n.d. 22 p.

> An acting edition with cast lists of two American productions; interleaved, with copious manuscript notes.

1636 MAUD'S PERIL: A PLAY IN FOUR ACTS. (Adelphi, 23 October 1867.) London: Lacy, n.d. 46 p.

> An acting edition with a cast list of the first London production, and a dedication. The Readex collection also includes an acting edition (Chicago: n.d., 28 p.).

1637 NOT GUILTY: A DRAMA IN FOUR ACTS. (Queen's, 13 February 1869.) London: Lacy, n.d. 65 p.

> An acting edition with a cast list of the first London production; numerous manuscript notes and deletions. The Readex collection also includes another copy (Chicago: n.d., 50 p.).

IV Biography

1638 Phillips, E. Watts. WATTS PHILLIPS: ARTIST AND PLAYWRIGHT. London: Cassell, 1891. 174 p.

> An account of Phillips' career pieced together mostly from contemporary sources, various theatrical correspondence, and playbills. An appendix includes a further sixteen of Phillips' letters.

PINERO, SIR ARTHUR WING (1855-1934)

I Collected Works

1639 Hamilton, Clayton, ed. THE SOCIAL PLAYS OF ARTHUR WING PINERO: EDITED WITH A GENERAL INTRODUCTION AND A CRITICAL PREFACE TO EACH PLAY. 4 vols. New York: Dutton, 1917-22; rpt. New York: AMS, 1967.

> Contents: volume one: THE SECOND MRS. TANQUERAY; THE NOTORIOUS MRS. EBBSMITH; volume two: THE GAY LORD QUEX; IRIS; volume three: LETTY; HIS HOUSE IN ORDER; volume four: THE THUNDERBOLT; MID-CHANNEL. This "LIBRARY EDITION of the weightiest and most important plays of . . . Pinero" is based on various previous editions, notably those issued by Heinemann and W.H. Baker. Hamilton includes cast lists of first productions and long prefaces on Pinero's career and the individual plays collected here. See item 1693, below.

1640 TWO PLAYS. London: Heinemann, 1930. x, 245 p.

> Contains DR. HARMER'S HOLIDAYS and CHILD MAN, and a foreword by Pinero.

II Acted Plays—Principal Titles

Heinemann issued a uniform edition of Pinero's plays, which is essentially a library edition, with only necessary stage directions. At the turn of the century, however, the stage directions burgeoned somewhat. An identical uniform series was issued by W.H. Baker in Boston.

1641 THE MONEY SPINNER: AN ORIGINAL COMEDY IN TWO ACTS. (Prince of Wales's, Manchester, 5 November 1880; St. James's, 8 January 1881.) London and New York: French, 1900. 43 p.

> An acting edition with cast lists of the Manchester and London productions.

1642 *THE SQUIRE: AN ORIGINAL COMEDY IN THREE ACTS. (St. James's, 29 December 1881.) London and New York: French, 1905. 81 p.

> An acting edition with a cast list of the first London production.

1643 IN CHANCERY: AN ORIGINAL FANTASTIC COMEDY IN THREE ACTS. (Lyceum, Edinburgh, 19 September 1884; Gaiety, 24 December 1884.) London and New York: French, 1905. 72 p.

> An acting edition with a cast list of the first London production.

1644 THE MAGISTRATE: A FARCE IN THREE ACTS. (Court, 21 March 1885.) London: Heinemann, 1892. xii, 164 p.

> Uniform edition, with an introductory note by M.C. Salaman, and a cast list of the first London production.

1645 THE SCHOOLMISTRESS: A FARCE IN THREE ACTS. (Court, 27 March 1886.) London: Heinemann, 1894. x, 165 p.

> Uniform edition, with an introductory note by M.C. Salaman, and a cast list of the first London production.

1646 THE HOBBY-HORSE: A COMEDY IN THREE ACTS. (St. James's, 25 October 1886.) London: Heinemann, 1892. x, 168 p.

> Uniform edition, with an introductory note by M.C. Salaman, and a cast list of the first London production.

1647 DANDY DICK: AN ORIGINAL FARCE IN THREE ACTS. (Court, 27 January 1887.) London: Privately printed, 1887. 93 p.

> A privately printed promptbook with a cast list of the first New York production. This was the promptbook used at the Boston Museum Theatre; interleaved with manuscript notes. The Readex collection also includes a Baker uniform edition.

1648 SWEET LAVENDER: A COMEDY IN THREE ACTS. (Terry's, 21 March 1888.) Boston: Baker, 1893. 184 p.

> Uniform edition.

1649 THE WEAKER SEX: A COMEDY IN THREE ACTS. (Theatre Royal, Manchester, 28 September 1888; Court, 16 March 1889.) Boston: Baker, 1894. 133 p.

> Uniform edition, with an introductory note by M.C. Salaman, and a cast list of the first London production. The text is the revised version for the London production.

1650 THE PROFLIGATE: A PLAY IN FOUR ACTS. (Garrick, 24 April 1889.) London: Heinemann, 1891. xix, 123 p.

> Uniform edition, with an introductory note by M.C. Salaman, an alternative ending to the play, and a cast list of the first London production.

1651 THE CABINET MINISTER: A FARCE IN FOUR ACTS. (Court, 23 April 1890.) Boston: Baker, 1892. x, 188 p.

> Uniform edition, with an introductory note by M.C. Salaman, and a cast list of the first London production.

1652 LADY BOUNTIFUL: A STORY OF YEARS: A PLAY IN FOUR ACTS. (Garrick, 7 March 1891.) London: Heinemann, 1891. xii, 185 p.

> Uniform edition, with an introductory note by M.C. Salaman, and a cast list of the first London production.

1653 THE TIMES: A COMEDY IN FOUR ACTS. (Terry's, 24 October 1891.) London: Heinemann, 1891. xi, 192 p.

> Uniform edition, with an introductory note by Pinero on the publication of plays.

1654 THE AMAZONS: A FARCICAL ROMANCE IN THREE ACTS. (Court, 7 March 1893.) Boston: Baker, 1895. 189 p.

> Uniform edition, with an introductory note by M.C. Salaman, and a cast list of the first London production.

1655 THE SECOND MRS. TANQUERAY: A PLAY IN FOUR ACTS. (St. James's, 27 May 1893.) Boston: Baker, 1894. 174 p.

> Uniform edition.

1656 THE NOTORIOUS MRS. EBBSMITH: A DRAMA IN FOUR ACTS. (Garrick, 13 March 1895.) London: Heinemann, 1895. iii, 224 p.

> Uniform edition.

1657 THE BENEFIT OF THE DOUBT: A COMEDY IN THREE ACTS. (Comedy,

16 October 1895.) London: Chiswick Press, 1895. 133 p.

Privately printed promptbook.

1658 TRELAWNY OF THE "WELLS": A COMEDIETTA IN FOUR ACTS. (Court, 20 January 1898.) London: Heinemann, 1925. 215 p.

Uniform edition. The Readex copy is the promptbook of the 1925 London revival, directed by Pinero; it includes a cast list, typescript, and manuscript additions and notes.

1659 THE GAY LORD QUEX: A COMEDY IN FOUR ACTS. (Globe, 8 April 1899.) London: Heinemann, 1900. 225 p.

Uniform edition.

1660 IRIS: A DRAMA IN FIVE ACTS. (Garrick, 21 September 1901.) Boston: Baker, 1902. 224 p.

Uniform edition.

1661 *LETTY: AN ORIGINAL DRAMA IN FOUR ACTS AND AN EPILOGUE. (Duke of York's, 8 October 1903.) London: Heinemann, 1904. 247 p.

Uniform edition.

1662 *HIS HOUSE IN ORDER: A COMEDY IN FOUR ACTS. (St. James's, 1 February 1906.) Boston: Baker, 1907. 204 p.

Uniform edition.

1663 *THE THUNDERBOLT: AN EPISODE IN THE HISTORY OF A PROVIN-CIAL FAMILY IN FOUR ACTS. (St. James's, 9 May 1908.) London: Heinemann, 1909. 270 p.

Uniform edition.

1664 *MID-CHANNEL: A PLAY IN FOUR ACTS. (St. James's, 2 September 1909.) London: Heinemann, 1922. 251 p.

Uniform edition.

1665 *PRESERVING MR. PANMURE: A COMIC PLAY IN FOUR ACTS. (Comedy, 19 January 1911.) London: Heinemann, 1912. 296 p.

Uniform edition.

1666 *THE "MIND THE PAINT" GIRL: A COMEDY IN FOUR ACTS. (Duke of York's, 17 February, 1912.) London: Heinemann, 1913. 234 p.

Uniform edition.

1667 *PLAYGOERS: A DOMESTIC EPISODE. (St. James's, 31 March 1913.)
London: French, 1913. 30 p.

> An acting edition with a cast list of the first London production.

1668 *THE BIG DRUM: A COMEDY IN FOUR ACTS. (St. James's, 1 September 1915.) Boston: Baker, 1915. viii, 213 p.

> Uniform edition, with a preface on the history of the play by Pinero.

1669 *THE FREAKS: AN IDYLL OF SUBURBIA IN THREE ACTS. (New, 14 February 1918.) London: Heinemann, 1922. 224 p.

> Uniform edition.

1670 *A SEAT IN THE PARK: A WARNING. (Winter Garden, 21 February 1922.) London and New York: French, 1922. 18 p.

> An acting edition with a cast list of the first London production.

1671 *THE ENCHANTED COTTAGE: A FABLE IN THREE ACTS. (Duke of York's, 1 March 1922.) Boston: Baker, 1949. 107 p.

> Uniform edition.

1672 *DR. HARMER'S HOLIDAYS. (Shubert-Belasco, Washington, 16 March 1931.) See item 1640.

IV Biography

1673 Dunkel, Wilbur D. "Pinero's Letters to R.M. Field." URLB, 1 (1945), 45–48.

> A descriptive account of twenty-three of Pinero's letters at the University of Rochester. Field was manager of the Boston Museum theatre, and Dunkel supplies some background information about the contemporary theatrical situation and Pinero's negotiations with Field. Only a few lines of the letters are quoted.

1674 Wearing, J.P. "Pinero's Letters in the Brotherton Collection of the University of Leeds." TN, 24 (1969-70), 74–79.

> Deals with Pinero's relationship with H.A. Jones as well as illustrating Pinero's views on the reception of several of his plays.

1675 _____. "Pinero the Actor." TN, 26 (1972), 133-39.

An account of Pinero's career as an actor, both in the provinces and in London; uses letters located at the University of
Texas.

1676 _____. "Pinero's Professional Dramatic Roles, 1874-1884." TN, 26
(1973), 140-44.

A listing of all Pinero's known roles; supplements item 1675.

1677 _____, ed. THE COLLECTED LETTERS OF SIR ARTHUR PINERO.
Minneapolis: University of Minnesota Press; London: Oxford University
Press, 1974. xii, 302 p.

A collection of 337 letters (mostly previously unpublished)
which illustrate the various phases of Pinero's life and work.

V Critical Studies

1678 Cook, Dutton, et. al. "Plays, Plagiarisms, and Mr. Pinero." THEATRE,
n.s. 5 (February 1882), 65-73.

Part of the debate over whether or not Pinero's THE SQUIRE
was plagiarized from Thomas Hardy's FAR FROM THE MAD-
DING CROWD.

1679 Cook, Dutton. "The Case of Mr. Pinero." THEATRE, n.s. 5 (April
1882), 202-4.

Cook details further evidence to prove Pinero's alleged
plagiarism in THE SQUIRE.

1680 Sharp, R. Farquharson. "Mr. Pinero and Farce." THEATRE, 29 (October 1892), 154-57.

Sharp takes issue with Pinero's definition of farce, and rightly
places THE TIMES and THE CABINET MINISTER as comedies
of manners.

1681 "A Morning with Mr. Pinero." ERA, 12 November 1892, p. 11.

An informal interview, covering various aspects of Pinero's
life and works.

1682 "Mr. Pinero and the Literary Drama." THEATRE, 31 (July 1893), 3-8.

This is something of an eulogy on Pinero's powers as a dramatist, which place him in the forefront of the theatrical world.
It also contains some useful references to the critical and

public reception of THE SECOND MRS. TANQUERAY.

1683 Hamilton, J. Angus. "Arthur Wing Pinero." MUNSEY'S MAGAZINE, 10 (July 1894), 247-51.

An inconsequential survey of Pinero's career to 1894, together with gossipy biographical information. The latter is largely unreliable (Hamilton, for example, gets both the date and place of Pinero's birth wrong).

1684 Fyfe, H. Hamilton. "Mr. Pinero's Plays as Literature." THEATRE, 35 (December 1895), 324-28.

A favorable, if discursive, review of some of Pinero's earlier work; Fyfe tries to establish that these plays possess literary qualities which remove them from mere staginess.

1685 Courtney, W.L. "The Idea of Comedy and Mr. Pinero's New Play." FORTNIGHTLY REVIEW, n.s. 61 (1897), 746-56.

Argues reasonably well that THE PRINCESS AND THE BUTTER-FLY is a new comic genre in form and spirit.

1686 Kobbe, Gustave. "The Plays of Arthur Wing Pinero." FORUM AND CENTURY, 26 (1899), 119-28.

An attempt to show Pinero's scope by examining THE AMA-ZONS and THE SECOND MRS. TANQUERAY in detail. However, Kobbe rarely rises above the level of recounting the plots of each play.

1687 Fyfe, H. Hamilton. ARTHUR WING PINERO PLAYWRIGHT: A STUDY. London: Greening, 1902. 250 p.

A not very perceptive critical estimate of Pinero's plays up to IRIS. There is a list of plays, with performance details and casts.

1688 Beers, Henry A. "The English Drama of To-Day." NORTH AMERICAN REVIEW, 180 (1905), 746-57.

A general and sometimes inaccurate survey of the state of English drama, which sees Pinero as the foremost dramatist of the time, followed by Shaw, Phillips, Yeats, and H.A. Jones.

1689 "Drama and Music." NATION (New York), 83 (1906), 211.

A review of the New York production of HIS HOUSE IN ORDER, with particular praise given to Pinero's technical and constructional abilities.

1690 Rideing, William H. "Some Women of Pinero's." NORTH AMERICAN REVIEW, 188 (1908), 38-49.

Rideing's judicious thesis--that Pinero's aim is "to measure fairly and to insist that what is condoned in a man shall not be condemned in a woman"--is unfortunately not developed or substantiated in the article.

1691 Courtney, W.L. "Realistic Drama." FORTNIGHTLY REVIEW, n.s. 93 (1913), 945-61; 1136-53; n.s. 94 (1913), 96-110.

The second paper discusses Pinero at some length as a "dramatist writing about his own country and his own times to paint not flattering portraits but veracious likenesses." The other two papers deal with the drama in a wider context.

1692 K., Q. "After the Play." NEW REPUBLIC, 13 (1917), 99.

The contention of this short piece is that Pinero "has taken the stage too seriously and life not seriously enough." But, because of the limited space, the argument remains assertive rather than fully proven and developed.

1693 Phelps, William Lyon. "Sir Arthur Pinero." BOOKMAN (New York), 47 (1918), 212-14.

A review of Clayton Hamilton's edition of Pinero's social plays.

1694 Spong, Hilda. "Working with Pinero, Barrie and Shaw: Well-known English-American Actress Compares the Methods of the Three Master Playwrights." THEATRE (New York), 32 (1920), 32, 34.

Not very reliable.

1695 Krutch, Joseph Wood. "Pinero the Timid." NATION (New York), 119 (1924), 551-52.

A strongly antipathetical review of a revival of THE SECOND MRS. TANQUERAY. Krutch sees Pinero as outmoded and failing to grasp the motivating forces of life.

1696 Wilson, Edmund. "Sixty-Five Years of Realism." NEW REPUBLIC, 43 (1925), 101.

A brief descriptive account of realism, provoked by a New York revival of TRELAWNY OF THE "WELLS."

1697 Holt, Edgar. "A Dramatist's Jubilee--Arthur Pinero." FORTNIGHTLY REVIEW, n.s. 123 (1928), 323-31.

An enthusiastic defense of Pinero as a good dramatist who sustained his abilities throughout his career. Particular, though uncritical, attention is given to plays written after 1902.

1698 Fyfe, Hamilton. SIR ARTHUR PINERO'S PLAYS AND PLAYERS. London: Benn, 1930. viii, 311 p.

A mixture of biography and criticism. Pinero had occasion to publicly rebuke Fyfe for some biographical inaccuracies, but spared him on the critical count.

1699 Weber, Carl J. "Plagiarism and Thomas Hardy." COLOPHON, n.s. 2, no. 3 (Summer 1937), 443-54.

A useful discussion of the plagiarism controversy surrounding THE SQUIRE and demonstrating Hardy's own "borrowings."

1700 Dunkel, Wilber Dwight. SIR ARTHUR PINERO: A CRITICAL BIOGRAPHY WITH LETTERS. Chicago: University of Chicago Press, 1941; rpt. Port Washington, N.Y.: Kennikat, 1967. 142 p.

A rather sketchy biography, and Dunkel's critical judgments are certainly not everyone's. He includes a number of Pinero's letters, but not always to good effect, and there are several errors in transcription.

1701 Stoakes, James P. "Arthur Wing Pinero and the Modern English Drama." Ph.D. Dissertation, University of Michigan, 1942. 255 p.

Stoakes provides sound historical material, but has little critical to say.

1702 _____. "The Reception of THE SECOND MRS. TANQUERAY." FSUS, 11 (1953), 89-94.

A disappointing article which fails to fulfill the promise of its title. Stoakes makes no attempt to synthesize previous materials to convey exactly the impact of the play on its contemporaries.

1703 Short, Ernest. "The British Drama Grows Up." QR, 295 (1957), 216-28.

Short gives a brief, lively account of the main features of Pinero's work and career and places both in historical context.

1704 Wellwarth, George E. "A Critical Study of the Reputation of Sir Arthur Wing Pinero in London and New York." Ph.D. Dissertation, University of Chicago, 1957.

> A moderately thorough-going account, with a useful appendix of productions of plays with cast lists.

1705 West, E.J. "The Playwright as Producer: Sir Arthur Pinero, the Autocrat-Dictator." UCSLL, no. 6 (1957), 79-102.

> A hostile account of Pinero's methods of directing his own plays.

1706 Pearson, Hesketh. "Pinero and Barrie: A Backstage View." THEATRE ARTS, 42 (July, 1958), 56-59.

> Pearson gives a biased account of Pinero as an autocrat in all matters, theatrical and personal. He views Barrie much more favorably.

1707 Carb, Nathan R.E., Jr. "The Social Plays of Arthur Wing Pinero, an Old Answer to a New Question." Ph.D. Dissertation, University of Pennsylvania, 1959. 257 p. (DA#59-4603)

> An unconvincing discussion of the social plays of Pinero's middle period (1889-1909). Carb argues that Pinero "stood squarely on the side of the social conventions of his day. Especially he approves the double standard of conduct for men and women." Such statements are demonstrably untrue.

1708 Kornbluth, Martin L. "Two Fallen Women: Paula Tanqueray and Kitty Warren." SHAVIAN, no. 14 (February 1959), 14-15.

> A very short article on the similarities of the two characters, with emphasis on Pinero's conventional resolution of the problem compared with Shaw's more unusual portrayal. The article's brevity precludes any significance emerging from this comparison.

1709 Davies, Cecil W. "Pinero: The Drama of Reputation." ENGLISH, 14 (Spring 1962), 13-17.

> This brief but suggestive article outlines Pinero's concern with reputation--the central theme of "all his great plays, comic and tragic."

1710 Milner, Brother Sylvester Edmund. "The Individual in Society: The Plays of Arthur Pinero." Ph.D. Dissertation, University of Notre Dame, 1969. 212 p. (DA#69-12791)

> Milner argues that Pinero's attitudes, themes, and methods do

not change throughout most of his career. He emphasises
Pinero's concern with exposing a society prepossessed with
the preservation of reputation and sees Pinero as a determin-
ist who holds to the belief "of the futility of striving to
overcome the prejudices and taboos in society."

1711 Wearing, J.P. "A Pinero Revival?" DRAMA, no. 94 (Autumn 1969),
40-42.

A brief survey of Pinero's plays, with mention of the newly
discovered play, LATE OF MOCKFORD'S.

1712 _____. "The Life and Achievement of Sir Arthur Wing Pinero (1855-
1934)." Ph.D. Dissertation, University of Wales, 1971. ix, 360 p.

An account of Pinero's life and works, drawing widely on
letters and manuscript materials. Appendices on the various
editions and manuscripts of the plays, location of letters,
Pinero's acting roles, and a list of productions and revivals.

1713 Lazenby, Walter. ARTHUR WING PINERO. New York: Twayne, 1972.
173 p.

Lazenby attempts to reestablish Pinero as a major figure in
the period 1885-1915. To this end he analyzes each of
Pinero's plays individually, grouping them according to type.
However, his treatment of each work amounts to little more
than plot-summary. The biographical information included is
based on earlier authors and is, therefore, sometimes inaccurate. Lazenby's bibliography of Pinero's plays is the most
complete to be published thus far, but it is also misleading
(he does not distinguish between manuscripts and handwritten
prompt copies--see pp. 166-67. Pinero's holograph manuscripts are generally located elsewhere than in the locations
cited).

1714 Ronning, Robert Thomas. "The Development of English Comic Farce in
the Plays of Sir Arthur Pinero." Ph.D. Dissertation, Wayne State University, 1972. 316 p. (DA#73-12587)

Ronning sees Pinero's greatest achievement as being in the
realm of comic farce rather than serious realistic drama. The
study also traces the roots of Pinero's farce to Robertsonian
comedy, Gilbert's early farces, and the French well-made
play.

1715 Wearing, J.P. "Two Early Absurd Plays in England." MD, 16, nos. 3
& 4 (1973), 259-64.

Pinero's farces are considered as first cousins to absurd drama,

and the article examines how, with only a slight shift in
emphasis, Pinero produced absurdist plays (PLAYGOERS and
A SEAT IN THE PARK).

PITT, GEORGE DIBDIN (1799-1855)

II Acted Plays—Principal Titles

1716 THE DRUNKARD'S DOOM; OR, THE LAST NAIL: A ROMANTIC DRAMA
IN TWO ACTS. (Victoria, 21 September 1832.) French's Standard
Drama, no. 345. New York: French, n.d. 24 p.

> An acting edition with a cast list of an 1850 American pro-
> duction.

1717 THE LAST MAN; OR, THE MISER OF ELTHAM GREEN. (Surrey, 22
July 1833.) Spencer's Boston Theatre, no. 94. Boston: William V.
Spencer, n.d. 24 p.

> An acting edition with cast lists of the first London and
> various American productions.

1718 THE JERSEY GIRL; OR, LES ROUGES VOLEURS: A MELODRAMA IN
TWO ACTS. (Surrey, 9 February 1835.) Lacy's Acting Edition, vol. 26.
London: Lacy, n.d. 28 p.

> With a cast list of the first London production.

1719 SIMON LEE; OR, THE MURDER OF THE FIVE FIELDS COPSE: A DO-
MESTIC DRAMA IN THREE ACTS. (City of London, 1 April 1839.)
London and New York: French, n.d. 41 p.

> An acting edition with a reproduction of the playbill for the
> first London production.

1720 SUSAN HOPLEY; OR, THE VICISSITUDES OF A SERVANT GIRL: A
DOMESTIC DRAMA IN THREE ACTS. (Victoria, 31 May 1841.) London: Davidson, n.d. 50 p.

> An acting edition with cast lists of two London productions
> and "Remarks" by D--G [George Daniel].

1721 THE BEGGAR'S PETITION; OR, A FATHER'S LOVE AND A MOTHER'S
CARE: A DRAMA IN THREE ACTS. (City of London, 18 October 1841.)
London and New York: French, n.d. 46 p.

> An acting edition with a reproduction of the playbill for the
> first London production. The Readex collection also contains
> a manuscript promptbook of this play.

1722 MARIANNE, THE CHILD OF CHARITY: A DOMESTIC DRAMA IN THREE ACTS. (Victoria, 30 December 1844.) London: Music Publishing Co., n.d. 43 p.

> An acting edition with "Remarks" by D--G [George Daniel]. The Readex copy is a promptbook (New York Public Library) with a few manuscript notes (and some missing pages).

PLANCHÉ, JAMES ROBINSON (1796-1880)

I Collected Works

1723 Croker, T.F., and Stephen Tucker, eds. THE EXTRAVAGANZAS OF J.R. PLANCHÉ, ESQ., (SOMERSET HERALD) 1825-1871. 5 vols. London: French, 1879.

> By no means Planché's complete works, but a large and representative collection, including some of his best and most popular plays: SUCCESS; OR, A HIT IF YOU LIKE IT (Adelphi, 12 December 1825); OLYMPIC REVELS; OR, PROMETHEUS AND PANDORA (Olympic, 3 January 1831); OLYMPIC DEVILS; OR, ORPHEUS AND EURYDICE (Olympic, 26 December 1831); HIGH, LOW, JACK AND THE GAME; OR THE CARD PARTY (Olympic, 30 September 1833); TELEMACHUS; OR, THE ISLAND OF CALYPSO (Olympic, 26 December 1834); RIQUET WITH THE TUFT (Olympic, 26 December 1836); PUSS IN BOOTS (Olympic, 26 December 1837); THE DRAMA'S LEVEE; OR, A PEEP AT THE PAST (Olympic, 16 April 1838); THE SLEEPING BEAUTY IN THE WOOD (Covent Garden, 20 April 1840); THE INVISIBLE PRINCE; OR THE ISLAND OF TRANQUIL DELIGHTS (Haymarket, 26 December 1846); THE GOLDEN BRANCH (Lyceum, 27 December 1847); THE SEVEN CHAMPIONS OF CHRISTENDOM (Lyceum, 9 April 1849); THE ISLAND OF JEWELS (Lyceum, 26 December 1849); MR. BUCKSTONE'S ASCENT OF MOUNT PARNASSUS (Haymarket, 28 March 1853); THE CAMP AT THE OLYMPIC (Olympic, 17 October 1853). There are prefaces, cast lists, and portraits of performers. THE EXTRAVAGANZAS is in the Readex collection, and some of the plays listed above are also available in single editions in Readex.

IV Biography

1724 Planché, James Robinson. THE RECOLLECTIONS AND REFLECTIONS OF J.R. PLANCHÉ. 2 vols. London: Tinsley, 1872. xv, 316; xii, 308 p.

> Lively and informative theatre history spanning some seventy years of the nineteenth century.

1725 Simpson, J. Palgrave. "James Robinson Planché." THE THEATRE, 3d
ser., 2 (1880), 95-99.

> A sympathetic obituary: "One of the brightest and most genial
> writers that ever shed sunlight on the British drama . . . there
> can be no doubt that he exercised a considerable influence on
> the English stage."

V Critical Studies

1726 Macmillan, Dougald. "Planché's Early Classical Burlesques." SP, 25
(1928), 340-45.

> Burlesques produced at the Olympic 1831-34.

1727 _____. "Some Burlesques with a Purpose, 1830-1870." PQ, 8 (1929),
255-63.

> "Though he wrote trifles of the lightest sort, he always en-
> deavoured to present, along with his tomfoolery, a sound
> moral principle dressed in a sparkling, if sometimes incon-
> gruous, costume."

1728 _____. "Planché's Fairy Extravaganzas." SP, 28 (1931), 790-98.

> A discussion of over twenty plays: "though these pieces
> . . . are frequently arrant nonsense, in them one finds
> often a truer key to the spirit of their age than in the
> works of persons of considerable greater literary respectabi-
> lity; and in the history of the stage of the early nineteenth
> century they must be considered."

1729 Nadeau, Albert Henry. "James Robinson Planché, Craftsman of Extravaganza." Ph.D. Dissertation, University of Michigan, 1955. 264 p.
(DA#00-12627)

1730 Reinhardt, Paul Denton. "James Robinson Planché and the Practice of
Historical Costume on the English Stage, 1823-1860." Ph.D. Dissertation,
University of Iowa, 1967. 371 p. (DA#67-09095)

1731 Rence, Robert Irving. "The Burlesque Techniques Employed by James
Robinson Planché in His Dramatic Works and Their Relationship to the
English Burlesque Tradition between Joseph Fielding and W.S. Gilbert."
Ph.D. Dissertation, University of Minnesota, 1967. 239 p. (DA#67-
14642)

1732 Reinhardt, Paul. "The Costume Design of James Robinson Planché (1796-
1880)." ETJ, 20 (1968), 524-44.

A detailed study of this important aspect of Planché's work for the theatre; illustrated.

1733 Bennett, Cleon Vernon. "James Robinson Planché: Victorian Craftsman." Ph.D. Dissertation, University of Wisconsin, 1971. 458 p. (DA#72-02618)

POCOCK, ISAAC (1782-1835)

II Acted Plays—Principal Titles

1734 HIT OR MISS! A MUSICAL FARCE IN TWO ACTS. (Lyceum, 26 February 1810.) London: W.H. Wyatt, 1810. 48 p.

Includes a cast list of the first London production and a prefatory note (thanking the performers) by Pocock.

1735 TWENTY YEARS AGO! A NEW MELO-DRAMATIC ENTERTAINMENT IN TWO ACTS. (Lyceum, 21 July 1810.) London: W.H. Wyatt, 1810. 40 p.

Includes a cast list of the first London production and a prefatory note by Pocock.

1736 THE MILLER AND HIS MEN: A MELO-DRAMA IN TWO ACTS. (Covent Garden, 21 October 1813.) 2nd ed. London: C. Chapple, 1813. 46 p.

Includes a cast list of the first London production; the Readex copy is a promptbook (New York Public Library), interleaved with manuscript notes.

1737 THE MAGPIE OR THE MAID? A MELO-DRAMA IN THREE ACTS. (Covent Garden, 15 September 1815.) London: John Miller, 1815. 52 p.

Includes a cast list of the first London production; the play is adapted from Caigniez's LA PIE VOLEUSE.

1738 ROBINSON CRUSOE; OR, THE BOLD BUCANIERS: A ROMANTIC MELO-DRAMA. (Covent Garden, 7 April 1817.) London: John Miller, 1817. 48 p.

With a cast list of the first London production; the play is adapted from Pixérécourt's ROBINSON CRUSOE.

1739 ROB ROY MACGREGOR; OR, AULD LANG SYNE! A MUSICAL DRAMA
IN THREE ACTS. (Covent Garden, 12 March 1818.) New York: D.
Longworth, 1818. 66 p.

> Includes cast lists of Covent Garden and New York produc-
> tions; the play is based on Scott's novel.

1740 MONTROSE; OR, THE CHILDREN OF THE MIST: A MUSICAL DRAMA
IN THREE ACTS. (Covent Garden, 14 February 1822.) London: W.
Simpkin and R. Marshall, 1822. 70 p.

> Includes a cast list of the first London production; the play
> is based on Scott's THE LEGEND OF MONTROSE.

1741 NIGEL; OR, THE CROWN JEWELS: A PLAY IN FIVE ACTS. (Covent
Garden, 28 January 1823.) London: n.p., 1823. 97 p.

> Includes a cast list of the first London production; the play
> is based on Scott's THE FORTUNES OF NIGEL.

1742 ALFRED THE GREAT; OR, THE ENCHANTED STANDARD: A MUSICAL
DRAMA IN TWO ACTS. (Covent Garden, 3 November 1827.) London:
John Miller, 1827. 45 p.

> Includes a cast list of the first London production and a
> prefatory note by Pocock.

1743 THE ROBBER'S WIFE: A ROMANTIC DRAMA IN TWO ACTS. (Covent
Garden, 22 October 1829.) London: Music Publishing Co., n.d. 40 p.

> An acting edition with a cast list of a Covent Garden 1830
> production and lengthy "Remarks" by D--G [George Daniel];
> the Readex copy is a promptbook, interleaved with manuscript
> notes.

POOLE, JOHN (1786-1872)

II Acted Plays—Principal Titles

1744 HAMLET TRAVESTIE, IN THREE ACTS: WITH ANNOTATIONS BY DR.
JOHNSON AND GEO. STEEVENS, ESQ. (New Theatre, 24 January
1811.) London: J.M. Richardson, 1810. xiii, 94 p.

> The author defends parodies in his preface; the piece went
> through five editions by 1814.

1745 THE HOLE IN THE WALL: A FARCE IN TWO ACTS. (Drury Lane, 23
June 1813.) London: J.M. Richardson, 1813. vii, 42 p.

Includes a cast list of the first London production and a preface by Poole defending farce.

1746 INTRIGUE: A COMIC INTERLUDE IN ONE ACT. (Drury Lane, 26 April 1814.) London: John Miller, 1814. 26 p.

Includes a cast list of the first London production and a preface in which the author singles out Miss Kelly "for a performance, as useful to me as it has been creditable to herself."

1747 A SHORT REIGN, AND A MERRY ONE: A PETITE-COMEDY IN TWO ACTS. (Covent Garden, 19 November 1819.) London: John Miller, 1819. 49 p.

Includes a cast list of the first London production.

1748 SIMPSON AND CO. A COMEDY IN ONE ACT. (Drury Lane, 4 January 1823.) London: Lacy, n.d. 42 p.

An acting edition with cast lists of Drury Lane and Princess' productions and "Remarks" by D--G [George Daniel].

1749 'TWOULD PUZZLE A CONJOURER: A COMIC DRAMA IN TWO ACTS. (Haymarket, 11 September 1824.) Modern Standard Drama, no. 47. New York: Wm. Taylor, n.d. 36 p.

An acting edition; the Readex copy is a promptbook (New York Public Library) with a few manuscript notes.

1750 PAUL PRY: A COMEDY IN THREE ACTS. (Haymarket, 13 September 1825.) Modern Standard Drama, no. 76. New York: Wm. Taylor, n.d. 69 p.

An acting edition with cast lists of London and New York productions and a brief editiorial introduction; the Readex copy is a promptbook (New York Public Library), inter-leaved with manuscript notes.

1751 THE SCAPEGOAT: A FARCE IN ONE ACT. (Covent Garden, 25 November 1825.) Lacy's Acting Edition, vol. 98. London: Lacy, n.d. 22 p.

With cast lists of 1825 and 1836 Covent Garden productions.

1752 LODGINGS FOR A SINGLE GENTLEMAN: A FARCE IN ONE ACT. (Haymarket, 15 June 1829.) London: Lacy, n.d. 30 p.

An acting edition with a cast list of the first London produc-tion.

1753 PATRICIAN AND PARVENU; OR, "CONFUSION WORSE CONFOUNDED":
A COMEDY IN FIVE ACTS. (Drury Lane, 21 March 1835.) London:
John Miller, 1835. x, 83 p.

> In a preface Poole expresses satisfaction that his attempt "to
> revive the public taste for entertainment offering no other
> claims to attention than plot, character, and dialogue" has
> been well received.

IV Biography

1754 Fitzgerald, Percy. "The Author of PAUL PRY." GM, 237 (1874), 336-
47.

RAYMOND, RICHARD JOHN (fl. 1818)

II Acted Plays—Principal Titles

1755 THE CASTLE OF PALUZZI; OR, THE EXTORTED OATH: A SERIOUS
DRAMA IN TWO ACTS. (Covent Garden, 27 May 1818.) 2nd ed.
London: William Sams, 1818. 53 p.

> Includes a cast list of the first London production and a
> preface in which the author says that the play "was written,
> accepted, and put into rehearsal, in the space of six days."

1756 CHERRY BOUNCE! A FARCE IN ONE ACT. (Sadler's Wells, 27 August
1821.) Duncombe's British Theatre, vol. 3. London: Duncombe, n.d.
18 p.

> An acting edition with a cast list of the first London produc-
> tion.

1757 ROBERT THE DEVIL! DUKE OF NORMANDY: A MUSICAL ROMANCE
IN THREE ACTS. (Coburg, 21 June 1830.) Cumberland's British Theatre,
vol. 33. London: Cumberland, n.d. 35 p.

> An acting edition with a cast list of a Covent Garden produc-
> tion and "Remarks" by D--G [George Daniel].

1758 THE DEUCE IS IN HER! A PETITE COMEDY IN ONE ACT. (Adelphi,
28 August 1830.) London: Duncombe, n.d. 24 p.

> An acting edition with a cast list of an unspecified production.

1759 THE FARMER'S DAUGHTER OF THE SEVERN SIDE; OR, MR. AND MRS.
TOODLES: A DOMESTIC DRAMA IN TWO ACTS. (Coburg, 11 April
1831.) London: Lacy, n.d. 42 p.

An acting edition with a cast list of the first London production (then with a different subtitle, THE BROKEN HEART).

1760 THE OLD OAK TREE: A DRAMA IN TWO ACTS. (English Opera House, 24 August 1835.) Duncombe's British Theatre, vol. 18. London: Duncombe, n.d. 40 p.

An acting edition with a cast list of the first London production.

1761 MRS. WHITE: A FARCE IN ONE ACT. (English Opera House, 23 June 1836.) London: Lacy, n.d. 25 p.

An acting edition with a cast list of the first London production.

1762 THE DISCARDED DAUGHTER: A DRAMA IN TWO ACTS. (Surrey, 5 April 1847.) Duncombe's British Theatre, vol. 59. London: Duncombe and Moon, n.d. 32 p.

An acting edition with a cast list of the first London production.

READE, CHARLES (1814-84)

II Acted Plays—Principal Titles

Note: All collaborations with Tom Taylor are listed under Taylor's name, (items 2098ff. below), regardless of the degree of collaboration each made.

1763 THE LADIES' BATTLE; OR, UN DUEL EN AMOUR: A COMEDY IN THREE ACTS. (Olympic, 7 May 1851.) London: Lacy, n.d. 41 p.

An acting edition with a cast list of the first London production, and a note on the play by Reade.

1764 ANGELO: A TRAGEDY IN FOUR ACTS. (Olympic, 11 August 1851.) London: Lacy, n.d. 24 p.

An acting edition with a cast list of the first London production.

1765 THE LOST HUSBAND: A DRAMA IN FOUR ACTS. (Strand, 26 April 1852.) Acting Edition, no. 86. London: Lacy, n.d. 36 p.

With a cast list of the first London production.

1766 GOLD! A DRAMA IN FIVE ACTS. (Drury Lane, 10 January 1853.) London: Lacy, n.d. 48 p.

> An acting edition with a cast list of the first London production.

1767 COURIER OF LYONS: A MELODRAMA, CONDENSED AND ALTERED FROM THE FRENCH. (Princess's, 26 June 1854; title altered to THE LYONS MAIL, Lyceum, 19 May 1877.) London: Dramatic Authors Society, 1854. vi, 53 p.

> An acting edition with a cast list of the first London production, and a preface on the play's composition.

1768 IT'S NEVER TOO LATE TO MEND: A DRAMA IN FOUR ACTS. (Theatre Royal, Leeds, 1864; Princess's, 4 October 1865.) London: n.d. 95 p.

> The author's promptbook, with many manuscript notes.

1769 DORA: A PASTORAL DRAMA IN THREE ACTS: FOUNDED ON TENNYSON'S POEM. (Adelphi, 1 June 1867.) Universal Stage, no. 50. Boston: Spencer, n.d. 33 p.

> An acting edition with three American cast lists.

1770 *THE WANDERING HEIR. (Amphitheatre, Liverpool, 10 September 1873; Queen's, 15 November 1873.) LC.

1771 *DRINK. (Princess's, 2 June 1879.) LC.

III Bibliographies

1772 Sadleir, Michael. EXCURSIONS IN VICTORIAN BIBLIOGRAPHY. London: Chaundy & Cox, 1922; rpt. Folcroft, Pa.: Folcroft Press, 1969. vii, 240 p.

> Sadleir's scholarly work devotes sections to Reade's fiction and drama. Most entries are annotated.

1773 Sutcliffe, Emerson Grant. "Charles Reade's Notebooks." SP, 27 (1930), 64-109.

> A useful, full, and descriptive account of Reade's notebooks, located in the London Library.

1774 Parrish, M.L., and Elizabeth V. Miller. WILKIE COLLINS AND CHARLES READE: FIRST EDITIONS DESCRIBED WITH NOTES. London: Constable, 1940; rpt. New York: Burt Franklin, 1968. x, 355 p.

A scholarly, annotated, and illustrated bibliography which
also lists posters and programs of Reade's plays. The original
title included the rider, IN THE LIBRARY AT DORMY HOUSE,
PINE VALLEY, NEW JERSEY.

1775 Burns, Wayne. "More Reade Notebooks." SP, 42 (1945), 824-42.

An account of four of Reade's notebooks in Princeton University Library.

1776 Martin, Robert B. "The Reade Collection." PULC, 17 (1956), 77-80.

A description of Princeton holdings.

1777 _____. "Manuscripts and Correspondence of Charles Reade." PULC,
19 (1957-58), 102-3.

The Princeton collection includes manuscripts of DORA, parts
of FOUL PLAY and IT'S NEVER TOO LATE TO MEND and
over 400 letters.

IV Biography

1778 Fields, Annie. "An Acquaintance with Charles Reade: with Letters
Hitherto Unpublished." CENTURY MAGAZINE, 29 (November 1884),
67-69.

A personal reminiscence, which reprints several letters,
mostly of a business nature.

1779 Reade, Charles L., and Rev. Compton Reade. CHARLES READE, DRAMA-
TIST, NOVELIST, JOURNALIST: A MEMOIR, COMPILED CHIEFLY
FROM HIS LITERARY REMAINS. 2 vols. London: Chapman and Hall,
1887.

The material not drawn directly from Reade is affectionate
and undiscriminating.

1780 Coleman, John. CHARLES READE AS I KNEW HIM. London: Treherne,
1903. xii, 428 p.

A typical volume of nineteenth-century personal reminiscence--
intimate and affable.

1781 Elwin, Malcolm. CHARLES READE: A BIOGRAPHY. London: Jonathan
Cape, 1931. 388 p.

A detailed biography, illustrated with letters and similar
documents. Appendices include an extensive bibliography
and a list of productions and revivals in London.

1782 Clareson, Thomas D. "Wilkie Collins to Charles Reade: Some Unpub-
lished Letters." VICTORIAN ESSAYS: A SYMPOSIUM ON THE OCCA-
SION OF THE CENTENNIAL OF THE COLLEGE OF WOOSTER IN
HONOR OF EMERITUS PROFESSOR WALDO H. DUNN. Eds. Warren D.
Anderson and Thomas D. Clareson. Kent, Ohio: Kent State University
Press, 1967. Pp. 107-24.

> A commentary on twenty-seven letters written by Collins to
> Reade and covering literary, social, and personal matters.
> An extensive letter deals with Collins's views on FREE LA-
> BOUR.

V Critical Studies

1783 Sutcliffe, Emerson Grant. "The Stage in Reade's Novels." SP, 27
(1930), 654-88.

> An extensive and perceptive study of the influence of Reade's
> theatrical experience on his novels. There are numerous, de-
> tailed references to the plays.

1784 Macmahon, Donald H. "Charles Reade as a Dramatist." Ph.D. Dissertation, Cornell University, 1936.

1785 _____. "The Composition and Early Stage History of MASKS AND
FACES." RS, 14, no. 4 (1946), 251-70.

> A fairly detailed study of the play, although the title of
> this article is misleading in its emphasis--there is more criti-
> cal evaluation and history than detail on the composition.

1786 Bond, William H. "NANCE OLDFIELD: An Unrecorded Printed Play by
Charles Reade." HLB, 1 (1947), 386-87.

> A bibliographical description and brief history of the produc-
> tion of the play.

1787 Brouse, Albert J. "Charles Reade: Dramatist." Ph.D. Dissertation,
Western Reserve University, 1956. 143 p.

1788 Fielding, K.J. "Charles Reade and Dickens--A Fight Against Piracy."
TN, 10 (1956), 106-11.

> Discusses efforts to protect dramatic copyright in the 1860's.

1789 Smith, Sheila M. "Realism in the Drama of Charles Reade." ENGLISH,
12 (1958), 94-100.

> "This article is partly concerned with the connexion between

> spectacular realism and serious social purpose in Reade's work,
> a connexion implied by his use of material from GOLD in
> IT IS NEVER TOO LATE TO MEND." The article also in-
> dicates how Reade used spectacular realism largely for sensa-
> tional effect and how "his efforts to produce serious social
> drama decreased after" IT'S NEVER TOO LATE.

1790 Burns, Wayne. CHARLES READE: A STUDY IN VICTORIAN AUTHOR-
SHIP. New York: Bookman Associates, 1961. 360 p.

> A detailed, documented study which mingles criticism and
> biography. Burns has made use of primary manuscript mate-
> rials, and there is a lengthy chapter on the plays.

REDE, WILLIAM LEMAN (1802-47)

II Acted Plays—Principal Titles

1791 THE RAKE'S PROGRESS: A MELODRAMA IN THREE ACTS. (City of
London, 28 January 1833.) Duncombe's British Theatre, vol. 12. London: Duncombe, n.d. 50 p.

> An acting edition (but no cast list); the Readex copy is a
> promptbook (New York Public Library) with a few manu-
> script notes.

1792 AN AFFAIR OF HONOUR: A FARCE [IN ONE ACT]. (Olympic, 12
March 1835.) London: John Miller, 1835. 19 p.

> Includes a cast list of the first London production. The
> Readex collection also has an acting edition of this play
> with "Remarks" by George Daniel.

1793 THE SKELETON WITNESS; OR, MURDER AT THE MOUND: A DOMES-
TIC DRAMA IN THREE ACTS. (Surrey, 27 April 1835.) French's Standard Drama, no. 197. New York: French, n.d. 44 p.

> An acting edition with cast lists of four American productions.

1794 CUPID IN LONDON; OR, SOME PASSAGES IN THE LIFE OF LOVE:
AN EXTRAVANGANZA IN TWO ACTS. (Queen's, 18 June 1835.)
Duncombe's British Theatre, vol. 17. London: Duncombe, n.d. 32 p.

> An acting edition with a cast list of the first London produc-
> tion.

1795 COME TO TOWN; OR, NEXT DOOR NEIGHBOURS! A FARCE IN ONE
ACT. (Strand, 25 April 1836.) Duncombe's British Theatre, vol. 21.

London: Duncombe, n.d. 26 p.

> An acting edition with a cast list of the first London production.

1796 THE FLIGHT TO AMERICA; OR, TEN HOURS IN NEW YORK! A DRAMA IN THREE ACTS. (Adelphi, 7 November 1836.) Duncombe's British Theatre, vol. 24. London: Duncombe, n.d. 43 p.

> An acting edition with a cast list of an unspecified production.

1797 PEREGRINATIONS OF PICKWICK: A DRAMA IN THREE ACTS. (Adelphi, 3 April 1837.) London: W. Strange, 1837. 32 p.

> An acting edition with cast lists of Adelphi and Surrey productions and a brief introduction by Rede.

1798 JACK IN THE WATER; OR, THE LADDER OF LIFE: A DOMESTIC BURLETTA IN THREE ACTS. (Olympic, 25 April 1842.) London: G.H. Davidson, n.d. 50 p.

> An acting edition with cast lists of Olympic and Strand productions in 1845 and "Remarks" by D--G [George Daniel].

1799 OUR VILLAGE; OR, THE LOST SHIP: A DOMESTIC DRAMA IN THREE ACTS. (Olympic, 17 April 1843.) Lacy's Acting Edition, vol. 88. London: Lacy, n.d. 48 p.

> With cast lists of Olympic and Marylebone productions and "Remarks" by D--G [George Daniel].

IV Biography

1800 "Recollections of Rede." NEW MONTHLY MAGAZINE AND HUMORIST, 1847, Part 2, pp. 102-9.

REECE, ROBERT (1838-91)

II Acted Plays—Principal Titles

1801 PROMETHEUS; OR, THE MAN ON THE ROCK! A NEW AND ORIGINAL EXTRAVAGANZA. (Royalty, 23 December 1865.) London: Lacy, n.d. 33 p.

> An acting edition with a cast list of the first London production.

1802 WHITTINGTON, JUNIOR, AND HIS SENSATION CAT: AN ORIGINAL CIVIC BURLESQUE. (Royalty, 23 November 1870.) London: Lacy, n.d. 37 p.

> An acting edition with a cast list of the first London production.

1803 DORA'S DEVICE: AN ORIGINAL COMEDY IN TWO ACTS. (Royalty, 11 January 1871.) London and New York: French, n.d. 37 p.

> An acting edition with a cast list of the first London production.

1804 PAQUITA; OR, LOVE IN A FRAME: AN ORIGINAL COMIC OPERA IN TWO ACTS. With J.E. Mallandain. (Royalty, 21 October 1871.) London: Lacy, n.d. 32 p.

> Libretto only, with a cast list of the first London production.

1805 THE VERY LAST DAYS OF POMPEII! A NEW CLASSICAL BURLESQUE. (Vaudeville, 13 February 1872.) London: Lacy, n.d. 26 p.

> An acting edition with a cast list of the first London production.

1806 MAY; OR, DOLLY'S DELUSION: A DOMESTIC DRAMA IN THREE ACTS. (Strand, 4 April 1874.) Standard Drama, no. 375. London and New York: French, n.d. 44 p.

> An acting edition with a cast list of the first London production.

1807 *GREEN OLD AGE: AN ORIGINAL MUSICAL IMPROBABILITY IN ONE ACT. (Vaudeville, 31 October 1874.) Acting Edition, no. 1535. London and New York: French, n.d. 24 p.

> Libretto only, with a cast list of the first London production.

1808 *VALENTINE AND ORSON: A NEW BURLESQUE DRAMA. (Gaiety, 23 December 1882.) London: 1882. 39 p.

> Libretto only, with a cast list.

ROBERTSON, THOMAS WILLIAM (1829-71)

I Collected Works

1809 THE PRINCIPAL DRAMATIC WORKS OF THOMAS WILLIAM ROBERTSON,

WITH A MEMOIR BY HIS SON. 2 vols. London: Sampson Low, 1889. lxxix, 789 p.

> Contents: volume one: BIRTH; BREACH OF PROMISE; CASTE; DAVID GARRICK; DREAMS; HOME; LADIES' BATTLE; M.P.; volume two: THE NIGHTINGALE; OURS; PLAY; PROGRESS; ROW IN THE HOUSE; SCHOOL; SOCIETY; WAR. This edition consists of a collection of French's acting editions together with cast lists of the various productions. The memoir provides useful biographical information, and there is also a list of Robertson's works.

II Acted Plays—Principal Titles

1810 THE CHEVALIER DE ST. GEORGE: A DRAMA IN THREE ACTS: ADAPTED FROM THE FRENCH OF MM. MELESVILLE & ROGER DE BEAUVOIR. (Princess's, 20 May 1845.) London: Lacy, n.d. 35 p.

> An acting edition with cast lists of the first Paris and London productions.

1811 NOEMIE: A DRAMA IN TWO ACTS: FROM THE FRENCH OF MM. DENNERY AND CLEMENT. (Princess's, 14 April 1846.) London and New York: French, n.d. 36 p.

> An acting edition, with several cast lists.

1812 THE LADIES' BATTLE: A COMEDY IN THREE ACTS: FROM THE FRENCH OF MM. SCRIBE AND LEGOUVE. (Haymarket, 18 November 1851.) London: Lacy, n.d. 43 p.

> An acting edition.

1813 FAUST AND MARGUERITE: A ROMANTIC DRAMA IN THREE ACTS: TRANSLATED FROM THE FRENCH OF MICHEL CARRÉ. (Princess's, 19 April 1854.) London: Lacy, n.d. 28 p.

> An acting edition with cast lists of the Paris and London productions.

1814 MY WIFE'S DIARY: A FARCE IN ONE ACT: TRANSLATED AND ADAPTED FROM "LES MEMOIRES DE DEUX JEUNES MARIÉES" BY MM. DENNERY AND CLAIRVILLE. (Olympic, 18 December 1854.) New York: De Witt, n.d. 15 p.

> An acting edition with cast lists of the first Paris and London productions.

1815 THE STAR OF THE NORTH: A DRAMA IN THREE ACTS. (Sadler's Wells, 5 March 1855.) London: Lacy, n.d. 36 p.

An acting edition.

1816 PEACE AT ANY PRICE! A FARCE IN ONE ACT. (Strand, 13 February 1856.) Acting Plays, no. 156. New York: De Witt, n.d. 10 p.

With a cast list of the first London production.

1817 THE HALF CASTE; OR, THE POISONED PEARL: A DRAMA IN THREE ACTS. (Surrey, 8 September 1856.) Acting Edition, no. 1441. London and New York: Lacy, n.d. 36 p.

With a cast list of the first London production.

1818 TWO GAY DECEIVERS; OR, BLACK, WHITE, AND GREY: A FARCE IN ONE ACT: TRANSLATED FROM EUGENE LABICHE'S "DEUX PROFONDS SCÉLÉRATS." (Strand, 1858.) Chicago: Dramatic Publishing Co., n.d. 11 p.

An acting edition with a cast list of the first London production.

1819 THE CANTAB: A FARCE IN ONE ACT. (Strand, 14 February 1861.) London and New York: French, n.d. 27 p.

An acting edition.

1820 DAVID GARRICK: A COMEDY IN THREE ACTS: (ADAPTED FROM THE FRENCH OF "SULLIVAN," WHICH WAS FOUNDED UPON A GERMAN DRAMATIZATION OF A PRETENDED INCIDENT IN GARRICK'S LIFE). (Prince of Wales's, Birmingham, April 1864; Haymarket, 30 April 1864.) London and New York: French, n.d. 36 p.

An acting edition with cast lists of the first London and New York productions; interleaved, with many manuscript notes.

1821 SOCIETY: A COMEDY IN THREE ACTS. (Prince of Wales's, Liverpool, 8 May 1865; Prince of Wales's, 11 November 1865.) London: Lacy, n.d. 65 p.

An acting edition, with cast lists of the first Liverpool and London productions.

1822 "OURS": A COMEDY IN THREE ACTS. (Prince of Wales's, Liverpool, 23 August 1866; Prince of Wales's, 15 September 1866.) London and New York: French, n.d. 56 p.

An acting edition with cast lists of the first London and New York productions; interleaved, with many manuscript notes.

1823 CASTE: AN ORIGINAL COMEDY IN THREE ACTS. (Prince of Wales's, 6 April 1867.) New York: French, n.d. 54 p.

> An acting edition with cast lists of the first productions in London and New York. The Readex collection also includes a manuscript promptcopy, located in New York Public Library.

1824 PLAY: AN ORIGINAL COMEDY IN FOUR ACTS. (Prince of Wales's, 15 February 1868.) London and New York: French, n.d. 489–542.

> An acting edition with a cast list of the first London production.

1825 HOME: A COMEDY IN THREE ACTS. (Haymarket, 14 January 1869.) London and New York: French, n.d. 235–74.

> An acting edition with a cast list of the first London production.

1826 SCHOOL: A COMEDY IN FOUR ACTS. (Prince of Wales's, 16 January 1869.) New York: De Witt, n.d. 40 p.

> An acting edition with cast lists of the first London and New York productions.

1827 DREAMS: A DRAMA IN FIVE ACTS. (Alexandra, Liverpool, 22 February 1869; Gaiety, 27 March 1869.) London and New York: French, n.d. 187–231.

> An acting edition with cast lists of the first Liverpool and London productions.

1828 A BREACH OF PROMISE: AN EXTRAVAGANT COMIC DRAMA IN TWO ACTS (ADAPTED FROM "LES AMOURS DE CLEOPATRA"). Acting Plays, no. 179. (Globe, 10 April 1869.) New York: De Witt, n.d. 20 p.

> With cast lists of first productions.

1829 *BIRTH: A NEW AND ORIGINAL COMEDY IN THREE ACTS. (Theatre Royal, Bristol, 5 October 1870.) Acting Edition, no. 1959. London and New York: French, n.d. 47 p.

> An acting edition with a cast list of the first Bristol production.

1830 WAR: A DRAMA IN THREE ACTS. (St. James's, 16 January 1871.) Standard Drama, no. 407. London and New York: French, n.d. 745–89.

> An acting edition with a cast list of the first London production.

1831 NOT AT ALL JEALOUS: A FARCE IN ONE ACT. (Court, 29 May 1871.) London: Lacy, n.d. 20 p.

> An acting edition.

1832 *A ROW IN THE HOUSE: A FARCE IN ONE ACT. (Toole's, 30 August 1883.) Acting Edition, no. 1917. London and New York: French, n.d. 20 p.

> With a cast list of the first London production.

IIa Unacted Plays

1833 BIRDS OF PREY; OR, A DUEL IN THE DARK: A DRAMA IN THREE ACTS. London: Lacy, n.d. 42 p.

> An acting edition.

1834 *ROBINSON CRUSOE: A BURLESQUE IN ONE ACT. London: Lacy, n.d. 63-84.

> An acting edition.

IV Biography

1835 Pemberton, T. Edgar. THE LIFE AND WRITINGS OF T.W. ROBERT-SON. London: Bentley, 1893. vi, 320 p.

> Largely a biographical and descriptive account, illustrated with lengthy contemporary extracts and letters. Typical of earlier theatre history, it lacks any critical incisiveness and documentation; nevertheless, interesting and valuable.

1836 Bulloch, John Malcolm. "Dame Madge Kendal's Robertson Ancestors." " N&Q, 163 (1932), 398-400; 418-20; 434-37.

> An account of some of T.W. Robertson's ancestors; interesting as biographical background; Robertson only mentioned in pass-ing.

V Critical Studies

1837 "Thomas William Robertson and the Modern Theatre." TEMPLE BAR, 44 (June 1875), 199-209.

> A brief, over-enthusiastic and very generalized attempt to give Robertson his due. Also includes some sketchy biography.

1838 Jones, W. Wilding. "Robertson as a Dramatist." THEATRE, n.s. 2 (July 1879), 355-60.

>A short, sympathetic, uncritical survey of the plays.

1839 Shaw, G.B. "Robertson Redivivus." SATURDAY REVIEW, 83 (19 June 1897), 685-87.

>Review of revival of CASTE; generally sympathetic, but pointing out that Robertson's innovative techniques in the 1860's had become commonplace by 1897, and thus much of the value of his work was lost.

1840 Dale, Harrison. "Tom Robertson: A Centenary Criticism." CONTEMPORARY REVIEW, 135 (March 1929), 356-61.

>A brief attempt to reassess and reestablish Robertson's reputation and contribution to the theatre. The biographical information and criticism are standard.

1841 Rahill, Frank. "A Mid-Victorian Regisseur." THEATRE ARTS MONTHLY, 13 (1929), 838-44.

>A short sympathetic account of Robertson's contribution to the development of realism in the theatre in an attempt to give Robertson his due.

1842 Savin, Maynard. THOMAS WILLIAM ROBERTSON: HIS PLAYS AND STAGECRAFT. Brown University Studies, vol. 13. Providence, R.I.: Brown University, 1950. ix, 146 p.

>Although this book bears strong traces of the dissertation style, it presents a fairly judicious account of Robertson's life, plays, ideas, and contribution to the theatre. There are useful appendices on Robertson's life, a list of plays (with cast lists), and a bibliography. There is no index.

1843 Durbach, Errol. "Remembering Tom Robertson (1829-1871)." ETJ, 24 (1973), 284-88.

RODWELL, GEORGE HERBERT BUONAPARTE (1800-1852)

II Acted Plays—Principal Titles

1844 WHERE SHALL I DINE? A FARCETTA IN ONE ACT. (Olympic, 17 February 1819.) London: Duncombe and Moon, n.d. 24 p.

>An acting edition with a cast list of a Covent Garden production.

1845 TEDDY THE TILER: A FARCE IN ONE ACT. (Covent Garden, 8 February 1830.) New York: E.B. Clayton, 1830. 22 p.

> An acting edition with cast lists of Covent Garden and three American productions; the Readex copy is a promptbook (New York Public Library).

1846 WAS I TO BLAME? A FARCE IN ONE ACT. (Adelphi, 13 December 1830.) Lacy's Acting Edition, vol. 32. London: Lacy, n.d. 19 p.

> With a cast list of the first London production.

1847 I'LL BE YOUR SECOND: A FARCE IN ONE ACT. (Olympic, 10 October 1831.) Lacy's Acting Edition, vol. 3. London: Lacy, n.d. 13 p.

> With a cast list of the first London production.

1848 THE CHIMNEY PIECE; OR, THE MARRIED MAID: A LAUGHABLE FARCE IN ONE ACT. (Drury Lane, 23 March 1833.) Turner's Dramatic Library. Philadelphia: Frederick Turner, n.d. 26 p.

> An acting edition with a cast list of the 1834 Chestnut St. theatre production and "Remarks" by E.T.W.

1849 MY WIFE'S OUT: AN ORIGINAL FARCE IN ONE ACT. (Covent Garden, 2 October 1843.) Lacy's Acting Edition, vol. 45. London: Lacy, n.d. 20 p.

> With a cast list of the first London production.

1850 HUSBANDS, WIVES, AND LOVERS: A FARCE IN ONE ACT. (Adelphi, 4 December 1843.) London: William Barth, n.d. 17 p.

> An acting edition with a cast list of the first London production.

1851 THE SEVEN MAIDS OF MUNICH; OR, THE GHOST'S TOWER: AN ORIGINAL MUSICAL ROMANCE IN ONE ACT. (Princess's, 19 December 1846.) No publication details.

> An acting edition with a cast list of the first London production.

SELBY, CHARLES (1801-63)

II Acted Plays—Principal Titles

1852 A DAY IN PARIS: A MUSICAL INTERLUDE IN ONE ACT. (Strand, 18 July 1832.) Fisher's Edition of Standard Farces. Philadelphia:

Turner & Fisher, n.d.   32 p.

An acting edition with cast lists of Strand and Victoria productions.

1853   ROBERT MACAIRE; OR, LES AUBERGES DES ADRETS!   A MELODRAMA
IN TWO ACTS.   (Victoria, 3 December 1834 [?].)   Duncombe's British
Theatre.   London: Duncombe, n.d.   34 p.

An acting edition with a cast list of a Covent Garden pro-
duction.   Nicoll (item 298) lists ROBERT MACAIRE; OR,
THE EXPLOITS OF A GENTLEMAN AT LARGE (Adelphi, 2
March 1835) and THE TWO MURDERERS; OR, THE AUBERGE
DES ADRETS (City, 1835).   The theatre and production date
given above come from the edition cited here.

1854   THE MARRIED RAKE: A FARCE IN ONE ACT.   (Queen's, 9 February
1835.)   French's American Drama, no. 71.   New York: French, n.d.
18 p.

An acting edition with cast lists of Philadelphia and New
York productions; the Readex copy is a promptbook (New
York Public Library).

1855   CATCHING AN HEIRESS: A FARCE IN ONE ACT.   (Queen's, 15 July
1835.)   Dicks' Standard Plays, no. 402.   [London: Dicks], n.d.   13 p.

An acting edition with a cast list of the first London production.

1856   LITTLE SINS & PRETTY SINNERS: AN INTERLUDE IN ONE ACT.
(Queen's, 12 January 1836.)   Duncombe's British Theatre, vol. 30.   London: Duncombe, n.d.   23 p.

An acting edition with a cast list of a Strand production in
1838.

1857   FREDERICK OF PRUSSIA; OR, THE MONARCH AND THE MIMIC: A
BURLETTA IN ONE ACT.   (Queen's, 24 July 1837.)   Duncombe's British
Theatre, vol. 27.   London: Duncombe, n.d.   29 p.

An acting edition with a cast list of the first London production; the Readex copy is a promptbook (New York Public
Library) interleaved with manuscript notes.

1858   THE KING'S GARDENER; OR, NIPPED IN THE BUD: A BURLETTA IN
ONE ACT.   (Strand, 1 April 1839.)   New British Theatre.   London:
Lacy, n.d.   22 p.

An acting edition with a cast list of the first London production.

1859 THE LOVES OF LORD BATEMAN AND THE FAIR SOPHIA! AN HIS-
TORICAL, PANTOMIMICAL, MELO-DRAMATICAL, BALLETICAL, BUR-
LESQUE BURLETTA IN ONE ACT. (Strand, 3 July 1839.) Duncombe's
British Theatre, vol. 37. London: Duncombe, n.d. 30 p.

   An acting edition with a cast list of the first London production.

1860 A LADY AND GENTLEMAN IN A PECULIARLY PERPLEXING PREDICA-
MENT! A BURLETTA IN ONE ACT. (English Opera House, 9 August
1841.) Duncombe's British Theatre, vol. 44. London: Duncombe, n.d.
27 p.

   An acting edition with a cast list of the first London production.

1861 THE BOOTS AT THE SWAN: A FARCE IN ONE ACT. (Strand, 8 June
1842.) French's Minor Drama, no. 2. New York: French, n.d. 29 p.

   An acting edition with cast lists of the first London and two
   subsequent American productions.

1862 THE MYSTERIOUS STRANGER: A DRAMA IN TWO ACTS. (Adelphi, 3
October 1844.) The Acting National Drama, vol. 10. London: National Acting Drama Office, 1844. 52 p.

   With a cast list of the first London production and a preface
   by Selby with a cryptic opening sentence: "It was my intention to have written a long article on 'Translations from the
   French,' and the power of the Lord Chamberlain, but as my
   piece has been triumphantly successful, in spite of its many
   crosses and delays, I think it better to let well alone, and
   confine myself to thanking the parties who have done me
   service."

1863 THE LIONESS OF THE NORTH; OR, THE PRISONER OF SCHLUSSEN-
BOURG: AN HISTORICAL DRAMA IN TWO ACTS. (Adelphi, 22
December 1845.) The Acting National Drama, vol. 12. London:
Nassau Steam Press, n.d.

   With a cast list of the first London production.

1864 TAKEN IN AND DONE FOR: AN ORIGINAL FARCE IN ONE ACT.
(Strand, 10 May 1849.) Modern Acting Drama. London: Chapman,
1849. 16 p.

   With a cast list of the first London production.

SERLE, THOMAS JAMES (1798-1889)

II Acted Plays—Principal Titles

1865 THE MAN IN THE IRON MASK: AN HISTORICAL PLAY IN FIVE ACTS. (Coburg, 16 January 1832.) Dicks' Standard Plays, no. 428. [London: Dicks], n.d. 24 p.

> An acting edition with a cast list of the first London production.

1866 THE MERCHANT OF LONDON: A PLAY IN FIVE ACTS. (Drury Lane, 26 April 1832.) London: W. Sams, 1832. iv, 115 p.

> Includes a cast list of the first London production, a dedication to Macready and a preface thanking the performers.

1867 THE GAMESTER OF MILAN: A PLAY IN THREE ACTS. (Victoria, 21 April 1834.) Duncombe's British Theatre, vol. 14. London: Duncombe, n.d. 44 p.

> An acting edition with a cast list of the first London production.

1868 A GHOST STORY: A DRAMA IN TWO ACTS. (Adelphi, 4 January 1836.) London: John Miller, 1836. 38 p.

> Includes a cast list of the first London production.

1869 THE PAROLE OF HONOUR: A DRAMA IN TWO ACTS. (Covent Garden, 4 November 1837.) London: W. Strange, 1837. 40 p.

> An acting edition with a cast list of the first London production.

1870 JOAN OF ARC, THE MAID OF ORLEANS: A HISTORICAL ROMANCE IN TWO ACTS. (Covent Garden, 28 November 1837.) London: W. Strange, 1837. 38 p.

> An acting edition with a cast list of the first London production.

1871 MASTER CLARKE: A PLAY IN FIVE ACTS. (Haymarket, 26 September 1840.) London: W.S. Johnson, 1840. iv, 88 p.

> Includes a cast list of the first London production and a preface by Serle, part of which is devoted to a plea for the abolition of the patent theatre monopoly.

SHEE, SIR MARTIN ARCHER (1769-1850)

II Acted Plays—Principal Titles

1872 ALASCO: A TRAGEDY IN FIVE ACTS. . . . EXCLUDED FROM THE STAGE BY THE AUTHORITY OF THE LORD CHAMBERLAIN. (Surrey, 5 April 1824.) London: Sherwood, Jones, and Co., 1824. lvi, 169 p.

> Shee's only play, but interesting because of its fierce and eloquent preface denouncing George Colman, Examiner of Plays, for refusing to license the play--it was performed unlicensed at the Surrey.

IV Biography

1873 Shee, Martin Archer. THE LIFE OF SIR MARTIN ARCHER SHEE. 2 vols. London: Longman, Green, Longman, and Roberts, 1860. xiv, 443; vii, 389 p.

> Volume one (page 365ff.) contains an account of the Lord Chamberlain's opposition to ALASCO (see item 1872).

SHEIL, RICHARD LALOR (1791-1851)

II Acted Plays—Principal Titles

1874 ADELAIDE; OR, THE EMIGRANTS: A TRAGEDY. (Crow St. Theatre, Dublin, 19 February 1814; Covent Garden, 23 May 1816.) Dublin: R. Coyne, 1814. vii, 74 p.

> Includes a dedication to Miss O'Neill, for whom the part of Adelaide was written.

1875 THE APOSTATE: A TRAGEDY IN FIVE ACTS. (Covent Garden, 3 May 1817.) London: John Murray, 1817. iv, 83 p.

> Includes a cast list of the first London production, a dedication to Miss O'Neill, and a preface in which Sheil explains the purpose of the play in order to "relieve himself from the imputation of having sought the illegitimate assistance of political allusion."

1876 BELLAMIRA; OR, THE FALL OF TUNIS: A TRAGEDY IN FIVE ACTS. (Covent Garden, 22 April 1818.) 3rd ed. London: John Murray, 1818. vi, 75 p.

> Includes a cast list of the first London production and a preface thanking the performers for their efforts.

1877 EVADNE; OR, THE STATUE: A TRAGEDY IN FIVE ACTS. (Covent Garden, 10 February 1819.) 4th ed. London: John Murray, 1819. vi, 86 p.

>Includes a cast list of the first London production and a preface in which Sheil explains the relationship of his play to Shirley's THE TRAITOR.

1878 *MONTONI; OR, THE PHANTOM. (Covent Garden, 3 May 1820.)

>Unpublished; manuscript is in the Huntington Library, LA 2147.

1878a DAMON AND PYTHIAS: A TRAGEDY IN FIVE ACTS. (Covent Garden, 28 May 1821.) London: John Warren, 1821. 70 p.

>Includes a cast list of the first London production and a dedication to Macready; the play is an altered and revised version of John Banim's play of the same name.

1879 *THE HUGUENOT. (Covent Garden, 11 December 1822.)

>Unpublished; manuscript is in the Huntington Library, LA 2267.

IV Biography

1879a McCullagh, W. Torrens. MEMOIRS OF THE RIGHT HONOURABLE RICHARD LALOR SHEIL. 2 vols. London: Hurst and Blackett, 1885. xii, 387; viii, 443 p.

SHELLEY, PERCY BYSSHE (1792-1822)

I Collected Works

1880 Herford, C.H., ed. THE DRAMATIC POEMS OF PERCY BYSSHE SHELLEY. ARRANGED IN CHRONOLOGICAL ORDER. New York: Brentano's, n.d. xi, 412 p.

>Contents: TASSO (a fragment); PROMETHEUS UNBOUND; THE CENCI; OEDIPUS TYRANNUS; HELLAS; AN UNFINISHED DRAMA; CHARLES THE FIRST. There is a brief but informative preface. This edition is available in the Readex collection (item 2517).

1881 Ingpen, Roger, and Walter E. Peck, eds. THE COMPLETE WORKS OF PERCY BYSSHE SHELLEY. 10 vols. The Julian Edition. London: Ernest Benn; New York: Gordian Press, 1965.

>Volume two has THE CENCI, PROMETHEUS UNBOUND, and OEDIPUS TYRANNUS; volume three has HELLAS; volume four has FRAGMENTS OF AN UNFINISHED DRAMA and CHARLES

THE FIRST. This edition of the Works also includes Shelley's letters (volumes 8-10) which contain numerous references to the plays. The editors supply useful editorial notes.

1882 Hutchinson, Thomas, ed. SHELLEY: POETICAL WORKS. London: Oxford University Press, 1968. xxiii, 918 p.

This edition contains PROMETHEUS UNBOUND, THE CENCI, OEDIPUS TYRANNUS, HELLAS, CHARLES THE FIRST, and FRAGMENTS OF AN UNFINISHED DRAMA. The editor supplies some brief notes on the text of each play and a useful list of the principal editions of Shelley's works.

1883 Rogers, Neville, ed. PERCY BYSSHE SHELLEY: SELECTED POETRY. Boston: Houghton Mifflin, 1968. xxxv, 488 p.

Contains THE CENCI, PROMETHEUS UNBOUND, OEDIPUS TYRANNUS, and HELLAS. There is helpful editorial matter with each play.

II Acted Plays—Principal Titles

1884 *THE CENCI: A TRAGEDY IN FIVE ACTS. (Grand Theatre, Islington, 7 May 1886.) London: C. and J. Ollier, 1819. xiv, 104 p.

1885 *Woodberry, George Edward, ed. THE CENCI. Boston and London: D.C. Heath, 1909. xxxv, 159 p.

This is a useful edition with good introductory material, including sections on the composition and publication of the play, a critical analysis of the play, Shelley's debt to Shakespeare, and the play's stage history. There are brief notes to the text and an appendix on the sources of THE CENCI. There is also a brief but helpful bibliography.

1886 *Hicks, Arthur C., and R. Milton Clarke, eds. A STAGE VERSION OF SHELLEY'S CENCI. Caldwell, Idaho: Caxton Printers, 1945. 156 p.

Based on the Bellingham Theatre Guilds's production, March 1940. "Through a detailed description of stage settings and business, only a part of which is indicated by Shelley, the editors have attempted to create a clear visual impression of the actual performance." There are nearly fifty pages of introductory discussion.

1887 *THE CENCI. Intro. Alfred Forman and H. Buxton Forman. Prologue. John Todhunter. New York: Phaeton Press, 1970. xvi, 107 p.

A reprint of the Shelly Society text of 1886.

1888 *Duerksen, Roland A., ed. THE CENCI. Indianapolis and New York: Bobbs-Merrill Co., 1970. xx, 121 p.

> The editor supplies an introduction, a select bibliography, and, as appendices, Mary Shelley's views on THE CENCI and Shelley's own views on his play (from the letters). This is a compact and useful edition of the play.

IIa Unacted Plays

1889 OEDIPUS TYRANNUS; OR, SWELLFOOT THE TYRANT: A TRAGEDY IN TWO ACTS. TRANSLATED FROM THE ORIGINAL DORIC. London: Published for the Author by J. Johnston, 1820. 45 p.

> "The burlesque was written in August, 1820, and published anonymously. It was suppressed and the edition destroyed, probably owing to a threat of prosecution from the Society for the Suppression of Vice; and only seven copies seem to have escaped." (Granniss [item 1898], p. 64.)

1890 PROMETHEUS UNBOUND: A LYRICAL DRAMA IN FOUR ACTS WITH OTHER POEMS. London: C. and J. Ollier, 1820. 222 p.

> With a preface by Shelley.

1891 *HELLAS: A LYRICAL DRAMA. London: Charles and James Ollier, 1822. xi, 60 p.

1892 *CHARLES THE FIRST. Published in POSTHUMOUS POEMS OF PERCY BYSSHE SHELLEY. London: John and Henry L. Hunt, 1824.

1893 *Wise, Thomas J., ed. HELLAS: A LYRICAL DRAMA BY PERCY BYSSHE SHELLEY. A REPRINT OF THE ORIGINAL EDITION PUBLISHED IN 1822. WITH THE AUTHOR'S PROLOGUE AND NOTES BY VARIOUS HANDS. London: Published for the Shelley Society by Reeves and Turner, 1886. lviii, 60 p.

1894 *Hughes, A.M.D., ed. SHELLEY: POEMS PUBLISHED IN 1820. Oxford: Clarendon Press, 1910. xxxii, 224 p.

> This is a useful edition of PROMETHEUS UNBOUND (and some miscellaneous poems) with notes, an introductory essay on the play, and a short life of Shelley.

1895 *Zillman, Lawrence John, ed. SHELLEY'S "PROMETHEUS UNBOUND": A VARIORUM EDITION. Seattle: University of Washington Press, 1959. xx, 792 p.

> An exhaustive study. Over 300 pages of critical notes and

several appendices, including one on contemporary reviews of PROMETHEUS UNBOUND. There is an extensive bibliography.

1896 * _____. SHELLEY'S "PROMETHEUS UNBOUND": THE TEXT OF THE DRAFTS. TOWARD A MODERN DEFINITIVE EDITION. New Haven and London: Yale University Press, 1968. 275 p.

1897 *FRAGMENTS OF AN UNFINISHED DRAMA. Published as above, items 1880-82.

III Bibliographies

1898 Granniss, Ruth S. A DESCRIPTIVE CATALOGUE OF THE FIRST EDITIONS IN BOOK FORM OF THE WRITINGS OF PERCY BYSSHE SHELLEY. New York: Grolier Club, 1922. 133 p.

IV Biography

1899 Dowden, Edward. THE LIFE OF PERCY BYSSHE SHELLEY. 2 vols. London: Kegan Paul, Trench & Co., 1886. xvi, 554; viii, 586 p.

The authorized Victorian biography.

1900 White, Newman Ivey. SHELLEY. 2 vols. New York: Alfred A. Knopf, 1940. xvi, 748; x, 642 p. Index numbered separately, cxlvii p.

An authoritative biography with extensive discussion of the plays.

1901 Jones, Frederick L., ed. THE LETTERS OF PERCY BYSSHE SHELLEY. 2 vols. Oxford: Clarendon Press, 1964. xxxvi, 457; xiv, 524 p.

The best edition of the letters; very well indexed with numerous references to the plays.

V Critical Studies

1902 Todhunter, John. A STUDY OF SHELLEY. London: Kegan Paul, 1880. vi, 293 p.

A chronological study of Shelley's works, including the drama.

1903 Bates, Ernest Sutherland. A STUDY OF SHELLEY'S DRAMA "THE CENCI." New York: Columbia University Press, 1908. x, 103 p.

An early analysis of the play, concluding that THE CENCI

is "a great work of art," but that Shelley "failed . . . in
his initial purpose of writing a play suitable for the stage."
More recent critics have forcefully disputed this latter claim.

1904 Kooistra, J. "Shelley's PROMETHEUS UNBOUND." NEOPHILOLOGUS,
1 (1916), 213-22.

Part of the essay compares the dramatic excellence of THE
CENCI with the dramatic inadequacies of PROMETHEUS UN-
BOUND.

1905 White, Newman I. "The Historical and Personal Background of Shelley's
HELLAS." SAQ, 20 (1921), 52-60.

A discussion of HELLAS ("of negligible worth merely as drama")
as an idealization of the Greek Revolution.

1906 _____. "Shelley's SWELL-FOOT THE TYRANT in Relation to Contemporary Political Satires." PMLA, 36 (1921), 332-46.

The essay identifies the political allusions in the play and
shows that Shelley "was sufficiently in touch with the numerous anonymous cartoons and political satires on the subject [the trial of Queen Caroline] to put out a satire of
his own remarkably like them in tone, incident, and
general paraphernalia."

1907 _____. "Shelley's CHARLES THE FIRST." JEGP, 21 (1922), 431-41.

A good discussion of various aspects of the play--its genesis,
why Shelley never completed it, its dramatic qualities, and
its relationship to other plays on the same subject.

1908 _____. "Shelley's PROMETHEUS UNBOUND, or Every Man His Own
Allegorist." PMLA, 40 (1925), 172-84.

The author takes issue with various allegorical interpretations
of PROMETHEUS UNBOUND and questions whether it is really
allegorical at all.

1909 Grabo, Carl. "PROMETHEUS UNBOUND": AN INTERPRETATION.
Chapel Hill: University of North Carolina Press, 1935. ix, 205 p.

A study of PROMETHEUS UNBOUND as a philosophical poem
rather than as a play.

1910 Irvine, St. John. "Shelley as a Dramatist." ESSAYS BY DIVERS
HANDS. BEING THE TRANSACTIONS OF THE ROYAL SOCIETY OF
LITERATURE OF THE UNITED KINGDOM. Ed. Hugh Walpole. London:

Oxford University Press, 1936. 77-106.

> A discussion of THE CENCI only; but Irvine argues that had Shelley "seriously applied his thoughts to the theatre, he would have become a great dramatist."

1911 White, Newman Ivey. THE UNEXTINGUISHED HEARTH. SHELLEY AND HIS CONTEMPORARY CRITICS. Durham, N.C.: Duke University Press, 1938. xvi, 397 p.

> There are substantial sections on THE CENCI and PROMETHEUS UNBOUND.

1912 Clarke, David Lee. "Shelley and Shakespeare." PMLA, 54 (1939), 261-87.

> There is substantial discussion of THE CENCI and reference also to PROMETHEUS UNBOUND, CHARLES THE FIRST, and OEDIPUS TYRANNUS.

1913 Watson, Sara Ruth. "Shelley and Shakespeare: An Addendum. A Comparison of OTHELLO and THE CENCI." PMLA, 55 (1940), 611-14.

> Parallels of imagery, plot, characterization, and structure.

1914 Wright, Walter Francis. "Shelley's Failure in CHARLES I." ELH, 8 (1941), 41-46.

> Wright argues that Shelley abandoned the play because, following Hume, he could not accept Cromwell's "ambitious tyranny" as an improvement over Charles's "well-meaning despotism" and hence the theme of liberty triumphing over tyranny floundered. Some of Wright's interpretations and judgments have been questioned by Cameron (item 1918).

1915 Pfeiffer, Karl G. "Landor's Critique of THE CENCI." SP, 39 (1942), 670-79.

> Landor's views are contained in a letter to Leigh Hunt. See also item 1917.

1916 Cameron, Kenneth Neill. "The Political Symbolism of PROMETHEUS UNBOUND." PMLA, 58 (1943), 728-53.

> A thorough and persuasive political interpretation of the drama.

1917 Super, R.H. "Landor's Critique of THE CENCI--A Correction." SP, 40 (1943), 101.

> Regarding Pfeiffer's dating and transcription of Landor's letter

to Hunt (item 1915).

1918 Cameron, Kenneth Neill. "Shelley's Use of Source Material in CHARLES I." MLQ, 6 (1945), 197-210.

A detailed analysis of four principal sources--Hume, Macaulay, Clarendon, Bulstrode Whitelocke--showing that from these sources comes only the framework of the play: "those qualities which make the play . . . a living work of literature, come from Shelley's own dramatic imagination and historical insight."

1919 Cameron, Kenneth N[eill], and Horst Frenz. "The Stage History of Shelley's THE CENCI." PMLA, 60 (1945), 1080-105.

An account of eleven productions of the play in England, Germany, France, Italy, Russia, Czechoslovakia, and the United States. See also item 1925.

1920 Havens, Raymond D. "HELLAS and CHARLES THE FIRST." SP, 43 (1946), 545-50.

Both works show that Shelley "was becoming less sure of the millenium, that the escape from reality into an ideal world no longer yielded him the satisfaction that it once did."

1921 Weaver, Bennett. "PROMETHEUS BOUND and PROMETHEUS UNBOUND." PMLA, 64 (1949), 115-33.

Shelley's debt to Aeschylus.

1922 White, William. "An Armenian Performance of Shelley's THE CENCI." MLN, 64 (1949), 178-79.

A performance by the Armenian Cultural Society of Los Angeles on 10 December 1933 (in Armenian!).

1923 Forman, Elsa. "Beatrice Cenci and Alma Murray." KSMB, 5 (1953), 5-10.

Comments on the first performance of THE CENCI by the daughter of Alma Murray; included is a portrait of the actress in the role of Beatrice.

1924 Rees, Joan. "The Preface to THE CENCI." RES, n.s. 8 (1957), 172-73.

Parallel passages in Shelley's preface and Plato's REPUBLIC.

1925 States, Bert O. "Addendum: The Stage History of Shelley's THE CENCI." PMLA, 72 (1957), 633-44.

> Ten productions of the play (including two on BBC Radio), 1936-53. See item 1919.

1926 Watson, Melvin R. "Shelley and Tragedy: The Case of Beatrice Cenci." KSJ, 7 (1958), 13-21.

> Concerned with these questions: "does she [Beatrice] possess a tragic flaw? is the motivation of her actions sufficient? is there any development of her character and is it logical? what, according to Shelley, is the essence of tragedy?"

1927 Whitman, Robert F. "Beatrice's 'Pernicious Mistake' in THE CENCI." PMLA, 74 (1959), 249-53.

> An analysis of Beatrice's character from which the author concludes that "If Beatrice is admirable, it is in spite of, not because of, her act of rebellion. By taking what she thought to be the law of God into her own hands, she acted as a brave and desperate human being--but she was wrong."

1928 Wilson, Milton. SHELLEY'S LATER POETRY: A STUDY OF HIS PRO-PHETIC IMAGINATION. New York: Columbia University Press, 1959. vi, 332 p.

> A major study of PROMETHEUS UNBOUND.

1929 Kessel, Marcel, and Bert O. States. "THE CENCI as a Stage Play." PMLA, 75 (1960), 147-49.

> A discussion arising out of States's earlier article (item 1925) about the quality of THE CENCI as drama.

1930 Marshall, William H. "CALEB WILLIAMS and THE CENCI." N&Q, 205 (1960), 260-63.

> A discussion of the degree of didacticism in each work.

1931 Rees, Joan. "Shelley's Orsino: Evil in THE CENCI." KSMB, 12 (1961), 3-6.

1932 Duerksen, Roland A. "Shelley and Shaw." PMLA, 78 (1963), 114-27.

> Duerksen includes in his discussion some brief comments on Shaw's opinion of THE CENCI, but the essay as a whole focuses on Shaw rather than Shelley.

1933 Smith, Paul. "Restless Casuistry: Shelley's Composition of THE CENCI." KSJ, 13 (1964), 77-85.

> The details of the composition of the play, drawn mainly from Shelley's letters and notebooks.

1934 Adams, Charles L. "The Structure of THE CENCI." DramS, 4 (1965), 139-48.

> Adams defends the play against the charge that it is structurally defective, paying particular attention to arguments that much of the play fails to advance the action in any way and that the focus of interest changes sharply with Count Cenci's death.

1935 Ridenour, George M., ed. SHELLEY: A COLLECTION OF CRITICAL ESSAYS. Twentieth Century Views Series. Englewood Cliffs, N.J.: Prentice-Hall, 1965. 182 p.

> The collection includes Frederick A. Pottle's "The Role of Asia in the Dramatic Action of Shelley's PROMETHEUS UNBOUND."

1936 Rieger, James. "Shelley's Paterin Beatrice." STUDIES IN ROMANTICISM, 4 (1965), 169-84.

1937 Wasserman, Earl R. SHELLEY'S "PROMETHEUS UNBOUND": A CRITICAL READING. Baltimore, Md.: Johns Hopkins Press, 1965. 222 p.

1938 Hurt, James R. "PROMETHEUS UNBOUND and Aeschylean Dramaturgy." KSJ, 15 (1966), 43-48.

> "Consideration of PROMETHEUS UNBOUND as a dramatic trilogy, inspired by the example of Aeschylus, will enable us to explain Shelley's plot development, his concept of the tragic hero, and his use of lyricism as a dramatic device more satisfactorily, perhaps, than other approaches have done."

1939 Donohue, Joseph W. "Shelley's Beatrice and the Romantic Concept of Tragic Character." KSJ, 17 (1968), 53-73.

> A detailed discussion of the influence of Guido's portrait of LA CENCI and the Actress Eliza O'Neill on the character of Beatrice; plates of Guido's portrait and of Miss O'Neill are included.

1940 Miller, Sara M. "Irony in Shelley's THE CENCI." UMSE, 9 (1968), 23-25.

1941 Woodings, R.B. "'A Devil of a Nut to Crack': Shelley's CHARLES THE FIRST." SN, 40 (1968), 216-37.

Woodings cracks it rather well; this is a good, comprehensive discussion of the play.

1942 McNiece, Gerald. SHELLEY AND THE REVOLUTIONARY IDEA. Cambridge, Mass.: Harvard University Press, 1969. x, 303 p.

The study is valuable for its study of Shelley's political ideas and the analysis of PROMETHEUS UNBOUND and HELLAS in this context.

1943 Otten, Terry. "Christabel, Beatrice, and the Encounter with Evil." BuR, 17, no. 2 (1969), 19-31.

A discussion of the parallel themes and devices in CHRISTABEL and THE CENCI.

1944 Steffan, Truman Guy. "Seven Accounts of the Cenci and Shelley's Drama." SEL, 9 (1969), 601-18.

1944a Woodings, R.B. "Shelley's Sources for CHARLES THE FIRST." MLR, 64 (1969), 267-75.

An extension of the discussion in Cameron's article (item 1918), with some useful reference to Shelley's notebooks. See also item 1941.

1945 Curran, Stuart. SHELLEY'S "CENCI." Princeton, N.J.: Princeton University Press, 1970. xviii, 298 p.

"The purpose of this book is to explore in detail the meaning, the range, and the influence of this solitary and singular tragedy" (preface). The play is discussed at length as a poem and as a play. Curran carefully and sympathetically analyses various productions of the play and includes some excellent illustrations (particularly of the 1959 Old Vic production).

1946 Del Prado, Wilma. "The Philosophy of PROMETHEUS UNBOUND." SLRJ, 1 (1970), 716-22.

1947 Peck, Mary Alice. "The Drama of Shelley and Browning: A Comparative Study." Ph.D. Dissertation, Miami University, 1970. 250 p. (DA#71-16923)

1948 Brophy, Robert J. "TAMAR, THE CENCI, and Incest." AL, 42 (1970-71), 241-44.

> Similarities between Robinson Jeffers's play and Shelley's.

1949 Coats, Sandra Whitaker. "Gothic Elements in Shelley's PROMETHEUS UNBOUND." Ph.D. Dissertation, Texas A & M University, 1971. 180 p. (DA#72-13210)

1950 Dyck, Sarah. "The Presence of that Shape: Shelley's PROMETHEUS UNBOUND." COSTERUS, 1 (1972), 13-80.

1951 Flagg, John Sewell. "PROMETHEUS UNBOUND" AND "HELLAS": AN APPROACH TO SHELLEY'S LYRICAL DRAMAS. Salzburg: Universitaet Salzburg, 1972. vii, 278 p.

> Originally a dissertation, Boston University, 1971.

1952 Johnson, Betty Freeman. "Shelley's CENCI and MRS. WARREN'S PROFESSION." SHAW REVIEW, 15 (1972), 26-34.

> A discussion of interesting literary connections between the plays.

1953 Labelle, M. "Artaud's Use of Shelley's THE CENCI: The Experiment in the 'Théâtre de la Cruauté.'" RLC, 46 (1972), 128-34.

> A discussion of Artaud's 1935 adaptation (LES CENCI) of Shelley's play.

1954 Singh, Sheila Uttam. SHELLEY AND THE DRAMATIC FORM. Salzburg: Universitaet Salzburg, 1972. 243 p.

> Originally a dissertation, London University.

1955 Turner, Justin G. "THE CENCI: Shelley vs. the Truth." ABC, 22 (1972), 5-9.

VI Journals and Newsletters

1956 BULLETIN OF THE KEATS-SHELLEY MEMORIAL, ROME. 1910-1913.

> Superseded by item 1957.

1957 KEATS-SHELLEY MEMORIAL BULLETIN, ROME. Keats-Shelley Memorial Association, 1950-- . Annual.

1958 KEATS-SHELLEY JOURNAL. KEATS, SHELLEY, BYRON, HUNT, AND
THEIR CIRCLES. New York: The Keats-Shelley Association of America,
1952-- . Annual.

> Includes book reviews and excellent current bibliographies.

SIMPSON, JOHN PALGRAVE (1807-87)

II Acted Plays—Principal Titles

1959 SECOND LOVE: AN ORIGINAL COMIC DRAMA IN THREE ACTS.
(Haymarket, 23 July 1856.) Boston Theatre, no. 65. Boston: Spencer,
n.d. 40 p.

> An acting edition with cast lists of the first London and New
> York productions.

1960 DADDY HARDACRE: A DRAMA IN TWO ACTS. (Olympic, 26 March
1857.) London and New York: French, n.d. 40 p.

> An acting edition with a cast list of the first London produc-
> tion.

1961 WORLD AND STAGE: AN ORIGINAL COMEDY IN THREE ACTS. (Haymarket, 12 March 1859.) London and New York: French, n.d. 76 p.

> An acting edition with a cast list of the first London produc-
> tion.

1962 A SCHOOL FOR COQUETTES: A COMEDIETTA IN ONE ACT. (Strand,
4 July 1859.) London: Lacy, n.d. 36 p.

> An acting edition with a cast list of the first London produc-
> tion.

1963 A SCRAP OF PAPER: A COMIC DRAMA IN THREE ACTS. (St. James's,
22 April 1861.) London and New York: French, n.d. 51 p.

> An acting edition with a cast list of the first London produc-
> tion.

1964 COURT CARDS: A COMIC DRAMA IN TWO ACTS. (Olympic, 25
November 1861.) London: Lacy, n.d. 44 p.

> An acting edition with a cast list of the first London produc-
> tion.

1965 SYBILLA; OR, STEP BY STEP: AN ORIGINAL COMIC DRAMA IN THREE
ACTS. (St. James's, 29 October 1864.) London: Lacy, n.d. 63 p.

An acting edition with a cast list of the first London production.

1966 SHADOWS OF THE PAST: A COMEDY DRAMA IN TWO ACTS. (Theatre Royal, Brighton, 1 November 1867; Prince of Wales's, Birmingham, 7 May 1869.) London and New York: French, n.d. 36 p.

An acting edition with a cast list.

1967 BROKEN TIES: DOMESTIC DRAMA IN TWO ACTS. (Olympic, 8 June 1872.) London and New York: French, n.d. 41 p.

An acting edition with a cast list of the first London production.

IV Biography

1968 [Simpson, John Palgrave]. LETTERS FROM THE DANUBE. 2 vols. London: Bentley, 1847. x, 338; viii, 312 p.

Something of a travelogue, which gives opportunity for speculative comment; includes a few pages on the drama (letter IX).

SOANE, GEORGE (1790-1860)

II Acted Plays—Principal Titles

1969 THE INNKEEPER'S DAUGHTER: A MELO-DRAMA IN TWO ACTS. (Drury Lane, 7 April 1817.) London: W. Simpkin and R. Marshall, 1817. iv, 67 p.

Includes a cast list of the first London production, a dedication to Frances Kelly, and a preface thanking the performers.

1970 THE FALLS OF CLYDE: A MELO-DRAMA IN TWO ACTS. (Drury Lane, 29 October 1817.) London: T. Rodwell, 1817. iii, 56 p.

Includes a cast list of the first London production and the author's preface thanking the performers.

1971 SELF-SACRIFICE; OR, THE MAID OF THE COTTAGE: A MELO-DRAMA IN TWO ACTS. (English Opera House, 19 July 1819.) London: John Lowndes, 1819. iv, 35 p.

Includes a cast list of the first London production and the author's preface thanking the performers.

1972 FAUSTUS: A ROMANTIC DRAMA IN THREE ACTS. Drury Lane, 16
     May 1825.) London: John Miller, 1825. 59 p.

> Includes a cast list of the first London production. The
> Readex collection has two other editions of this play, one
> a promptbook with manuscript notes.

1973 PRIDE SHALL HAVE A FALL: A COMEDY IN FIVE ACTS. (Coburg,
     30 July 1832.) London: Hurst, Robinson & Co., 1824. 115 p.

> A promptbook (New York Public Library) with numerous
> manuscript notes and alterations; an intended cast list for
> a first production is printed, but the play was not acted
> until eight years later.

1974 THE YOUNG REEFER: A FARCE IN TWO ACTS. (Queen's, 27 April
     1835.) London: Cumberland, n.d. 38 p.

> An acting edition with a cast list of the first London produc-
> tion and "Remarks" by D--G [George Daniel].

1975 ZARAH: A ROMANTIC DRAMA IN TWO ACTS. (Queen's, 7 September
     1835.) Cumberland's British Theatre, no. 266. London: Cumberland,
     n.d. 31 p.

> An acting edition with a cast list of the first London produc-
> tion and "Remarks" by D--G [George Daniel].

1976 HAYDÉE; OR, THE SECRET: A COMIC OPERA IN THREE ACTS. (Strand,
     3 April 1848.) London: Davidson, 1848. 38 p.

> Includes a cast list of a Covent Garden 1848 production and
> a brief anonymous preface; the opera is based on Scribe's
> HAYDÉE. Music by Auber.

IIa Unacted Plays

1977 THE BOHEMIAN: A TRAGEDY IN FIVE ACTS. London: C. Chapple,
     1817. 139 p.

> Includes a brief preface by Soane: "The publication of an
> unacted play is generally considered as a declaration of war
> against theatrical managers, as an appeal from their taste to
> that of the public--for myself, this certainly is not the
> case. . . ."

V Critical Studies

1978 Bowman, W.P.   "Some Plays by George Soane." MLN, 54 (1939), 278–79.

> Identifies Soane as the author of five plays listed by Nicoll (item 298) as of unknown authorship.

SOMERSET, CHARLES A. (fl. 1827-34)

II Acted Plays—Principal Titles

1979 CRAZY JANE: A ROMANTIC PLAY IN THREE ACTS. (Surrey, 19 June 1827.) Cumberland's Minor Theatre, vol. 2. London: Cumberland, n.d. 57 p.

> An acting edition with a cast list of the first London production and "Remarks" by D--G [George Daniel].

1980 THE ROEBUCK; OR, GUILTY AND NOT GUILTY: A COMEDY IN THREE ACTS. (Surrey, 1 October 1827.) Duncombe's British Theatre, vol. 2. London: Duncombe, n.d. 40 p.

> An acting edition with a cast list of the first London production.

1981 DAY AFTER THE FAIR: A BURLETTA. (Olympic, 5 January 1829.) French's Minor Drama, no. 123. New York: French, n.d. 33 p.

> An acting edition with cast lists of Surrey and New York productions.

1982 HOME! SWEET HOME! OR, THE SWISS FAMILY: AN OPERA IN TWO ACTS. (Covent Garden, 19 March 1829.) London: Duncombe, n.d. 24 p.

> An acting edition with a cast list of the first London production; the opera is adapted from the German. Music by Bishop.

1983 SHAKESPEARE'S EARLY DAYS: A DRAMA IN TWO ACTS. (Covent Garden, 29 October 1829.) Lacy's Acting Edition, vol. 93. London: Lacy, n.d. 48 p.

> With a cast list of the first London production and "Remarks" by D--G [George Daniel].

1984 THE FEMALE MASCARONI; OR, THE FAIR BRIGANDS: AN OPERATIC DRAMA IN TWO ACTS. (Surrey, 12 February 1831.) London: Cumberland, n.d. 40 p.

> An acting edition with a cast list of the first London production and "Remarks" by D--G [George Daniel].

1985 THE MISTLETOE BOUGH; OR, THE FATAL CHEST: A MELO-DRAMA IN TWO ACTS. (Garrick, 1834.) Ames' Series of Standard and Minor Drama, no. 34. Clyde, Ohio: Ames' Publishing Co., n.d. 22 p.

> An acting edition with a cast list of the first London production. (The play was also published with the alternative subtitle, YOUNG LOVEL'S BRIDE.)

1986 THE SEA: A NAUTICAL DRAMA IN TWO ACTS. (Queen's, 1834.) Cumberland's Minor Theatre, no. 56. London: Davidson, n.d. 42 p.

> An acting edition with a cast list of the first London production and "Remarks" by D--G [George Daniel].

SOUTHEY, ROBERT (1774-1843)

I Collected Works

1987 THE POETICAL WORKS OF ROBERT SOUTHEY. COLLECTED BY HIMSELF. 10 vols. London: Longman, Brown, Green, and Longmans, 1837-38.

> WAT TYLER is in volume two, with a brief preface by Southey.

IIa Unacted Plays

1987a THE FALL OF ROBESPIERRE (1794). See item 951, above.

1988 WAT TYLER: A DRAMATIC POEM. A NEW EDITION. WITH A PREFACE SUITABLE TO RECENT CIRCUMSTANCES. London: W. Hone, 1817. xxiii, 70 p.

IV Biography

1989 Southey, Charles Cuthbert. THE LIFE & CORRESPONDENCE OF THE LATE ROBERT SOUTHEY. 6 vols. London: Longman, Brown, Green & Longmans, 1849-50.

1990 Simmons, Jack. SOUTHEY. London: Collins, 1945. 256 p.

> A readable biography with some attention given to WAT TYLER.

1991 Curry, Kenneth, ed. NEW LETTERS OF ROBERT SOUTHEY. 2 vols. New York and London: Columbia University Press, 1965.

> There are a few references to WAT TYLER in these letters.

1992 _____. "The Published Letters of Southey: A Checklist." BNYPL, 71 (1967), 158-64.

> ". . . attempts to give a complete listing of all the books and articles in which one or more letters of Robert Southey have been published for the first time."

V Critical Studies

1993 Hoadley, Frank Taliaferro. "The Controversy over Southey's WAT TYLER." SP, 38 (1941), 81-96.

> A comprehensive account of the controversy stirred up in Parliament and the press over the publication of Southey's allegedly seditious play.

1994 Zall, Paul M. "Lord Eldon's Censorship." PMLA, 68 (1953), 436-43.

> Discusses, in part, the Lord Chancellor's refusal to grant Southey an injunction against the unauthorized publication of WAT TYLER.

1995 Carnall, Geoffrey. ROBERT SOUTHEY AND HIS AGE. THE DEVELOPMENT OF A CONSERVATIVE MIND. Oxford: Clarendon Press, 1960. viii, 233 p.

> Carnall places WAT TYLER in the context of Southey's political development.

1996 Madden, Lionel, ed. ROBERT SOUTHEY: THE CRITICAL HERITAGE. London and Boston: Routledge & Kegan Paul, 1972. xix, 492 p.

> There are interesting sections on WAT TYLER and the controversy following its publication.

STEVENSON, ROBERT LOUIS (1850-94)

I Collected Works

1997 THREE PLAYS. With W.E. Henley. London: D. Nutt, 1892. 250 p.

Contains DEACON BRODIE, BEAU AUSTIN, and ADMIRAL GUINEA. Acting editions with cast lists.

1998 THE PLAYS OF W.E. HENLEY AND R.L. STEVENSON: DEACON BRODIE, BEAU AUSTIN, ADMIRAL GUINEA, ROBERT MACAIRE. London: Heinemann, 1896. xii, 303 p.

With cast lists of the various performances. The Readex collection reproduces each play except ADMIRAL GUINEA.

1999 Henley, W.E. PLAYS WRITTEN IN COLLABORATION WITH R.L. STEVENSON. London: D. Nutt, 1908. 303 p.

This is volume seven of THE WORKS OF W.E. HENLEY, and includes DEACON BRODIE, BEAU AUSTIN, ADMIRAL GUINEA, and ROBERT MACAIRE. The texts printed are acting editions, and there is a brief note on the publication history of each play.

2000 DEACON BRODIE OR THE DOUBLE LIFE AND OTHER PLAYS. London: Heinemann; New York: Scribner's, 1922. 414 p.

Volume six of the Vailma edition. Contains DEACON BRODIE, BEAU AUSTIN, ADMIRAL GUINEA, MACAIRE, and THE HANGING JUDGE.

2001 PLAYS. London: Heinemann, 1924. x, 294 p.

Volume twenty-four of the Tusitala edition. Contains DEACON BRODIE, BEAU AUSTIN, ADMIRAL GUINEA, ROBERT MACAIRE, and THE HANGING JUDGE. Where appropriate, performance details are given.

II Acted Plays—Principal Titles

2002 *BEAU AUSTIN: A PLAY IN FOUR ACTS. With W.E. Henley. (Haymarket, 3 November 1890.) Edinburgh: 1884. 46 p.

A privately printed acting edition with a dedication to George Meredith.

2003 ADMIRAL GUINEA: A DRAMA IN FOUR ACTS. With W.E. Henley.
(Avenue, 29 November 1897.) London: Heinemann, 1897. 104 p.

   A library edition, with some stage directions.

2004 *MACAIRE: A MELODRAMATIC FARCE IN THREE ACTS. With W.E.
Henley. (Her Majesty's, 2 May 1901.) Edinburgh: 1885. 40 p.

   A privately printed acting edition with a dedication to A.
   Egmont Hake.

2005 *MACAIRE: A MELODRAMATIC FARCE IN THREE ACTS. London:
Heinemann, n.d. 22 p.

   An acting edition.

III Bibliographies

2006 Slater, J. Herbert. ROBERT LOUIS STEVENSON: A BIBLIOGRAPHY
OF HIS COMPLETE WORKS. London: Bell, 1914. vii, 46 p.

   Semischolarly, with annotations.

2007 FIRST EDITIONS OF THE WORKS OF ROBERT LOUIS STEVENSON 1850-
1894 AND OTHER STEVENSONIANA: EXHIBITED AT THE GROLIER
CLUB FROM NOVEMBER 5 TO NOVEMBER 28, 1914. New York:
Grolier Club, 1915. xviii, 87 p.

   An annotated, unscholarly, illustrated exhibition catalog.
   With an article on Stevenson's stay at Saranac in 1887-88.

2008 PRIDEAUX, Col. W.F. A BIBLIOGRAPHY OF THE WORKS OF ROBERT
LOUIS STEVENSON: A NEW AND REVISED EDITION, EDITED AND
SUPPLEMENTED BY MRS. LUTHER S. LIVINGSTON. London: Frank
Hollings, 1927. viii, 401 p.

   Scholarly, with annotations and illustrations.

2009 McKay, George L., comp. A STEVENSON LIBRARY CATALOGUE OF
A COLLECTION OF WRITINGS BY AND ABOUT ROBERT LOUIS STEVEN-
SON FORMED BY EDWIN J. BEINECKE. 6 vols. New Haven: Yale
University Library, 1951-64.

   A scholarly, annotated bibliography of Yale's holdings, which
   include much manuscript material.

2010 ROBERT LOUIS STEVENSON: A CATALOGUE OF THE HENRY E.
GERSTLEY STEVENSON COLLECTION, THE STEVENSON SECTION OF
THE MORRIS L. PARRISH COLLECTION OF VICTORIAN NOVELISTS,
AND ITEMS FROM OTHER COLLECTIONS IN THE DEPARTMENT OF

RARE BOOKS AND SPECIAL COLLECTIONS OF THE PRINCETON UNIVERSITY LIBRARY. Princeton: Princeton University Library, 1971. xi, 130 p.

Useful for manuscript materials.

IV Biography

2011 VAILMA LETTERS: BEING CORRESPONDENCE ADDRESSED BY ROBERT LOUIS STEVENSON TO SIDNEY COLVIN, NOVEMBER 1890-OCTOBER 1894. London: Methuen, 1895. xx, 366 p.

2012 Colvin, Sidney, ed. THE LETTERS OF ROBERT LOUIS STEVENSON TO HIS FAMILY AND FRIENDS. 2nd ed. 2 vols. London: Methuen, 1900. xliv, 375; xiii, 384 p.

2013 Balfour, Graham. THE LIFE OF ROBERT LOUIS STEVENSON. 2 vols. New York: Scribner's, 1908. xi, 255; 275 p.

The official biography, written by Stevenson's cousin. Volume two contains, as an appendix, a chronological list of Stevenson's writings.

2014 Colvin, Sidney, ed. LETTERS AND MISCELLANIES OF ROBERT LOUIS STEVENSON: NEW LETTERS. New York: Scribner's, 1912. xiii, 338 p.

2015 ROBERT LOUIS STEVENSON: A BOOKMAN EXTRA NUMBER. London: Hodder and Stoughton, 1913. 208 p.

An illustrated miscellany of articles, written by contemporaries, associates, and friends.

2016 Colvin, Sidney, ed. THE LETTERS OF ROBERT LOUIS STEVENSON. 4 vols. London: Heinemann; New York: Scribner's, 1923.

Volumes 20-23 of the Vailma edition of Stevenson's collected works.

2017 Masson, Robert. THE LIFE OF ROBERT LOUIS STEVENSON: WITH NUMEROUS ILLUSTRATIONS REPRODUCING PHOTOGRAPHS, MANUSCRIPT LETTERS AND A DRAWING IN BLACK AND WHITE. New York: F.A. Stokes, 1923. xvii, 358 p.

A weightier biography than Balfour's (item 2013).

2018 Colvin, Sir Sidney, ed. THE LETTERS OF ROBERT LOUIS STEVENSON. 5 vols. London: Heinemann, 1924.

Volumes 31-35 of the Tusitala edition of Stevenson's collected works.

2019 Hellman, George S. THE TRUE STEVENSON: A STUDY IN CLARIFICA-TION. Boston: Little, Brown, 1925. xiv, 253 p.

Hellman was a collector of Stevensonia, and on the basis of manuscript materials attempts to correct the record on Stevenson. There is a chapter on Stevenson's relationship with Henley.

2020 Ferguson, DeLancey, and Marshall Waingrow, eds. R.L.S.: STEVENSON'S LETTERS TO CHARLES BAXTER. New Haven: Yale University Press, 1956. xxiv, 385 p.

A scholarly edition. Baxter was a close friend of Stevenson, and these letters are useful for their unreserved, detailed information.

2021 Wood, James Playsted. THE LANTERN BEARER: A LIFE OF ROBERT LOUIS STEVENSON: ILLUSTRATED BY SAUL LAMBERT. New York: Pantheon, 1965. 182 p.

A readable, though not overly scholarly biography.

V Critical Studies

2023 Pinero, Arthur Wing. "Robert Louis Stevenson as a Dramatist." Intro. Clayton Hamilton. PAPERS ON PLAYMAKING, 4. New York: Dramatic Museum of Columbia University, 1914. 78 p.

2024 Swinnerton, Frank. R.L. STEVENSON: A CRITICAL STUDY. New York: G.H. Doran, 1923. 195 p.

This edition is a slightly revised version of Swinnerton's 1914 study. In the chapter on the plays he criticizes Stevenson's inability to visualize a scene, to construct "for real dramatic effect."

2025 Steuart, John A. ROBERT LOUIS STEVENSON: A CRITICAL BIOGRAPHY. 2 vols. Boston: Little, Brown, 1924. xxi, 419; 352 p.

Steuart's work is not as critical as the title implies and amounts to little more than a diffuse, discursive biography.

2026 Chesterton, G.K. ROBERT LOUIS STEVENSON. 1928; rpt. New York: Sheed and Ward, 1955. 175 p.

Written in Chesterton's usual fashion, this book attempts to correct the dismissive attitude too readily adopted towards Stevenson.

2026a Eigner, Edwin M. ROBERT LOUIS STEVENSON AND ROMANTIC
TRADITION. Princeton: Princeton University Press, 1966. xiii, 258 p.

> Although the plays are only mentioned in passing, Eigner has
> some interesting points to make, and indicates some interrela-
> tionships between the plays and the fiction.

STIRLING, EDWARD (1809-94)

II Acted Plays—Principal Titles

2027 MARGARET CATCHPOLE, THE HEROINE OF SUFFOLK; OR, THE
VICISSITUDES OF REAL LIFE: A DRAMA IN THREE ACTS. (Surrey,
24 March 1835.) London: Lacy, n.d. 50 p.

> An acting edition with a cast list of the first London produc-
> tion.

2028 THE PICKWICK CLUB; OR, THE AGE WE LIVE IN! A BURLETTA EX-
TRAVAGANZA IN THREE ACTS. (City of London, 27 March 1837.)
Turner's Dramatic Library. Philadelphia: Frederick Turner; New York:
Turner & Fisher, n.d. 60 p.

> An acting edition with a cast list of an unspecified produc-
> tion and a brief preface.

2029 THE BLUE JACKETS; OR, HER MAJESTY'S SERVICE! A FARCE IN ONE
ACT. (Adelphi, 5 October 1838.) Duncombe's British Theatre, vol. 31.
London: Duncombe, n.d. 23 p.

> An acting edition with a cast list of the first London produc-
> tion; the Readex copy is a promptbook (New York Public
> Library) interleaved with manuscript notes.

2030 GRACE DARLING; OR, THE WRECK AT SEA: A DRAMA IN TWO ACTS.
(Adelphi, 3 December 1838.) London: Chapman and Hall, n.d. 32 p.

> An acting edition with a cast list of the first London produc-
> tion.

2031 THE LITTLE BACK PARLOUR: A FARCE IN ONE ACT. (English Opera
House, 17 August 1839.) Duncombe's British Theatre, vol. 38. London:
Duncombe, n.d. 18 p.

> An acting edition with a cast list of the first London produc-
> tion.

2032 THE SERPENT OF THE NILE; OR THE BATTLE OF ACTIUM! A MELO-
DRAMA IN TWO ACTS. (Adelphi, 20 April 1840.) Duncombe's British
Theatre, vol. 41. London: Duncombe, n.d.

> An acting edition with a cast list of the first London produc-
> tion.

2033 ALINE, THE ROSE OF KILLARNEY! A DRAMA IN THREE ACTS.
(Strand, 10 July 1843.) London: Lacy, n.d. 42 p.

> An acting edition with a cast list of the first London produc-
> tion; the Readex copy is a promptbook (New York Public
> Library) interleaved with manuscript notes.

2034 THE BOHEMIANS; OR, THE ROGUES OF PARIS: A DRAMA IN THREE
ACTS. (Adelphi, 6 November 1843.) Dicks' British Drama, no. 98.

> An acting edition; the play is based on Sue's LES MYSTÈRES
> DE PARIS.

2035 THE SEVEN CASTLES OF THE PASSIONS: A DRAMA OF ENCHANT-
MENT IN TWO ACTS. (Lyceum, 21 October 1844.) [London: W.
Barth], n.d. 32 p.

> An acting edition with some very detailed scene descriptions
> and a cast list of the first London production; the Readex
> copy is a promptbook (New York Public Library) interleaved
> with manuscript notes.

2036 LESTELLE; OR, THE WRECKER'S BRIDE: A DRAMA IN THREE ACTS.
(Surrey, 21 August 1845.) Cumberland's British Theatre. London: Lacy,
n.d. 36 p.

> An acting edition with a cast list of the first London produc-
> tion.

2037 THE BOULD SOGER BOY: A FARCE IN ONE ACT. (Olympic, 6
November 1848.) Duncombe's British Theatre. London: Duncombe, n.d.
19 p.

> An acting edition with a cast list of the first London produc-
> tion (?).

IV Biography

2038 Stirling, Edward. OLD DRURY LANE: FIFTY YEARS' RECOLLECTIONS
OF AUTHOR, ACTOR, AND MANAGER. 2 vols. London: Chatto and
Windus, 1881. vi, 364; 370 p.

SWINBURNE, ALGERNON CHARLES (1837-1909)

I Collected Works

2039 THE TRAGEDIES OF ALGERNON CHARLES SWINBURNE IN FIVE
VOLUMES. London: Chatto and Windus, 1905.

> Contents: volume one: THE QUEEN-MOTHER, ROSAMOND;
> volume two: CHASTELARD, BOTHWELL (I and II); volume
> three: BOTHWELL (III-V); volume four: MARY STUART;
> volume five: LOCRINE, THE SISTERS, MARINO FALIERO,
> ROSAMUND.

2040 Gosse, Sir Edmund, and Thomas James Wise, eds. THE COMPLETE
WORKS OF ALGERNON CHARLES SWINBURNE. The Standard Bonchurch
edition. London: Heinemann, 1925; rpt. New York: Russell and Russell,
1968.

> Volumes 7-10 contain the dramatic works. Volume seven:
> THE QUEEN-MOTHER, ROSAMOND, ATALANTA IN CA-
> LYDON, ERECHTHEUS; volume eight: CHASTELARD, BOTH-
> WELL (I and II); volume nine: BOTHWELL (III-V), MARY
> STUART; volume ten: MARINO FALIERO, LOCRINE, THE
> SISTERS, ROSAMUND, THE DUKE OF GANDIA.

II Acted Plays—Principal Titles

2041 LOCRINE: A TRAGEDY. (St. George's Hall, 20 March 1899.) New
York: J.B. Alden, c. 1887. viii, 138 p.

> With a dedication in verse to Alice Swinburne.

IIa Unacted Plays

2042 CHASTELARD: A TRAGEDY. London: E. Moxon, 1865. 219 p.

2043 ATALANTA IN CALYDON: A TRAGEDY. Boston: Ticknor and Fields,
1866. 113 p.

2044 BOTHWELL: A TRAGEDY. London: Chatto and Windus, 1874. 532 p.

2045 MARY STUART: A TRAGEDY. London: Chatto and Windus, 1881.
[vii], 203 p.

2046 *ATALANTA IN CALYDON: A FACSIMILE OF THE FIRST EDITION: WITH A PREFACE BY DR. GEORGES LAFOURCADE. London: Oxford University Press, 1930. xxii, 111 p.

III Bibliographies

2047 Wise, Thomas J. A BIBLIOGRAPHY OF THE WRITINGS IN PROSE AND VERSE OF ALGERNON CHARLES SWINBURNE. 2 vols. London: R. Clay, 1919; rpt. London: Dawsons, 1966. xvi, 507; xvi, 407 p.

> Although compiled on a "scholarly" basis, with annotations and illustrations, this work is not always accurate.

2048 _____. A BIBLIOGRAPHY OF THE WRITINGS IN PROSE AND VERSE OF ALGERNON CHARLES SWINBURNE. 1925; rpt. New York: Russell and Russell, 1968. xii, 575 p.

> Volume twenty of the Bonchurch edition of the complete works.

IV Biography

2049 Gosse, Edmund. THE LIFE OF ALGERNON CHARLES SWINBURNE. New York: Macmillan, 1917. xi, 363 p.

> Useful source material, but a somewhat biased early biography.

2050 Gosse, Sir Edmund, and Thomas James Wise, eds. THE COMPLETE WORKS OF ALGERNON CHARLES SWINBURNE: XVIII: LETTERS. 20 vols. London: Heinemann, 1925; rpt. New York: Russell and Russell, 1968.

> The Bonchurch edition, now superseded by Lang, item 2051.

2051 Lang, Cecil Y., ed. THE SWINBURNE LETTERS. 6 vols. New Haven: Yale University Press, 1959.

> The definitive, scholarly edition.

2052 Hyder, Clyde K., ed. SWINBURNE AS CRITIC. London and Boston: Routledge, 1972. xii, 324 p.

> A useful anthology of Swinburne's own criticism; the section on drama includes criticism of Congreve, Shakespeare, Lamb, Chapman, Jonson, Marlowe, and Webster.

2053 Peattie, Roger W. "Swinburne and His Publishers." HLQ, 36 (1972), 45-54.

A brief account of Swinburne's stormy dealings with his publishers. Contains a few references to the plays.

2054 Lebourgeois, John Y. "Swinburne and Simeon Solomon." N&Q, 218 (March 1973), 91-95.

Discusses the decline in their friendship in the light of Solomon's homosexual propensities.

V Critical Studies

2055 Wratislaw, Theodore. ALGERNON CHARLES SWINBURNE: A STUDY. London: Greening, 1900. viii, 212 p.

This study, typical of literary criticism of the period, merely heaps hyperbole on hyperbole.

2056 Drinkwater, John. SWINBURNE: AN ESTIMATE. London and Toronto: Dent, 1913. ix, 215 p.

Drinkwater's chapter on the dramas is one of the more perceptive of earlier critical essays and is valuable in examining Swinburne from a theatrical, practical perspective.

2057 Nicolson, Harold. SWINBURNE. London: Macmillan 1926; rpt. Hamden, Conn.: Archon Books, 1969. viii, 207 p.

While Nicolson mentions most of Swinburne's drama only in passing, he is clearly enthusiastic about ATALANTA and devotes a major chapter to it. By and large, however, he resorts to plot telling and fails to bring any acute analytical judgment to the play.

2058 Welby, T. Earle. A STUDY OF SWINBURNE. London: Faber and Gwyer, 1926. xii, 274 p.

Although Welby devotes two chapters to the dramas, his criticism is vague and generalized. His "bibliographical note" contains useful, annotated entries.

2059 Chew, Samuel C. SWINBURNE. 1929; rpt., Hamden, Conn.: Archon Books, 1966. xi, 335 p.

Although an extensive chapter deals with the tragedies, Chew's criticism tends strongly toward the vaguely impressionistic and narrative.

2060 Granville-Baker, Harley. "Some Victorians Afield: II: The Poet as Dramatist." THEATRE ARTS MONTHLY, 13 (1929), 361-72.

Granville-Baker points to Tennyson's mechanical approach to drama as being his main weakness. Tennyson adopted the Elizabethan mode without realizing the source of its inner vitality (rhetoric). Swinburne, however, relied on his instinctive, natural rhetoric; but his work is ultimately not drama, even though it is made of the stuff of drama.

2061 Rutland, William R. SWINBURNE: A NINETEENTH CENTURY HELLENE: WITH SOME REFLECTIONS ON THE HELLENISM OF MODERN POETS. Oxford: Blackwell, 1931. viii, 410 p.

Most of Rutland's book considers ATALANTA and ERECHTHEUS; the approach is largely historical, and investigates at some length the original sources of the dramas.

2062 Hyder, Clyde Kenneth. SWINBURNE'S LITERARY CAREER AND FAME. Durham, N.C.: Duke University Press, 1933. xi, 388 p.

This work chronicles the critical reception of Swinburne's work, and is heavily documented with notes and bibliography extending over 100 densely packed pages.

2063 Chandler, Josephine. "The So-called Elizabethan Tragedies of Swinburne: A Study of Literary Assimilation." Ph.D. Dissertation, University of California, 1935.

2064 Maurer, Oscar. "Swinburne vs. Furnivall." UNIVERSITY OF TEXAS STUDIES IN ENGLISH, 31 (1952), 86-96.

2065 Lang, Cecil Y. "The First Chorus of Swinburne's ATALANTA." YULG, 27 (1952-53), 119-22.

Reproduction and discussion of an early holograph draft.

2066 Mayfield, John S. "Two Presentation Copies of Swinburne's ATALANTA IN CALYDON." PBSA, 49 (1955), 360-65.

An interesting account of how C.A. Howell came to possess two copies of the first edition. Incidentally throws light on Swinburne's life, and touches on some bibliographical problems.

2067 Want, M.S. "A New Approach to the Dramatic Works of Swinburne." Ph.D. Dissertation, Leeds University, 1955-56.

2068 Baum, Paull F. "The Fitzwilliam Manuscript of Swinburne's ATALANTA, Verses 1038-1204." MLR, 54 (1959), 161-78.

> Close examination of manuscript changes to demonstrate creative process.

2069 Boswell, Grace Hadaway. "Swinburne's Mary, Queen of Scots, and the Historical Mary." Ph.D. Dissertation, University of Georgia, 1960. 244 p. (DA#40-4648)

> A comparison of Mary in CHASTELARD, BOTHWELL, and MARY STUART with the historical Mary, whose virtues are sympathetically exaggerated.

2070 Hargreaves, H.A. "Swinburne's Greek Plays and God, 'The Supreme Evil.'" MLN, 76 (1961), 607-16.

> Discusses "Swinburne's bitter attack upon the divine treatment of man" in ATALANTA and ERECHTHEUS. Useful both in surveying the critical field and suggesting parallels and similarities between Swinburne's text and Old Testament writers.

2071 Lang, Cecil Y. "ATALANTA in Manuscript." YULG, 37 (1962), 19-24.

> A short account of the various, scattered manuscripts, together with a transcription of a "missing" chorus reproduced from an autograph manuscript.

2072 Cassidy, John A. ALGERNON C. SWINBURNE. New York: Twayne, 1964. 186 p.

> Useful general information, but only a few pages devoted to the plays.

2073 Dahl, Curtis. "Autobiographical Elements in Swinburne's Trilogy on Mary Stuart." VP, 3 (1965), 91-99.

> "The trilogy reflects Swinburne at three widely separated eras in his career and thus, conversely, provides insight into him at those points."

2074 _____. "Swinburne's Mary Stuart: A Reading of Ronsard." PLL, 1 (1965), 39-49.

> Sees Swinburne's trilogy receiving unity from the numerous allusions to Ronsard, and this "symbolic use of the France of Ronsard . . . raises his trilogy from a mere dramatized biography or psychological study into a tragic criticism of life as he sees it."

2075 _____. "Macaulay, Henry Taylor, and Swinburne's Trilogy." PLL, 2 (1966), 166–69.

>Suggests that a plan for a trilogy on Mary Queen of Scots outlined by Macaulay to Henry Taylor, and relayed by the latter to Swinburne, may have inspired Swinburne's own trilogy.

2076 _____. "The Composition of Swinburne's Trilogy on Mary Queen of Scots." TSL, 12 (1967), 103–10.

>Uses evidence from Swinburne's letters, "supplemented by scattered chronological evidence hitherto uncollected," to date the composition of the trilogy.

2077 Kinneavy, Gerald B. "Character and Action in Swinburne's CHASTE-LARD." VP, 5 (1967), 31–39.

>A close explication, which sees Chastelard as a passive, ideal lover and all the dynamic action as stemming from Mary.

2078 Fuller, Jean Overton. SWINBURNE: A CRITICAL BIOGRAPHY. London: Chatto and Windus, 1968. 319 p.

>Chiefly valuable for the fresh manuscript materials incorporated into the biographical account. Critical aspects devoted to the drama are confined to plot summary and lengthy quotation.

2079 McGinnis, Robert M. "Swinburne's CHASTELARD and Wilde's SALOMÉ: Victorian Experiment in the Theatre of Cruelty." KOMOS, 2 (1969), 32–36.

2080 Hyder, Clyde K., ed. SWINBURNE: THE CRITICAL HERITAGE. New York: Barnes and Noble, 1970. li, 255 p.

>Provides contemporary responses to Swinburne's work and includes reviews of ATALANTA, CHASTELARD, and ERECHTHEUS.

2081 Wilson, F.A.C. "Swinburne's Victorian Huntress: Autobiographical Traces in ATALANTA IN CALYDON." KOMOS, 2 (1970), 118–25.

2082 Lougy, Robert E. "Thematic Imagery and Meaning in ATALANTA IN CALYDON." VP, 9 (1971), 17–34.

>A close discussion of the imagery to illuminate theme and character motivation.

2083 Mathews, Richard. "Heart's Love and Heart's Division: The Quest for Unity in ATALANTA IN CALYDON." VP, 9 (1971), 35-48.

"ATALANTA depicts the yearning of the human soul for unity through love, and the ultimate futility of this wish. In doing so, it sets forth many of the themes and impulses which inform Swinburne's whole oeuvre."

2084 Wymer, Thomas. "Swinburne's Tragic Vision in ATALANTA IN CALYDON." VP, 9 (1971), 1-16.

By eschewing the traditional concentration on the classicism of ATALANTA, Wymer attempts to present the work as the "tragic struggle of the youthful quest for freedom . . . against the old-age forces of repression." This conflict is embodied in Meleager and Althaea.

2085 McGann, Jerome J. SWINBURNE: AN EXPERIMENT IN CRITICISM. Chicago and London: University of Chicago Press, 1972. xi, 321 p.

A novel critical approach: a "dialogue form has been adopted because it illustrates, in a dramatic and recreative fashion, the absurd limits of analytic knowledge." Thus, McGann's "debaters," using extensive quotation from previous critics, examine and discuss Swinburne's work--with provocative results.

2086 Jordan, John O. "The Sweet Face of Mothers: Psychological Patterns in ATALANTA IN CALYDON." VP, 11 (1973), 101-14.

"ATALANTA . . . is a profound study of the ambivalent relationship of mother and son. Within a broader context of generational conflict, the play focuses specifically on Meleager's quest for identity and his efforts to liberate the brand, a symbol of erotic and creative powers, from his mother's control."

2087 Sypher, Francis Jacques, Jr. "Victoria's Lapse from Virtue: A Lost Leaf from Swinburne's LA SOEUR DE LA REINE." HLB, 21 (1973), 349-55.

A discussion of a recently discovered fragment of Swinburne's French comic drama.

2088 Wilson, F.A.C. "Swinburne and Kali: The Confessional Element in ATALANTA IN CALYDON." VP, 11 (1973), 215-28.

Wilson, like Jordan (item 2086), explores the psychological, autobiographical basis of the play and accounts for Swinburne's masochism.

2089 Workman, Gillian. "LA SOEUR DE LA REINE and Related 'Victorian Romances' by Swinburne." HLB, 21 (1973), 356-64.

>A further discussion of this piece and variants.

TALFOURD, THOMAS NOON (1795-1854)

I Collected Works

2090 THE DRAMATIC WORKS OF SIR THOMAS NOON TALFOURD. TO WHICH ARE ADDED, A FEW SONNETS AND VERSES. 11th ed. London: Edward Moxon, 1852. xii, 369 p.

>Includes ION, THE ATHENIAN CAPTIVE, and GLENCOE.

II Acted Plays—Principal Titles

2091 ION: A TRAGEDY IN FIVE ACTS. (Covent Garden, 26 May 1836.) 2nd ed. London: Moxon, 1836. vi, 120 p.

>With an essay by Talfourd on his friend, Dr. Valpy. The Readex collection also contains a privately printed [1835] text of ION, which is Edwin Booth's promptbook, with a few manuscript notes.

2092 *ION: A TRAGEDY IN FIVE ACTS. New York: George Dearborn, 1837. x, 109 p.

>Includes a preface by the publishers.

2093 THE ATHENIAN CAPTIVE: A TRAGEDY IN FIVE ACTS. (Haymarket, 4 August 1838.) London: Moxon, 1838. x, 103 p.

>Includes a cast list of the first London production and a preface by Talfourd.

2094 GLENCOE; OR, THE FATE OF THE MACDONALDS: A TRAGEDY IN FIVE ACTS. (Haymarket, 23 May 1840.) 2nd ed. London: Moxon, 1840. xiii, 98 p.

>Includes a cast list of the first London production, an "Advertisement" to the second edition, and a preface by Talfourd.

IV Biography

2095 Biographical Notes in N&Q, 194 (1949), 282, 350; and 195 (1950), 20.

V Critical Studies

2096 Newdick, Robert S. "A Victorian Demosthenes (A Study of Thomas Noon Talfourd as an Orator)." QJS, 25 (1939), 580-96.

2097 Ward, William S. "An Early Champion of Wordsworth: Talfourd." PMLA, 68 (1953), 992-1000.

> Discusses Talfourd's poetry, not the plays.

TAYLOR, TOM (1817-80)

I Collected Works

2098 HISTORICAL DRAMAS. London, 1877. viii, 466 p.

> Contents: THE FOOL'S REVENGE, JEANNE D'ARC, 'TWIXT AXE AND CROWN, LADY CLANCARTY, ARKWRIGHT'S WIFE, ANNE BOLEYN, and PLOT AND PASSION. Acting editions, with prefaces and cast lists.

II Acted Plays—Principal Titles

2099 A TRIP TO KISSENGEN: AN ORIGINAL FARCE IN ONE ACT. (Lyceum, 14 November 1844.) London: W. Barth, n.d. 28 p.

> An acting edition with a cast list of the first London production.

2100 "TO PARENTS AND GUARDIANS! AT JUBILEE HOUSE ESTABLISHMENT, CLAPHAM, YOUNG GENTLEMEN ARE, &C. &C.": AN ORIGINAL COMIC DRAMA IN ONE ACT. (Lyceum, 14 September 1846.) American Drama, no. 127. New York: French, n.d. 24 p.

> An acting edition with cast lists of two New York productions. The Readex collection also includes a later edition of the play (London, c. 1883, Dicks' Standard Plays, no. 997).

2101 MASKS AND FACES; OR, BEFORE AND BEHIND THE CURTAIN: A COMEDY IN TWO ACTS. With Charles Reade. (Haymarket, 20 November 1852.) London: Bentley, 1854. 71 p.

> An acting edition with a cast list of the first London production; interleaved, with manuscript notes.

2102 PLOT AND PASSION: A DRAMA (FOUNDED ON THE FRENCH) IN THREE ACTS. (Olympic, 17 October 1853.) Acting Plays, no. 61. New York: De Witt, n.d. 39 p.

   With cast lists of the first London and New York productions.

2103 TO OBLIGE BENSON: A COMEDIETTA IN ONE ACT: ADAPTED FROM THE FRENCH. (Olympic, 6 March 1854.) Minor Drama, no. 86. London and New York: French, n.d. 24 p.

2104 TWO LOVES AND A LIFE: A DRAMA IN FOUR ACTS. With Charles Reade. (Adelphi, 20 March 1854.) Boston Theatre, no. 56. Boston: Spencer, n.d. 48 p.

   An acting edition with several cast lists.

2105 THE KING'S RIVAL; OR, THE COURT AND THE STAGE: A DRAMA IN FIVE ACTS. With Charles Reade. (St. James's, 2 October 1854.) American Drama, no. 33. New York: French, n.d. 50 p.

   An acting edition with several cast lists.

2106 "STILL WATERS RUN DEEP": AN ORIGINAL COMEDY IN THREE ACTS. (Olympic, 14 May 1855.) London and New York: French, n.d. 58 p.

   An acting edition with a cast list of the first London production.

2107 RETRIBUTION: A DOMESTIC DRAMA IN FOUR ACTS. (Olympic, 12 May 1856.) French's Standard Drama, no. 151. No publication details. 30 p.

   An acting edition with cast lists of the first London and New York productions.

2108 A SHEEP IN WOLF'S CLOTHING: A DOMESTIC DRAMA IN ONE ACT. (Olympic, 19 February 1857.) London and New York: French, n.d. 34 p.

   An acting edition with a cast list of the first London production; interleaved, with manuscript notes.

2109 VICTIMS: AN ORIGINAL COMEDY IN THREE ACTS. (Haymarket, 8 July 1857.) Standard Drama, no. 186. New York: French, n.d. 44 p.

   An acting edition with cast lists of the first London and New York productions.

2110 GOING TO THE BAD: AN ORIGINAL COMEDY IN TWO ACTS.
(Olympic, 5 June 1858.) London: Lacy, n.d. 72 p.

> An acting edition with a cast list of the first London production.

2111 OUR AMERICAN COUSIN: A DRAMA IN FOUR ACTS (Laura Keene's,
New York, 18 October 1858; Haymarket, 11 November 1861.) No
publication details. 1869. 46 p.

> An acting copy with a cast list of the first New York production.

2112 THE CONTESTED ELECTION: A COMEDY IN THREE ACTS. (Haymarket, 29 June 1859.) Manchester: T. Chambers, 1868. 60 p.

> An acting edition; interleaved, with numerous manuscript notes and alterations.

2113 THE FOOL'S REVENGE: A DRAMA IN THREE ACTS. (Sadler's Wells,
18 October 1859.) London: Lacy, n.d. 58 p.

> An acting edition with a preface by Taylor on the play's composition, and a cast list of the first London production.

2114 UP AT THE HILLS: AN ORIGINAL COMEDY OF INDIAN LIFE IN TWO
ACTS. (St. James's, 29 October 1860.) London: Lacy, n.d. 60 p.

> An acting edition with a cast list of the first London production; interleaved, with manuscript notes.

2115 THE TICKET OF LEAVE MAN: A DRAMA IN FOUR ACTS. (Olympic,
27 May 1863.) Acting Edition, no. 329. London and New York:
French, n.d. 56 p.

> With cast lists of the first London and New York productions.

2116 THE HIDDEN HAND: A DRAMA IN FOUR ACTS (FREELY ADAPTED
FROM "L'AIEULE" OF MM. D'ENNERY AND EDMOND). (Olympic, 2
November 1864.) London and New York: French, n.d. 60 p.

> An acting edition with a cast list of the first London production.

2117 SETTLING DAY: A STORY OF THE TIME IN FIVE ACTS. (Olympic,
4 March 1865.) London: Lacy, n.d. 84 p.

> An acting edition with a cast list of the first London production.

2118 NEW MAN AND OLD ACRES: AN ORIGINAL COMEDY IN THREE
ACTS. With Augustus W. Duborg. (Theatre Royal, Manchester, 20
August 1869; Haymarket, 25 October 1869.) London and New York:
French, n.d. 76 p.

> An acting edition with a cast list of the first London produc-
> tion. The Readex collection also includes a De Witt acting
> edition, no. 115.

2119 TWIXT AXE & CROWN; OR, THE LADY ELIZABETH: AN HISTORICAL
PLAY. (Queen's, 22 January 1870.) London and New York: French,
n.d. 72 p.

> An acting edition with a preface on the composition of the
> play, and a cast list of the first London production.

2120 JOAN OF ARC: AN ORIGINAL HISTORICAL PLAY IN FIVE ACTS.
(Queen's, 10 April 1871.) Chicago: Sergel, n.d. 41 p.

> An acting edition with a cast list of the first London produc-
> tion.

2121 LADY CLANCARTY; OR, WEDDED AND WOOED: A TALE OF THE
ASSASSINATION PLOT, 1696: AN ORIGINAL DRAMA IN FOUR ACTS.
(Olympic, 9 March 1874.) London and New York: French, n.d.
68 p.

> An acting edition with a cast list of the first London produc-
> tion.

III Bibliographies

2122 Rayner, Colin, and Jack Reading. "Tom Taylor: Manuscript Plays."
TN, 19 (1965), 83-89.

> Catalogs, describes, and annotates sixty-seven manuscript
> plays by or associated with Taylor and located in the British
> Theatre Museum.

IV Biography

2123 Sheehan, John. "Tom Taylor." DUBLIN UNIVERSITY MAGAZINE, 90
(August 1877), 142-58.

> Focuses maninly on Taylor's university career.

2124 Hughes, Thomas. "In Memoriam." MACMILLAN'S MAGAZINE, 42
(August 1880), 298-301.

> Obituary.

V Critical Studies

2125 Tolles, Winton. TOM TAYLOR AND THE VICTORIAN DRAMA. 1940;
rpt., New York: AMS, 1966. vii, 299 p.

> A judicious account of Taylor's work which Tolles sees as a
> significant contribution to the drama 1840–80. After placing
> Taylor in historical context, his work is examined by genre.
> A useful bibliography lists plays and nondramatic work.

TENNYSON, ALFRED LORD (1809-92)

I Collected Works

2126 THE WORKS OF ALFRED LORD TENNYSON: VI: QUEEN MARY;
HAROLD. Boston and New York: Houghton Mifflin, 1904. 306 p.

> Riverside edition, based on the Cambridge edition.

2127 THE WORKS OF ALFRED LORD TENNYSON: VII: BECKET; THE
FALCON; THE CUP; THE PROMISE OF MAY; CROSSING THE BAR.
Boston and New York: Houghton Mifflin, 1904. 323 p.

> See item 2126.

2128 Tennyson, Hallam, ed. DEMETER AND OTHER POEMS: ANNOTATED
BY ALFRED LORD TENNYSON. London: Macmillan, 1908. vii,
421 p.

> Volume seven of the standard Eversley edition. Contains
> THE CUP and THE PROMISE OF MAY.

2129 _____. QUEEN MARY AND HAROLD: ANNOTATED BY ALFRED
LORD TENNYSON. London: Macmillan, 1908. 381 p.

> Volume eight of the Eversley edition.

2130 _____. BECKET AND OTHER PLAYS: ANNOTATED BY ALFRED LORD
TENNYSON. London: Macmillan, 1908. [viii], 539 p.

> Volume nine of the Eversley edition. Also includes THE
> FALCON and THE FORESTERS.

2131 THE POEMS AND PLAYS OF ALFRED LORD TENNYSON. New York:
Random House, 1938. xviii, 1,133 p.

> Contains all the plays.

2132 POEMS AND PLAYS. Oxford Standard edition. London: Oxford University Press, 1965. xvi, 868 p.

>Contains all the plays.

II Acted Plays—Principal Titles

2133 QUEEN MARY: A DRAMA. (Lyceum, 18 April 1876.) London: H.S. King, 1875. viii, 278 p.

2134 THE CUP, AND THE FALCON. (FALCON, St. James's, 18 December 1879; CUP, Lyceum, 3 January 1881.) London: Macmillan, 1884. 146 p.

>With cast lists of the first London productions.

2135 THE PROMISE OF MAY (Globe, 11 November 1882.) in LOCKSEY HALL SIXTY YEARS AFTER. London and New York: Macmillan, 1884. 201 p.

2136 THE FORESTERS, ROBIN HOOD AND MAID MARIAN. (Lyceum, 17 March 1892.) London and New York: Macmillan, 1892. 155 p.

2137 BECKET. (Lyceum, 6 February 1893.) London: Macmillan, 1885. 213 p.

>With a dedication to the Earl of Selbourne.

2138 *Poteat, Mary, ed. "A Critical Edition of Tennyson's BECKET." Ph.D. Dissertation, Duke University, 1935.

IIa Unacted Plays

2139 HAROLD: A DRAMA. (Author's Edition, from Advance Sheets.) Boston: J.R. Osgood, 1877. 170 p.

III Bibliographies

2140 [Shepherd, Richard Herne]. THE BIBLIOGRAPHY OF TENNYSON: A BIBLIOGRAPHICAL LIST OF THE PUBLISHED AND PRIVATELY-PRINTED WRITINGS OF ALFRED (LORD) TENNYSON POET LAUREATE FROM 1827 TO 1894 INCLUSIVE: WITH HIS CONTRIBUTIONS TO ANNUALS, MAGAZINES, NEWSPAPERS, AND OTHER PERIODICAL PUBLICATIONS AND A SCHEME FOR A FINAL DEFINITIVE EDITION OF THE POET'S WORKS. London: [Printed for subscribers only], 1896; rpt. New York:

Haskell House, 1970. vii, 88 p.

A short, unscholarly bibliography with annotations.

2141 Thomson, J.C., ed. BIBLIOGRAPHY OF THE WRITINGS OF ALFRED, LORD TENNYSON. Wimbledon: J. Thomson, 1905; rpt. London: H. Pordes, 1967. 72 p.

Unscholarly, with annotations and turn-of-the-century selling prices.

2142 Wise, Thomas J. A BIBLIOGRAPHY OF THE WRITINGS OF ALFRED, LORD TENNYSON. 2 vols. London: Printed for Private Circulation, 1908; rpt. in one volume. London: Dawsons, 1967.

Extensive, annotated, illustrated, but unreliable.

2143 Tennyson, Charles, and Christine Fall. ALFRED TENNYSON: AN ANNOTATED BIBLIOGRAPHY. Athens: University of Georgia Press, 1967. viii, 126 p.

Useful. Lists some of the more interesting secondary sources, especially first night reviews.

IV Biography

2144 Tennyson, Hallam. ALFRED LORD TENNYSON: A MEMOIR BY HIS SON. 2 vols. New York: Macmillan, 1897. xxiii, 516; vii, 551 p.

2145 Hallam, Lord Tennyson, ed. TENNYSON AND HIS FRIENDS. London: Macmillan, 1911. xiii, 503 p.

An extensive miscellany of memoirs and criticisms of Tennyson.

2146 Tennyson, Sir Charles B.L. ALFRED TENNYSON. New York: Macmillan, 1949. xv, 579 p.

The standard biography.

V Critical Studies

2147 Brody, G.M. TENNYSON'S "QUEEN MARY": A CRITICISM. Edinburgh and London: Maclachan and Stewart, [1875]. 44 p.

2148 "QUEEN MARY: A Drama by Alfred Tennyson." ATHENAEUM, 26 June 1875, pp. 845–48.

Concludes that the play imperils Tennyson's reputation and that it should discourage him from further efforts.

2149 "Tennyson's QUEEN MARY." QR, 139 (July 1875), 231-48.

> The play has literary quality, but lacks dramatic impulse.

2150 [Jebb, R.C.]. "Notes on Mr. Tennyson's QUEEN MARY," MACMILLAN'S MAGAZINE, 32 (September 1875), 434-41.

> Despite reservations that Tennyson should have avoided the topic altogether, the play is praised as a "noble drama," the distinctive quality of which is its subtle study of character.

2150a "The Dramas of Alfred Tennyson." EDINBURGH REVIEW, 145 (April 1887), 383-415.

2151 Egan, M.F. "ST. THOMAS OF CANTERBURY and BECKET." CATHOLIC WORLD, 42 (December 1885), 383-95.

2152 "Lord Tennyson's BECKET." MACMILLAN'S MAGAZINE, 51 (1885), 287-94.

> Sympathetic review of the play, but regarding it as the product of a poet not at the height of his powers.

2153 Lambert, Agnes. "Aspects of Tennyson: III, The Real Thomas Beckett." NINETEENTH CENTURY, 33 (1893), 273-92.

> Comparison of various historical portrayals with Tennyson's characterization.

2154 SOUVENIR OF BECKET, BY ALFRED, LORD TENNYSON: FIRST PRESENTED AT THE LYCEUM THEATRE, 6TH FEBRUARY, 1893, BY HENRY IRVING: ILLUSTRATED BY J. BERNARD P.ARTRIDGE, W. TELBIN, J. HARKER, & HAWES CRAVEN. London: "Black and White," n.d. Unpaged.

> Cast list of the production, with illustrations.

2155 Luce, Morton. A HANDBOOK TO THE WORKS OF ALFRED LORD TENNYSON. London: George Bell, 1895. vii, 454 p.

> Brief chapter on the plays, commenting on each in turn.

2156 Block, Louis J. "The Dramatic Sentiment and Tennyson's Plays." POET-LORE, 8 (1896), 512-27.

> Generalized examination, prefaced by sweeping, undeveloped dramatic theories.

2157 "Tennyson as Dramatist." ACADEMY, 52 (14 August 1897), 134-35.

Tennyson is seen as inferior to Browning, and his success due
as much to actors and producers as to any intrinsic quality in
the plays.

2158 Lang, Andrew. ALFRED TENNYSON. 2nd ed. Edinburgh and London:
Blackwood, 1901; rpt. New York: AMS, 1970. vii, 233 p.

The section on the dramas is written "conscious of entire
ignorance of the stage and of lack of enthusiasm for the
drama." Critical judgement accords with this stance.

2159 James, Henry. "Tennyson's Drama" in VIEWS AND REVIEWS: NOW
FIRST COLLECTED: INTRODUCTION BY LEROY PHILLIPS. Boston:
Ball Publishing, 1908. ix, 241 p.

James's view of QUEEN MARY is that it is something of a
tour de force rather than the height of achievement. HAROLD
is given short shrift, as minor drama.

2160 Baker, Arthur E. A TENNYSON DICTIONARY: THE CHARACTERS
AND PLACE-NAMES CONTAINED IN THE POETICAL AND DRAMATIC
WORKS OF THE POET, ALPHABETICALLY ARRANGED AND DESCRIBED
WITH SYNOPSES OF THE POEMS AND PLAYS. London: Paul, Trench,
Trubner, 1916; rpt. New York: Haskell House, 1967. vii, 296 p.

2161 Japikse, Cornelia Geertrui Hendrika. THE DRAMAS OF ALFRED LORD
TENNYSON. Amsterdam: H.J. Paris, 1926. [ii], 167 p.

This appallingly written work is nonsensical, vague, and
completely wrongheaded.

2162 Hutton, W.H. "Two Unfamiliar Plays." CHURCH QUARTERLY REVIEW,
3 (1931), 314-27.

Consideration of HAROLD.

2163 Eidson, John Olin. "The Reception of Tennyson's Plays in America."
PQ, 35 (1956), 435-43.

2164 Shannon, Edgar F., Jr., and W.H. Bond. "Literary Manuscripts of
Alfred Tennyson in the Harvard College Library." HLB, 10 (1956), 254-
74.

Illustrated and scholarly, with some reference to the plays.

2165 Buckley, Jerome Hamilton. TENNYSON: THE GROWTH OF A POET.
Cambridge, Mass.: Harvard University Press, 1960. xiii, 298 p.

Views Tennyson's work in its biographical context and for
intrinsic qualities. The plays receive a sound evaluation
within this framework.

2166 Richardson, Joanna. THE PRE-EMINENT VICTORIAN: A STUDY OF
TENNYSON. London: Jonathan Cape, 1962. 313 p.

Leans heavily on the biographical side without displaying
much critical insight. Undocumented.

2167 Lally, Sr. Mary Aquin. "A Comparative Study of Five Plays on the
Becket Story, by Tennyson, Binyon, Eliot, Anouilh, and Fry." Ph.D.
Dissertation, University of Notre Dame, 1963. 224 p. (DA#63-7328)

Tennyson's play is seen as exemplifying "some typical defects
of the nineteenth-century 'well-made' play in which the plot
is the formative principle."

2168 Marshall, George O., Jr. A TENNYSON HANDBOOK. New York:
Twayne, 1963. 291 p.

A useful source of basic facts concerning such matters as
publication and production details. Occasional critical
comment is interpolated.

2169 Rehak, Louise Rouse. "On the Use of Martyrs: Tennyson and Eliot on
Thomas Becket." UTQ, 33 (1963-64), 43-60.

An interesting comparison. Tennyson's play is seen to possess
psychological realism, political objectivity, and ironic mani-
pulation of Becket's career. His theatrical sense and characterization are deficient.

2170 Eidson, John Olin. "The First Performance of Tennyson's HAROLD."
NEQ, 37 (1964), 387-90.

Gives new information.

2171 _____. "Tennyson's First Play on the American Stage." AL, 35 (1964),
519-28.

Critical history of the productions of QUEEN MARY in America.

2172 _____. "Tennyson's THE FORESTERS on the American Stage." PQ, 43
(1964), 549-57.

Critical history of Daly's highly successful New York production, and the subsequent American tour.

2173 _____. "Tennyson's BECKET on the American Stage." EMERSON SOCIETY QUARTERLY, no. 39 (Quarter 2, 1965), 15-20.

Historical account of Irving's American tours of 1893-94 and 1895-96.

2174 _____. "Tennyson's Minor Plays in America." AN&Q, 4, no. 2 (1965), 19-21.

Surveys the American critical reception of THE FALCON, THE CUP, and THE PROMISE OF MAY.

2175 Kissane, James D. ALFRED TENNYSON. New York: Twayne, 1970. 183 p.

Only a short section in a chapter considering Tennyson as a dramatic poet is devoted to the plays. The judgments and evaluation there are much too generalized to be of any real significance.

2176 Ricks, Christopher. TENNYSON. New York: Macmillan, 1972. xiii, 349 p.

Although the book is interesting as a critical biography, the plays themselves are cursorily dismissed in less than a paragraph.

VI Journals and Newsletters

2177 TENNYSON RESEARCH BULLETIN. Lincoln, Eng.: Tennyson Society, 1967-- .

An annual bulletin, modest in length and scope.

THOMAS, BRANDON (1856-1914)

II Acted Plays—Principal Titles

2178 THE COLOUR-SERGEANT: A PLAY IN ONE ACT. (Princess's, 26 February 1885.) London and New York: French, 1905. 20 p.

An acting edition with a cast list of the first London production.

2179 *CHARLEY'S AUNT. (Bury St. Edmund's, 29 February 1892; Royalty, 21 December 1892.) London: French, 1935. 107 p.

An acting edition with illustrations and a cast list of the first London production. Text slightly altered "in order to change certain mannerisms of 1892."

2179a *CHARLEY'S AUNT. Ed. E.R. Wood. London: Heinemann, 1969. xi, 115 p.

With useful introduction and notes.

IV Biography

2180 Brandon-Thomas, Jevan. CHARLEY'S AUNT'S FATHER: A LIFE OF BRANDON THOMAS. London: Douglas Saunders and MacGibbon and Kee, 1955. 232 p.

A readable account, with some very occasional criticism. It fills in many of the small, anecdotal details of the genesis of Thomas's work, drawing on contemporary documents. Unfortunately no sources are given for the latter.

TOBIN, JOHN (1770-1804)

II Acted Plays—Principal Titles

2181 THE HONEY MOON: A COMEDY IN FIVE ACTS. (Drury Lane, 31 January 1805.) London: Longman, Hurst, Rees, and Orme, 1805. 81 p.

Includes a cast list of the first London production.

2182 THE CURFEW: A PLAY IN FIVE ACTS. (Drury Lane, 19 February 1807.) 3rd ed. London: Richard Phillips, 1807. 62 p.

Includes a cast list of the first London production.

2183 THE SCHOOL FOR AUTHORS: A COMEDY IN THREE ACTS. (Covent Garden, 5 December 1808.) London: Longman, Hurst, Rees, and Orme, 1808. 45 p.

Includes a cast list of the first London production.

2184 THE FARO TABLE; OR, THE GUARDIANS: A COMEDY. (Drury Lane, 5 November 1816.) London: John Murray, 1816. 54 p.

Includes a cast list of the first London production.

IV Biography

2185 Benger, [Elizabeth Ogilvy]. MEMOIRS OF MR. JOHN TOBIN.

AUTHOR OF "THE HONEY-MOON." WITH A SELECTION FROM HIS UNPUBLISHED WRITINGS. London: Longman, Hurst, Rees, Orme, and Brown, 1820. xiii, 444 p.

> The memoirs take up less than half the volume; the texts of four plays take up the rest--THE TRAGEDY, A FRAGMENT; THE INDIANS, A PLAY; YOURS OR MINE? A COMIC OPERA (Covent Garden, 23 September 1816); and THE FISHER-MAN, AN OPERA (Drury Lane, 20 October 1819).

WEBSTER, BENJAMIN NOTTINGHAM (1797-1882)

II Acted Plays—Principal Titles

2186 HIGHWAYS AND BY-WAYS: A FARCE IN TWO ACTS. (Drury Lane, 15 March 1831.) New York: E.B. Clayton, n.d. 36 p.

> An acting edition with cast lists of the first London and a New York production and "Remarks" by D--G [George Daniel].

2187 PAUL CLIFFORD, THE HIGHWAYMAN OF 1770: A DRAMA IN THREE ACTS. (Coburg, 12 March 1832.) Cumberland's Minor Theatre, no. 47. London: Davidson, n.d. 76 p.

> An acting edition with a cast list of the first London produc-tion and "Remarks" by D--G [George Daniel]; the play is adapted from Bulwer-Lytton's novel.

2188 THE OLD GENTLEMAN: A COMEDY IN ONE ACT. (Olympic, 19 November 1832.) Duncombe's British Theatre, vol. 13. London: J. Duncombe, n.d. 24 p.

> An acting edition with a cast list of the first London produc-tion.

2189 THE MODERN ORPHEUS; OR, MUSIC THE FOOD OF LOVE: A FARCE IN ONE ACT. (Covent Garden, 15 April 1837.) The Acting National Drama, vol. 1. London: Chapman and Hall, 1837. 23 p.

> With a cast list of the first London production and "An Origi-nal Biographical Sketch" of the actor William Farren.

2190 THE VILLAGE DOCTOR: A DRAMA IN TWO ACTS. (Haymarket, 24 July 1839.) The Acting National Drama, vol. 7. London: Chapman and Hall, n.d. 42 p.

> With a cast list of the first London production; the Readex

copy is a promptbrook (New York Public Library) with manuscript notes.

2191 CAUGHT IN A TRAP: A COMEDIETTA IN TWO ACTS. (Haymarket,
25 November 1843.) The Acting National Drama, vol. 10. London:
Webster, n.d. 44 p.

With a cast list of the first London production.

2192 THE MISERIES OF HUMAN LIFE: A FARCE IN ONE ACT. (Haymarket,
27 November 1845.) The Acting National Drama, vol. 11. London:
National Acting Drama Office, n.d. 24 p.

2193 PIERROT, THE MARRIED MAN; THE POLICHINELLO, THE GAY SINGLE
FELLOW: AN ITALIAN PANTOMIME IN TWO PARTS AND TEN
TABLEAUX. (Adelphi, 27 December 1847.) The Acting National Drama,
vol. 14. London: National Acting Drama Office, n.d. 12 p.

With a cast list of the first London production.

2194 BELPHEGOR, THE MOUNTEBANK; OR, THE PRIDE OF BIRTH: A
DRAMA IN THREE ACTS. (Adelphi, 13 January 1851.) The Acting
National Drama, vol. 17. London: National Acting Drama Office,
n.d. 67 p.

With a cast list of the first London production; the Readex
copy is a promptbook (New York Public Library) with manuscript notes.

2195 THE MAN OF LAW: A COMEDY IN FOUR ACTS. (Haymarket, 9
December 1851.) The Acting National Drama, vol. 17. London: National Acting Drama Office, n.d. 56 p.

With a cast list of the first London production; the Readex
copy is defective, missing pages 1-5.

WIGAN, ALFRED SYDNEY (1814-78)

II Acted Plays—Principal Titles

2196 WATCH AND WARD: A FARCE IN ONE ACT. (Lyceum, 28 October
1844.) London: W. Barth, n.d. 27 p.

An acting edition with a cast list of the first London production and a copyright warning (see item 2198).

2197 A MODEL OF A WIFE: A FARCE IN ONE ACT. (Lyceum, 27 January 1845.) London: Lacy, n.d. 16 p.

> An acting edition with a cast list of the first London production.

2198 LUCK'S ALL! A FARCE IN TWO ACTS. (Lyceum, 23 June 1845.) London: W. Barth, n.d. 31 p.

> An acting edition with a cast list of the first London production and a warning to provincial theatre managers that they may not produce the play without first obtaining written permission from the author's agent--a result of copyright legislation in the 1843 Theatres Act.

2199 THE LOAN OF A WIFE: A FARCE IN ONE ACT. (Lyceum, 29 June 1846.) Duncumbe's British Theatre, vol. 56. London: Duncombe, n.d. 25 p.

> An acting edition with a cast list of the first London production.

2200 FIVE HUNDRED POUNDS REWARD; OR, DICK TURPIN THE SECOND: A COMIC DRAMA IN TWO ACTS. (Lyceum, 28 January 1847.) Dicks' Standard Plays, no. 1003. London: Dicks, n.d. 15 p.

> An acting edition with a cast list of the first London production.

WILDE, OSCAR (1854-1900)

I Collected Works

2201 THE PLAYS OF OSCAR WILDE. 4 vols. Boston and London: J.W. Luce, 1905-8.

> Contents: volume one: LADY WINDERMERE'S FAN, A WOMAN OF NO IMPORTANCE; volume two: THE IMPORTANCE OF BEING EARNEST, AN IDEAL HUSBAND; volume three: THE DUCHESS OF PADUA, VERA; OR, THE NIHILISTS, SALOMÉ, and A FLORENTINE TRAGEDY. Cast lists, where appropriate, are given as well as a list of Wilde's corrections and additions to VERA. Volume four contains an introductory note by Robert Ross on the fate of some of Wilde's manuscripts and on the completion of A FLORENTINE TRAGEDY by Thomas Sturge Moore.

2202 Ross, Robert, ed. THE FIRST COLLECTED EDITION OF THE WORKS OF

OSCAR WILDE 1908–1922. 14 vols. London: Methuen, 1908; rpt. in 15 vols. New York: Barnes and Noble, 1969.

> Mason (item 2214) describes the first collected edition fully on pages 459–90. The plays are contained in volumes 1–6. The reprint edition adds a fifteenth volume, FOR LOVE OF THE KING: A BURMESE MASQUE, originally published by Methuen in London, 1922.

2203 Maine, G.F., ed. THE WORKS OF OSCAR WILDE. London and Glasgow: Collins, 1948; 2nd ed., 1966. 1,216 p.

> The second edition is expanded and more accurate (notably the text of DE PROFUNDIS). It contains all the plays and an introduction by Vyvyan Holland, but lacks much critical apparatus.

2204 PLAYS: LADY WINDERMERE'S FAN, A WOMAN OF NO IMPORTANCE, AN IDEAL HUSBAND, THE IMPORTANCE OF BEING EARNEST, SALOMÉ. Harmondsworth: Penguin, 1958. 348 p.

> With cast lists of the original productions.

2205 FIVE PLAYS: WITH AN INTRODUCTION BY HESKETH PEARSON. New York: Bantam, 1961. xvi, 300 p.

> Contains the major plays. Pearson's introduction gives some flavor to brief histories of the plays, and there is a short bibliographical note.

II Acted Plays—Principal Titles

2206 VERA; OR, THE NIHILISTS: A DRAMA IN A PROLOGUE AND FOUR ACTS. (Union Square, New York, 20 August 1883.) No publication details. 1902. 75 p.

> Privately printed. See Mason (item 2214), pages 249–281; 551–52.

2207 THE DUCHESS OF PADUA. (Broadway, New York, 26 January 1891). New York: F.M. Buckles, 1906. 120 p.

2208 LADY WINDERMERE'S FAN: A PLAY ABOUT A GOOD WOMAN. (St. James's, 20 February 1892.) Paris: 1903. xvi, 132 p.

2209 A WOMAN OF NO IMPORTANCE. (Haymarket, 19 April 1893.) London: Bodley Head, 1894. xvi, 154 p.

2210 AN IDEAL HUSBAND, BY THE AUTHOR OF LADY WINDERMERE'S FAN. (Haymarket, 3 January 1895.) London: Leonard Smithers, 1899. xvi, 213 p.

2211 THE IMPORTANCE OF BEING EARNEST: A TRIVIAL COMEDY FOR SERIOUS PEOPLE BY THE AUTHOR OF LADY WINDERMERE'S FAN. (St. James's, 14 February 1895.) London: Leonard Smithers, 1899. xvi, 152 p.

2212 *Holland, Vyvyan, ed. THE ORIGINAL FOUR-ACT VERSION OF "THE IMPORTANCE OF BEING EARNEST." London: Methuen, 1957. xiv, 114 p.

2213 SALOMÉ: A PLAY. (Bijou, Bayswater, 10 May 1905.) New York: F.M. Buckles, 1906. 60 p.

IIa Unacted Plays

2213a FOR LOVE OF THE KING: A BURMESE MASQUE. London: Methuen, 1922. [v], 39 p.

> See item 2263a for evidence on the authencity of this piece.

III Bibliographies

2214 Mason, Stuart [Christopher Millard]. BIBLIOGRAPHY OF OSCAR WILDE. London: T.W. Laurie, 1914.; New ed. Intro. Timothy d'Arch Smith. London: Betram Rota, 1967. [vi], xxxix, 605 p.

> This remains a very useful tool for Wilde studies. There are sections on original editions and authorized reprints, collected editions, and selections, as well as details of Wilde's periodical publications and studies of Wilde. It is well illustrated, with many extracts from Wilde's correspondence, and fully annotated throughout.

2215 Cowan, Robert Ernest, and William Andrews Clark, Jr., et al., eds. THE LIBRARY OF WILLIAM ANDREWS CLARK, JR.: WILDE AND WILDEIANA. 5 vols. San Francisco: [Printed by J.H. Nash], 1922-31.

> Volume one deals specifically with the plays--a bibliographical and critical account of the library housed in the University of California at Los Angeles.

2216 Finzi, John Charles, comp. OSCAR WILDE AND HIS LITERARY CIRCLE: A CATALOGUE OF MANUSCRIPTS AND LETTERS IN THE WILLIAM ANDREWS CLARK MEMORIAL LIBRARY. Berkeley and Los Angeles: University of California Press, 1957. xxxiv, plus listings.

A companion to item 2215, listing 2,892 items acquired by
the library from 1929 to 1957. Contains several illustrations;
indexes of subjects, addresses, Wilde's correspondents; and
author/title list of manuscript works.

2217 Lawler, Donald L. "Oscar Wilde in the NEW CAMBRIDGE BIBLIOG-
RAPHY OF ENGLISH LITERATURE." PBSA, 67, no. 2 (1973), 172-88.

An exhaustive and highly informed examination of the NCBEL
listings of Wilde, indicating the numerous errors and omissions
there, and providing a lengthy list of corrections and additions.
Indispensable.

IV Biography

2218 Gide, André. OSCAR WILDE: A STUDY: WITH INTRODUCTION,
NOTES AND BIBLIOGRAPHY BY STUART MASON. Oxford: Holywell
Press, 1905. xiii, 110 p.

Personal recollections. The notes also contain some interesting
information, and are more reliable than most earlier works.

2219 Sherard, Robert Harborough. THE LIFE OF OSCAR WILDE. New York:
T. Werner Laurie, 1906. xvi, 470 p.

An early biography written by a friend with an exceptionally
puritanical bias. Sherard viewed Wilde's homosexuality as a
form of "insanity" and thus gives minimal attention to the
vital decade of Wilde's life. Lord Alfred Douglas, for
example, is not even mentioned.

2220 Douglas, Lord Alfred. OSCAR WILDE AND MYSELF. New York:
Duffield, 1914. vii, 306 p.

A hostile account of their relationship. Douglas, under the
impression that Wilde had turned against him since his im-
prisonment, here repudiates his former admiration of the man
and his work.

2221 Harris, Frank. OSCAR WILDE: HIS LIFE AND CONFESSIONS: (WITH
MEMORIES OF OSCAR WILDE BY G. BERNARD SHAW). 2 vols. New
York, 1918. vii, 612, 32 p.

An often fanciful and fictitious biography, many details of
which have been discredited by subsequent, more accurate
work.

2222 AFTER READING: LETTERS OF OSCAR WILDE TO ROBERT ROSS. London: C.W. Beaumont, 1921. 60 p.

Written during the summer of 1897.

2223 Harris, Frank, and Lord Alfred Douglas. NEW PREFACE TO "THE LIFE AND CONFESSIONS OF OSCAR WILDE". London: Fortune Press, 1925. 55 p.

> Intended to correct some of the more blatant errors of Harris's 1918 work, this preface was to precede a new edition of the biography. Because of differences between Harris and Douglas, it was finally published by Douglas, and is chiefly useful for its additional written evidence.

2224 Raymond, Jean Paul, and Charles Ricketts. OSCAR WILDE: RECOLLECTIONS. London: Nonesuch Press, 1932. 60 p.

> "Raymond" is a creation of Ricketts's imagination to whom he addresses a series of letters which contain genuine recollections of Wilde.

2225 Reinier, G.J. OSCAR WILDE. London: Davies, 1933. 164 p.

> A sound, straightforward account, which takes an enlightened and well-informed view of Wilde's homosexuality. There are also a few critical comments and a short, annotated bibliography.

2226 Silver, Rollo G. "Oscar Makes a Call." COLOPHON, part 20 (1935). No pagination. 4 p.

> An account of Wilde's visit to Walt Whitman in 1882 in the latter's own words.

2227 O'Sullivan, Vincent. ASPECTS OF WILDE. New York: Holt, 1936. vi, 213 p.

> O'Sullivan, who knew Wilde personally, attempts to "place an historical figure in an historical position." While many of the anecdotes and sketches are interesting, the book emerges as a rag-bag of characterizations and incidents and lacks overall coherence. The facts are undocumented and there is no index.

2228 Sherard, Robert Harborough. BERNARD SHAW, FRANK HARRIS & OSCAR WILDE. London: T. Werner Laurie, 1937. 319 p.

> Sherard's objective is to expose the patent absurdities and errors of Harris's biographies of Wilde.

2229 Brasol, Boris. OSCAR WILDE: THE MAN, THE ARTIST, THE MARTYR. New York: Scribner's, 1938. xviii, 402 p.

> This sympathetic biography is franker in its treatment of Wilde's homosexuality than most earlier studies. However, it only occasionally adds to our knowledge. Of most use

is the "chronological index" which gives a detailed, year-
by-year record of Wilde's career, personal and literary.

2230 Douglas, Lord Alfred. OSCAR WILDE: A SUMMING UP: WITH AN
INTRODUCTION BY DEREK HUDSON. London: Duckworth, 1940 and
1950. xiv, 142 p.

A much more evenly tempered biography in which Douglas
admits and reverses his earlier hostility. Douglas's preamble
on homosexuality, Wilde and himself, is too protestingly verbose.

2231 Snider, Rose. "Oscar Wilde's Progress Down East." NEQ, 13 (1940),
7-23.

Wilde's visit to Maine and the Canadian Maritime provinces
in 1882. Draws mainly on contemporary newspaper reports.

2232 Winwar, Frances. OSCAR WILDE AND THE YELLOW 'NINETIES. Garden City, N.Y.: Blue Ribbon Books, 1941. xviii, 381 p.

This is based largely on earlier biographies, although it
touches on the cultural background fairly extensively. It
has a blunt foreword in which Lord Alfred Douglas corrects
Winwar's errors about his relationship with Wilde.

2233 Pearson, Hesketh. OSCAR WILDE: HIS LIFE AND WIT. New York
and London: Harper, 1946. 345 p.

Pearson recreates Wilde "first and foremost as a genial wit
and humorist" and succeeds admirably in his task. His treatment is sympathetic and eminently readable. No documentation.

2234 Wilson, Edmund. "Oscar Wilde: 'One Must Always Seek What Is Most
Tragic.'" NEW YORKER, 29 June 1946, pp. 65-70.

Review of Pearson's biography (item 2233). Wilson also takes
the opportunity to develop the theory that Wilde invited his
own catastrophe.

2235 "An Unwise Forgery?" PULC, 8 (1947), 90-91.

A brief note on a forged Wilde letter linked with T.J. Wise's
faked edition of Browning's PAULINE.

2236 Wimberly, Lowry Charles. "Oscar Wilde Meets Woodberry." PRAIRIE
SCHOONER, 21 (1947), 108-16.

Wilde's 1882 visit to the University of Nebraska.

2237 Wyndham, Horace. "When Oscar Wilde was Editor." LIFE AND LETTERS AND THE LONDON MERCURY, 55 (1947), 201-4.

A short account of Wilde's editorship of THE WOMAN'S WORLD.

2238 Hyde, H. Montgomery, ed. THE TRIALS OF OSCAR WILDE: REGINA (WILDE) V. QUEENSBURY; REGINA V. WILDE AND TAYLOR. London: Hodge, 1948. [ix], 384 p.

A near-verbatim report of the three trials, with an extensive introduction and appendices which provide valuable background information.

2239 Broad, Lewis. THE FRIENDSHIPS & FOLLIES OF OSCAR WILDE. London: Hutchinson, 1954. 264 p.

Straightforward, but adding little new material. Broad does amplify on the friendships with Ross and Sherard usefully. There is an annotated bibliography.

2240 Holland, Vyvyan. SON OF OSCAR WILDE. New York: Dutton, 1954. xvii, 237 p.

The autobiography of one of Wilde's sons, which relates some of the effects of Wilde's life upon his own family. Useful appendices consisting of thirty-three of Wilde's letters and some unpublished "poems in prose."

2241 Furnell, John. THE STRINGED LUTE: AN EVOCATION IN DIALOGUE OF OSCAR WILDE. London: Rider, 1955. xvii, 198 p.

Covering the years 1891-1900, this work consists of a dramatic dialogue which uses Wilde's words whenever possible. However, it adds nothing to previously published works.

2242 Hyde, H. Montgomery. "An Afternoon with Max." SPECTATOR (London), 197 (1956), 445-47.

Account of an interview with Max Beerbohm, with his reminiscences of Wilde and other notables.

2243 Wilson, Asher. "Oscar Wilde and LOYALTIES." ETJ, 11 (1959), 208-11.

An interesting article which demonstrates parallels between Wilde's trial and Galsworthy's LOYALTIES.

2244 Holland, Vyvyan. OSCAR WILDE: A PICTORIAL BIOGRAPHY. London: Thames and Hudson, 1960. 144 p.

A brief, sound biography which covers the salient points of
Wilde's life; with numerous illustrations.

2245 Burke, Rev. Edmund. "Oscar Wilde: The Final Scene." LONDON
MAGAZINE, n.s. 1 (May 1961), 37-43.

An account of Wilde's death-bed conversion to Catholicism,
based on the written evidence of Fr. Cuthbert Dunne who
administered the last rites.

2246 Pearson, Hesketh. "Oscar Wilde and his Actors." THEATRE ARTS, 45
(1961), 63-64; 75.

Some useful information on the actors with whom Wilde
worked. However, some of the anecdotes have been al-
ready overworked.

2247 Harrod, Roy. "Oscar Wilde." TLS, 27 July 1962, p. 541.

Indirect reminiscences of Wilde with whom Harrod's mother
was personally acquainted.

2248 Hart-Davis, Rupert, ed. THE LETTERS OF OSCAR WILDE. London:
Hart-Davis, 1962. xxv, 958 p.

An excellently edited volume which contains indispensable
information. It also prints the only accurate version of
DE PROFUNDIS. See item 2298.

2249 Croft-Cooke, Rupert. BOSIE: THE STORY OF LORD ALFRED DOUGLAS:
HIS FRIENDS AND ENEMIES. Indianapolis: Bobbs-Merrill, 1963.
414 p.

The most balanced and accurate version of Wilde's relationship with Douglas.

2250 Hyde, H. Montgomery. OSCAR WILDE: THE AFTERMATH. London:
Methuen, 1963. xxi, 221 p.

A well-documented account of Wilde's prison life, drawn
from official government sources and records, as well as
the standard biographies.

2251 Monteiro, George. "A Contemporary View of Henry James and Oscar
Wilde, 1882." AL, 35 (1963-64), 528-30.

Quotes in full a letter written by Harriet Loring recording
her impressions of James's and Wilde's visit to Washington,
D.C.

2252 Gollin, Richard M. "Beerbohm, Wilde, Shaw, and 'The Good-Natured
Critic': Some New Letters." BNYPL, 68 (1964), 83-99.

A lucid commentary on a group of fourteen letters, written
to Edward Rose, of which one is by Wilde after his release
from prison. This last "is especially interesting for its
insistence, three times repeated, that prison was good for
his career as an artist."

2253 Austin, Arthur D. "Regina v. Queensbury." UR, 32 (1966), 179-86.

A clear and concise analysis of Wilde's trial which views
Queensbury's lawyer as much more subtle and adroit in his
cross-examination of Wilde than had been thought previously.

2254 Jullian, Philippe. OSCAR WILDE. Trans. Violet Wyndham. London:
Constable, 1969. 420 p.

Despite the benefit of recent research, there is little new
here, although the book is sound and reliable.

2255 Burkhart, Charles. "Ada Leverson and Oscar Wilde." ELT, 13 (1970),
193-200.

A useful account of their relationship.

2256 Clive, H.P. "Oscar Wilde's First Meeting with Mallarmé." FRENCH
STUDIES, 24 (1970), 145-49.

Evidence to correct previous conjectures about when this
meeting took place.

2257 Taylor, Welford Dunaway. "A 'Soul' Remembers Oscar Wilde." ELT,
14 (1971), 43-48.

A discussion of Amelie Rives's fictionalization of her brief
association with Wilde in her novel SHADOWS OF FLAMES.

2258 Croft-Cooke, Rupert. THE UNRECORDED LIFE OF OSCAR WILDE.
London: W.H. Allen, 1972. x, 289 p.

In his opening chapter Croft-Cooke reviews earlier biographies
and their respective weaknesses, as well as some of the legends
surrounding Wilde. The remainder of this flowing biography is
characterized by its frank treatment of Wilde's life, notably
his homosexuality. The latter aspect is unbiased, and set
against the racy world of underground London at the close of
the century. Cooke also knew Lord Douglas for the last
twenty-five years of the latter's life.

V Critical Studies

2259 Leadman, Wilfred M. "The Literary Position of Wilde." WESTMINISTER

REVIEW, 166 (1906), 201-8.

Nothing directly on the plays, but of interest as an early
attempt to estimate Wilde impartially and to rehabilitate him.

2260 Ingleby, Leonard Cresswell. OSCAR WILDE. London: T. Werner
Laurie, n.d. [1907]. viii, 400 p.

The biographical aspects of this book are sympathetic to
Wilde. Also interesting is the bibliography of references
to Wilde in PUNCH from 1881-1906. Criticism of the plays
is genial, and illustrated with lengthy quotation.

2261 Esdaile, Arundell. "The New Hellenism." FORTNIGHTLY REVIEW,
n.s. 88 (1910), 706-22.

A review of Ross's edition of the works and of Sherard's
biography. The review also has a brief biographical sketch
and makes some incidental comments on the plays.

2262 Ransome, Arthur. OSCAR WILDE: A CRITICAL STUDY. 3rd ed.
London: Methuen, 1913. vi, 234 p.

The original edition involved Ransome in a libel suit with
Lord Douglas, which he won, although in subsequent editions
he chose to omit various biographical passages. As a critical
study, the work is too brief and lacks any real analysis.

2263 Shanks, Edward. "Oscar Wilde." LONDON MERCURY, 10 (1924),
278-87.

Wilde viewed as a second-rate writer whose personal reputation has inflated his literary standing. Shanks tries to prove
Wilde possesses little more than a surface glitter cast by his
felicity with paradox and wit. The analysis is, however,
not incisive.

2263a Millard, C.S. [Stuart Mason]. "Who wrote 'For Love of the King'?"
Birmingham: Juckes, [1925]. 4 p.

A scarce pamphlet with strong evidence that the play might
not be Wilde's.

2264 Braybrooke, Patrick. OSCAR WILDE: A STUDY. London: Braithwaite
& Miller, 1930; rpt. Folcroft Press, 1970. 150 p.

Braybrooke's intention is to show "the value of Wilde as a
serious thinker," and he devotes chapters to him as dramatist,
dialectician, story writer, novelist, poet, and essayist. The
book fails to match the scope of these pretensions.

2265 Symons, Arthur. A STUDY OF OSCAR WILDE. London: C.J. Sawyer, 1930. 89 p.

> Touches on most aspects of Wilde's work, but too brief to give more than a few generalizations.

2266 Lavrin, Janks. ASPECTS OF MODERNISM: FROM WILDE TO PIRAN-DELLO. London: Stanley Nott, 1935. 247 p.

> The section on Wilde sees him as afraid of and averse to the realities of life and taking refuge in a world of decadence, sensations, and art for art's sake.

2267 Snider, Rose. SATIRE IN THE COMEDIES OF CONGREVE, SHERIDAN, WILDE AND COWARD. University of Maine Studies, 2nd ser., no 42. Orono: University of Maine Press, 1937; rpt. New York: Phaeton, 1972. x, 135 p.

> Wilde is seen as a writer of comedies of manners and hence a satirist. His satire is judged to be more elusive than that of the others, but "finds expression in the verbal achievements of his characters."

2268 Kingsmill, Hugh. "The Intelligent Man's Guide to Oscar Wilde." FORT-NIGHTLY, n.s. 144 (1938), 296-303.

> A brief, objective history of Harris's books on Wilde, indi-cating the faults and deceptions in them.

2269 Kernahan, Coulson. "Wilde and Heine." DUBLIN MAGAZINE, 15 (1940), 19-26.

> Some comparison between the lives and work of the two men. Kernahan knew Wilde personally, and one letter between them is quoted fully.

2270 Nethercot, Arthur H. "Oscar Wilde and the Devil's Advocate." PMLA, 59 (1944), 833-50.

> The works are seen as autobiographical, revealing a schizoid personality. Wilde both flaunts his doctrines and life at the public and then confesses and repents his behavior. See item 2271.

2271 _____. "Oscar Wilde on His Subdividing Himself." PMLA, 60 (1945), 616-17.

> A follow-up to item 2270, quoting a previously unpublished letter of Wilde's to substantiate the theory of Wilde "splitting himself into different and often antithetical persons in his published works."

2272 Agate, James. "Oscar Wilde and the Theatre." MASQUE, no. 3 (1947), 5-23.

A brief, inimical survey of the plays with nothing in the way of analytical substantiation.

2273 Roditi, Edouard. OSCAR WILDE. Norfolk, Conn.: New Directions, 1947. 256 p.

Roditi sees the plays as a cheap commercialization of Wilde's artistic capabilities, concluding that the "comedies . . . suggest that his life, as a serious creative artist, had perhaps ended before his trials and tribulations, and that his only future . . . was that of the successful writer."

2274 Auden, W.H. "A Playboy of the Western World: St. Oscar, the Homintern Martyr." PARTISAN REVIEW, 17 (1950), 390-94.

A review of item 2275 and an occasion to toss out some of Auden's own suggestions on Wilde.

2275 Woodcock, George. THE PARADOX OF OSCAR WILDE. New York: Macmillan, 1950. 250 p.

The controlling notion is of Wilde as a "schizoid type," with examples drawn from Wilde's life, writings, and the people who significantly influenced him (Pater and Ruskin). The plays are not central to Woodcock's interesting, though un-documented book. No index.

2276 Ervine, St. John. OSCAR WILDE: A PRESENT TIME APPRAISAL. London: Allen and Unwin, 1951. 336 p.

This is an antipathetical and thoroughly bigoted piece of work. Ervine makes much of Wilde's homosexuality, which he attributes to Robert Ross's "degenerate" influence.

2277 Mercier, Vivian. "The Fate of Oscar Wilde." COMMONWEAL, 61 (1955), 528-30.

A brief review of the state of Wilde studies on the centenary of his birth.

2278 Vordtriede, Werner. "A Dramatic Device in FAUST and THE IMPORTANCE OF BEING EARNEST." MLN, 70 (1955), 584-85.

Wilde's indebtedness in Act II of EARNEST.

2279 Bergler, Edmund. "SALOMÉ: The Turning Point in the Life of Oscar Wilde." PSYCHOANALYTIC REVIEW, 43 (1956), 97-103.

2280 Foster, Richard. "Wilde as Parodist: A Second Look at THE IMPOR-
TANCE OF BEING EARNEST." CE, 18 (1956-57), 18-23.

> Argues the opposite case to Reinert (item 2282) and, while
> seeing elements of farce and comedy of manners in the play,
> maintains it is a parody in that the characters <u>know</u> they are
> in a play and consciously parody such notions as romantic love.

2281 Peckham, Morse. "What Did Lady Windermere Learn?" CE, 18 (1956-
57), 11-14.

> Concludes that Lady Windermere fails to learn anything be-
> cause she does not question the standards by which she judges.
> A suggestive, but unrigorous article.

2282 Reinert, Otto. "Satiric Strategy in THE IMPORTANCE OF BEING
EARNEST." CE, 18 (1956-57), 14-18.

> See item 2280. Demonstrates that the play is a farce in
> which the characters are totally unconscious of the ramifica-
> tions of their speech and action.

2283 Ganz, Arthur F. "The Dandiacal Drama: A Study of the Plays of Oscar
Wilde." Ph.D. Dissertation, Columbia University, 1957. 293 p. (DA#58-
1338)

> Views the dandy as central to the plays--"the advocate of the
> supremacy of artistic form."

2284 Reinert, Otto. "The Courtship Dance in THE IMPORTANCE OF BEING
EARNEST." MD, 1 (1958-59), 256-57.

> A brief discussion of a "systematic symmetry of action" in the
> second half of Act II and the first scene of Act III of EARNEST.

2285 James, Norman. "Oscar Wilde's Dramaturgy." Ph.D. Dissertation, Duke
University, 1959. 258 p. (DA#60-265)

> An examination of the evolution of Wilde's dramaturgy, seeing
> a decrease in the influence of Augier and Dumas fils and the
> development of a more relaxed style more clearly Wilde's own.

2286 Ryals, Clyde de L. "Oscar Wilde's SALOMÉ." N&Q, 204 (1959), 56-
57.

> Discusses the legends surrounding the composition of SALOMÉ
> and establishes that the play was solely Wilde's, although he
> did receive assistance from Pierre Louys purely in matters of
> grammar.

2287 Ganz, Arthur. "The Divided Self in the Society Comedies of Oscar Wilde." MD, 3 (1960), 16-23.

> An interesting, useful discussion of Wilde's dualistic attitude towards society, which, in rejecting society's mores, he alternately supplicates and disdains.

2288 Zagona, H.G. THE LEGEND OF SALOMÉ AND THE PRINCIPLE OF ART FOR ART'S SAKE. Geneva and Paris: Ambilly-Annemasse, 1960. 141 p.

2289 Partridge, E.B. "The Importance of Not Being Earnest." BUCKNELL REVIEW, 9 (1960-61), 143-58.

> Sees the play as a defense of "the life of the imagination in the subtlest of all ways--by embodying it in a play so trivial and absurd that it makes fun of itself."

2290 Dyson, A.E. "The Socialist Aesthete." LISTENER, 66 (24 August 1961), 273-74.

> Deals briefly but usefully with Wilde's ironic persona, his theories of art and socialism, all of which Dyson sees as contributions to Wilde's merciless attack on hypocrisy or moral posing.

2291 Wadleigh, Paul Custer. "Form in Oscar Wilde's Comedies: A Structural Analysis." Ph.D. Dissertation, Indiana University, 1962. 284 p. (DA#62-5087).

> This thesis views earlier critical estimates of Wilde's artistry as unjust and attempts to demonstrate his skillful composition.

2292 Toliver, Harold E. "Wilde and the Importance of 'Sincere and Studied Triviality.'" MD, 5 (1962-63), 389-99.

> Centers on the notion that the theme of EARNEST is that irony and skepticism are sincere and earnest pursuits.

2293 Ellmann, Richard. "Romantic Pantomime in Oscar Wilde." PARTISAN REVIEW, 30 (1963), 342-55.

> Sees Wilde as "greater than any of his works," and also places him in his age.

2294 Nethercot, Arthur H. "Prunes and Miss Prism." MD, 6 (1963), 112-16.

> Suggests allusions hidden in Miss Prism's name and in particular points to a connection with Dickens's LITTLE DORRIT.

2295 White, William. "A Bribe for Oscar Wilde." AN&Q, 2 (1963), 38-39.

> An account of a letter which offered a bribe to the Governor
> of Pentonville Prison to connive at Wilde's escape.

2296 Freedman, Morris. "The Modern Tragicomedy of Wilde and O'Casey."
CE, 25 (1963-64), 518-27.

> Not a fruitful comparison of the two dramatists, since Wilde's
> tragicomic elements could easily have been determined in-
> dependently. Freedman sees the dominant theme in Wilde as
> being the boredom and despair of the individual in a society
> which emphasizes only the superficial.

2297 Ganz, Arthur. "The Meaning of THE IMPORTANCE OF BEING EARN-
EST." MD, 6 (1963-64), 42-52.

> A persuasive explication of the theme of EARNEST: "the
> world of perfect Wildean dandyism" where no distinction is
> made between physical and moral failings, between the ex-
> ternal and the internal.

2298 Wilson, Harry. "Epistolary Autobiography: The Letters of Oscar Wilde."
SAQ, 63 (1964), 406-13.

> Review of Hart-Davis's edition of Wilde's letters (item 2248),
> seen as Wilde's real masterpieces.

2299 Brockett, O.G. "J.T. Grein and the Ghost of Oscar Wilde." QJS,
52 (1966), 131-38.

> An account of the libel suit provoked by Grein's 1918 pro-
> duction of SALOMÉ.

2300 Gregor, Ian. "Comedy and Oscar Wilde." SoR, 74 (1966), 501-21.

2301 Raafat, Z. "The Literary Indebtedness of Wilde's SALOMÉ to Sardou's
THEODORA." RLC, 40 (1966), 453-66.

> This heavily documented article attempts to draw both direct
> and indirect parallels between the two plays and hints at
> Wilde's dependency on other French models in his later plays.

2302 Ryskamp, Charles, ed. WILDE AND THE NINETIES: AN ESSAY AND
AN EXHIBITION BY RICHARD ELLMANN, E.D.H. JOHNSON AND
ALFRED L. BUSH. Princeton: Princeton University Library, 1966. viii,
64 p.

> Contains brief essays--"The Critic as Artist as Wilde" and
> "The Eighteen Nineties: Perspectives."

2303 Wadleigh, Paul C. "EARNEST at St. James's Theatre." QJS, 52 (1966), 58-62.

> Straightforward account of the production and reception, drawn from secondary accounts and not radically new.

2304 Ellmann, Richard. EMINENT DOMAIN: YEATS AMONG WILDE, JOYCE, POUND, ELIOT AND AUDEN. London and New York: Oxford University Press, 1967. vii, 159 p.

> A short account of the biographical and literary interchange between Wilde and Yeats.

2305 San Juan, Epifanio, Jr. THE ART OF OSCAR WILDE. Princeton: Princeton University Press, 1967. ix, 238 p.

> Although this book smacks of the dissertation and is pedantic stylistically, it does occasionally yield some fresh insights into Wilde's work. It is littered with footnotes which repay investigation.

2306 Mikhail, E.H. "Oscar Wilde and his First Comedy." MD, 10 (1967-68), 394-96.

> A brief account of the dating and writing of LADY WINDERMERE.

2307 Ellmann, Richard. "Overtures to Wilde's SALOMÉ." YEARBOOK OF COMPARATIVE AND GENERAL LITERATURE, 17 (1968), 17-28.

> Offers some "fugitive" "subliminal" associations of Wilde's which lie beneath the surface. Considerable biographical background information, particularly Wilde's association with Ruskin and Pater.

2308 Mikhail, E.H. "The French Influences on Oscar Wilde's Comedies." RLC, 42 (1968), 220-33.

> Mikhail evaluates the more general, technical influences of French drama and indicates more specific instances. Special attention is given to LADY WINDERMERE and A WOMAN OF NO IMPORTANCE.

2309 Recoulley, Alfred Lunsford III. "Oscar Wilde, the Dandy-Artist: A Study of Dandyism in the Life and Works of Oscar Wilde, with Particular Attention Given to the Intellectual Bases of Wilde's Dandyism." Ph.D. Disseration, University of North Carolina at Chapel Hill, 1968. 495 p. (DA#69-10196)

2310 Mikhail, E.H. "The Four-Act Version of THE IMPORTANCE OF BEING EARNEST." MD, 11 (1968-69), 263-66.

> An account of variants.

2311 _____. "Self-Revelation in AN IDEAL HUSBAND." MD, 11 (1968-69), 180-86.

> Draws parallels between Wilde's life and the play, with emphasis on the autobiographical portrayal of Lord Goring.

2312 Bader, Earl Delbert. "The Self-Reflexive Language: Uses of Paradox in Wilde, Shaw, and Chesterton." Ph.D. Dissertation, Indiana University, 1969. 226 p. (DA#70-7419)

> Looks at the manner in which the paradoxist reminds his audience of the artificiality of language and the writer's own theatricality.

2313 Ellmann, Richard. OSCAR WILDE: A COLLECTION OF CRITICAL ESSAYS. Englewood Cliffs, N.J.: Prentice-Hall, 1969. viii, 180 p.

> A useful collection which also touches on the life of Wilde. Wide range of well-known contributors.

2314 Beckson, Karl, ed. OSCAR WILDE: THE CRITICAL HERITAGE. London: Routledge & Kegan Paul. 1970. xiv, 434 p.

> An excellent, extensive collection of reviews which makes readily accessible the contemporary critical reception of Wilde's work. Beckson provides good explanatory headnotes to many of the items.

2315 Berland, Ellen. "Form and Content in the Plays of Oscar Wilde." Ph.D. Dissertation, Columbia University, 1970. 255 p. (DA#72-33407)

> Examines the thematic content of the plays against the background of various influences--melodrama, Decadent and Symbolist movements, the well-made play.

2316 Breugelmans, R. "The Reconciliation of Opposites in the Mythopoesis of Wilde, George and Hofmannsthal." PROCEEDINGS: PACIFIC NORTHWEST CONFERENCE ON FOREIGN LANGUAGES, TWENTY-FIRST ANNUAL MEETING. Ed. Ralph W. Baldner. April 3-4, 1970. Victoria, B.C.: University of Victoria, 1970.

2317 Hunt, Jean Mary. "The Comic Spirit and Oscar Wilde." Ph.D. Dissertation, Brown University, 1970. 169 p. (DA#71-13884)

> Applies the comic theory (of providing escape from various restraints) to Wilde and sees the dandy as both Wilde's mouthpiece and an autobiographical reflection.

2318 Jordan, Robert J. "Satire and Fantasy in Wilde's THE IMPORTANCE OF BEING EARNEST." ARIEL, 1, no. 3 (1970), 101-9.

Examination of the satiric content (the reversal of the usual Victorian male and female relationship). Interesting is Jordan's contention that while the young people are "terribly elegant, exquisitely sophisticated adults . . . much of their behaviour and many of their attitudes are redolent of the world of the child."

2319 Shafer, Elizabeth. "The Wild, Wild West of Oscar Wilde." MONTANA MAGAZINE OF WESTERN HISTORY, 20, no. 2 (1970), 86-89.

A brief, breezily readable account of Wilde's visit to Colorado in 1882.

2320 Ware, James M. "Algernon's Appetite: Oscar Wilde's Hero as Restoration Dandy." ELT, 13 (1970), 17-26.

A reading of EARNEST "intended to show merely that Algernon's hunger is reminiscent of appetite-satisfaction motifs found in several Restoration comedies of manners, and that Wilde returned in this play to the tone of the purest--that is, Etheregean--comedy of manners."

2321 Pine, Richard. "The Personality of Wilde." DULBIN MAGAZINE, 9, no. 2 (1971-72), 52-59.

A vaguely written generalization which adds nothing to an understanding of the man or the work.

2322 Borowitz, Helen Osterman. "Visions of Salomé." CRITICISM, 14, no. 1 (1972), 12-21.

2323 Chamberlin, J.E. "Oscar Wilde and the Importance of Doing Nothing." HUDR, 25, no. 2 (1972), 194-218.

A wide ranging discussion of Wilde's embodiment of Taoist thought into his work. Sees the concept of "actionless activity" as a "moment of paradoxical intensity or creative insight" which informs Wilde's output. Incidental reference to the plays.

2324 Fox, Steven James. "Art and Personality: Browning, Rosetti, Pater, Wilde and Yeats." Ph.D. Dissertation, Yale University, 1972. 314 p. (DA#72-22885)

The chapter devoted to Wilde reveals how his "achievement derives from Pater. Wilde dramatizes Pre-Raphaelite or Paterian personality, and popularizes the principles implicit in the works of his predecessors, but his contribution to an art of personality is minimal."

2325 Fussell, B.H. "The Masks of Oscar Wilde." SR, 80, no. 1 (1972), 124-39.

> A biographical and critical overview of Wilde's work which interprets the latter in the light of Wilde's posings, particularly his mask of the dandy.

2326 Joost, Nicholas, and Franklin E. Court. "SALOMÉ, the Moon, and Oscar Wilde's Aesthetics: A Reading of the Play." PLL, 8, supplement (1972), 96-111.

> A close, interesting interpretation of the play which views the moon as the central, controlling image of the play. In particular the moon "symbolizes for the principal characters the unique vision that each has of Salomé herself."

2327 Livingstone, Brenda Mae. "Oscar Wilde and the Tragic Mode." Ph.D. Dissertation, University of California, Riverside, 1972. 271 p. (DA#72-22051)

> Sees Wilde using tragic elements intermittently. He abandoned the mode for EARNEST, but returned to the dual approach in A FLORENTINE TRAGEDY and SALOMÉ.

2328 Nassaar, Christopher Suhayl. "Into the Demon Universe: A Literary Exploration of Oscar Wilde." Ph.D. Dissertation, University of Wisconsin, 1972. 256 p. (DA#72-11252)

> Accepts Ellmann's premise that Wilde changed psychologically and artistically after his initial homosexual experience in 1886 and examines his succeeding works in that light.

2329 Roy, Emil. BRITISH DRAMA SINCE SHAW: WITH A PREFACE BY HARRY T. MOORE. Carbondale and Edwardsville: Southern Illinois University Press; London and Amsterdam: Feffer and Simons, 1972. xiii, 143 p.

> A chapter is devoted to a discussion of Wilde, whose importance is based solely on EARNEST, examined here in some detail.

WILKS, THOMAS EGERTON (1812-54)

II Acted Plays—Principal Titles

2330 THE BROTHERS; OR, THE WOLF AND THE LAMB. (Haymarket, 23 June 1832.) London Acting Drama, no. 31. London: W. Strange, n.d. 26 p.

> With a cast list of a St. James's production; the play was originally acted with the subtitle as the main title.

2331 THE SEVEN CLERKS; OR, THE THREE THIEVES AND THE DENOUNCER: AN ORIGINAL ROMANTIC DRAMA IN TWO ACTS. (Surrey, 3 November 1834.) French's American Drama: The Acting Edition, no. 115. New York: French, n.d. 27 p.

> With cast lists of Boston, New York, and Philadelphia productions.

2332 STATE SECRETS; OR, THE TAILOR OF TAMWORTH: A FARCE IN ONE ACT. (Surrey, 12 September 1836.) London: Lacy, n.d. 18 p.

> An acting edition with a cast list of the first London production.

2333 LORA DARNELY; OR, THE KEEP OF CASTLE HILL! AN ORIGINAL ROMANTIC DRAMA IN TWO ACTS. (Surrey, 11 September 1837.) Duncombe's British Theatre, vol. 32. London: Duncombe, n.d. 39 p.

> An acting edition with a cast list of the first London production and a note indicating that the play was performed with the title of THE KING AND THE FREEBOOTER for the first six nights.

2334 THE KING'S WAGER; OR, THE COTTAGE AND THE COURT: A DRAMA IN THREE ACTS. (Victoria, 5 December 1837.) London: Lacy, n.d. 71 p.

> An acting edition with a cast list of the first London production.

2335 THE CROWN PRINCE; OR, THE BUCKLE OF BRILLIANTS: A DRAMA IN TWO ACTS. (Sadler's Wells, 16 July 1838.) French's Minor Drama, no. 100. New York: French, n.d. 26 p.

> An acting edition; the Readex copy is a promptbook (New York Public Library), interleaved, with manuscript notes.

2336 THE WREN BOYS; OR, THE MOMENT OF PERIL: A DRAMA IN TWO ACTS. (City of London, 8 October 1838.) Dicks' Standard Plays, no. 404. No publication details. 18 p.

> An acting edition with a cast list of the first London production.

2337 BEN THE BOATSWAIN: A NAUTICAL DRAMA IN THREE ACTS. (Surrey, 19 August 1839.) London: Lacy, n.d. 38 p.

> An acting edition with a cast list of the first London production; the Readex copy is a promptbook (New York Public Library).

2338 BAMBOOZLING: AN ORIGINAL FARCE IN ONE ACT. (Olympic, 16
May 1842.) Dicks' Standard Plays, no. 627. London: Dicks, n.d.
19 p.

> An acting edition with a cast list of the first London produc-
> tion.

2339 SIXTEEN STRING JACK; OR, THE KNAVE OF KNAVES' ACRE: A
ROMANTIC ORIGINAL DRAMA IN TWO ACTS. (Sadler's Wells, 28
November 1842.) New British Theatre (Late Duncombe's), no. 505.

> An acting edition with a cast list of a City of London pro-
> duction.

2340 THE AMBASSADOR'S LADY; OR, THE ROSE AND THE RING! A
ROMANTIC DRAMA IN TWO ACTS. (Strand, 7 August 1843.) Duncombe's British Theatre, vol. 47. London: Duncombe, n.d. 38 p.

> An acting edition with a cast list of the first London produc-
> tion.

2341 THE ROLL OF THE DRUM: A ROMANTIC DRAMA IN THREE ACTS.
(Adelphi, 16 October 1843.) London: Lacy, n.d. 33 p.

> An acting edition with a cast list of the first London produc-
> tion; the Readex copy is a promptbook (New York Public
> Library), interleaved, with manuscript notes.

2342 KENNYNGTON CROSSE; OR, THE OLD HOUSE ON THE COMMON.
A LEGEND OF LAMBETH: AN ORIGINAL ROMANTIC DRAMA IN TWO
ACTS. (Surrey, 12 June 1848.) London: Lacy, n.d. 48 p.

> An acting edition with a cast list of the first London produc-
> tion and a reproduction of the playbill.

WILLS, WILLIAM GORMAN (1828-91)

II Acted Plays—Principal Titles

2343 CHARLES THE FIRST: AN HISTORICAL TRAGEDY IN FOUR ACTS.
(Lyceum, 28 September 1872.) Edinburgh and London: Blackwood, 1873.
83 p.

> A revised version of the stage text, with a cast list of the
> first London production, a preface, and an appendix on
> Cromwell by Wills.

2344 *EUGENE ARAM. (Lyceum, 19 April 1873.) LC.

2345 *OLIVIA. (Court, 30 March 1878.) LC.

2346 *VANDERDICKEN. With Percy Fitzgerald. (Lyceum, 8 June 1878.) LC.

2347 *IOLANTHE. (Lyceum, 20 May 1880.) LC.

2348 *WILLIAM AND SUSAN. (St. James's, 9 October 1880.) LC.

2349 *FAUST: IN A PROLOGUE AND FIVE ACTS: ADAPTED AND AR-RANGED FOR THE LYCEUM THEATRE: FIRST PART OF GOETHE'S TRAGEDY. (Lyceum, 19 December 1885.) [London: c. 1886?]. 58 p.

　　Printed prompt copy.

2350 *A CHAPTER FROM DON QUIXOTE. (Lyceum, 4 May 1895.) LC.

IV Biography

2351 Wills, Freeman. W.G. WILLS: DRAMATIST AND PAINTER. London: Longmans, 1898. 284 p.

　　A discursive and largely anecdotal biography, with a little critical investigation of Wills's work. A chronological table of acted plays is also given.

V Critical Studies

2352 Stottlar, James F. "A Victorian Stage Adapter at Work: W.G. Wills 'Rehabilitates' the Classics." VS, 16, no. 4 (1973), 401-32.

　　A detailed and thorough examination of Wills's historical dramas which indicates some of the reasons for the return of fashionable audiences to the theatre in the '70's and '80's and the part Wills played in bringing about that phenomenon.

WORDSWORTH, WILLIAM (1770-1850)

I Collected Works

2353 De Selincourt, E., and Helen Darbishire, eds. THE POETICAL WORKS OF WILLIAM WORDSWORTH. 5 vols. Oxford: Clarendon Press, 1940-49.

　　The standard edition. Wordsworth's only play, THE BORDERERS, first published in 1842, but never acted, is in volume one. De Selincourt reprints Wordsworth's origi-nal preface and provides valuable textual and critical notes.

III Bibliographies

2354 Wise, Thomas J. A BIBLIOGRAPHY OF THE WRITINGS IN PROSE AND
VERSE OF WILLIAM WORDSWORTH. London: Privately printed, 1916.
xv, 268 p.

> Wise gives a bibliographical description of POEMS, CHIEFLY
> OF EARLY AND LATE YEARS, 1842, in which THE BOR-
> DERERS was first published.

IV Biography

2355 Legouis, Emile. THE EARLY LIFE OF WILLIAM WORDSWORTH, 1770–
1798: A STUDY OF 'THE PRELUDE.' Trans. J.W. Matthews. Pref.
note. Leslie Stephen. New York: Scribner, 1897. xvi, 477 p.

> Legouis includes an early but still persuasive and influential
> discussion of THE BORDERERS.

2356 De Selincourt, Ernest, ed. THE EARLY LETTERS OF WILLIAM AND
DOROTHY WORDSWORTH (1787-1805). Oxford: Clarendon Press, 1935.
xviii, 578 p.

> Includes some interesting letters on THE BORDERERS; a revised
> edition, edited by Chester L. Shaver, was published in 1967
> (Oxford: Clarendon Press).

2357 Meyer, George Wilbur. WORDSWORTH'S FORMATIVE YEARS. London
and Ann Arbor: Oxford University Press and University of Michigan
Press, 1943. vii, 265 p.

> There is a long chapter on THE BORDERERS which begins by
> describing the play as "all but unintelligible."

2358 Moorman, Mary. WILLIAM WORDSWORTH: A BIOGRAPHY. 2 vols.
Oxford: Clarendon Press, 1957-65. xvi, 632; xvi, 632 p.

> There is discussion of THE BORDERERS in volume one of this
> definitive biography.

2359 Gordon, William A. "Autobiography and Identity: Wordsworth's THE
BORDERERS." TSE, 20 (1972), 71-86.

V Critical Studies

2360 Allen, B. Sprague. "Analogues of Wordsworth's THE BORDERERS."
PMLA, 38 (1923), 267-77.

> An interesting review of various anti-Godwinian novels, "the
> aim of which is identical with that of THE BORDERERS."

2361 Campbell, Oscar James, and Paul Mueschke. "THE BORDERERS as a Document in the History of Wordsworth's Aesthetic Development." MP, 23 (1925-26), 465-82.

Only incidentally concerned with THE BORDERERS as a play.

2362 MacGillivray, J.R. "Wordsworth's THE BORDERERS." TLS, 25 December 1930, p. 1101.

A letter arguing that Marmaduke (originally called Mortimer) in the play represents Wordsworth himself.

2363 Fausset, Hugh I'A. "Wordsworth's BORDERERS." ADELPHI, n.s. 2 (July 1931), 337-48.

A general discussion of the play; not an important article.

2364 MacGillivray, J.R. "The Date of Composition of THE BORDERERS." MLN, 49 (1934), 104-11.

MacGillivray corrects the dating from 1795-96 to 1796-97, a conclusion which has been generally accepted.

2365 Smith, John Harrington. "Genesis of THE BORDERERS." PMLA, 49 (1934), 922-30.

A discussion of the relationship between some travel literature written by William Gilpin and the Gothicism of Wordsworth's play.

2366 Watson, H.F. "THE BORDERERS and THE ANCIENT MARINER." TLS, 28 December 1935, p. 899.

Parallels between the two works.

2367 Beatty, Arthur. "THE BORDERERS and THE ANCIENT MARINER." TLS, 29 February 1936. p. 184.

Supplements item 2366.

2368 Watson, H.F. "Historic Detail in THE BORDERERS." MLN, 52 (1937), 577-79.

Watson shows that Wordsworth used "actual historical characters and incidents" in the play.

2369 Hayden, Donald. "Toward an Understanding of Wordsworth's THE BORDERERS." MLN, 66 (1951), 1-6.

THE BORDERERS is neither pro-Godwinian nor anti-Godwinian in its political ideas, but is a "transitional play" which represents the "working out of Wordsworth's problems rather than a statement of his solution."

2370 Smith, Charles J. "The Effect of Shakespeare's Influence on Wordsworth's THE BORDERERS." SP, 50 (1953), 625-39.

> Smith argues that the "real weakness" of THE BORDERERS lies in its imitativeness of Shakespearean tragedy, in characters, scenes, and dialogue.

2371 Knieger, Bernard. "Wordsworth and Coleridge as Playwrights." CLAJ, 6 (1962), 57-63.

2372 Hartmann, Geoffrey H. "Wordsworth, THE BORDERERS, and 'Intellectual Murder.'" JEGP, 62 (1963), 761-68.

> A discussion of Oswald as "the first explicit proponent in literature of intellectual murder; that is to say, of a murder planned by the intellect for an intellectual result."

2373 Sharrock, Roger. "THE BORDERERS: Wordsworth on the Moral Frontier." DUJ, 56 (1964), 170-83.

2374 Thorslev, Peter L. "Wordsworth's BORDERERS and the Romantic Villain-Hero." SIR, 5 (1966), 84-103.

> Principally a discussion of Oswald--"a character far more profound and more interesting than the villains in the Gothic dramas of [Wordsworth's] contemporaries."

2375 Pollin, Burton R. "Permutations of Names in THE BORDERERS, or Hints of Godwin, Charles Lloyd, and a Real Renegade." WCircle, 4, no. 1 (1973), 31-35.

> A discussion of some of the sources of THE BORDERERS.

VI Journals and Newsletters

2376 THE WORDSWORTH CIRCLE. Philadelphia: Temple University, 1970-- .

> A quarterly, publishing articles and notes on Wordsworth, Coleridge, Hazlitt, de Quincey, Lamb, and Southey.

Chapter 4

BIBLIOGRAPHIES AND REFERENCE WORKS

We have included here important bibliographies and reference works which contain material on nineteenth-century English drama and theatre even though their overall scope might be much broader. We also list, of course, those works which relate directly to nineteenth-century theatre studies.

2377 Baker, David Erskine; Isaac Reed; and Stephen Jones. BIOGRAPHIA DRAMATICA; OR, A COMPANION TO THE PLAYHOUSE. 4 vols. in 3. London: Longman, 1812; rpt. Graz, Austria: Akademische Druck-u. Verlagsanstalt, 1967.

An early handbook useful for the first decade of the century.

2378 [Genest, John]. SOME ACCOUNT OF THE ENGLISH STAGE FROM THE RESTORATION IN 1660 TO 1830. 10 vols. Bath, Eng.: Thomas Rodd, 1832.

Coverage of the nineteenth century begins with volume seven. The account, in note form, deals with each theatre individually and chronologically and attempts to give at least some information on the day-to-day details of productions (cast changes, reception, etc.). Still the most valuable record available of early nineteenth-century productions.

2379 Pascoe, Charles E. OUR ACTORS AND ACTRESSES: THE DRAMATIC LIST: A RECORD OF THE PERFORMANCES OF LIVING ACTORS AND ACTRESSES OF THE BRITISH STAGE. 2nd ed. London: D. Bogue, 1880; rpt. New York: Blom, 1969. iv, 432 p.

Pascoe's biographical dictionary, first published in 1879, limits itself to the more prominent actors and actresses. However, most entries are very extensive and frequently include contemporary newspaper accounts of particular performances.

2380 Lowe, Robert W. A BIBLIOGRAPHICAL ACCOUNT OF ENGLISH THEATRICAL LITERATURE FROM THE EARLIEST TIMES TO THE PRESENT. 1888; rpt. Detroit: Gale Research Co., 1966. xi, 384 p.

Arranged generally by subject, this is a copiously annotated
bibliography of theatrical literature. It lacks an index. See
also item 2458 which incorporates and largely supersedes this
work.

2381 French, Samuel. DESCRIPTIVE CATALOGUE OF PLAYS AND DRAMATIC
WORKS: WITH A COMPLETE LIST OF AMATEUR PLAYS AND ARTICLES
. . . 1891-92. London: French, [1892]. 48 p.

2382 Reid, Erskine, and Herbert Compton. THE DRAMATIC PEERAGE, 1891:
PERSONAL NOTES AND PROFESSIONAL SKETCHES OF THE ACTORS
AND ACTRESSES OF THE LONDON STAGE. London: General Pub-
lishing Co., and Dodd, Eyton and Co., [1892]. 266 p.

Short biographical sketches of notable theatrical figures active
at the close of the century.

2383 "The ERA Interviews." ERA, 28 November 1896, p. 8.

A list of interviews with leading theatrical figures. Although
informal, the interviews provide useful information about the
life and work of each subject.

2384 "The ERA Biographies." ERA, 2 January 1897, p. 8.

A list of brief biographies (of actors, actresses, and other
theatrical figures) which appeared in earlier issues of the
ERA.

2385 Clapp, John Bouve, and Edwin Francis Edgett. PLAYS OF THE PRESENT.
New York: Dunlap Society, 1902; rpt. New York: Blom, 1969. ix,
331 p. [with 34 unnumbered pages of plates].

An alphabetical listing of significant plays performed on the
London and New York stages in the latter half of the century.
A cast list and brief history of each play is given, as well
as such incidental information as adaptations, plot summaries,
and the like.

2386 Adams, W. Davenport. A DICTIONARY OF THE DRAMA: A GUIDE
TO THE PLAYS, PLAYWRIGHTS, PLAYERS, AND PLAYHOUSES OF THE
UNITED KINGDOM AND AMERICA, FROM THE EARLIEST TIMES TO
THE PRESENT. Vol. 1, A-G. London: Chatto and Windus, 1904,
rpt. New York: Franklin, n.d. viii, 627 p.

Unfortunately, only volume one was ever published. It
contains much valuable and useful information and repays
careful search.

2387 Parker, John. THE GREEN ROOM BOOK. 4 eds. London: T. Sealey Clark, 1906-9. Continued as WHO'S WHO IN THE THEATRE.

See item 2389.

2388 Eldredge, H.J., comp. "THE STAGE" CYCLOPEDIA: A BIBLIOGRAPHY OF PLAYS. London: "The Stage," 1909; rpt. New York: Franklin, 1970. 503 p.

A listing of about 30,000 plays (not the 50,000 claimed), arranged alphabetically, together with place and date of production. Revivals included. Useful (the only attempt of its kind), but inaccuracies are bound to be present in a work of this kind.

2389 Parker, John, ed. WHO'S WHO IN THE THEATRE: A BIOGRAPHICAL RECORD OF THE CONTEMPORARY STAGE. 15 eds. London: Pitman, 1912-72.

An invaluable tool for biographical records, plays, long runs, playbills, and so forth. The accuracy of biographical informa- tion depends on the returns from the actors concerned. Con- tinues item 2387.

2389a SUBJECT INDEX TO PERIODICALS. London: Library Association, 1915- 61.

Superseded by BRITISH HUMANITIES INDEX. See item 2431.

2390 DRAMATIC COMPOSITIONS COPYRIGHTED IN THE UNITED STATES 1870 TO 1916. 2 vols. Washington, D.C.: Government Printing Office, 1918.

Lists 56,089 items, registering various information necessary for securing American copyright. Arranged by title and author, this work includes many English playwrights.

2391 ANNUAL BIBLIOGRAPHY OF ENGLISH LANGUAGES AND LITERATURE. London: Modern Humanities Research Association, 1921-- .

An annual, extensive bibliography, arranged by topic, period, and author.

2392 MODERN LANGUAGES ASSOCIATION INTERNATIONAL BIBLIOGRAPHY OF BOOKS AND ARTICLES ON THE MODERN LANGUAGES AND LITERATURES. New York: MLA, 1921-- . Annual

The most extensive annual bibliography. Arranged by country and period. Before 1956 lists works by American scholars only.

2393 Firkins, Ina Ten Eyck, ed. INDEX TO PLAYS, 1800-1926. New York: H.W. Wilson, 1927. 307 p.

A guide to available editions of plays by nineteenth- and twentieth-century authors. Arranged by author, title, and subject. Supplement issued in 1935.

2394 PLAYS. A GUIDE TO THE WORKS IN THE LIBRARY OF THE NATIONAL OPERATIC AND DRAMATIC ASSOCIATION. London: Noda, 1929. 167 p.

A list of about 1,500 plays and musical works, many of them from the nineteenth century, forming a guide for prospective producers. A brief plot outline is given with many of the plays.

2395 French, Samuel. FRENCH'S CATALOGUE, 1933. London: French, [1933]. 220 p.

A catalog of plays from the famous theatrical publisher.

2396 Ehrsam, Theodore G.; Robert H. Deily; and Robert M. Smith. BIBLI-OGRAPHIES OF TWELVE VICTORIAN AUTHORS. New York: H.W. Wilson, 1936. 362 p.

Includes sections on Stevenson, Swinburne, and Tennyson.

2397 Gilder, Rosamond, and George Freedley. THEATRE COLLECTIONS IN LIBRARIES AND MUSEUMS: AN INTERNATIONAL HANDBOOK. New York: Theatre Arts, 1936. 182 p.

Full descriptions and information given on major world collections.

2398 Rhodes, R. Crompton. "The Early Nineteenth-Century Drama." LI-BRARY, 4th ser., 16 (1936), 91-112; 210-31.

A full discussion, based largely on Rhodes's own collection, of the various anthologies of plays issued by several publishers in the nineteenth century. An important study.

2399 "The Romantic Movement: A Selective and Critical Bibliography." ELH (annually, 1937-49); PQ (annually, 1950-64); ELN (annually, 1965--).

Extensive and annotated.

2400 Sper, Felix. THE PERIODICAL PRESS OF LONDON, THEATRICAL AND LITERARY, EXCLUDING THE DAILY NEWSPAPER, 1800-1830: A HAND-LIST. Boston: F.W. Faxon, 1937. 58 p.

2401 Macmillan, Dougald. CATALOGUE OF THE LARPENT PLAYS IN THE HUNTINGTON LIBRARY. San Marino, Calif: Huntington Library, 1939. xv, 442 p.

> Arranged chronologically, the catalog lists some 2,500 manuscripts of plays submitted to the Lord Chamberlain's Office for licensing from 1737-1823. Full details are given for each entry. See item 2436 for LC plays, 1824-51.

2402 Peck, Louis Francis. "M.G. Lewis and the Larpent CATALOGUE." HLQ, 5 (1941-42), 382-84.

> Annotations on six hitherto unattributed manuscripts listed in item 2401.

2403 Ewing, Majl. "The Authorship of Some Nineteenth-Century Plays." MLN, 57 (1942), 466-68.

> Corrections to Nicoll, item 298.

2404 Biella, Arnold. "Additions and Corrections to the Bibliography of 19th Century Drama." PQ, 21, no. 3 (1943), 299-322.

> Additions and corrections to Nicoll's handlist, item 298.

2405 Ewing, Majl. "Notes on Nicoll's Hand-list for 1800-1850." MLN, 58 (1943), 460-64.

> Additions and corrections to Nicoll, item 298.

2406 Loewenberg, Alfred. ANNALS OF OPERA 1597-1940: COMPILED FROM THE ORIGINAL SOURCES: WITH AN INTRODUCTION BY EDWARD J. DENT. 1943. 2nd rev. ed. New York: Rowman and Littlefield, 1970. xxv, 1,756 cols.

> Arranged chronologically, this work gives extensive information on each opera (composer, librettist, number of acts, details of first night) together with the history of subsequent performances.

2407 Pearce, Ethel. "THE LARPENT PLAYS: Additions and Corrections." HLQ, 6 (1943), 491-94.

> See item 2401.

2408 Tobin, James Edward. "More English Plays: 1800-1850." PQ, 23 (1944), 320-32.

> Additions and corrections to Nicoll, item 298.

2409 Troubridge, St. Vincent. "Notes on XIX CENTURY DRAMA 1800-1850." N&Q, 187 (1944), 189.

    Additions to Nicoll, item 298.

2410 Templeman, William D., ed. BIBLIOGRAPHIES OF STUDIES IN VICTORIAN LITERATURE FOR THE THIRTEEN YEARS 1932-1944. Urbana: University of Illinois Press, 1945. ix, 450 p.

    A cumulation of the annotated annual bibliography which appeared in MP. Continued in items 2424-25, 2448.

2411 Tobin, James E. "Early Nineteenth Century Drama." N&Q, 188 (1945), 156-58; 184-85.

    Additions and corrections to Nicoll, item 298.

2412 Troubridge, St. Vincent. "Early XIXth Century Plays." TN, 1 (1945-47), 62-67.

    Supplements Nicoll, item 298.

2413 Wade, Allan. "Early XIXth Century Plays." TN, 1 (1945-47), 27-32; 42-43.

    Supplements Nicoll, item 298.

2414 Stone, M.W. "Unrecorded Plays Published by William West." TN (1946), 33-34.

    West published juvenile drama between 1811-32, most of which was listed in an essay in VARIA, 1894. Stone adds to that list.

2415 Byrne, M. St. Clare. CATALOGUE OF AN EXHIBITION PRESENTED BY THE ARTS COUNCIL OF GREAT BRITAIN AND THE SOCIETY FOR CULTURAL RELATIONS WITH THE U.S.S.R. 1947. A PICTORIAL HISTORY OF SHAKESPEAREAN PRODUCTION IN ENGLAND 1576-1946. 1947; rpt. New York: Books for Libraries, 1970. 36 p.

2416 Troubridge, St. Vincent, and Allan Wade. "Early XIXth Century Plays." TN, 3 (1948-49), 13-17; 31-33, 56-59; 76-80.

    Supplements Nicoll, item 298. See also TN, 4 (1949-50), 24; 40-43; 68-71; 81-85 for further supplements.

2417 INDEX TO THESES ACCEPTED FOR HIGHER DEGREES IN THE UNIVERSITIES OF GREAT BRITAIN AND IRELAND. London: Aslib, 1950-- . Annual.

The entries give author, title, and university arranged according to subject. There are no annotations.

2418 Loewenberg, Alfred, comp. THE THEATRE OF THE BRITISH ISLES EX-
CLUDING LONDON: A BIBLIOGRAPHY. London: Society for Theatre
Research, 1950. ix, 75 p.

An indispensable guide to materials on provincial theatres.
Arranged alphabetically by place.

2419 THE PLAYER'S LIBRARY; THE CATALOGUE OF THE LIBRARY OF THE
BRITISH DRAMA LEAGUE. London: Faber, 1950. xvi, 1,115 p.

Supplements issued in 1951, 1954, 1956. Arranged by author,
with some bibliographical detail, together with synopses of
cast and scenery. Essentially designed for amateur drama
groups as an aid in casting, but can have scholarly uses too.

2420 Hartnoll, Phyllis, ed. THE OXFORD COMPANION TO THE THEATRE.
3 eds. London: Oxford University Press, 1951-67.

Brief, useful articles on every aspect of the theatre; the third
edition corrects most of the errors of earlier editions.

2421 Troubridge, St. Vincent. "Some Pseudonyms of Dramatic Authors, 1800-
1900." TN, 6 (1951-52), 63-64.

2422 Baker, Blanch M. THEATRE AND ALLIED ARTS: A GUIDE TO BOOKS
DEALING WITH THE HISTORY, CRITICISM, AND TECHNIQUE OF THE
DRAMA AND THEATRE AND RELATED ARTS AND CRAFTS. New York:
Wilson, 1952; rpt. New York: Blom, 1967. xiv, 536 p.

A moderately comprehensive bibliography of all periods.
Annotated.

2423 ENCICLOPEDIA DELLO SPETTACOLO. 9 vols. and supplements. Rome:
Casa Editrice le Maschere, 1954-66.

Extensive in scope and lavishly illustrated.

2424 Wright, Austin, ed. BIBLIOGRAPHIES OF STUDIES IN VICTORIAN
LITERATURE FOR THE TEN YEARS 1945-1954. Urbana: University of
Illinois Press, 1956. [v], 310 p.

A cumulation of the annotated annual bibliographies which
first appeared in MP. Continues item 2410. See also items
2425, 2448.

2425 "Victorian Bibliography." VS, 1957-- . Annual.

> Provides an extensive annual bibliography, arranged by sub-
> ject and author. Annotated. Continues item 2424. See
> also items 2410, 2448.

2426 ABSTRACTS OF ENGLISH STUDIES. Boulder, Colo., 1958-- . Annual
cumulations.

> Arranged by country, period, and authors. Well annotated.

2427 Stott, Raymond Toole, CIRCUS AND ALLIED ARTS: A WORLD BIBLI-
OGRAPHY 1500-1970. 4 vols. Derby, Eng.: Harpur and Sons, 1958-71.

> An indispensable reference work for all research in circus
> history.

2428 Youngs, Olive E.B. "Important Articles on the Theatre in the TIMES
LITERARY SUPPLEMENT, 1902-1956." ThR, 1, no. 1 (1958), 42-48;
1, no. 2 (1958), 34-44.

2429 Nicoll, Allardyce. A HISTORY OF ENGLISH DRAMA 1660-1900:
VOLUME VI: A SHORT-TITLE ALPHABETICAL CATALOGUE OF PLAYS
PRODUCED OR PRINTED IN ENGLAND FROM 1660 TO 1900. Cam-
bridge: At the University Press, 1959. xii, 565 p.

> An important index to Nicoll's hand lists of plays (items 298,
> 321, and 431).

2430 Stratman, Carl J. "Additions to Allardyce Nicoll's Hand-list of Plays:
1800-1818." N&Q, 206 (1961), 214-17.

> Deals with tragedies. See Nicoll, item 298.

2431 BRITISH HUMANITIES INDEX. London: Library Association, 1962-- .
Annual.

> Superseded SUBJECT INDEX TO PERIODICALS (1915-61),
> item 2389a above. Arranged largely by subject, with ade-
> quate cross-references. Also covers some daily and weekly
> publications.

2432 Jackson, Allan S., and John C. Morrow. "Handlist of Aqua-Dramas
Produced at Sadler's Wells, 1804-1824." OSUTCB, no. 9 (1962), 38-
47.

2433 THE LIBRARY OF CONGRESS CATALOGS: THE NATIONAL UNION
CATALOG OF MANUSCRIPT COLLECTIONS 1959-- . Ann Arbor,
Mich.: J.W. Edwards, 1962; Hamden Conn.: Shoe String, 1964; Wash-

ington, D.C.: Library of Congress, 1965-- .

Several volumes published since 1962. They attempt to list
and locate all manuscripts in the United States, among which
are numerous collections of nineteenth-century English dramatists. Useful for advanced research.

2434 Stratman, Carl J. A BIBLIOGRAPHY OF BRITISH DRAMATIC PERIODI-
CALS 1720-1960. New York: New York Public Library, 1962. 58 p.

A chronologically arranged listing of 674 periodicals. Locations of holdings are also provided, as is an alphabetical
index. See also item 2470.

2435 _____. "English Tragedy: 1819-1823." PQ, 41 (1962), 465-74.

Supplements Nicoll, item 298.

2436 BRITISH MUSEUM: CATALOGUE OF ADDITIONS TO THE MANU-
SCRIPTS: PLAYS SUBMITTED TO THE LORD CHAMBERLAIN 1824-1851:
ADDITIONAL MANUSCRIPTS 42865-43038. London: British Museum,
1964. viii, 359 p.

The catalog describes the contents of each volume of manuscripts and provides cross-references by author and title indexes. A primary source for plays of the period and ex-
tremely useful. See item 2401 for LC plays, 1737-1823. LC
plays for the period after 1851 are in the British Library, but
are uncataloged.

2437 Shattuck, Charles H. THE SHAKESPEARE PROMPTBOOKS: A DESCRIP-
TIVE CATALOGUE. Urbana and London: University of Illinois Press,
1964. ix, 553 p.

An important bibliographical catalog which describes promptbooks used for Shakespearean productions from 1620 to 1961.
Arranged chronologically and alphabetically.

2438 Faxon, Frederick Winthrop; Mary E. Bates; and Anne C. Sutherland, eds.
CUMULATED DRAMATIC INDEX 1909-1949: A CUMULATION OF THE
F.W. FAXON COMPANY'S DRAMATIC INDEX. 2 vols. Boston: G.K.
Hall, 1965.

An extensive index to material in periodicals for the period
1909-49, arranged in one continuous index. Covers dramatists, plays, and actors.

2438a PALMER'S INDEX TO THE TIMES NEWSPAPER 1790-1905. Vaduz, Switzerland: Kraus Reprint, 1965.

> This multivolumed index is an excellent source of information on all theatrical matters of the nineteenth century.

2439 Houghton, Walter E., ed. THE WELLESLEY INDEX TO VICTORIAN PERIODICALS, 1824-1900: VOLUME I: TABLES OF CONTENTS AND IDENTIFICATION OF CONTRIBUTORS WITH BIBLIOGRAPHIES OF THEIR ARTICLES AND STORIES. Toronto: Toronto University Press; London: Routledge, 1966. 1,194 p.

> See also item 2467 (Volume II).

2440 Sharp, Harold S., and Marjorie Z. Sharp. INDEX TO CHARACTERS IN THE PERFORMING ARTS: AN ALPHABETICAL LISTING OF 30,000 CHARACTERS. 5 vols. New York: Scarecrow, 1966-69.

> An invaluable guide in tracking down characters.

2441 Stratman, Carl J. BIBLIOGRAPHY OF ENGLISH PRINTED TRAGEDY 1565-1900. Carbondale: Southern Illinois University Press, 1966. xx, 843 p.

> "The entries are restricted to English printed tragedies written in England, Scotland, or Ireland, from the beginnings of formal tragedy in England, to the end of the nineteenth century, together with the various adaptations of each work." Shakespeare is included. The 6,852 main entries, arranged by author, give full bibliographical details and the library location of each work. Useful appendices on anthologies and the location of manuscripts.

2442 _____. DRAMATIC PLAY LISTS 1591-1963. New York: New York Public Library, 1966. 44 p.

> Fully annotated guide to bibliographies of "actual play titles." Arranged chronologically.

2443 Cheshire, David. THEATRE: HISTORY, CRITICISM AND REFERENCE. London: Clive Bingley, 1967. 131 p.

> A general descriptive bibliography which deals with aspects of the theatre only; books on drama are omitted. A useful starting place, with well-written descriptions.

2444 Hunter, Frederick J., comp. A GUIDE TO THE THEATRE AND DRAMA COLLECTIONS AT THE UNIVERSITY OF TEXAS. Austin: Humanities Research Center, University of Texas at Austin, 1967. 85 p.

> A not very scholarly and nonindexed guide to one of the

larger theatrical collections, rich in nineteenth- and twentieth-century British and American drama.

2445 THE NEW YORK PUBLIC LIBRARY: THE RESEARCH LIBRARIES: CATA-LOG OF THE THEATRE AND DRAMA COLLECTIONS: PART 1: DRAMA COLLECTION: AUTHOR LISTING. 6 vols. Boston: G.K. Hall, 1967.

The New York Public Library is rich in printed and manuscript materials and all its catalogs are worth searching.

2446 THE NEW YORK PUBLIC LIBRARY: THE RESEARCH LIBRARIES: CATA-LOG OF THE THEATRE AND DRAMA COLLECTIONS: PART 1: DRAMA COLLECTION: LISTING BY CULTURAL ORIGIN. 6 vols. Boston: G.K. Hall, 1967.

2447 THE NEW YORK PUBLIC LIBRARY: THE RESEARCH LIBRARIES: DICTIO-NARY CATALOG OF THE MANUSCRIPT DIVISION. 2 vols. Boston: G.K. Hall, 1967.

2448 Slack, Robert C., ed. BIBLIOGRAPHIES IN VICTORIAN LITERATURE FOR THE TEN YEARS 1955-1964. Urbana, Chicago, and London: University of Illinois Press, 1967. xvii, 461 p.

A cumulation of the annotated annual bibliographies which first appeared in MP and VS. See also items 2410, 2424-25.

2449 Taylor, John Russell, THE PENGUIN DICTIONARY OF THE THEATRE. London: Methuen, 1967. 295 p.

Not a serious rival of THE OXFORD COMPANION (item 2420).

2450 Levitt, Paul M. "The Well-Made Problem Play: A Selective Bibliography." ELT, 11 (1968), 190-94.

A brief introduction justifies the study of problem plays. The bibliography (sixty items) is arranged alphabetically by author.

2451 Rickards, Sandra L. "The Authorship of FOUR STAGES OF LIFE." N&Q, 15 (1968), 422-23.

Corrects and supplements information in Nicoll on this hitherto anonymous play of 1862.

2452 Stump, Walter Ray. "Indiana University Acquires New Collection of Nineteenth Century Plays." TN, 22 (1968), 120-21.

Brief account of the acquisition of over 6,000 plays.

2453 Gassner, John, and Edward Quinn, eds. THE READER'S ENCYCLOPEDIA OF WORLD DRAMA. New York: Crowell, 1969. xi, 1,030 p.

> A general encyclopedia whose scope "is the drama as litera-
> ture, not as theater. It contains no entries on actors, the-
> atrical troupes, costumes, scenery, or playhouses."

2454 Litto, Frederic M. AMERICAN DISSERTATIONS ON THE DRAMA AND THE THEATRE: A BIBLIOGRAPHY. Kent, Ohio: Kent State University Press, 1969. ix, 519 p.

> Arranged by complete description, author, "key-word-in-
> context," and subject. Five-year cumulations are planned.

2455 THE NEW YORK PUBLIC LIBRARY: ASTOR, LENNOX AND TILDEN FOUNDATIONS: THE RESEARCH LIBRARIES: DICTIONARY CATALOG OF THE HENRY W. AND ALBERT A. BERG COLLECTION OF ENGLISH AND AMERICAN LITERATURE. 5 vols. Boston: G.K. Hall, 1969.

2456 Watson, George, ed. THE NEW CAMBRIDGE BIBLIOGRAPHY OF ENGLISH LITERATURE: VOL. 3: 1800-1900. Cambridge: At the University Press, 1969. xxiv, 1,956 cols.

> Drama is dealt with in cols. 1111-96. Generally a good
> starting point, the bibliography is unannotated and occa-
> sionally wildly inaccurate.

2457 Shattuck, Charles H. "The Shakespeare Promptbooks: First Supplement." TN, 24 (1969-70), 5-17.

> Over fifty additions to Shattuck's 1965 catalog (item 2438),
> mostly from the nineteenth century.

2458 Arnott, James Fullarton, and John William Robinson. ENGLISH THE-ATRICAL LITERATURE 1559-1900: A BIBLIOGRAPHY, INCORPORATING ROBERT W. LOWE'S A BIBLIOGRAPHICAL ACCOUNT OF ENGLISH THEATRICAL LITERATURE PUBLISHED IN 1888. London: Society for Theatre Research, 1970. xxii, 486 p.

> A thorough revision of Lowe's work (see item 2380) with
> improved arrangement (by general topics), bibliographical
> description, and location. Two useful indexes (author and
> title).

2459 CATALOG OF PRINTED BOOKS OF THE FOLGER SHAKESPEARE LI-BRARY, WASHINGTON, D.C. 28 vols. Boston: G.K. Hall, 1970.

> Despite its title the Folger has extensive holdings in
> nineteenth-century drama, both in printed books and manu-
> scripts. Well worth investigation for advanced research.

2460 CATALOG OF MANUSCRIPTS OF THE FOLGER SHAKESPEARE LIBRARY, WASHINGTON, D.C. 3 vols. Boston: G.K. Hall, 1971.

2461 Ewen, David. THE NEW ENCYCLOPEDIA OF THE OPERA. New York: Hill and Wang, 1971; London: Vision Press, 1973. viii, 759 p.

   A useful companion, with about 5,000 entries.

2462 Hunter, Frederick J. DRAMA BIBLIOGRAPHY: A SHORT-TITLE GUIDE TO EXTENDED READING IN DRAMATIC ART FOR THE ENGLISH-SPEAKING AUDIENCE AND STUDENTS IN THEATRE. Boston: G.K. Hall, 1971. x, 239 p.

   An unannotated and rather elementary bibliography; arranged by broad topic area.

2463 Breed, Paul F., and Florence M. Sniderman. DRAMATIC CRITICISM INDEX: A BIBLIOGRAPHY OF COMMENTARIES ON PLAYWRIGHTS FROM IBSEN TO THE AVANTGARDE. Detroit: Gale Research Co., 1972. vii, 1,022 p.

   Mainly on the twentieth century, but some entries on H.A. Jones, Pinero, Wilde, and Shaw.

2464 "Handlist of Books in Guildhall Library on the London Theatre." GUILDHALL MISCELLANY, 4 (April 1972), 121-35.

2465 Hartnoll, Phyllis, ed. THE CONCISE OXFORD COMPANION TO THE THEATRE. London: Oxford University Press, 1972. ix, 640 p.

   Not simply an abridgement of the complete work, since some entries have been enlarged or rewritten. A useful, if not absolutely reliable work.

2466 Holden, David Franklin. "Analytical Index and Annotated Bibliography to MODERN DRAMA: Volumes I-XIII." Ph.D. Dissertation, University of Kansas, 1972. 532 p. (DA#72-32891)

   Divided into three indexes: general, contributors, book reviews.

2467 Houghton, Walter E., ed. THE WELLESLEY INDEX TO VICTORIAN PERIODICALS, 1824-1900: VOL. II. Toronto: Toronto University Press; London: Routledge, 1972. xxii, 1,221 p.

   See also item 2439 (volume I). A third volume of this work is planned.

2468 McGRAW-HILL ENCYCLOPEDIA OF WORLD DRAMA: AN INTERNA-
TIONAL REFERENCE WORK IN FOUR VOLUMES. 4 vols. New York:
McGraw-Hill, 1972.

> Deals with dramatists only, each having sections dealing
> with biography, critical evaluation, synopses of major
> works, a play listing, and a bibliography. Lesser drama-
> tists are treated more concisely.

2469 "The Macmillan Archive." BRITISH MUSEUM QUARTERLY, 36, nos. 3
and 4 (1972), 74-80.

> Describes briefly the correspondence and papers of the
> Macmillan publishing house. Forty volumes concern poets
> and dramatists.

2470 Stratman, C.J. BRITAIN'S THEATRICAL PERIODICALS, 1720-1967: A
BIBLIOGRAPHY. New York: New York Public Library, 1972. xxiv,
160 p.

> See also item 2434.

2471 Tonkin, Jennifer. "Theatre Material in the John Johnson Collection of
Printed Ephemera, Bodleian Library, Oxford." TN, 26, no. 2 (1972),
72-75.

> A descriptive account of the collection, which is largely
> nineteenth-century playbills and programs.

2472 COMPREHENSIVE DISSERTATION INDEX 1861-1972. 37 vols. Ann
Arbor, Mich.: Xerox University Microfilms, 1973.

> A cumulated index to DISSERTATION ABSTRACTS. Volumes
> 29-30 deal with literature, 31 with the theatre.

2473 Conolly, L.W., and J.P. Wearing. "Nineteenth Century Theatre Research: A Bibliography." NCTR, 1973-- . Annual.

> Comprehensive listing of nineteenth-century theatre and drama
> studies. The bibliography attempts to cover the entire English-
> speaking stage of the period.

2474 Highfill, Philip H.; Kalman A. Burnim; and Edward A. Langhans. A
BIOGRAPHICAL DICTIONARY OF ACTORS, ACTRESSES, MUSICIANS,
DANCERS, MANAGERS AND OTHER STAGE PERSONNEL IN LONDON,
1660-1800. 4 vols. to date. Carbondale and Edwardsville: Southern
Illinois University Press, 1973-- .

> An essential reference work for its own period, this dictionary
> also contains information on actors, and others, whose careers
> extended into the nineteenth century.

2475 McCallum, Heather.   THEATRE RESOURCES IN CANADIAN COLLEC-
TIONS.   Ottawa: National Library of Canada, 1973.   iii, 113 p.

Contains information on nineteenth-century English theatre
research collections in Canadian archives.

Chapter 5

ANTHOLOGIES OF PLAYS

For a fuller description of the complicated bibliographical problems of nineteenth-century play anthologies, readers should consult the important study by R.C. Rhodes, item 2398, above. We have attempted to include here all of the important anthologies and series, but the list is not exhaustive. The arrangement is chronological.

2476 THE REJECTED THEATRE; OR, A COLLECTION OF DRAMAS WHICH HAVE BEEN OFFERED FOR REPRESENTATION BUT DECLINED BY THE MANAGERS OF THE PLAYHOUSES. Ca. 15 nos. London: 1814.

> Title varies: THE ORIGINAL AND REJECTED THEATRE; THE NEW BRITISH THEATRE.

2477 Dibdin, Thomas., ed. THE LONDON THEATRE: A COLLECTION OF THE MOST CELEBRATED DRAMATIC PIECES: CORRECTLY GIVEN, FROM COPIES USED IN THE THEATRES. 26 vols. London: Whittingham and Arliss, 1815-18. Vols. 22-26 published by Sherwood, Neely and Jones.

2478 Oxberry, William, ed. THE NEW ENGLISH DRAMA, WITH PREFATORY REMARKS, BIOGRAPHICAL SKETCHES, AND NOTES . . . WITH . . . STAGE DIRECTIONS. 20 vols. London: 1818-25.

2479 DUNCOMBE'S NEW ACTING DRAMA. 12 nos. London: [John Duncombe], 1821-25.

> See Rhodes, pages 215-16.

2480 DOLBY'S BRITISH THEATRE. Ca. 59 nos. London: [Thomas Dolby, 1823-25].

> See Rhodes, pages 104-6.

2481 THE LONDON STAGE: A COLLECTION OF THE MOST REPUTED

TRAGEDIES, COMEDIES, OPERAS, MELO-DRAMAS, FARCES, AND INTERLUDES: ACCURATELY PRINTED FROM ACTING COPIES, AS PERFORMED AT THE THEATRES ROYAL, AND CAREFULLY COLLATED AND REVISED. 4 vols. London: Sherwood and Jones, [ca. 1824].

2482 CUMBERLAND'S BRITISH THEATRE, WITH REMARKS, BIOGRAPHICAL AND CRITICAL, BY D.--G. [GEORGE DANIEL]: PRINTED FROM THE ACTING COPIES, AS PERFORMED AT THE THEATRE ROYAL, LONDON. 48 vols. London: Cumberland, [1826-61].

See Rhodes, pages 106-11.

2483 CUMBERLAND'S MINOR THEATRE, WITH REMARKS BIOGRAPHICAL AND CRITICAL, BY D.--G. [GEORGE DANIEL]: PRINTED FROM THE ACTING COPIES, AS PERFORMED AT THE METROPOLITAN MINOR THEATRES. 16 vols. London: Cumberland, [1828-43].

Available in the Readex collection. See Rhodes, pages 111-12.

2484 DUNCOMBE'S EDITION; THE NEW BRITISH THEATRE. 67 vols.? London: Duncombe, [1828-52].

Rhodes, pages 212-15, lists the title as DUNCOMBE'S BRITISH THEATRE.

2485 RICHARDSON'S NEW MINOR DRAMA: WITH REMARKS BIOGRAPHICAL AND CRITICAL, BY W.T. MONCRIEFF. 4 vols. London: Richardson, 1828-31.

2486 DUNCOMBE'S MINOR THEATRE. 24 nos. London: [John Duncombe], 1834.

See Rhodes, pages 216-18. Full title appears to be DUNCOMBE'S MINOR BRITISH DRAMA: COPYRIGHT PLAYS, AS ACTED IN ALL THE LONDON THEATRES.

2487 THE LONDON ACTING DRAMA. Ca. 31 nos. London: [Printed by W. Strange], 1837-38.

See Rhodes, pages 218-20.

2488 Webster, B.N., ed. THE ACTING NATIONAL DRAMA. 18 vols. London: Chapman and Hall, 1837-[59].

See Rhodes, pages 222-24.

2489 PATTIE'S PLAY OR WEEKLY ACTING DRAMA. Ca. 45 nos. London: [James Pattie], 1838-39.

See Rhodes, pages 227-28.

2490 PATTIE'S UNIVERSAL STAGE OR THEATRICAL PROMPT BOOK. 100
nos. London: [James Pattie], 1839-45.

>See Rhodes, pages 224-27. From approximately number 32
onward continued by William Barth and eventually absorbed
by Lacy.

2491 Hilsenberg, Ludwig, et al. THE MODERN ENGLISH COMIC THEATRE;
WITH NOTES IN GERMAN. 6 ser. Leipzig, Germany: 1843-?.

2492 Webster, R., ed. THE SERIES OF DRAMATIC ENTERTAINMENTS PER-
FORMED BY ROYAL COMMAND . . . AT WINDSOR CASTLE 1848-9
. . . PRINTED VERBATIM FROM THE AUTHORISED VERSION; WITH
FAC-SIMILES OF THE BILLS OF PERFORMANCE AND A CORRECTED
LIST OF THE ROYAL PERSONAGES AND THE NOBILITY AND GENTRY
PRESENT ON EACH OCCASION. London: Mitchell, 1849. 372 p.

2493 LACY'S ACTING EDITION OF PLAYS, DRAMAS, EXTRAVAGANZAS,
FARCES. 165 vols. London: Lacy, 1850-1917.

>Bought by French in 1872. See Rhodes, pages 230-31.

2494 THE BRITISH DRAMA: ILLUSTRATED. 12 vols. London: Dicks, 1864-
72.

2495 THE BRITISH DRAMA. 12 vols. London: Dicks, 1866-?.

>See Rhodes, pages 228-29.

2496 Scott, Clement. DRAWING-ROOM PLAYS AND PARLOUR PANTO-
MIMES. London: S. Rivers, 1870. 360, xii p.

>Contents: "An Induction" by E.L. Blanchard; J.P. Simpson,
TWO GENTLEMEN AT MIVART'S; Gilbert, A MEDICAL MAN;
Hood, HARLEQUIN LITTLE RED RIDING-HOOD; OR, THE
WICKED WOLF AND THE WIRTUOUS WOODCUTTER; Chelt-
nam, FIRESIDE DIPLOMACY; Reece, INGOMAR; OR, THE
NOBLE SAVAGE; Sketchley, MONEY MAKES THE MAN;
Thompson, THE HAPPY DESPATCH; Archer and Brough, AN
ELIGIBLE SITUATION; Scott, THE PET-LAMB, THE LAST
LILY; Blanchard, THE THREE TEMPTATIONS; Sterry, KATH-
ERINE AND PETRUCHIO; OR, THE SHAMING OF THE
TRUE; Daryl, HIS FIRST BRIEF; A.B., THE GIRLS OF THE
PERIOD.

2497 DEWITT'S ACTING EDITION OF PLAYS, DRAMAS, FARCES, EXTRAVA-
GANZAS . . . AS PERFORMED AT THE VARIOUS THEATRES. 21 vols.
New York: R.M. De Witt, [1873?-83].

2498 DICKS' STANDARD PLAYS. Nos. 1-1074. London: Dicks, [1874-1907].

    See Rhodes, pages 229-30.

2499 Brown, Calvin Smith, ed. THE LATER ENGLISH DRAMA. New York: A.S. Barnes, 1898. xx, 571 p.

    Includes Knowles, VIRGINIUS, and Bulwer-Lytton, THE LADY OF LYONS and RICHELIEU.

2500 FRENCH'S ACTING EDITION: (SENSATION SERIES). Nos. 1-10. London and New York: French, [1899-1903].

2501 Bates, Alfred, ed. THE DRAMA: ITS HISTORY, LITERATURE AND INFLUENCE ON CIVILIZATION: VOL. XVI: BRITISH DRAMA. London: Athenian Society, 1903; rpt. New York: AMS, 1970. viii, 344 p.

    Contents: Tobin, THE HONEYMOON; Bulwer-Lytton, MONEY; Robertson, SOCIETY; Gilbert, SWEETHEARTS. With a general history of drama in the nineteenth century.

2502 Moses, Montrose, J., ed. REPRESENTATIVE BRITISH DRAMAS: VICTORIAN AND MODERN. 1918. Rev. ed. Boston: Little, Brown, 1931. xvi, 996 p.

    Includes: Knowles, VIRGINIUS; Jerrold, BLACK-EY'D SUSAN; Bulwer-Lytton, RICHELIEU; Boucicault, LONDON ASSURANCE; Browning, A BLOT IN THE 'SCUTCHEON; Taylor, THE TICKET-OF-LEAVE MAN; Robertson, CASTE; Gilbert, H.M.S. PINAFORE; Jones, THE MASQUERADERS; Wilde, THE IMPORTANCE OF BEING EARNEST; Pinero, THE GAY LORD QUEX. In addition to substantial introductions to each play, there are cast lists and bibliographies.

2503 Rowell, George, ed. NINETEENTH CENTURY PLAYS. 1953. 2nd ed. Oxford: Oxford University Press, 1972. xiv, 567 p.

    "The texts here printed aim at reproducing the play as originally performed," although Rowell has collated various versions for BLACK-EY'D SUSAN and MONEY. Contents: Jerrold, BLACK-EY'D SUSAN; Bulwer-Lytton, MONEY; Taylor and Reade, MASKS AND FACES; Boucicault, THE COLLEEN BAWN; Hazlewood, LADY AUDLEY'S SECRET; Taylor, THE TICKET-OF-LEAVE MAN; Robertson, CASTE; Albery, TWO ROSES; Lewis, THE BELLS; Grundy, A PAIR OF SPECTACLES. A brief biography of each dramatist is given, together with the cast list of the first London production.

2504 Brings, Lawrence Martin, ed. GAY NINETIES MELODRAMAS: A COL-
LECTION OF OLD-FASHIONED MELODRAMAS OF THE GAY NINETIES
PERIOD. Minneapolis: T.S. Denison, 1963. 351 p.

> Modern plays written mostly as parodies of genuine nineteenth-
> century melodramas.

2505 Booth, Michael, ed. HISS THE VILLAIN: SIX ENGLISH AND AMERI-
CAN MELODRAMAS. London: Eyre and Spottiswoode, 1964. 390 p.

> Includes: Pocock, THE MILLER AND HIS MEN; Haines, MY
> POLL AND MY PARTNER JOE; Phillips, LOST IN LONDON;
> Lewis, THE BELLS. There is a long and valuable introduc-
> tion on melodrama together with biographical notes on the
> authors, and cast lists of first productions.

2506 Bailey, J.O. BRITISH PLAYS OF THE NINETEENTH CENTURY: AN
ANTHOLOGY TO ILLUSTRATE THE EVOLUTION OF THE DRAMA.
New York: Odyssey, 1966. ix, 535 p.

> There is a lengthy and useful introduction and texts of
> Maturin, BERTRAM; OR, THE CASTLE OF ST. ALDSBRAND;
> Bulwer-Lytton, RICHELIEU; Marston, THE PATRICIAN'S
> DAUGHTER; Browning, PIPPA PASSES; Boucicault, LONDON
> ASSURANCE; Taylor, OUR AMERICAN COUSIN; Holcroft, A
> TALE OF MYSTERY; Buckstone, LUKE THE LABOURER; Jerrold,
> THE RENT-DAY; Boucicault, AFTER DARK; Mrs. Henry Wood,
> EAST LYNNE; Jones, THE SILVER KING; Robertson, CASTE;
> Gilbert, ENGAGED; Shaw, WIDOWERS' HOUSES; Jones,
> THE MASQUERADERS; Pinero, THE NOTORIOUS MRS. EBB-
> SMITH.

2507 Ashley, Leonard R.N., ed. NINETEENTH CENTURY BRITISH DRAMA:
AN ANTHOLOGY OF REPRESENTATIVE PLAYS. Glenview, Ill.: Scott,
Foresman, 1967. 700 p.

> Contents: Shelley, THE CENCI; Jerrold, BLACK-EY'D
> SUSAN; Bulwer-Lytton, THE LADY OF LYONS; Boucicault,
> LONDON ASSURANCE; Robertson, CASTE; Lewis, THE BELLS;
> Palmer, EAST LYNNE; Gilbert, H.M.S. PINAFORE; Yeats,
> THE COUNTESS CATHLEEN; Pinero, THE SECOND MRS.
> TANQUERAY; Wilde, THE IMPORTANCE OF BEING EARNEST;
> Jones, MICHAEL AND HIS LOST ANGEL; Hankin, DRA-
> MATIC SEQUELS. There are brief introductions to each play,
> cast lists, biographical and bibliographical notes.

2508 Corrigan, Robert W., ed. LAUREL BRITISH DRAMA: THE NINETEENTH
CENTURY. New York: Dell, 1967. 464 p.

> Contents: Boucicault, LONDON ASSURANCE; Lewis, THE
> BELLS; Gilbert, PATIENCE; Pinero, THE SECOND MRS.

TANQUERAY; Shaw, ARMS AND THE MAN; Wilde, THE IMPORTANCE OF BEING EARNEST. One attractive feature of this inexpensive collection is that each play is prefaced by a useful critical essay, respectively by Boucicault, Gordon Craig, Gilbert, Shaw, Eric Bentley, and Mary McCarthy.

2509 Rowell, George, ed. LATE VICTORIAN PLAYS, 1890–1914. 1968. 2nd ed. London: Oxford University Press, 1972. xviii, 507 p.

Plays of interest are: Pinero, THE SECOND MRS. TANQUERAY; Jones, THE LIARS.

2510 Booth, Michael R., ed. ENGLISH PLAYS OF THE NINETEENTH CENTURY: I: DRAMAS 1800–1850. Oxford: Clarendon Press, 1969. xi, 315 p.

Booth's series of plays is the most scholarly available. He provides good introductions to the drama generally and to each play, and gives cast lists and provenances of texts. Contents: Pocock, THE MILLER AND HIS MEN; Knowles, VIRGINIUS; Jerrold, BLACK-EYED SUSAN; Walker, THE FACTORY LAD; Bulwer-Lytton, RICHELIEU.

2511 _____. ENGLISH PLAYS OF THE NINETEENTH CENTURY: II: DRAMAS 1850–1900. Oxford: Clarendon Press, 1969. vii, 427 p.

Contents: Boucicault, THE CORSICAN BROTHERS; Taylor, THE TICKET-OF-LEAVE MAN; Boucicault, THE SHAUGHRAUN; Pinero, THE SECOND MRS. TANQUERAY; Jones, MRS. DANE'S DEFENCE.

2512 _____. ENGLISH PLAYS OF THE NINETEENTH CENTURY: III: COMEDIES. Oxford, Clarendon Press, 1973. viii, 476 p.

Contents: Colman, JOHN BULL; Bulwer-Lytton, MONEY; Taylor and Dubourg, NEW MEN AND OLD ACRES; Gilbert, ENGAGED; Chambers, THE TYRANNY OF TEARS.

2513 _____. ENGLISH PLAYS OF THE NINETEENTH CENTURY: IV: FARCES. Oxford: Clarendon Press, 1973. vii, 384 p.

Contents: Kenney, RAISING THE WIND; Jerrold, MR. PAUL PRY; Mathews, PATTER VERSUS CLATTER; Murray, DIAMOND CUT DIAMOND; Coyne, HOW TO SETTLE ACCOUNTS WITH YOUR LAUNDRESS; Morton, BOX AND COX; Brough and Halliday, THE AREA BELLE; Gilbert, TOM COBB; Pinero, THE MAGISTRATE.

2514 Kauvar, Gerald B., and Gerald C. Sorenson, eds. NINETEENTH-CENTURY ENGLISH VERSE DRAMA. Rutherford, Madison, and Teaneck:

Fairleigh Dickinson University Press, 1973.   355 p.

> Contains individual introductions to and texts of Wordsworth, THE BORDERERS; Coleridge, REMORSE; Byron, MANFRED; Shelley, THE CENCI; Keats, OTHO THE GREAT; Arnold, EMPEDOCLES ON ETNA; Browning, KING VICTOR AND KING CHARLES; Tennyson, BECKET; Swinburne, ATALANTA IN CALYDON.

2515 Booth, Michael R., ed.   THE MAGISTRATE AND OTHER NINETEENTH-CENTURY PLAYS.   London: Oxford University Press, 1974.   xxi, 461 p.

> Based on items 2510-13, this anthology contains: Colman the Younger, JOHN BULL; Pocock, THE MILLER AND HIS MEN; Walker, THE FACTORY LAD; Coyne, HOW TO SETTLE ACCOUNTS WITH YOUR LAUNDRESS; Morton, BOX AND COX; Boucicault, THE CORSICAN BROTHERS; Gilbert, EN-GAGED; Pinero, THE MAGISTRATE; Jones, MRS. DANE'S DEFENCE.

2516 Kilgarriff, Michael, ed.   THE GOLDEN AGE OF MELODRAMA: TWELVE 19TH CENTURY MELODRAMAS.   London: Wolfe, 1974.   499 p.

> Contents: Holcroft, A TALE OF MYSTERY; Planché, THE VAMPIRE; Buckstone, LUKE THE LABOURER; Jerrold, FIFTEEN YEARS OF A DRUNKARD'S LIFE; Haines, THE OCEAN OF LIFE; MARIA MARTIN; Pitt, THE STRING OF PEARLS (SWEE-NEY TODD); Oxenford, EAST LYNNE; H.J. Byron and Boucicault, LOST AT SEA; Wills, EUGENE ARAM; Gilbert, DAN'L DRUCE; Potter, TRILBY. The editor provides bio-graphical introductions and contemporary press notices. He has abridged the plays by "filleting" some of the longer speeches.

2517 Nicoll, Allardyce, and George Freedley, eds.   ENGLISH AND AMERI-CAN DRAMA OF THE 19TH CENTURY.   New York: Readex Micro-print Corporation.   In progress.

> For once, a publisher's blurb is accurate: "This collection represents a more complete assembly of all the plays of the nineteenth century in the English language than the holdings of any single institution in the United States or Europe." The collection consists of several thousand plays in microprint, including acting editions, promptbooks and manuscript copies. It is an indispensable research collection.

2518 NINETEENTH CENTURY ENGLISH AND AMERICAN DRAMA.   Louis-ville: Falls City Microcard.   In progress.

This is a series of microprint reproductions similar in aim
to that published by the Readex Microprint Corporation (item
2517), though it seems an unnecessary duplication and is not
yet as comprehensive as the Readex collection.

Chapter 6

THE THEATRES

This chapter is divided into three sections: General Works, London Theatres, and Provincial Theatres. Since some theatres are discussed in works on actors or general theatre history listed in other chapters of this bibliography, it is important that readers check the names of theatres in the index for such references. For a more extensive listing of contemporary works on the theatres, readers should consult Arnott and Robinson's ENGLISH THEATRICAL LITERATURE 1559-1900, item 2458, above.

A. GENERAL WORKS

2519 Oulton, W.C. A HISTORY OF THE THEATRES OF LONDON, CONTAINING AN ANNUAL REGISTER OF NEW PIECES, REVIVALS, PANTOMIMES, &C. WITH OCCASIONAL NOTES AND ANECDOTES. BEING A CONTINUATION OF VICTOR'S & OULTON'S HISTORIES, FROM THE YEAR 1795 TO 1817 INCLUSIVE. 3 vols. London: C. Chapple, W. Simpkin and R. Marshall, 1818.

> Contains reviews (but no cast lists) of productions at Covent Garden, Drury Lane, Haymarket, and the English Opera House, as well as some summaries of each season's affairs and other miscellaneous information.

2520 Dibdin, Charles. HISTORY AND ILLUSTRATIONS OF THE LONDON THEATRES: COMPRISING AN ACCOUNT OF THE ORIGIN AND PROGRESS OF THE DRAMA IN ENGLAND; WITH HISTORICAL AND DESCRIPTIVE ACCOUNTS OF THE THEATRES ROYAL, COVENT GARDEN, DRURY LANE, HAYMARKET, ENGLISH OPERA HOUSE, AND ROYAL AMPHITHEATRE. London: Proprietors of the ILLUSTRATIONS OF LONDON BUILDINGS, 1826. 94 p.

> Contains brief but fairly detailed technical descriptions of each theatre; illustrated with plates, line drawings, and plans.

2521 Brayley, Edward Wedlake. HISTORICAL AND DESCRIPTIVE ACCOUNTS
OF THE THEATRES OF LONDON . . . ILLUSTRATED WITH A VIEW OF
EACH THEATRE, ELEGANTLY COLOURED, DRAWN AND ENGRAVED
BY THE LATE DANIEL HAVELL. London: J. Taylor, [1827]. vi, 92 p.

2522 Rede, Leman Thomas. THE ROAD TO THE STAGE, CONTAINS CLEAR
AND AMPLE INSTRUCTIONS FOR OBTAINING THEATRICAL ENGAGE-
MENTS; WITH A LIST OF THE PROVINCIAL THEATRES, NAMES OF THE
MANAGERS, AND PARTICULARS AS TO SALARIES, RULES, FINES, &C.;
AN ACCOUNT OF THINGS NECESSARY ON AN OUTSET IN THE PRO-
FESSION, HOW AND WHERE OBTAINED; AND A CLEAR ELUCIDATION
OF ALL THE TECHNICALITIES OF THE HISTRIONIC ART: TO WHICH
IS ADDED, A LIST OF LONDON THEATRES; COPIES OF THEIR RULES
AND ARTICLES OF ENGAGEMENT; AN ACCOUNT OF THE DRAMATIC
AUTHORS' SOCIETY; THE MEMBERS, SCALE OF PRICES, AND A COPY
OF THE DRAMATIC COPYRIGHT ACT. New ed. London: J. Onwhyn.
1836. viii, 100 p.

   See item 2668, below.

2523 Williams, Michael. SOME LONDON THEATRES PAST AND PRESENT.
London: Sampson Low, 1883. 215 p.

2524 Baker, H. Barton. HISTORY OF THE LONDON STAGE AND ITS
FAMOUS PLAYERS (1576-1903). London: Routledge, 1904; rpt. New
York and London: Blom, 1969. xiv, 557 p.

   A revision and expansion of Baker's 1889 edition. The account outlines, in the briefest terms, the highlights of the
   history of individual theatres. While not always accurate,
   it is among the better early theatrical histories.

2525 Sherson, Erroll. LONDON'S LOST THEATRES OF THE NINETEENTH
CENTURY: WITH NOTES ON PLAYS AND PLAYERS SEEN THERE. London: John Lane, 1925; rpt. New York: Blom, 1969. [ix], 392 p.

   This remains a valuable account of theatres, productions,
   casts, etc., of London theatres which have disappeared since
   the nineteenth century. However, sources are undocumented.

2526 Morice, Gerald. "A Record of Some XIX-Century London Theatres."
N&Q, 185 (1943), 223-24.

   This note is a roll call of destroyed and damaged London
   theatres, although there is some interesting detail in the
   narration. See also correspondents' notes, ibid., pages 295,
   326, 354 and volume 186, pages 56, 212.

2527 Harting, Hugh. "A Record of Some XIX-Century London Theatres." N&Q, 186 (1944), 175-76.

    Additional notes to items 2526 and 2528.

2528 Morice, Gerald. "A Further Record of Some XIX-Century London Theatres." N&Q, 186 (1944), 108-10.

2529 R., S. [Sybil Rosenfeld]. "Pictorical Records of Provincial Theatres." TN, 2 (1948), 66-69.

    Discusses the holdings of provincial art galleries, museums, and libraries--"the paucity of material available is astonishing," but Liverpool Public Library has a good collection of illustrations of the city's nineteenth-century theatres.

2530 Southern, Richard. THE GEORGIAN PLAYHOUSE. London: Pleiades Books, 1948. 72 p.

    Southern includes a chapter describing some nineteenth-century Georgian provincial theatres; there are many line drawings and plates.

2531 Leacroft, Richard. "The Remains of the Theatres at Ashby-de-la-Zouch and Loughborough." TN, 4 (1950), 12-21.

    Leacroft discusses the architectural aspects of the rectangular pit at these theatres in the first half of the nineteenth century. Illustrated.

2532 _____. "The Remains of the Fisher Theatres at Beecles, Bungay, Lowestoft, and North Walsham." TN, 5 (1951), 82-87.

    A continuation of item 2531 and examines a "horse-shoe" pit.

2533 Wilson, A.E. EAST END ENTERTAINMENT. London: Arthur Barker, 1954. 240 p.

    Readable, though undocumented, accounts of such theatres as the Pavilion, City, Garrick (Whitechapel), Effingham Saloon, City of London, Britannia Saloon, Queen's, Theatre Royal (Stratford East), Borough, and Dalston.

2534 Smith, William C., comp. THE ITALIAN OPERA AND CONTEMPORARY BALLET IN LONDON 1789-1820: A RECORD OF PERFORMANCES AND PLAYERS WITH REPORTS FROM THE JOURNALS OF THE TIME. London: Society for Theatre Research, 1955. xviii, 191 p.

    An invaluable calendar of operas and ballets produced at

Covent Garden, King's Theatre, and the Pantheon.

2535 Armstrong, William A. "The Art of the Minor Theatres in 1860." TN, 10 (1955-56), 89-94.

2536 Speaight, George. "Illustration of Minor Theatres." TN, 12 (1957-58), 94-96.

2537 Cox, Antony Hippisley. "The Lesser Known Circuses of London." TN, 13 (1958-59), 89-100.

A well-documented and illustrated account of circuses in pleasure gardens and theatres in London.

2538 Macomber, Philip Alan. "The Iconography of London Theatre Auditorium Architecture, 1660-1900." Ph.D. Dissertation, Ohio State University, 1959. 644 p. (DA#59-5864)

A discussion of the bearing theatre architecture has on the form and style of the plays produced.

2539 Bligh, N.M. "Mirror Curtains." TN, 15 (1961), 56.

With a print of the mirror curtain at the Surrey theatre and brief discussion of other such curtains.

2540 Mander, Raymond, and Joe Mitchenson. THE THEATRES OF LONDON. Illus. Timothy Birdsall. London: Hart-Davis, 1961. 292 p.

Together with item 2545, this is an invaluable guide to London theatres. This volume deals with existing theatres, outlining their histories, major productions, and so forth. Often draws on nineteenth-century accounts. Appendices give a "Chronological List of the Theatres of London." There is no index.

2541 Morley, Malcolm. "More on the Minor Theatre." TN, 19 (1964), 29.

2542 Carter, Rand. "The Architecture of English Theatres: 1760-1860." Ph.D. Dissertation, Princeton University, 1966. 171 p. (DA#66-13298)

2543 Saxon, A.H. "Shakespeare and the Circuses." ThS, 7 (1966), 59-79.

A scholarly, illustrated account of some of the more popular representations of Shakespearean plays in the nineteenth century. Saxon concentrates on the productions of William Cooke at Astley's (1853-60) and Charles Kean at the Princess's (1850-59).

2544 Stokes, J.A.A. "The Non-Commercial Theatres in London and Paris in the Late Nineteenth Century and the Origins of the Irish Literary Theatre and Its Successor." Ph.D. Dissertation, Reading University, 1967-68.

2545 Mander, Raymond, and Joe Mitchenson. THE LOST THEATRES OF LONDON. London: Hart-Davis, 1968. 576 p.

> Complement to item 2540, covering theatres no longer in existence.

2546 Howard, Diana. LONDON THEATRES AND THE MUSIC HALLS 1850-1950. London: Library Association, 1970. xiii, 291 p.

> This directory attempts to give information on every theatre and music hall which existed during the period. The information is arranged under such headings as building details, management, literature, location of materials, and other sources. Of necessity this work is incomplete, but it is certainly one of the most valuable reference tools to date.

2547 Leacroft, Richard. THE DEVELOPMENT OF THE ENGLISH PLAYHOUSE. London: Eyre Methuen; Ithaca, Cornell University Press, 1973. 354 p.

> Leacroft describes the development of the theatre from the beginnings to the early twentieth century. There are numerous illustrations.

B. INDIVIDUAL LONDON THEATRES

London theatres tended to change their names from time to time. For clarification of these sometimes baffling changes, Nicoll's notes on London theatres in volumes 4 and 5 of A HISTORY OF ENGLISH DRAMA [items 298 and 321, above] should be consulted. General Works, A. above, also often contains valuable supplementary information.

ALHAMBRA

2547a Walker, Kathrine Sorley. "Georges Jacobi and Alhambra Ballet." TN, 1 (1945-47), 82-83.

> Jacobi was musical director of the Alhambra, 1871-97.

AQUARIUM

2548 Munro, John M. "Queer Fish at the Aquarium: The Failure of a Victorian Compromise." DRAMA AND THEATRE, 9 (1970-71), 75-80.

A general description of the various entertainments and exhibits offered by the Aquarium.

ASTLEY'S

2549 Disher, M. Willson. GREATEST SHOW ON EARTH: AS PERFORMED FOR OVER A CENTURY AT ASTLEY'S (AFTERWARDS SANGER'S) ROYAL AMPHITHEATRE OF ARTS, WESTMINSTER BRIDGE ROAD. London: G. Bell, 1937; rpt. New York: Blom, 1969. xiv, 306 p.

A well-illustrated history, which draws considerably on contemporary sources

CATHERINE STREET

2550 Morley, Malcolm, and George Speaight. "The Minor Theatre in Catherine Street." TN, 18 (1964), 117-20.

A brief history of this private theatre, also known as the Temple of Arts, Harmonic Theatre, Theatre Mechanique, Argus Subscription Theatre, Theatre of Variety, Royal Pantheon, and the Royal Victorian Saloon.

COBURG

See OLD VIC.

COVENT GARDEN

2551 Wyndham, Henry Saxe. THE ANNALS OF COVENT GARDEN THEATRE FROM 1732 TO 1897. 2 vols. London: Chatto and Windus, 1906.

A pedestrian account of events and personalities on a brief year-by year basis. Two appendices list patentees, lessees, and managers and a chronology of principal events.

2552 Shawe-Taylor, Desmond. COVENT GARDEN. London: Max Parrish, [1948]. 70 p.

2553 Rosenthal, Harold. TWO CENTURIES OF OPERA AT COVENT GARDEN; WITH A FOREWORD BY THE EARL OF HAREWOOD. London: Putnam, 1958. xv, 849 p.

This work is particularly exhaustive in documenting the history of opera productions down to 1957. There is an invaluable appendix listing production details of operas staged between 1847 and 1957. Also see item 2555.

2554 Dewart, William H. "Covent Garden's Calendar, 1803-1808." Ph.D. Dissertation, University of Florida, 1960. 119 p. (DA#60-5152)

Gives a complete list of plays produced by J.P. Kemble based on account books and the like in the British Library. Dewart also compares this five-year period with Garrick's tenancy of Drury Lane from 1747-52.

2555 Rosenthal, Harold. OPERA AT COVENT GARDEN: A SHORT HISTORY. London: Gollancz, 1967. 192 p.

Covers the period 1732-1966 and deals only with opera productions. It is a lively account and touches on several important aspects--managers, conductors, performers, audiences, and policies. There is a useful appendix of operas produced 1847-1966. Also see item 2553.

2556 Sheppard, F.H.W., ed. SURVEY OF LONDON: VOL. XXXV: THE THEATRE ROYAL DRURY LANE AND THE ROYAL OPERA HOUSE COVENT GARDEN. London: Athlone Press, 1970. xvi, 132, 68 p.

An excellently documented, scholarly work on both theatres, limited to a discussion of managements, buildings, and sites (performances mentioned only incidentally). Well-illustrated with plans and photographs.

DALY'S

2557 Forbes-Winslow, D., et al. DALY'S: THE BIOGRAPHY OF A THEATRE. London: W.H. Allen, 1944. 220 p.

A random, unorganized, undocumented, and anecdotal account of the theatre and its productions.

DRURY LANE

Also see item 2556, above.

2558 Kenney, Charles Lamb. POETS AND PROFITS AT DRURY LANE THEATRE: A THEATRICAL NARRATIVE: SUGGESTED BY F.B. CHATTERTON. London: Aubert's Printing Works, 1875. 58 p.

2559 Doran, John. IN AND ABOUT DRURY LANE AND OTHER PAPERS: REPRINTED FROM THE PAGES OF THE "TEMPLE BAR" MAGAZINE. 2

vols. London: Richard Bentley, 1881. 316; 349 p.

Rather leisurely, "gentlemanly," chapters on such topics as
Master Betty, Macready, private theatricals, and French
drama.

2560 Stirling, Edward. OLD DRURY LANE: FIFTY YEARS' RECOLLECTIONS
OF AUTHOR, ACTOR AND MANAGER. 2 vols. London: Chatto and
Windus, 1881. vi, 363; 369 p.

2561 FIVE YEARS AT OLD DRURY LANE, 1879-1884, BEING A RECORD OF
THE PRODUCTIONS AT THE NATIONAL THEATRE DURING THE PAST
FIVE YEARS OF THE MANAGEMENT OF AUGUSTUS HARRIS. Drury
Lane Theatre: [Alfred Gibbons], 1884. 32 p.

A brief but interesting compilation of productions from November 1879 to December 1883, with cast lists and information on
a variety of matters--receipts, runs, reviews, sets, etc.

2562 "Subscription List Prospectus." THE TIMES, 29 May 1897, p. 8.

Gives details of proposed management, objectives, costs.

2563 MacQueen-Pope, W.J. THEATRE ROYAL DRURY LANE. London: W.H.
Allen, 1945. 350 p.

A readable, though undocumented, history, focusing on
players and managers.

2564 Forsyth, Gerald. "Notes on Pantomime, with a List of Drury Lane Pantomimes 1879-1914." TN, 2 (1947), 22-30.

The list of pantomimes is prefaced by some general reminiscences (Forsyth attended the theatre from 1885 onwards). The
list is taken from playbills and gives authors and principal
performers, but not exact dates and runs.

2565 Skinner, Quentin. "Sheridan and Whitbread at Drury Lane 1809-1815."
TN, 17 (1962-63), 40-46; 74-79.

Using manuscript materials from the Samuel Whitbread papers
at Southill, Skinner gives a detailed account of the rebuilding
of Drury Lane and the many attendant problems. He also attempts to redress the balance of previous accounts which
placed Whitbread in a poor light.

2566 Dobbs, Brian. DRURY LANE: THREE CENTURIES OF THE THEATRE
ROYAL, 1663-1971. London: Cassell, 1972. xiv, 226 p.

An uneven work which deals eccentrically with the various

phases of the theatre's history and is ultimately disappointing and unsatisfying.

2567 Nelson, Alfred L., and B. Gilbert Cross. "The Drury Lane Portico, 1820." NCTR, 1 (1973), 107-8.

A brief discussion of the history of the design.

EMPIRE

2567a Guest, Ivor. THE EMPIRE BALLET. London: Society for Theatre Research, 1962. 111 p.

Includes an appendix of ballets produced, 1884-1915.

ENGLISH OPERA HOUSE

See LYCEUM.

GAIETY

2568 "Gaiety Theatre Company." ERA, 27 August 1892, p. 9; 3 September 1893, p. 9.

Financial report for the year ending 30 June 1892 and as such useful for its detailed balance sheet. Also a report of the annual general meeting discussing policy.

2569 Hollingshead, John. GAIETY CHRONICLES. London: Constable, 1898. xvi, 493 p.

2570 _____. "GOOD OLD GAIETY": AN HISTORIETTE AND A REMEMBRANCE. London: Gaiety Theatre Co., 1903. 79 p.

A personal, anecdotal account by the theatre's first manager. Liberally illustrated with photographs of actors.

2571 MacQueen-Pope, W. GAIETY: THEATRE OF ENCHANTMENT. London: W.H. Allen, 1949. 498 p.

This embroidered history is more suitable for those looking for light, pleasurable reading than for scholarly, documented work. The author is knowledgeable, however, and useful information is tucked away in these pages.

2572 Jupp, James. THE GAIETY STAGE DOOR: THIRTY YEARS' REMINIS-

CENCES OF THE THEATRE. Boston: Small, Maynard & Company, n.d. 352 p.

Jupp was stage doorkeeper at the Gaiety in the 1890's.

GARRICK

2573 Troubridge, St. Vincent. "Minor Victorian Playhouses." N&Q, 179 (1940), 195.

A short account of the Garrick in 1875. See also note by Gerald Morice, ibid., page 119-20.

HAMPSTEAD

2574 Davidson, Pamela. "Theatre in Hampstead in the Early Nineteenth Century." N&Q, 17 (1970), 168-69.

A brief descriptive account, which concentrates on the years 1805-29.

HAYMARKET, THEATRE ROYAL

2575 Maude, Cyril, and Ralph Maude. THE HAYMARKET THEATRE: SOME RECORDS & REMINISCENCES. London: Richards, 1903. vii, 240 p.

This is a deliberately random history of the theatre and its people, told anecdotally.

2576 Leverton, W.H. THROUGH THE BOX-OFFICE WINDOW: MEMORIES OF THE HAYMARKET THEATRE. WITH A FOREWORD BY MARIE TEMPEST. London: T. Werner Laurie, 1932. 245 p.

Leverton was box office keeper at the Haymarket for fifty years, from 1882.

2577 MacQueen-Pope, W. HAYMARKET: THEATRE OF PERFECTION. London: W.H. Allen, 1948. 394 p.

A genial, though incomplete and undocumented guide to the theatre, its managers, productions, and actors.

KING'S HAYMARKET

2578 Waters, E. A STATEMENT OF MATTERS RELATIVE TO THE KING'S THEATRE. London: J. Ebers, 1818. 27 p.

This pamphlet is Waters's own account and defense of his
management of the King's Theatre and the financial difficulties he found himself in which provoked a "public"
examination of his activities. It also contains numerous
documents, selected by Waters, to substantiate his position.

2579 Ebers, John. SEVEN YEARS OF THE KING'S THEATRE. London: Ains-
worth, 1828. xxviii, 395 p.

A personal account of his management of the King's from
1821-27 with considerable information on productions.
Useful appendices on various aspects of management, especially financial.

2580 Nalbach, Daniel. THE KING'S THEATRE 1704-1867: LONDON'S FIRST
ITALIAN OPERA HOUSE. London: Society for Theatre Research, 1972.
xii, 164 p.

Deals with the first two theatres which went under this title,
and for each devotes chapters to managers, architecture, and
artists and audiences. A brief epilogue sketches out the last
150 years. Much detailed, well-documented information.

LONDON BRIDGE

2581 Morley, Malcolm. "Drama at London Bridge." TN, 14 (1960), 119-22.

Drama at this illegal playhouse from 8 April 1833-13 April
1835. Morley also discusses the Railroad Theatre (31 May
1837-19 June 1837) and Simpson's Minor Theatre (1830's).

LYCEUM (ENGLISH OPERA HOUSE)

There is also much about the Lyceum under Henry Irving, chapter 7, B, below.

2582 A DESCRIPTION OF THE ENGLISH OPERA-HOUSE, IN THE STRAND:
ERECTED A.D. 1816: OPENED FOR THE ENCOURAGEMENT OF NA-
TIVE TALENT, AND AS A SCHOOL FOR ENGLISH MUSIC, ON THE
15TH OF JUNE IN THE SAME YEAR, UNDER THE EXPRESS SANCTION
OF HIS MAJESTY: TOGETHER WITH A SHORT ACCOUNT OF THE
FIRST ESTABLISHMENT OF THE ENGLISH OPERA. London: J. Miller,
1816. 20 p.

A short, though fairly detailed account of Samuel James
Arnold's opera house built on the site of the Old Lyceum.

2583 Scott, Clement. FROM "THE BELLS" TO "KING ARTHUR": A CRITICAL

RECORD OF THE FIRST-NIGHT PRODUCTIONS AT THE LYCEUM THE-
ATRE FROM 1871 TO 1895. London: Macqueen, 1897. vii, 444 p.

>An anthology of Scott's newspaper reviews of productions at
>the Lyceum, 1871-95. He includes cast lists, illustrations,
>and appendices on important revivals (with cast lists) and
>parts played by Irving.

2584 Brereton, Austin. THE LYCEUM AND HENRY IRVING. London and
New York: Larence and Bullen, 1903. xvi, 351 p.

>A straightforward chronological account which covers the
>inception of the theatre as well as Irving's years. Liberally
>illustrated from contemporary sources.

2585 Wilson, A.E. THE LYCEUM. London: Yates, 1952. 208 p.

>Uses extensive quotations from contemporary sources to furnish
>a straightforward account.

2586 Rosenfeld, Sybil. "Early Lyceum Theatres." TN, 18 (1964), 129-34.

>A series of notes on theatres bearing the Lyceum title during
>the period 1765-1816.

2587 Hughes, Alan. "Henry Irving's Finances: The Lyceum Accounts, 1878-
1899." NCTR, 1 (1973), 79-87.

>A detailed investigation of the Lyceum account books which
>demonstrates closely Irving's income from and expenditure on
>productions, and refutes earlier relations of Irving's bankruptcy.

2587a _____. "The Lyceum Staff: A Victorian Theatrical Organization."
TN, 28 (1974), 11-17.

LYRIC, HAMMERSMITH

2588 Barker, B. Ashley. "The Lyric Theatre, Hammersmith." TN, 24 (1969-
70), 118-22.

>Brief illustrated history of the first theatre situated in Brad-
>more Grove (from 1888-95).

(ROYAL) MARYLEBONE

See also OLD MARYLEBONE and ROYAL WEST LONDON theatres.

2589 F., I.K. [Ifan Kyrle Fletcher]. "The Royal Marylebone Theatre." TN, 17 (1962), 7-9.

> The main feature is a list of notable actors who performed here from 1837-57. An additional list (for 1858-86) is provided by Diana Barron, "The Royal West London Theatre," TN, 18 (1964), 126.

NEW QUEEN'S

See ROYAL ALBION

NEW ROYAL BRUNSWICK

2590 Wellwarth, George E. "The Disappearance of the New Royal Brunswick Theatre; or, The Mystery of the Iron Roof." TN, 22 (1967-68), 56-63.

> An account of the destruction of the theatre three days after it opened in 1828.

OLD MARYLEBONE

See also (ROYAL) MARYLEBONE and ROYAL WEST LONDON theatres.

2591 Morley, Malcolm. THE OLD MARYLEBONE THEATRE. St. Marylebone Society Publication, no. 2. London: [St. Marylebone Society], 1960. 40 p.

OLD VIC

2592 Booth, John. A CENTURY OF THEATRICAL HISTORY, 1816-1916: THE OLD VIC. London: Stead's Publishing House, 1917. 72 p.

> The brevity of this history precludes all but the sketchiest of detail, most of which is undocumented. It touches on all the salient facts, however.

2593 Newton, H. Chance. THE OLD VIC AND ITS ASSOCIATIONS. London: Fleetway Press [1923]. 86 p. Illus.

2594 Hamilton, Cicely, and Lilian Baylis. THE OLD VIC. London: Cape, 1926. 285 p.

> There is much of interest in this genial and leisurely history, although the work falls short of scholarly standards.

2595 Fagg, Edwin. THE OLD "OLD VIC": A GLIMPSE OF THE OLD THE-
ATRE, FROM ITS ORIGIN AS "THE ROYAL COBURG," FIRST MANAGED
BY WILLIAM BARRYMORE, TO ITS REVIVAL UNDER LILIAN BAYLIS.
[London]: Vic Well's Association, 1936. 124 p.

> Dips into the various periods of the theatre's history to give
> something of its flavor.

2596 Dent, Edward J. A THEATRE FOR EVERYBODY: THE STORY OF THE
OLD VIC AND SADLER'S WELLS. London and New York: T.V. Board-
man, 1946. 167 p.

> A lightweight history of both theatres, with emphasis on the
> work of Cons and Baylis.

OLYMPIC

2596a Sands, Mollie. "The Olympic Theatre and the Windsor Theatrical Scan-
dal." TN, 26 (1971-72), 8-15.

> Concerns Charles Kean's loss of the directorship of the Royal
> Theatricals in 1857.

OPERA COMIQUE

2597 "The Opera Comique Theatre." ERA, 15 October 1898, p. 11.

> A history of the theatre from 1871-98, with details of manage-
> ments, productions, and costs.

ORANGE

See ROYAL ALBION.

PAVILION

See ROYAL WEST LONDON.

PORTMAN

See ROYAL WEST LONDON.

PRINCE OF WALES'S

2598 Lorenzen, Richard LeRoy. "A History of the Old Prince of Wales's Theatre, London, 1772-1903." Ph.D. Dissertation, Ohio State University, 1968. (DA#69-4929)

> Lorenzen draws on primary materials in such locations as the Enthoven Collection, the British Library and the Greater London Council. There are chapters on managers, plays, physical layout, and an overall view of the theatre in relation to contemporary theatrical activity.

2599 _____. "The Old Prince of Wales's Theatre: A View of the Physical Structure." TN, 25 (1971), 132-45.

> An extensively illustrated documentation of this theatre, 1772-1903.

PRINCESS'S

> See entires under Charles Kean, items 2875 ff., for information on this theatre.

RAILROAD

> See LONDON BRIDGE.

ROYAL ALBION

2600 Rosenfeld, Sybil. "Two Westminster Theatres." TN, 12 (1957-58), 19-21.

> The Royal Albion or New Queen's, Windmill Street, and the Orange Theatre, Queen Street. Illustrated.

ROYAL CIRCUS

2601 Tuttle, George Palliser. "The History of the Royal Circus, Equestrian and Philharmonic Academy, 1782-1816, St. George's Fields, Surrey, England." Ph.D. Dissertation, Tufts University, 1972. 416 p. (DA#72-30285)

> Managers mentioned in the study include Charles Dibdin the Elder, Charles Hughes, Giuseppe Grimaldi, Delphini, Thomas Read, John Palmer, James Jones, J.C. Cross, Elliston, James

Dunn, and Thomas Dibdin.

ROYAL CLARENCE

2602 Byrne, M. St. Clare. "Supplement to the Playbill." TLS, 29 June 1933, p. 445.

> A short account of the history of the Royal Clarence and Westminster theatres, gleaned from sketchy newspaper reports.

ROYAL KENT

2603 Bligh, N.M. "The Royal Kent Theatre, Kensington." TN, 13 (1959), 124-28.

> Records of the theatre from 1831-50; with an illustration of the theatre.

2604 Morley, Malcolm. "More About the Royal Kent Theatre." TN, 14 (1960), 43-44.

ROYAL WEST LONDON

2605 Baily, Leslie J.R. "The Royal West London Theatre in the Nineteenth Century." N&Q, 187 (1944), 182-84.

> Brief history of a former theatre which occupied the site of the Royal West London in the period 1832-47 and known variously as the Pavilion, Portman, and Marylebone.

2606 Morice, Gerald. "Some Fresh Notes on the Royal West London Theatre in the Nineteenth and Twentieth Centuries." N&Q, 188 (1945), 250-52.

> Deals with the period 1838-1940.

2607 Morley, Malcolm. ROYAL WEST LONDON THEATRE: A SEQUEL TO "THE OLD MARYLEBONE THEATRE." St. Marylebone Society Publication, no. 6. London: St. Marylebone Society, 1962. 44 p.

SADLER'S WELLS

See also item 2596, above.

2608 Rosenfeld, Sybil. "A Sadler's Wells Scene Book." TN, 15 (1961), 57-62.

Designs by Robert C. Andrews, Luke Clint, and John Henderson Grieve for Sadler's Wells under Charles Dibdin's management.

2609 Jackson, Allan S., and John C. Morrow. "Aqua Scenes at Sadler's
Wells Theatre, 1804-1824." OSUTCB, no. 9 (1962), 22-47.

An interesting and well-illustrated account of Sadler's Wells
major attraction in the early nineteenth century. The authors
provide a list of aqua drama producers, 1804-24.

2610 Morrow, John Charles. "The Staging of Pantomime at Sadler's Wells
Theatre, 1828-1860." Ph.D. Dissertation, Ohio State University, 1963.
393 p. (DA#64-1286)

"The purpose of this study was to isolate and explain the
primary theatrical appeals of extravaganza pantomime."
Morrow utilizes primary source materials and also emphasizes
the technical production side of the topic.

2611 Arundell, Dennis. THE STORY OF SADLER'S WELLS 1683-1964. London: Hamilton, 1965. xiv, 306 p.

An account of performers and productions, often interspersed
with interesting anecdotal material. The study lacks documentation and occasionally falls back on mere cataloging
of events.

ST. JAMES'S

2612 Beard, Harry R. "Some Notes on John Braham (1774?-1856) at the St.
James's Theatre." TN, 10 (1955-56), 86-89.

2613 Macqueen-Pope, W. ST. JAMES'S: THEATRE OF DISTINCTION; WITH
A FOREWORD BY VIVIEN LEIGH. London: Allen, 1958. 256 p.

A genial, theatreman's history, concentrating on George
Alexander's management. Contemporary reviews of plays,
playbills, and other information are often given, although
the information is not always reliable.

2614 Duncan, Barry. THE ST. JAMES'S THEATRE: ITS STRANGE AND COM-
PLETE HISTORY 1835-1957. London: Barrie and Rockliff, 1964. xxiii,
407 p.

A dull, year-by-year account which is mostly a mixture of
anecdotes and cast lists. Undocumented and unreliable. Ap-

pendices on main managements, debuts, long runs, and first-nights.

SIMPSON'S MINOR THEATRE

See LONDON BRIDGE.

STRAND

2615 Morley, Malcolm. "The First Strand Theatre." TN, 18 (1964), 100-102.

A brief history of the first theatre, from 1832 to 1906.

VAUDEVILLE

2616 Rendle, T. Macdonald. JUBILEE OF THE VAUDEVILLE THEATRE, 1870-1920. London: J. Miles, [1920]. 33 p.

Illustrated.

VAUXHALL GARDENS

2617 Southworth, James Granville. VAUXHALL GARDENS: A CHAPTER IN THE SOCIAL HISTORY OF ENGLAND. New York: Columbia University Press, 1941. xi, 199 p.

This is a well-documented account of the Gardens during the eighteenth and nineteenth centuries, covering both social and theatrical aspects. A lengthy chapter is given over to entertainments. Illustrated.

WESTMINSTER

See ROYAL CLARENCE.

C. PROVINCIAL THEATRES

ABERDEEN

2618 Angus, J. Keith. A SCOTCH PLAY-HOUSE: BEING THE HISTORICAL RECORDS OF THE OLD THEATRE ROYAL, MARISCHAL STREET, ABER-

DEEN. Aberdeen: D. Wyllie and Son, 1878. 69 p.

BATH

2619 Penley, Belville S. THE BATH STAGE: A HISTORY OF DRAMATIC REPRESENTATIONS IN BATH. London and Bath: William Lewis, 1892. xv, 180 p.

2620 Rosenfeld, Sybil. "An Act Drop at Bath." TN, 21 (1967), 168.

A note on J.H. Grieve's first act drop (1827).

BIRMINGHAM

2621 Pemberton, T. Edgar. THE BIRMINGHAM THEATRES: A LOCAL RETROSPECT. Birmingham and London: Cornish Bros. and Simpkin, Marshall, Hamilton, Kent & Co., [1890]. i, 216 p.

A series of reminiscences, originally written for the BIRMINGHAM DAILY MAIL. Gives some useful accounts of London stars touring the provinces.

2622 _____. THE THEATRE ROYAL, BIRMINGHAM, 1774-1901: A RECORD AND SOME RECOLLECTIONS. Birmingham: Printed by Cord Bros., 1901. 64 p.

2623 Levy, E. Laurence. BIRMINGHAM THEATRICAL REMINISCENCES, 1879-1920. Birmingham: J.G. Hammond, [1922]. 255 p.

Illustrated.

2624 Rhodes, Raymond Crompton. THE THEATRE ROYAL, BIRMINGHAM, 1774-1924: A SHORT HISTORY. Birmingham: Moody Bros., 1924. 56 p.

Illustrated.

2625 Cunningham, John E. THEATRE ROYAL: THE HISTORY OF THE THEATRE ROYAL BIRMINGHAM. Oxford: George Ronald, 1950. 158 p.

Considering that the author had a lot of primary material at his disposal, the result is disappointing and generalized. The book fails to give a vivid impression of one of the major theatrical centers outside London.

BRIGHTON

2626 Porter, Henry C. THE HISTORY OF THE THEATRES OF BRIGHTON
FROM 1774 TO 1885. Brighton: King and Thorne, 1886. xiv, 206 p.

BRISTOL

2627 Jenkins, Richard. MEMOIRS OF THE BRISTOL STAGE, FROM THE
PERIOD OF THE THEATRE AT JACOB'S WELL, DOWN TO THE PRESENT
TIME; WITH NOTICES, BIOGRAPHICAL AND CRITICAL, OF SOME OF
THE MOST CELEBRATED COMEDIANS WHO HAVE APPEARED ON ITS
BOARDS. Bristol: Printed for the author by W.H. Somerton, 1826.
xii, 103 p.

2628 "An Old Playhouse: The Theatre Royal, Bristol--No. II." ERA, 29 July
1893, p. 13.

2629 Watts, Guy Tracey. THEATRICAL BRISTOL. Bristol: Holloway and Son,
1915. xi, 131 p.

2630 Powell, G. Rennie. THE BRISTOL STAGE: ITS STORY. Bristol: 1919.
204 p.

2631 Board, M.E. THE STORY OF THE BRISTOL STAGE 1490-1925. London:
Fountain Press, [1926]. vi, 57 p.

> Much too short to encompass adequately the scope of the title.
> Comprises a brief annual listing of the main features of each
> year, but little else.

2632 Joseph, Bertram L. "Famous Theatres: I: The Theatre Royal, Bristol."
DramS, 2 (1962), 139-45.

> A very brief account of the history of the theatre and its
> productions from 1766 to the present. Scarcely any attention
> is paid to the nineteenth century.

2633 Barker, Kathleen. "The Theatre Proprietor's Story." TN, 18 (1964), 79-
91.

> Drawing on four volumes of minute books for the Theatre
> Royal, Barker gives a brief history of the theatre from
> 1764 to 1925.

2634 _____. ENTERTAINMENT IN THE NINETIES. Bristol: Bristol Branch
of the Historical Association, 1973. 20 p.

A brief, lively account of theatrical activities in Bristol during the 1890's, a period which Miss Barker sees as being the last belonging to earlier traditions. The account is divided into sections dealing with drama and opera, pantomime, music hall, popular entertainment, and film.

2635 Kilburn, Michael. "Nineteenth Century Timber Stage Machinery at the Theatre Royal." ARCHITECTURAL REVIEW, 153 (February, 1973), 131.

Illustrated with two diagrams.

2636 Barker, Kathleen. THE THEATRE ROYAL, BRISTOL, 1766-1966: TWO CENTURIES OF STAGE HISTORY. London: Society for Theatre Research, 1974. xii, 278 p.

A very detailed history, drawn from wide-ranging contemporary sources, notably letters, minute books, newspaper accounts. The whole adds up to a substantial understanding of one of the most significant provincial theatres.

BURY ST. EDMUNDS

2637 Rosenfeld, Sybil. "William Wilkins and the Bury St. Edmunds Theatre." TN, 13 (1958-59), 20-25.

CANTERBURY

2638 Rosenfeld, Sybil. "A Project for an Iron Theatre." TN, 11 (1956-57), 19-20.

In Canterbury, 1859. Illustrated.

EAST ANGLIA

2639 Burley, T.L.G. PLAYHOUSES AND PLAYERS OF EAST ANGLIA. Norwich: Jarrold, 1928. xi, 180 p.

One of the better studies of provincial theatrical activity, concentrating largely on the Theatre Royal, Norwich. There is, in a short space, considerable detailed information on managements and performers, the latter frequently including London stars.

EDINBURGH

2640 Dibdin, James C. THE ANNALS OF THE EDINBURGH STAGE WITH AN ACCOUNT OF THE RISE AND PROGRESS OF DRAMATIC WRITING IN SCOTLAND. Edinburgh: Richard Cameron, 1888. viii, 511 p.

> Extends over the period up to 1888 and provides a detailed history of an important center. Dibdin makes frequent reference to playbills, accounts, and other primary material. Useful appendix listing the principal members of the Theatre Royal Company from 1769 to 1851.

EXETER

2641 Cotton, William. THE STORY OF THE DRAMA IN EXETER DURING ITS BEST PERIOD, 1787 TO 1823; WITH REMINISCENCES OF EDMUND KEAN. Exeter: Hamilton; London: Adams and William Pollard, 1887. 66 p.

> Quite an effective account, drawing on newspaper reports. Useful, too, for Kean's early provincial career.

2642 Delderfield, Eric R. CAVALCADE BY CANDLELIGHT: THE STORY OF EXETER'S FIVE THEATRES, 1725-1950. Exmouth, Eng.: Raleigh Press, 1950. 169 p.

> Good account of destruction of Exeter Theatre in 1887, but otherwise too short to cover the ground adequately.

GLOUCESTERSHIRE

2643 Hannam-Clark, Theodore. DRAMA IN GLOUCESTERSHIRE (THE COTS-WOLD COUNTY): SOME ACCOUNT OF ITS DEVELOPMENT FROM THE EARLIEST TIMES TILL TO-DAY. Gloucester: Minchin and Gibbs; London: Simpkin, Marshall, 1928. 240 p.

> A rag-bag of facts, with little overall coherence, but worth dipping into on the off-chance.

HULL

2644 Sheppard, Thomas. THE EVOLUTION OF THE DRAMA IN HULL AND DISTRICT. Hull: A. Brown, 1927. xii, 253 p.

2644a Brokaw, John W. "An Inventory of Gas Lighting Equipment in the Theatre Royal, Hull, 1877." ThS, 1-5 (1974), 29-37.

IPSWICH

2645 Lingwood, Harold Robert. IPSWICH PLAYHOUSES: CHAPTERS OF
LOCAL THEATRICAL HISTORY. Ipswich: East Anglian Daily Times,
1936. 40 p.

LIVERPOOL

2646 Broadbent, R.J. ANNALS OF THE LIVERPOOL STAGE FROM THE
EARLIEST PERIOD TO THE PRESENT TIME; TOGETHER WITH SOME AC-
COUNT OF THE THEATRES AND MUSIC HALLS IN BOOTLE AND BIR-
KENHEAD. Liverpool: Howell, 1908. 393 p.

> A useful catalog of productions and performers, often re-
> cording the provincial tours of leading stars or the early
> careers of later notables.

MANCHESTER

2647 Hodgkinson, J.L., and Rex Pogson. THE EARLY MANCHESTER THEATRE.
·London: Blond, for the Society for Theatre Research, 1960. xii, 189 p.

MARGATE

2648 Morley, Malcolm. MARGATE AND ITS THEATRES, 1730-1965: WITH A
FOREWORD BY C.B. PURDOM. London: Museum Press, 1966. 176 p.

> A readable account, with more flavor than fact. It contains
> useful information on the Thorne family.

NEWCASTLE

2649 Oswald, Harold. THE THEATRES ROYAL IN NEWCASTLE UPON TYNE:
DESULTORY NOTES RELATING TO THE DRAMA AND ITS HOMES IN
THAT PLACE. Newcastle upon Tyne: Northumberland Press, 1936.
viii, 160 p.

NORTHAMPTON

2650 Warwick, Lou. THEATRE UN-ROYAL; OR, "THEY CALLED THEM CO-
MEDIANS": A HISTORY OF THE THEATRE, SOMETIME ROYAL, MARE-
FAIR, NORTHAMPTON (1806-84 AND 1887). Northampton: Lou War-
wick, 1974. 279 p.

Journalistic and undocumented, but full of detail.

NORTH SHIELDS

2651 King, Robert. NORTH SHIELDS THEATRES: A HISTORY OF THE THE-
ATRES AT NORTH SHIELDS AND THE ADJOINING VILLAGE OF TYNE-
MOUTH FROM 1765: INCLUDING AN ACCOUNT OF THE TRAVELLING
BOOTHS, WITH ILLUSTRATIONS. Gateshead, Eng.: Northumberland
Press, 1948. 163 p.

NORWICH

2652 Harcourt, Bosworth. THEATRE ROYAL, NORWICH: THE CHRONICLES
OF AN OLD PLAYHOUSE. Norwich: Norfolk News Co., 1903. viii,
96 p.

Covers, in note form, 1826 to 1900.

2653 Eshleman, Dorothy H., ed. THE COMMITTEE BOOKS OF THE THEATRE
ROYAL NORWICH, 1768-1825. London: Society for Theatre Research,
1970. 182 p.

A scholarly edition. The books show in detail the minutiae
of theatre management and provide useful insights into the
workings of a provincial theatre. See also item 2639.

RICHMOND (SURREY)

2654 Bingham, Frederick. A CELEBRATED OLD PLAYHOUSE: THE HISTORY
OF RICHMOND THEATRE IN SURREY FROM 1765 TO 1884. London:
H. Vickers, 1886. 42 p.

RICHMOND (YORKSHIRE)

2655 Southern, Richard, and Ivor Brown. THE GEORGIAN THEATRE, RICH-
MOND, YORKSHIRE: THE STORY OF THE THEATRE. Richmond:
Georgian Theatre (Richmond) Trust, 1962. 25 p.

A brief discussion of the theatre and its repertory, well
illustrated with sketches and ground-plans.

SCOTLAND

2656 Lawson, Robb. THE STORY OF THE SCOTS STAGE. Paisley, Scotland:

Alexander Gardner, 1917. 303 p.

>Attempts to cover theatres in Aberdeen, Edinburgh, Arbroath, Dundee, Glasgow, and Perth. Consequently very cursory.

WAKEFIELD

2657 Senior, William. THE OLD WAKEFIELD THEATRE. Wakefield, Eng.: W.H. Milnes, 1894. 144 p.

WALES

2658 Price, Cecil. THE ENGLISH THEATRE IN WALES IN THE EIGHTEENTH AND EARLY NINETEENTH CENTURIES. Cardiff: University of Wales Press, 1948. x, 202 p.

>A detailed, scholarly study of theatrical activity in Wales, useful for its account of local conditions and of visiting London actors. A further large amount of historical material is packed into six appendices.

2659 _____. "The History of the English Theatre in Wales, 1844-1941." Ph.D. Dissertation, University of Wales, 1952-53.

2660 _____. "Some Welsh Theatres 1844-1870." NATIONAL LIBRARY OF WALES JOURNAL, 12 (1961), 156-76.

>Accounts of theatrical activity in various Welsh towns.

WOLVERHAMPTON

2661 "Grand Theatre, Wolverhampton." ERA, 8 December 1894, p. 11.

>A full description of the theatre, opened 1894, with dimensions, seating capacity, etc.

WORTHING

2662 Odell, M.T., comp. THE OLD THEATRE, WORTHING: THE THEATRE ROYAL, 1807-1855. Aylesbury, Eng.: G.W. Jones, 1938. 163 p.

2663 _____. MR. TROTTER OF WORTHING AND THE BRIGHTON THEATRE (THE THEATRE ROYAL, 1814-1819). Worthing: Aldridge Press, 1944. 102 p.

2664 _____. MORE ABOUT THE OLD THEATRE WORTHING: (THE THEATRE ROYAL, 1807-1885). Worthing: Aldridge Bros., 1945. 134 p.

Chapter 7

ACTING AND MANAGEMENT

This chapter is divided into two sections: General Works and Individual Actors, Actresses, and Managers. For a more extensive listing of contemporary works on acting and management and on individual performers and managers, readers should consult Arnott and Robinson's ENGLISH THEATRICAL LITERATURE 1559-1900, item 2458, above.

A. GENERAL WORKS

2665 [Hill, Aaron]. THE ACTOR; OR, GUIDE TO THE STAGE; EXEMPLI-
FYING THE WHOLE ART OF ACTING: IN WHICH THE DRAMATIC
PASSIONS ARE DEFINED, ANALYZED, AND MADE EASY OF ACQUIRE-
MENT. THE WHOLE INTERSPERSED WITH SELECT AND STRIKING EX-
AMPLES FROM THE MOST POPULAR MODERN PIECES. London: John
Lowndes, 1821. 30 p.

2666 THE BIOGRAPHY OF THE BRITISH STAGE: BEING CORRECT NARRA-
TIVES OF THE LIVES OF ALL THE PRINCIPAL ACTORS & ACTRESSES,
AT DRURY-LANE, COVENT-GARDEN, THE HAYMARKET, THE LYCEUM,
THE SURREY, THE COBURG, AND THE ADELPHI THEATRES. INTER-
SPERSED WITH ORIGINAL ANECDOTES AND CHOICE AND ILLUSTRA-
TIVE POETRY. TO WHICH IS ADDED, A COMIC POEM, ENTITLED
"THE ACTRESS". London: Sherwood, Jones & Co., 1824. xii, 295 p.

2667 Terry, D. BRITISH THEATRICAL GALLERY: A COLLECTION OF WHOLE
LENGTH PORTRAITS, WITH BIOGRAPHICAL NOTICES. London: H.
Berthoud, 1825. [76] p.

> Terry's book contains color portraits and biographical essays
> on a number of well-known and minor nineteenth-century
> performers.

2668 Rede, Leman Thomas. THE ROAD TO THE STAGE; OR, THE PER-
FORMER'S PRECEPTOR. CONTAINING CLEAR AND AMPLE INSTRUC-

TIONS FOR OBTAINING THEATRICAL ENGAGEMENTS; WITH A LIST
OF ALL THE PROVINCIAL THEATRES, THE NAMES OF THE MANAGERS,
AND ALL PARTICULARS AS TO THEIR CIRCUITS, SALARIES, &C. WITH
A DESCRIPTION OF THE THINGS NECESSARY ON AN OUTSET IN THE
PROFESSION, WHERE TO OBTAIN THEM, AND A COMPLETE EXPLANA-
TION OF ALL THE TECHNICALITIES OF THE HISTRIONIC ART! London:
Joseph Smith, 1827. iv, 106 p.

>An important guide for prospective actors in the nineteenth
>century; it went through several editions.

2669 Galt, John. THE LIVES OF THE PLAYERS. 2 vols. London: Henry
Colburn and Richard Bentley, 1831. viii, 316; 308 p.

>Includes essays on George Frederick Cooke, Mrs. Jordan,
>John Philip Kemble, John Emery, and Mrs. Siddons.

2670 Old Stager, An. [James Shirley Hodson]. A COMPLETE GUIDE TO
THE STAGE, AND MANUAL FOR AMATEURS AND ACTORS; CONTAIN-
ING A LIST OF THE PRINCIPAL LONDON AND PROVINCIAL THEATRES,
WITH THE NAMES OF THEIR MANAGERS, ETC., ALSO INSTRUCTIONS
IN THE VARIOUS REQUISITES FOR THE STAGE, TOGETHER WITH
SUCH USEFUL INFORMATION AND ADVICE AS RENDER IT OF THE
HIGHEST VALUE TO THE YOUNG ARTIST. London: Henry Beal,
[1851]. 36 p.

>In a preface the author acknowledges his debt to Rede's work,
>item 2668.

2671 Russell, W. Clark. REPRESENTATIVE ACTORS. A COLLECTION OF
CRITICISMS, ANECDOTES, PERSONAL DESCRIPTIONS, ETC. ETC. RE-
FERRING TO MANY CELEBRATED BRITISH ACTORS FROM THE SIXTEENTH
TO THE PRESENT CENTURY; WITH NOTES, MEMOIRS, AND A SHORT
ACCOUNT OF ENGLISH ACTING. London: Frederick Warne, [1872].
xv, 496 p.

>Short essays on a number of nineteenth-century performers;
>no protraits.

2672 Fitzgerald, Percy. THE ROMANCE OF THE ENGLISH STAGE. 2 vols.
London: Richard Bentley, 1874. xii, 334; 328 p.

>Includes brief biographical sketches of a number of actors
>including, from the nineteenth century, Mrs. Siddons, Edmund
>Kean, Cooke, Elliston, and Master Betty.

2673 Lewes, George Henry. ON ACTORS AND THE ART OF ACTING. London: Smith, Elder & Co., 1875; rpt. New York: Grove Press, [1957].
xiv, 278 p.

>Lewes's aim was to arrive at some objective assessment of the

abilities and methods which comprise good acting. To this end, he has useful comments on, among others, the Keans, Macready, Elizabeth Farren, the Keeleys, and Charles Mathews.

2674 Baker, Henry Barton. OUR OLD ACTORS. 2 vols. London: Richard Bentley, 1878. xii, 402; x, 379 p.

Volume two has essays on many nineteenth-century performers, with portraits.

2675 Cook, Dutton. HOURS WITH THE PLAYERS. 2 vols. London: Chatto and Windus, 1881. vi, 277; 263 p.

Biographies of eighteenth and nineteenth-century performers, volume two being devoted to the nineteenth century.

2676 Brereton, Austin. SOME FAMOUS HAMLETS FROM BURBAGE TO FECHTER: WITH AN APPENDIX GIVING EXTRACTS FROM THE CRITICISMS ON "HAMLET" BY GOETHE, COLERIDGE, SCHLEGEL, HAZLITT, ULRICI, ETC. London: David Bogue, 1884. viii, 74 p.

Brereton gives brief accounts of fifteen interpretations of Hamlet, including, from the nineteenth century, those by the Kembles, the Keans, Macready, Booth, and Fechter.

2677 Matthews, James Brander, and Laurence Hutton. ACTORS AND ACTRESSES OF GREAT BRITAIN AND THE UNITED STATES FROM THE DAYS OF DAVID GARRICK TO THE PRESENT TIME. 5 vols. New York: Cassell, 1886.

2678 Marston, Westland. OUR RECENT ACTORS: BEING RECOLLECTIONS, CRITICAL, AND IN MANY CASES, PERSONAL, OF LATE DISTINGUISHED PERFORMERS OF BOTH SEXES. WITH SOME INCIDENTAL NOTICES OF LIVING ACTORS. 2 vols. London: Sampson Low, Marston, Searle & Rivington, 1888. xviii, 288; xix, 310 p.

A good survey of leading and minor performers of the nineteenth century, but lacking portraits.

2679 Goddard, Arthur. PLAYERS OF THE PERIOD: A SERIES OF ANECDOTAL, BIOGRAPHICAL, AND CRITICAL MONOGRAPHS OF THE LEADING ENGLISH ACTORS OF THE DAY. 2 vols. London: Dean and Son, 1891. 368; 316 p.

Volume one: Irving, Wilson Barrett, Beerbohm Tree, E.S. Willard, Bancroft, Toole; volume two: John Hare, Charles Wyndham, Edward Terry, W.H. Kendal, Charles Warner, Arthur Cecil, Thomas Thorne, William Terriss, George Grossmith, Henry Neville, Lionel Brough, Rutland Barrington.

Numerous plates and line drawings.

2680 Dircks, Rudolph. PLAYERS OF TO-DAY. London: Simpkin, Marshall, Hamilton, Kent & Co.; Newcastle-upon-Tyne: Andrew Reid, [1892]. xxii, 150 p.

With numerous photographic portraits.

2681 Whyte, Frederic. ACTORS OF THE CENTURY: A PLAY-LOVER'S GLEANINGS FROM THEATRICAL ANNALS. London: George Bell, 1898. xii, 204 p.

A survey of the leading performers of the nineteenth century, with numerous plates.

2682 Pond, J.B. ECCENTRICITIES OF GENIUS: MEMORIES OF FAMOUS MEN AND WOMEN OF THE PLATFORM AND STAGE. New York: G.W. Dillingham, 1900. xxvi, 564 p.

Includes very brief and inconsequential accounts of Irving and Ellen Terry.

2683 Robins, Edward. TWELVE GREAT ACTORS. New York and London: G.P. Putnam's Sons, 1900. xiv, 474 p.

Nineteenth-century actors discussed are J.P. Kemble, Edmund Kean, Junius Brutus Booth, Macready, Charles Mathews, Fechter, Edward Sothern. Illustrated.

2684 _____. TWELVE GREAT ACTRESSES. New York and London: G.P. Putnam's Sons, 1900. x, 446 p.

Nineteenth-century English actresses discussed are Mrs. Siddons, Mrs. Jordan, Fanny Kemble, and Adelaide Neilson. Illustrated.

2685 Scott, Clement. SOME NOTABLE HAMLETS OF THE PRESENT TIME (SARAH BERNHARDT, HENRY IRVING, WILSON BARRETT, BEERBOHM TREE, AND FORBES ROBERTSON). London: Greening, 1900. 193 p.

Reprints of reviews which first appeared in the DAILY TELE-GRAPH and the NEW YORK HERALD. The cast of each production is also given. Useful additions are illustrations by W.G. Mein and a brief account by L.A. Greening of Scott's work as a drama critic and playwright.

2686 Fyvie, John. COMEDY QUEENS OF THE GEORGIAN ERA. London: Constable, 1906. xii, 445 p.

Useful mainly for a long chapter on Mrs. Jordan.

2687 Matthews, Brander, and Laurence Hutton, eds. THE LIFE AND ART OF EDWIN BOOTH AND HIS CONTEMPORARIES. Boston: L.C. Page, 1906. 317 p.

> Contains short essays on sixteen performers, mainly American. English performers discussed are the Bancrofts, the Boucicaults, Irving, the Kendals, Ellen Terry, and Toole.

2688 Fyvie, John. TRAGEDY QUEENS OF THE GEORGIAN ERA. New York: Dutton, 1909; rpt. New York: Blom, 1972. x, 316 p.

> A "haphazard collection of biographical sketches" (preface). Includes Mrs. Siddons, Julia Glover, Eliza O'Neill.

2689 Armstrong, Cecil Ferard. A CENTURY OF GREAT ACTORS 1750-1850. London: Mills & Boon, 1912; rpt. New York: Blom, 1971. [vi], 412 p.

> Includes chapters on Cooke, J.P. Kemble, Edmund Kean, Macready, Charles Kean, Master Betty, Munden, Grimaldi, Charles Mathews, Robson. There is a portrait of each actor and a short bibliography.

2690 Simpson, Harold, and Mrs. Charles Braun. A CENTURY OF FAMOUS ACTRESSES 1750-1850. London: Mills & Boon, [1913]. [viii], 380 p.

> A "collection of character studies; little pen-pictures of the famous women of the theatre" (preface). Includes Mrs. Jordan, Mrs. Siddons, Fanny Kemble, Eliza O'Neill, Helen Faucit, Ellen Tree. An appendix lists the chief characters played by each actress.

2691 THE ART OF ACTING. A DISCUSSION BY CONSTANT COQUELIN, HENRY IRVING AND DION BOUCICAULT. Publications of the Dramatic Museum of Columbia University, Papers on Acting, II. New York: Columbia University Press, 1926. 93 p.

2692 Boucicault, Dion. THE ART OF ACTING. WITH AN INTRODUCTION BY OTIS SKINNER. Publications of the Dramatic Museum of Columbia University, Papers on Acting, I. New York: Columbia University Press, 1926. 63 p.

> With notes on Boucicault by Brander Matthews.

2693 Kemble, Frances Anne. ON THE STAGE. WITH AN INTRODUCTION BY GEORGE ARLISS. Publications of the Dramatic Museum of Columbia University, Papers on Acting, III. New York: Columbia University Press, 1926. 35 p.

> Fanny Kemble's theory of dramatic art with references to

some of her contemporaries and predecessors, with notes by
Brander Matthews.

2694 Newton, H. Chance. CUES AND CURTAIN CALLS, BEING THE THE-
ATRICAL REMINISCENCES OF H. CHANCE NEWTON ("CARADOS" OF
"THE REFEREE"). WITH AN INTRODUCTION BY SIR JOHNSTON
FORBES-ROBERTSON. London: John Lane, The Bodley Head, 1927.
xiv, 306 p.

Memories of Irving and his sons, Phelps, Tree, Wilson Barrett,
and other actors. Illustrated.

2695 Skinner, Otis. MAD FOLK OF THE THEATRE: TEN STUDIES IN
TEMPERAMENT. Indianapolis: Bobbs-Merrill, 1928. 297 p.

Unoriginal sketches of (from the nineteenth century) Mrs. Jordan, Cook, Edmund Kean, Junius Brutus Booth. Illustrated.

2696 West, Edward Joseph. "Histrionic Methods and Acting Traditions on the
London Stage from 1870 to 1890: Studies in the Conflict of the Old and
the New Schools of Acting." Ph.D. Dissertation, Yale University, 1940.
582 p. (DA#72-01065)

2697 _____. "From a Player's to a Playwright's Theatre: The London Stage,
1870-1890." QJS, 28 (1942), 430-36.

West blames Robertson for making actors "domesticated animals"
performing "parlor tricks" for their masters (Pinero, Jones,
Grundy, etc.) instead of acting. "The disappearance of the
old school actor, with the concurrent development of the new
school non-actor . . . made possible . . . the so called
'dramatic renascence' of the nineties, which was not a sudden
efflorescence of dramatic genius, but rather a floral wreath
upon the grave of histrionic genius."

2698 Agate, James, ed. THESE WERE ACTORS: EXTRACTS FROM A NEWS-
PAPER CUTTING BOOK 1811-1833. London: Hutchinson, 1943; rpt.
New York: Blom, 1969. 150 p.

Agate provides a useful commentary to link together this
series of newspaper extracts dealing with Mrs. Siddons, Fanny
Kemble, J.P. Kemble, Edmund Kean, and Macready, among
others. The book lacks an index.

2699 West Edward Joseph. "The London Stage, 1870-1890. A Study in the
Conflict of the Old and New Schools of Acting." UNIVERSITY OF
COLORADO STUDIES, ser. B, 2, no. 1 (May 1943), 31-84.

A more detailed version of item 2697.

2700 Sprague, Arthur Colby. SHAKESPEARE AND THE ACTORS. THE STAGE
BUSINESS IN HIS PLAYS (1660-1905). Cambridge, Mass.: Harvard
University Press, 1944. xxvi, 440 p.

> The nineteenth-century actors receiving most attention are
> Benson, Edwin Booth, Cooke, Helen Faucit, Irving, the
> Keans, the Kembles, Macready, Phelps, Mrs. Siddons, and
> Beerbohm Tree. One unfortunate limitation of the study is
> that Sprague was restricted to promptbooks and other sources
> available in American libraries only. Nonetheless, this is
> still a valuable work, extensively documented, scholarly and
> readable. Illustrated.

2701 Downer, Alan S. "Players and Painted Stage: Nineteenth Century
Acting." PMLA, 61 (1946), 522-76.

> A substantial and important study of the development of acting
> styles and techniques throughout the century. The big names
> are there--Kemble, Kean, Macready, Irving--but so are some
> lesser, but still significant, ones--Charles Dillon and Alfred
> Wigan, for example. Downer also examines the views of
> nineteenth-century actors on their profession, and has scores
> of useful references.

2702 James, Henry. THE SCENIC ART: NOTES ON ACTING & THE DRAMA,
1872-1901. Ed. Allan Wade. New Brunswick: Rutgers University Press,
1948. xxv, 384 p.

> A collection of James's writings on drama and the theatre;
> there is a useful appendix of notes on actors, actresses,
> playwrights, plays, and theatres mentioned by James.

2703 Pallette, Drew B. "The English Actor's Fight for Respectability." TA,
7 (1948-49), 27-34.

> An interesting article, citing many contemporary sources,
> which discusses social attitudes (including the church's)
> toward actors in the final decades of the nineteenth century.

2704 Darlington, W.A. THE ACTOR AND HIS AUDIENCE. London: Phoenix
House, 1949. 188 p.

> Chapters on Mrs. Siddons, Kean, and Irving.

2705 West, Edward Joseph. "The Original Robertsonians: Competency, a
Touch of Genius, and the Make-Up Box." SM, 16 (1949), 253-71.

> A discussion of the acting of the Bancrofts ("both sound
> products of the old school training") and John Hare ("an
> example of the untrained player welcomed by the new stage
> because of talents in mimetic realism"). West cites many

contemporary opinions of these actors.

2706 Pearson, Hesketh. THE LAST ACTOR-MANAGERS. London: Methuen, 1950. xii, 84 p.

Sketches of Forbes-Robertson, Beerbohm Tree, George Alexander, Frank Benson, Lewis Waller, John Martin-Harvey, H.B. Irving, Laurence Irving, and Oscar Asche. The book is extensively illustrated from the Mander and Mitchenson theatre collection.

2707 Lelyveld, Toby Bookholtz. "Shylock on the Stage: Significant Changes in the Interpretation of Shakespeare's Jew." Ph.D. Dissertation, Columbia University, 1951. 196 p. (DA#00-02541)

2708 Sprague, Arthur Colby. SHAKESPEARIAN PLAYERS AND PERFORMANCES. Cambridge, Mass.: Harvard University Press, 1953. xiv, 222 p.

Includes chapters on J.P. Kemble as Hamlet, Mrs. Siddons as Lady Macbeth, Edmund Kean as Othello, Macready as Macbeth, Irving as Shylock, Edwin Booth as Iago. William Poel and the Elizabethan Stage Society are also discussed. The study is illustrated and well-documented.

2709 Carlisle, Carol Jones. "The Nineteenth-Century Actors VERSUS the Closet Critics of Shakespeare." SP, 51 (1954), 599-615.

"It is the purpose of this paper to present some of the views of nineteenth-century actors concerning the interpretative and critical possibilities of their act as applied to Shakespeare's plays and concerning the suitability of these plays to stage productions." Actors discussed include J.P. Kemble, Macready, Helen Faucit, Irving, Knowles, Fanny Kemble.

2710 Mander, Raymond, and Joe Mitchenson. THE ARTIST AND THE THEATRE: THE STORY OF THE PAINTINGS COLLECTED AND PRESENTED TO THE NATIONAL THEATRE BY W. SOMERSET MAUGHAM. London: Heinemann, 1955. xxii, 280 p.

The collection consists of forty-two portraits of eighteenth- and nineteenth-century actors and actresses, including William Farren, Charles Mathews, J.B. Buckstone, and Edmund Kean.

2711 Edwards, Charlene Frances. "The Tradition for Breeches in the Three Centuries that Professional Actresses Have Played Male Roles on the English-Speaking Stage." Ph.D. Dissertation, University of Denver, 1957.

2712 Kern, R.C. "The Actor-Manager System in the Nineteenth Century." Ph.D. Dissertation, Bristol University, 1957-58.

2713 Joseph, Bertram. THE TRAGIC ACTOR. London: Routledge & Kegan Paul, 1959. xvi, 415 p.

> Covers from the Elizabethan period to the end of the nine-teenth century. Includes discussion of the Kembles, Edmund Kean, Macready, Phelps, Irving, and Forbes-Robertson. There is a select bibliography with numerous plates and line drawings.

2714 Lelyveld, Toby. SHYLOCK ON THE STAGE. Cleveland: Western Reserve University Press, 1960. [x], 149 p.

> Includes discussion of Edmund Kean, Edwin Booth, and Irving. Illustrated; bibliography.

2715 Pugliese, Rudolph Edward. "A Promptbook Investigation of Macbeth Productions by the Foremost English Producers from 1800 to 1850." Ph.D. Dissertation, Ohio State University, 1961. 233 p. (DA#61-2841)

> Pugliese compares the productions of J.P. Kemble with those of Macready in the first quarter of the century, and those of Phelps and Charles Kean in the second quarter.

2716 Rosenberg, Marvin. THE MASKS OF OTHELLO: THE SEARCH FOR THE IDENTITY OF OTHELLO, IAGO, AND DESDEMONA BY THREE CENTURIES OF ACTORS AND CRITICS. Berkeley and Los Angeles: University of California Press, 1961. xii, 313 p.

> This is an intelligent and thorough attempt at the notoriously difficult problem of reconstructing performances. The nine-teenth century is well represented, but Rosenberg's task is made more difficult than it need be by the lack of illustrations.

2717 Golding, Alfred Siemon. "The Theory and Practice of Presentational Acting in the Serious Drama of France, England and Germany During the Eighteenth and Nineteenth Centuries." Ph.D. Dissertation, Columbia University, 1962. 151 p. (DA#62-02863)

2718 Meisel, Martin. "Perspectives on Victorian and Other Acting: The Actor's Last Call, or, No Curtain Like the Shroud." VS, 6 (1962-63), 355-60.

> A review article on items 2714, 2716, 2901, 2969.

2719 Hass, Thomas Booth. "Kean, Irving, Tree: Shakespearean Production

Aesthetics." Ph.D. Dissertation, University of Wisconsin, 1963.

2720 Booth, Michael R. "The Acting of Melodrama." UNIVERSITY OF TORONTO QUARTERLY, 34 (1964), 31-48.

A spirited and erudite defense of melodramatic acting.

2721 Meldrum, Ronald Murray. "Changing Attitudes Toward Selected Characters of Shakespeare." Ph.D. Dissertation, University of Arizona, 1965. 238 p. (DA#65-10377)

Some attention is paid to the work of the Kembles, Kean, and Macready.

2722 Tinapp, Richard A. "An Historical Study of Selected American and British Stage Directors, 1869 to 1890." Ph.D. Dissertation, Northwestern University, 1966. 523 p. (DA#67-04276)

Discusses the work of Boucicault and Irving.

2723 Bishop, Conrad Joy. "Melodramatic Acting: Concept and Technique in the Performance of Early Nineteenth Century English Melodrama." Ph.D. Dissertation, Stanford University, 1967. 269 p. (DA#67-11018)

2724 Lorenzen, Richard L. "Managers of the Old Prince of Wales's Theatre." TN, 24 (1969-70), 32-36.

For the period 1772-1882.

2725 Cole, Toby, and Helen Krich Chinoy, eds. ACTORS ON ACTING: THE THEORIES, TECHNIQUES, AND PRACTICES OF THE GREAT ACTORS OF ALL TIMES AS TOLD IN THEIR OWN WORDS. New rev. ed. New York: Crown Publishers, 1970. xviii, 715 p.

This is a useful collection, with good nineteenth-century representation; substantial bibliography. Originally published 1949.

2726 Donaldson, Frances. THE ACTOR-MANAGERS. Chicago: Henry Regnery, 1970. 195 p.

Covers the work of the Bancrofts, Irving, George Alexander, Forbes-Robertson, Tree, and Gerald du Maurier. There are several plates and a brief bibliography.

2727 Macht, Stephen Robert. "The Development of Acting Training at the London Academy of Music and Dramatic Art from 1861 to 1969." Ph.D. Dissertation, Indiana University, 1970. 272 p. (DA#70-26937)

2728 _____. "The Origin of the London Academy of Music and Dramatic Art." TN, 26 (1971-72), 19-30.

> The early history of the oldest extant acting school in England, founded in 1861.

2729 Favorini, Attilio. "The Old School of Acting and the English Provinces." QJS, 58 (1972), 199-208.

2730 Stedman, Jane W. "General Utility: Victorian Author-Actors from Knowles to Pinero." ETJ, 24 (1972), 289-301.

> Includes discussion of the acting of Knowles, Pinero, Robertson, Brandon Thomas, J.B. Buckstone, Boucicault, H.J. Byron, Mark Lemon, F.C. Burnand, and Gilbert.

2731 Rubin, Lucille S. "Voices of the Past: David Garrick, John Philip Kemble, Edmund Kean, 1741-1833." Ph.D. Dissertation, New York University, 1973. 264 p. (DA#73-19957)

B. INDIVIDUAL ACTORS, ACTRESSES, AND MANAGERS

ALDRIDGE, IRA (Actor, 1807-67)

2732 MEMOIR AND THEATRICAL CAREER OF IRA ALDRIDGE, THE AFRICAN ROSCIUS. London: Onwhyn, [1848?]. 28 p.

2732a Marshall, Herbert, and Mildred Stock. IRA ALDRIDGE, THE NEGRO TRAGEDIAN. Carbondale and Edwardsville: Southern Illinois University Press, 1958. viii, 355 p.

> A thorough study of the life and art of this neglected American-born actor who made his name on the English stage. Amply illustrated.

ALEXANDER, SIR GEORGE [GEORGE ALEXANDER GIBB SAMSON] (Actor-Manager, 1858-1918)

2733 "Mr. George Alexander at Home." ERA, 3 June 1893, p. 9.

> An informal interview which gives useful information on Alexander's life and work.

2734 Mason, A.E.W. SIR GEORGE ALEXANDER & THE ST. JAMES'S THEATRE. London: Macmillan, 1935; rpt. New York: Blom, 1969. x, 247 p.

A comprehensive, though not exhaustive, account of Alexander's achievements. Appendices give a list of plays produced at the St. James's 1891-1916.

ANDERSON, JAMES R. (Actor, 1811-95)

2735 _____. AN ACTOR'S LIFE. London: Walter Scott Publishing Co., 1902. xxvi, 356 p.

Reprinted from the NEWCASTLE WEEKLY CHRONICLE; with an introduction by W.E. Adams.

ARCHER, FRANK [F.B. ARNOLD] (Actor, 1845-1917)

2736 _____. AN ACTOR'S NOTEBOOKS: BEING SOME MEMORIES, FRIENDSHIPS, CRITICISMS AND EXPERIENCES OF FRANK ARCHER. London: Stanley Paul, [1912]. 345 p.

Covers the second half of the nineteenth century and deals with many theatre personalities of the period. Forty-two plates.

ARLISS, GEORGE (Actor, 1868-1946)

2737 _____. ON THE STAGE: AN AUTOBIOGRAPHY BY GEORGE ARLISS. London: John Murray, 1928. 341 p.

2738 _____. GEORGE ARLISS: BY HIMSELF. London: John Murray, 1940. xii, 349 p.

These are mainly reminiscences of Arliss's film career.

ASCHE, OSCAR [JOHN STRANGER HEISS] (Actor, 1871-1936)

2739 _____. OSCAR ASCHE: HIS LIFE, BY HIMSELF. London: Hurst & Blackett, [1929]. 256 p.

BAKER, SARAH (Manager, 1736/7-1816)

See item 285.

BANCROFT, SIR SQUIRE (1841-1926) AND LADY MARIE EFFIE (1839-1921)
(Actor-Managers)

2740 _____ . MR. & MRS. BANCROFT ON AND OFF THE STAGE. WRIT-
TEN BY THEMSELVES. 8th ed. London: Richard Bentley and Son,
1891. 410 p.

>The autobiography of the Bancrofts, first published in 1888.

2741 _____ . THE BANCROFTS: RECOLLECTIONS OF SIXTY YEARS. London: John Murray, 1909. xii, 462 p.

>The Bancrofts reminisce; thirty-seven plates and very useful
>index.

2742 Buzecky, Robert Conrad. "The Bancrofts at the Prince of Wales's and
Haymarket Theatres, 1865-1885." Ph.D. Dissertation, University of
Wisconsin, 1970. 261 p. (DA#70-12718)

BANNISTER, JOHN (Actor, 1760-1836)

2743 Adolphus, John. MEMOIRS OF JOHN BANNISTER, COMEDIAN. 2
vols. London: Richard Bentley, 1839. xix, 400; xi, 386 p.

BARNES, J.H. (Actor, 1850-1925)

2744 _____ . FORTY YEARS ON THE STAGE. London: Chapman and Hall,
1914. vi, 320 p.

>Memoirs of an undistinguished actor, but like many such
>volumes it is interesting for the light it sheds on more
>illustrious members of the profession (in this case, for ex-
>ample, Forbes-Robertson, Irving, the Kendals, Ellen Terry).

BARRETT, WILSON [WILLIAM HENRY BARRETT] (Actor-Manager, 1847-1904)

See items 2679, 2685.

BARRINGTON, RUTLAND [GEORGE RUTLAND FLEET] (Actor, 1853-1922)

2745 _____ . RUTLAND BARRINGTON: A RECORD OF THIRTY-FIVE YEARS'
EXPERIENCE ON THE ENGLISH STAGE . . . WITH A PREFACE BY SIR

WILLIAM S. GILBERT. London: G. Richards, 1908. 270 p.

2746 _____. MORE RUTLAND BARRINGTON, BY HIMSELF. London: G. Richards, 1911. 233 p.

BATEMAN, KATE (1843-1917) AND ELLEN (1844-1936) (Actresses)

2747 Badal, Robert Samuel. "Kate and Ellen Bateman: A Study in Precocity." Ph.D. Dissertation, Northwestern University, 1971. 183 p. (DA#72-07751)

BEDFORD, PAUL JOHN (Actor, ca. 1792-1871)

2748 _____. RECOLLECTIONS AND WANDERINGS OF PAUL BEDFORD. FACTS, NOT FANCIES. London: Strand Printing and Publishing Co., 1867. 132 p.

   Memoirs of a well-known comedian, first published in 1864.

BELTON, FRED (Actor, 1815-89)

2749 _____. RANDOM RECOLLECTIONS OF AN OLD ACTOR. BY FRED BELTON. London: Tinsley Brothers, 1880. 248 p.

BENSON, SIR FRANK ROBERT (Actor-Manager, 1858-1939)

2750 Benson, Lady [Constance]. MAINLY PLAYERS: BENSONIAN MEMORIES. Intro. Arthur Machen. London: Thornton Butterworth, 1926. 313 p.

   Reminiscences by Benson's wife, whom he married in 1886.

2751 Benson, Frank. MY MEMORIES. London: E. Benn, 1930; rpt. New York: Blom, 1971. x, 322 p.

2752 Trewin, J.C. BENSON AND THE BENSONIANS. Foreword. Dorothy Green. London: Barrie and Rockliff, 1960. xvi, 302 p.

   A good biography of Benson. Illustrated.

2753 Rostron, David. "F.R. Benson's Early Productions of Shakespeare's Roman Plays at Stratford." TN, 25 (1970-71), 46-54.

   Benson's work at Stratford in the 1890's was viewed by London critics with condescension and indifference, but seen by Midlands critics as "significantly successful."

2754 Toth, John William. "The Actor-Manager Career of Sir Frank Robert Benson in Perspective: An Evaluation." Ph.D. Dissertation, Ohio State University, 1971. 328 p. (DA#71-27577)

BERNHARDT, SARAH (French actress, 1845-1923)

2755 Skinner, Cornelia Otis. MADAME SARAH. Boston: Houghton Mifflin, 1967. 356 p.

2756 Taranow, Gerda. SARAH BERNHARDT: THE ART WITHIN THE LEGEND. Princeton: Princeton University Press, 1972. xviii, 287 p.

2757 Richardson, Joanna. SARAH BERNHARDT. London: Hale, 1973. 207 p.

BERTRAM, JAMES GLASS

See Paterson, Peter.

BETTY, WILLIAM HENRY WEST (Actor, 1791-1874)

2758 Harley, George Davies [George Davies]. AN AUTHENTIC BIOGRAPHI-CAL SKETCH OF THE LIFE, EDUCATION, AND PERSONAL CHARACTER, OF WILLIAM HENRY WEST BETTY, THE CELEBRATED YOUNG ROSCIUS. London: Richard Phillips, 1804. 76 p.

> One of several books and pamphlets published in 1804 and 1805 giving accounts, mostly adulatory, of the boy who first appeared on the London stage at the age of thirteen, enjoyed a rapturous reception for a brief period and then faded into oblivion. A full list of the contemporary publications about him is given by Arnott and Robinson (item 2458, pp. 233-36).

2759 Playfair, Giles. THE PRODIGY: A STUDY OF THE STRANGE LIFE OF MASTER BETTY. London: Secker & Warburg, 1967. 190 p.

> A balanced account, with a bibliography and several plates.

BOND, JESSIE (Actress, 1833-1942)

2760 _____. THE LIFE AND REMINISCENCES OF JESSIE BOND, THE OLD

SAVOYARD. AS TOLD BY HERSELF TO ETHEL MACGEORGE. London: John Lane, 1930. xvi, 244 p.

> Memoirs of a long-time Savoy performer. The book includes several plates of the actress in Gilbert and Sullivan roles.

BOOTH, JUNIUS BRUTUS (Actor, 1796-1852)

2761 _____. MEMOIRS OF JUNIUS BRUTUS BOOTH, FROM HIS BIRTH TO THE PRESENT TIME; WITH AN APPENDIX, CONTAINING ORIGINAL LETTERS FROM PERSONS OF RANK AND CELEBRITY; AND COPIOUS EXTRACTS FROM THE JOURNAL KEPT BY MR. BOOTH DURING HIS THEATRICAL TOUR ON THE CONTINENT. London: Chapple, Miller, Rowden and E. Wilson, 1817. 86 p.

2762 [Clarke, Asia Booth]. PASSAGES, INCIDENTS, AND ANECDOTES IN THE LIFE OF JUNIUS BRUTUS BOOTH (THE ELDER). New York: Carleton, 1866. 184 p.

2763 _____. THE ELDER AND THE YOUNGER BOOTH. Boston: James R. Osgood, 1882. 194 p.

> Biographies of Junius Brutus and Edwin Booth. Illustrated.

2764 Roman, Lisbeth Jane. "The Acting Style of Junius Brutus Booth." Ph.D. Dissertation, University of Illinois, 1968. 185 p. (DA#69-10832)

BOSTOCK, EDWARD HENRY (Circus performer, 1858-1940)

2765 _____. MENAGERIES, CIRCUSES AND THEATRES. London: Chapman and Hall, 1927. viii, 305 p.

> A well-illustrated autobiography of the "Barnum of British Circuses."

BROOKE, GUSTAVUS VAUGHAN (Actor, 1818-66)

2766 Lawrence, W.J. THE LIFE OF GUSTAVUS VAUGHAN BROOKE, TRAGEDIAN. Belfast: W. & G. Baird, 1892. x, 283 p.

> A good biography by a reliable theatre historian.

BROOKFIELD, CHARLES HALLAM ELTON (Actor, 1857-1913)

2767 _____. RANDOM REMINISCENCES. London: Nelson, [1911]. 377 p.

Humorous and irreverent memoirs, with a chapter on music halls.

BROUGH, LIONEL (Actor, 1836-1900)

See item 2679.

BUCKSTONE, JOHN BALDWIN (Actor, Manager, Playwright, 1802-79)

See items 768, 769.

BUNN ALFRED (Manager, Playwright, 1798-1860)

See items 803, 804, 805.

BUTLER, MRS. FRANCES

See Kemble, Frances Anne.

CALVERT, ADELAIDE HELEN (Actress, 1837-1921)

2768 _____. SIXTY-EIGHT YEARS ON THE STAGE. London: Mills & Boon, 1911. viii, 273 p.

Some reflections on provincial theatres, mainly Manchester. Several plates.

CALVERT, CHARLES ALEXANDER (Actor, 1828-79)

See item 154.

CAMPBELL, MRS. PATRICK [BEATRICE STELLA TANNER] (Actress, 1865-1940)

2769 _____. MY LIFE AND SOME LETTERS. Toronto: Ryerson Press, [1922]. [viii], 359 p.

Her life and career up to 1920.

2770 Dent, Alan, ed. BERNARD SHAW AND MRS. PATRICK CAMPBELL: THEIR CORRESPONDENCE. New York: Knopf, 1952. xviii, 385 p.

Letters written between 1899 and 1939.

2771 Dent, Alan. MRS. PATRICK CAMPBELL. London: Museum Press, 1961. 335 p.

Sixty-two short, chatty chapters of biography. There are some interesting plates, a bibliography, and index.

CAVE, JOSEPH ARNOLD (Music hall manager, 1823-1912)

2772 Soutar, Robert, ed. A JUBILEE OF DRAMATIC LIFE AND INCIDENT OF JOSEPH A. CAVE. London: T. Vernon, [1894]. 218 p.

CECIL, ARTHUR (Actor, 1844-96)

2773 Child, Harold. A POOR PLAYER: THE STORY OF A FAILURE. Cambridge: At the University Press, 1939. 109 p.

Reminiscences of a minor actor of the 1890's.

CHEVALIER, ALBERT (Music hall actor, 1861-1923)

2774 _____. ALBERT CHEVALIER: A RECORD, BY HIMSELF. Ed. Bryan Daly. London: J. Macqueen, 1895. xii, 295 p.

2775 _____. BEFORE I FORGET: THE AUTOBIOGRAPHY OF A CHEVALIER D'INDUSTRIE. London: T.F. Unwin, 1901. xvi, 257 p.

COATES, ROBERT (Actor, 1772-1848)

2776 Robinson, John R., and Hunter H. Robinson. THE LIFE OF ROBERT COATES, BETTER KNOWN AS "ROMEO" AND "DIAMOND" COATES THE CELEBRATED "AMATEUR OF FASHION." London: Sampson Low, Marston & Co., 1891. viii, 255 p.

Biography of an amateur actor who achieved some notoriety on the stage for a brief spell and then, like Master Betty, faded into obscurity.

COLEMAN, JOHN (Actor-Manager, 1831-1904)

2777 _____. FIFTY YEARS OF AN ACTOR'S LIFE. 2 vols. London: Hutchinson, 1904.

> Largely anecdotal autobiography.

COMPTON, HENRY CHARLES MACKENZIE (Actor, 1805-77)

2778 Compton, Charles, and Edward Compton, eds. MEMOIR OF HENRY COMPTON. London: Tinsley Bros., 1879. viii, 348 p.

> Contains anecdotes and recollections of Compton by, among others, Madge Robertson, Irving, Charles Mathews, Planché, Tom Taylor, and Toole.

CONQUEST, BENJAMIN OLIVER (1805-72) AND FAMILY (Actors)

2779 Fleetwood, Frances. CONQUEST: THE STORY OF A THEATRE FAMILY. In collaboration with Betty Conquest. London: W.H. Allen, 1953. xiv, 282 p.

COOKE, GEORGE FREDERICK (Actor, 1756-1812)

2780 Dunlap, William. MEMOIRS OF GEORGE FRED. COOKE, ESQ. LATE OF THE THEATRE ROYAL, COVENT GARDEN. 2 vols. London: Henry Colburn, 1813. xiv, 344; vi, 362 p.

> A biography drawn from Cooke's diaries and Dunlap's personal knowledge of Cooke. Since Dunlap's predominant aim was to render service to "the cause of morality" his biography should be read with caution.

2781 Wilmeth, Don B. "The Posthumous Career of George Frederick Cooke." TN, 24 (1969-70), 68-74.

> The history of Cooke's mortal remains, with emphasis on his much-travelled skull. Fourteen interesting plates, including one of Cooke's teeth. All in all, a rather esoteric piece of theatre history.

2782 _____. "Cooke Among the Yankee Doodles." THEATRE SURVEY, 14, no. 2 (1973), 1-32.

> A description and assessment of Cooke's career in America. An appendix gives details of Cooke's performances and receipts in American theatres, 1810-12. Illustrated.

COWELL, JOSEPH (Actor, 1792-1863)

2783 _____. THIRTY YEARS AMONG THE PLAYERS OF ENGLAND AND
AMERICA: INTERSPERSED WITH ANECDOTES AND REMINISCENCES OF
A VARIETY OF PERSONS, DIRECTLY OR INDIRECTLY CONNECTED WITH
THE DRAMA DURING THE THEATRICAL LIFE OF J. COWELL, COME-
DIAN. New York: Harper, n.d. 103 p.

CRAIG, EDWARD HENRY GORDON (Actor, Designer, 1872-1966)

2784 Rose, Enid. GORDON CRAIG AND THE THEATRE: A RECORD AND
AN INTERPRETATION. London: Sampson Low, Marston & Co., n.d.
xii, 250 p.

> The opening chapters deal with Craig's nineteenth-century
> acting career.

2785 Craig, Edward Gordon. INDEX TO THE STORY OF MY DAYS: SOME
MEMOIRS OF EDWARD GORDON CRAIG, 1872-1907. London: Hulton
Press, 1957. viii, 308 p.

> Engagingly frank memoirs, with many recollections of Ellen
> Terry and Henry Irving, as well as accounts of Craig's own
> early acting career.

2786 Craig, Edward. GORDON CRAIG: THE STORY OF HIS LIFE. London:
Gollancz, 1968. 398 p.

> An authoritative biography by Craig's son. Deals at length
> with the nineteenth-century part of Craig's life and theatrical
> career, necessarily involving his mother, Ellen Terry, and
> father, E.W. Godwin. The book is extensively illustrated
> and well documented.

CRESWICK, WILLIAM (Actor, 1813-88)

2787 _____. AN AUTOBIOGRAPHY: A RECORD OF FIFTY YEARS OF THE
PROFESSIONAL LIFE OF THE LATE WILLIAM CRESWICK. London: J.
Henderson, 1889. 128 p.

DAWSON, JAMES (Actor-Manager, fl. 1865)

2788 _____. THE AUTOBIOGRAPHY OF MR. JAMES DAWSON. Truro,
Eng.: Netherton, 1865. viii, 171 p.

> An actor-manager's life in the provinces, especially Cornwall.

DONALDSON, WALTER ALEXANDER (Actor, 1793-1877)

2789 _____. FIFTY YEARS OF AN ACTOR'S LIFE; OR, THESPIAN GLEAN-
INGS. London: T.H. Lacy, 1858. 56 p.

2790 _____. RECOLLECTIONS OF AN ACTOR. London: John Maxwell,
1865. viii, 360 p.

> Memoirs of an experienced provincial actor; reprinted in
> 1881 as FIFTY YEARS OF GREEN-ROOM GOSSIP.

DOUGLASS, ALBERT (Actor, 1864-1940?)

2791 _____. MEMORIES OF MUMMERS AND THE OLD STANDARD THEATRE.
Liverpool: J.A. Thompson, 1924. 138 p.

2792 _____. FOOTLIGHT REFLECTIONS: THE MUSINGS OF ONE WHO
HAS SPENT 60 YEARS IN THE THEATRICAL PROFESSION. London: S.
French, 1934. 145 p.

DUCROW, ANDREW (Circus manager, 1793-1842)

2793 Saxon, A.H. "Andrew Ducrow, England's Mime on a Moving Stage.
The Years in France." ThR, 13 (1973), 15-21.

> Ducrow's career before he took over the management of
> Astley's.

2794 _____. "The Tyranny of Charity: Andrew Ducrow in the Provinces."
NCTR, 1 (1973), 95-105.

DYER, ROBERT (Actor)

2795 _____. NINE YEARS OF AN ACTOR'S LIFE. London: Longman, Rees,
Orme, Brown, 1883. xiv, 241 p.

> Memoirs of a provincial actor.

EAST, JOHN M. (1860-1924) AND CHARLES ALEXANDER (1863-1914)
(Actor-Managers)

2796 East, John M. 'NEATH THE MASK: THE STORY OF THE EAST FAMILY.
London: Allen & Unwin, 1967. 356 p.

The careers of John and Charles East "serve to illustrate life in the melodramatic theatre of the 1890s" (preface).

ELLERSLIE, ALMA (Actress)

2797 _____. THE DIARY OF AN ACTRESS OR REALITIES OF STAGE LIFE. Ed. H.C. Shuttleworth. London: Griffith, Farran, Okeden & Welsh, 1885. 160 p.

Memoirs of a provincial actress.

ELLIS, GEORGE CRESSALL (Stage manager, 1809-75)

2798 Shattuck, Charles H. "A Victorian Stage Manager: George Cressall Ellis." TN, 22 (1967-68), 102-12.

"For the theatre historian, the information about early Victorian theatre practice which is embedded in Ellis's promptbooks is of incalcuable worth." Shattuck gives an account of Ellis's career, including his work with Macready and Charles Kean.

ELLISTON, ROBERT WILLIAM (Actor-Manager, 1774-1831)

2799 Raymond, George. MEMOIRS OF ROBERT WILLIAM ELLISTON. 2 vols. London: John Mortimer, 1844-45; rpt. 2 vols. in 1, New York: Blom, 1969. xxxvi, 438; x, 554 p.

An interesting biography of this controversial and eccentric figure, splendidly illustrated by Cruikshank. Volume two has a list of characters (with dates and theatres) played by Elliston; he also managed Drury Lane for seven years and is an important man in the history of the early nineteenth-century theatre.

2800 Murray, Christopher Noel. "The Great Lessee: The Management Career of Robert William Elliston (1774-1831)." Ph.D. Dissertation, Yale University, 1969. 399 p. (DA#70-16312)

2801 _____. "Elliston's Coronation Spectacle, 1821." TN, 25 (1970-71), 57-64.

Elliston's celebration of the coronation of George IV; three plates.

EMERY, JOHN (Actor, 1777-1822)

   See item 2669.

FAUCIT, HELEN SAVILLE (Actress, ca. 1817-98)

2802 Martin, Sir Theodore. HELENA FAUCIT (LADY MARTIN). 2nd ed.
   Edinburgh and London: Blackwood, 1900. xii, 416 p.

      A detailed biography by Helen Faucit's husband; five plates
      and a helpful index.

FORBES-ROBERTSON, SIR JOHNSTON (Actor, 1853-1937)

2803 _____. A PLAYER UNDER THREE REIGNS. London: T. Fisher Unwin,
   1925. 292 p.

      Autobiography, with several plates.

GLOVER, JAMES M. (Composer, Conductor, 1861-1931)

2804 _____. JIMMY GLOVER, HIS BOOK. London: Methuen, 1912.
   286 p.

      Glover enjoyed a long association with Drury Lane; his
      autobiography contains a list of Drury Lane productions
      1879-1911.

2805 _____. JIMMY GLOVER AND HIS FRIENDS. London: Chatto &
   Windus, 1913. xi, 325 p.

2806 _____. HIMS: ANCIENT AND MODERN; BEING THE THIRD BOOK
   OF JIMMY GLOVER. London: Unwin, 1926. 256 p.

GLOVER, JULIA (Actress, 1781-1850)

   See item 2688.

GRAHAM, JOE (Actor, fl. 1875)

2807 _____. AN OLD STOCK-ACTOR'S MEMORIES. Intro. Dame Madge
   Kendal. London: John Murray, 1930. xiv, 305 p.

Graham's career began in 1861 and, as he says, "For over half a century there were few leading lights of the English-speaking stage with whom I had not the honour of close association." Twelve plates are included.

GRANVILLE-BARKER, HARLEY (Actor-Manager, 1877-1946)

2808 Davis, Mary Louise. "Reading List on Harley Granville-Barker." BB, 7 (1912-13), 130-32.

2809 Downer, Alan S. "Harley Granville-Barker." SR, 55 (1947), 627-45.

A general assessment of Granville-Barker's achievements as an actor and producer, with special emphasis, quite properly, on his Shakespearean productions.

2810 Purdom, C.B. HARLEY GRANVILLE BARKER: MAN OF THE THEATRE, DRAMATIST AND SCHOLAR. London: Rockliff, 1955. xiv, 322 p.

A very thorough biography with several illustrations and three appendices--a list of characters played by Granville-Barker (1891-1911), a list of his productions (1900-1915) and a copious bibliography of his writings.

2811 Kelly, Helen Marie Terese. "The Granville-Barker Shakespeare Productions: A Study Based on the Promptbooks." Ph.D. Dissertation, University of Michigan, 1965. 382 p. (DA#66-06631)

2812 Elberson, Stanley Denton. "The Nature of Harley Granville Barker's Productions in America in 1915." Ph.D. Dissertation University of Oregon, 1968. 340 p. (DA#69-00010)

GRIMALDI, JOSEPH (Clown, 1778-1837)

2813 Miles, Henry Downes. THE LIFE OF JOSEPH GRIMALDI; WITH ANECDOTES OF HIS CONTEMPORARIES. London: Christopher Harris, 1838. 194 p.

2814 Tulin, Miriam S. "Mr. Grimaldi in the English Pantomime." Ph.D. Dissertation, Yale University, 1943.

2815 Findlater, Richard. GRIMALDI, KING OF CLOWNS. London: MacGibbon & Kee, 1955. 240 p.

2816 Dickens, Charles. MEMOIRS OF JOSEPH GRIMALDI. Illus. George

Cruikshank. Ed. Richard Findlater. London: MacGibbon & Kee, 1968. 311 p.

Originally published in 1838. Findlater adds an introduction on "Grimaldi and His World," notes, and three appendices, one of them usefully outlining the history of the publication of the MEMOIRS and the whereabouts of the original manuscript.

GRIMSTON, WILLIAM HUNTER

See Kendal, William Hunter.

GROSSMITH, GEORGE (Actor, Singer, 1847-1912)

2817 _____. A SOCIETY CLOWN: REMINISCENCES BY GEORGE GROSSMITH. Bristol: J.W. Arrowsmith; London: Simpkin, Marshall & Co., 1888. 192 p.

Includes an interesting chapter on Grossmith's Gilbert and Sullivan performances.

2818 Grossmith, George, and Weedon Grossmith. THE DIARY OF A NOBODY. Bristol: J.W. Arrowsmith, [1892]. 300 p.

2819 Grossmith, George. PIANO AND I: FURTHER REMINISCENCES BY GROSSMITH. Bristol: J.W. Arrowsmith; London: Simpkin, Marshall, Hamilton, Kent & Co., 1919. 200 p.

GROSSMITH, WALTER WEEDON (Actor, 1852-1910)

2820 _____. FROM STUDIO TO STAGE: REMINISCENCES OF WEEDON GROSSMITH, WRITTEN BY HIMSELF. London: John Lane, 1913. 367 p.

There is a good deal in these reminiscences about Irving, with whom Grossmith acted. Thirty-two plates.

HAINES, JOHN THOMAS (Actor, Playwright, 1798-1843)

2821 Wewiora, G.E. "J.T. Haines in Manchester, 1828-29." TN, 27 (1972-73), 89-94.

HARE, SIR JOHN (Actor-Manager, 1844-1921)

2822 Pemberton, T. Edgar. JOHN HARE, COMEDIAN, 1865-1895. A BI-
OGRAPHY. London: Routledge, 1895. vi, 202 p.

> An account of Hare as actor-manager at the Prince of Wales's,
> the Court, St. James's, and the Garrick theatres. There are
> several plates of Hare in various roles.

HAWTREY, SIR CHARLES HENRY (Actor-Manager, 1858-1923)

2823 Maugham, W. Somerset, ed. THE TRUTH AT LAST FROM CHARLES
HAWTREY. London: Butterworth, 1924. 352 p.

HICKS, SIR EDWARD SEYMOUR (Actor-Manager, 1871-1949)

2824 _____. SEYMOUR HICKS: TWENTY-FOUR YEARS OF AN ACTOR'S
LIFE, BY HIMSELF. London: Alston Rivers, 1910. ix, 321 p.

2825 _____. BETWEEN OURSELVES. London: Cassell, 1930. 252 p.

2826 _____. NIGHT LIGHTS. London: Cassell, 1938. 244 p.

2827 _____. ME AND MY MISSUS: FIFTY YEARS ON THE STAGE. London: Cassell, 1939. 276 p.

> The "missus" is Ellaline Terriss.

2828 _____. VINTAGE YEARS WHEN KING EDWARD THE SEVENTH WAS
PRINCE OF WALES. London: Cassell, 1943. 184 p.

HODSON, HENRIETTA (Actress-Manager, 1841-1910)

2829 _____. A LETTER FROM MISS HENRIETTA HODSON, AN ACTRESS,
TO THE MEMBERS OF THE DRAMATIC PROFESSION: BEING A RELA-
TION OF THE PERSECUTIONS WHICH SHE HAS SUFFERED FROM MR.
WILLIAM SCHWENCK GILBERT. [London, 1877.] 22 p.

> A personal dispute between the actress and Gilbert. See item
> 1207.

HOLBROOK, ANN CATHERINE (Actress, 1781-1837)

2830 _____. THE DRAMATIST; OR MEMOIRS OF THE STAGE. WITH THE
LIFE OF THE AUTHORESS, PREFIXED AND INTERSPERSED WITH A
VARIETY OF ANECDOTES, HUMOUROUS AND PATHETIC. Birmingham:
Printed by Martin and Hunter, 1809. 68 p.

An interesting description of the hardships suffered by some
members of the acting profession in the early nineteenth
century; this is an enlarged edition of Holbrook's MEMOIRS
OF AN ACTRESS, published in 1807.

HOLLINGSHEAD, JOHN (Manager, 1827-1904)

2831 _____. MY LIFETIME. 2 vols. London: Sampson Low, Marston &
Co., 1895. xvi, 255; viii, 250 p.

Memoirs of the founder of the Gaiety theatre (which he
managed for nearly twenty years) and the man who first
staged Ibsen in England--although Hollingshead has disap-
pointingly little to say about this momentous occasion.

2832 Gibson, Frank A. "John Hollingshead--A Notable Victorian."
DICKENSIAN, 62 (1966), 37-46.

Mainly on Hollingshead's relationship with Dickens.

2833 Olshen, Barry N. "John Hollingshead and the Restoration Comedy of
Manners." NCTR, 2 (1974), 1-10.

Hollingshead's Gaiety versions of Vanbrugh's RELAPSE and
Congreve's LOVE FOR LOVE.

IRVING, HENRY (Actor-Manager, 1838-1905)

2834 Russell, Edward R. IRVING AS HAMLET. London: Henry S. King,
1875. 54 p.

A detailed, and laudatory, description (without illustrations)
of Irving's Lyceum performance.

2835 [Archer, William, and Robert William Lowe]. THE FASHIONABLE
TRAGEDIAN: A CRITICISM. Edinburgh and Glasgow: Thomas Gray,
1877. 24 p.

The authors claim that "it is by no means difficult to prove,
beyond the possibility of rational contradiction from any one
who is not entirely blinded by fashion, that Mr. Irving is in

fact one of the worst actors that ever trod the British stage in
so-called 'leading' characters." Archer and Lowe put the
blame firmly on the long run. There are ten unflattering cartoons of Irving [by G.R. Halkett]. A second, slightly revised,
edition of this attack on Irving was published in 1877; copies
were withdrawn following rumors of legal action.

2836 Archer, William. HENRY IRVING, ACTOR AND MANAGER: A CRITI-
CAL STUDY. 2nd ed. London: Field and Tuer, [1883]. 108 p.

A more sympathetic appreciation than that in item 2835, but
Archer regrets that Irving, unlike Macready, "confines his
efforts almost entirely to the drama of the past." Gordon
Craig (item 2785, page 67) claims that "much that the good
Archer write of Irving in this booklet is not true."

2837 Brereton, Austin. HENRY IRVING: A BIOGRAPHICAL SKETCH. London: David Bogue, 1883. xi, 136 p.

Irving's life and career up to his departure for America in
1883. Illustrated.

2838 Daly, Frederic [Frederic Louis Austin]. HENRY IRVING IN ENGLAND
AND AMERICA 1838-84. London: T. Fisher Unwin, 1884. viii, 300 p.

2839 Hatton, Joseph. HENRY IRVING'S IMPRESSIONS OF AMERICA, NAR-
RATED IN A SERIES OF SKETCHES, CHRONICLES, AND CONVERSA-
TIONS. 2 vols. London: Sampson Low, Marston, Searle & Rivington,
1884. xii, 297; viii, 272 p.

2840 Calvert, Walter. SOUVENIR OF SIR HENRY IRVING. London: Henry
J. Drane, Chant & Co., [1895]. 48 p.

This "anecdotal, biographical, and critical monograph" is
valuable mostly for its numerous illustrations, some of them
sketches, some photographs.

2841 Fitzgerald, Percy. SIR HENRY IRVING: A RECORD OF OVER TWENTY
YEARS AT THE LYCEUM. New ed. London: Chatto & Windus, 1895.
viii, 149 p.

"Having known the actor from the very commencement of his
career; having seen him in all his characters; having written
contemporaneous criticisms of these performances--I may be
thought to be at least fairly qualified for undertaking such
a task" (preface). First published in 1893.

2842 Russell, Percy. SIR HENRY IRVING. London: S. Champness, [1895].
63 p.

2843 Hiatt, Charles. HENRY IRVING: A RECORD AND REVIEW. London: George Bell and Sons, 1899. xiv, 282 p.

> A straightforward biography, superseded by later studies, but still valuable if only for its seventy-five plates. An appendix lists parts played by Irving in London, with dates of first performances.

2844 Brereton, Austin. HENRY IRVING. London: Anthony Treherne, 1905. vii, 75 p.

> Mainly a collection of articles written shortly after Irving's death. A first chapter (by Brereton) covers the actor's life up to 1870 and was revised by Irving himself shortly before his death. Illustrated.

2845 Fitzgerald, Percy. SIR HENRY IRVING: A BIOGRAPHY. Philadelphia: George W. Jacobs, [1906]. xvi, 319 p.

> A sympathetic biography with numerous plates, many of them of Irving in various roles.

2846 Hatton, Joseph. SIR HENRY IRVING; HIS ROMANTIC CAREER ON AND OFF THE STAGE. London: G. Newnes, 1906.

2847 MacFall, Haldane. SIR HENRY IRVING. Boston: John W. Luce, 1906. 128 p.

> Includes drawings of Irving by Gordon Craig and others.

2848 Stoker, Bram. PERSONAL REMINISCENCES OF HENRY IRVING. 2 vols. New York and London: Macmillan, 1906. xiii, 372; vii, 385 p.

> Stoker was Irving's close friend for nearly thirty years, as well as being his business manager. His account of his association with Irving is essential to any understanding of the actor's character and art. Numerous plates.

2849 Brereton, Austin. THE LIFE OF HENRY IRVING. 2 vols. London: Longmans, Green, and Co., 1908. xx, 381; x, 364 p.

> A very full biography by one of Irving's closest friends. There are numerous plates and line drawings, a list of part played by Irving, a bibliography, and a good index. The work is superseded to some extent by Laurence Irving's biography (item 2859), but is still worth consulting in view of Brereton's intimacy with his subject.

2850 Pollock, Walter Herries. IMPRESSIONS OF HENRY IRVING GATHERED IN PUBLIC AND PRIVATE DURING A FRIENDSHIP OF MANY YEARS.

London: Longmans, 1908; rpt. New York: Blom, 1971. vii, 140 p.

2851 Stoker, Bram. "Irving and Stage Lighting." THE NINETEENTH CEN-
TURY AND AFTER, 69 (1911), 902-12.

An interesting account of Irving's innovations at the Lyceum
(including the difficulties encountered with electric lighting).

2852 Craig, Gordon. HENRY IRVING. New York: Longmans, Green and
Co., 1930. ix, 232 p.

An assessment of Irving's achievements as an actor, manager,
and director by a devotee of Irving and a famous man of the
theatre himself. Illustrated.

2853 Jones, Henry Arthur. THE SHADOW OF HENRY IRVING. London:
Richards, 1931; rpt. New York: Blom, 1969. 111 p.

Jones did not live to complete the book. The last chapter
is in note form only. Jones's daughter explains in a brief
preface that the conclusion was to have been "a sweeping
indictment of the fact that, during his long and honourable
career, he [Irving] did practically nothing to help English
authors or to advance the cause of modern English drama."
Ellen Terry thought the completed part of the book to be
"the most penetrating and fascinating" study of Irving (preface).

2854 Walbrook, H.M. "Henry Irving." FORTNIGHTLY, n.s. 143 (1938),
203-11.

An unremarkable appreciation of the actor on the 100th
anniversary of his birth.

2855 Saintsbury, H.A., and Cecil Palmer, eds. WE SAW HIM ACT: A
SYMPOSIUM ON THE ART OF HENRY IRVING. London: Hurst &
Blackett, 1939. 424 p.

Views of some of Irving's contemporaries on his performances
in several roles between September 1871 and April 1903.
Illustrated.

2856 West, Edward Joseph. "Henry Irving, 1870-90." STUDIES IN SPEECH
AND DRAMA IN HONOR OF ALEXANDER M. DRUMMOND. Ithaca:
Cornell University Press, 1944; rpt. New York: Russell & Russell, 1968.
167-96

A critical survey of Irving's achievement in the context of
opposition from the "new realistic school of acting and production."

2857 R., S. [Sybil Rosenfeld]. "An Irving Collection." TN, 4 (1949-50), 63.

> At the Russell-Cotes Art Gallery, Bournemouth.

2858 Shuttleworth, Bertram. "Irving's Macbeth." TN, 5 (1950-51), 28-31.

> Irving's part-book for his 1875 production of MACBETH.

2859 Irving, Laurence. HENRY IRVING, THE ACTOR AND HIS WORLD. London: Faber, 1951. 734 p.

> An authoritative biography by the actor's grandson. The author makes use of much new material, including over 1,000 letters to Irving. Irving's 1891 Address to the Philosophical Institution, Edinburgh, is printed in an appendix, and another appendix gives a "complete list of parts played by Henry Irving." There are numerous interesting illustrations of Irving and his circle. Bibliography and index.

2860 Beck, Martha Ryan. "A Comparative Study of Prompt Copies of Hamlet Used by Garrick, Booth and Irving." Ph.D. Dissertation, University of Michigan, 1956. 729 p. (DA#57-2269)

> Uses the promptbook of Irving's 1878 production.

2861 Novick, Julius Lerner. "Henry Irving and 'Natural Acting.'" Ph.D. Dissertation, Yale University, 1966. 118 p.

2862 Kline, Herbert Walter. "Henry Irving and the Lyceum Theatre Company in America." Ph.D. Dissertation, University of Illinois, 1967. 215 p. (DA#68-01790)

2863 Schaffer, Byrn Smith. "The Stage Management of Henry Irving in America 1883-1904." Ph.D. Dissertation, Ohio State University, 1967. 242 p. (DA#67-16333)

2864 Willems, Virginia Alison Wright. "Henry Irving and the Meininger." Ph.D. Dissertation, University of Wisconsin, 1970. 294 p. (DA#71-02254)

2865 Rouder, Wendy Phyllis. "Henry Irving's MACBETH." Ph.D. Dissertation, University of Illinois, 1971. 190 p. (DA#72-07042)

2866 Hughes, Alan. "Henry Irving's Tragedy of Shylock." ETJ, 24 (1972), 249-64.

A careful study of the text, production and reviews of Irving's 1879 production of THE MERCHANT OF VENICE, which ran for 250 nights. An appendix prints a lighting plot for the production.

2867 _____. "Henry Irving's Finances: The Lyceum Accounts, 1878-1899." NCTR, 1 (1973), 79-87.

Figures show that, contrary to popular belief, Irving was not driven by financial need to sell the Lyceum in 1899.

IRVING, HENRY BRODRIBB (Actor-Manager, 1870-1919)

2868 Wotton, Mabel E. H.B. IRVING: AN APPRECIATION. London: Cassell, 1912. 48 p.

2869 Brereton, Austin. "H.B." AND LAURENCE IRVING. Boston: Small, Maynard and Co., 1923. 239 p.

Biography of Henry Irving's two sons.

JORDAN, DOROTHY (Actress, 1761-1816)

2870 Boaden, James. THE LIFE OF MRS. JORDAN; INCLUDING ORIGINAL PRIVATE CORRESPONDENCE, AND NUMEROUS ANECDOTES OF HER CONTEMPORARIES. 2 vols. London: Edward Bull, 1831. xv, 368; xiv, 364 p.

"Having had the pleasure of Mrs. Jordan's personal acquaintance for some years, and having paid unwearied attention to her professional exertions from their very commencement in London" (preface), Boaden claims some authority for writing this biography.

2871 Sergeant, P.W. MRS. JORDAN: CHILD OF NATURE. London: Hutchinson, 1913. viii, 356 p.

2872 Jerrold, Clare. THE STORY OF DOROTHY JORDAN. London: E. Nash, 1914. x, 429 p.

2873 Aspinall, A., ed. MRS. JORDAN AND HER FAMILY; BEING THE UNPUBLISHED CORRESPONDENCE OF MRS. JORDAN AND THE DUKE OF CLARENCE, LATER WILLIAM IV. London: Arthur Barker, 1951. xxvii, 295 p.

2874 Fothergill, Brian. MRS. JORDAN: PORTRAIT OF AN ACTRESS. London: Faber, 1965. 334 p.

> A well-researched biography; includes eight plates and a list of characters played by Mrs. Jordan 1785-1809.

KEAN, CHARLES (Actor-Manager, 1811-68)

2875 Cole, John William. THE LIFE AND THEATRICAL TIMES OF CHARLES KEAN, INCLUDING A SUMMARY OF THE ENGLISH STAGE FOR THE LAST FIFTY YEARS AND A DETAILED ACCOUNT OF THE MANAGE-MENT OF THE PRINCESS'S THEATRE, FROM 1850 TO 1859. 2 vols. London: Richard Bentley, 1859. xii, 368; viii, 398 p.

> Useful, but published nearly ten years before Kean's death.

2876 Dunkel, Wilbur B. "Kean's Portrayal of Cardinal Wolsey." TN, 6 (1951-52), 80-82.

> Charles Kean's reply to criticism of his portrayal of Wolsey in HENRY VIII at the Princess's in 1855.

2877 Hardwick, J.M.D., ed. EMIGRANT IN MOTLEY. THE JOURNEY OF CHARLES AND ELLEN KEAN IN QUEST OF A THEATRICAL FORTUNE IN AUSTRALIA AND AMERICA, AS TOLD IN THEIR HITHERTO UNPUB-LISHED LETTERS. Foreword. Anthony Quayle. London: Rockliff, 1954. xx, 260 p.

> The 1863-66 Australian and American tour.

2878 Threlkeld, Budge. "A Study of the Management of Charles Kean at the Princess's Theatre, 1850-1859." Ph.D. Dissertation, Ohio State University, 1955. 315 p. (DA#56-294)

> The author includes a daily calendar of Kean's productions and stresses his innovative practices regarding directing and scenery.

2879 Wilson, Mardis Glen, Jr. "The Box Set in Charles Kean's Productions of Shakespearean Tragedy." OSUTCB, 5 (1958), 7-26.

> At the Princess's, 1850-59. Illustrated.

2880 _____. "Charles Kean: A Study in Nineteenth Century Production of Shakespearean Tragedy." Ph.D. Dissertation, Ohio State University, 1958. 527 p.

2881 Garnham, Mary. "Letters from Charles Kean." DRAMA, n.s., no. 64 (1962), 28-32.

Letters (1855-59) to John Walter Huddleston showing, among other things, Kean's "lifelong zest for historical accuracy in his productions."

2882 Wells, Stanley. "Burlesques of Charles Kean's WINTER'S TALE." TN, 16 (1962), 78-83.

Burlesques of the famous production which opened at the Princess's on 28 April 1856 and ran for 102 performances.

2883 Byrne, Muriel St. Clare. "Charles Kean and the Meininger Myth." ThR, 6 (1964), 137-53.

The author takes issue with those theatre historians who argue or accept that the German company of Duke George of Saxe-Meiningen established "the basic principles which have governed modern productions in the realistic theatre ever since." She shows that the Duke owed a great debt in the art of mise-en-scène to Kean and, before him, Macready. This is a carefully reasoned and persuasive essay, with fifteen plates. See also items 334 and 343.

2884 Denning, Anthony. "Charles Kean and the Meininger Myth." ThR, 7 (1964), 46-47.

A note on item 2883.

2885 Wilson, M. Glen. "George Henry Lewes as Critic of Charles Kean's Acting." ETJ, 16 (1964), 360-67.

Wilson's argument is that "Lewes is a questionable authority as a critic of Charles Kean," mainly because of a personal feud between the two men. Lewes's hostility was aroused because he was suspended from the free list at the Princess's for failing to review the theatre's plays in the LEADER.

2886 Blakeley, Clyde. "A Reconstruction of the Masque Scene from Charles Kean's THE TEMPEST." OSUTCB, no. 13 (1966), 38-45.

The production of 1857. Illustrated.

2887 Wilson, M. Glen. "OSU Theatre Collection Studies on Charles Kean with Notes on a Scene from Kean's HENRY VIII." OSUTCB, no. 13 (1966), 27-37.

A description of doctoral dissertations on Kean written at Ohio State University and notes on the Folger promptbooks of HENRY VIII.

2888 _____. "Charles Kean's Production of RICHARD II." ETJ, 19 (1967),

41-51.

> The 1857 production, which enjoyed 112 performances.
> Illustrated.

2889 Edden, Valerie, ed. THE WINTER'S TALE. CHARLES KEAN, 1856.
London: Cornmarket Press, 1970. [vi], 105 p.

> A facsimile reprint of the text of Kean's 1856 production
> at the Princess's, with a preface and historical and explana-
> tory notes by Kean. There is a brief introduction by the
> editor.

2890 Rittenhouse, David. "A Victorian WINTER'S TALE." QQ, 77 (1970),
41-55.

> On Kean's 1856 production.

2891 Vander Yacht, Douglas R. "Queen Victoria's Patronage of Charles Kean,
Actor-Manager." Ph.D. Dissertation, Ohio State University, 1970.
207 p. (DA#71-07586)

2892 Wright, Martin, ed. THE TEMPEST, CHARLES KEAN, 1857. London:
Cornmarket Press, 1970. [viii], 74 p.

> Facsimile reprint of the text of Kean's 1857 production at
> the Princess's, with a preface and explanatory notes by Kean:
> "the scenic appliances of the play are of a more extensive
> and more complicated nature than have ever yet been attempted
> in any theatre in Europe; requiring the aid of above one hun-
> dred and forty operatives nightly."

> Cornmarket Press has also published in the same series facsimile
> reprints of Kean's 1855 HENRY VIII (1970), 1856 MIDSUMMER
> NIGHT'S DREAM (1970), 1857 RICHARD II (1970), 1858
> MERCHANT OF VENICE (1971), 1859 HAMLET (1971), and
> 1859 HENRY V (1971).

2893 Marker, Frederick J. "The First Night of Charles Kean's THE
TEMPEST--From the Notebook of Hans Christian Andersen." TN, 25
(1970-71), 20-23.

> Andersen's account of the 1857 production. Two plates.

2894 Wilson, M. Glen. "Charles Kean at the Princess's Theatre: A Financial Report." ETJ, 23 (1971), 51-61.

> A detailed analysis of Kean's financial affairs during his
> management of the Princess's, 1850-59.

KEAN, EDMUND (Actor, 1789?-1833)

2895 Phippen, Francis. AUTHENTIC MEMOIRS OF EDMUND KEAN, OF THE THEATRE ROYAL, DRURY LANE; CONTAINING A SPECIMEN OF HIS TALENT AS COMPOSITION. London: J. Roach, 1814. 112 p.

2896 [Procter, Bryan Waller]. THE LIFE OF EDMUND KEAN. 2 vols. London, 1835. xlvii, 216; vii, 280 p.

 A sympathetic biography which recognizes Kean the tragedian as "decidedly of the very first order."

2897 Hawkins, F.W. THE LIFE OF EDMUND KEAN, FROM PUBLISHED AND ORIGINAL SOURCES. 2 vols. London: Tinsley Bros., 1869. xxiii, 420; xiii, 430 p.

2898 Molloy, J. Fitzgerald. THE LIFE AND ADVENTURES OF EDMUND KEAN TRAGEDIAN 1787-1833. 2 vols. London: Ward and Downey, 1888. xii, 298; viii, 286 p.

 Draws on materials from John Forster's projected (but never written) life of Kean, and on Henry Irving's private collection of Keaniana.

2899 Hillebrand, Harold Newcomb. EDMUND KEAN. New York: Columbia University Press, 1933; rpt. New York: AMS Press, 1966. x, 387 p.

 A careful study, giving responsible attention to Kean's theatrical and personal life. Well illustrated and indexed, but no bibliography.

2900 Playfair, Giles. KEAN. New York: Dutton, 1939. xii, 346 p.

 Random documentation and the absence of a table of contents create inconveniences for the reader. But the study is important, for the author draws on new material from private collections (apparently unknown to Hillebrand) and makes good use of the resources of some English provincial libraries. Playfair also presents persuasive evidence about the date of Kean's birth (pages v-vii) and includes a useful genealogy.

2901 Berstl, Julius. THE SUN'S BRIGHT CHILD: THE IMAGINARY MEMOIRS OF EDMUND KEAN. London: Hammond, 1946. 192 p.

 A fictional biography. "It was my aim to delineate clearly by omissions and simplifications the significance of this kaleidoscopic life" (preface).

2902 Disher, Maurice Willson. MAD GENIUS: A BIOGRAPHY OF EDMUND KEAN WITH PARTICULAR REFERENCE TO THE WOMEN WHO MADE AND UNMADE HIM. London: Hutchinson, 1950. 196 p.

Disher claims (page 11) that "nobody has succeeded in telling the whole truth" about Kean. This fictionalized biography is interesting reading, though it is not the best way to discover the truth. The author does, however, make use of new material (e.g., the diaries of James Winston) and there are forty illustrations.

2903 Rulfs, Donald J. "The Romantic Writer and Edmund Kean." MLQ, 11 (1950), 425-37.

A summary, with ample quotation, of the reactions of Hazlitt, Keats, Hunt, Byron, Coleridge, Shelley, and Wordsworth to Kean's acting.

2904 Downer, Alan S., ed. OXBERRY'S 1822 EDITION OF KING RICHARD III WITH THE DESCRIPTIVE NOTES RECORDING EDMUND KEAN'S PERFORMANCE MADE BY JAMES H. HACKETT. London: Society for Theatre Research, 1959. xxiv, 100, vii p.

A facsimile reprint, with a useful introduction by Downer and an appendix with a bibliography and supplementary notes.

2905 Macqueen-Pope, W. EDMUND KEAN: THE STORY OF AN ACTOR. Illus. Robert Hodgson. Edinburgh: Thomas Nelson and Sons, 1960. 84 p.

Apparently intended for a popular, perhaps juvenile, audience.

2906 Carlisle, Carol J. "Edmund Kean on the Art of Acting." TN, 22 (1967-68), 119-20.

A few statements made by Kean to the American artist, John Neagle.

2907 Van Maanen, W. "Kean: From Dumas to Sartre." NEOPHILOLOGUS, 56 (1972), 221-30.

French plays based on the life of Kean.

KEELEY, ROBERT (Actor, 1796-1869) AND MARY ANN (Actress, 1806-99)

2908 Goodman, Walter. THE KEELEYS ON THE STAGE AND AT HOME. London: Richard Bentley, 1895. xiv, 357 p.

Biographies of popular performers who also managed the

Lyceum from 1844 to 1847.

KELLY, FRANCES MARIA (Actress, Singer, 1790-1882)

2909 Holman, L.E. LAMB'S "BARBARA S--." THE LIFE OF FRANCES MARIA
KELLY, ACTRESS. London: Methuen, 1935. xi, 117 p.

"It is because of Lamb's admiration for Fanny Kelly that
most interest attaches to her name. But there are two
other reasons for preserving some record of her life. She
was a versatile actress of deserved popularity, and of almost unblemished character, who performed for many years
as a leading lady at Drury Lane; and she made a valuable
contribution to the history of the theatre by establishing
the first authentic School of Dramatic Art" (preface).
Holman's biography includes eight plates and a short index.

2910 Staples, Leslie C. "Fanny Kelly." DICKENSIAN, 38 (1942), 153-58.

An outline of her life with some emphasis on her friendship
with Dickens.

2911 Francis, Basil. FANNY KELLY OF DRURY LANE. London: Theatre
Book Club, 1950. xvi, 207 p.

A more thorough biography than Holman's, with thirty-one
plates, a bibliography, and a list of Fanny Kelly's roles.

KELLY, MICHAEL (Actor, Singer, Composer, 1762-1826)

2912 [Hook, Theodore, ed.]. REMINISCENCES OF MICHAEL KELLY, OF THE
KING'S THEATRE, AND THEATRE ROYAL DRURY LANE, INCLUDING
A PERIOD OF NEARLY HALF A CENTURY; WITH ORIGINAL ANEC-
DOTES OF MANY DISTINGUISHED PERSONS, POLITICAL, LITERARY,
AND MUSICAL. 2 vols. London: Henry Colburn, 1826. xxiii, 354;
404 p.

2913 Ellis, S.M. THE LIFE OF MICHAEL KELLY, MUSICIAN, ACTOR, AND
BON VIVEUR, 1762-1826. London: Gollancz, 1930. 400 p.

A survey of theatrical and social life of the late eighteenth
and early nineteenth centuries as well as a life of Kelly.
It corrects and adds to Hook's edition of Kelly's REMINIS-
CENCES. There are many interesting plates.

KEMBLE, CHARLES (Actor-Manager, 1775-1854)

2914 Lane, R.J., ed. CHARLES KEMBLE'S SHAKESPEARE READINGS: THE
SELECTED PLAYS READ BY HIM IN PUBLIC. 2nd ed. London: George
Bell, 1879. ix, 932 p.

A short preface by the editor gives an account of Kemble's
public readings. First published 1870.

2915 Williamson, Jane. CHARLES KEMBLE: MAN OF THE THEATRE.
Lincoln: University of Nebraska Press, 1970. xii, 267 p.

A soundly researched and meticulously documented biography.
Includes a good bibliography of printed and manuscript sources.
With five plates and a useful index.

KEMBLE, FRANCES ANNE (Actress, 1809-93)

2916 Butler, Frances Anne. JOURNAL, BY FRANCES ANNE BUTLER. 2 vols.
London: John Murray, 1835; rpt. New York: Blom, 1970. vii, 313;
298 p.

Record of Kemble's life in America, 1832-34, published under
her married name.

2917 Kemble, Frances Anne. A YEAR OF CONSOLATION. 2 vols. New
York: Wiley & Putnam, 1847. 136; 171 p.

A record of "the happy year" Frances Kemble spent in Italy,
1846.

2918 _____. RECORD OF A GIRLHOOD. 3 vols. London: Richard Bentley
and Son, 1878. 299; 336; 321 p.

Frances Kemble's autobiography to 1834. The lack of an
index makes access to the information in this bulky work
difficult.

2919 _____. RECORDS OF LATER LIFE. New York: Henry Holt, 1882.
676 p.

Letters to various people, October 1834-April 1848. There
is an index.

2920 _____. FURTHER RECORDS, 1848-1883. A SERIES OF LETTERS BY
FRANCES ANNE KEMBLE. 2 vols. New York: Henry Holt, 1891; rpt.
New York: Blom, 1972. ix, 323; viii, 280 p.

2921 Wright, William Aldis, ed. LETTERS OF EDWARD FITZGERALD TO FANNY KEMBLE 1871-1883. London: Richard Bentley and Son, 1895. 269 p.

> This collection is not particularly informative on theatrical matters, but it is revealing about the long Kemble-Fitzgerald friendship.

2922 Kemble, Frances Anne. ON THE STAGE. WITH AN INTRODUCTION BY GEORGE ARLISS. Publications of the Dramatic Museum of Columbia University, Papers on Acting III. New York: Columbia University Press, 1926. 35 p.

> In his introduction Arliss offers the interesting thesis that Fanny Kemble "had a certain latent contempt for the actor as an artist." Certainly Kemble's essay shows little enthusiasm for the stage. There are some biographical notes by Brander Matthews.

2923 Bobbé, Dorothie. FANNY KEMBLE. New York: Minton, Balch & Co., 1931. ix, 351 p.

> The first full-length biography, drawing extensively on primary sources. Eight plates and a good bibliography.

2924 Driver, Leota S. FANNY KEMBLE. Chapel Hill: University of North Carolina Press, 1933; rpt. New York: Negro Universities Press, 1969. xiv, 148 p.

> A sound biography, thoroughly researched and conscientiously documented. Eight plates and a helpful index.

2925 Armstrong, Margaret. FANNY KEMBLE: A PASSIONATE VICTORIAN. New York: MacMillan, 1938. vi, 387 p.

> Lengthy, but totally lacking in documentation. In such a biography it is difficult to distinguish between fact and fiction.

2926 Oliver, Egbert S. "Melville's Goneril and Fanny Kemble." NEQ, 18 (1945), 489-500.

> Melville's caricature of Fanny Kemble as Goneril in THE CONFIDENCE-MAN.

2927 Gibbs, Henry. AFFECTIONATELY YOURS, FANNY: FANNY KEMBLE AND THE THEATRE. London: Jarrolds, [1947]. 192 p.

> The author, quite properly, attempts to see his subject "not so much as an actress without reference to time as an actress in relation to a particular period in theatrical history." But

the brief bibliography betrays limited reading in nineteenth-century theatre history, and there is no other documentation in the book.

2928 Melchiori, Barbara. "Fanny Kemble in Rome, with Some Unpublished Letters." EM, 20 (1969), 269-89.

2929 Wister, Fanny Kemble, ed. FANNY, THE AMERICAN KEMBLE. HER JOURNALS AND UNPUBLISHED LETTERS. Tallahassee: South Pass Press, 1972. xv, 227 p.

2930 Wright, Constance. FANNY KEMBLE AND THE LOVELY LAND. New York: Dodd, Mead & Co., 1972. xii, 242 p.

The "Lovely Land" is America. Thirteen plates and a good bibliography.

KEMBLE, JOHN PHILLIP (Actor-Manager, 1757-1823)

2931 AN AUTHENTIC NARRATIVE OF MR. KEMBLE'S RETIREMENT FROM THE STAGE: INCLUDING FAREWELL ADDRESS, CRITICISMS, POEMS, &C. SELECTED FROM VARIOUS PERIODICAL PUBLICATIONS; WITH AN ACCOUNT OF THE DINNER GIVEN AT THE FREEMASON'S TAVERN, JUNE 27, 1817; AN ALPHABETICAL LIST OF THE COMPANY PRESENT; SPEECHES OF LORD HOLLAND, MR. KEMBLE; MR. CAMPBELL'S ODE; TO WHICH IS PREFIXED AN ESSAY, BIOGRAPHICAL AND CRITICAL. London: John Miller, 1817. xxvii, 78 p.

The contents of this interesting rag-bag on Kemble's retirement from the stage are accurately described in the title.

2932 Williams, John Ambrose. MEMOIRS OF JOHN PHILIP KEMBLE, ESQ. WITH AN ORIGINAL CRITIQUE ON HIS PERFORMANCE. London: John Bowley Wood, 1817. 80 p.

2933 Boaden, James. MEMOIRS OF THE LIFE OF JOHN PHILIP KEMBLE, ESQ. INCLUDING A HISTORY OF THE STAGE, FROM THE TIME OF GARRICK TO THE PRESENT PERIOD. 2 vols. London: Longman, Hurst, Rees, Orme, Brown and Green, 1825. x, 477; 595 p.

2933a Child, Harold. THE SHAKESPERIAN PRODUCTIONS OF JOHN PHILIP KEMBLE. London: Oxford University Press, 1935. 22 p.

2934 Baker, Herschel. JOHN PHILIP KEMBLE: THE ACTOR IN HIS THEATRE. Cambridge, Mass.: Harvard University Press, 1942. viii, 414 p.

A valuable study, with a useful bibliography.

2935 Holmes, Martin. "Portrait of a Celebrity." TN, 11 (1957), 53-55.

A Derby porcelain statuette of Kemble as Richard III.

2936 Donohue, Joseph W. "Kemble's Production of MACBETH (1794). Some Notes on Scene Painters, Scenery, Special Effects, and Costumes." TN, 21 (1966-67), 63-74.

2937 McAleer, John J. "John Kemble--Shakespeare's First Great Producer." ShN, 17 (1967), 17.

A brief sketch of Kemble, assessing his "service to Shakespeare."

2938 Donohue, Joseph W. "Kemble and Mrs. Siddons in MACBETH: The Romantic Approach to Tragic Character." TN, 22 (1967-68), 65-86.

A synthesis of a number of late eighteenth- and early nineteenth-century performances which "epitomize ideas about tragic experience which pervade the literary criticism and philosophical enquiry of the time."

2939 Rostron, David. "John Philip Kemble's CORIOLANUS and JULIUS CAESAR: An Examination of the Prompt Copies." TN, 23 (1968-69), 26-34.

The promptbooks (in the Garrick Club) of Kemble's 1806 CORIOLANUS and 1812 JULIUS CAESAR.

2940 Brown, John Russell, ed. TWELFTH NIGHT. J.P. KEMBLE, 1811. London: Cornmarket Press, 1971. [vi], 76 p.

A facsimile reprint of Kemble's 1811 production at Covent Garden, with a brief introduction by the editor.

2941 Edden, Valerie, ed. THE WINTER'S TALE. J.P. KEMBLE, 1811. London: Cornmarket Press, 1972. [vi], 80 p.

A facsimile reprint of Kemble's 1811 production at Covent Garden, with a brief introduction by the editor. Cornmarket Press has also published in the same series Kemble's 1789 HENRY V (1971), 1789 TEMPEST (1972), 1794 MACBETH (1972), 1796 MEASURE FOR MEASURE (1970), 1800 HAMLET (1971), and 1806 CORIOLANUS (1970).

2942 Pentzell, Raymond J. "Kemble's Hamlet Costume." ThS, 13 (1972), 81-85.

An engraving in the Harvard Theatre Collection.

KENDAL, MRS. MADGE (Actress, 1849-1935)

2943 _____. DRAMATIC OPINIONS. Boston: Little, Brown, 1890. xiv, 180 p.

>   There are a good many opinions in here, but the book is mainly autobiographical.

2944 Pemberton, T. Edgar. THE KENDALS: A BIOGRAPHY. London: C. Arthur Pearson, 1900. x, 340 p.

>   Mrs. Kendal requested Pemberton to "ignore me as much as you possibly can," but inevitably, and rightly, this biography is as much about Madge Kendal as it is about her husband.

2945 Kendal, Mrs. [Madge]. DAME MADGE KENDAL. BY HERSELF. London: John Murray, 1933. x, 214 p.

>   Rambling reminiscences with several plates and a good index.

2946 West, Edward Joseph. "Actress Between Two Schools: The Case of Madge Kendal." SM, 11 (1944), 105-14.

>   A critical survey of Madge Kendal's career. West sees her as an actress who betrayed the "old school" that displayed "magnificence of voice and gesture and carriage" for the "new school" of "scenic and mimetic realism, superficial and minuteness of playing."

2947 Barker, Kathleen. "Madge Robertson--Product of a Famous Training School." NCTR, 2 (1974), 11-21.

>   Discusses Madge Robertson's career with the Bristol and Bath Stock Company in the late 1850's and early 1860's.

KENDAL, WILLIAM HUNTER (Actor-Manager, 1843-1917)

See item 2944.

KINGSTON, GERTRUDE (Actress-Manager, 1866-1937)

2948 _____. CURTSEY WHILE YOU'RE THINKING. London: Williams & Norgate, 1937. 307 p.

LANGTRY, LILLIE (Actress-Manager, 1853-1929)

2949 _____. THE DAYS I KNEW. Foreword. Richard Le Gallienne. London: Hutchinson, 1925. 319 p.

LEE, HENRY (Actor-Manager, 1766-1836)

2950 _____. MEMOIRS OF A MANAGER; OR, LIFE'S STAGE WITH NEW SCENERY. 2 vols. Taunton, Eng.: W. Bragg, 1830. viii, 183; iv, 178 p.

> A rambling account of the career of a provincial actor-manager, mainly in the south of England.

LENO, DAN [GEORGE GALVIN] (Music hall performer, 1860-1904)

2951 Wood, Jay Hickory. DAN LENO: HIS BOOK. London: Methuen, 1905. xiv, 285 p.

> Extensively illustrated reminiscences of the famous music hall and pantomime performer.

LESLIE, FRED [FREDERICK HOPSON] (Actor, Singer, 1855-92)

2952 Vincent, W.T. RECOLLECTIONS OF FRED LESLIE. Intro. Clement Scott. 2 vols. London: Kegan Paul, Trench, Truebner & Co., 1894. xviii, 259; 272 p.

LLOYD, MARIE [MATILDA WOOD] (Music hall performer, 1870-1922)

2953 Jacob, Naomi. OUR MARIE. London: Hutchinson, 1936. 287 p.

2954 Farson, Daniel. MARIE LLOYD AND MUSIC HALL. London: Tom Stacey, 1972. 176 p.

MACREADY, WILLIAM CHARLES (Actor-Manager, 1793-1873)

2955 Littleton, R.H. BIOGRAPHY OF WILLIAM C. MACREADY, TRAGEDIAN. London: Vickers, [1851?]. 24 p.

2956 Pollock, Frederick, ed. MACREADY'S REMINISCENCES AND SELECTIONS FROM HIS DIARIES AND LETTERS. 2 vols. London: MacMillan, 1875. xii, 476; x, 486 p.

Contains autobiography to 1826; extracts from the diaries, 1827-51; letters to Sir Frederick and Lady Pollock, 1852-67. Toynbee's edition of the diaries (item 2960) is more complete and authoritative for the years 1833-51.

2957 Pollock, Lady. MACREADY AS I KNEW HIM. London: Remington & Co., 1885. [viii], 141 p.

Personal reminiscences by a close friend, especially in later years.

2958 Archer, William. WILLIAM CHARLES MACREADY. London: Kegan Paul, Trench, Truebner & Co., 1890. vii, 224 p.

A careful study, with extensive reference to playbills and newspapers. Archer provides a list, with casts, of productions at Covent Garden and Drury Lane under Macready's management.

2959 Price, W.T. A LIFE OF WILLIAM CHARLES MACREADY. New York: Brentano's, 1894. vi, 201 p.

2960 Toynbee, William, ed. THE DIARIES OF WILLIAM CHARLES MACREADY. 2 vols. London: Chapman and Hall, 1912. xvi, 512; vi, 543 p.

"[M]ost often seen as the querulous chafing of an oversensitive egoist, but actually a precise account of an artist's development, from which can be derived a clear idea of his proposed goal and guiding principles" (Downer, EMINENT TRAGEDIAN, p. vi [item 2972]). Numerous portraits of Macready's acquaintances are included. This is an important source for early Victorian theatre history, but there is a less-than-adequate index.

2961 Downer, Alan. "The Making of a Great Actor--William Charles Macready." TA, 7 (1948-49), 59-83.

A critical survey of Macready's career, more fully developed in Downer's monograph on the actor (item 2972).

2962 Barker, Kathleen, and Joseph MacLeod. "The Macready Prompt Books at Bristol." TN, 4 (1949-50), 76-81.

Twenty-seven promptbooks at the Theatre Royal.

2963 Trewin, J.C. MR. MACREADY: A NINETEENTH-CENTURY TRAGEDIAN AND HIS THEATRE. London: Harrap, 1955. 267 p.

A solid biography with several plates, bibliography and good index.

2964 Reed, Joseph W. "Browning and Macready: The Final Quarrel."
PMLA, 75 (1960), 597-603.

> An account of disagreements about the text of A BLOT IN
> THE 'SCUTCHEON, including details of Macready's revisions.

2965 Shattuck, Charles H. "Macready's Comus: A Prompt-Book Study."
JEGP, 60 (1961), 731-48.

> The Drury Lane 1843 production.

2966 _____. "Macready Prompt-Books." TN, (1961), 7-10.

> Ten promptbooks in the Folger Shakespeare Library.

2967 Bassett, Abraham Joseph. "The Actor-Manager Career of William Charles
Macready." Ph.D. Dissertation, Ohio State University, 1962. 514 p.
(DA#63-04638)

2968 Shattuck, Charles H., ed. MR. MACREADY PRODUCES "AS YOU LIKE
IT": A PROMPT-BOOK STUDY. Urban, Ill.: Beta Phi Mu, 1962.
Unpaged.

> A facsimile reprint of Macready's promptbook for his 1842
> production of AS YOU LIKE IT, with an introduction and
> commentary by Shattuck: "Macready's aims were to reduce
> the bulk of the text to practical dimensions for performance
> . . . to expurgate such parts as would offend his extremely
> decorous audience . . . to restore the order of the scenes
> and to get rid of flagrant corruptions which the theatrical
> profession had foisted upon the play during the preceding
> century."

2969 _____. WILLIAM CHARLES MACREADY'S "KING JOHN." Urbana:
University of Illinois Press, 1962. [vi], 75 p.

> A facsimile reprint of Macready's promptbook for the 1842
> revival of KING JOHN. The editor's aim, an important
> one and ably carried out, is "to reconstruct a living event
> within the covers of a book--so that we can know again,
> almost exactly, what was said and done, heard and seen,
> upon that long-forgotten stage." There are thirty-four very
> helpful illustrations.

2970 Bassett, Abraham J. "Macready's CORIOLANUS; An Early Contribution
to Modern Theatre." OSUTCB, no. 13 (1966), 14-26.

> The 1838 production at Covent Garden. Illustrated.

2971 Collins, Philip. "W.C. Macready and Dickens: Some Family Recollections." DICKENS STUDIES, 2 (1966), 51-56.

Recollections by Macready's grand-daughter of passages in Macready's diaries (the manuscript of which she helped Macready's son destroy) about Dickens.

2972 Downer, Alan S. THE EMINENT TRAGEDIAN: WILLIAM CHARLES MACREADY. Cambridge, Mass.: Harvard University Press, 1966. xvi, 392 p.

A probably definitive account of Macready's career, in which Downer shows Macready to have been "the founder of modern theatre practice." This is a thorough and scholarly work covering Macready's career as an actor, manager, and director. There are fourteen plates and several line drawings, a full index, but no bibliography.

2973 Trewin, J.C., ed. THE JOURNAL OF WILLIAM CHARLES MACREADY 1832-1851. London: Longmans, 1967. xxxiv, 315 p.

Pollock's edition (item 2956) was emasculated for fear of offending living persons; Toynbee's (item 2960) was more inclusive, but still incomplete; in 1914 the manuscript of the diary was destroyed by Macready's son. Trewin has abridged both Pollock and Toynbee and "tried to establish the places and circumstances in which Macready wrote." Trewin also makes use of sixty-four manuscript pages which survived the 1914 destruction and prints extracts from them for the first time. This is a sensible and useful abridgement, well-illustrated and competently indexed.

2974 Murray, Christopher. "Macready, Helen Faucit, and Acting Style." TN, 23 (1968-69), 21-25.

Discusses the principles of acting on which Macready based his training of Helen Faucit: "The fact that Helen Faucit, and all Macready's protegees, triumphed over mediocrity and won greatness, proves the success of Macready as a teacher . . . ."

MANLY, T.H. WILSON (Actor-Manager, fl. 1825)

2975 Rosenfeld, Sybil. "The Theatrical Notebooks of T.H. Wilson Manly." TN, 7 (1952-53), 2-12, 43-45.

A detailed and informative account of a provincial circuit manager's affairs in the 1820's.

MARTIN-HARVEY, SIR JOHN (Actor-Manager, 1863-1944)

2976 Edgar, George. MARTIN HARVEY: SOME PAGES OF HIS LIFE. London: G. Richards, 1912. 339 p.

2977 Martin-Harvey, Sir John. THE BOOK OF MARTIN HARVEY. Ed. R.N. G.-A. London: Henry Walker, [1930]. xvi, 176 p.

A collection of papers and addresses by Martin-Harvey.

2978 _____. THE AUTOBIOGRAPHY OF SIR JOHN MARTIN-HARVEY. London: Low, Marston, 1933. xix, 563 p.

2979 Disher, Maurice Willson. THE LAST ROMANTIC: THE AUTHORISED BIOGRAPHY OF SIR JOHN MARTIN-HARVEY. Foreword. D.L. Murray. London: Hutchinson, [1948?]. 270 p.

MATHEWS, CHARLES (Actor, 1776-1835)

2980 Arnold, S.J. FORGOTTEN FACTS IN THE MEMOIRS OF CHARLES MATHEWS, COMEDIAN, RECALLED IN A LETTER TO MRS. MATHEWS, HIS BIOGRAPHER. London: Ridgway, [1839]. 52 p.

A reply to certain criticisms of Arnold made by Mrs. Mathews in item 2981.

2981 Mathews, Mrs. [Anne Jackson]. MEMOIRS OF CHARLES MATHEWS. 2nd ed. 4 vols. London: Richard Bentley, 1839.

Autobiography for Mathews' early career; thereafter continued by his wife. Appendices include the evidence Mathews presented to the 1832 Select Committee on Dramatic Literature, and a list of characters he played, totalling 665 (but no theatres or dates are given). See also Mrs. Mathews' ANECDOTES OF ACTORS, 1844, a supplementary volume to the MEMOIRS.

2982 Hartnoll, Phyllis. "A Note on Some Letters of the Elder Mathews." TN, 1 (1945-47), 22.

220 letters to his second wife.

MATHEWS, CHARLES JAMES (Actor-Manager, 1803-78)

2983 Dickens, Charles [Jr.], ed. THE LIFE OF CHARLES JAMES MATHEWS. 2 vols. London: Macmillan, 1879. xii, 324; xii, 336 p.

"With but very few exceptions every letter or paper included or quoted in these volumes was found in the box marked 'Materials for the book [autobiography],' which was entrusted to my care by CHARLES MATHEWS' family after his death" (preface). Two appendices give miscellaneous speeches and addresses by Mathews, a list of plays produced under Mathews' management at Covent Garden and the Lyceum, and a list of plays in which Mathews acted (neither list is complete).

2984 Butler, James H. "The Ill-Fated American Theatrical Tour of James Mathews and His Wife, Madame Vestris." ThR, 8, no. 1 (1966), 23-36.

The 1838 tour, with a calendar of performances.

2985 Haugen, Clair Oliver. "Covent Garden and the Lyceum Theatre Under the Charles J. Mathewses." Ph.D. Dissertation, University of Wisconsin, 1968. 310 p. (DA#68-09080)

2986 Klepac, Richard Lee. "'At Home With Charles Mathews': A Comedian and His Theatre." Ph.D. Dissertation, University of Missouri, 1970. 237 p. (DA#71-03550)

MAUDE, CYRIL (Actor-Manager, 1862-1951)

2987 _____. THE HAYMARKET THEATRE: SOME RECORDS AND REMINIS-CENCES. London: G. Richards, 1903. vii, 239 p.

Maude managed the Haymarket in the 1890's.

2988 _____. BEHIND THE SCENES WITH CYRIL MAUDE. London: John Murray, 1927. xii, 331 p.

MELLON, HARRIOT (Actress, 1777-1837)

2989 Baron-Wilson, Mrs. Cornwell. MEMOIRS OF HARRIOT, DUCHESS OF ST. ALBANS. 2 vols. London: H. Colburn, 1839. xvi, 362; vii, 354 p.

2990 Pearce, Charles E. THE JOLLY DUCHESS: HARRIOT MELLON, AFTER-WARDS MRS. COUTTS, AND THE DUCHESS OF ST. ALBANS. London: Stanley Paul, 1915. xx, 332 p.

MOORE, MARY (Actress-Manager, 1862-1931)

2991 _____. CHARLES WYNDHAM AND MARY MOORE. Edinburgh: Printed for Private Circulation, 1925. xi, 288 p.

> Wyndham was Mary Moore's second husband; her first was the playwright, James Albery.

MORTON, CHARLES (Music hall manager, 1819-1904)

2992 Morton, William, and H.C. Newton. SIXTY YEARS OF STAGE SERVICE, BEING A RECORD OF THE LIFE OF CHARLES MORTON, "THE FATHER OF THE HALLS." London: Gale & Polden, 1905. viii, 208 p.

MUNDEN, JOSEPH SHEPHERD (Actor, 1758-1832)

2993 [Munden, Thomas Shepherd]. MEMOIRS OF JOSEPH SHEPHERD MUNDEN, COMEDIAN. BY HIS SON. London: Richard Bentley, 1846. 330 p.

MURRAY, ALMA (Actress, 1854-1945)

2994 Mosely, B.L. MISS ALMA MURRAY AS BEATRICE CENCI. A PAPER . . . READ AND DISCUSSED BEFORE THE SHELLEY SOCIETY ON THE 9TH OF MARCH, 1887. London: Reeves and Turner, 1887. 24 p.

NEILSON, LILIAN ADELAIDE [ELIZABETH ANN BROWN] (Actress, 1846-80)

2995 De Leine, M.A. LILIAN ADELAIDE NEILSON. A MEMORIAL SKETCH, PERSONAL AND CRITICAL. London: Newman and Co., 1881. 64 p.

2996 Holloway, Laura C. ADELAIDE NEILSON: A SOUVENIR. New York and London: Funk & Wagnalls, 1885. 58 p.

> With eight photographs of the actress.

NEVILLE, HENRY (Actor-Manager, 1837-1910)

> See item 2679.

O'NEILL, ELIZA (Actress, 1791-1872)

2997 Jones, Charles Inigo. MEMOIRS OF MISS O'NEILL; CONTAINING HER PUBLIC CHARACTER, PRIVATE LIFE, AND DRAMATIC PROGRESS, FROM HER ENTRANCE UPON THE STAGE; WITH A FULL CRITICISM OF HER DIFFERENT CHARACTERS, APPROPRIATE SELECTIONS FROM THEM, AND SOME ACCOUNT OF THE PLAYS SHE HAS PREFERRED FOR HER REPRESENTATIONS. London: D. Cox, 1816. iv, 100 p.

PATERSON, PETER [JAMES GLASS BERTRAM] (Actor, 1824-92)

2998 _____. GLIMPSES OF REAL LIFE AS SEEN IN THE THEATRICAL WORLD AND IN BOHEMIA: BEING THE CONFESSIONS OF PETER PATERSON, A STROLLING COMEDIAN. Edinburgh: William P. Nimmo, 1864. xii, 352 p.

> Mainly a story of hard work and bad pay, this autobiography ends with the firm advice to "would-be dramatic heroes" of "DON'T GO UPON THE STAGE." The book contains interesting accounts of the less glamorous sides of theatrical life, including, for example, booth theatricals.

PAXTON, SYDNEY [SAMUEL PAXTON HOOD] (Actor, 1860-1930)

2999 _____. STAGE SEE-SAWS; OR, THE UPS AND DOWNS OF AN ACTOR'S LIFE. BEING SOME OF THE EXPERIENCES OF SYDNEY PAXTON. London: Mills & Boon, 1917. viii, 243 p.

PENLEY, WILLIAM SYDNEY (Actor-Manager, 1852-1912)

3000 _____. PENLEY ON HIMSELF. THE CONFESSIONS OF A CONSCIENTIOUS ARTIST. Bristol, Eng.: J.W. Arrowsmith, 1896. 196 p.

PHELPS, SAMUEL (Actor-Manager, 1804-78)

3001 Coleman, John, and Edward Coleman. MEMOIRS OF SAMUEL PHELPS. London: Remington & Co., 1886. 331 p.

3002 Phelps, W. May, and John Forbes-Robertson. THE LIFE AND LIFE-WORK OF SAMUEL PHELPS. London: Sampson Low, Marston, Searle, & Rivington, 1886. xi, 436 p.

> A substantial biography in which many playbills of Phelps's performances and productions are reprinted, as are many of

his letters. There are some illustrations and a good index.

3003 West, Edward Joseph. "The Victorian Voice on the Stage: Samuel
Phelps, 'A Faultless Elocutionist.'" QJS, 31 (1945), 29–34.

A description of Phelps's "quiet and restrained technique,"
in contrast to the "mutterers of modern comedy and intrigue-
drama" and the "violent interpretations of Irving and his
imitators."

3004 Allen, Shirley S. "Samuel Phelps, Last of a Dynasty." TA, (1946),
55–70.

A discussion of Phelps as "the last of the old school" of
actors in the tradition of Betterton, Kemble, Kean, and
Macready.

3005 _____. "Samuel Phelps and His Management of Sadler's Wells Theatre."
Ph.D. Dissertation, Bryn Mawr College, 1949. 208 p.

3006 Staples, Leslie C. "The Ghost of a French Hamlet." DICKENSIAN,
52 (1956), 71–76.

Discusses a quarrel between Phelps and Fechter during Fechter's
management of the Lyceum in 1863. Phelps was asked what
part he would play in HAMLET; he replied, "Hamlet. Do
you think I'll play the Ghost to a blasted Frenchman?"

3007 Weiner, Albert B. "Samuel Phelps' Staging of MACBETH." ETJ, 16
(1964), 122–33.

At Sadler's Wells, 27 May 1844, and five times revived; a
study of four extant promptbooks and contemporary reviews.

3008 Bangham, Paul Jerald. "Samuel Phelps's Production of RICHARD III:
An Annotated Prompt Book." Ph.D. Dissertation, Ohio State University,
1965. 214 p. (DA#66-01754)

3009 Pugliese, Rudolph E. "The Beginning of Modern Directorial Principles."
OSUTCB, no. 13 (1966), 46–53.

A comparison of some of Phelps's promptbooks with some of
those of J.P. Kemble, Macready, and Charles Kean.

3010 Foulkes, Richard. "Samuel Phelps's A MIDSUMMER NIGHT'S DREAM,
Sadler's Wells--October 8th, 1853." TN, 23 (1968-69), 55–60.

3011 Allen, Shirley S. SAMUEL PHELPS AND SADLER'S WELLS THEATRE.

Middletown, Conn.: Wesleyan University Press, 1971. xvi, 354 p.

A substantial biography, well-researched and well-documented. There are nineteen plates, a useful select bibliography, and two appendices which record the plays produced at Sadler's Wells 1844-62 with the number of times each was performed.

3012 Engle, Ronald G., and Daniel J. Watermeier. "Phelps and His German Critics." ETJ, 24 (1972), 237-47.

Reviews from German newspapers of Phelps's productions in Berlin, Leipzig, and Hamburg, 1859.

POEL, WILLIAM (Actor-Manager, 1852-1934)

3013 WILLIAM POEL AND HIS STAGE PRODUCTIONS, 1880-1932. London: 1932.

A list of productions, with a portrait.

3014 NOTES ON SOME OF WILLIAM POEL'S STAGE PRODUCTIONS. London: A.W. Patching, 1933.

3015 Sprague, Arthur Colby. "Shakespeare and William Poel." UTQ, 17 (1947-48), 29-37.

A review of Poel's productions.

3016 Speaight, Robert. WILLIAM POEL AND THE ELIZABETHAN REVIVAL. London: Heinemann, for the Society for Theatre Research, 1954. 302 p.

An authoritative study of Poel's career. Three appendices (compiled by Allan Gomme) give a chronological list of Poel's stage activities 1878-1934, a bibliography of articles on Poel and a bibliography of Poel's own writings.

3017 Schear, Bernice Elaine Larson. "The Contribution of William Poel to the Presentation of Verse Drama." Ph.D. Dissertation, University of Kansas, 1961. 349 p. (DA#61-5060)

3018 Glick, Claris. "William Poel: His Theories and Influence." SQ, 15 (1964), 15-25.

Poel's revivals of Elizabethan drama, 1881-1934.

3019 Michaeloff, Gonnie. "William Poel: His Theatre Work and Lectures in the United States in 1916." Ph.D. Dissertation, Louisiana State University, 1967. 191 p. (DA#67-14002)

3020 Schultz, Stephen Charles. "The Contribution of William Poel to the Modern Theory of Shakespearean Acting." Ph.D. Dissertation, University of Iowa, 1972. 354 p. (DA#73-683)

REEVE, JOHN (Actor, 1799-1838)

3021 Banister, Douglas. LIFE OF MR. JOHN REEVE, WITH ORIGINAL ANEC-DOTES, AND PORTRAIT BY WAGEMAN. London: Richardson and Son, [1838]. 16 p.

ROBERTS, ARTHUR (Actor, Music hall performer, 1852-1933)

3022 _____. THE ADVENTURES OF ARTHUR ROBERTS BY RAIL, ROAD AND RIVER. TOLD BY HIMSELF AND CHRONICLED BY R. MORTON. Bristol, Eng.: J.W. Arrowsmith, 1895. 198 p.

3023 _____. FIFTY YEARS OF SPOOF. London: John Lane, 1927. 255 p.

A volume of reminiscences, with illustrations.

ROBERTSON, AGNES KELLY [MRS. DION BOUCICAULT] (Actress, 1833-1916)

See item 2687.

ROBERTSON, MADGE

See Kendal, Madge.

ROBSON, FREDERICK [THOMAS ROBSON BROWNBILL] (Actor, 1821-64)

3024 Sala, George Augustus. ROBSON: A SKETCH. London: John Camden Hotten, 1864. 64 p.

3025 Mackie, Craven. "Frederick Robson and the Evolution of Realistic Acting." ETJ, 23 (1971), 160-70.

An outline of Robson's career, citing several contemporary critics.

RYLEY, SAMUEL WILLIAM (Actor, 1759-1837)

3026 _____. THE ITINERANT; OR MEMOIRS OF AN ACTOR. 9 vols.
London: Taylor and Hessey (vol. 1); Sherwood, Neely, and Jones (vols.
2-9), 1808-27.

> Colorful, if lengthy, memoirs; they are useful, as many such
> memoirs are, for showing the trials and tribulations of a pro-
> vincial actor's life.

SIDDONS, SARAH (Actress, 1755-1831)

3027 [Ballantyne, James]. CHARACTERS BY MRS. SIDDONS. [Edinburgh:
1812.] 42 p.

> Criticisms of Mrs. Siddons's performances, 1805-12, all but
> one reprinted from the EDINBURGH COURANT.

3028 Boaden, James. MEMOIRS OF MRS. SIDDONS. INTERSPERSED WITH
ANECDOTES OF AUTHORS AND ACTORS. 2 vols. London: Henry
Colburn, 1827. xxvii, 382; xii, 394 p.

> J.M. Kemble, Mrs. Siddons's nephew, asked whether it was
> not "abominable that such a fellow should perfectly unautho-
> rised sit down, to scribble on a subject of all others the most
> ticklish, when in addition to the drawback of knowing nothing
> whatever of his hero, he adds that of knowing very little
> more of his own language" (Parsons, THE INCOMPARABLE
> SIDDONS, page viii [item 3032]). The book nonetheless went
> through several editions and contains much useful information
> on Mrs. Siddons.

3029 Campbell, Thomas. LIFE OF MRS. SIDDONS. London: Edward Moxon,
1839; rpt. New York: Blom, 1972. xii, 378 p.

> First published 1834. The "official" biography. Mrs. Siddons
> left her memoranda, letters, and diary to Campbell for the
> biography. "How, with the ample material at his command,
> Campbell wrote so bad a life, it is difficult to conceive"
> (Kennard, MRS. SIDDONS, page v [item 3031]). Kennard's
> own book is not an obvious improvement, however.

3030 Fitzgerald, Percy. THE KEMBLES. AN ACCOUNT OF THE KEMBLE
FAMILY, INCLUDING THE LIVES OF MRS. SIDDONS, AND HER
BROTHER JOHN PHILIP KEMBLE. 2 vols. London: Tinsley Bros.,
[1871]. xxiv, 353; vi, 414 p.

> Fitzgerald has an interesting preface on the inadequacies of
> previous biographies; his own is certainly more thorough and

more readable.

3031 Kennard, Mrs. A. MRS. SIDDONS. London: W.H. Allen, 1887.
viii, 268 p.

Draws generously on Mrs. Siddons's letters. There are no
illustrations, no bibliography, no index.

3032 Parsons, Mrs. Clement. THE INCOMPARABLE SIDDONS. London:
Methuen, 1909. xx, 298 p.

More thorough and reliable than any previous biography, but
it has its shortcomings. For example: "To me, the majority
of old playbills seem dead leaves on the Tree of Useless
Knowledge, and, therefore, I have not weighted my book
with the thousand obtainable details of first night dates of
forgotten tragedies, the number of nights each ran, the number of Mrs. Siddons's appearances season by season, etc."
Theatre history has, fortunately, progressed beyond this kind
of indifference to detail. There are twenty plates and a
short bibliography.

3033 Jenkin, H.C. Fleeming. MRS. SIDDONS AS LADY MACBETH AND
AS QUEEN KATHARINE. WITH AN INTRODUCTION BY BRANDER
MATTHEWS. New York: Dramatic Museum of Columbia University,
1915. 113 p.

3034 Eaton, Walter Prichard. "Professor is Thrilled." THEATRE ARTS
MONTHLY, 10 (1926), 473-78.

A Scottish professor's notes on Mrs. Siddons's Lady Macbeth
at Covent Garden in 1809.

3035 Royde-Smith, Naomi. THE PRIVATE LIFE OF MRS. SIDDONS: A
PSYCHOLOGICAL INVESTIGATION. London: Gollancz, 1933. 319 p.

Of little value to the serious student of theatre history.

3036 Lennep, William Van, ed. THE REMINISCENCES OF SARAH KEMBLE
SIDDONS, 1773-1785. Cambridge, Mass.: Printed at the Widener
Library, 1942. x, 33 p.

From the Harvard Theatre Collection manuscript; a limited
edition of 237 copies.

3037 Ffrench, Yvonne. MRS. SIDDONS: TRAGIC ACTRESS. London: Derek
Verschoyle, 1954. xvi, 256 p.

A revised edition of the study first published in 1936. It is
a straightforward, sparsely documented biography largely

superseded by Manvell's study (item 3040).

3038 Clark, William Smith. "'The Siddons' in Dublin." TN, 9 (1954-55), 103-11.

Includes an account of Sarah Siddons's 1802 visit to Dublin.

3039 Haycraft, Molly Costain. FIRST LADY OF THE THEATRE: SARAH SIDDONS. New York: Julian Messner, 1958. 192 p.

Fictionalized biography.

3040 Manvell, Roger. SARAH SIDDONS: PORTRAIT OF AN ACTRESS. New York: G.P. Putnam's Sons, 1971. xii, 385 p.

A thorough, well-documented, well-illustrated biography. There are eight interesting appendices, a select bibliography, an index of plays and parts in which Mrs. Siddons appeared, and a good general index.

3041 Jonson, Marian. A TROUBLED GRANDEUR: THE STORY OF FN-GLAND'S GREAT ACTRESS, SARAH SIDDONS. Boston: Little, Brown, 1972. xiii, 238 p.

3042 McMahon, P.M. "The Tragical Art of Sarah Siddons: An Analysis of Her Acting Style." Ph.D. Dissertation, Yale University, 1972. 319 p. (DA#72-31448)

SOLDENE, EMILY (Music hall performer, 1840-1912)

3043 _____. MY THEATRICAL AND MUSICAL RECOLLECTIONS. London: Downey & Co., 1897. xviii, 315 p.

SOTHERN, EDWARD ASKEW (Actor, 1826-81)

3044 Pemberton, T. Edgar. A MEMOIR OF EDWARD ASKEW SOTHERN. London: Richard Bentley and Son, 1889. iv, 314 p.

Memoirs of a comedian popular on both sides of the Atlantic. Illustrated.

STIRLING, FANNY [MARY ANNE KEHL] (Actress, 1815-95)

3045 Allen, Percy. THE STAGE LIFE OF MRS. STIRLING, WITH SOME SKETCHES OF THE 19TH CENTURY THEATRE. Intro. Sir Frank R. Benson. London: T.F. Unwin, 1922. 244 p.

> An appendix lists some of the principal parts played by Mrs.
> Stirling, with dates of her first appearance in each part.

SULLIVAN, BARRY (Actor, 1821-91)

3046 Lawrence, W.J. BARRY SULLIVAN: A BIOGRAPHICAL SKETCH. London: W. & G. Baird, 1893. 98 p.

3047 Sillard, Robert M. BARRY SULLIVAN AND HIS CONTEMPORARIES. A HISTRIONIC RECORD. 2 vols. London: T. Fisher Unwin, 1901. xii, 275; viii, 257 p.

> A detailed account of a much-travelled actor's life (Ireland,
> Scotland, English provinces, America, Australia). It includes
> a list of characters played by Sullivan, but without theatres
> or dates. No index; few illustrations.

TEMPEST, MARIE (Actress, 1864-1912)

3048 Bolitho, Hector. MARIE TEMPEST: HER BIOGRAPHY. Philadelphia: J.B. Lippincott, 1937. 320 p.

> There is a record of the actress's appearances and a good
> index.

TERNAN, T.L. (Actor, 1799-1846)

3049 Morley, Malcolm. "The Theatrical Ternans." DICKENSIAN, 54 (1958), 38-43, 95-106, 155-63; 55 (1959), 36-44, 109-17, 159-68; 56 (1960), 41-46, 76-83, 153-57; 57 (1961), 29-35.

> An extensive account of the professional and private lives
> of T.L. Ternan, the actor, and his family, in London, the
> provinces, and abroad.

TERRISS, ELLALINE (Actress, 1871-1971)

3050 _____. ELLALINE TERRISS, BY HERSELF AND WITH OTHERS. London: Cassell, 1928. 299 p.

> A volume of reminiscences.

3051 _____. JUST A LITTLE BIT OF STRING. London: Hutchinson, 1955.

296 p.

> Autobiography. Illustrated.

TERRISS, WILLIAM [WILLIAM CHARLES JAMES LEWIN] (Actor, 1847-97)

3052 Smythe, Arthur J. THE LIFE OF WILLIAM TERRISS, ACTOR. Intro.
Clement Scott. Westminster: Constable, 1898. xxviii, 212 p.

> A well-illustrated biography of the popular Adelphi actor,
> father of Ellaline Terriss.

TERRY, EDWARD O'CONNOR (Actor-Manager, 1844-1912)

See item 2679.

TERRY, DAME ELLEN ALICE (Actress, 1847-1928)

3053 Hiatt, Charles. ELLEN TERRY AND HER IMPERSONATIONS. London:
George Bell and Sons, 1898; rpt. New York: Blom, 1972. x, 274 p.

> Written before the completion of Ellen Terry's career and
> hence limited in its judgments. There are several plates
> of the actress in various roles.

3054 Scott, Clement. ELLEN TERRY. 2nd ed. New York: Frederick A.
Stokes, 1900. vi, 150 p.

> Adulation, not criticism. Numerous plates. First published
> 1900.

3055 Pemberton, T. Edgar. ELLEN TERRY AND HER SISTERS. London: C.
Arthur Pearson, 1902. [viii], 314 p.

> Deals (briefly) with the stage career of Kate, Marion, and
> Florence Terry as well as extolling Ellen Terry's career.
> Twenty plates.

3056 St. John, Christopher. ELLEN TERRY. London: John Lane, 1907.
viii, 97 p.

3057 Terry, Ellen. THE STORY OF MY LIFE. London: Hutchinson, 1908.
viii, 381 p.

> Interesting not only for the insights it gives into Ellen Terry's
> career, but also for the light it throws on other theatre per-

sonalities of the time, especially Henry Irving. Numerous plates.

3058 Craig, Edward Gordon. ELLEN TERRY AND HER SECRET SELF. TO-GETHER WITH A PLEA FOR G.B.S. New York: Dutton, 1932. xiv, 205, 29 p.

Written, says Craig, because Shaw detracted from Ellen Terry's fame by permitting, "through his blind vanity and jealousy," the publication of the Ellen Terry-Shaw correspondence and by writing a preface to the letters "in which he descends here and there not to salute, but to insult the dead" (see item 3061). The appended "Plea for G.B.S." further attacks Shaw for allowing publication of the correspondence and says his motive was to link their names "as twin stars in the dramatic firmament, and thus put Irving's shapely nose out of joint." Edith Craig claims that the latter part of her brother's biography is "inadequate, and at times inaccurate" (ELLEN TERRY'S MEMOIRS, page x [item 3059]), but Craig claims in his preface that his sister "never knew" Ellen Terry (who was, of course, their mother).

3059 Terry, Ellen. ELLEN TERRY'S MEMOIRS. New York: G.P. Putnam's Sons, 1932. xvi, 367 p.

An extended version of Terry's THE STORY OF MY LIFE (item 3057). Preface, notes, and additional biographical chapters are by Edith Craig and Christopher St. John. The additional chapters cover the period 1906-28.

3060 West, Edward Joseph. "Ellen Terry--Histrionic Enigma." COLORADO-WYOMING JOURNAL OF LETTERS (April 1940), 39-62.

A survey of Ellen Terry's career arguing that her greatness was based on "the sound training of the old school."

3061 St. John, Christopher, ed. ELLEN TERRY AND BERNARD SHAW: A CORRESPONDENCE. London: Reinhardt & Evans, 1949. xxxviii, 434 p.

This edition includes Shaw's preface to the original edition of 1931 and explanatory notes by the editor.

3062 Steen, Marguerite. A PRIDE OF TERRYS: FAMILY SAGA. London: Longmans, 1962. xvi, 412 p.

The story of many Terrys--not all of them of the theatre--but the central character is Ellen Terry. Numerous plates.

3063 Manvell, Roger. ELLEN TERRY. London: Heinemann, 1968. x, 390 p.

The most recent biography. There are three interesting
appendices: Ellen Terry's notes for her interpretation of
Lady Macbeth; the parts played by Ellen Terry at the
Lyceum in association with Irving; and her notes on the
principal non-Shakespearean plays in which she appeared
at the Lyceum. There is a short select bibliography and
a good index.

TERRY, FLORENCE (Actress, 1854-96)

See items 3055, 3062.

TERRY, KATE (Actress, 1844-1924)

3064 Barker, Kathleen. "The Terrys and Godwin in Bristol." TN, 22 (1967-
68), 27-43.

The Terrys' performances in Bristol, August 1862-October
1864, and Godwin's criticisms.

TERRY, MARION (Actress, 1852-1930)

See items 3055, 3062.

THORNE, THOMAS (Actor, 1841-1918)

See item 2679.

TOOLE, JOHN LAURENCE (Actor-Manager, 1830-1906)

3065 Hatton, Joseph. REMINISCENCES OF J.L. TOOLE. Illus. Alfred
Byran and W.H. Margetson. 2 vols. London: Hurst and Blackett,
1889. xx, 295; xii, 305 p.

Memoirs of a minor but successful actor and manager, friend,
and acquaintance of many of the leading theatre people of
his day.

3066 Pinero, A.W. "J.L. Toole: A Great Comic Actor: The Natural Man."
The TIMES, 12 March 1932, pp. 13-14.

TREE, SIR HERBERT BEERBOHM (Actor-Manager, 1853-1917)

3067 _____, ed. SHAKESPEARE'S COMEDY "THE TEMPEST," AS ARRANGED FOR THE STAGE BY HERBERT BEERBOHM TREE. London: J. Miles, 1904. xvi, 63 p.

> The text of Tree's 1904 production at His Majesty's, with an introduction by Tree. There are some impressive color illustrations by Charles A. Buchel.

3068 Cran, Mrs. George. HERBERT BEERBOHM TREE. London and New York: John Lane, 1907. viii, 110 p.

> With a list of Tree's principal productions and several illustrations.

3069 Tree, Beerbohm. THOUGHTS AND AFTER-THOUGHTS. London: Cassell, 1913. [vi], 316 p.

> A miscellany of essays, mainly on Shakespeare.

3070 Beerbohm, Max, ed. HERBERT BEERBOHM TREE. London: Hutchinson, [1921]. xii, 314 p.

> Contains a long essay by Tree's widow and a series of shorter pieces from friends and relatives. There are numerous plates and line drawings.

3071 Pearson, Hesketh. BEERBOHM TREE: HIS LIFE AND LAUGHTER. New York: Harper & Brothers, 1956. [xii], 205 p.

> Pearson extravagantly praises Tree as "the most intelligent and versatile actor-manager in the record of the British stage." Family documents as well as recollections of many of Tree's friends are drawn upon. There are several plates, a brief bibliography, and a list of plays produced by Tree at the Haymarket and His Majesty's 1887-1917.

3072 Paulus, Gretchen. "Beerbohm Tree and 'The New Drama.'" UTQ, 27 (1957-58), 103-15.

> "More at home in the old world than the new, Tree still persisted in making generous gestures towards the important modern plays which came his way"--particularly AN ENEMY OF THE PEOPLE at the Haymarket in 1893.

3073 Rosenfeld, Sybil. "Some Experiments of Beerbohm Tree." NCTR, 2 (1974), 75-83.

> Tree's productions of Maeterlinck's THE INTRUDER, Ibsen's

ENEMY OF THE PEOPLE, and Brieux' FALSE GODS.

VANDENHOFF, GEORGE (Actor, 1813-85)

3074 _____. DRAMATIC REMINISCENCES; OR, ACTORS AND ACTRESSES IN ENGLAND AND AMERICA. Ed., with preface. Henry Seymour Carleton. London: Thomas Cooper and John Camden Hotten, 1860. xvi, 318 p.

> Published in America as LEAVES FROM AN ACTOR'S NOTE BOOK. Vandenhoff performed with Madame Vestris and on other occasions rubbed shoulders with the great.

VESTRIS, MADAME ELIZA LUCY (Actress-Manager, 1797-1856)

3075 Pearce, Charles E. MADAME VESTRIS AND HER TIMES. London: Stanley Paul, 1923; rpt. New York and London: Blom, 1969. 314 p.

> A substantial, but incomplete biography (e.g., sketchy treatment of the 1838 American tour). It is well-illustrated and includes a list of Mde. Vestris's appearances at the Olympic, 1831-39.

3076 Waitzkin, Leo. THE WITCH OF WYCH STREET. A STUDY OF THE THEATRICAL REFORMS OF MADAME VESTRIS. Cambridge, Mass.: Harvard University Press, 1933. 67 p.

> An early attempt ot assess the influence of Mde. Vestris in the English theatre. Superseded by later studies.

3077 Armstrong, William A. "Madame Vestris: A Centenary Appreciation." TN, 11 (1956-57), 11-18.

> A valuable and concise assessment of Mde. Vestris's contributions to the English stage. Two plates.

3078 Williams, Clifford John. MADAME VESTRIS, A THEATRICAL BIOGRAPHY. London: Sidgwick & Jackson, 1973. xiv, 240 p.

3079 Appleton, William W. MADAME VESTRIS AND THE LONDON STAGE. New York and London: Columbia University Press, 1974. 231 p.

> Similar in scope to Williams's study, but generally more detailed and comprehensive.

WALLER, LEWIS [WILLIAM WALLER LEWIS] (Actor-Manager, 1860-1915)

3080 _____. PARTS I HAVE PLAYED. Westminster: Abbey Press, 1909.

With thirty photographs and a biographical sketch by R. de Cordova.

WARD, DAME GENEVIEVE (ACTRESS, 1838-1922)

3081 Gustafson, Zadel Barnes. GENEVIEVE WARD: A BIOGRAPHICAL SKETCH FROM ORIGINAL MATERIAL DERIVED FROM HER FAMILY AND FRIENDS. London: David Bogue, [1881]. xv, 208 p.

3082 Ward, Genevieve, and R. Whiteing. BOTH SIDES OF THE CURTAIN. London: Cassell, 1918. 291 p.

WARNER, CHARLES (Actor, 1846-1909)

See item 2679.

WEBSTER, BENJAMIN NOTTINGHAM (Actor-Manager, 1797-1882)

3083 Downer, Alan. "The Diary of Benjamin Webster." TA (1945), 47-64.

A description of and extracts from Webster's diary, which covers the years 1825-50.

3084 Webster, Margaret. THE SAME ONLY DIFFERENT: FIVE GENERATIONS OF A GREAT THEATRE FAMILY. New York: Knopf, 1969. xviii, 396, xiv p.

Reminiscences about the important contribution made to the nineteenth-century theatre by the Webster family (including Dame May Whitty). The author draws on many family papers and her study is well-illustrated and indexed; documentation is lacking.

3085 Nichols, Harold James. "Ben Webster's Management of the Haymarket Theatre, 1837-1853." Ph.D. Dissertation, Indiana University, 1971. 428 p. (DA#72-06816)

WEBSTER, CLARA (Dancer, d. 1844)

3086 Guest, Ivor. VICTORIAN BALLET-GIRL: THE TRAGIC STORY OF
CLARA WEBSTER. London: Adam and Charles Black, 1957. [v], 136 p.

> A biography of the dancer who was burned to death on the
> stage of Drury Lane in December 1844.

WHITTY, DAME MAY (Actress, 1865-1948)

See item 3084.

WILLARD, EDWARD SMITH (Actor, 1853-1915)

See item 2679.

WINSTON, JAMES (Manager, Stage manager, 1779?-1843)

3087 Nelson, Alfred L. "James Winston in Paris, 1824 (An Extract from His
Diary)." ThR, 10, (1970), 141-55.

3088 _____. "The Winston Diaries." TN, 25 (1970-71), 5-10.

> A general description of the diaries of a man closely involved
> in the affairs of the London theatre, especially Drury Lane,
> in the early nineteenth century. See also item 3190.

WYNDHAM, SIR CHARLES (Actor-Manager, 1837-1919)

3089 Pemberton, T. Edgar. SIR CHARLES WYNDHAM, A BIOGRAPHY.
London: Hutchinson, 1904. 362 p.

3090 Shore, Florence T. SIR CHARLES WYNDHAM. London: John Lane,
1908. viii, 88 p.

YOUNG, CHARLES MAYNE (Actor, 1777-1856)

3091 Young, Julian Charles. A MEMOIR OF CHARLES MAYNE YOUNG,
TRAGEDIAN, WITH EXTRACTS FROM HIS SON'S JOURNAL. 2 vols.
London and New York: MacMillan, 1871. xviii, 374; ix, 368 p.

Chapter 8

THE CRITICS

This chapter includes only works <u>about</u> nineteenth-century theatre critics. For works by contemporary (and modern) critics, see chapters 1 and 2 above, which deal specifically with literary history and criticism. The critics also may be found in chapter 3, under the individual authors about whom they write.

A. GENERAL WORKS

3092 Emerson, Elizabeth. "English Dramatic Critics of the Nineties and the Acting of the 'New Theatre.'" Ph.D. Dissertation, Bryn Mawr, 1953. 297 p. (DA#54-498)

> An assessment of Clement Scott, Henry James, William Archer, and Shaw.

B. INDIVIDUAL CRITICS

AGATE, JAMES (1877-1947)

3093 Ballen, Leighton M. "The Theatre Criticism of James Agate." Ph.D. Dissertation, University of Illinois, 1955.

ARCHER, WILLIAM (1856-1924)

3094 Archer, Lt. Col. C. WILLIAM ARCHER: LIFE, WORK AND FRIEND-SHIPS. New Haven: Yale University Press, 1931. 451 p.

> A competent, solid biography, interspersed with Archer's correspondence.

3095 Cairns, Paul Edward. "William Archer as a Critic of Modern English Drama, 1882-1914." Ph.D. Dissertation, University of Michigan, 1956.

403 p. (DA#75-225)

3096 Thompson, Marjorie. "William Archer: Dramatic Critic 1856-1924." TN, 11 (1956-57), 6-11.

Archer's career reflects the "rise of dramatic criticism from shoddy journalism to a respected branch of letters."

3097 Baylen, Joseph O. "A Note on William Archer and THE PALL MALL GAZETTE, 1888." UMSE, 4 (1963), 21-26.

Deals briefly with Archer's work for the GAZETTE and his relationship with its editor, W.T. Stead. Includes one letter.

3098 _____. "William Archer, W.T. Stead, and the Theatre: Some Unpublished Letters." UMSE, 5 (1964), 91-103.

Archer's influence in converting Stead into a supporter of the theatre and of the compaign to abolish censorship.

3099 Schmid, Hans. THE DRAMATIC CRITICISM OF WILLIAM ARCHER. Cooper Monograph, no. 9. Bern: Francke Verlag, 1964. 111 p.

Marred by a stilted style and too many remnants of the dissertation.

3100 Darlington, W.A. "Of Critics, and Untidy Playwrights." DAILY TELE-GRAPH (London), 15 January 1973, p. 9.

Archer and A.B. Walkley.

BEERBOHM, MAX (1872-1956)

3101 Buckley, Anthony John. "The Dramatic Criticism of Max Beerbohm." Ph.D. Dissertation, Cornell University, 1962. 233 p. (DA#68-03500)

3102 Huss, Roy. "Max Beerbohm's Drawings of Theatrical Figures." TN, 21 (1966-67), 75-86; 102-19; 169-80.

Illustrated.

3103 McElderry, B.R. MAX BEERBOHM: New York: Twayne, 1972. 185 p.

A general introduction, including an assessment of Beerbohm as a critic. There is a selected bibliography.

GREIN, J.T. (1862-1935)

3104 Orme, Michael [Mrs. Alice Grein]. J.T. GREIN: THE STORY OF A
PIONEER, 1862-1935. Foreword. Conal O'Riordan. Rev. George
Bernard Shaw. London: John Murray, 1936. 360 p.

3105 Schoonderwoerd, N. J.T. GREIN: AMBASSADOR OF THE THEATRE
1862-1935: A STUDY IN ANGLO-CONTINENTAL THEATRICAL RELA-
TIONS. Assen, Netherlands: Van Gorcum, 1963. xi, 356 p.

In addition to providing a biography of Grein, this extensively documented book gives valuable accounts of the Independent Theatre and the theatrical traffic between England
and the Continent.

HAZLITT, WILLIAM (1778-1830)

3106 Ireland, Alexander. LIST OF THE WRITINGS OF WILLIAM HAZLITT
AND LEIGH HUNT: CHRONOLOGICALLY ARRANGED WITH NOTES,
DESCRIPTIVE, CRITICAL AND EXPLANATORY AND A SELECTION OF
OPINIONS REGARDING THEIR GENIUS AND CHARACTERISTICS BY
DISTINGUISHED CONTEMPORARIES AND FRIENDS AS WELL AS BY
SUBSEQUENT CRITICS: PRECEDED BY A REVIEW OF AND EXTRACTS
FROM BARRY CORNWALL'S "MEMORIALS OF CHARLES LAMB"; WITH
A FEW WORDS ON WILLIAM HAZLITT AND HIS WRITINGS, AND A
CHRONOLOGICAL LIST OF THE WORKS OF CHARLES LAMB. 1868;
rpt. New York: Burt Franklin, 1970. xxiv, 233 p.

3107 Keynes, Geoffrey. BIBLIOGRAPHY OF WILLIAM HAZLITT. London:
Nonesuch Press, 1931. xx, 137 p.

Scholarly, annotated and illustrated.

3108 Howe, P.P. THE LIFE OF WILLIAM HAZLITT: WITH AN INTRODUC-
TION BY FRANK SWINNERTON. London: Hamish Hamilton, 1947; rpt.
Westport, Conn.: Greenwood Press, 1972. xxvi, 433 p.

Standard biography.

3109 Wilkerson, Leon Cogswell. "The Eighteenth Century Background of
Hazlitt's Criticism." Ph.D. Dissertation, Vanderbilt University, 1954.
372 p.

3110 Whitley, Alvin. "Hazlitt and the Theatre." STUDIES IN ENGLISH, 34
(1955), 67-100.

3111 Albrecht, W.P. "Hazlitt's Preference for Tragedy." PMLA, 71 (1956),
1042-51.

An analysis of Hazlitt's theory of imagination "as it affects his definitions and evaluation of both tragedy and comedy."

3112 Klingopulos, G.D. "Hazlitt as Critic." EIC, 6 (1956), 386-403.

Includes some comments on Hazlitt's dramatic criticism.

3113 Sikes, Herschel M. "William Hazlitt's Theory of Literary Criticism and Its Contemporary Application." Ph.D. Dissertation, New York University, 1957. 213 p.

Appraisal of Hazlitt on Wordsworth, Coleridge, Byron, Keats, Shelley, Southey, Hunt, Lamb, and others.

3114 Barnett, Sylvan, and W.P. Albrecht. "More on Hazlitt's Preference for Tragedy." PMLA, 73 (1958), 443-45.

A continuation of Albrecht's discussion in item 3111.

3115 Linck, Alice E. Meyer. "The Psychological Basis of Hazlitt's Criticism." Ph.D. Dissertation, University of Kansas, 1961. 251 p. (DA#61-5053)

Sees a common psychological basis to Hazlitt's criticism, which can be approached through his unified conception of fancy, wit, reason, and imagination.

3116 Plasberg, Elaine. "William Hazlitt: The Structure and Application of his Critical Standards." Ph.D. Dissertation, Boston University, 1961. 298 p.

3117 Baker, Herschel. WILLIAM HAZLITT. Cambridge, Mass.: Harvard University Press, 1962. xiv, 530 p.

Places Hazlitt in his literary, political, and philosophical milieu, with a lengthy discussion of his dramatic criticism.

3118 Goodwin, George Vincent. "The Comic Theories of Hazlitt, Lamb, and Coleridge." Ph.D. Dissertation, University of Illinois, 1962. 187 p. (DA#62-2918)

3119 Jones, David L. "Hazlitt and Leigh Hunt at the Opera House." SYMPOSIUM, 16 (1962), 5-16.

Comparison of Hazlitt's and Hunt's opera criticism for the EXAMINER--Hazlitt being antipathetic, Hunt enthusiastic.

3120 Albrecht, William Price. HAZLITT AND THE CREATIVE IMAGINATION.

Lawrence: University of Kansas Press, 1965. 203 p.

3121 Donohue, Joseph. "Hazlitt's Sense of the Dramatic: Actor as Tragic Character." SEL, 5 (1965), 705-21.

3122 Perry, David Scott. "Hazlitt, Lamb and the Drama." Ph.D. Dissertation, Princeton University, 1966. 440 p. (DA#66-9633)

3123 Park, C. "Hazlitt's Literary Criticism: Its Foundations in Philosophy and Painting." Ph.D. Dissertation, University of Cambridge, 1967-68.

3124 Powers, Harvey Marcellus. "The Theatrical Criticism of Arthur Murphy, Leigh Hunt, and William Hazlitt: A Study in Changing Tastes." Ph.D. Dissertation, Cornell University, 1968. 227 p. (DA#68-16762)

3125 Wardle, Ralph M. HAZLITT. Lincoln: University of Nebraska Press, 1971. xiii, 530 p.

Scholarly biography.

HORNE, R.H. (1803-84)

3126 Laird, Robert Glen. "The New Spirit of the Age: Richard Henry Horne." Ph.D. Dissertation, Yale University, 1973. 231 p. (DA#73-19029)

Besides examining Horne's four major dramas, Laird looks at A NEW SPIRIT OF THE AGE, which is Horne's recognition of the place and "importance of the artist in a newly literate age."

HUNT, LEIGH (1784-1859)

3127 Monkhouse, Cosmo. LIFE OF LEIGH HUNT. London: Walter Scott, 1893. 250, xv p.

Includes an extensive bibliography of Hunt's work.

3128 Miller, Barnette. LEIGH HUNT'S RELATIONS WITH BYRON, SHELLEY AND KEATS. 1910; rpt. Folcroft, Pa.: Folcroft Press, 1969. vii, 169 p.

Largely biographical.

3129 Blunden, Edmund C. LEIGH HUNT'S "EXAMINER" EXAMINED: COMPRISING SOME ACCOUNT OF THAT CELEBRATED NEWSPAPER'S CON-

TENTS, &C. 1808-25 AND SELECTIONS, BY OR CONCERNING
LEIGH HUNT, LAMB, KEATS, SHELLEY, AND BYRON, ILLUSTRATING
THE LITERARY HISTORY OF THAT TIME, FOR THE MOST PART PRE-
VIOUSLY UNREPRINTED. London: Cobden-Sanderson, 1928. xi,
263 p.

3130 _____. LEIGH HUNT: A BIOGRAPHY. London: Cobden-Sanderson,
1930. xiii, 402 p.

3131 Brewer, Luther A. MY LEIGH HUNT LIBRARY: THE FIRST EDITIONS.
1932; rpt. New York: Franklin, 1970. xlv, 391 p.

   Well-annotated bibliography of an important collection.

3132 Young, Percy M. "Leigh Hunt--Music Critic." MUSIC AND LETTERS,
25 (1944), 86-94.

3133 Fleece, Jeffrey A. "Leigh Hunt's Theatrical Criticism." Ph.D. Dissertation, University of Iowa, 1952. 166 p.

   Places Hunt in his theatrical milieu as well as comparing
   him with Hazlitt.

3134 Mackerness, Edward D. "Leigh Hunt: Musical Journalism." MONTHLY
MUSICAL RECORD, 86 (1956), 212-22.

3135 Trewin, J.C. "Leigh Hunt as a Drama Critic." KSMB, 10 (1959), 14-
19.

3136 Fenner, Theodore Lincoln. "Leigh Hunt on Opera: The EXAMINER
Years." Ph.D. Dissertation, Columbia University, 1967. 364 p. (DA#
68-8578)

   Covers the years 1808 to 1822.

3137 _____. LEIGH HUNT AND OPERA CRITICISM: THE "EXAMINER"
YEARS, 1808-1821. Lawrence: University of Kansas Press, 1972. xiv,
353 p.

LAMB, CHARLES (1775-1834)

3138 Houghton, Walter E. "Lamb's Criticism of Restoration Comedy." ELH,
10 (1943), 61-72.

   An appreciation of Lamb's "highly sensitive interpretation."

3139 Barnet, Sylvan. "Charles Lamb's Contribution to the Theory of Dramatic Illusion." PMLA, 69 (1954), 1150-59.

    Demonstrates Lamb's realization of the degree to which dramatic illusion must vary in comedy and tragedy, and argues that his degree of sophistication in this concept places him as an important dramatic critic.

3140 Patterson, C.I. "Lamb, Shakespeare and the Stage Reconsidered." EUQ, 20 (1964), 101-7.

3141 Ades, John I. "Charles Lamb, Shakespeare, and Early Nineteenth-Century Theatre." PMLA, 85 (1970), 514-26.

    This revaluation of Lamb's Shakespearean criticism demonstrates "that it is derived from an awareness of the limitations of the London theatre of Lamb's time and of its audience, and by extension, of the limitations inherent in transforming any script into performance."

LEWES, G.H. (1817-78)

3142 Doremus, Robert B. "George Henry Lewes: A Descriptive Biography, with Especial Attention to his interest in the Theatre." Ph.D. Dissertation, Harvard University, 1940. 304 p.

3143 Kaminsky, Alice R. "George Henry Lewes: A Victorian Literary Critic." Ph.D. Dissertation, New York University, 1952. 199 p.

3144 _____. GEORGE HENRY LEWES AS LITERARY CRITIC. Syracuse, N.Y.: Syracuse University Press, 1968. xi, 220 p.

Chapter 9

STAGE DESIGN, SCENIC ART, AND COSTUME

3145 Planché, James Robinson. HISTORY OF BRITISH COSTUME FROM THE
EARLIEST PERIOD TO THE CLOSE OF THE EIGHTEENTH CENTURY.
3rd ed. London: George Bell, 1874. xxiv, 416 p.

> A pioneering work, first published in 1834, which was in-
> fluential in encouraging authentic costuming on the English
> stage.

3146 Lloyds, F. PRACTICAL GUIDE TO SCENE PAINTING AND PAINTING
IN DISTEMPER. WITH ILLUSTRATIONS DRAWN BY THE AUTHOR.
London: George Rowney, [1875]. 97 p.

3147 Planché, James Robinson. A CYCLOPAEDIA OF COSTUME OR DICTIO-
NARY OF DRESS, INCLUDING NOTICES OF CONTEMPORANEOUS
FASHIONS ON THE CONTINENT; AND A GENERAL CHRONOLOGI-
CAL HISTORY OF THE COSTUMES OF THE PRINCIPAL COUNTRIES OF
EUROPE, FROM THE COMMENCEMENT OF THE CHRISTIAN ERA TO
THE ACCESSION OF GEORGE THE THIRD. 2 vols. London: Chatto
and Windus, 1876-79. 975 p.

> A large, scholarly and magnificently illustrated work.

3148 Bowen, Cyril. PRACTICAL HINTS ON STAGE COSTUME, INCLUDING
INSTRUCTIONS AND PATTERNS FOR MAKING HATS, BOOT TOPS,
SWORD BELTS, LACE ORNAMENTS, BALLET SHIRTS, AND OTHER
NECESSARY ARTICLES OF COSTUME GENERALLY SUPPLIED BY THE
ACTOR HIMSELF. London and New York: French, ca. 1881. 36 p.

3149 Lawrence, W.J. "The Pioneers of Modern English Stage Mounting:
William Capon." MAGAZINE OF ART, 18 (1895), 289-92.

> Capon was an unadventurous designer who worked with J.P.
> Kemble.

3150 Archer, William. "The Limitations of Scenery." MAGAZINE OF ART, [19] (1896), 432-36.

> Archer discusses productions of Shakespeare and contemporary plays in the light of his axiom that "scenery should as nearly as possible express to the eye the locality which was present to the author's imagination, without distracting the attention of the audience from the action of the play, either by too great ingenuity and luxury or by ludicrous and grotesque inadequacy."

3151 Lawrence, W.J. "Scenery on a Tour." MAGAZINE OF ART, [19] (1896), 476-79.

> Praise for the Shakespearean settings of F.R. Benson; criticism for the Elizabethan Stage Society "whose attempts to put back the clock of Time fully three centuries must be viewed as mere midsummer madness."

3152 Strange, Edward F. "The Scenery of Charles Kean's Plays and the Great Scene-Painters of His Day." MAGAZINE OF ART (1902), 454-59; 514-18.

> Discusses drawings by several artists for Kean's productions from 1848 to 1859 with many excellent illustrations.

3153 Harker, Joseph Cunningham. STUDIO AND STAGE. Intro. Sir Johnston Forbes-Robertson. London: Nisbet & Co., 1924. 283 p.

> Includes a discussion of the history of scene painting and stage decoration in England.

3154 Gamble, William B. THE DEVELOPMENT OF SCENIC ART AND STAGE MACHINERY: A LIST OF REFERENCES IN THE NEW YORK PUBLIC LIBRARY. Rev. ed. New York: New York Public Library, 1928. 128 p.

> A revised version of a list originally published in BNYPL, June-November, 1919.

3155 Southern, Richard. "Trick-Work in the English Nineteenth Century Theatre." LIFE AND LETTERS TO-DAY, 21 (1939), 94-101.

> A brief article for the general reader, mainly on stage traps.

3156 Linton, Calvin Darlington. "Shakespearean Staging in London from Irving to Gielgud." Ph.D. Dissertation, Johns Hopkins University, 1940. 304 p.

3157 Thomas, Russell B. "Spectacle in the Theatres of London from 1767 to 1802." Ph.D. Dissertation, University of Chicago, 1942. 255 p.

3158 Abegglen, Homer N. "The Methods of Staging in London Theatres in the Last Half on the Nineteenth Century." Ph.D. Dissertation, Western Reserve University, 1945.

3159 McDowell, John H. "Historical Development of the Box Set." TA, 4 (1945), 65–83.

> McDowell considers European, English, and American developments from the last decade of the eighteenth century. Illustrated.

3160 S., R. [Richard Southern]. "Benwell on Victorian Scene Painting." TN, 1 (1945–47), 61–62.

3161 Van Lennep, William. "Dykwynkyn of Old Drury." TA (1946), 62–72.

> The costume designs of Richard Wynne Keene (Drury Lane costume designer from 1852 to 1880) for E.L. Blanchard's pantomime HARLEQUIN HUDIBRAS, Drury Lane, 27 December 1852.

3162 Harbron, Dudley. THE CONSCIOUS STONE: THE LIFE OF EDWARD WILLIAM GODWIN. London: Latimer House, 1949. xviii, 190 p.

> There is not a great deal in this biography about this important designer's work for the theatre, but the author does provide a useful chapter on Godwin's part in the Bancrofts' revival of THE MERCHANT OF VENICE.

3163 S., R. [Richard Southern]. "The Picture-Frame Proscenium of 1880." TN, 5 (1950–51), 59–61.

> The Bancrofts' Haymarket proscenium.

3164 Southern, Richard. CHANGEABLE SCENERY: ITS ORIGIN AND DEVELOPMENT IN THE BRITISH THEATRE. London: Faber, 1952. 411 p.

> An authoritative study which brings together a wealth of material about nineteenth-century scenic design and mechanics. Many valuable illustrations.

3165 Armstrong, William A. "Peter Nicholson and the Scenographic Art." TN, 8 (1953-54), 91–96.

> Nicholson's theories favored verisimilitude rather than decoration in stage settings.

3166 Larson, Orville K. "A Commentary on the 'Historical Development of the Box Set' (THEATRE ANNUAL, 1945)." TA, 12 (1954), 28-36.

See item 3158.

3167 Watters, Don Albert. "The Pictorial in English Theatrical Staging, 1773-1833." Ph.D. Dissertation, Ohio State University, 1954. 388 p. (DA# 00-12252)

3168 Speaight, George. "Early Multiple Settings in England." TN, 9 (1954-55), 15.

The setting for the last scene of Fitzball's WALTER BRAND at the Surrey, 26 December 1833 (with an illustration).

3169 Miesle, Frank L. "The Staging of Pantomime Entertainments on the London Stage, 1715-1808." Ph.D. Dissertation, Ohio State University, 1955. 376 p. (DA#00-14478)

3170 Williams, Dallas S. "Gordon Craig's Theory of the Theatre as Seen through THE MASK." Ph.D. Dissertation, Louisiana University, 1955. 266 p. (DA#00-1235)

3171 Rosenfeld, Sybil. "Scene Designs of William Capon." TN, 10 (1955-56), 118-22.

With nine plates of Capon's sketches, which "confirm the evidence of his studied antiquarianism and meticulous attention to detail."

3172 Forsyth, Gerald. "Wilhelm: A Noted Victorian Theatrical Designer." TN, 11 (1956-57), 55-58.

The work of John Charles Pitcher (1858-1925). Eight plates.

3173 Adelsperger, Walter Charles. "Aspects of Staging of Plays of the Gothic Revival in England." Ph.D. Dissertation, Ohio State University, 1959. 295 p. (DA#60-1168)

3174 Lacy, Robin Thurlow. "An Encyclopedia of Scenographers, 534 BC to 1900 AD." Ph.D. Dissertation, University of Denver, 1959.

3175 Eddison, Robert. "Capon and Goodman's Fields." TN, 14 (1960), 127-32.

3176 Wickman, Richard Carl. "An Evaluation of the Employment of Panoramic Scenery in the Nineteenth-Century Theatre." Ph.D. Dissertation, Ohio

State University, 1961. 376 p. (DA#62-824)

3177 Banks, Howard Milton. "A Historical Survey of the Mise-en-Scène Employed in Shakespearean Productions from the Elizabethan Period to the Present." Ph.D. Dissertation, University of Southern California, 1963. 821 p. (DA#63-01549)

3178 Hamblin, Junius M. "The Artistic Approach of the Grieve Family to Selected Problems of Nineteenth Century Scene Painting." Ph.D. Dissertation, Ohio State University, 1966. 332 p. (DA#67-06318)

3179 Johnson, Raoul Fenton. "United States and British Patents for Scenic and Lighting Devices for the Theatre from 1861 to 1915." Ph.D. Dissertation, University of Illinois, 1966. 278 p. (DA#66-07759)

3180 "Edward Gordon Craig, Artist of the Theatre 1872-1966. A Memorial Exhibition in the Amsterdam Gallery." BNYPL, 71 (1967), 431-67; 524-41.

   With an introduction by Donald Oenslager and the catalog (presenting "a chronological survey of Craig's work in the theatre, with biographical commentary and several quotations from Craig and his contemporaries interspersed") compiled by Arnold Rood.

3181 Fletcher, Ifan Kyrle, and Arnold Rood. EDWARD GORDON CRAIG: A BIBLIOGRAPHY. London: Society for Theatre Research, 1967. 117 p.

3182 Campbell, Lily Bess. "A History of Costuming on the English Stage Between 1660 and 1823." COLLECTED PAPERS OF LILY B. CAMPBELL. New York: Russell & Russell, 1968. 103-39.

3183 Allen, Ralph G. "Kemble and Capon at Drury Lane, 1794-1802." ETJ, 23 (1971), 22-35.

   A description and appreciation of Capon's work which anticipated the "theatrical revolution" of Charles Kean and Saxe-Meiningen by almost fifty years.

3184 Rothgeb, John Reese. "The Scenographic Expression of Nature (1545-1845): The Development of Style." Ph.D. Dissertation, Case Western Reserve University, 1971. 396 p. (DA#72-6328)

3185 Rosenfeld, Sybil. "Scene Designs by Hodgins the Younger." TN, 27, no. 1 (1972), 22-25.

Hodgins painted scenes at Covent Garden from 1796-1826, and this article provides a brief history of his work, together with a list of plays for which he designed scenes. Illustrated.

3186 _____. A SHORT HISTORY OF SCENE DESIGN IN GREAT BRITAIN. Oxford: Blackwell, 1973. xviii, 214 p.

Three chapters of this extensively illustrated book are devoted to the nineteenth century.

Chapter 10

PERIODICALS

For a more detailed list of nineteenth-century theatre periodicals, readers should consult Arnott and Robinson's ENGLISH THEATRICAL LITERATURE 1559-1900, item 2458, above, and Stratman's BIBLIOGRAPHY OF BRITISH DRAMATIC PERIODICALS, item 2434, above.

3187 Dutton, Thomas, ed. THE DRAMATIC CENSOR: OR WEEKLY THEATRICAL REPORT. COMPRISING A COMPLETE CHRONICLE OF THE BRITISH STAGE, AND A REGULAR SERIES OF THEATRICAL CRITICISM, IN EVERY DEPARTMENT OF THE DRAMA. London: Sold by J. Roach and C. Chapple, 1800-1801.

A weekly and then monthly journal, containing mainly summaries and reviews of Covent Garden and Drury Lane productions.

3188 THE THEATRICAL REPERTORY. CONTAINING CRITICISMS ON THE PERFORMANCES WHICH WERE REPRESENTED AT DRURY-LANE AND COVENT GARDEN THEATRES, DURING THE SEASON 1801-2. WITH OCCASIONAL OBSERVATIONS ON OTHER PLACES OF PUBLIC ENTERTAINMENT. London: Printed by T. Woodfall, [1802].

Published in weekly numbers from 19 September 1801 to 28 June 1802. Playbills are reprinted, followed by critiques; this is a useful guide to daily performances for these months.

3189 [Winston, James]. THE THEATRIC TOURIST; BEING A GENUINE COLLECTION OF CORRECT VIEWS, WITH BRIEF AND AUTHENTIC HISTORICAL ACCOUNTS OF ALL THE PRINCIPAL PROVINCIAL THEATRES IN THE UNITED KINGDOM. REPLETE WITH USEFUL AND NECESSARY INFORMATION TO THEATRICAL PROFESSORS, WHEREBY THEY MAY LEARN HOW TO CHUSE AND REGULATE THEIR COUNTRY ENGAGEMENTS; AND WITH NUMEROUS ANECDOTES TO AMUSE THE READER. London: T. Woodfall, 1805. 72 p.

Originally published in eight parts, THE THEATRIC TOURIST

contains brief accounts of British provincial theatres with magnificent color plates.

3190 Nelson, Alfred Lewis, Jr. "James Winston's THEATRIC TOURIST: A Critical Edition, with a Biography and a Census of Winston Material." Ph.D. Dissertation, George Washington University, 1968. 474 p. (DA#68-11762)

See also C.B. Hogan, "The Manuscript of Winston's THEATRIC TOURIST." TN, 1 (1947), 86-95; John E. Cunningham, "The Origin of THE THEATRIC TOURIST." TN, 4 (1949-50), 38-40; Philip H. Highfill, "Folger Library Manuscripts Relating to THE THEATRIC TOURIST." TN, 20 (1965-66), 121-26; Alfred L. Nelson, "The Periodicity of THE THEATRIC TOURIST." TN, 21 (1966-67), 59-62.

3191 Holcroft, Thomas. THE THEATRICAL RECORDER. 2 vols. London: C. Mercier, 1805-6.

Published monthly, January-December 1805. Contents include English translations of foreign plays, articles on new productions, and essays on, for example, actors, dramatic composition, and the German stage. Illustrated (but not profusely).

3192 Williams, J.M., ed. THE DRAMATIC CENSOR; OR, CRITICAL AND BIOGRAPHICAL ILLUSTRATION OF THE BRITISH STAGE. FOR THE YEAR 1811. INVOLVING A CORRECT REGISTER OF EVERY NIGHTS PERFORMANCES AT OUR METROPOLITAN THEATRES, AND PUBLISHED WITH A VIEW TO SUSTAIN THE MORALITY AND DIGNITY OF THE DRAMA. London: Printed by G. Brimmer, [1812].

Published monthly; includes some substantial reviews, occasional cast lists, and comments arising out of the theatrical events of the year.

3193 THE THEATRICAL INQUISITOR; OR, LITERARY MIRROR. 1812-20.

A substantial monthly containing reviews of current London productions and serious essays on matters theatrical (the minor theatres, the history of English drama, etc.). It is an excellent source for information on the early nineteenth-century theatre. It appeared with various imprints.

3194 Dutton, Thomas. THE MONTHLY THEATRICAL REPORTER; OR, LITERARY MIRROR. London: J. Roach, [1814-15].

Published in ten monthly parts between October 1814 and July 1815. It contains reviews of productions at Covent Garden and Drury Lane, critiques of various actors and actresses, and miscellaneous notes aimed at reforming a stage which Dutton saw as being "in a state of . . . disgraceful prostitution, vileness, and contemptiblilty."

3195 COVENT-GARDEN THEATRICAL GAZETTE. Ed. W. Legget. Nos. 1-148, 9 September 1816 to 9 April 1817.

Published up to six days a week, containing "a complete Analysis of the whole of the Evening's Entertainments, with the names of the Characters, Performers, &C. &C. . . ." Reprints playbills and gives descriptive analyses of Covent Garden productions.

3196 Kenrick, Thomas. THE BRITISH STAGE, AND LITERARY CABINET. 6 vols. London: Published for the Proprietors by J. Chappel, 1817-22.

A monthly publication containing a wide variety of interesting theatrical information: notices of London and provincial productions, essays on performers (with excellent color portraits), book reviews, and miscellaneous articles. Indexed.

3197 THE CORNUCOPIA; OR, LITERARY AND DRAMATIC MIRROR, CONTAINING CRITICAL NOTICES OF THE DRAMA, AND A VARIETY OF INTERESTING SUBJECTS UNDER THE HEAD OF MISCELLANIES. London: J. Jameson, 1821.

The colored engravings (one in each monthly issue) of scenes from plays are of interest, but the rest of this slight journal is of limited value. It appeared in thirteen numbers, September 1820 to September 1821.

3198 THE DRAMA; OR, THEATRICAL POCKET MAGAZINE . . . CONTAINING ORIGINAL DRAMATIC BIOGRAPHY, ESSAYS, CRITICISMS, POETRY, REVIEWS, ANECDOTES, BON MOTS, CHIT CHAT; WITH OCCASIONAL NOTICES OF THE COUNTRY THEATRES. 7 vols. London: T. and J. Elvey, 1821-25.

A monthly with many interesting points of view and much useful information; indexed (but not fully).

3199 THE THEATRICAL OBSERVER. London: E. Thomas, 1821-76.

A daily, later called THE THEATRICAL OBSERVER; AND DAILY BILLS OF THE PLAY, which reviews productions at Drury Lane, Covent Garden, and the Haymarket, and reprints playbills from these theatres. It is an important source of information for the history of the patent theatres.

3200 THE THEATRICAL EXAMINER; OR, CRITICAL REMARKS ON THE DAILY PERFORMANCES, WITH THE BILLS OF THE PLAY. 9 vols. London: T. Holt, J. Fitzwilliam & Co. and W. Barrow, 1828-31.

A daily publication of playbills and reviews for several
London theatres, but good runs are hard to come by.

3201 [Oxberry, William, and Catherine Oxberry, eds.]. OXBERRY'S DRAMAT-
IC BIOGRAPHY, AND HISTRIONIC ANECDOTES. 7 vols. London:
George Virtue and John Duncombe, 1825-27.

> Published weekly from 1 January 1825 to 12 August 1827.
> Offered to readers as "a cheap and interesting medium of
> learning of their several theatrical favourites." Each bi-
> ography is accompanied by a portrait.

3202 THE WEEKLY DRAMATIC REGISTER, A CONCISE HISTORY OF THE
LONDON STAGE . . . COMPILED FROM THE THEATRICAL OBSERVER.
3 vols. London: E. Thomas, 1825-27.

> A weekly publication concentrating on short reviews of pro-
> ductions at London theatres (only occasionally including the
> minors). There are memoirs of some actors and later issues
> contain news from the provincial theatres and miscellaneous
> theatrical news and comment.

3203 THE DRAMATIC MAGAZINE, EMBELLISHED WITH NUMEROUS EN-
GRAVINGS OF THE PRINCIPAL PERFORMERS. 3 vols. London: Whittaker, Treacher, & Co., 1829-31.

> "The object of the Dramatic Magazine will be . . . to
> afford a complete history of the modern stage; but in addi-
> tion to this, the Editors purpose abridging from numerous
> publications a history of the British drama, including a bi-
> ography of all the principal performers from its commence-
> ment" (preface). THE DRAMATIC MAGAZINE is a sub-
> stantial monthly with detailed reviews of London productions
> (including some attention to the minor theatres), provincial
> and foreign intelligence, and, as promised, essays on the
> history of drama.

3204 THE BRITISH STAGE; OR, DRAMATIC CENSOR. London: J. Duncombe,
[1831].

> Published monthly, April-June 1831. Includes reviews of
> current London productions, memoirs of actors and actresses,
> and miscellaneous notes. A short-lived and not very im-
> portant journal.

3205 ACTORS BY DAYLIGHT; OR, PENCILINGS IN THE PIT. CONTAINING
CORRECT MEMOIRS OF UPWARDS OF FORTY OF THE MOST CELE-
BRATED LONDON PERFORMERS; ORIGINAL TALES, POETRY, AND
CRITICISMS: THE WHOLE FORMING A FAITHFUL ACCOUNT OF THE

LONDON STAGE FOR THE LAST TWELVE MONTHS. 2 vols. London: J. Pattie and W.M. Clarke, [1838-39].

> Published weekly from 3 March 1838 to 17 March 1839. In each issue there is a memoir and a full-length portrait of an actor or actress. There are also brief notices of current London productions and other miscellaneous items.

3206 ACTORS BY GASLIGHT; OR, 'BOZ' IN THE BOXES. London: M. Hetherington and W. Strange, 1838.

> Published in weekly numbers, April-December 1838. Each issue consists mainly of stories based on popular plays of the time.

3207 THE ERA. 103 vols. [London: The Era Office, 1838-1939].

> This weekly theatrical newspaper is invaluable for reviews, news, and general theatrical information and gossip. Also of value are the assorted advertisements by and for actors and companies.

3208 THE THEATRICAL JOURNAL, AND STRANGER'S GUIDE. 1839-73.

> A weekly publication with some general essays, reviews of London productions, and news from the provinces and abroad. It appeared with various imprints.

3209 THE THEATRICAL CHRONICLE; OR, THESPIAN SKETCH BOOK AND DRAMATIC REVIEW; WITH NOTES OF LONDON LIFE. 1840-43; 1848-49.

> A weekly publication with biographies and portraits of actors, reviews of London productions, news from provincial theatres, and editorials on matters of general theatrical interest.

3210 THE MANCHESTER DRAMATIC AND MUSICAL REVIEW. Nos. 1-43, 14 November 1846 to 4 September 1847.

> Issued weekly, with occasional supplements. It contains reviews of London productions, with occasional notices of provincial theatre affairs and essays on miscellaneous theatre topics. There is also esoteric Manchester news, like notices of French and Latin plays at the Manchester Free Grammar School (3 April 1847).

3211 THE THEATRICAL TIMES. A WEEKLY MAGAZINE OF THESPIAN BIOGRAPHY, ORIGINAL DRAMATIC ESSAYS, PROVINCIAL, CONTINENTAL, AMERICAN, METROPOLITAN THEATRICALS; A COMPLETE RECORD OF PUBLIC AMUSEMENTS, WITH ORIGINAL PORTRAITS OF EMINENT

LIVING ACTORS. 4 vols. London: S. Grieves, 1846-51.

As the subtitle indicates, the interests of this journal are wide-ranging. It contains a great deal of information about the mid-nineteenth-century theatre.

3212 THE STAGE-MANAGER; OR A JOURNAL OF DRAMATIC LITERATURE AND CRITICISM. 1849-50.

A weekly journal (known towards the end of its run as THE LITERARY REVIEW AND STAGE MANAGER) concerned with dramatic theory and history as well as current theatre activity. Each issue usually has an engraving of an author, performer, or scene from a current production. It appeared with various imprints.

3213 Ledger, Edward; Frank Desprez; and Alfred Barnard, eds. THE ERA ALMANACK. London: "The Era," 1868-1919.

An annual publication packed with information about the theatre: biographies of authors and actors, reviews, histories of theatres, calendars of performances, etc., and much advertising which provides interesting, often esoteric, information about the theatre.

3214 THE ENTR'ACTE ALMANACK AND THEATRICAL & MUSIC HALL ANNUAL. 34 vols. London: W.H. Combes, 1873-1906.

Also called THE ENTR'ACTE AND LIMELIGHT ALMANACK, and, from 1886, THE ENTR'ACTE ANNUAL. It is a light-hearted publication important for its numerous cartoons of theatrical personalities, many of them by Alfred Bryan.

3215 ILLUSTRATED SPORTING AND DRAMATIC NEWS. 1874-1943.

A weekly, then fortnightly, journal with criticism and information on the theatre.

3216 FIGARO PROGRAMME. London: [Alfred Wilcox], 1874-77.

A weekly journal (which underwent several name changes) containing a fairly short drama section comprised of miscellaneous theatrical news and notes.

3217 THE THEATRE. A MONTHLY REVIEW AND MAGAZINE. 1877-97.

Originally a weekly review, THE THEATRE was for some years edited by Clement Scott. It is a substantial and serious journal containing essays on important aspects of the theatre (censorship, copyright, etc.) as well as reviews, biographies of actors (with many handsome photographs), and news of foreign theatre.

3218 Pascoe, Charles Eyre; William H. Rideing; T. Walter Wilson; Austin
Brereton; and Cecil Howard, eds. DRAMATIC NOTES. AN ILLUSTRA-
TED HANDBOOK OF THE LONDON THEATRES. 14 vols. London:
Gay and Bird, 1879-93.

An annual publication with summaries of events at London's
theatres, plus lists of new plays and important revivals in
London, and (in some volumes) lists of provincial productions. There are useful indexes to each volume.

3219 UNDER THE CLOCK. A WEEKLY JOURNAL FOR PLAYGOERS. 1884-
85.

Published in 64 numbers between 30 January 1884 and 20
April 1885. UNDER THE CLOCK contains miscellaneous
news items and gossip about the theatre. Each issue carries
a portrait of an actor or actress.

3220 THE DRAMATIC REVIEW. A JOURNAL OF THEATRICAL, MUSICAL,
AND GENERAL CRITICISM. [London: The Proprietors], 1885-94.

Published weekly, 512 numbers in all. It is an important
publication, the earlier issues containing articles by Archer,
Shaw, Godwin, and others. Each issue carries advertise-
ments by individual theatres, reviews of London and provincial productions, book reviews, and notes of general
theatrical interest.

3221 THE PLAY-PICTORIAL. AN ILLUSTRATED MONTHLY JOURNAL. 1902-
39.

Contains photographs and information on many nineteenth-
century actors and actresses whose careers extended into the
twentieth century.

3222 THE MASK. A MONTHLY JOURNAL OF THE ART OF THE THEATRE.
Ed. Gordon Craig. 1908-29; rpt. New York: Kraus Reprint, 1967.

3223 QUARTERLY JOURNAL OF SPEECH. New York: Speech Communica-
tion Association, 1915-- .

From time to time QJS publishes articles relating to the
nineteenth-century theatre.

3224 THEATRE ANNUAL: A PUBLICATION OF INFORMATION AND RE-
SEARCH IN THE ARTS AND HISTORY OF THE THEATRE. New York:
Theatre Library Association, 1942-- .

3225 THEATRE NOTEBOOK. A QUARTERLY JOURNAL OF THE HISTORY
AND TECHNIQUE OF THE BRITISH THEATRE. London: Society for
Theatre Research, 1945-- .

> A journal which has done much to stimulate and publish re-
> search in the theatre history of the nineteenth century and
> other periods.

3226 EDUCATIONAL THEATRE JOURNAL. Washington, D.C.: American
Theatre Association, 1949-- .

> A quarterly journal covering a wide variety of world theatre
> topics, sometimes including essays on the English nineteenth-
> century theatre.

3227 THEATRE STUDIES [Formerly OHIO STATE UNIVERSITY THEATRE COL-
LECTION BULLETIN]. Columbus: OSU Theatre Research Institute,
1954-- .

> Publishes articles based, for the most part, on its own ex-
> tensive theatre archives.

3228 THEATRE RESEARCH/RECHERCHES THÉÂTRALES. THE JOURNAL OF
THE INTERNATIONAL FEDERATION FOR THEATRE RESEARCH. 1958-- .

> Published three times a year, this is a bilingual journal
> which includes essays on all aspects of world theatre history.

3229 THEATRE SURVEY. THE AMERICAN JOURNAL OF THEATRE HISTORY.
Pittsburgh: American Society for Theatre Research, 1960-- .

> A semiannual journal.

3230 THEATRE DOCUMENTATION. Sao Paulo: University of Sao Paulo,
1968-72.

> Publishes articles (mainly of a bibliographical nature) and
> information on all aspects of theatre arts.

3231 THEATRE QUARTERLY. London: TQ Publications, 1971-- .

> A British journal which publishes essays on all aspects of
> the theatre, the emphasis being on modern theatre. It is
> usually extensively illustrated. See item 3234.

3232 NINETEENTH CENTURY THEATRE RESEARCH. Edmonton, Alberta and
Tuscon, Ariz.: L.W. Conolly and J.P. Wearing, 1973-- .

> A semiannual journal founded "to encourage such scholarship
> as will add to present limited knowledge and understanding
> of all aspects of the nineteenth-century theatre in the English-

speaking world." There is an annual bibliography and each issue contains articles, news of work in progress, notes and queries, and book reviews.

3233 PANTO! THE JOURNAL OF THE BRITISH PANTOMIME ASSOCIATION. London: The British Pantomime Association, 1973-- .

Publishes articles on nineteenth-century pantomime.

3234 THEATREFACTS: INTERNATIONAL THEATRE REFERENCE. London: TQ Publications, 1974-- .

Published quarterly as companion periodical to THEATRE QUARTERLY (item 3231); a useful bibliographical source.

GENERAL INDEX

This index is alphabetized letter by letter and numbers refer to entry numbers. Indexed are names of actors, actresses, managers, theatres, and authors. Subject areas and titles of particular interest and importance to the study of English drama and theatre are also indexed.

General Index

Archer, Frank 2736
Archer, Thomas 630
Archer, William 47, 54, 60, 77-80, 84-86, 88, 91, 102, 120, 122, 156, 421, 432, 830, 1368, 2835-36, 2958, 3094-3100, 3150, 3220
Architecture, theatre 134, 318, 352, 428, 2542
Ariail, J.M. 708
Arliss, George 2693, 2737-38
Armstrong, Cecil Ferard 113, 167, 2689
Armstrong, Margaret 2925
Armstrong, William A. 2535, 3077, 3165
Arnold, Matthew 118, 2514
Arnold, Samuel James 464-71, 1585, 2582, 2980
Arnold, W.T. 95
Arnott, James Fullerton 2458
Arthur, George 224
Arundell, Dennis 2611
Asche, Oscar 2706, 2739
Ashe, Dora Jean 965-66
Ashley, Leonard R.N. 2507
Ashton, Thomas L. 891
Aspinall, A. 2873
Astin, Marjorie 1562
Astley's Theatre 2549
Atkinson, Colin Bernard 1354
Auden, W.H. 2274
Audiences 134, 142, 222, 287, 397, 437
Augier, Emile 2285
Austin, Arthur D. 2253
Ayre, Leslie 1281

B

Babcock, R.W. 832
Badal, Robert Samuel 2747
Bader, Earl Delbert 2312
Badstuber, Alfred 486
Bailey, J.O. 1400, 2506
Baillie, Joanna 252, 472-90
Baily, Leslie 1213, 1284
Baily, Leslie J.R. 2605
Bair, George Eldridge 290
Baker, Arthur E. 2160

Baker, Blanche M. 2422
Baker, David Erskine 2377
Baker, G.P. 1382
Baker, H. Barton 2524, 2674
Baker, Herschel 2934, 3117
Baker, Sarah 285
Baker, Seymour O. 257
Balfe, Michael 800-802
Balfour, Graham 2013
Ball, Patricia M. 975
Ball, Robert Hamilton 230
Ballantyne, James 3027
Ballen, Leighton M. 3093
Ballet 324, 351, 414, 424, 2534, 2567a
Balmforth, Ramsden 197
Bancroft, Lady Marie 2687, 2705, 2726, 2740-42, 3162
Bancroft, Sir Squire 306, 830, 2679, 2687, 2705, 2726, 2740-42, 3162
Bangham, Paul Jerald 3008
Banim, John 1878a
Banister, Douglas 3021
Banks, Howard Milton 3177
Banks, Thomas Wilson 973
Bannister, John 2743
Baring, Maurice 184, 1225
Barish, Jonas A. 399
Barker, B. Ashley 2588
Barker, Kathleen 880, 2633-34, 2636, 2947, 2962, 3064
Barnard, Alfred 3213
Barnes, J.H. 2744
Barnet, Sylvan 3114, 3139
Barnett, Charles Zachery 491-98
Barnett, Howard A. 716
Barnett, Morris 499-506
Baron-Wilson, Mrs. Cornwell 2989
Baron-Wilson, Margaret 1475
Barrett, Lawrence 711
Barrett, Wilson 2679, 2685, 2694
Barrie, J.M. 114, 194, 204-5, 373, 1694, 1706
Barrington, Rutland 2679, 2745-46
Barron, Diana 2589
Barrymore, William 507-13, 2595
Barth, William 2490
Bartholomeusz, Dennis 377
Bartholomew, James Reece 812

Bassett, Abraham Joseph 2967, 2970
Bate, Walter Jackson 1407
Bateman, Ellen 2747
Bateman, Kate 2747
Bates, Alfred 2501
Bates, Arlo 645
Bates, Ernest Sutherland 1903
Bates, Mary E. 2438
Bath 189, 2619-20
Baum, Joan Mandell 378
Baum, Paull F. 2068
Baxter, Charles 2020
Baylen, J.O. 3097-98
Baylis, Lilian 2594-95
Bayly, Thomas Haynes 514-26
Beard, Harry R. 2612
Beatty, Arthur 2367
Beaudry, Harry Richard 1411
Beaumont, Cyril W. 187
Beaumont and Fletcher 258
Beazley, Samuel 527-34
Bebbington, W.B. 840
Beck, Martha Ryan 2860
Beckson, Karl 2314
Bedford, Paul John 2748
Beerbohm, Max 123, 139-40, 1219,
    1393, 2252, 3070, 3101-3
Beers, Henry A. 103, 1688
Bell, E.G. 791
Belton, Fred 2749
Benbow, William 883
Benefit system 361
Benger, Elizabeth Ogilvy 2185
Bennett, Cleon Vernon 1733
Bennett, John B. 15
Benson, Lady Constance 2750
Benson, Sir F.R. 2700, 2706, 2750-
    54, 3151
Bentley, Eric 2508
Bergler, Edmund 2279
Berland, Ellen 2315
Bernard, Bayle 1496
Bernard, William Bayle 535-47
Bernhardt, Sarah 75, 94, 184, 2685,
    2755-57
Berstl, Julius 2901
Bertram, James Glass. See Paterson,
    Peter
Betjeman, Sir John 347

Bettany, W.A. Lewis 1391
Betty, Master 2559, 2672, 2689,
    2758-59
Bhalla, Alok 861
Biblical drama. See Religious Drama
Biederstedt, Joan 1139
Bingham, Frederick 2654
BIOGRAPHY OF THE BRITISH STAGE,
    THE 2666
Birmingham 2621-25
Bishop, Conrad Joy 2723
Bjornson, Bjornstjerne 170
Blake, William 245, 885
Blakeley, Clyde 2886
Blanchard, E.L. 548-55, 2496, 3161
Blanchard, William 555
Blathwayt, Raymond 1385
Bleackley, Horace 215
Bligh, N.M. 2539, 2603
Block, Louis J. 2156
Blunden, Edmund C. 3129-30
Boaden, James 2870, 2933, 3028
Board, M.E. 2631
Boas, Frederick S. 225, 704
Boas, Guy 1249
Bobbe, Dorothie 2923
Bolitho, Hector 3048
Bond, Jessie 2760
Bond, W.H. 2164
Bond, William H. 1786
Booth, Edwin 317, 404, 2091,
    2676, 2687, 2700, 2708,
    2714, 2860
Booth, John 2592
Booth, Junius Brutus 230, 2683,
    2695, 2761-64
Booth, Michael R. 340-41, 356,
    436, 2505, 2510-13, 2515,
    2720
Borough Theatre 2533
Borowitz, Helen Osterman 2322
Borsa, Mario 156
Bostock, Edward Henry 2765
Boswell, Grace Hadaway 2069
Boucicault, Dion 26, 35, 306, 366,
    556-611a, 1078, 2502-3,
    2506-8, 2511, 2515-16, 2687,
    2691-92, 2722, 2730
Bouslog, Charles S. 968

General Index

Bowen, Cyril 3148
Bowley, Victor E.A. 198
Bowman, W.P. 1978
Boyer, Robert D. 1279
Bradbrook, M.C. 342
Bradley, Kathleen Harris. See Field, Michael
Braham, John 2612
Brandon-Thomas, Jevan 2180
Brasol, Boris 2229
Braun, Mrs. Charles 2690
Braybrooke, Patrick 2264
Brayley, Edward Wedlake 2521
Breeches parts 305
Breed, Paul F. 2463
Brereton, Austin 61, 2584, 2676, 2837, 2844, 2849, 2869, 3218
Brestensky, Dennis F. 730
Breugelmans, R. 2316
Brewer, Luther A. 3131
Bridgeman, Cunningham 1222
Brieux, Eugene 170, 3073
Brighton 2626
Brings, Lawrence Martin 2504
Brinton, Carrie 188
Brinton, Selwyn 156
Briscoe, Walter A. 830
Bristol 189, 285, 2627-36
Britannia Saloon 2533
BRITISH DRAMA, THE 2494-95
BRITISH HUMANITIES INDEX 2431
BRITISH MUSEUM: CATALOGUE OF ADDITIONS TO THE MANU-SCRIPTS 2436
BRITISH STAGE, THE 3204
BRITISH STAGE AND LITERARY CABI-NET, THE 3196
Broad, Lewis 2239
Broadbent, R.J. 148-49, 2646
Brockett, Oscar G. 423, 2299
Brody, G.M. 2147
Brokaw, John Wilkie 769, 2644a
Brook, Donald 281
Brooke, Gustavus Vaughan 2766
Brooke, Stopford 828
Brookfield, Charles H.E. 2767
Brooks, Charles William Shirley 612-19
Brophy, Robert J. 1948
Brough, Lionel 2679

Brough, Robert Barnabas 620-30
Brough, William 620-24, 631-33, 2496, 2513
Broughton, Frederick W. 634-37
Broughton, Leslie Nathan 673
Brouse, Albert J. 1787
Brown, Calvin 147, 2499
Brown, Eluned 133, 138
Brown, Ivor 2655
Brown, John Russell 410, 2940
Brown, T. Allston 101
Browne, Edith A. 1220
Browning, Oscar 644
Browning, Robert 212, 417, 638-738, 1136, 1947, 2235, 2324, 2502, 2506, 2514, 2964
Bryan, Alfred 69
Buchanan, Robert 739-57
Buck, J.D. 685
Buckley, Anthony John 3101
Buckley, Jerome Hamilton 2165
Buckstone, J.B. 25, 37, 758-69, 2506, 2516, 2710, 2730
Bulloch, John Malcolm 1211, 1218, 1392, 1836
Bulwer-Lytton, Sir Edward George 23, 26, 35, 37, 145, 212, 313, 355, 538, 770-97, 1148, 2499, 2501, 2503, 2506-7, 2510, 2512
Bunn, Alfred 798-805, 895
Burgis, Nina 1085
Burke, Rev. Edmund 2245
Burke, John David 402
Burkhart, Charles 2255
Burlesque 71, 181, 282, 296, 319, 329
Burletta 420, 425
Burley, T.L.G. 2639
Burnand, F.C. 35, 71, 364, 1242, 2730
Burnim, Kalman A. 2474
Burns, Wayne 1775, 1790
Burton, E.J. 323
Bury St. Edmunds 2637
Bush, Alfred L. 2302
Butler, James H. 2984
Butler, Maria Hogan 851
Buzecky, Robert Conrad 2742
Byers, William Franklin 333

General Index

Jones, John B. 1262, 1267-69, 1274
Jones, Leonidas M. 1409
Jones, Stephen 2377
Jones, W. Wilding 1838
Jonson, Marian 3041
Joost, Nicholas 2326
Jordan, Anne 600
Jordan, Dorothy 2669, 2684, 2686, 2690, 2695, 2870-74
Jordan, John O. 2086
Jordan, Robert J. 2318
Joseph, Bertram L. 2632, 2713
Joseph, M.K. 857
Jullian, Philippe 2254
Jump, John D. 892
Jupp, James 2572
Juvenile drama 214, 238-39, 244-46, 259, 264, 270-71, 279, 289, 304, 357, 386, 416. See also Toy theatre

K

K., Q. 1692
Kahan, Stanley 316
Kahn, Arthur D. 881
Kaminsky, Alice R. 3143-44
Kauvar, Gerald B. 2514
Kean, Charles 25, 34, 64, 85, 154, 230, 306, 380, 385, 407, 505, 570-71, 879, 1507, 2543, 2596a, 2673, 2676, 2689, 2700, 2715, 2798, 2875-94, 3009, 3152, 3183
Kean, Edmund 31, 65, 74, 133, 190, 225, 230, 344, 350, 505, 867, 2641, 2672-73, 2676, 2683, 2689, 2695, 2698, 2700-2701, 2704, 2708, 2710, 2713-14, 2719, 2721, 2731, 2895-907, 3004
Keats, John 144, 290, 378, 412, 1404-11, 1956-58, 2514, 2903, 3128-29
Keats-Shelley Journals 1956-58
Keeley, Mrs. 25, 762, 2673, 2908
Keeley, Robert 2908
Keene, Richard Wynne 3161
Kelly, Miss 469, 1746
Kelly, Frances 34, 49, 1969, 2909-11

Kelly, Helen Marie Terese 2811
Kelly, Michael 2912-13
Kelly, Richard M. 1355
Kemble, Charles 29, 344, 402, 1412-14, 2914-15
Kemble, F.A. 54
Kemble, Fanny 2684, 2690, 2693, 2698, 2709, 2916-30
Kemble, J.P. 133, 183, 377, 385, 2554, 2669, 2676, 2683, 2689, 2698, 2700-2701, 2708-9, 2713-14, 2721, 2731, 2931-42, 3004, 3009, 3030, 3149
Kemble, Stephen 1541, 2676
Kendal, Madge 55, 1240, 1836, 2687, 2744, 2943-47
Kendal, W.H. 2679, 2687, 2744, 2944
Kennard, Mrs. A. 3031
Kennedy, Virginia Wadlow 957
Kenney, Charles Lamb 2558
Kenney, James 1415-26, 2513
Kenrick, Thomas 3196
Kent 189, 285
Kenyon, Frederic G. 674
Kern, R.C. 2712
Kernahan, Coulson 2269
Kernodle, George R. 293
Kessel, Marcel 1929
Keynes, Geoffrey 3107
Kilburn, Michael 2635
Kilgarriff, Michael 2516
Kimberley, M.E. 398
Kincaid, Arthur 735
Kincaid, Margaret 736
King, Lucille 833
King, Robert 2651
King, Roma A. 648, 727
Kingsmill, Hugh 2268
King's Theatre 414, 2534, 2578-80
Kingston, Gertrude 2948
Kinnaird, Douglas 821
Kinneavy, Gerald B. 2077
Kissane, James D. 2175
Klein, John W. 846
Klepac, Richard Lee 2986
Kline, Herbert Walter 2862
Klingopulos, G.D. 3112
Knickerbocker, Leslie 678

494